Renaissance
and
Reformation
1500–1620

Renaissance and Reformation 1500–1620

A Biographical Dictionary

Edited by
JO ELDRIDGE CARNEY

The Great Cultural Eras of the Western World
Ronald H. Fritze, Series Adviser

GREENWOOD PRESS
Westport, Connecticut • London

Library of Congress Cataloging-in-Publication Data

Renaissance and Reformation, 1500–1620 : a biographical dictionary / edited by Jo
Eldridge Carney.
     p. cm.—(The great cultural eras of the Western world)
   Includes bibliographical references and index.
   ISBN 0–313–30574–9 (alk. paper)
    1. Europe—Biography—Dictionaries. 2. Renaissance—Biography—Dictionaries. 3.
Reformation—Biography—Dictionaries. I. Carney, Jo Eldridge, 1954– II. Series.
CT759.R46   2001
920.04—dc21   99–462063

British Library Cataloguing in Publication Data is available.

Library of Congress Catalog Card Number: 99–462063
ISBN: 0–313–30574–9

First published in 2001

Greenwood Press, 88 Post Road West, Westport, CT 06881
An imprint of Greenwood Publishing Group, Inc.
www.greenwood.com

Printed in the United States of America

The paper used in this book complies with the
Permanent Paper Standard issued by the National
Information Standards Organization (Z39.48–1984).

10 9 8 7 6 5 4 3 2 1

For Sandy, Alex, Julie, and Annie

Contents

Introduction

This series of reference books, The Great Cultural Eras of the Western World, is intended to provide brief, introductory information about various individuals who have made outstanding contributions to the culture of Western civilization. A biographical dictionary covering the years 1500–1620 assumes a particular interest since this is a period of greater emphasis on individual achievement and self-expression. This is also the period that comprises the Renaissance and the Reformation, two watershed movements in the history of cultural, political, and religious change.

As both a term and a concept, the Renaissance has recently undergone scrutiny from scholars. The more traditionally held view of the Renaissance has been that it was a period in European civilization in which enormous progress was made intellectually, culturally, and politically; that it involved, quite literally, a rebirth of interest in classical texts, arts, and ideas; and that this movement originated in fourteenth-century Italy and then spread to other parts of Europe in the next two centuries. Furthermore, this phenomenon was seen as a major departure from the relatively unsophisticated, perhaps even barbaric, Middle Ages. This approach was advanced by nineteenth-century historians Jules Michelet and Jakob Burckhardt and achieved greater currency in the twentieth century. Now, however, many scholars prefer the phrase "early modern" to the term "Renaissance" as more accurate and inclusive, since many medieval historians have naturally objected to the ideological implications of the more traditional view of the Renaissance, while other scholars, resisting the idea of rigid periodization, have sought to emphasize the idea of continuity from one era to the next, instead of change; even the term "early modern" has also been considered problematic since it emphasizes the idea of modernity. While the reevaluation of our views of what constitutes the Renaissance has provided fruitful reassessment of our historical perspectives, the term itself will probably not disappear, even if its usage becomes more fluid.

This was indeed an exciting, tumultuous, chaotic, and productive age. In 1500 there was increasing dissatisfaction from various corners of Europe with the Catholic church, but Catholicism still provided a unified religion for most of western Europe; in 1517 that changed dramatically when Martin Luther nailed his ninety-five theses to the church door in Wittenberg, initiating the Reformation and the emergence of numerous Protestant sects during the next century. Changing religious beliefs resulted in different views of humankind's place in the cosmos; concurrently, this era also brought about new ways of thinking about the universe itself and dramatic developments in the history of science. Nicolaus Copernicus's ideas of heliocentricity challenged Ptolemy's geocentric model of the universe and paved the way for the further discoveries of astronomers Tycho Brahe, Johannes Kepler, and Galileo Galilei. Other scholars, such as Andreas Vesalius, Gabriele Fallopio, Gerardus Mercator, and Niccolò Tartaglia initiated new approaches in medicine, physics, cartography, geography, and mathematics. All of these developments involved an increasing emphasis on observation and experiment, thus providing a critical transition to modern scientific practice.

This period also saw great strides in the development of the printing press, an invention that had a revolutionary influence on the dissemination of information and increasing literacy rates. The far-reaching humanist movement, beginning with Italian scholars but quickly adopted by their counterparts in northern Europe, emphasized the recovery and translation of ancient texts, strove to apply the lessons of antiquity to improvement of their present world, and granted more emphasis to individual human conduct and achievement. The study of antiquity had great bearing on the visual arts, particularly in an appreciation of the human form. The proliferation of literature in the Renaissance was also indebted to classical genres such as comedy, tragedy, epic, and satire. Artists and writers, however, did not merely duplicate ancient formulas; they moved beyond the inspiration provided by models of antiquity and created their own masterpieces of remarkable innovation and beauty. Moreover, painters, sculptors, and architects themselves came to be seen as creative artists rather than merely skilled craftsmen; whereas artistic achievements in the medieval period had tended to be communal and anonymous, Renaissance artists began signing their canvases and proclaiming their individual styles. Likewise, authors increasingly sought publication and wider distribution of their works, and many authors continued to advocate the use of the vernacular in literature in a spirit of patriotism and hope that their works would be accessible to a larger audience.

While the humanist movement was inextricably connected with the greatest triumphs of Renaissance culture, it was also often in conflict with the aims of the Reformation. Much of the period's great art was created through the direct patronage of the Catholic clergy, especially the popes; however, this artistic production often came at the expense of spiritual concerns. Humanist emphasis on the autonomous individual and free will also came into conflict with the Calvinist doctrine of predestination and man's natural depravity. Furthermore, the humanist interest in classical models was often found suspect by Protestant reformers as a celebration of pagan ideals.

Cultural production in sixteenth-century Europe flourished in spite of—and because of—the contradictions and tensions of the age. We can come closer to understanding this era by learning more about the individuals who contributed to the radical transformations of their time. These men and women were responding to their changing world; at the same time, the changes were produced because of these remarkable individuals. The exchange was dynamic and reciprocal, and the resulting cultural production was astounding.

For the purposes of this volume, culture has been defined broadly to include figures who have made contributions to the fields of art and architecture, music, philosophy, religion, political and social thought, science, mathematics, literature, history, and education. While the focus of other biographical dictionaries has typically been on political and military figures, the aim of this volume is to highlight individual cultural achievement rather than political influence, though there is often considerable overlap.

Certainly the most outstanding personalities of the Renaissance are featured here: Michelangelo, Shakespeare, Luther, Galileo, Erasmus. However, the volume also includes subjects perhaps not as prominent in the historical canon: for example, the Flemish geographer and astronomer Reiner Gemma Frisius, the English travel writer Thomas Coryate, the Muslim scholar Leo Africanus, and the German abbess Caritas Pirckheimer. Compiling a list of individuals who have made significant cultural contributions was a relatively satisfying task; the far greater challenge was to make the regrettable deletions. Particularly for this time period, so rich in artistic and literary achievement and religious and intellectual development, this volume could have been twice the size, but for obvious practical reasons, that was not possible. Any editor must accept the responsibility and regret for any sins of omission.

This volume does aim, however, at a fair, if not equal, distribution in terms of discipline and geography. We may have coined the word "interdisciplinary" in our century, but we certainly did not invent the concept. Trying to provide equal representation for all of the disciplines in an age of nonspecialization was a delightfully problematic task. To what discipline does Sir Walter Raleigh belong? Or Pietro Bembo? Or Vittoria Colonna? Many of these subjects truly were Renaissance men—and women: Girolamo Cardano was a physician by profession but made significant contributions to literature and to mathematics; Giambattista Della Porta was a popular playwright but devoted much of his attention to pursuits in the name of science. Gil de Vicente was a master goldsmith as well as an actor, musician, poet, and playwright. Disciplinary categories were not as distinct for this era as they are today, but one of the pleasures of reading about many of these subjects is the reminder of their versatility. Given the larger cultural developments of the Renaissance, much attention is given to artistic and literary achievement, but the subjects in this volume represent important contributions in many areas of cultural production.

The geographical distribution represented by these subjects also reminds us that the Renaissance was not merely synonymous with Italy. While we cannot deny Italy's profound accomplishments in the sixteenth century as well as its profound influence on the rest of Europe, we must also acknowledge the exciting and innovative developments in other areas as well: in Nuremberg, Hans Sachs produced hundreds of literary works, including plays, chronicles, satires, and poetry; in Poland, the poet Jan Kochanowski wrote some of the finest lyric poetry of the century; in Spain, the composer Tomás Luis de Victoria created unparalleled works of Renaissance vocal music. It is probably more useful to speak not of one Renaissance, but of many.

Furthermore, while this volume is composed of separate, individual biographies, readers will soon become aware of how truly "connected" these outstanding personalities were; between many of these figures there were few degrees of separation. In spite of the difficulties of travel, many of these people were surprisingly mobile: witness the Italian artist Giuseppe Arcimboldo's tenure at the court of Rudolf II's Habsburg court in Prague, Philip II of Spain's invitation to the Flemish Antonio Mor to serve as his court painter, or the French humanist Isaac Casaubon's move to England at the behest of the Archbishop of Canterbury. In the absence of actual travel, ideas and knowledge still spread with an amazing facility; in England, Anne Cook Bacon translated the sermons of Italian Calvinist preacher Bernardino Ochino, while John Florio became a leading Italian scholar though he may never have set foot in Italy. Cultural exchange and influence across borders was impressive, and the traffic did not simply flow in one direction.

This reference guide is meant to provide ready-reference introductions to the many fascinating men and women whose cultural contributions made the Renaissance such a remarkable phenomenon. This volume offers over 350 entries written by 72 scholars; individual entries range from 250 to 1,000 words in length and include bibliographic references for further reading. Cross-references to other subjects are indicated by an asterisk. An overview of particularly significant achievements and events is provided in the Chronology, and the Bibliography provides classified suggestions for further reading.

All of the entries in this volume were written by devoted and conscientious scholars. I thank all of the contributors for their superb scholarship, their good will, and, in most cases, their punctuality. I would especially like to thank Barbara Boyle, Michael Medwick, Rosemary Poole, Thomas Olsen, Karen Nelson, Connie Evans, Iain Maclean, Heather Murray, Patricia White, Debbie Barrett-Graves, and Catherine Pontoriero for their willingness to offer further assistance and support beyond their initial contributions.

I would also like to thank The College of New Jersey for research support; our excellent library staff and interlibrary loan department for their gracious help; and especially librarian Melissa Hofmann for her cheerful pursuit of often-elusive materials. For his technological expertise, sense of humor, and generosity, Douglas Skipper Carney will forever be a hero. Ron Fritze has been a kind and helpful series editor, and Cynthia Harris at Greenwood a most supportive general editor.

To my dear friend Carole Levin I owe gratitude that can never be sufficiently expressed; her generosity of spirit and intellect are overwhelming. Finally, I thank my husband, Sandy, and our children, Alex, Julie, and Annie, for their love and understanding, and, of course, their patience.

Chronology

1498–1500	Michelangelo, *Pietà*.
1501–4	Michelangelo, *David*.
1504	Jacopo Sannazaro, *Arcadia*.
1505	Pietro Bembo, *Gli Asolani*.
1509	Henry VIII becomes king of England.
	Desiderius Erasmus, *Praise of Folly*.
1509–11	Raphael, *The School of Athens* and *Disputa*.
1513	Leo X elected pope.
1515	François I becomes king of France.
1516	Charles V becomes king of Spain.
	Ludovico Ariosto, *Orlando furioso*.
	Sir Thomas More, *Utopia*.
1516–18	Titian, *Assumption of the Virgin*.
1517	Martin Luther posts his ninety-five theses on the door of the church in Wittenberg.
1519	Charles V becomes Holy Roman emperor.
1523	Margaret More Roper's translation of Erasmus's *Precatio dominica*.
	Juan Luis Vives, *On the Instruction of a Christian Woman*.
1525–26	William Tyndale, English New Testament.
1526	Albrecht Dürer, *Four Apostles*.
	Leo Africanus, *The History and Description of Africa*.
1528	Baldesar Castiglione, *The Courtier*.
1529	Albrecht Altdorfer, *Battle of the Issus*.
1530	Heinrich Agrippa von Nettesheim, *On the Vanity of the Arts and Sciences*.

1531	Sir Thomas Elyot, *The Boke Named the Governour*.
1532	Correggio, *Jupiter and Io*.
	Niccolò Machiavelli's *Prince* published posthumously.
1532–34	François Rabelais, *Gargantua and Pantagruel*.
1533	Hans Holbein, *The Ambassadors*.
1534	Pietro Aretino, *I ragionamenti*.
	Baccio Bandinelli, *Hercules and Cacus*.
1536	John Calvin, *Institutes of the Christian Religion*.
1538	Vittoria Colonna, *Rime spirituali*.
1543	Nicolaus Copernicus, *On the Revolutions of the Celestial Spheres*.
	Andreas Vesalius, *On the Structure of the Human Body*.
1543–44	Benvenuto Cellini, *Nymph of Fontainebleau*.
1544	Maurice Scève, *Délie*.
1545	Girolamo Cardano, *Ars magna*.
1548	Tintoretto, *Miraculous Rescue of a Christian Slave by St. Mark*.
	Titian, *Charles V on Horseback*.
1549	Thomas Cranmer, *Book of Common Prayer*.
	Joachim Du Bellay, *Defense and Illustration of the French Language*.
1550	Giorgio Vasari, *Lives of the Artists* (first edition).
1551 (c.)	Giovanni Della Casa, *Il Galateo*.
1552	Bartolomé de Las Casas, *Brief Account of the Destruction of the Indies*.
1554	Giovanni Palestrina dedicates his first book of masses to Pope Julius III.
1556	Charles V abdicates from the throne of Spain and the Holy Roman Empire.
1557	Martin Bucer's *De regno Christi* published posthumously.
1558	Elizabeth I becomes queen of England.
	John Knox, *The First Blast of the Trumpet against the Monstrous Regiment of Women*.
	Marguerite de Navarre's *Heptameron* published posthumously.
1558–59	Jorge de Montemayor, *Diana*.
1561	Gabriele Fallopio, *Anatomical Observations*.
	Thomas Hoby's translation of *The Courtier*, by Baldesar Castiglione.
c. 1562	St. Teresa of Ávila, *Book of Her Life*.
1563	John Foxe, *The Book of Martyrs*.
1566–68	Pieter Bruegel, *Peasant* series.
1570	Andrea Palladio, *Four Books on Architecture*.
1572	Luís Camões, *Os Lusíadas* (The Lusiads).
1573	Paolo Veronese, *Feast in the House of Levi*.

1575	Torquato Tasso, *Gerusalemme liberata.*
1576	Jean Bodin, *Six Books of the Republic.*
1578	Guillaume Du Bartas, *Première semaine ou la création du monde.*
	Pierre de Ronsard, *Sonnets for Hélène* and *Sonnets and Madrigals for Astrea.*
1579	Stephen Gosson, *The School of Abuse.*
1580	Michel de Montaigne, *Essais.*
1581	Torquato Tasso, *Gerusalemme liberata.*
1584	Reginald Scot, *Discovery of Witchcraft.*
1586	Dirck Coornhert, *Ethics, or the Art of Living Well.*
1586–88	El Greco, *Burial of Count Orgaz.*
1589	Richard Hakluyt, *The Principal Navigations, Voyages, and Discoveries of the English Nation.*
1590	José de Acosta, *Historia natural y moral de las Indias.*
	Christopher Marlowe's *Tamburlaine* plays published.
	Edmund Spenser, *Fairie Queene*, Books I–III.
1591	Sir Philip Sidney, *Astrophil and Stella.*
1594	Richard Hooker, *Laws of Ecclesiastical Polity*, Books I–V
1597	Matteo Alemán, *Guzmán de Alfarache.*
	Sir Francis Bacon, *Essays.*
1598	King James VI of Scotland, *Basilikon Doron.*
	John Stow, *Survey of London.*
1600	William Gilbert, *De magnete.*
1600–1608	William Shakespeare, *Hamlet, Othello, Macbeth, King Lear.*
1602	Tycho Brahe, *First Exercises in a Restored Astronomy.*
1605	Miguel de Cervantes, *Don Quixote*, part I.
1607	Francis Beaumont, *The Knight of the Burning Pestle.*
	Claudio Monteverdi, *Orfeo.*
1609–14	Peter Paul Rubens, *Raising of the Cross* and *Descent from the Cross.*
c. 1610	Caravaggio, *David with the Head of Goliath.*
1611	King James Authorized Version of the Bible.
	Aemilia Lanyer, *Salve Deus Rex Judaeorum.*
1613	Elizabeth Cary, *The Tragedy of Mariam.*
1613–14	John Webster, *The Duchess of Malfi.*
1615	William Camden, *Annals of English and Irish History in the Reign of Queen Elizabeth.*
1616	Ben Jonson, *Works.*
1618	Juan de la Cruz, St. John of the Cross, *Dark Night of the Soul.*
1620	Francis Bacon, *Novum organum.*

A

ABATE, NICCOLÒ DELL' (c. 1509/12–c. 1571)

Niccolò dell'Abate was one of several Italian artists who worked in France in the sixteenth century. Born in the Emilia region, he moved permanently to France and worked at court, primarily at Fontainebleau, where he became proficient at realizing in fresco the designs for large-scale mural decorations of his countryman, Francesco Primaticcio.*

Niccolò's earliest work is found in his native Modena. By 1530 he is documented in the regional capital, Bologna, executing independent commissions in fresco and in oil. Niccolò went to France in 1552 at the behest of Henri II, who, like his father, François I,* cultivated a taste for the Italian style. Primaticcio probably engineered the invitation to Niccolò because of his familiarity with illusionistic decorative painting in northern Italy, from that of Andrea Mantegna to more recent developments by Correggio.*

Niccolò undertook customary court assignments and, within Primaticcio's workshop, began fresco decoration for Fontainebleau in the Salle de Bal and the Galerie d'Ulysse. He settled in France with his family, his sons Giulio Camillo and Cristoforo becoming his apprentices. His association with Primaticcio and Fontainebleau continued throughout his life. Niccolò also worked on the triumphal entry to Paris in 1571 of Charles IX and Elisabeth of Austria and made drawings for retables executed in enamel by Léonard Limousin for the Sainte-Chapelle, Paris (now Paris, Louvre). He also executed decorations for several private Parisian hotels, including that of the Guise. Niccolò extended the influence of Italian style in France and, as a painter of domestic interiors—where he pioneered in the inclusion of landscape—helped invent an influential decorative style that became popular throughout Europe.

Bibliography

S. Béguin, "Emilia and Fontainebleau: Aspects of a Dialogue," In *The Age of Correggio and the Carracci: Emilian Painting of the Sixteenth and Seventeenth Centuries,* 1986.

E. Brugerolles and D. Guillet, *The Renaissance in France: Drawings from the Ecole des Beaux-Arts, Paris*, 1995.

Sheila ffolliott

ACOSTA, JOSÉ DE (c. 1540–1600)

José de Acosta, a Spanish Jesuit historian, wrote the earliest European study on Mexico and western South America, *Historia natural y moral de las Indias* (Natural and Moral History of the Indies, 1590). In *De procuranda Indorum salute* (1576), Acosta was one of the first Europeans to write at length about European missionary activity in the Americas.

José de Acosta worked as a preacher, teacher, and leader of the Jesuits in Peru for fourteen years. When Acosta arrived in Lima in 1572, he immediately addressed the problem of converting the native population to Christianity. He learned the native language, Quechua, in Cuzco and examined firsthand the situation of the Indians. In *De procuranda Indorum salute* Acosta argued that the native peoples were capable of being evangelized. He wrote the first book to be published in Peru, a catechism written in local native languages (1584). While he believed that Spain fulfilled the will of divine providence in its conquest of the Americas, he complained to the king about colonial policies that burdened the native population.

Acosta sought to educate Europeans about the native peoples of the Americas and their natural surroundings in his *Historia natural*. Acosta described the geography, the climate, and the plant and animal life of Mexico and Peru. He depicted the culture of the indigenous peoples: their economic, educational, political, and religious beliefs and institutions. He asserted that the native peoples had reached a high level of cultural development that could be perfected by the introduction of Christianity.

Acosta's depiction of the native peoples evinces a mixture of forward-thinking notions about universal human dignity with condescending Eurocentric attitudes. He argued for universal human equality while also characterizing native peoples as childish, barbaric, and unintelligent. His *Historia natural* was widely read by educated Spaniards and was translated into other European languages. Through *De procuranda Indorum salute* and *Historia natural* Acosta contributed in a fundamental way to the formation of European attitudes toward native Americans as Europe sought to incorporate them and their lands into its orbit of influence in the sixteenth and seventeenth centuries.

Bibliography

E. O'Gorman, *Cuatro historiadores de Indias*, 1989.

Evelyn Toft

AERTSEN, PIETER (1519–1573)

Pieter Aertsen, nicknamed "Langhen Pier" because of his height, was best known for introducing still-life and genre scenes as subjects worthy of painting.

Karel van Mander, the first northern European art historian, provides much of what we know about Aertsen.

Aertsen was born in Amsterdam and trained with Alart Claessen before moving to Antwerp, where he married and entered the painters' guild in 1533. Before 1557 Aertsen returned to Amsterdam, where he remained for the rest of his life. Although Aertsen received many important commissions to paint religious altarpieces—the major livelihood for artists of his time—iconoclasts, objecting to depictions of sacred subjects, destroyed many of his explicitly religious works in a massive uprising in 1566. Aertsen is best known for his kitchen scenes, such as butcher stalls or fruit and vegetable vendors, with large robust figures and realistic depictions of foodstuffs in vibrant natural colors, a subject that anticipates two significant categories of Dutch painting a generation later: still life and genre, or scenes of everyday life.

On first view, Aertsen's unusual paintings appeal for the artist's treatment of new, realistic subject matter, but a closer look reveals that in some, Aertsen retains an interest in traditional religious narrative. Many of his genre and still-life paintings contain biblical subjects in the background, while more prosaic images of fruit, vegetables, or meat loom prominently in the foreground. In one such still life, a scene of Christ in the house of Martha and Mary appears in the background, and in his 1551 *Butcher's Stall*, fresh beef flesh hanging in the foreground of a butcher's stall overshadows the religious subject of the *Rest on the Flight into Egypt*.

Aertsen, like his more famous countryman Pieter Bruegel,* also captured colorful, lively scenes of peasant life in paintings such as *The Country Feast* (1551), *The Egg Dance* (1552), and *Country Gathering* (1557). Although free-spirited and even erotic in tone, these paintings were probably moralizing admonitions against loose behavior. Aertsen contributed a unique style of painting for his generation, combining brilliant color with monumentality in describing simple, humble people and the goods of daily life with immediacy and dignity.

Bibliography

K.P.F. Moxley, *Pieter Aertsen, Joachim Beuckelaer, and the Rise of Secular Painting in the Context of the Reformation*, 1977.

Susan H. Jenson

AGRICOLA, GEORG (1494–1555)

Georg Agricola, a German humanist and classicist, was best known for his contributions to earth sciences. This friend of Desiderius Erasmus* advanced contemporary knowledge of mining, metallurgy, and geology, in part by reclaiming some lost knowledge of classical authors, but more importantly by relying upon observation and experimentation and rejecting the erroneous theories of ancient authorities, thereby earning the title "the father of mineralogy."

Born in Saxony, Agricola attended various schools before entering the University of Leipzig, where he studied classics and philosophy. He taught classics briefly and published a short treatise on humanistic pedagogy before returning to the university to study medicine. However, due to theological disputes at Leipzig, the Catholic Agricola moved to Italy in 1523 to study medicine, natural science, and philosophy at Bologna, Padua, and Venice. He worked for three years helping to edit the works of Galen and Hippocrates, while also developing interests in politics and economics.

He returned to Germany and worked as a physician and apothecary in the busiest mining district of central Europe, where he sought to discover new medicinal uses for ores and minerals. Here he began writing about various aspects of mining and metallurgy, ranging from the occupational hazards of mining and smelting to the equipment, practices, and labor conditions prevalent in the region. He even wrote about the care of animals used in mining. With the aid of a letter of recommendation from Erasmus, Agricola became an established author, writing on subjects from politics to natural science. Furthermore, thanks to his knowledge of minerals and geology, he grew wealthy from his shares in mining operations, and his prosperity afforded him the opportunity to write extensively on the principles of geology and mineralogy. Aside from one speech in favor of German religious and political unity against the Turks, Agricola maintained a relatively low political profile during the religious wars of the period, though he did serve as one of the few Catholic representatives to the Protestant court of the duke of Saxony.

His contributions include *De re metallica* (On Metallurgy, 1556), which ranges from ancient history of mining, sociology and labor relations, surveying, engineering, smelting, and even glass making to what we would now call metallurgy and geology. His most scientific contributions occur in *De natura fossilium* (On the Nature of Minerals, 1546), in which Agricola classifies minerals according to their physical form, as chemistry had not yet advanced to a point that would allow for chemical classification of minerals. He may have been the first to differentiate between elements and compounds and is credited with having been one of the first to apply the experimental approach to the natural sciences. Also, he helped to undermine the previously unquestioned authority of the ancient writers on earth science by regularly debunking their claims about minerals that clashed with his own careful observations.

Bibliography

O. Hannaway, "Georgius Agricolus as Humanist," *Journal of the History of Ideas* 53 (1992): 553–60.

Tim McGee

AGRICOLA, JOHANN (1494–1566)

Johann Agricola was an influential German Reformer who broke with Martin Luther* over antinomianism, the issue of whether Christians were held to obey the Mosaic Law. Agricola went to school in Braunschweig and began his university career in Wittenberg in 1515–16. He soon established a close association with Martin Luther. Luther persuaded Agricola to change his course of study from medicine to theology, and he subsequently received a bachelor's degree in that subject in 1519. Agricola was a secretary at the famous Leipzig Debate of 1519 between Luther and the scholar Johann Eck; he also participated with Luther in the famous burning of the papal bull the following year.

In 1525 he became head of a new grammar school at Eisleben and a preacher at the Church of St. Nicholai. He was appointed the preacher of electoral Saxony's delegation at the Diets of Speyer (1525, 1526) and Augsburg (1530). At Eisleben Agricola began to assert his antinomianism. He condemned the Ten Commandments as an unnecessary carryover from the Old Testament and too similar to the Catholic doctrine of good works. In 1527 he attacked Luther's colleague Philip Melanchthon* for the inclusion of the Decalogue in Reformed theology. When Agricola returned to Wittenberg in 1536, the controversy raged violently. Luther responded against him with five disputations and a treatise, *Against the Antinomians*. Under persecution for his attacks on Luther's position, in 1540 Agricola went to Berlin, where he retracted his views. In the same year he was made court preacher by the Protestant prince Joachim II of Brandenburg. Luther, however, remained adamant in his rejection of his former disciple.

In 1548, following Emperor Charles V's* victory over the Protestants, Agricola was selected to help draft a provisional religious settlement between Protestants and Catholics, the Augsburg Interim. His role damaged his reputation among Lutherans, although Agricola himself thought that he had helped the Lutheran cause.

Agricola wrote several theological works, including biblical commentaries and a catechism. He published a small collection of German proverbs that were illustrated with a commentary. Agricola was also a skilled theologian; his career provides fitting evidence to the controversies within Reformed circles during the first generation of the Reformation.

Bibliography

G. R. Elton, *Reformation Europe, 1517–1559*, 1963.
G. Kawerau, *Johann Agricola von Eisleben: Ein Beitrag zur Reformationsgeschichte*, 1881, rpt., 1977.

Andrew G. Traver

AGRICOLA, MICHAEL (1508–1557)

Michael Agricola was a reformist bishop who helped introduce Lutheran worship to the vernacular culture of Finland. Born on the southern coast of Finland, Agricola attended school in Viipuri (Viborg). He arrived in Turku (Åbo) in 1528 and became secretary to Bishop Martin Skytte (1528–50), a pious Catholic reformist. Bishop Skytte did not oppose the evangelical piety of the Reformers; rather, he fostered it and throughout the 1530s sent talented young students to Wittenberg for study. This decision had lasting implications for the Reformation in Finland.

Due to Skytte, Agricola left for Wittenberg in 1536 and remained there for three years. He heard Martin Luther* lecture on Genesis and Philip Melanchthon* on the Greek classics. In 1539 he received the master's degree and returned to Finland. He then accepted a position as headmaster of a Latin school in Turku, the most respected in Finland. Nine years later he became an assistant to Skytte. After Skytte's death, Agricola succeeded to his position. When war broke out between Russia and Sweden in 1555, Agricola became increasingly involved in the diplomatic negotiations between the two countries. He died in 1557 while returning from Moscow on a peace mission.

Through his extensive writings, Agricola laid the foundation of Finnish orthography. He is known as the father of Finnish literature. His first printed book was an alphabet that included a translation of Luther's *Small Catechism*. He published a biblical prayer book in 1544 that consisted of a short calendar and a collection of prayers from the Bible, Luther, Erasmus,* and Catholic mystics such as Thomas à Kempis. As early as his time at Wittenberg, Agricola had worked on a Finnish translation of the New Testament; it was published in 1548. He also translated Psalms into Finnish and produced church manuals and missals in the vernacular.

Although Agricola was a Reformer, he proceeded cautiously. He accepted various forms of religious life and doctrine and remains a prime representative of the tolerant attitude in Finnish religious thinking in the early Reformation period. As a Reformer, Agricola laid the foundation for the national development and independence of the Finnish church, even though the country would remain a part of Sweden until the nineteenth century.

Bibliography

O. Grell, ed., *The Scandinavian Reformation*, 1995.

Andrew G. Traver

AGRIPPA VON NETTESHEIM, HEINRICH CORNELIUS (1486–1535)

Heinrich Cornelius Agrippa von Nettesheim, a Neoplatonist with a penchant for mysticism, excelled in such wide-ranging professions as university professor, soldier, physician, lawyer, astrologer, and occult philosopher. His many enemies, however, marred the successes of his tumultuous career by maligning him as a magician and a heretic.

Born in Cologne, Agrippa matriculated from the city's university in 1499 and began his career as a professor of philosophy and theology at the University of Dole in 1509. Agrippa's public lectures on Johannes Reuchlin's *De verbo mirifico* earned him a doctorate of theology, but they also attracted the attention of Burgundy's Franciscan provincial superior, who accused Agrippa of heresy. Agrippa left Dole and traveled to London before serving Emperor Maximilian I as both a minor secretary and a soldier during the French-Italian wars from

1511 to 1518. Amid military engagements, Agrippa continued his occult studies and taught theology courses at the Universities of Pavia and Turin.

Agrippa subsequently accepted a position as ambassador and legal advisor for the city of Metz. While there, he became a close friend of Father Deodatus and visited his Celestine monastery regularly to give lectures and discuss theology. Bitter conflict, however, characterized Agrippa's relationship with the city's Dominican leaders, who decried his enthusiastic support for Jacques Lefèvre's* *De una ex tribus Maria* and his successful defense of a woman dubiously accused of witchcraft.

Agrippa left Metz in 1520 and served as physician to Louise of Savoy from 1524 to 1527, when disputes with his employer forced him to become Margaret of Austria's advisor and historiographer. While in Antwerp, he obtained an imperial privilege to publish several of his works, including his most famous, *De incertitudine et vanitate scientiarum* (On the Vanity of the Arts and Sciences, 1530). Doubting the book's orthodoxy, Princess Margaret sent it for review to the theology faculty at Louvain, which charged Agrippa with heresy.

Unemployed and in debt, Agrippa returned to Cologne in 1531 in order to publish *De occulta philosophia* (Occult Philosophy). The efforts of Cologne's inquisitor and Faculty of Theology to prevent its publication enraged Agrippa, and he accused both of denouncing the ideas of reformers like himself, Reuchlin, and Desiderius Erasmus* before undertaking a proper preliminary investigation. In order to escape creditors, Agrippa moved his family to Bonn, where he published his remaining works, including a commentary on Ramon Lull's *Ars brevis* (1533) and a volume entitled *Collected Orations* (1535). After a brief period of imprisonment, Agrippa moved to Grenoble, where he died in 1535.

Agrippa's conviction that God manifests himself in the created world explains his enthusiastic inquiry into the fields of alchemy, astrology, medicine, and geology. His research contributions in these areas include a clinical description of the plague, the development of medicines, a report on firearms and war engines, and a work on mining and minerals. Agrippa's desire to bring humanity closer to God also explains his career-long interest in religious matters ranging from the essence of faith to church politics. Agrippa, who radically opposed Scholastic theology, championed a new, humanistic theology that would ascertain the true meaning of God's word through a comparison of similar biblical texts, an analysis of Hermetic writings, and the commentaries of church-sanctioned authorities.

Bibliography

C. Nauert, Jr., *Agrippa and the Crisis of Renaissance Thought*, 1965.

Whitney Leeson

ALBRET, JEANNE D' (1528–1572)

Queen of Navarre and mother of France's monarch Henri IV, Jeanne d'Albret was a champion of Calvinism in both France and Navarre. The only surviving child of Henri d'Albret and Marguerite de Navarre,* Jeanne d'Albret was born on 16 November 1528. Throughout her early life, Jeanne remained a pawn in the political struggles between her father and her uncle, François I,* the king of France, concerning Henri's desire to reestablish Navarre as a separate country. After much political wrangling and one dissolved marriage to the duke of Cleves, in 1548 Jeanne married Antoine de Bourbon, duc de Vendôme, heir to the French throne in the event that the king had no sons. The couple had only two children who survived infancy, Henri and Catherine.

Upon her father's death in 1555, Jeanne became queen of Navarre, and through her insistence, Antoine was made king. The two of them continued Henri's attempts to establish Navarre as a separate country, but gradually Jeanne became committed to a new cause, Calvinism, to which she converted openly in 1560. Her mother, Marguerite, although Catholic, had been known for her beliefs in reform and for her protection of Protestant leaders. Jeanne was to eclipse her mother's role and become one of the leaders of the Calvinist movement in France and Navarre.

Her influence as one of the highest-ranked Calvinists in France inspired many to convert to the new religion, and Jeanne aspired to make Navarre a Protestant country. Her decision led her into great difficulties with Catholic France and Spain, and when Pope Pius IV excommunicated Jeanne in 1563, only the objections of Catherine de' Medici,* queen mother of France, who protested that the pope was transgressing on French sovereignty, protected her. In exchange for that aid, Jeanne was forced to make concessions that curtailed her personal and national independence.

When civil wars broke out in France between the Catholics and Protestants, Jeanne originally remained neutral. However, as pressure mounted on her sovereignty, she became one of the leaders of the third civil war, serving as both propagandist and military leader. Upon the war's ending, conditional on the marriage negotiations between Jeanne's son Henri and Marguerite de Valois,* the king's sister, Jeanne acted as a diplomat, working out the tortuous details of the peace and a marriage she opposed. The incredible strain of the negotiations weakened Jeanne, and she fell prey to one of the bouts of tuberculosis that had plagued her throughout her life; she died on 9 June 1572. Although rumors surfaced that Catherine de' Medici had her poisoned, the idea was almost universally discredited. Her death was a great loss to the Protestant cause, and years later, in order to assume the French throne, her son Henri converted to Catholicism.

Bibliography

N. L. Roelker, *Queen of Navarre: Jeanne d'Albret, 1528–1572*, 1968.

Erin Sadlack

ALEMÁN, MATEO (1547–c. 1615)

Mateo Alemán was one of the great novelists of the Spanish Golden Age, primarily known for his picaresque novel *Guzmán de Alfarache* (1597) and for the biography *San Antonio de Padua* (1604). Alemán was the son of a doctor assigned to the royal prison at Seville. He graduated from the University of Maese Rodrigo in Seville in 1564 and reentered the university to study medicine, although his studies were discontinued after the death of his father. With the assistance of two loans, Alemán began a career in business. The terms of the loans stipulated repayment within one year; in addition, one loan included the requirement of marriage to Catalina de Espinosa, with whom he was involved. Neither loan was repaid within one year, and although Alemán avoided marriage with de Espinosa for a time, he was eventually forced to honor the agreement rather than subject himself to a prison term. Alemán did not live with his wife for long, but they remained business partners for thirty years.

Alemán returned to the University of Maese Rodrigo in 1580 to study law. It is believed that his studies were for the purpose of learning how to circumvent the law rather than practice it. Alemán did not complete the school term and was imprisoned for his debts. After his release from prison, Aleman attempted to emigrate to Mexico but was denied permission because he was unable to prove that he was not of Jewish descent. In 1583 Alemán took a temporary position as a judge. His primary duty was to collect debts owed by deceased court employees. Alemán was imprisoned again when it was learned that his means of recovering these funds from the employees' families were illegal and immoral. In 1593 Alemán was appointed judge for a second time and investigated the abhorrent working conditions to which slaves were subjected in the quicksilver mines.

Alemán's picaresque novel *Guzmán de Alfarache* is a satirical and pessimistic commentary on Spanish life and society, filled with historical and literary allusions. Although the novel was completed in 1597, it was not actually in print for another year. *San Antonio de Padua* was written several years after Alemán narrowly escaped death when he was struck in the head by a burning cannon plug. Alemán was not injured, but he is said to have invoked the name of St. Anthony at the time of the incident. He wrote the biography as a means of expressing his gratitude to the saint for his protection.

In 1608 Alemán was permitted to emigrate to Mexico with his mistress and several of his children, where he received the protection and patronage of Archbishop García Guerra. Alemán's last known work, *Suceso de F. Frai García Gera* (1613), was written as a tribute to the clergyman.

Bibliography

D. McGrady, *Mateo Alemán*, 1968.

Barbara Boyle

ALTDORFER, ALBRECHT (c. 1480–1538)

Albrecht Altdorfer, one of the first true landscape painters, was born in or near Regensburg in Bavaria, where he spent most of his life, and where he was a leading member of the Danube school of painting. A man of property, he was active in civic affairs, for several years serving both as city architect and as a member of the Regensburg city council. Altdorfer was a councillor when Regensburg adopted Lutheranism in 1533. But Regensburg had earlier demonstrated other sympathies. After expelling the Jews in 1519, the city demolished their synagogue and in its place erected a shrine to the Madonna, selling images—some of which were made by Altdorfer himself—and encouraging pilgrimages. Martin Luther* criticized the city, writing that this shrine and several others must be leveled. Albrecht Dürer* also commented in 1523 that a "specter against Holy Scripture" had arisen at Regensburg.

Altdorfer's small painting of *The Danube near Regensburg* (c. 1530) is often cited as the first true landscape painting, but his work also reflects popular interest in the customs and way of life of the ancient Germanic inhabitants, ideas based on the *Germania* of Tacitus. Altdorfer included exotic architecture along with natural forms in several paintings; because he was city architect of Regensburg, this is perhaps not surprising. Probably his best-known painting is *Battle of the Issus* of 1529, depicting the battle in 333 B.C. between Alexander the Great and Darius of Persia, which can also be read as a political commentary on an event in Altdorfer's own time, the defeat of the Turks at Vienna in 1529. Altdorfer's contribution to painting was innovative and long-lived, for he helped establish a school of romantic landscape painting that would influence European artists for generations, particularly the Dutch, German, and British landscape painters of the seventeenth through the nineteenth centuries.

Bibliography

S. Schama, *Landscape and Memory*, 1995.
C. Wood, *Albrecht Altdorfer and the Origins of Landscape*, 1993.

Rosemary Poole

AMYOT, JACQUES (1513–1593)

Jacques Amyot was a French humanist, bishop, and scholar famous for his translation of classical texts, most notably Plutarch's *Lives*, or *Les vies des hommes illustres*. Amyot was born of humble parentage in Melun, France, and was educated at the University of Paris and at Bourges. An excellent scholar, he studied Greek with the humanists Danes and Toussain. Marguerite de Navarre* assisted him in becoming a professor of Latin and Greek at Bourges, where he taught for about six years.

Amyot first came to the attention of François I* when he translated Heliodorus's *Aethiopica* in 1547. As a reward for his accomplishment, Amyot was given the abbey of Bellozane and was commissioned to complete his translation of Plutarch's *Lives*, which he did in 1559. While Amyot was in Italy, where he studied for the next four years at the libraries of St. Mark and the Vatican, he rediscovered and later translated lost books of Diodorus Siculus. Amyot is also known for playing a small role in the Council of Trent, an ecumenical council convened from 1545 to 1563 with the purpose of reforming the Catholic church.

Upon his return to France, Amyot was appointed tutor in 1554 to the sons of Henri II, later Charles IX and Henri III. Upon his ascension in 1560, one of Charles IX's first acts as king was to confer upon Amyot the position of grand almoner, a high dignitary of the church responsible for the clergy attached to the court and for supervising charitable works. Amyot became bishop of Auxerre in 1570, where he remained until his death in 1593. Under the reign of Henri III, Amyot was appointed commander of the Order of the Holy Spirit, an honor usually reserved for members of the nobility. These positions offered Amyot the opportunity to devote himself to classical literature. Through his translations, Amyot made the words of the ancients remarkably accessible to his contemporaries. Also regarded as an elegant stylist, Amyot is equally recognized for increasing the versatility of the French language.

Amyot's *Lives* was subsequently translated into English by Sir Thomas North in 1579 and became the source for the Roman plays of William Shakespeare.* The *Lives* had an immense influence upon French literature as well; this work was a source for the tragedies of Pierre Corneille and was quoted by Montaigne* in his *Essais*. In addition to the *Lives*, Amyot also translated *The Seven Books* of Diodorus Siculus (1554), *Daphnis and Chloe* of Longus (1559), and the *Moralia* of Plutarch (1572).

Bibliography

A. Tilley, *The Literature of the French Renaissance*, vol. 1, 1959.

Heather J. Murray

ANDREA DEL SARTO (1486–1530)

Born Andrea d'Agnolo, Andrea del Sarto was the most successful painter in Florence in the second and third decades of the sixteenth century; his art exemplifies the High Renaissance style and led the way into the development of Mannerism. Born in Florence, Andrea trained with Piero di Cosimo and established himself as an independent artist in 1508. Although his teacher worked in an early Renaissance style, Andrea's exposure to the art of Leonardo da Vinci, Michelangelo,* and Raphael* in the early years of the sixteenth century led him to become a leading proponent of High Renaissance painting by 1510. He primarily produced religious works, both frescoes and panels, although he achieved some success as a portraitist as well; more than fifty paintings plus numerous drawings survive from his short career.

His earliest important commission was for a series of frescoes in the Church of the Scalzi in Florence; the first of these was painted perhaps as early as 1507, and he continued to work intermittently on the cycle until 1526. In 1510 Andrea was paid for five frescoes of the life of St. Filippo Benizi in the atrium of Santissima Annunziata in Florence. In both cycles we can see the remnants of an early Renaissance approach in the use of detailed landscapes and lively figures, but Andrea also explored the High Renaissance formula of idealized naturalism: figures' anatomies were well understood; space was clearly indicated;

and compositions were balanced and grand. At the same time, he imparted to the formula his own particular touch of intimacy and gentleness.

By the second decade of the century High Renaissance classicism was beginning to seem dated, and Andrea started to add a more expressive element to his art. A series of panel paintings produced between 1512 and 1518, including his most famous altarpiece, *Madonna of the Harpies* (Florence, Uffizi, 1517), showed him exploring more vivid colors, less predictable compositions, and more complicated figural poses.

Andrea was invited to Paris in 1518, where François I* established him as court painter. Upon his return to Florence a year later, he embarked on a new phase in his work, abandoning a naturalistic approach for a more calculated and artificial style that would lead into the elegant forms of Mannerism. The paintings of the 1520s are monumental compositions, the figures are heroic and graceful, forms are sculptural and expressive, and there is a marked use of chiaroscuro.

Andrea del Sarto's career bridged the gap from the early Renaissance tradition through the High Renaissance to Mannerism. While he was not one of the greatest innovators of the early sixteenth century, his notable skills, exquisite sensitivity, and depth of feeling led him to produce an art that served as a model for many later artists.

Bibliography

J. Shearman, *Andrea del Sarto*, 2 vols., 1965.

Jane C. Long

ANDREWES, LANCELOT (1555–1626)

Lancelot Andrewes was a renowned English prelate, preacher, and theologian who shared Archbishop William Laud's Arminianism. Born in London in 1555 to Thomas and Joan Andrewes, he attended the Cooper's Free School, Merchant Taylors' School, and Pembroke Hall, Cambridge, obtaining the B.A. (1575), M.A. (1578), an appointment as catechist (1578), ordination as deacon (1580), B.D. (1585), D.D. (c. 1588), and mastership (1589–1605), plus an M.A. (1581) from Jesus College, Oxford. After serving as chaplain to the earl of Huntingdon, president of the Council of the North, he obtained the living at St. Giles, Cripplegate, London, and prebends at St. Paul's and Southwell in 1589, thanks to Sir Francis Walsingham. He was chaplain to Queen Elizabeth* and Archbishop John Whitgift and received a prebend (1597) and deanery (1601) at Westminster Abbey, but rejected the bishoprics of Salisbury (1596) and Ely (1599), being unwilling to alienate their revenues. However, he served James I* as bishop of Chichester (1605–9), Ely (1609–19), and Winchester (1619–26); lord almoner (1605–19); dean of the Chapel Royal (1619–26); at the Hampton Court Conference (1604); with the Authorized Version of the Bible (1607–11); and as a privy councillor. He died on 26 September 1626.

Andrewes was a good administrator, generous benefactor, and opponent of corruption, but avoided politics. A linguist (Latin, Greek, Hebrew, and fifteen modern languages), learned in patristic literature, and a brilliant preacher, Andrewes (like Richard Hooker*) defended the via media, rejecting both transubstantiation and predestination. He incurred Puritan ire for favoring "high-church" worship and the Arminian belief in free will. His writings are voluminous, though few appeared during his lifetime. Most famous are *Tortura torti* (1609), a reply to Cardinal Robert Bellarmine's attack on the oath of allegiance instituted after the Gunpowder Plot, and *Preces privatae* (A Manual for Private Devotions), posthumously published prayers.

Bibliography

K. Fincham, *Prelate as Pastor: The Episcopate of James I*, 1990.
N. Lossky, *Lancelot Andrewes the Preacher (1555–1626): The Origins of the Mystical Theology of the Church of England*, trans. Andrew Louth, 1991.

William B. Robison

ANGHIERA, PIETRO MARTIRE D' (PETER MARTYR D'ANGHERA) (1457–1526)

An Italian humanist, author, and member of the Spanish Council of the Indies, Peter Martyr was among the first Europeans to publicly contemplate the consequences of a "New World"; he might even be credited with inventing the whole concept. The reactions generated by Columbus's 1492 voyage, in turn, provoked greater interest in "discovery" among the chattering classes of late-fifteenth- and early-sixteenth-century western Europe. Martyr, the author of *De orbe novo*, a series of newsletters circulated in manuscript to prominent churchmen, including the pope, after 1494 and published posthumously in several languages, set the tone of the discussion in Renaissance and pro-Spanish terms.

Martyr was a native of Milan, but Queen Isabella attracted him to the resurgent Spanish court to tutor young aristocrats, and it was there that the educator first received the news of Columbus's first voyage. While Columbus clung to his belief that he had arrived at the outskirts of the Indies, Martyr quickly realized that the admiral had stumbled upon lands and peoples hitherto unknown in Europe.

The enormity of "discovery" could only be comprehended, even by the intelligentsia, in familiar terms. Martyr's reports try to make sense of American Indians with biblical and classical references. His "savages," some of them part human, lived in an idyll but with little semblance of European law or sense of decency; scarcely clad, they were full of sexual desire and even stooped to cannibalism. Notwithstanding its "strange" denizens, the "New World" also offered the chance to recheck some of the claims made by antiquity. Martyr's accounts continually stressed the possible American locations of ancient legends, such as the Fountain of Youth that intrepid explorers might seize.

America and its inhabitants never ceased to fascinate, and Martyr's house became a nerve center for information on the newfound territories where government officials, aristocrats, churchmen, seafarers, cartographers, diplomats—anyone interested in the expansion of Spanish interests in the Western Hemisphere—could meet and discuss the "discoveries." Martyr himself accepted a policy role when he joined the Council of the Indies, and he was appointed bishop of Jamaica, in recognition of his promotion of America, in 1499.

The intellectual excitement generated notions of finding fabulous cities of gold and the mass conversion or overthrow of pagan kingdoms that also were in accord with the current of *conquistador* thinking in *reconquista* Spain. In 1513 Juan Ponce de León tramped through Florida in his fruitless quest for the source of eternal youth. But eight years later Hernán Cortés, espousing God, gold, and glory, completed his remarkable conquest of Mexico. The defeat of the Aztecs and the Spanish acquisition of the wealth of Central America suddenly made the realization of Martyr's American dreams of conversion and conquest feasible.

Bibliography

P. Martyr d'Anghera, *The Decades of the Newe Worlde on West India*, 1966.

Louis Roper

ANGUISSOLA, SOFONISBA (1532/35–1625)

Sofonisba Anguissola, the daughter of a provincial nobleman in Cremona, achieved fame throughout Europe for her portrait paintings. Sofonisba's original use of genrelike scenes in her drawings and paintings received international acclaim, as much for their beauty as for their invention.

Amilcare Anguissola, a provincial nobleman, provided his eldest daughter, Sofonisba, along with her five talented sisters—Elena, Lucia, Europa, Anna Maria, and Minerva—with training in humanist studies, such as Latin, music, and painting. Amilcare further arranged to provide Sofonisba and her sister Elena with professional painting lessons. Both Sofonisba and Elena studied under the local Mannerist painter Bernardino Campi for approximately three years (1546–49). After Campi moved to Milan in 1549, Sofonisba, who showed significant promise, continued her artistic training with the Mannerist painter Bernardino Gatti.

In the history of female portrait painters, Sofonisba, a gifted artist, inspired other Renaissance women, such as Irene di Spilimbergo (1541–1559) and Lavinia Fontana* (1552–1614) to emulate her accomplishments. During a long career that spanned approximately seven decades, Sofonisba earned the praise of the art critic Giorgio Vasari,* the encouragement and advice of the Renaissance sculptor and architect Michelangelo Buonarroti,* and the patronage of Philip II,* the king of Spain. During her stay at Philip's court, Pope Pius IV asked for and received from Sofonisba a portrait of Queen Isabella of Valois, such was Sofonisba's fame as a portrait artist. In 1624 Anthony Van Dyck visited Sofonisba in Palermo, where she had retired with her second husband, Orazio Lomellino, after living in Genoa for some years. The esteem Van Dyck had for

Sofonisba is evident. He included in his *Italian Sketchbook* both a sketch of Sofonisba and a written entry.

Of Sofonisba's considerable oeuvre, approximately fifty paintings that can be securely attributed to her have survived. Unfortunately, a number of the paintings she is thought to have produced at the Spanish court remain either unsigned or undocumented, making attribution difficult. Other works executed during Sofonisba's residence at the Spanish court were destroyed in a seventeenth-century fire.

Sofonisba's position as Queen Isabella's court painter does, however, provide an important link. Her presence at the Spanish court for approximately ten or more years probably assisted in disseminating the artistic trends of northern Italy into Spain. One of the first Italian artists to specialize in portrait paintings, Sofonisba transformed the limitations imposed upon her as a woman into an opportunity. With each painting, she strove to explore the personality of her subject fully. Particularly noteworthy is the number of self-portraits that Sofonisba painted throughout her long career. Her output rivals that of other major artists, such as Albrecht Dürer* and Rembrandt van Rijn, who are similarly noted for their numerous self-portrait studies.

A sketch Sofonisba drew in response to a suggestion from Michelangelo attained universal acclaim. Sofonisba's sketch of her brother Asdrubale being bitten by a crab circulated for nearly half a century before going on to provide inspiration for Caravaggio's* oil painting entitled *Boy Being Bitten by a Lizard*.

Bibliography

S. Ferino-Pagden and M. Kusche, *Sofonisba Anguissola: A Renaissance Woman*, 1995.
I. S. Perlingieri, *Sofonisba Anguissola: The First Great Woman Artist of the Renaissance*, 1992.

Debbie Barrett-Graves

ARAGONA, TULLIA D' (1510–1556)

Tullia d'Aragona wrote poetry as well as a popular treatise on human love; she was also a well-known courtesan and controversial acquaintance of many of Italy's prominent literary figures. Tullia was born in Rome around 1510, the illegitimate daughter of Giulia Campana, herself a courtesan. According to Campana, Tullia's father was a prominent cardinal of Aragona. Like her mother, Tullia was well trained in the musical skills that were paramount among the attractions of the *cortegiane oneste*, or higher-class courtesans. Her accomplishments suggest that she received a fine education; numerous contemporaries praised her eloquence and intellect.

Tullia's life was marked by mobility, perhaps due to greater government restrictions on courtesans; she and her mother lived in Rome, Siena, Venice, Ferrara, and Florence. Tullia counted many aristocrats and men of letters among her acquaintances, though not all of them were her admirers: she was denounced by satirists Pietro Aretino* and Agnolo Firenzuola.* She was praised, however, by the humanist Sperone Speroni,* in whose *Dialogo di amore* (Dialogue on Love) she appears as a principal interlocutor; she also met the poet Vittoria Colonna* after a church sermon by the Capuchin preacher Bernardino Ochino.* One of the most important relationships of her life was with the author Girolamo Muzio, her friend and lover; he dedicated several works to her and assisted Tullia in publishing her own writing. In 1543 she married one Silvestro Guicciardini, apparently as a formality to protect her from the accusations leveled against women of her profession. She also became close friends with the Florentine author Benedetto Varchi, with whom she formed a literary academy. When Tullia was denounced as a courtesan, she escaped the usual punishment of wearing a yellow veil in public because Varchi defended her as an established poet.

Perhaps to prove her status as a writer, Tullia published an anthology of 130 poems in 1547, dedicated to Eleanora of Toledo,* wife of Duke Cosimo de' Medici.* Along with Tullia's own poems, this popular edition included works by her admirers and acquaintances. With her treatise *Dialogo della infinità d'amore* (Dialogue on the Infinity of Love), which also appeared in 1547, Tullia added a woman's voice to the current debate on the subject of human love, arguing for the importance of the physical as well as the spiritual aspects of love. She also wrote a 30,000-line poem in octaves about a chivalrous adventurer. Tullia's fortunes were less prosperous in her final years; she died in 1556 in Rome.

Bibliography

T. d'Aragona, *Dialogue on the Infinity of Love*, eds. R. Russell and B. Merry, 1997.

Jo Eldridge Carney

ARCADELT, JACQUES (c. 1505–1568)

A composer and singer known primarily for his Italian madrigals, Jacques Arcadelt was probably born in France, and French was probably his native language. His music first appears shortly after 1530. He was in Florence at the court of Alessandro de' Medici for much of that decade, but came to Rome by 1539. He joined the papal chapel, the Cappella Sistina, in 1540 and left in 1551 for France. He was the single most prolific composer in the chapel during his tenure. Arcadelt served Charles of Lorraine (later archbishop of Rheims) as early as 1544 until 1562 and also perhaps served the French king as well. He died in retirement in Paris. Among the offices he held at his death were canonries at St. Germain l'Auxerrois, Notre Dame in Paris, and Rheims.

The publication of his first book of madrigals in 1538 is most important, for it marks the beginnings of true commercialism in music. Beginning with Gardano in Venice, most major Italian music printers reproduced this collection for over one hundred years. At first the madrigals were for the entertainment of the middle and upper classes, but later they came to be used for pedagogy. Their light, engaging style is largely responsible for their popularity. His French chansons employed the same style. Arcadelt's output, besides the countless number of madrigals, includes over 120 secular chansons, 3 masses, 24 motets, 3 lamentation lessons, a magnificat, and 2 French sacred settings.

His motets reveal a style that has the breadth and seriousness that one expects from church music, yet with the clear phrase articulations one finds in the madrigal. Despite fugal imitation, the text settings are clear. Arcadelt uses contrasting chordal sections for further textual emphasis. At least nine of his motets were composed for the Cappella Sistina, notably *Domine non secundum peccata*, the tract for Ash Wednesday, *Pater noster*, and *Corona aurea*, which was performed at coronations and investitures into the eighteenth century. His masses were also probably composed in Rome, as they are based on models found in the Cappella Sistina's repertory.

Bibliography

J. Arcadelt, *Opera omnia*, ed. A. Seay, Corpus Mensurabilis musicae 31, 10 vols., 1965–71.

A. Seay, "Jacques Arcadelt," in *The New Grove Dictionary of Music and Musicians*, ed. S. Sadie, vol. 1, 1980: 546–50.

Mitchell Brauner

ARCIMBOLDO, GIUSEPPE (c. 1527–1593)

Popular among his contemporaries for curious, if not bizarre, allegorical portraits depicting humans as compositions of everyday objects, Giuseppe Arcimboldo built his reputation while he was the favored painter at the imperial Habsburg court in Prague. Born in Milan to a distinguished family, Arcimboldo completed early works there of an ordinary sort, designing stained glass and executing paintings for the cathedral while he was apprenticed to his father, Biagio. By 1562 the artist was in the Habsburg lands of Austria and Bohemia, where his art began to reflect his own distinctive style, and where he completed his most famous works. He was celebrated as a designer of state ceremonies, festivals, and balls during the reigns of Emperors Maximilian II and Rudolf II.* He also earned attention as a designer of architectural and theatrical decoration, a creator of magnificent waterworks and fountains, and an advisor in such matters as silk manufacture and museum collections. In 1587 he returned to his home city, where he remained active in Rudolf's employ. He was made count palatine in 1592 and died in Milan the following year.

Art historians have termed his allegorical paintings "composite heads" because of his depictions of books, weapons, implements of various kinds, and (most famously) plant and animal products in his portraits of human subjects. Two series of four portraits each stand out as his masterworks: *Seasons* of 1563 (*Spring, Summer, Fall, Winter*) and *Elements* of 1566 (*Water, Fire, Earth, Air*). *Seasons* makes use of spring flowers, ripening grains, autumnal fruit, and empty branches and fallen leaves, while *Elements* makes similar use of related images.

Arcimboldo's reputation declined soon after his death, his works becoming objects of ridicule or indifference until his "rediscovery" by the surrealists in the twentieth century. More recently, his works have been interpreted as "serious jokes," reflecting the Renaissance fascination with artifice, paradox, and humor to render harmonious apparently disharmonious elements. Such themes were particularly welcome in the Habsburg court, where, as the accompanying poems of Giovanni Battista Fontana make clear, Arcimboldo's "composite heads" were understood as imperial allegories for the harmonious rule of a far-flung and diverse empire.

Bibliography

D. Craig, *The Life and Works of Arcimboldo*, 1966.
T. D. Kaufmann, *The School of Prague*, 1988.

Edmund M. Kern

ARETINO, PIETRO (1492–1556)

One of the more versatile and prolific writers in the Italian vernacular, Pietro Aretino made a significant impact on the literary, political, social, and artistic worlds of sixteenth-century Italy. Born in Arezzo, Italy, Aretino came under the protection of the nobleman Luigi Bacci at an early age, where he grew up in a cultivated atmosphere and probably received occasional lessons. Aretino continued his unconventional humanist education in Perugia under the protection of the humanist Francesco Bontempi, coming into contact with men of letters, intellectuals, and artists and publishing his first collection of works in 1512. In 1517 Aretino went to Rome under the patronage of Agostino Chigi and subsequently under Cardinal Giulio de' Medici, later elected Pope Clement VII. At the court of Rome, Aretino developed his skill at political and clerical gossip in the form of pasquinades and lampoons. During his stay there, Aretino also drafted *La cortegiana* (The courtesan), in which he satirized the papal court and Baldesar Castiglione's* manual for courtly behavior, *Il cortegiano* (The Courtier). While Aretino is frequently described as an anticlassical, antihumanistic, and scurrilous author who proudly boasted of never having studied Latin, *La cortegiana* reveals a rich heritage of sources, including Virgil, Desiderius Erasmus,* and the contemporary humanistic treatise. In 1524 Aretino had to briefly flee Rome owing to his publication of a series of erotic sonnets to accompany sixteen pornographic engravings designed by Giulio Romano.* During this period, Aretino was successfully presented to François I,* king of France, who in 1533 sent Aretino a golden chain.

After practically being assassinated on the order of Bishop Giberti, who had been offended by Aretino's writings, Aretino left Rome in 1525 and went to Mantua for a brief period under the patronage of Federico Gonzaga II,* the marquis of Mantua, where he composed the satiric comedy *Il marescalco* (The Farrier). Aretino then took permanent refuge in Venice, where he gained security with the protection of the doge, international respect, and a network of contacts with the Venetian patriciate as he consolidated his power with his influential publications. Amid his literary output, Aretino also gave voice to his caustic version of "truthful" political reporting in the form of satire and knowledgeable commentary on the contemporary political scene in the local broadsheets. In 1534 Aretino published the first part of *I ragionamenti*, a series of dialogues in which prostitutes vividly discuss their profession. Like many of his other works, this play interweaves literary and historical plots with a satirical target as it parodies the literary form of the dialogue and Neoplatonic theories then in vogue as embodied in Pietro Bembo's* *Gli Asolani*. Aretino also composed religious works that appear to reflect the current religious taste that responded to the atmosphere of the religious Reformation with its restlessness, need for rehabilitation, and desire for renewed personal faith.

Much of Aretino's fame comes from his collection of letters published at intervals beginning in 1537. The letters, which show a mixture of gossip, flattery, praise, and criticism as they simultaneously document the political and cultural life of the time, received a very wide circulation. While outwardly they seem spontaneously written, they are actually well-planned and composed set pieces that combine historical truth with literary fiction. Owing to Aretino's acknowledged lack of Latin culture, critics have tended to dismiss his letters from the long Latin tradition from which they derive. Many of these letters contain insightful comments on the figurative arts, and Aretino himself befriended several artists, including Titian,* from whom he commissioned his portrait and whose career he actively promoted, helping to spread the artist's reputation. In response to Aretino's artistic expertise, Ludovico Dolce made Aretino one of the protagonists in his important sixteenth-century treatise on painting, memorializing his artistic knowledge and career.

Because of his influential letters, lewd works, never-ending desire for prestige, and notoriety as revealed in his sobriquet, the "Scourge of Princes," coined by Ludovico Ariosto* in *Orlando Furioso* in 1532, Aretino's reputation as a writer has frequently been underrated. His language, however, reveals a humanistic learning of the arts and letters, and his comedies uncover literary myths through their historical satirical targets, which he often reinforced with classical models. Because of Aretino's responsiveness to public demand and knowledge of the contemporary literary scene, his works found wide readership.

Bibliography

P. Aretino, *Selected Letters*, trans. George Bull, 1976.
C. Cairns, *Pietro Aretino and the Republic of Venice*, 1985.

Mary Pixley

ARIOSTO, LUDOVICO (1474–1533)

One of the greatest Italian authors and a major Renaissance humanist, Ludovico Ariosto was a pioneering dramatist and author of the great romance epic *Orlando Furioso*. Ariosto's career was shaped by the fortunes of the Este court in the northern Italian city-state of Ferrara, which reached its zenith of cultural and political importance during his lifetime. Born in Reggio, Ludovico was the eldest son of a trusted and unscrupulous courtier of Ercole d'Este, the second duke of Ferrara. Destined by his father for the law, Ariosto studied half-heartedly while participating enthusiastically in the city's burgeoning cultural life. When he was finally freed to pursue his literary interests in 1494, he became a luminary in the circle of brilliant young men studying with the humanist scholar Gregorio da Spoleto. During this happy period, Ariosto made a name for himself with his smooth, accomplished Latin poetry and in 1498 began his lifelong friendship with the influential Italian humanist Pietro Bembo.*

His happiness came to an end in 1500 with the death of his father, leaving Ariosto responsible for an extensive family. In 1503 he entered the service of Cardinal Ippolito d'Este, brother of Duke Alfonso, Ercole's son. Thus began the lifelong service to the Este court that made Ariosto's great works possible, since it was through such noble patronage that literature was produced and disseminated in this age. At the same time, it was a source of constant exasperation, since the Este princes continually deflected him from his writing with their diplomatic business. Yet his frequent travels also allowed him to meet and maintain relationships with many of the day's leading humanists. By the late 1510s Ariosto had become a central figure in Ferrara, both as a diplomat and as poet and dramatist for court festivities. In 1513 he hoped for new patronage when his friend Giovanni de' Medici became Pope Leo X,* but his hopes were dashed, and he continued with the Este.

In 1516, after much polishing, *Orlando Furioso* (The Madness of Roland) was published in forty cantos to great acclaim. But family obligations, financial worries, and the whims of his patrons continued to haunt the poet. Ariosto broke with Cardinal Ippolito in 1517 rather than follow him to Hungary and entered the employ of the steadier Duke Alfonso in 1519. Continuing financial problems led him to accept appointment as governor of the Garafagnana region northwest of Ferrara even as the second edition of *Orlando Furioso* was coming out in 1521. Ariosto held this thankless job for the next five years, trying to manage the unruly, feuding inhabitants of the region and frequently serving as Alfonso's scapegoat. Upon his return to Ferrara, he was finally able to live in relative peace and prosperity, marrying his longtime mistress, Alessandra Benucci, rewriting and supervising the performance of his great comedies at court, and seeing the final version of *Orlando Furioso*, in forty-six cantos, through the press in 1532. During the 1520s he also wrote his seven autobiographical satires. The famous inscription upon his house may still be read today: "Parva sed apta mihi, sed nulla obnoxia, sed non sordida, parta meo tamen aere Domus" (A small house but suitable for me, dependent upon no one, nor mean, and yet the result of my own earnings). Ariosto died in 1533 and by his own request was buried quietly in his parish church.

Ariosto's fame as a major writer would have been assured by his satires and comedies alone, but *Orlando Furioso* puts him on the level of Dante and Petrarch in Italian letters. Based upon Matteo Boiardo's unfinished romance epic

Orlando Innamorato (Roland in Love), *Orlando Furioso* outdoes its predecessor in sophistication, complexity, and epic scope. The tale of the futile love that drives the great knight Orlando insane is intertwined with Charlemagne's war against the pagans and the dynastic love of Ruggiero and the lady knight Bradamante, who are destined to marry and found the Este dynasty. In elegant stanzas of beautiful eight-line ottava rima, the poem treats the headlong chase of individual desire, the national drive for imperial control, and the sweep of providential history with both high seriousness and amused irony, implicating the poet himself and his own age in the grandeur and folly of the human condition. In its synthesis of medieval romance and Virgilian epic, *Orlando Furioso* is heir to the greatest preceding literary traditions, looks forward to Tasso's* *Gerusalemme liberata*, Spenser's* *Fairie Queene*, and Milton's *Paradise Lost*, and stands as one of the great works of world literature.

Bibliography

R. Griffin, *Ludovico Ariosto*, 1974.
W. Gundersheimer, *Ferrara: The Style of a Renaissance Despotism*, 1973.
R. J. Rodini, "Selected Bibliography of Ariosto Criticism: 1986–1993," *Annali d'Italianistica* 12 (1994): 299–317.

Katherine Hoffman

ASCHAM, ROGER (1515–1568)

Roger Ascham played his role in English thought and politics during the reigns of the Tudor monarchs and is best remembered as the author of *The Scholemaster*, one of the first educational treatises written in the vernacular in Europe. Born at Kirby Wiske, Yorkshire, Ascham, virtually adopted by Sir Humphrey Wingfield, who had him tutored, was sent to St. John's College, Cambridge, in 1530, where he studied under Sir John Cheke. Here he mastered classical literature and developed an eloquent Latin style that, combined with his penmanship, led to important opportunities, including appointment as university orator and tutor for Henry VIII's* daughters Mary* and Elizabeth.*

When Ascham earned his bachelor of arts in 1534, he was elected a fellow of St. John's. When he was awarded the master's degree in 1537, he began to lecture at the university. In 1545 he published *Toxophilus*, a dialogue on exercise and recreation, placing special emphasis on the English longbow. Written in English and dedicated to Henry VIII, the book pleased the king, an avid archer, who granted Ascham an annual pension. From 1550 to 1553, as secretary to Sir Richard Morison, ambassador to Charles V,* Ascham visited continental courts, schools, and scholars. When this diplomatic group was recalled to England after Edward VI died in 1553, Ascham returned to Cambridge and wrote *Report and Discourse of the Affaires and State of Germany*. In spite of his Protestantism, the Catholic queen Mary made him her Latin secretary. After Mary died in 1558, he continued as secretary and tutor to Queen Elizabeth until he died.

In 1563 he began *The Scholemaster* and completed it just before he died in

December 1568. Mainly concerned with the education of proper Christian gentlemen, the study of classical literature as the foundation of liberal learning, and the "double-translation" method for teaching Latin, the work also attacks medieval romances, Italian books, and travel and discusses wit and literary imitation. Its purity of diction and its sentence structure define its place in the development of English prose, and its content, drawn from classical and contemporary sources, ensures Ascham's stature as a Renaissance humanist educator worthy of note.

Bibliography

L. V. Ryan, *Roger Ascham*, 1963.

Al Geritz

ASKEW, ANNE (1521–1546)

Anne Askew, burned as a heretic in the reign of Henry VIII,* was a woman of exceptional bravery. She was also forthright and articulate and had the foresight to keep a record of her travails as a testament to her faith, though we do not know how much of what was posthumously published was revised from Anne's actual words. Anne was well born and well educated; she was the daughter of Sir William Askew in Lincolnshire.

Anne's older sister Martha was betrothed to a local farmer, Thomas Kyme, whose father owned extensive lands, and on Martha's death in 1539, Anne's father insisted that she marry him instead. It was a disastrously unhappy marriage. Anne was already a committed Protestant. Kyme was appalled by his wife's beliefs, her conflicts with priests, and her refusal to be silenced. Despite the couple having two children, Kyme finally threw Anne out, but when he reconsidered, she refused to return. According to Askew, Kyme was not a true Christian, and thus their marriage was invalid. Anne left Lincolnshire to seek an annulment from her marriage and a community of the faithful in London. Anne found her community and gained introduction to some of the women who surrounded Henry VIII's sixth wife, Katherine Parr, who was also sympathetic to Reformed ideas.

In 1545 Anne's outspoken denial of transubstantiation led to her arrest and an examination for heresy, but her evasive answers to the questions placed made it difficult to condemn her. The intervention of several influential friends finally led to her freedom. Anne apparently began to keep records of her examinations as a way to bear witness to her faith; these were eventually published after her death. Anne was arrested again the following year. When she refused to recant, she was convicted of heresy and condemned to death. She was then moved from Newgate Prison to the Tower of London for further questioning.

In 1546 it was clear that Henry VIII's health was failing, and the conservative faction at court was in a desperate power struggle with those of Reformed leanings. Thomas Wriothesley, lord chancellor, Stephen Gardiner, bishop of Winchester, and Richard Rich, solicitor general, attempted to force Anne to incriminate Catherine Parr and other Protestant ladies at court. To try to force her to implicate others, Anne was placed on the rack. When the lieutenant of the Tower refused to continue racking her, Wriothesley and Rich continued the job themselves.

Anne absolutely refused to recant or to name anyone else. She was so hurt by the torture that she had to be carried to the stake at Smithfield, where she was burned on 16 July 1546. Anne's brilliant answers to her examinations were publicized early in the reign of Henry's son Edward VI less than a year after her death by the Protestant polemicist John Bale.* Anne's words were available to an even wider audience in the Elizabethan period because of her place of honor as one of the martyrs in John Foxe's* *Acts and Monuments*.

Bibliography

E. Beilin, ed., *The Examinations of Anne Askew*, 1996.
D. Wilson, *A Tudor Tapestry: Men, Women, and Society in Reformation England*, 1972.

Carole Levin

B

BACON, ANNE COOK (c. 1528–1610)

Anne Cook Bacon was recognized during the late sixteenth century for her prowess as a translator of religious works. Bacon and her sisters—Mildred Cook Cecil, Elizabeth Cook Hoby, Katherine Cook Kiligrew, and Margaret Cook—were educated privately in the humanist tradition. Their father, Sir Anthony Cook, was tutor to Edward VI, a task with which Anne is thought to have assisted him. Sir Anthony Cook later presented the Act of Uniformity to the House of Lords. Anne Cook married Sir Nicholas Bacon, lord keeper of the privy seal and a member of Elizabeth's Privy Council, and raised two sons, Sir Anthony and Sir Francis Bacon,* philosopher, essayist, and lord chancellor.

Anne Cook Bacon's translation of *Apologia ecclesiae anglicanae* (Apology for the Church of England) remains among the finest translations of this tract. Attributed to John Jewel, the *Apologia* was written in Latin in 1562 to explain and justify the English church's reforms to continental theologians. It focused especially upon areas criticized by Roman Catholics. The Convocation of 1563 ordered that it be "in all cathedral and collegiate churches, and also in private houses." Bacon's version, first printed in 1564, became the definitive translation, and in 1565 Thomas Harding, the Roman Catholic divine, used Bacon's edition as the basis for his *Confutation of a Booke Intituled an Apologie of the Church of England.* In addition, Bacon translated the sermons of the Italian Calvinist Bernardino Ochino*; her own translations of his sermons "concerning the predestination and election of God" were printed probably in 1548 and 1551, and her work, along with that of Richard Argentine, was published in collections of Ochino's sermons, probably in 1551 and 1570. Her letters to her sons also survive and are printed in modern editions of Francis Bacon's letters.

Bibliography

A. C. Bacon, in *The Early Modern Englishwoman: Printed Writings, 1500–1640,* vol. 1, 1998.

M. E. Lamb, "The Cooke Sisters: Attitudes toward Learned Women in the Renaissance," in *Silent But for the Word: Tudor Women as Patrons, Translators, and Writers of Religious Works*, ed. M. Hannay, 1985: 107–25.

Karen Nelson

BACON, FRANCIS (1561–1626)

Francis Bacon was a lawyer, man of letters, and philosopher in the Elizabethan and Jacobean eras. Although he eventually became lord chancellor of England, he is best known for his *Essays* and writings concerning the "new philosophy," or modern science.

Born in London, Bacon was the younger son of Sir Nicholas Bacon, lord keeper, and Anne Cook Bacon.* In 1573 he entered Trinity College, Cambridge, and completed his education at Gray's Inn, from which he was admitted barrister in 1582. Bacon began a parliamentary career in 1584 after his uncle, Elizabeth's lord treasurer Sir William Cecil, failed to help him enter royal service. In 1593 he damaged his prospects by opposing a war subsidy, and despite the sponsorship of the earl of Essex, whose service he had entered in 1591, Bacon was passed over for attorney general in 1594 and for solicitor general the next year. He was, however, made one of the queen's learned counsel, and following Essex's disastrous rebellion in 1601, he helped to secure his former patron's conviction for treason. This prompted such public ill will that Bacon was obliged to publish an *Apology* for his efforts in 1604.

Following James I's* accession in 1603, Bacon was knighted; he also served on a commission to discuss union with Scotland and dedicated his *Advancement of Learning* to the king in 1605. Preferment finally came with the post of solicitor general in 1607 and of attorney general in 1613. Bacon was then named lord keeper in 1617; sponsored by George Villiers, later duke of Buckingham, he became lord chancellor and Baron Verulam in 1618. As chancellor he prosecuted Sir Walter Raleigh* in 1618 and the earl of Suffolk in 1619. In 1620 he published his most famous work, *Novum organum*, and in 1621 he was created Viscount St. Albans. Shortly after this last promotion Bacon confessed to charges of bribery and corruption and was fined, imprisoned, and forbidden any state office. Although the king remitted the fine and a general pardon was eventually published, Bacon's career as a public servant was over. In 1626, after an experiment to see if snow would stop a fowl from decaying, Bacon caught a chill and died.

Much of Bacon's philosophical writing works to widen the breach between medieval Scholasticism, with its emphasis on abstract concepts and application of Aristotelian formulas, and the emerging "new philosophy," which concentrated on inductive reasoning through experimentation with physical phenomena. To Bacon, the goal of philosophy was to develop practical knowledge, which would then extend the limits of humanity's power in nature and lead to the development of new arts and sciences. While he did not exclude the importance of metaphysics, he felt that the way to truth began with observing nature directly.

In *Novum organum* Bacon provides his most important contribution to modern scientific thought by examining a set of "idols," or false notions that possess the mind. The greatest obstacle Bacon identifies is the medieval conviction that truth could be discerned by applying logical reasoning to a small number of observations. Bacon insists that the natural philosopher accumulate as many examples as possible, eliminate all inessential factors, and draw conclusions from whatever conditions remain. While his method fails to allow for the concept of the controlling hypothesis or the impossibility of exhausting all potentialities, its insistence on examining a wide range of situations makes it a cornerstone of modern scientific thought.

Bacon's most important literary works are the *Essays* (1597), *The History of the Reign of King Henry VII* (1622), and *The New Atlantis* (1627). The *Essays*, the first exercise in this genre in English, speak to many aspects of human life, including politics, marriage, education, and travel, and are more concerned with examining questions about their subjects than in producing conclusions about them. *The History of the Reign of King Henry VII* glorifies Henry as a wise, cautious Solomon who brought England peace and unity out of civil war and presents him as the type of king James should strive to become. *The New Atlantis* is a futuristic utopia where work is conducted by a scientific society and provides a model for what would become the Royal Society.

While Bacon achieved high office under James I and participated as a lawyer in some of his time's most influential trials, his most important contributions came in the realm of natural philosophy. The empirical method he advocated had much to do with the development of modern science in the seventeenth century, and his approach to weighing and examining evidence can be seen in his political and literary works as well as his scientific ones. His intellectual concepts show him to be in advance of most thinkers of his time.

Bibliography

F. Anderson, *Francis Bacon: His Career and His Thought*, 1962.
J. Epstein, *Francis Bacon: A Political Biography*, 1977.
P. Zagorin, *Francis Bacon*, 1998.

Kevin Lindberg

BAÏF, JEAN-ANTOINE DE (1532–1589)

Less well known than his fellow poets of the Pléïade school, Jean-Antoine de Baïf remained a faithful member of the group and produced an astonishing number and variety of works in his lifetime. The results of his musical research, his metrical experiments, and his proposed spelling reforms were not widely adopted, but together with his collected poetry they embody the versatility and enthusiastic pursuit of knowledge and invention characteristic of the French Renaissance.

The natural son of the author Lazare de Baïf, Jean-Antoine received an excellent early education, then studied the classics and modern Italian literature at the Collège de Coqueret in Paris under the renowned humanist Jean Dorat. Baïf joined Pierre de Ronsard* and Joachim Du Bellay,* fellow students at Coqueret, in forming the influential French poetic circle entitled the Pléïade.

In 1552 Baïf published the two books of his *Amours* for Méline, a *canzoniere* of Petrarchan-style love poetry written for an idealized woman. Baïf wrote the four books of his *Amours de Francine* (1555) for Françoise de Gennes, a young woman he met in Poitiers. In his love poetry, Baïf follows the Italian models— Petrarch, above all—that were well known and widely used by French Renaissance poets.

Baïf took orders in the church and received an ecclesiastical income that supplemented his inheritance and allowed him to devote all of his time to writing. Charles IX eventually named Baïf royal secretary, which allowed him to live with the king's entourage in Paris.

In 1567 Baïf published his comedy in verse *Le brave* (The Braggart), a loose adaptation of Plautus's *Miles gloriosus*. The play met with success when it was staged at the Hôtel de Guise in 1567. Along with his poetry, this and several translations by Baïf of classical plays point to the poet's desire to experiment in all genres. Also in 1567 Baïf published a short scientific and didactic poem, *Le premier des météores*, dedicated to Catherine de' Medici.* The volume reflects the increasing popularity of scientific writings, and of astrology in particular, in Baïf's day, as well as the poet's own interest in scientific truth, which for him superseded poetic imagination.

Along with Thibaut de Courville, and with Charles IX's approval and protection, Baïf founded the Académie de poésie et de musique in 1570. A principal aim of the academy, in keeping with the Pléïade's early doctrine, was to explore the close link between poetry and music. As a part of his work within the academy, Baïf continued his research on rhythm and rhyme and created new metrical patterns based on Greek poetry, as well as a new, reformed system of spelling based on phonetics. In 1572 Baïf published his collected *Oeuvres en rime* in four volumes. In 1574 he published his *Etrénes de poézie fransoëze an vers mezurés*, printed using his new system of orthography. Baïf's spelling reforms never took hold, but he continued to use them in his own work until his death. In 1574 Henri III elevated the status of the academy, renamed the Académie du Palais, making it one of the most important cultural institutions in France. Under the influence of the new king, however, the focus of the academy's work shifted from that of music and poetry to eloquence in the service of morality.

In 1576 Baïf published the first edition of his last collection, entitled *Mimes, enseignemens, et proverbes*. Following a popular sixteenth-century trend, Baïf's *Mimes* use proverbs, popular expressions, fables, and rhyming adages for both the pleasure and the moral edification of the reader. The collection also includes political *satires* and *épîtres*. In the final years of his life, surrounded by civil wars in France, Baïf turned his interest to religious questions and texts. He translated the Psalter into metrical verse, into Latin verse, and into French rhyming verse.

Bibliography

M. Augé-Chiquet, *La vie, les idées, et l'oeuvre de Jean-Antoine de Baïf*, 1969.
J.-A. de Baïf, *Le brave*, ed. Simone Maser, 1979.
J.-A. de Baïf, *Mimes, enseignemens, et proverbes*, ed. Jean Vignes, 1992.

Karen S. James

BALE, JOHN (1495–1563)

John Bale was an evangelical Reformer, dramatist, and bishop of Ossory. He was born on 21 November 1495 in Suffolk and by the age of twelve had entered the Carmelite friary of Norwich. In 1514 he began to study at Cambridge; he eventually became a doctor of divinity. Until 1530 he remained faithful to the Catholic church, but then he began to waver, and in 1536 he officially left the Carmelite order and took a wife, Dorothy. During the 1530s he also began to write plays, which he continued to do for the remainder of his life, although only five are extant: *King Johan, God's Promises, John's Preaching, The Temptation of Our Lord*, and *Three Laws*.

In 1540 his strongest supporter, Thomas Cromwell, fell out of favor with Henry VIII* and was executed. Subsequently Bale fled England, first to the Netherlands, then to Germany. During his eight years in exile he continued to write both plays and polemics vilifying the Catholics and praising the first Protestant martyrs, including William Thorpe and Anne Askew.* The accession of Edward VI persuaded Bale to return to England, and in 1552 the king appointed him bishop of Ossory in Ireland. Bale vigorously attempted to implement Protestantism, but met hostile resistance from both the people and the clergy there. Mary I's* accession in 1553 induced him once again to flee to Strasbourg, where he published an account of his persecution, the *Vocation*. He began to work closely with John Foxe* and accompanied him to Wesel, Germany, where each continued to write, Foxe on the *Acts and Monuments* (in Latin), and Bale on the *Catalogus*, a history of the English church and people that also contains an account of his own life.

After Mary's death, Bale returned to England, but did not resume his position at Ossory. He continued to revise his most well-known work, *King Johan*, which may have been performed for Queen Elizabeth* at Ipswich in 1561. On 15 November 1563 he died and was buried in the nave of Canterbury Cathedral. Bale was best known for his dramatic, polemical, and autobiographical writings, which have continued to provide a religious and political perspective from one who was both a recorder of and a participant in the Reformation.

Bibliography

P. Happe, *John Bale*, 1996.

Jean Akers

BANDELLO, MATTEO (1485–1561)

Matteo Bandello was a Dominican priest and courtier whose life and *novelle* reveal the vicissitudes of the tumultuous political environment of sixteenth-century Italy. Bandello, born in Castelnuovo Scrivia in Lombardy, was educated from age twelve by his uncle Vincenzo, vicar general of the Dominican order, at the Milanese monastery S. Maria delle Grazie. He studied law and theology at Pavia, but favored literature, history, and Platonic philosophy. He made his first religious vows in Genoa, probably in 1504.

Cosmopolitan perspectives were opened to him on an inspection tour of monasteries throughout Italy with his uncle. In Florence he composed love poetry for "Viola" (Violante Borromeo); at Rome he knew courtesan culture and was introduced to the famous courtesan Imperia; in Naples Matthias Corvinus's widow, Beatrice d'Aragona, became his protector after his uncle Vincenzo died there. Bandello returned to Lombardy, where he befriended humanists and the poets Cecilia Gallerana and Camilla Scrampa and attached himself to the household of Alessandro Bentivoglio and Ippolita Sforza. Enmeshed in the struggle for control of Milan between King Louis XII of France and the Sforza, after the French victory at Marignano (1515), he had to flee to the Gonzaga court at Mantua. He remained there until 1522 as secretary to Isabella d'Este* and composed poetry to a second platonic love, "Mincia." After the French withdrawal from Milan, Bandello returned briefly but fled a second time when Spanish troops advanced on the city after the French defeat at Pavia (1525). His house sacked and his books and manuscripts dispersed, he became an itinerant courtier. From 1526 he worked first for Federigo Gonzaga di Bozzolo, then for Giovanni delle Bande Nere while making the acquaintance of Niccolò Machiavelli,* next for Ranuccio Farnese, and by 1528 for Cesare Fregoso at Verona while participating in intellectual circles at the houses of the Canossa, Saula, and Serego. In 1537 he met Lucrezia Gonzaga and celebrated her in verse; on a subsequent trip to France he dedicated other compositions to Marguerite de Navarre.* When Fregoso died in 1541, Bandello stayed on to serve his widow, Costanza Rangone, accompanying her eventually to Bordeaux. In 1550 he was given a benefice and lived quietly in France until his death in 1561.

Of significant literary note are Bandello's 240 *novelle*, composed over many years. They are divided into four parts. The first three were edited by Bandello himself and were published in Lucca by Busdraghi (1554); the fourth appeared posthumously at Lyons (1573). Bandello introduces each tale with a dedicatory letter to a prominent individual; once thought to be authentic biographical indicators, these letters are now understood to be mere literary conventions. The tales, rather, convey aspects of real life: the dismantling of the Italian state system, the divisive impact of the Reformation, the encroachment of the Turks in eastern Europe, and the tenor of life across social classes. They draw upon the interest of humanist and vernacular writers in classical literature and ancient and recent history: the rape of Lucretia, the marriages of Henry VIII,* and most famously a version of the story of Romeo and Juliet that served as one of Shakespeare's sources.

Bibliography

T. Griffith, *Bandello's Fiction: An Examination of the Novelle*, 1955.

Luci Fortunato DeLisle

BANDINELLI, BACCIO (BARTOLOMEO BRANDINI) (1493–1560)

A Florentine sculptor patronized by the Medici for nearly twenty-one years, Baccio Bandinelli is best known for producing *Hercules and Cacus* as the pendant to Michelangelo's* *David*; together they flanked the entrance to the Palazzo della Signoria, the town hall of Florence. Born in Florence in 1493, Bandinelli was taught by his father, a Medicean goldsmith, and then entered the workshop of Giovanni Francesco Rustici, a Tuscan sculptor of some reputation who had trained under Andrea del Verrocchio and who also worked for the Medici, a happy circumstance that undoubtedly helped further to pave the way for Bandinelli establishing his own relationship with the Medici. A sculptor of questionable talent who sought to emulate Michelangelo from an early age, he had an uncanny ability for acquiring ambitious commissions, only to leave many of them unfinished. Bandinelli's works are largely derivative of either classical models or contemporary masters, an acceptable characteristic based on "imitation" for an artist of the time. His works are noted for employing figures in contrived and often-awkward poses rendered with a ponderous heaviness and sterile hyperbole that is in actuality the antithesis of all that Michelangelo's sculpture represents.

Bandinelli's first major commission came in 1515 for a statue of St. Peter for Florence Cathedral, followed by work on the decorations for the entry of Leo X* into Florence and numerous commissions for Medici dukes and high clergy, including *Orpheus and Cerberus* (c. 1519), a full-size copy of the Hellenistic masterpiece the *Laocoön* (1520–24), and the tombs of Popes Leo X and Clement VII (1536–41) and of Duke Cosimo I's* father, Giovanni delle Bande Nere, in 1540. In Genoa after the expulsion of the Medici from Florence in 1527, he began work on a statue of Andrea Doria. Around 1529 he was made a knight of the Order of S. Iago and also established an academy commemorated in engravings by Agostino Veneziano and Eneo Vico. The shifting political fortunes of the Medici caused the commission for *Hercules and Cacus* to be batted back and forth between Bandinelli and Michelangelo (to whom it had been awarded originally in 1508) until the Medici return to Florence, when Bandinelli was instructed to complete the sculpture. It was unveiled in 1534 to scathing criticism for its bulging musculature, which was later described by Benvenuto Cellini* as resembling a "sack of melons." Cellini's arrival in Florence marked the end to Bandinelli's near monopoly on Medici patronage of sculpture. The rivalry and resultant acrimony that existed between the two men is thoroughly described by Cellini in his autobiography as well as by Bandinelli in his own

Memoriale, an account of his family and career. These two works, combined with Giorgio Vasari's* colorful life of the artist, provide significantly more information about the life and character of Bandinelli than is known about many artists of the period. Throughout his career Bandinelli was reviled by his contemporaries for his lack of artistic ability and inspiration, for his arrogance and virulent tongue, and for his sly business practices. One of his last works, *Christ and Nicodemus* (c. 1554–59), made for his own memorial chapel in SS. Annunziata in Florence, is perhaps one of his most sympathetic works, representing himself in the guise of Nicodemus, just as his lifelong model Michelangelo had done.

Bibliography

J. Poeschke, *Michelangelo and His World: Sculpture of the Italian Renaissance*, 1996.
J. Pope-Hennessy, *Italian High Renaissance and Baroque Sculpture*, 1970.

Rachel Hostetter Smith

BARBARO, DANIELE (1514–1570)

An influential Italian humanist, Daniele Barbaro had an important impact on the culture, art, and architecture of northern Italy in the sixteenth century through his publications, designs for decorative programs, and patronage of the arts. Born in Venice, Italy, into a distinguished patriciate family, Daniele pursued education at the University of Padua, receiving his degree in 1540. While there, he met Benedetto Varchi and Sperone Speroni,* with whom he founded the Accademia degli Infiammati. During this period he wrote his *Dialogo della eloquenza* (Dialogue on Eloquence) and finished his great-uncle Ermolao's commentaries on the *Ethics* of Aristotle. Between 1548 and 1550 he became the Venetian ambassador to England, and in 1550 he was elected patriarch elect of Aquileia and attended the Council of Trent. In 1556 Daniele published his own translated and commented edition of Vitruvius's *De architectura* (On Architecture). Using his experience with Aristotelian analysis and Platonic view of the elements, order, and universal harmony, Daniele showed his mastery of the disciplines Vitruvius felt a true architect should possess, including music, mathematics, philosophy, history, and rhetoric, as he interrelated the scientific and humanistic disciplines. This translation of the very popular ancient architectural treatise made the work available even to those without a formal education. At about the same time, Daniele and his brother Marcantonio commissioned the Villa Barbaro at Maser, designed by the architect Andrea Palladio* and decorated with frescoes by Paolo Veronese.* The fresco program, authored by Barbaro, reflected his intellectual interests as it simultaneously related the family, state, and church to the universal harmony of the cosmos. Barbaro's skill in devising iconographical schemes was also called upon for decorative programs in the ducal palace. Regarded as a great intellectual through his scholarly endeavors and influential publications, Barbaro was held in high esteem by Venetian statesmen, and in recognition of this he was named official historian to the Republic of Venice in 1560.

Bibliography

O. Logan, *Culture and Society in Venice, 1470–1790*, 1972.

Mary Pixley

BARCLAY, ALEXANDER (c. 1475–1552)

Alexander Barclay was a humanist, a priest, a poet, and a translator. Tradition holds that he was born in Scotland, although scholars propose either Gloucestershire or Lincoln. He was ordained in Exeter as deacon and priest in 1508. During this period he resided at the College of St. Mary, Ottery. By 1515 Barclay had taken vows at the Benedictine monastery of Ely. Barclay offers topical allusions to this monastery in his *Ship of Fools* and in his eclogues.

Barclay's continued project of translating and publishing the works of continental humanists remains his most important work. He is especially known for his translation of *Das Narrenschiff*, written by Sebastian Brant and translated into Latin by Jakob Locher. Barclay's version, *The Ship of Fools*, was first printed in 1509. His eclogues, based on those by Baptista Spagnoli of Mantua and by Aeneas Silvius (later Pope Pius II) were first published in 1518. Other translations include *The Castle of Labor* (1505), from Pierre Gringore's *Le chasteau de labour; The Life of St. George* (1515), from Baptista Spagnoli of Mantua's *Georgius; The Mirror of Good Manners* (1518), from Dominicus Mancinus's *Libellus de quattuor virtutibus*; and *The Battle of Jurgith* (1522), from Sallust's *Bellum Jugurthinum*. Barclay published instructions for writing and speaking French (1521) and, according to John Bale's* *Catalogus*, wrote or translated lives of St. Catherine, St. Margaret, and St. Ethelreda, all of which have been lost.

Bibliography

W. Nelson, "Introduction," in *The Life of St. George*, by A. Barclay, 1955.

Karen Nelson

BARCLAY, WILLIAM (1546–1608)

William Barclay was a Scottish scholar and lawyer who was known for his legal texts dealing with the rights of kings, the state, and the temporal powers of the pope, works that aroused controversy from both the Roman Catholic (Robert Bellarmine) and the Protestant (Samuel Rutherford) sides. Barclay studied at King's College, Aberdeen, Paris, and Bourges, at which institution he studied law under Jacques Cujas and received a doctorate. He was then invited by his uncle, the Jesuit Edmund Hay, to teach law at a new university at Pont-à-Mousson in Lorraine, where he was appointed by the duke of Lorraine and made a counsellor of state. After marriage to a French woman, he spent the years 1603–4 in England, where King James I* offered him positions on condition that he become Anglican. He refused, returned to France, and was appointed professor and then dean of law at Angers, where he died in 1608.

His major works were *De regno et regali potestate* (Concerning the Kingship and Royal Power, 1600) and *De potestate papae* (Concerning the Power of the Pope, 1609). In the former he strongly defended the rights of kings and rejected the arguments of Hubert Languet, Jean Boucher, and George Buchanan,* the last mentioned of whom had argued in his *De iure regni* (Concerning the Rights of kings) that the people hold extensive powers against the king. King James VI of Scotland (James I of England) used Barclay to support his own divine-right theory. The latter work, Barclay's *De potestate papae*, published posthumously by his son John in London, attacked the papal claim to authority in temporal matters, a position sharply rejected by Robert Bellarmine.

Bibliography

J. N. Figgis, *The Theory of the Divine Right of Kings*, 1896 (1965).

Iain S. Maclean

BASSANO, JACOPO DA (c. 1510–1592)

One of the least well known of the important artists of Venetian painting, Jacopo da Bassano played a role in the renewal of painting in the Veneto in the second half of the sixteenth century. From Bassano, Italy, Jacopo grew up in his father's art workshop. In 1533 he visited Venice, where he remained impressed by the art of Bonifacio de' Pitati, in whose shop he worked, and by Titian's* paintings, as evidenced by the forms and rapid and fluid brushwork visible in Jacopo's art. Instead of remaining in Venice, Jacopo preferred to pursue his painting career in the provincial town of Bassano. But Jacopo's interest in the art of other painters and the prints of their work he collected kept him from an isolated rural mentality, and his art shows an awareness of the developments in northern Europe and in central Italy, in particular the art of Raphael.* By 1541 Jacopo received government support in the form of an exemption from paying city taxes because of the excellence of his art. His *Adoration of the Shepherds* (1546, London, Hampton Court) combines a certain naturalism with finely drawn, graceful, and attenuated figures of Mannerist descent.

Throughout his career, Jacopo experimented while remaining sensitive to many artistic currents. In the 1560s he combined his loose brushwork with a deeper interest in coloristic, luminous, and chiaroscuro effects. For his later bucolic visions of country life and rustic biblical subjects, often portrayed as nocturnal scenes, Jacopo harmonized a pastoral simplicity and emphasis on genre details with a sophisticated artifice. With the help of his sons, he led an incredibly productive workshop. Remaining apart from the Venetian art scene, his special brand of rustic poetry that balanced mannerist stylism, observation of nature, and expressive brushstroke found favor in Venice and the surrounding countryside both among collectors and artists.

Bibliography

B. L. Brown and P. Marini, eds., *Jacopo Bassano, c. 1510–1592*, exhibition catalog, 1993.

Mary Pixley

BEAUMONT, FRANCIS (c. 1585–1616)

Francis Beaumont is best known for his partnership with John Fletcher,* chief dramatist, after William Shakespeare's* retirement, to the King's Men. His satiric wit and sensibility differed markedly from Fletcher's, however, and deserve the separate and appreciative notice recent scholarship has afforded them.

Beaumont was born in Leicestershire, England, the third son of a justice of the court of common pleas and a member of a prominent recusant family. Following a brief period at Oxford, he entered the Inner Temple, presumably to study his father's profession, but he never became a lawyer. Instead, he began writing satirical verse, ranging from the Ovidian *Salamacis and Hermaphroditus* (1602) to the biting, even shocking poems on the deaths of acquaintances. His earliest unaided play, *The Knight of the Burning Pestle* (1607), although unsuccessful when first presented, was, when published several years later, highly praised. It is today his most popular solo work. In these early works Beaumont's tart and cutting observations of the new and middle-class world around him brought him considerable notice. His detachment may well have been sharpened by his position both as a recusant and a younger son, both conditions having left him outside the path of economic success his position in a well-connected family might otherwise have provided him.

Between 1605 and 1613 Beaumont lived and worked closely with John Fletcher, producing many other dramas, including *Philaster, The Maid's Tragedy*, and *A King and No King*. Their popular collaboration provided a balance between Beaumont's penchant for satire and Fletcher's interest in weightier, more lyrical material. Their work achieved its preeminence in their own time for having articulated on stage what Philip Finkelpearl has called "the inauguration of the postheroic age" during James I's* reign.

In 1613 Beaumont retired from the theater following his marriage to Ursula Isley, an heiress from Kent. Evidently Beaumont suffered an apoplectic attack, or stroke, during that same year and wrote no more afterwards. He fathered two daughters, one born posthumously, and died in 1616. He was only the third poet, after Geoffrey Chaucer and Edmund Spenser,* to be buried in Westminster Abbey.

Bibliography

L. Bliss, *Francis Beaumont*, 1987.
F. Bowers, ed., *The Dramatic Works in the Beaumont and Fletcher Canon*, 16 vols., 1966–96.
P. J. Finkelpearl, *Court and Country Politics in the Plays of Beaumont and Fletcher*, 1990.

Robin Farabaugh

BECCAFUMI, DOMENICO (c. 1486–1551)

Domenico Beccafumi had a significant role in the development of the Mannerist style in sixteenth-century painting in central Italy. Noted as a painter in Siena in 1507, Beccafumi probably studied painting in a mediocre workshop there. Around 1510–12 Beccafumi went to Rome for the first time. The impact of his Roman experience was immediate and long-lasting, with references to the art of Raphael,* Michelangelo,* Baldassare Peruzzi,* and antique Rome visible in his art. Beccafumi was also heavily influenced by the Florentine artist Fra Bartolomeo, as seen in his painting of the *Stigmatization of Saint Catherine* (c. 1515, Siena, Pinacoteca). In 1519 Beccafumi began creating a series of designs for the pavement of the cathedral of Siena. A probable second trip to Rome updated Beccafumi on the latest innovations there, as evidenced in his *St. Michael Evicting the Rebel Angels* (c. 1524, Siena, Pinacoteca), which shows the influence of Michelangelo's *Last Judgment*. At the same time, Beccafumi balanced the Roman influence with his own personal style consisting of liquid and loose brushstrokes, vivid colors, contrasts of light and shadow, elongated figures, and an evanescent elegance.

Testifying to his growing reputation, in 1529 the Sienese government commissioned Beccafumi to provide some decorations for the communal palace and entrusted him with the organization of the festive decorations for the entrance of Emperor Charles V,* and Andrea Doria invited Beccafumi to Genoa to participate in the decoration of his palace. As a mature artist in the 1530s, Beccafumi felt free to experiment, and the fantastic element may be seen as overtaking reality in his art as he adopted an irrational system of lighting with sudden bursts of light, exaggerated contrasts, and transparent color. This unrealistic use of light combined with Beccafumi's fluid and loose painting manner and unique mixture of Roman classical learning and anticlassical experimentation gave his art an impalpable and elusive quality, making him a highly original painter.

Bibliography

Domenico Beccafumi e il suo tempo, exhibition catalog, 1990.

Mary Pixley

BECON, THOMAS (c. 1513–1567)

A preacher and propagandist whose career stretched from the reign of Henry VIII* to that of Elizabeth I,* Thomas Becon contributed to the progress and success of the Reformation in England. Becon appears to have been born in Norfolk and to have entered Cambridge University in 1527. Influenced by Hugh Latimer, Becon quickly became known as a Protestant Reformer. Ordained as a priest in 1533, he eventually ran afoul of the anti-Protestant Six Articles of 1539 with his preaching and was ordered to recant in 1541. He then retired to Kent, where he wrote a number of dialogues under the pseudonym Theodore

Basille. After being forced to recant again in 1543, Becon wrote devotional works and poetry while traveling quietly in England's midlands.

Upon Edward VI's accession in 1547, Becon gained a chaplaincy in Lord Protector Edward Somerset's household. Archbishop Thomas Cranmer* also appointed him one of Canterbury's six preachers. During Edward's reign Becon contributed the "Homily against Adultery" to the *Book of Homilies* and wrote the most popular of his works, *The Sick Man's Salve*, which demonstrates how to die a peaceful Christian death.

Soon after the Catholic Mary I* came to the throne in 1553, Becon was imprisoned for a time, after which he joined several Protestants in exile on the Continent. This community smuggled anti-Catholic pamphlets into England, where they sold readily. Influenced by his fellow exiles, Becon's contributions, including *An Humble Supplication unto God for the Restoring of His Holy Word unto the Church of England*, demonstrate an invective that would become uncharacteristic of his later work. Becon returned to England after Mary's death and Elizabeth's accession in 1558, and in 1564 he produced a folio collection of his works. He eventually became canon of Canterbury, where he died in 1567.

Bibliography

D. S. Bailey, *Thomas Becon and the Reformation of the Church in England*, 1952.

Kevin Lindberg

BELLEAU, RÉMY (c. 1528–1577)

Pierre de Ronsard's* designation of Rémy Belleau as a "painter of nature" secured his membership in the group of French poets known as the Pléïade, whose other members were Jean-Antoine de Baïf,* Joachim Du Bellay,* Étienne Jodelle,* Jacques Peletier Du Mans, Pierre de Ronsard, and Pontus de Tyard. Little is known of Belleau's childhood, apart from his birth in Nogent-le-Routrou and the patronage he received from Chrétophle de Choiseul, abbot of Mureaux, who helped further his education at the Collège de Boncourt in Paris. His studies in Greek under Marc-Antoine Muret,* Ronsard's celebrated commentator, culminated in Belleau's translation of Anacreon's *Odes* (1556), which was followed by *Petites hymnes de son invention*, poems about various abstract or concrete objects—the glowworm, snails, shadows, time—evoking a cosmic lyricism. If these works elicited Ronsard's praise and secured his membership in the Pléïade, others became jealous of the attention Ronsard showed him. After a period of interest in the Reformation, Belleau left for the French campaign against Naples with René de Lorraine in 1557, returning to France to write occasional poetry at the court of Charles IX and later Henri III, dividing his time among Champagne, Lorraine, and Paris. His stay in Joinville-en-Bassigny from 1563 to 1566 was the most calm, studious part of his life, thanks to the marquis of Elbeuf. During this period Belleau wrote a pastoral composition in verse and prose, which he published as *La Bergerie* (1565), later reediting it in

1572. His volume of lapidary poems, *Les amours et nouveaux eschanges des pierres precieuses, verius et proprietez d'icelles* (1576), demonstrates Belleau's talent for precise description as he renders in minute detail a portrait of each different kind of gem and its origins, influences, and properties. Like many of his contemporaries, Belleau was convinced that each gem represented a different celestial element, the mastery of which can give man a happy and healthy life. Before his death in the Hôtel de Guise during one of his brief trips to Paris in 1577, Belleau completed an adaptation of *Ecclésiaste* and a paraphrase of the *Cantique des cantiques*. His sole dramatic work, *La reconnue*, an unfinished comedy, was published posthumously in 1578. Ronsard's epitaph of his friend Belleau is perhaps most telling: "Don't engrave, industrious hands, stones to cover Belleau, for he himself has built his tomb in his *Pierres precieuses*."

Bibliography

J. Braybrook, "Science and Myth in the Poetry of Remy Belleau," *Renaissance Studies* 5, no. 3 (September 1991): 277–87.

Nancy Erickson Bouzrara

BEMBO, PIETRO (1470–1547)

Scholar, courtier, and, later in life, cardinal, Pietro Bembo was one of the foremost arbiters of Italian and Latin literary style of the sixteenth century. Bembo was the son of the Venetian diplomat Bernardo Bembo, himself a significant personality in his native city's intellectual and political community. Pietro studied Greek under Constantine Lascaris at Messina and philosophy under Pietro Pompanazzo at Padua and later fell in with the circle of scholars associated with the Venetian printer Aldus Manutius. Bembo resided in Ferrara from 1498, where he began a passionate, though epistolary, romance with Lucrezia Borgia, the wife of Alfonso d'Este. It was to her that Bembo dedicated his well-known *Gli Asolani* (1505), a dialogue on earthly and platonic love written in his trademark polished Italian. In 1506 he was lured to the celebrated court of Urbino, where his scholarly ability, gentility, and pleasant manner made him a popular figure and, eventually, a principal speaker in Baldesar Castiglione's* *Il cortegiano* (The Courtier).

In 1512 Bembo moved to Rome in the company of Giuliano de' Medici and was appointed papal secretary to Leo X,* Giuliano's brother, shortly afterwards. He was a natural addition to the community of artists, scholars, and socialites that Leo took pains to foster. Like his employer, Bembo tended to value the literary grace of pagan antiquity over the moral imperatives of Christianity; a famous anecdote has him advising Jacopo Sadoleto to avoid studying the Epistles of St. Paul too closely lest he become corrupted by their inferior style. An ubiquitous member of a distinguished circle that included Raphael,* Vittoria Colonna,* and the affluent Agostino Chigi, Bembo also became enamored of a young Roman woman named Morosina. Their long and affectionate relationship lasted twenty-two years, eventually producing three children.

Bembo remained in the papal service until 1519, when, in poor health, he retired to Padua to pursue his cultural interests. In 1522 he took minor orders and used the income from his ecclesiastical benefices to finance his household, which became a notable repository for fine art, antiquities, and books, as well as a popular haunt for artists and literati. It was while he was at the height of his influence in 1530 that he accepted a commission to pen the history of Venice (published in 1551) and was appointed librarian of St. Mark's Cathedral soon after. It may have been Morosina's death in 1535, however, that wrought a fundamental change in his personality. In time, he began to regard his religious duties with a more serious eye, applying himself to the scriptural study that he had once disdained. He was made a cardinal by Pope Paul III in 1539, bishop of Gubbio two years later, and lived as a model churchman until his death in 1547.

Bembo's fame derives largely from his role as the most influential dictator of style in Latin and Italian letters of his time. His endorsement of Ciceronian style as the standard for excellence in Latin manifests itself in the technical perfection of his correspondence and poetry and is outlined in his *De imitatione* (1513). Perhaps his most significant work was his *Prose della volgar lingua* (Prose in the vernacular tongue). Published in 1525, this was a significant contribution to the movement to establish the fourteenth-century Tuscan vernacular of Petrarch and Boccaccio as the model for Italian literary endeavor. Aside from his *Gli Asolani*, Bembo's other major works include *De Aetna* (1496) and *Le rime* (1530), as well as his editions of Petrarch's poetry (1501) and Dante's *Commedia* (1502), which he guided into print through the Aldine press.

Bibliography

P. Bembo, *Gli Asolani*, trans R. Gottfried, 1954.
G. Braden, "Applied Petrarchism: The loves of Pietro Bembo," *Modern Language Quarterly* 57 (September 1996).

Michael J. Medwick

BESS OF HARDWICK (c. 1527–1608)

A loyal friend and servant to Queen Elizabeth I,* Bess of Hardwick became one of the wealthiest women of Elizabethan England. She was a grand matriarch committed to securing position and affluence for her family.

Born at Hardwick Hall in Derbyshire, Hardwick was daughter to John Hardwick and Elizabeth Leake. She was married in 1543 to Robert Barley. This was the first and shortest of her four marriages. Barley died in 1544. In the years following his death Hardwick served as lady-in-waiting to Lady Dorset. In 1547 Hardwick married William Cavendish, treasurer of the Chamber. Together the couple had six children. Both Hardwick and Cavendish were ambitious and began acquiring lands and estates. Hardwick was also acquiring a keen financial intellect. Cavendish had a profitable career until he was accused of pilfering funds in 1557. Cavendish died later that year, leaving Hardwick with a sub-stantial debt to the throne.

When Elizabeth I took the throne in 1558, Hardwick was appointed lady-in-waiting. While at court, Hardwick married Sir William St. Loe, captain of the guard and later chief butler of England. St. Loe was very generous to Hardwick and to her children. With St. Loe, Hardwick built up an impressive estate at Chatsworth. His death in 1565 left her a very wealthy widow.

Hardwick entered her fourth and final marriage in 1567, this time to George Talbot, earl of Shrewsbury. Shrewsbury was a widower with seven children, reputed to be the richest nobleman in England. Indeed, the arrangement focused on finance; in order to allow both Hardwick and Shrewsbury's children to benefit from the amalgamation of wealth, Hardwick arranged for the marriage of two of her children to two of Shrewsbury's children. This way, the union would profit future generations on both sides of the family. All three marriages seemed congenial until duty to the queen put a strain on Shrewsbury. He accused Hardwick of manipulating him and stealing his possessions. The couple separated for two years, and only at the insistence of the queen did they reconcile in 1587.

During this separation Hardwick began developing Hardwick Hall into the grand estate that bears her name. Widowed again in 1590, Hardwick returned there with an assortment of family, including her granddaughter, Lady Arabella Stuart. Hardwick died a very old woman in 1608. She left her children well endowed, and Hardwick Hall still stands as a tribute to its mistress.

Bibliography

D. N. Durant, *Bess of Hardwick: Portrait of an Elizabethan Dynast*, 1978.
E. C. Williams, *Bess of Hardwick*, 1959.

Michele Osherow

BEZA, THEODORE (1519–1605)

A French Protestant biblical scholar, Reformed diplomat, and theologian who served as a professor at John Calvin's* Geneva Academy from 1558 to 1595, Theodore Beza made major contributions to New Testament textual studies and was a creative formulator of Reformed doctrine. He produced a critical edition of the Greek New Testament text, further developed Calvin's doctrine of pre-destination, and became, after Calvin's death in 1564, his successor as leader of the Genevan church and of the Reformed movement.

Beza came from an old French Catholic family in Vézelay in Burgundy and while being educated under M. Melchior Wolmar, a Protestant, came into con-tact with John Calvin, who was a frequent visitor to his tutor. From 1535 to 1539 he studied law in Orléans in preparation for an ecclesiastical career. Mov-ing to Paris in 1540, he published some minor literary works and, after formally renouncing Roman Catholicism in 1548, moved to Geneva and married Claudine Denossos. In 1549 he was appointed professor of Greek at Lausanne and in 1558 accepted Calvin's offer of a professorship at the Geneva Academy. Despite his academic responsibilities, he remained active in the affairs of the French Reformed church, participating in the 1561 Poissy colloquy between Catholics and Huguenots, and in 1562, when civil war broke out, he sought help from German Protestant rulers. He participated in numerous theological controversies, on the nature of free will with Sebastian Castellio, against Laelius Socinus on the doctrine of the Trinity, and against Lutheran ubiquitarians on the nature of the Eucharist.

His first major theological work was *De haereticis a civili magistratu puniendis* (Heretics to Be Punished by the Civil Magistrate), written in 1554 to defend the actions of the Genevan magistrates in condemning Michael Servetus* to death by public burning for denying the doctrine of the Trinity. In 1559 he published a defense of Reformed beliefs in his *Confession de la foi chrétienne* (Confession of the Christian Faith), a confession that was swiftly translated into Latin (1560) and various European languages. As a result of ongoing disputes with the Lutherans on the nature of the Eucharist, Beza produced a series of apologetic works between 1559 and 1593 on the question of Christ's spiritual presence in the Sacrament. In 1574 his *Du droit magistrats* (The Right of Magistrates) argued, against accepted medieval political tradition, that subordinate government officials had the authority to depose a tyrannical ruler. However, his major academic contribution was in the field of biblical studies. His edition of the New Testament, first published in Latin with annotations in 1556 (with the Greek text included in the 1565 edition), went through five editions during his lifetime. Beza intended this edition to replace that produced by Desiderius Erasmus,* which he regarded as textually and doctrinally defective. Beza's New Testament text was based on the text produced by Henricus Stephanus (Henri Estienne) in 1550 and included variants from hitherto-unknown manuscripts such as the Codex Bezae. He also published an edition of the Psalms left incomplete by Clément Marot.* Beza's Scripture text was widely used in Europe and served as a primary source for the translators of the Authorized King James Version.

Bibliography

I. D. Backus, *The Reformed Roots of the English New Testament: The Influence of Theodore Beza on the English New Testament*, 1980.
J. S. Bray, *Theodore Beza's Doctrine of Predestination*, 1975.

Iain S. Maclean

BODIN, JEAN (1529/30–1596)

Jean Bodin was the first political theorist of the early modern period to emphasize the concept of sovereignty. In his *Six Books of the Republic* (1576), Bodin examined difficult conditions in his native France and called for the establishment of one center of unimpeachable political authority.

Jean Bodin was born and received his initial education in Angers, France. He subsequently studied law, history, languages, mathematics, and astronomy at

Toulouse, later securing a teaching post in law. Throughout Bodin's adult life France was racked by civil and religious strife and was led by weak and ineffectual monarchs. At the core of his most influential work, the *Six Books of the Republic*, is a search for a lasting solution to this endemic instability. At the time of its publication in 1576, Bodin was serving as a deputy to the Third Estate of the French Estates General, the chief legislative forum under the monarch. Only four years earlier, the Catholic majority in Paris had set upon the minority Protestant population of the city and had massacred upwards of 10,000 men, women, and children. In the aftermath of such a disaster, it is no surprise that Bodin's *Six Books* was a popular and influential work, being published in ten French editions, together with three Latin ones, before the author's death in 1596. It was first translated into English in 1606.

Bodin was a Roman Catholic, but he argued that continued persecution of the Protestant minority was not only divisive but also counterproductive. In his mind, religion was a personal matter, and so long as the sovereignty of the state was not threatened on the basis of religious principles, forms of worship were best left to the discretion of the individual believer. Despite this exceptional expression of tolerance in an age of persecution, a view shared by a small group of thinkers known as Politiques, Bodin never acknowledged any right to resistance on the part of aggrieved religious minorities. To permit such a right implied that there was a power in society higher than that of the sovereign.

Six Books of the Republic defines sovereignty as the unabridged and undivided power to make law for the entire nation. This sovereign law always supersedes local tradition and customary law. According to Bodin, in the absence of this untrammeled power, no state can long survive as an integral unit, and he was doubtless thinking here of the situation in his own country. Bodin was not concerned with the precise location of this sovereign power. For example, it might be exercised under a monarchy, an aristocracy, or a democracy. But he did reject the idea that sovereignty can in any respect be divided or shared. In a monarchy like France, Bodin's sovereign king does not simply follow the medieval model of the ruler as the dispenser of justice; instead, a proactive king makes law for the well-being of the community, appoints all inferior magistrates, decides issues of war and peace, and serves as a court of final appeal in all religious, civil, and criminal cases. All power exercised on behalf of the ruler was in the end merely a delegation of sovereign authority, not an authority distinct from the sovereign.

It is important to acknowledge that Bodin was not in favor of unrestricted and absolute monarchy. He firmly believed that the legitimate ruler must always rule in conformity with natural and divine law. Like the divine King of Kings, the legitimate sovereign monarchy must temper power with justice. The ruler must also respect deeply held custom and, above all, property rights. The ruler will also seek the advice and consent of the representative estates of the realm, especially when the issue of taxation is to be addressed.

For Bodin, the purpose of civil society was not merely the advancement of material or utilitarian good. Rather, the sovereign power must be exercised on behalf of Christians who seek to live in harmony and pursue their goal of salvation without hindrance. In this key respect Bodin's theories were informed by theological considerations, and it would be left to subsequent thinkers to shift his dynamic idea of sovereignty into the secular realm of politics.

Bibliography

J. H. Franklin, *Jean Bodin and the Rise of Absolutist Theory*, 1973.

William Spellman

BOEHME, JAKOB (1575–1624)

Jakob Boehme, after a series of mystical experiences, turned from shoemaking and devoted the rest of his life to preaching and writing about God. Boehme's accounts of his mystical experiences later became a major influence upon other religious movements, such as the Quakers.

Boehme was born and lived much of his life in Görlitz, near the Black Forest in Germany. While gazing at the reflection of the sun in a jar of pewter, Boehme interpreted this to be the manifestation of divine truth. This truth, as he would later write in his letters, was that the universe is a theater wherein an eternal conflict between spirit and matter is waged. Boehme argued that matter is the source and embodiment of all evil; however, without matter, even the divine spirit would not exist. Thus the divine spirit needs matter to exist, and yet matter is what leads to evil—hence the inevitable, necessary conflict between spirit and matter.

When critics confronted Boehme and questioned the authority of the claims he was making, Boehme usually responded by stating that the mystical experiences that revealed these truths were not really "his" experiences but the God in him. "Not I," Boehme would write, "the I that I am, know these things, but God knows them IN me." This ultimately led Boehme to argue and preach that true salvation is achieved only when the limited "I" and "self" of a person are transcended, such as Boehme believed occurred during his mystical experiences.

Of the intellectuals who were later influenced by Boehme, perhaps the most significant is F.W.J. Schelling. Schelling was particularly influenced by Boehme's claim that the identity and limits of the self must be overcome, and in doing so, one then comes to recognize the true nature of the relationship between the divine and the worldly. The Quaker movement was also deeply influenced by the writings of Boehme. Boehme represents an important minor tradition within traditional religion—the Gnostic, mystical tradition—and is likely to continue to be associated with other mystics and Gnostics, such as Meister Eckart, Giordano Bruno,* and Paracelsus.*

Bibliography

D. Walsh, *The Mysticism of Innerworldy Fulfillment*, 1983.

Jeffrey A. Bell

BRAHE, TYCHO (1546–1601)

The founder of modern observational astronomy, Tycho Brahe led the transition from ancient to modern astronomy that occurred after the introduction of Nicolaus Copernicus's* heliocentric model of the universe. His reputation as the foremost astronomer of his day rested upon a number of cosmological discoveries, the establishment of a new standard for astronomical instrumentation, and a series of technical studies of the heaven's movements.

Tycho's fascination with astronomy began when he witnessed a partial eclipse on 21 August 1560. For three years thereafter, he eagerly studied astronomy and mathematics in Copenhagen until his uncle sent him to Leipzig University to broaden his studies. Rhetoric and philosophy, however, did not appeal to Tycho, and his determination to pursue astronomical studies only increased when he obtained copies of the planetary tables of King Alfonso X of Castile and the Prussian tables compiled by one of Copernicus's assistants. Tycho learned how to determine the positions of the planets using the tables and soon detected systematic errors in the data. Ill-designed instruments accounted for the discrepancies, and so Tycho compiled a table by which to correct his observations. Thus by age sixteen Tycho had already learned that systematic observation coupled with improved instrumentation could reduce or eliminate inaccuracies in astronomical tables.

King Frederick II of Denmark endowed Tycho with the island of Hven and funds for building two state-of-the-art observatories known as Uraniborg or "the city of the heavens" and Stjerneborg or "the city of the stars," as well as an annual pension to support his research efforts. Tycho's most memorable cosmological discoveries were a new, fixed star, which appeared in the constellation of Cassiopeia on 1 November 1572, and the arrival of the 1577 comet. Both the appearance of a new star and a comet running a course in the ether high above the moon ran counter to Aristotelian logic, which maintained a strict dichotomy between a changing earthly sphere and an unchanging heavenly sphere. Based on his comet studies, Tycho dismissed Aristotle's concept of solid planetary spheres. He proposed instead the Tychonic world system, an earth-centered model capable of representing all astronomical phenomena without positing belief in a moving earth, for which no proof yet existed. Tycho also realized the immediate necessity of producing a new star catalog to record celestial changes occurring since Ptolemy's second-century record of the heavens.

In 1581 Tycho began working on his star catalog, a ten-year project that required a plethora of specialized instruments capable of producing the most precise measurements possible. During the 1580s Tycho completed his solar theory, studies of refraction, and his lunar theory. Forced to leave Hven in 1597, Tycho moved to Prague, where Johannes Kepler* joined him as an assistant in 1600. When Tycho died in October 1601, the long-delayed star catalog was still not ready for the presses, and it was Kepler who oversaw the final publication in 1602 of his mentor's *Astronomiae instauratae progymnasmata* (First exercises in a Restored Astronomy).

Bibliography

V. Thoren, *The Lord of Uraniborg: A Biography of Tycho Brahe*, 1990.

Whitney Leeson

BRANTÔME (PIERRE DE BOURDEILLE) (c. 1540–1614)

Pierre de Bourdeille, better known as Brantôme, was a career courtier and soldier whose salacious and detailed accounts of life at court provide a portrait of aristocratic France during the reigns of François I* and Henri II. Born around 1540 to a noble family, Pierre de Bourdeille was raised at the court of Marguerite de Navarre* with his grandmother, Louise de Vivonne, who figures as one of the characters in Marguerite's famous work *The Heptameron*. In 1556 Henri II granted de Bourdeille the abbey at Brantôme as a benefice, by which name he was known thereafter. Although he received three additional such benefices, he never took ecclesiastical orders and remained an active courtier and soldier for the first forty years of his life. He fought in several military campaigns, including a religious crusade to Malta. Brantôme may have flirted with Protestant ideas, although it is certain that he fought on the Catholic side of the civil war of 1569 and remained Catholic for the rest of his life, if indeed he had ever converted. Brantôme was an active courtier; however, in 1582 his eldest brother, André, the governor of Perigord, died, and Brantôme quarreled with Henri III over the succession. As a result, he broke with Henri, went into a self-imposed exile, and determined to enter the service of the king of Spain. He began writing his book *Les dames galantes*, an account of life at court, in an effort to raise money to carry out these intentions. Unfortunately, in 1584 a riding accident caused him serious injury, leaving him a semi-invalid for the rest of his life and isolating him from court.

After the accident, Brantôme continued his writing as his only link to the courtly exploits of his past. First published posthumously in 1665, the works reflect his disappointment in his lack of advancement while still at court. However, they are a rich recounting of that life, especially the numerous scandals and gossip of the various courts to which he was attached. The biographies contained therein are of varying accuracy, and many of the stories are borrowed from other sources; nonetheless, the works overall grant a vivid picture of a Renaissance court.

Bibliography

R. Cottrell, *Brantôme: The Writer as Portraitist of His Age*, 1970.

Erin Sadlack

BRIÇONNET, GUILLAUME (c. 1472–1534)

Guillaume Briçonnet was an influential Catholic reformer who through his Meaux Group created a uniquely French approach to the Reformation. Briçonnet was the second of the five surviving children of Guillaume Briçonnet; his family had a long tradition of service to the kings of France. The elder Briçonnet was the counsellor of the French king Charles VIII. After his wife's death, he entered holy orders and received several ecclesiastical dignities, including the position of cardinal. The younger Briçonnet received a humanist education and studied law.

Briçonnet accepted the position of bishop of Lodève in 1489 while still a student. He became the queen's chaplain in 1496 and a canon of Paris in 1503. He succeeded his father as the abbot of Saint-Germain-des-Prés and became bishop of Meaux in 1516. Briçonnet held these and other offices concurrently. He also served the French king in various capacities. King Louis XII sent him to Rome in 1507 on a diplomatic mission. Briçonnet later took part in the Council of Pisa (1511) and negotiated the Concordat of Bologna with Pope Leo X* on behalf of King François I* (1516–17).

Briçonnet attempted to reform his diocese of Meaux. He made frequent visitations, encouraged devotion to the Eucharist and the Virgin Mary, and promoted a religous revival by means of sermons and tracts printed in the episcopal residence. Finding his priests lacking or absent, he divided his diocese into thirty-two preaching positions and encouraged scriptural preaching in the vernacular. After Jacques Lefèvre d'Étaples's* French translation of the New Testament was published in 1523, Meaux became a center of religious revivalism in France that was protected by François I's sister Marguerite de Navarre.*

Briçonnet created the Meaux Group, bringing noted humanists such as Lefèvre into his diocese for biblical studies and preaching. While Briçonnet sought to combine humanism with biblical study in order to reform the church outside of his diocese, several members of the Meaux Group became attracted to Lutheran theology and began to question the veneration of saints, purgatory, and prayers for the dead. Although Briçonnet himself had condemned Lutheranism, he still had to appear twice before the Parlement of Paris on suspicion of heresy. During François I's captivity in Spain following the disastrous Battle of Pavia (1525), the Parisian Faculty of Theology and the Parlement of Paris joined forces and had the Meaux Group dispersed.

Through the Meaux Group, Briçonnet created a French approach to the Reformation. Briçonnet wanted the French church to be reformed but argued that such a reform needed to be conducted at the episcopal level.

Bibliography

J. Farge, *Orthodoxy and Reform in Early Reformation France*, 1985.
M. Veissiere, *L'evêque Guillaume Briçonnet (1470–1534)*, 1986.

Andrew G. Traver

BRONZINO, IL (1503–1572)

Agnolo di Cosimo di Mariano Tori, better known as "Il Bronzino," is commonly regarded as a principal figure of sixteenth-century Italian Mannerist painting. He was born in Monticelli, in the vicinity of Florence, and served an apprenticeship under the artist Rafaelino del Garbo. But it was his close friendship and lifelong professional association with Pontormo* beginning around 1517 that strongly influenced Bronzino's early artistic persona. In time, however, he gradually emerged from his master's influence to develop an increasingly refined, cerebral style of painting.

After a stint in the service of the duke of Urbino, Bronzino returned to Florence, where he continued to collaborate with Pontormo while taking on independent work. In 1539 he was commissioned to assist with the wedding decorations for the marriage of Cosimo I* and Eleanora of Toledo.* The success of his efforts led to his employment as the official painter and portraitist of the Medici court, an appointment that produced many of his most representative works. The pronounced use of chiaroscuro and the formal, aristocratic poise evident in earlier portraits like that of *Guidobaldo della Rovere* (1532) were showcased and refined in his portraits of *Cosimo I* (date uncertain) and his family. His portrait of Cosimo's illegitimate daughter, *Bia de' Medici* (before 1542), is frequently noted for its almost lapidarian stillness and beauty. Portraiture aside, Bronzino's major accomplishment during this phase of his career was the Chapel of Eleanora, in the Palazzo Vecchio, which he meticulously decorated in fresco between 1540 and 1546. Bronzino's other paintings often reflect the sophisticated composition and awkward, highly stylized posturings typical of Mannerism, such as the erudite and erotic *Allegory of Venus, Cupid, Time, and Folly* (before 1545).

Bronzino was eventually eclipsed in the Medici court by Giorgio Vasari,* but his professional reputation remained intact. He continued to receive commissions, mostly for religious pieces that were influenced by his study of the anatomical work of Michelangelo* and Raphael.* Aside from painting, Bronzino also pursued his interest in poetry by publishing a number of his own works between 1555 and 1560 and dedicating others to his patron Cosimo I. He remained active until his death in 1572.

Bibliography

A. Cecchi, *Bronzino*, 1996.

Michael J. Medwick

BRUEGEL (BRUEGHEL), PIETER (c. 1526/27–1569)

Pieter Bruegel, a painter and graphic artist, was the first and most outstanding member of several generations of artists in his family. He was born near Breda in the Netherlands. Both the contemporary Italian art historian Giorgio Vasari* and Bruegel's fellow countryman Karel van Mander mention Bruegel; van Mander describes the artist as "Pier den Droll" because his works always evoked laughter.

Bruegel may have trained with Pieter Coecke van Aelst,* whose daughter he married a number of years later. However, more significant for his artistic development were his years spent between 1555 and 1563 with the printer Hieronymus Cock, for whom he designed engravings. Some of the prints produced in Cock's shop Bruegel engraved in the style of Hieronymus Bosch, the Dutch artist of the previous generation famous for his phantasmagoric scenes.

Although Bruegel painted religious scenes, the traditional subject of most paintings up to his generation, he was best known in his own time and is still known today for his realistic depictions of folklore and peasant life, neither condescending nor sentimental in vein. Several large paintings, which the artist may have intended as a series, catalog courtship and marriage. The group includes a kermis, or peasant festival, and a *Peasant Wedding Feast* where the nuptial feast takes place in a barn, with puddings and pies distributed to the guests from a barn door. The series, painted between 1566 and 1568, concludes with a jubilant, romping *Peasant Dance*.

In an earlier series (1565) of paintings depicting the seasons, peasants engage in various timely labors: hunting, haymaking, and harvesting corn. These scenes capture the essence of each period of the year, particularly in *Hunters in the Snow*, a painting that evokes better than any painting before that time the frosty, icy chill of winter in its dark forms and figures set against a stark white and silvery gray landscape. By contrast, in *Wheat Harvest*, summer shimmers in an even golden light, with bright patches of red and orange dotting the parched yellow swathes of wheat to suggest the broiling heat of midday. Bruegel further displayed his virtuosity by painting scenes teeming with life and activity in encyclopedic works, such as his *Children's Games* of 1560 describing a great variety of youthful pastimes and his earlier work of 1559, *Netherlandish Proverbs*, showing the myriad follies of adults.

Bruegel's biographer, Karel van Mander, asserted that the artist liked to dress up as a peasant and participate in peasant activities. However, Bruegel was almost certainly well educated; we know that he traveled throughout Italy between 1551 and 1554, and he counted among his colleagues the cartographer Abraham Ortelius, the publisher Christopher Plantin, the humanist Dirck Coornhert,* and the poet Dominicus Lampsonius. Wealthy merchants, Cardinal Antoine de Granvelle, and the Habsburg royal family collected Bruegel's work— many of the artist's best-known works are today in the Vienna Kunsthistonisches Museum.

Bruegel was one of the most intriguing artists of the sixteenth century, and his influence lived after him, not only through the work of his sons, artists who became well known in their own right, but through other artists who emulated his style, in particular Bruegel's genre and landscape scenes. Some later artists even spuriously signed their drawings or engravings as by Bruegel, presumably because such works demanded higher prices.

Scholars still debate whether or not Bruegel's works held hidden political or religious meaning. According to van Mander, he instructed his wife to burn many of his works shortly before he died in 1569 because he thought that they might put his family in jeopardy.

Bibliography

Walter S. Gibson, *Bruegel*, 1977.

Susan H. Jenson

BRUNO, GIORDANO (1548–1600)

Remembered best as a Renaissance magician and as a victim of intellectual intolerance, during his life, Giordano Bruno fashioned a Neoplatonic natural philosophy that saw the universe as an infinite, organic, and living emanation from God. Although his works are magical in sentiment, they prefigured many of the tenets of modern science, rejecting tradition and espousing rationalism.

Little is known of Bruno's earliest years following his birth in the Neapolitan town of Nola in 1548. By 1565 he entered the famous Dominican house of San Domenico Maggiore, and despite early suspicions of heresy, Bruno's superiors allowed his ordination as a priest in 1572. Fears soon resurfaced, and a trial was initiated against him. After escaping to Rome, he found himself once again subject to an investigation. By 1576 he had left the Dominican order and had fled to points north.

Thus began a fifteen-year period of wandering. Bruno's open rejection of contemporary religious ideas and received philosophical traditions brought him into trouble with both secular and religious authorities, be they Catholic or Protestant. In 1581 his life became a bit more stable—although no less controversial—when he received the protection of King Henri III of France. In Paris he published on the arts of memory, turning to a deeply magical understanding of the problem. Moving to England as part of the French embassy of 1583, he remained there and wrote his most systematic works, six Italian dialogues that argued in detail for a new understanding of the cosmos—a magical, infinite universe of multiple worlds harmoniously united by emanations from God.

The final fifteen years of Bruno's life comprised more of the same. He departed England in 1585 and traveled widely through Germany and Bohemia, continuing to publish on old themes as well as new ones, most notably, an atomic theory on the nature of matter. By 1591 he took up residence in the relatively liberal Republic of Venice upon the invitation of a powerful patrician. Within a year Bruno's protector denounced him to the Inquisition. He was imprisoned in Rome for the last eight years of his life, determined to convince church authorities that his views were correct. Finally, he refused to recant and was burned for heresy in 1600.

Since Bruno's ideas were so radical, it is hard to measure any direct influence upon his contemporaries. He defended the heliocentricity of Nicolaus Copernicus* and extended it into a theory of an infinite universe, arguing that the Bible had no astronomical authority. He advanced a monistic metaphysics of the world in which form and matter combined through a generative force manifesting itself in every living thing. He outlined a moral theory of virtue, elevating philosophical reason and relegating religion to a secondary role for the instruction of the ignorant. He rejected Aristotelian physics in favor of atomism. He used reason to concoct a mysterious blend of magical spiritualism.

Although certain parallels can be found in the works of Galileo* and Johannes Kepler,* most contemporaries were either unaware of his work or rejected him out of hand. Abrupt and intolerant in his tone, Bruno found few disciples. While modern scientists might find aspects of Bruno's thought in harmony with their own, his works appealed to few contemporaries beyond a small group of like-minded Neoplatonists. Yet Bruno's elaboration of universal harmonies is not wholly unlike Isaac Newton's later, more prosaic one.

Bibliography

H. Gatti, *Giordano Bruno and Renaissance Science*, 1999.
F. A. Yates, *Giordano Bruno and the Hermetic Tradition*, 1964.

Edmund M. Kern

BRY, THEODORE DE (1528–1598)

Flemish engraver Theodore de Bry made famous representations of American Indians that were among the first artistic impressions of "New World" peoples produced in Europe. De Bry operated in the international Protestant circle that was interested in overseas trade, colonization, and exploration. In 1587 he traveled from his Frankfurt home to London and received the commission from Sir Walter Raleigh* to engrave plates based upon the drawings made by John White of the indigenous inhabitants of "Virginia." These became part of the set of elaborate illustrations that accompanied his series depicting European voyages to the Americas, Africa, and Asia. Published in thirteen parts between 1590 and 1634, de Bry's *Grands Voyages* included, in addition to White's drawings and Thomas Hariot's description of the English colony at Roanoke, Jean de Léry's 1555–56 narrative of his visit to Brazil, the drawings of Jacques Le Moyne of the natives of Florida and the description of the ill-fated Huguenot colony there, Girolamo Benzoni's *Historia del Mondo Nuovo* (History of the New World), and other accounts. A less ambitious series, the *Petits Voyages*, focused on the activities of the Dutch in the Arctic, Africa, and East Asia.

American Indians, as depicted in de Bry's interpretation of indigenous life in Virginia and Florida, were well muscled and noble—innocent savages—who engaged in their daily routines without apparent self-consciousness. But the engraver also chose to include illustrations of the natives of Central and South America as practitioners of human sacrifice and cannibalism, and he offered portrayals of the bizarre, such as the Brazilians whose heads purportedly grew beneath their shoulders. What armchair readers in the early modern period, who gobbled up such accounts, made of all this remains unclear, but at the least they must have obtained a sense that European visitors regarded Americans with a mixture of fascination and disquiet.

Bibliography

T. de Bry, *Thomas Hariot's Virginia*, 1966.

Louis Roper

BUCER, MARTIN (1491–1551)

Martin Bucer, a Protestant Reformer, was most famous for his efforts to mediate religious differences, both between his fellow Reformers and between Protestants and Catholics. Born in Schlettstadt (Selestat), Alsace, to a family of humble means, Bucer reluctantly entered the Dominican order at the age of fifteen so that he could receive an education. His studies at Heidelberg led him to the works of the humanist scholar Desiderius Erasmus,* and in 1518 he began a correspondence with Martin Luther.* He left the Dominicans in 1521 and, after briefly serving one of the electors of the holy Roman emperor, was appointed pastor in Landstuhl; he then married Elisabeth Silbereisen, a former nun, becoming one of the first ordained priests among the Reformers to marry.

Excommunicated in 1523 for recommending the study of the German Bible and advancing Lutheran views, Bucer fled to Strasbourg and joined the many Reformation sympathizers in that city. Strasbourg was particularly well situated for Bucer's purposes, lying between southern Germany and Switzerland, where the Swiss Reformer Huldrych Zwingli* held sway, and northern Germany, an area heavily influenced by Martin Luther. A dispute between these two famous Reformers arose after 1524 over the nature of Christ's presence in the Host at Communion. Bucer attempted to effect a compromise between Zwingli's humanist view that Christ's presence was largely spiritual and Luther's more traditional belief that the presence in the bread and wine was more concrete. At the end of a colloquy to resolve the dispute, Luther refused to compromise with Bucer and Zwingli. In an attempt to mend this and other rifts in the Reform movement, Bucer participated in virtually every conference focusing on religious questions held in Switzerland and Germany from 1524 to 1548.

The 1530s saw Bucer rise from a relatively uninfluential Protestant divine who nevertheless showed great potential to an eminent figure in the Reformation. He acted as an ecclesiastical consultant in several towns in southwest Germany and became a trusted and useful advisor to Philip of Hesse—unfortunately also contributing to that landgrave's infamous bigamy. Bucer reorganized the ecclesiastical order of Hesse and was a motivating force behind instituting and organizing the Reformed church in Strasbourg.

In 1541 Bucer participated in the Diet of Regensburg, the goal of which was to reach an agreement between Protestants and Catholics on certain issues—for example, the doctrine of sin and issues of the Mass and Communion. The ultimate goal was the reconciliation and reunification of the church, but the resistance to compromise on both sides proved too great for any hope of a lasting peace. In that same year, Bucer's wife and several of his children died of the plague; a year later he married the widow of Wolfgang Capito, a noted Hebrew scholar and fellow Reformer who also had a reputation as a mediator of religious disputes.

The 1540s saw Bucer pushing doggedly for reform, beginning with an attempt—which ultimately failed—to work with Hermann von Weid, the archbishop of Cologne, to implement a moderate church reform in that city. In the course of the decade, the combination of the judgments of the Council of Trent and the attempts by Holy Roman Emperor Charles V* to force unity on the princes of Germany resulted in the Augsburg Interim of 1548, a compromise with which Bucer disagreed. The Interim succeeded in suppressing the discussion of theology to an extent unacceptable to Bucer, and at the invitation of Thomas Cranmer,* archbishop of Canterbury, he sought refuge in England in 1549.

His last years in England were active. Cranmer sought Bucer's advice repeatedly, and a professorship of divinity at Cambridge was arranged for his livelihood. Bucer was asked to contribute criticism to the first edition of *The Book of Common Prayer*, warned the religious community in England against importing the continental dispute over the Communion into the British Isles, and completed his greatest work, *De regno Christi*, in October 1550 (published posthumously in 1557).

Bucer was a prolific writer, producing over ninety works in his lifetime, from sermons to treatises on theology to detailed plans of religious reform. He influenced many other religious thinkers than those already mentioned, including Peter Martyr Vermigli, John Calvin,* and Philip Melanchthon,* and was second only to Erasmus among major foreign Protestant divines invited to England in the sixteenth century. His most enduring claim to fame is the ceaseless effort he devoted to promoting a constant equitable dialogue between religious factions in the early years of the Protestant Reformation.

Bibliography

H. Eells, *Martin Bucer*, 1931.

Richard J. Ring

BUCHANAN, GEORGE (1506–1582)

George Buchanan, a humanist scholar and convert to Calvinism, was the author of *De jure regni apud Scotos* (The Right of the Kingdom in Scotland, 1579). This book defended the deposition of Queen Mary Stuart* in 1567 and argued in favor of the right to resist ungodly rulers.

Buchanan was educated first at Aberdeen, Scotland, and later at Paris, where he subsequently taught and distinguished himself as an author of Latin poems and plays. He returned to his native Scotland in 1561, abandoning Roman Catholicism for the Calvinist teachings of John Knox.* During the 1570s and 1580s he was employed as a propagandist for the government, and it was during these decades that his most important work was published.

Buchanan's resistance theory was composed in response to dramatic events that had recently overtaken his country. In 1567 a revolt had taken place against Queen Mary of Scotland, a Roman Catholic who had outraged Scottish Protestant nobles by marrying the earl of Bothwell, the alleged murderer of Mary's second husband, Lord Darnley. In the aftermath of the queen's expulsion, her infant son was installed as James VI,* and a regency government was established under the Protestant earl of Moray. Catholic opinion in Europe was out-raged at this turn of events; in response, the new government sought to justify its actions in print. Buchanan was enlisted for the important work.

Buchanan's first contribution was *A Detection of the Doings of Mary, Queen of Scots* (1571), a hostile biography designed to injure the deposed queen's reputation by making her complicit in the murder of her husband and thus unfit to govern as a Christian prince. This work was followed by *De jure regni*, which was first published in 1579 but circulated in manuscript before this date. The book, which was dedicated to the boy king James VI, was reissued several times both in Scotland and on the Continent, and it remained in print into the eighteenth century.

In *De jure* Buchanan argued that legitimate monarchs gain their power by popular consent. In his view, rulers were charged with the maintenance of justice as established in law, and the authors of the law are the estates of the realm acting on behalf of the entire nation. On the other hand, tyrants are defined as those who secure power without the consent of their subjects, or who exercise their power in opposition to the known rule of law. Tyrants rule in pursuit of their own selfish interests; legitimate monarchs always place the welfare of the larger community of the realm first. Resistance to tyrants is always justified, even to the extreme of using military force or assassination. Buchanan's call for a general revolt and even tyrannicide is more radical than anything proposed by continental resistance theorists in the late sixteenth century.

Bibliography

I. D. McFarlane, *Buchanan*, 1981.

William Spellman

BUDÉ, GUILLAUME (1467–1540)

A contemporary of Desiderius Erasmus,* Guillaume Budé, one of France's leading humanists, served at the court of François I* and was instrumental in founding the Collège de France, a center for humanist teaching. Budé, who belonged to a family of government functionaries, began training for a career at court by studying the arts in Paris and the law in Orléans. However, he never finished his law degree, and around 1491 he began to study the classics intensively. Although he received some tutoring from various Hellenists, Budé was mainly self-taught.

At the behest of the chancellor, Charles VIII appointed Budé secretary of the king in 1497; however, he resigned sometime between 1502 and 1506, probably because the job interfered with his studies. He began to translate works of Greek literature into French; the study of ancient languages was becoming more popular, and Budé's reputation grew.

In 1508 Budé published his *Annotationes in Pandectas* (Annotations on the Pandects), a commentary on the first twenty-four books of Justinian, which also contained a severe attack on the legal profession and its methods. Although the work was poorly organized and difficult to follow, it was well received, and in 1515 he published *De asse*, a work on classical weights, measures, and coinage. In both works Budé included many useful annotations and quotations from the classics, as well as political, social, and economic commentary on French affairs.

At this point, Budé began to reenter public life. François I, who had assumed the throne in 1515, wanted to cultivate the cultural reputation of his court. Accordingly, he preferred appointing educated men to important positions; the time was auspicious for a humanist to succeed in courtly affairs. In 1519 Budé presented François with his work *Institution du prince*, which belonged to the "mirror of princes" genre, describing the duties and proper behavior of a ruler. Budé published several other works in his lifetime, including a Greek lexicon titled *Commentarii linguae graecae* (Commentary on the Greek Language) and a book on philology, *De philologia*. In addition, he continued his letters to other humanists, such as Erasmus and Thomas More.*

Throughout his life Budé wavered between the active and contemplative life. However, he continued to serve François, attending him at court and acting as a foreign envoy. Although Budé became disgusted at his lack of progress in courtly life and withdrew from court for a time, he returned and received the prestigious office of master of the king's library. In addition, he was appointed master of requests, a magisterial position, and provost of the merchants of Paris. However, these positions were largely honorary in nature, and he did little actual work at them.

More importantly, during this period, Budé, with the help of Marguerite de Navarre,* the king's sister, was instrumental in persuading François to endow royal lectureships in humanist topics such as Greek, Hebrew, and mathematics. He also convinced François to commit himself further and establish a royal college that would focus on these subject areas and oppose the strictly conservative Sorbonne. With François's permission and Marguerite's support, the institution in time became the Collège de France, a center of humanist learning.

Budé died in August 1540, but he left behind a rich legacy of humanist studies. His influence inspired much of the resurgence of classical languages in France, and it was he who helped develop France's growing literary and cultural reputation. His translations and compendia of classical works became widely used as textbooks in various fields of learning, and scholars throughout Europe celebrated his achievements. Above all, his fame ultimately enabled him to persuade François to support the foundation of the Collège de France, which has enriched the culture and learning of France for centuries.

Bibliography

D. McNeil, *Guillaume Budé and Humanism in the Reign of Francis I*, 1975.

Erin Sadlack

BULL, JOHN (1562–1628)

The English composer and musician John Bull was recognized by his contemporaries as the most skillful keyboard performer of his day, but his personal life was less esteemed. His career playing the organ and virginal with the musicians of the Chapel Royal lasted for twenty years, during which time he composed both religious and secular pieces. In 1596 Elizabeth I* recommended Bull as lecturer in music at newly founded Gresham College; unable to write lectures in Latin, he was granted special permission to use English. Since one of the requirements was residency at the college, and his assigned rooms were occupied, he battered down a wall to hasten the previous tenant's departure.

In recognition of his talent, Bull was granted doctorates in music from Cambridge and Oxford; his portrait still stands in the Bodleian Library. Favored by Elizabeth I, James I,* and the latter's heir Henry, he served as music tutor to James's daughter Elizabeth and wrote an anthem to celebrate her marriage. He also enjoyed the patronage of many wealthy Roman Catholics, for whom the virginal was a favorite instrument. One of his better-known pieces is "Lord Lumley's Pavan," for an aristocrat who also patronized William Byrd.* Bull collaborated with Byrd on a collection entitled *Parthenia* that contained some of the earliest keyboard duets (c. 1612). The following year he fled to Antwerp in disgrace, pursued by the king's wrath and a letter from the archbishop of Canterbury informing Archduke Albert that Bull was charged with adultery and other "grievous crimes." Bull apparently had had a long history of sexual episodes, including one that resulted in a forced marriage that in turn cost him his position at Gresham College. The archduke protected Bull, who became the organist of Antwerp Cathedral in 1617; in his application, he claimed that his exile was not for adultery but for adhering to the Catholic faith. It is not recorded that anyone believed this assertion. Bull remained in Antwerp until his death in 1628, known to contemporaries as a brilliant composer and performer with "more music than honesty."

Bibliography

D. Wulstan, *Tudor Music*, 1985.

Jean Graham

BULLINGER, HEINRICH (1504–1575)

Heinrich Bullinger was a Swiss Reformer and theologian, active in the composition of the First and Second Helvetic Confessions, developer of the Reformed doctrine of the covenant, and in 1531 successor to Huldrych Zwingli* as chief pastor at Zurich. He was born in Bremgarten, the fifth child of Henry Bullinger, parish priest and dean, and Anna Widerkehr. He was educated at Emmerich, where he was influenced by the *Devotio moderna*, the devotional teachings characteristic of the northern Renaissance, and the University of Cologne, graduating with degrees in 1520 and 1522, before teaching from 1523 to 1529 at the Cistercian school at Kappel at the personal invitation of its abbot, Wolfgang Joner. Earlier, in 1520, he had come under the influence of Martin Luther's* works, especially *The Babylonian Captivity of the Church* and *On Christian Liberty*, and of Philip Melanchthon's* *Loci communes*, influences that led to his conversion first to Lutheranism and then to a modified form of Zwinglianism. In 1529 he was married to Anne Widlischweiler, a former nun. After the military defeat of the Protestants at Kappel in October 1531 and the deaths of Zwingli and Joner, Bullinger was forced to move his family to Zurich, where he was appointed Zwingli's successor.

Apart from John Calvin,* Bullinger was the leading theologian on Swiss and continental reform. He had a formative role in the composition of the First and Second Helvetic Confessions, of 1536 and 1566, respectively, and of the Consensus Tigurinus of 1549. These confessional statements provided both a national and a continental platform for Reform movements. He rejected, in numerous controversies, the Lutheran doctrine of the Eucharist and wrote two well-known refutations of Anabaptism. In 1571 he published a reply to the bull *Regnans in excelsis*, by which the pope excommunicated Elizabeth I* of England. The reply went through numerous editions in Latin, German, and English. His collection of sermons, published under the name *Decades* because of their tenfold division, became a standard Reformed work in Europe, England, and Scotland, as well as later among the early Puritan settlers of the American colonies.

Bullinger made significant contributions to Reformed theology, apologetics, and thought, particularly through his articulation of the concept of the covenant and in his broader understanding of the doctrine of predestination. In his early work *De testamento* (Concerning the Covenant, 1534) he argued for the unity and continuity of one covenant stretching from the one concluded by God with Abraham through to the renewed covenant in Jesus Christ. While there remained a single covenant, the external structures or practices might change through time. Consequently, little sharp distinction was drawn between the secular and the sacred, and God's election was to some extent modified by human adherence to the covenantal laws. Bullinger was a prolific writer, producing over eighty publications on a wide range of biblical and theological issues.

Bibliography

J. W. Baker, *Heinrich Bullinger and the Covenant*, 1980.
G. W. Bromiley, ed. *Zwingli and Bullinger*, Library of Christian Classics, 1953.

Iain S. Maclean

BURBAGE, RICHARD (1567–1619)

The greatest actor of his time, Richard Burbage originated many famous roles of the English stage, including Hamlet, Oberon, Othello, Lear, Volpone, Ferdinand in John Webster's* *Duchess of Malfi*, and Hieronimo in Thomas Kyd's* *Spanish Tragedy*. Born into a theatrical family, the son of James Burbage, a theatrical entrepreneur, and younger brother to Cuthbert, a business manager, young Richard began as a boy actor at the Theatre, the first open-air playhouse, built by his father in 1576. In 1594 Richard Burbage joined the Lord Chamberlain's Men, later the King's Men. William Shakespeare* also joined the company around this time. With Richard Burbage as the star and Shakespeare's plays as the major property, the Lord Chamberlain's Men became a profitable, popular company and a powerful force. Unlike their rivals the Admiral's Men, who employed a manager, eight actors of the Lord Chamberlain's Men, including Burbage and Shakespeare, invested in and received profits from the company.

When the Theatre's lease expired in April 1597, Burbage decided to build a playhouse on land across the Thames. Legend has it that on 28 December 1598, workmen dismantled the Theatre and floated the oak timber frames across the Thames to build the Globe, which was completed in 1599. In 1608 Burbage and his brother gained control of Blackfriars, an indoor theater. With this acquisition, for the first time, one company had command of two theaters, enabling the Lord Chamberlain's Men to work both summer and winter, day and night.

Burbage's skill as an actor was one of superb voice and stage presence. Unlike his rival, Edward Alleyn, a large, physical, melodramatic actor famous for playing Marlowe's* Dr. Faustus, Burbage had range. Women swooned over him; men imitated him in the streets. The nature of the Renaissance stage provided a place for his genuine intimacy with the players and familiarity with the audience. His acting was considered realistic and sophisticated, so realistic, in fact, that playing the death of Hamlet, Burbage was thought to be truly dying. Not wanting to move into a more administrative capacity, Burbage worked as an actor until his death in 1619.

Bibliography

A. Gurr, *Playgoing in Shakespeare's London*, 1987.

Megan S. Lloyd

BURGKMAIR, HANS (1473–1531)

Hans Burgkmair, the son of the prominent Augsburg painter Thoman Burgkmair, studied both under his father and with Martin Schongauer in Colmar. He became a friend of Albrecht Dürer* and, like Dürer, made full use of the print medium, introducing the chiaroscuro woodcut in the north. He also shared Dürer's great interest in the new ideas of the Italian Renaissance and responded particularly to the work of Venetian painters.

Achieving the status of master painter in 1498, Burgkmair probably married in the same year the sister of Hans Holbein the Elder, thus linking himself with the Holbein family of painters, who were also close neighbors in Augsburg. Burgkmair was well traveled, spending much time in Italy, particularly in Venice, which was an important center of printing and humanistic studies. His work shows the influence of both Italian and Netherlandish art. Known for his woodcuts as well as for his portraits and religious paintings, Burgkmair settled in Augsburg, a rich and cosmopolitan city where his status was as high as that of Albrecht Dürer in Nuremberg.

Through his prints, Burgkmair came to the attention of Emperor Maximilian

I, for whom he made ninety-two genealogical woodcuts. He was also one of several artists called upon to illuminate Maximilian's Prayer Book and participated in the illustrations for the emperor's autobiographical romance, the *Weisskunig*. With Dürer and others, he made woodcut designs for elaborate triumphal processions and arches for the emperor. Apart from his work for the emperor, Burgkmair is perhaps best known for his *St. John Altarpiece* of 1518, now in Munich, a work that blended Italianate and northern styles.

Burgkmair also participated in the growing dialogue between the German humanists and painters, encouraged by such men as Conrad Celtis, Maximilian's librarian. At Celtis's death, both Burgkmair and Dürer paid tribute, Burgkmair with a portrait woodcut of Celtis. Burgkmair's portraits and portrait woodcuts strongly influenced those of Hans Holbein the Younger,* but he was important also as an intellectual, a purveyor and supporter of the new humanism, and an eminent role model for Hans Holbein the Younger.

Bibliography

A. von Bartsch, *Sixteenth Century German Artists: Hans Burgkmair the Elder, Hans Schaufelein, Lucas Cranach the Elder*, 1980.
H. M. Kaulbach, "Trial Sheets for Maximilian I," *Burlington Magazine*, May 1995: 313–14.

Rosemary Poole

BYRD, WILLIAM (c. 1543–1623)

William Byrd was one of the most prominent composers of sixteenth-century England; in addition, he was known as a versatile musician, able to perform on many instruments. He probably began his musical career as a choirboy, either in Queen Mary's* Chapel Royal or at St. Paul's Cathedral with his two older brothers. Byrd served as organist of Lincoln Cathedral from 1563 until he joined Elizabeth I's* Chapel Royal in 1572. His compositions bear some resemblance to those of his teacher, Thomas Tallis.* With Tallis he was so favored by Elizabeth that in 1575 the monarch granted the two composers a monopoly on printed music and music paper; the venture was a business failure, producing only one publication, their joint *Cantiones sacrae* (Sacred songs, 1575), which did not sell. When Tallis died ten years later, he left his share to Byrd's youngest son, Thomas, Tallis's godson. William Byrd later sold his share to his own pupil, Thomas Morley.* Both Byrd and Morley were famous for writing madrigals and secular dance music. Byrd also collaborated with John Bull,* publishing a collection entitled *Parthenia* (c. 1612).

Byrd adhered to the Roman Catholic faith despite its unpopularity in the England of his time. He was apparently forced to withdraw from publication his *Gradualia* (1605), a collection of motets based on the Roman Catholic liturgy. With his wife Juliana, their children Rachael, Elizabeth, and Christopher, and at least one of their servants, Byrd was prosecuted on several occasions for absenting himself from Anglican services. However, none of the cases reached trial, since Byrd was protected by the queen. Nor did Byrd's Catholic ties prevent him from setting to music many poems of Sir Philip Sidney,* a strong Protestant. Christopher Byrd later married the sister of a Catholic chaplain.

Byrd's instrumental music, of which he published little, was virtually unknown until the twentieth century. However, both vocal and instrumental compositions are creative and imaginative while drawing on English musical tradition. Equally at ease composing in Latin and English, Byrd claimed in his *Psalmes, Songs, and Sonnets* (1611) that his goal was one of matching his music "to the life of the words."

Bibliography

J. Harley, *William Byrd: Gentleman of the Chapel Royal*, 1997.

Jean Graham

C

CALMO, ANDREA (1510–1571)

Like Ruzzante,* Andrea Calmo was both actor and playwright. In many ways he may be considered as the heir of Ruzzante and the link to the commedia dell'arte. His first comedy, produced in 1540, was *La Rodiana* (The Woman from Rhodes). This was followed by *Il Saltuzza*, a comedy featuring two servants, one male and one female, who try to outwit each other. These pieces are more to be regarded as farces than as regular comedies, with little or no characterization. Their humor depends more on the repetition of the same thoughts and gestures by the same stereotyped characters. Calmo is credited with the creation of the stock character Pantalone, the avaricious old man usually outfoxed by his servant, who would become a staple of the commedia dell'arte.

La pozione (The Potion) is an adaptation of Niccolò Machiavelli's* *Mandragola*, in the manner of a farce. The central character is a parasite who helps the student gain the merchant's wife. In the play *Fiorina*, in imitation of Ruzzante's homonymous play, the protagonist renounces her coquetry and settles for a comfortable life with the old suitor, Coccolin. The farce entitled *Spagnola* (1549) has many elements that anticipate the commedia dell'arte.

Calmo made exuberant use of various languages and dialects—Venetian, Paduan, Bergamask, Dalmatian, Greco-Venetian, and even Turkish. This linguistic variety also characterizes his *Egloghe pastorali*, produced in 1553, which are more in the classic pastoral form. Perhaps Calmo's most interesting work is his collection of imaginary letters, bizarre conversations with historical personages that contain fables and fantastic stories, songs, and proverbs. The last book of the collection is addressed to courtesans. The letters are written in an archaic Venetian and are of interest for their chronicling of the customs of the day.

Bibliography

P. Vescovo, *Da Ruzante a Calmo*, 1996.

Charles Fantazzi

CALVIN, JOHN (1509–1564)

A dominant figure of the Protestant Reformation, John Calvin was a preacher, biblical scholar, and theologian. Although his Reform movement was centered in Geneva, Calvin's influence extended throughout all of Europe in the sixteenth century.

John Calvin was born in Noyon, France, and initially set out on a course of training that would prepare him for an ecclesiastical position in the Catholic church. However, after studying theology in Paris, he switched to the study of law at Orléans. By the early 1530s Calvin had come under the influence of the French humanist movement, and his earliest publication was a Latin commentary on Seneca's *De clementia* (1532). At this time Calvin also began to associate with a group that favored reform in the church, and by 1534 he had clearly identified himself with the Protestant movement in France. Faced with the threat of persecution, Calvin left his native land and ended up in Basel, where in 1536 he published what would become one of the most important works of the Protestant Reformation, the *Christianae religionis institutio* (Institutes of the Christian Religion).

Later that same year Calvin found himself in Geneva, where Guillaume Farel insisted that Calvin stay and help carry out the reform of the church. Calvin and Farel set out to work immediately, but after various conflicts with the civil magistrates, they were forced into exile in 1538. This time Calvin settled in Strasbourg, where Martin Bucer,* another leading Protestant Reformer, had a decisive influence on Calvin's thought. During this Strasbourg period Calvin married and also published an expanded French edition of the *Institutes* (1541) that became a seminal work in the development of the French language. Calvin's literary production during his stay in Strasbourg was impressive; it included his extensive *Commentary on the Book of Romans*, as well as a strong defense of Protestantism in response to the challenge of Jacopo Sadoleto, a Catholic cardinal.

In 1541, with the success of the Reformation in Geneva in jeopardy, Calvin was called back to the city, and although he never enjoyed complete freedom from conflict with the city magistrates, he was now given greater control over the reform of the church. Calvin set out to make Geneva into a model Christian commonwealth. The *Ecclesiastical Ordinances* (1541) provided the blueprint for Calvin's organization of the church in Geneva, and Calvin continued to press for an independent ecclesiastical structure that was free from subjection to civil authority and free to exercise religious and moral supervision over the citizens of Geneva. To this end, Calvin instituted the consistory, a body of church leaders (elders and ministers) that was responsible for ecclesiastical discipline. Calvin also worked to rid Geneva of all remnants of the Catholic religion and to establish a Reformed style of worship that emphasized simplicity, the preaching of the Word, and psalm singing. By the 1550s Calvin had become the leader of an international Reformed, or Calvinist, movement. Calvin himself carried on an extensive correspondence with Protestant leaders throughout Europe, and

Geneva developed into a hub for Protestant publishing and printing. A gifted organizer, Calvin was instrumental in the establishment of the Genevan Academy (1559), which functioned as a training ground for Calvinist pastors and missionaries and became a center of Protestant higher education.

In addition to his duties as a pastor, preacher, and teacher, Calvin continued to write extensively throughout his years in Geneva. He revised and expanded the *Institutes* until it appeared in the definitive 1559 edition, wrote commentaries on almost all of the books of the Bible, and engaged in polemical exchange with both Catholics and Protestants. In the *Institutes*, a magisterial statement of Protestant doctrine, Calvin demonstrated his deep learning and articulated the central themes of his theology: the absolute authority of Scripture, the sovereignty of God, the complete depravity of human beings, salvation and faith as divine gifts, and, in this context, his well-known doctrine of predestination. Calvin also emphasized the need for a biblical piety and for a disciplined and active Christian life, lived in obedience to God's will. Calvin's political thought provided the foundation for a theory of resistance that would develop into an important force within European politics. Calvinism expanded rapidly in the mid-sixteenth century, and by 1560 Calvinist congregations were located throughout much of Europe, from Poland to Scotland. Calvin's encouragement of these churches often enabled them to survive as underground and persecuted communities. Eventually, Calvin's influence extended, via Puritanism, across the Atlantic as well. In the end, Calvin must be regarded as one of the most significant religious thinkers and actors of the sixteenth century. His impact was enormous.

Bibliography

W. J. Bouwsma, *John Calvin: A Sixteenth-Century Portrait*, 1988.
A. McGrath, *A Life of John Calvin: A Study in the Shaping of Western Culture*, 1990.
M. Prestwich, ed., *International Calvinism, 1541–1715*, 1985.

Michael A. Hakkenberg

CAMDEN, WILLIAM (1551–1623)

William Camden was important both as an antiquarian and a historian, as exemplified, respectively, by his topographical survey *Britannia* and his *Annales rerum Anglicarum et Hibernicarum regnante Elizabetha* (Annals of English and Irish History in the Reign of Queen Elizabeth). Born in London on 2 May 1551 to painter Sampson Camden and his wife Elizabeth, he was educated at Christ's Hospital, St. Paul's School (1564–66), and Oxford University (1566–71)—at Magdalen, Broadgates Hall (Pembroke), and Christ Church—though without receiving the bachelor of arts. Returning to London in 1571 and devoting himself to antiquarian studies, he became second master at Westminster School in 1575 and headmaster in 1593, where Ben Jonson* and other notables were his students. Queen Elizabeth* appointed him Clarenceux king-of-arms in 1597, prompting a scholarly feud with York Herald Ralph Brooke. His publications include *Britannia* (1586), a Greek grammar (1597), a list of Westminster Abbey epitaphs (1600), an edition of early English chronicles (1603), assorted *Remains* (1605), an account of the Gunpowder Plot trial (1607), and the first part (to 1588) of *Annales* (1615); the latter part appeared posthumously, as did a short history of James I's* reign, various Society of Antiquaries papers, and his correspondence. He died on 9 November 1623 and is buried in Westminster Abbey.

Camden knew many contemporary scholars, including Sir Robert Cotton,* John Selden, and Sir Henry Spelman in England and Isaac Casaubon,* Abraham Ortelius, and Jacques-Auguste de Thou on the Continent. His *Britannia* continues a tradition including the ancients Strabo and Varro, the Renaissance Italian Flavio Biondo, and Englishmen John Leland and William Lambarde. The first edition addresses only Roman Britain, but Camden gradually enlarged subsequent editions to include the Anglo-Saxon and Danish periods. Though not directly challenging Geoffrey of Monmouth, Camden rejected the more fantastic elements of British legend. Camden traveled extensively but relied more on secondary sources than Leland. Camden's *Annales*, which Cotton may have helped write, represents a second tradition including Polybius, Tacitus, and the Renaissance scholars Leonardo Bruni, Francesco Guicciardini,* and de Thou. Camden revived the previously abandoned project in 1608 for King James, who was dissatisfied by George Buchanan* and de Thou's accounts of his mother, Mary Stuart* (Mary Queen of Scots). A continuous, complex narrative based on primary sources, it avoids fictional speeches, recognizes the contingent (as opposed to teleological) nature of history, defends the Anglican establishment, and praises Elizabeth's, and by implication James's management of Parliament and diplomacy. The Camden Society, founded in 1838, honors him with quality editions of primary sources.

Bibliography

H. Trevor-Roper, *Queen Elizabeth's First Historian: William Camden and the Beginnings of English "Civil History,"* 1971.

D. R. Woolf, *The Idea of History in Early Stuart England: Erudition, Ideology, and "The Light of Truth" from the Accession of James I to the Civil War*, 1990.

                                                                William B. Robison

CAMERARIUS, JOACHIM (1500–1574)

Joachim Camerarius, a German classicist and theologian, edited and translated works of numerous classical authors, wrote biographies of contemporary humanists, helped reorganize the universities at Tübingen and Leipzig, and had a moderating influence on Lutheranism in the Augsburg Diets. The son of an episcopal official, Camerarius was born in Franconia and studied at the universities in Leipzig and Erfurt, where he joined the humanist circle. He went on to Wittenberg in 1521, where he became a pupil of Philip Melanchthon* and a renowned scholar of classical Greek. In a distinguished academic career, he advanced from rector of the gymnasium in Nuremberg to a professorship at the

University of Tübingen and then to dean at the University of Leipzig. He published over 150 works, mostly editions and translations of Greek authors, including Homer, Sophocles, Herodotus, Thucydides, Aristotle, Ptolemy, and Galen. In addition to his classical works, he wrote biographies of Eobanus Hessus, Duke George of Anhalt, and Philip Melanchthon. He worked to promote religious compromise, serving in 1530 as a deputy of the city at the Diet of Augsburg, where he helped write the Augsburg Confession. He participated in discussions with François I* in 1535 and Maximilian II in 1568 regarding reuniting Catholics and Protestants.

By supporting Luther in the 1520s, he contributed to the initial success of Protestantism, and by advocating flexibility and compromise, he exerted a peaceful influence during a period of religious strife. Through his administration and promotion of classical studies, Camerarius helped turn Tübingen and Leipzig into leading Protestant universities.

Bibliography

M. Forster in *The Oxford Encyclopedia of the Reformation*, ed., H. J. Hillerbrand, 1995: 249.

Tim McGee

CAMÕES, LUÍS VAZ DE (c. 1524/25–1580)

Luís Vaz de Camões, nicknamed the "Portuguese Virgil," was the greatest lyric poet of Portugal, and indeed of sixteenth-century Europe, and the author of the epic national poem *Os Lusíadas* (The Lusiads or, literally, The Portuguese, 1572). This work commemorated the nation and the navigator Vasco da Gama's discovery of the sea route to India via the Cape of Storms or Good Hope. Camões's writings, both epic and lyric, had a lasting impact on Portuguese, Brazilian, English, southern African, and European literature.

Despite conflicting and unreliable biographical sources, it is known that Camões was born in Lisbon to an impoverished minor aristocratic family. He acquired a comprehensive classical and contemporary knowledge through his formal training at the College of All Saints in Coimbra, gaining the bachelor's degree in 1542, and through his own experiences in North Africa and the Iberian Peninsula. However, offending the court through an ill-managed love affair with Catharina de Ataíde, daughter of the royal chamberlain, he was exiled in 1546. In 1547 he went to Ceuta, returning briefly to Portugal before leaving with Cabral in 1553 for India. He spent the next seventeen years in the Far East, Goa on the Indian coast, the Mekong Delta, and Mozambique. He returned to Portugal in 1570, published *Os Lusíadas* in 1572, the first vernacular epic of modern times, and received in consequence almost universal acclaim and a royal pension. The epic was well received not only by the Portuguese court and in Spain (Spanish translation in 1580), but also across Europe, in particular by the Italian Torquato Tasso* and later by Humboldt.

Camões's poetic works include lyric poems, drama, and epic. The title of

Camões's *Os Lusíadas* was taken from the Roman name for Portugal, Lusitania. The epic poem, modeled on the *Aeneid*, relates and praises the great deeds of the Portuguese, especially their victories over the enemies of Christianity. This national epic is infused with a crusading spirit, describing the courage and exploits of earlier Portuguese explorers. The poem itself, in ten cantos of 1,102 stanzas, begins with a dedication to King Sebastian before proceeding to describe the voyages of Vasco da Gama. The epic describes this voyage on a literal and on a mythological level as a conflict among the Olympian deities. In this manner Camões attained a remarkable synthesis of indigenous, national, and classical themes, extolling the adventurous life and, inter alia, exhorting divided European Christian monarchs to unite against the threatening advances of Islam in southern Europe.

While Camões's dramatic works have remained relatively unknown outside of the Iberian Peninsula, his sonnets, odes, and elegies are highly regarded. His epic is considered the greatest synthesis of classical and Christian themes ever written and is the source of his claim to be the greatest sixteenth-century poet.

Bibliography

A.F.G. Bell, *Luis de Camões*, 1923.
L. V. de Camões, *The Lusíads*, trans. L. White, 1997.
A. B. Giamatti, *The Earthly Paradise and the Renaissance Epic*, 1966.

Iain S. Maclean

CAMPION, THOMAS (1567–1620)

The English poet, composer, and physician Thomas Campion (or Campian) exemplifies the basically collaborative nature of Renaissance literature and music. Campion's parents were gentry who died when he was a child. He was sent to Cambridge at age fourteen, but apparently left without a degree. He was admitted to Gray's Inn at age nineteen, but rather than becoming a lawyer, he began to write poetry in Latin and drama such as masques; he may also have performed in some of these entertainments. He became friends with the composers John Dowland* and Philip Rosseter, both of whom began setting Campion's poems to music around 1600. Campion wrote a dedicatory epigram to Dowland's *First Booke of Songs* (1597). Campion began to write poems in English for Rosseter to use as lyrics, and then to compose his own music, which Rosseter published in his *Book of Ayres* (1601).

Campion's main goal in composing music was that the words should be heard, and with their correct stresses. His *Observations in the Art of English Poesie* (1602) dismissed rhyme as old-fashioned, an idea well in advance of its time and refuted to general contemporary satisfaction by Samuel Daniel's* *Defense of Ryme* (1603). Campion's other idea has never caught on: to use Latin meters for English poetry. Apparently having exhausted the modest 260 pounds he had inherited from his mother, Campion studied medicine at the University of Caen, finishing his degree in 1605 or 1606. Returning to England, he practiced medicine while continuing to publish poetry and music, frequently in collaboration with Rosseter: *Songs of Mourning* (for Prince Henry, 1613), *Two Books of Ayres* (c. 1613), *The Third and Fourth Books of Ayres* (c. 1617), *Ayres That Were Sung and Played at Brougham Castle* (1618), and two volumes of Latin epigrams and elegies (1619). His book of musical theory, *A New Way of Making Fowre Parts in Counterpoint* (c. 1618), was dedicated to Prince Charles (later Charles I).

In competition with Samuel Daniel and Ben Jonson,* Campion wrote masques for the court, with sets and costumes designed in at least two cases by the prominent Inigo Jones. *The Caversham Entertainment* was performed for the queen, and *The Lord's Masque* for the wedding of Princess Elizabeth. Both were published in 1613, as was *The Masque on St. Stephen's Night*, which was commissioned for the wedding of Lady Frances Howard to Robert Carr, the earl of Somerset, one of the king's favorites. Soon after the wedding, the couple was charged with the fatal poisoning of Sir Thomas Overbury,* who had opposed his friend Somerset's marriage and Lady Frances's divorce from her first husband. Campion was cleared of complicity in the murder, but his friend and patron Sir Thomas Monson was imprisoned in the Tower for over a year.

Campion apparently never married. On his death in 1620, he left his estate of twenty pounds to Rosseter, with the wish that it had been more. Campion's lyric poems in English have been admired by later critics and poets; his music has been performed and adapted frequently in recent years.

Bibliography

W. Davis, *Thomas Campion*, 1987.
C. Wilson, *Words and Notes Coupled Lovingly Together: Thomas Campion, A Critical Study*, 1989.

Jean Graham

CARAVAGGIO (MICHELANGELO MERISI) (1571–1610)

One of the most influential Italian painters of the seventeenth century, Michelangelo da Caravaggio, so called after the Lombard hometown of his family, where he spent much of his youth, is almost equally as notorious for his volatile and violent temperament as he is noteworthy for his achievements as an artist. He, with the Carracci* family of Bolognese painters whose revival of classical style presents a strong contrast with Caravaggio's naturalism, is credited with inspiring the transformation of Italian painting in the seventeenth century, which would later become identified as the baroque era.

Although Caravaggio never established a workshop to cultivate pupils, as did many of his contemporaries, the originality and power of his works spawned a following that spread throughout Europe in the decades following his death. The *caravaggisti*, or *tenebristi*, as they are also called because of the obscure darkness out of which the figures appear to emerge—the hallmark of Caravaggio's mature style—include such notable painters as the Italians Orazio Gentileschi and his daughter Artemesia,* Giovanni Baglione, Bartolommeo Manfredi, Carlo Saraceni, and Giovanni Caracciolo, the Frenchman Georges de la Tour, the Spaniard José de Ribera, and Gerrit von Honthorst and Hendrick Terbruggen in the Netherlands, who in turn had an influence on the art of Rembrandt, as well as Peter Paul Rubens* in Flanders following his Italian travels. A veritable who's who of seventeenth-century painters, this list of admirers is even more remarkable for a painter whose career spanned less than two decades and whose paintings were rejected more often than is commonly perceived because of the ways in which he radically reinterpreted both secular and sacred subjects.

Caravaggio was born in 1571, probably in Milan, where his father worked as a steward of the Sforza, a family whose protection Caravaggio would enjoy throughout his life. The first in his family to take up painting, he was apprenticed at thirteen to Simone Peterzano in Milan, a painter virtually unknown today. Caravaggio's art was clearly affected by the religious and artistic climate of post-Tridentine Milan, which promoted art as an instructional and devotional agent, as well as by the Lombard tradition of naturalism, which reflected an interest in light effects and the expression of intense emotion. He visited Venice, where he encountered the influence of Tintoretto* and Jacopo da Bassano* sometime before his arrival in Rome in late 1592 or early 1593. Caravaggio struggled for several years before his genre paintings *Cardsharps* (c. 1594–95) and *The Fortune Teller* (c. 1594–95) caught the eye of Cardinal del Monte, who subsequently became his patron. The intimate three-quarters view of one, two, or three figures was typical of his early work in Rome, works that were sometimes charged with heightened emotion or erotic overtones.

With his first major commissions for the three paintings of the life of St. Matthew for the Contarelli Chapel, S. Luigi dei Francesi (1599–1602), and *The Conversion of St. Paul* and *The Crucifixion of St. Peter* in the Cerasi Chapel, S. Maria del Popolo (1600–1601), several of the works for which he is now best known, Caravaggio transformed the sharp and appealing immediacy of those early works into high drama and pathos, introducing his trademark bold lighting of figures pushed to the foreground and against the frame, distilling the presentation to include only the most essential components of the subject that convey its central meaning. From an early date, his contemporaries remarked how he painted directly from life, intent upon the observation of nature. Frequently criticized, sometimes viciously, for a lack of "decorum" in the way he treated his subjects in his paintings (e.g., *Death of the Virgin*), Caravaggio elected to present sacred figures in the guise of simple Italian peasant folk with the physical flaws and distinct features of real people, thus creating figures of palpable presence and rejecting the convention of reverential distance that was so commonly expected.

As his stature as an artist grew, so did his reputation for having a mercurial temperament and regular scrapes with the law. In 1606 Caravaggio fled Rome after killing a man in a swordfight and reappeared in Naples some months later. He spent the remaining four years of his life in exile from Rome, as a wanted man, moving from Naples to Malta, where he was inducted into the Knights of Malta under the sponsorship of a powerful patron who admired his painting. All the while he painted, sometimes at what appears to have been a breakneck speed, creating works that reveal a thoughtful maturity and fundamental humanity—but remain little known as a result of their remote locations—as if in response to his own adversity. Once again, he had to flee Malta, first to Sicily, then to Naples, all the while seeking a papal pardon that would allow him to return to Rome. In July 1610, the pardon finally arranged, he headed for Rome, but was stricken with fever en route and died. In painting his self-portrait as the decapitated head of Goliath in *David with the Head of Goliath* (c. 1610), one of his last paintings, Caravaggio presents a graphic yet poignant and eerily prophetic image of the demise of a giant.

After the widespread influence of his paintings in the seventeenth century, Caravaggio fell into disrepute and was all but forgotten until the twentieth century, when the originality of his artistic vision was rediscovered. Since then, his work has enjoyed a growing audience, resulting in a burgeoning body of literature on the man and his art. Perennially controversial, the frank sensuality of many of Caravaggio's paintings, such as *Boy with a Fruitbasket* (c. 1593–94), which reveals Caravaggio's capacity to breathe life into even a bunch of fruit, *Bacchus* (c. 1597), with its bold invitation, and his provocative *Cupid* (c. 1601–2), with his playful grin, has generated assertions in recent scholarship of Caravaggio's homosexual leanings, claims that are equally as vigorously disputed. Archival research has brought to light new information resulting in a reconsideration of some of the details of his career, and new technologies have allowed for a better understanding of his working methods based upon the analysis of his paintings. Composing directly on the canvas, Caravaggio worked with remarkable speed to bring about the dramatic naturalism that is the essence of his art.

Bibliography

H. Hibbard, *Caravaggio*, 1983.
C. Puglisi, *Caravaggio*, 1998.

Rachel Hostetter Smith

CARDANO, GIROLAMO (1501–1576)

One of the most prolific writers of sixteenth-century Italy, Girolamo Cardano is best known for his contributions to medical literature and mathematical scholarship. He was born in Pavia on 24 September 1501, the illegitimate son of Fazio Cardano, a jurisconsult, and Chiara Micheri, a younger widow. According to Cardano, the physiological, emotional, and astrological circumstances surrounding his nativity were less than auspicious. His parents had attempted to abort the pregnancy through drugs, and he was prone to chronic poor health from his early childhood. Neither parent lavished affection on their son, but

Girolamo seems to have experienced a somewhat warmer relationship with his father than with his mother.

It was Fazio who taught his son the rudiments of arithmetic, geometry, and even some principles of the astrological sciences. Instead of the legal career that his father envisioned, however, Cardano gravitated toward medicine. He began his studies at Pavia when he was nineteen, then continued at the University of Padua, where he took his doctorate in medicine in 1526. His first professional appointment was in the town of Saccolongo, near Padua. While he was in residence there, in an act typical of his profound belief in portents and signs, he married Lucia Bandarini because of her likeness to a woman in one of his dreams. The marriage produced three children.

After a brief stay in Gallarate, Cardano moved his family to Milan in 1534, where he taught mathematics, astronomy, dialectics, and Greek while he was employed as the physician of the city's poorhouse. The success of his medical practice quickly made him Milan's most esteemed physician; his reputation across Europe would eventually be second only to that of Andreas Vesalius.* By his fifties, Cardano had already received invitations from several European courts, most of which he declined. In 1552, however, he undertook the principal journey of his life when he traveled to Scotland to treat John Hamilton, the asthmatic archbishop of Edinburgh, visiting the English court on his return. He held the chair in medicine at the University of Pavia from 1543 to 1559 (with a seven-year interruption) and also at the University of Bologna from 1562 to 1570.

Much of Cardano's notoriety was the product of his long and extraordinarily prolific publishing career. Including his medical treatises, he wrote over 130 printed works on subjects ranging from music to morality and from gambling to astrology. His encyclopedic *De subtilitate* found a widespread audience and saw ten reprints during his lifetime. His *Practica arithmeticae* (1539) and the celebrated *Ars magna* or *The Rules of Algebra* (1545) established him as a mathematician of considerable ability. The latter work also sparked Niccolò Tartaglia's* bitter dispute with Cardano, to whom he had confided his solution for cubic equations. When Cardano learned that Tartaglia's accomplishment duplicated the work of an earlier mathematician, he published it (with attribution) in *Ars magna*. The controversy aside, *Ars magna* is frequently cited as the signature work of his body of publications.

Cardano's professional felicity did not translate to his domestic affairs, however. In 1560 he unsuccessfully petitioned to save his eldest son from execution for poisoning his wife. His daughter's premature death and his younger son's criminal behavior also stained much of his life with grief. In 1570, while teaching at Bologna, he was arrested by the Inquisition for heresy, possibly for having cast and published the horoscope of Christ. He recanted and was thereafter prohibited to teach or publish. Afterwards, he moved to Rome, where he was pensioned by Pope Pius V for the remaining years of his life. At the age of seventy-four, Cardano wrote his autobiographical *De propria vita* (The Book of

My Life), a candid assessment of his life, habits, and work, and died later that same year on 20 September 1576.

Bibliography

M. Fierz, *Girolamo Cardano (1501–1576): Physician, Natural Philosopher, Mathematician, Astrologer, and Interpreter of Dreams*, trans. Helga Niman, 1983.
N. Siraisi, *The Clock and the Mirror: Girolamo Cardano and Renaissance Medicine*, 1997.

Michael J. Medwick

CARO, ANNIBAL (1507–1566)

Annibal Caro proved himself a competent administrator and diplomat in the service of a succession of cardinals. Notorious for his literary debates and quarrels with his contemporaries, Caro excelled as a man of letters. A dramatist, a poet, and an accomplished translator of classical languages, Caro exemplified the life of a sixteenth-century Italian courtier.

Caro, born in 1507 at Civitanova Marche, Italy, studied in his early youth at Florence, where he first served as tutor to Monsignor Giovanni Gaddi's nephew Lorenzo Lenzi and then as secretary to Gaddi himself. After Caro moved to Rome, his connection with Gaddi placed him in contact with the educated luminaries who comprised the followers of the reigning Farnese pope, Paul III, who ruled from 1534 to 1549. Caro temporarily served Monsignor Guidiccioni, a close friend and ally of the Farnese family. Upon Gaddi's death, Guidiccioni proved instrumental in obtaining a secretarial position for Caro with Pierluigi Farnese (assassinated 1547), Pope Paul's eldest son. Caro's only play, *Gli straccioni* (The scruffy scoundrels), written around 1543, may have been a condition of his employment with Pierluigi. Caro's play is noteworthy for its engaging dialogue and natural action.

After Pierluigi's assassination, Caro returned to Rome, where Pope Paul III's influential nephew, Cardinal Alessandro Farnese, employed him as his secretary. Caro worked for Alessandro until 1563, when he was able to devote himself solely to literary pursuits. Alessandro Farnese, also the patron of Pietro Bembo* and Giorgio Vasari,* commissioned Caro's *Canzoniere* in 1553, a poetic sequence written in praise of the Farnese family and the royal house of France. Lodovico Castelvetro's* criticism of Caro's poetry incited Caro's systematic persecution of Castelvetro. In response to Castelvetro's criticism of his work, Caro sought to defame Castelvetro by calling him indecent names and by issuing a series of pamphlets attacking him.

When Caro's collected letters were printed in Venice (c. 1572–74), they earned praise from his contemporaries for the elegant rhetorical style in which they were written. In addition, Caro's translation of Virgil's *Aeneid*, published in 1581, written in vernacular blank verse, remained in use as a standard text in Italian schools until recently.

Bibliography

A. Caro, *The Scruffy Scoundrels (Gli Straccioni)*, trans. M. Ciavolella and D. Beecher, 1980.
M. Herrick, *Italian Comedy in the Renaissance*, 1960.

Debbie Barrett-Graves

CARON, ANTOINE (1521–1599)

The multifaceted Antoine Caron—painter, draughtsman, and deviser of court entertainments—typifies the court artist of the later sixteenth century. Caron began painting religious art in his birthplace, Beauvais. In the 1540s he found work at court under Henri II, principally at the Château of Fontainebleau, where, beginning under François I,* artists from Italy and France collaborated on lavish interior decoration projects. Caron, working with Francesco Primaticcio* and Niccolò dell'Abate,* absorbed the latest artistic ideas.

Caron remained at court throughout the Valois era. Among his most important works are two albums of drawings intended for enlargement into tapestries (Paris, Louvre and Bibliothèque Nationale). These were gifts to Henri II's widow, Catherine de' Medici,* from a courtier, Nicolas Houel. Caron made drawings to accompany a manuscript biography of the ancient queen Artemesia (a model for Catherine, the queen regent) that Houel composed in 1562. He also illustrated Houel's *History of the Kings of France*.

In the 1570s Caron helped organize Parisian entertainments for three of Catherine de' Medici's children, including the triumphal entry of Charles IX, the wedding of Henri and Marguerite de Valois,* and the reception of the Polish ambassadors come to offer their crown to the duke of Anjou. He also documented such events in drawings.

Caron developed a personal style within the Mannerist idiom, his works featuring numerous elongated figures populating monumentally conceived theatrical spaces. He championed the Catholic cause, and paintings like *The Massacre of the Triumvirate* (Paris, Louvre) allegorize the contemporary religious wars in an antique setting. Caron's career as a painter, however, is less well defined than that as a draftsman. In addition to the models for tapestries, Caron furnished drawings for printmakers to market and to illustrate an influential publication on iconography. Caron not only helped invent the imagery of the Valois; his drawings of court festivals also provide important visual records of this ephemeral, but significant aspect of Renaissance court culture.

Bibliography

R. Strong, *Art and Power: Renaissance Festivals, 1450–1650*, 1984.
S. J. Turner, "Antoine Caron," in *The Dictionary of Art*, 5:813–15, 1996.
F. Yates, *The Valois Tapestries*, 1959.

Sheila ffolliott

CARRACCI, LUDOVICO (1555–1619), AGOSTINO (1557–1602), and ANNIBALE (1560–1609)

The Carracci are credited with restoring painting from the corrupt style of the Mannerists to the heights once achieved by the great Renaissance masters, especially Raphael.* They trained some of the leading Italian baroque painters, like Domenichino and Guido Reni, who then disseminated the Carracci's ideas throughout Italy. As a result, by the late 1620s theirs became the favored style among artists and patrons.

The brothers Agostino and Annibale and their cousin Ludovico were born in Bologna to a tailor and a butcher, respectively. Ludovico trained with the Mannerist Prospero Fontana, Agostino with Bartolomeo Passerotti of the same school, and Annibale seems to have received his training from Ludovico. In 1582, dissatisfied with the state of painting, the Carracci opened a private academy. Students from other shops began to attend because the Carracci academy offered a more progressive learning environment. Here they were provided with a forum where new ideas could be exchanged. Anatomy lessons were given by a trained doctor, and competitions and prizes were also part of the curriculum. Students were encouraged to draw from nature and participate in pictorial games from which Annibale developed the art of caricature.

In Bologna the Carracci collaborated on three fresco cycles: the Palazzo Fava completed in 1584, the Palazzo Magnani in 1590, and the Palazzo Sampieri in 1594. In these years the Carracci also created some of the most appealing altarpieces of the period, like the *San Ludovico Altarpiece* painted by Annibale around 1589, the *Bargellini Madonna* of 1588 and the *Cento Madonna* of 1591 created by Ludovico, and *The Last Communion of St. Jerome* of around 1592, Agostino's most celebrated work. These altarpieces, with their sense of immediacy and figures that appeal to the viewer, visually and emotionally, were well suited for the agenda of the Counter-Reformation.

In 1582 Archbishop Paleotti of Bologna wrote *Intorno alle imagini sacre e profanei* (On Sacred and Profane Paintings) dealing with appropriate subjects in religious art. Following the prescriptions of the Council of Trent, Paleotti criticized the ambiguity of subject and style in Mannerist paintings and called instead for works that were easily understood by the viewer and inspired piety and devotion. The Carracci were the first in Bologna to meet these demands with their altarpieces.

In 1595 Annibale left for Rome to work for Odoardo Farnese at the Farnese Palace. Agostino and Ludovico remained in Bologna and continued to manage the academy. From 1597 to 1608 Annibale painted the crowning glory of his career, the *Farnese Ceiling*. In 1597 Agostino joined him in Rome and assisted him on this project. *Cephalus and Aurora* and *Galatea* are usually attributed to him. In 1600 Agostino had a falling-out with Annibale and left for Parma to work for Duke Ranuccio Farnese. He died prematurely in 1602. Three years later Annibale suffered a mental breakdown and died in 1609. Ludovico lived until 1619, until which time he remained active as a painter and teacher in Bologna.

The Carracci's students—Reni, Domenichino, Giovanni Lanfranco, Francesco Albani, and Sisto Badalocchio—followed Annibale to Rome and worked as his assistants. After Annibale's death, they developed careers of their own and carried on their teachers' legacy. Because of this, the Carracci style remained popular until the end of the seventeenth century and even beyond.

Bibliography

A.W.A. Boschloo, *Annibale Carracci in Bologna*, 1974.
National Gallery of Art and Metropolitan Museum of Art, *The Age of Correggio and the Carracci*, 1986.
D. Posner, *Annibale Carracci*, 1971.

Lilian H. Zirpolo

CARVER, ROBERT (16th century)

Robert Carver or Carvor is now acknowledged as Scotland's greatest composer, but his work was unpublished and unrecorded until the early 1990s, and the details of his life are largely conjectural. His birthdate has been variously given as 1484/85 and 1487/88; his death is unrecorded, but he was alive in 1568. Some documents list him as "Carvor alias Arnot," leading to speculation that he may have been the natural son of David Arnot, archdeacon of Lothian and later bishop of Whithorn and the Chapel Royal of Scotland, located at Stirling. Alternatively, Bishop Arnot may have been his patron. Carver's father may have been David Kervour, who worked on the construction of the Chapel Royal. Associated with Scone Abbey, the Chapel Royal, and Stirling Parish Church, Carver was probably in the Augustinian order. He may have been educated at the University of Louvain, which lists a "Robert from St. Johnstone" (Perth, near Scone) on the matriculation roll in 1504. It has also been suggested that Carver was the Robert Arnot who was a burgess of Stirling, holding offices of bailie, council member, and master of work in Stirling between 1519 and 1550.

Five masses and two motets signed by Carver are the highlights of the *Carver Choirbook*, a manuscript largely in his hand. The other compositions are anonymous, except for one by Franco-Flemish Guillaume Dufay. Carver's *Five-Part Mass* is based on the lament of Jacob when he believes that his son Joseph has been slain by wild beasts; various explanations have been advanced for the choice of this obscure text, including the conjecture that Carver lost a son in the plague. The complexity of the vocal parts in Carver's music—one motet is in nineteen parts—suggests the influence of the Gaelic vocal tradition in addition to familiarity with contemporary English and continental music.

Bibliography

D. J. Ross, *Musick Fyne: Robert Carver and the Art of Music in Sixteenth Century Scotland*, 1993.

I. Woods, "Towards a Biography of Robert Carvor," *Music Review* 49, no. 2 (May 1988): 83–101.

Jean Graham

CARY, ELIZABETH, LADY FALKLAND (c. 1585–1639)

Among the most remarkable learned women in early modern England, Elizabeth Cary is best known for writing *The Tragedy of Mariam*, the first female-authored play published in English (1613), and for her strong religious convictions. We know more about Cary than about many early modern figures, thanks to a biography written by one of her daughters. Structured around Cary's spiritual life, particularly her conversion to Catholicism in 1626, the *Life* is itself an important document—the first female-authored biography of a woman in English. An avid reader, Cary learned French, Spanish, Italian, Latin, and Hebrew at a young age, translating Seneca's epistles and Abraham Ortelius's geography. In 1602 she was married to Henry Cary; the arranged match was apparently neither happy nor affectionate. Nine of their children survived to adulthood, including Lucius, a prominent intellectual and royalist in the English Civil War. After years of religious doubts, Cary converted to Catholicism in 1626, while her husband was serving as lord deputy in Ireland. When her conversion became public, Cary was pressured by Charles I and various courtiers to recant and was confined briefly to her residence. Her mother refused to aid her; her husband denounced her in letters from Ireland, cut off financial support, emptied the house, and took away the children. Cary and her servant, Bessie Poulter, survived with the help of friends and fellow Catholics. Henry and Elizabeth may have reconciled by his death in 1633; afterwards, she lived again with most of her children.

Although works of piety and devotion were deemed suitable for women, works of religious controversy were not. Cary nevertheless read Catholic and Protestant polemicists extensively; she translated the works of Cardinal Jacques Davy Du Perron and wrote one herself. Cary harbored priests (a crime), saw four daughters convert and join a Catholic convent in Lille, and abducted her two youngest sons from Lucius's home and sent them abroad (illegally) for Catholic training. For several decades her home was frequented by Anglican clergy, Catholic priests, students, and others who valued intellectual discussions of religious issues. Cary died of a respiratory illness in 1639.

Cary was praised in her time for her learning and writing. *The Tragedy of Mariam* evidently circulated in manuscript before it was printed and may have influenced Shakespeare's *Othello* and the anonymous *The Second Maiden's Tragedy*. In addition to *Mariam*, an elegy on the Duke of Buckingham's death, and probably a history of Edward II, Cary also wrote works not yet recovered: translations, poems, hymns to female saints and the Virgin Mary, and a play about Tamburlaine.

Bibliography

B. Weller and M. Ferguson, eds., *The Tragedy of Mariam the Fair Queen of Jewry: with "The Lady Falkland: Her Life,"* 1995.

Gwynne Kennedy

CASAUBON, ISAAC (1559–1614)

A leading scholar and teacher, the French classicist and Protestant theologian Isaac Casaubon epitomizes the spirit of Renaissance humanism and the Reformation. Born to French Huguenot refugees in Geneva, Casaubon was educated, until age eighteen, by his father. Then he attended the Academy of Geneva, where his work as a classical scholar earned him an appointment to teach Greek. He remained in Geneva until 1596, becoming acquainted with many who visited this Swiss Calvinist center. In 1596, after the Edict of Nantes granted civil rights and limited freedom of worship to French Protestants, Casaubon taught at the University of Montpellier. At this time Casaubon produced his editions of and commentaries on the classical authors Diogenes Laertius, Athenaeus, Theophrastus, and Aristotle.

In 1600 Casaubon, called to the court of France, was named one of the Protestant commissioners to judge the accuracy of the patristic quotations in a treatise against the Mass. Protestant scholars blamed Casaubon for siding with Catholic commissioners in this controversy, a decision that plagued Casaubon for much of his life. When he was presented to Henri IV by Catholics eager for Casaubon's conversion, he was denied a professorship at the Royal College because he refused to convert, but was granted a post at the Royal Library. Within a few years, throughout northern Europe, Casaubon's reputation as a scholar spread.

Because of his study of early Christian theology and Catholic pressure on him to convert, Casaubon became disillusioned with Calvinist doctrine and attracted to the Church of England. When Henri IV's assassination in 1610 heightened religious unrest, Casaubon accepted the invitation of Richard Bancroft, archbishop of Canterbury, to come to England. Warmly received by James I,* Lancelot Andrewes* (bishop of Ely), and others, Casaubon was converted to the Church of England and was given a living at Canterbury Cathedral. Although he kept his appointment in France, he took English citizenship in 1611 and never returned to France. He spent his last years writing to defend the English church against Catholicism and refuting the massive anti-Protestant history of Christianity, *Annales ecclesiastici* (Annals of the Church) by Cesare Baronio. He died in London and was buried in Westminster Abbey. Casaubon's involvement in religious controversy as he was torn between continental Calvinists and Catholics and his excellence in the activities Renaissance humanists promoted— the edition of and commentary on classical texts—both testify to his stature as a noteworthy figure.

Bibliography

M. Pattison, *Isaac Casaubon, 1559–1614*, 2nd ed., 1892.

Al Geritz

CASTELVETRO, LODOVICO (1505–1571)

Lodovico Castelvetro, a prominent critic and linguist, stands out as the man who systematically arranged the supposed Aristotelian unities of time, place, and action. Castelvetro lived the life of a sixteenth-century humanist devoted to the study of letters.

Castelvetro, born in 1505 in Modena, Italy, expressed an early passion for the study of humanistic letters. He pursued a course of study at the Universities of Bologna, Ferrara, Padua, and Siena. Bowing to his father's wishes, Castelvetro earned a doctorate of law at Siena before moving to Rome, where his family hoped that his maternal uncle, Giovanni Maria della Porta, would be able to use his political connections to advance his nephew's career.

Finding life in Rome unbearable, around the time of its sack in 1527 by the imperial forces of Charles V,* Castelvetro returned to Modena, where he found intellectual satisfaction in the company of the humanists allied with Giovanni Grilenzono's circle of friends. Castelvetro and Grilenzono studied ancient languages while also practicing vernacular languages. Under Castelvetro's leadership, humanist scholarship flourished in Modena, with Castelvetro's contemporaries referring to him as "another Socrates."

Castelvetro's association with the allegedly heretical Academy of Modena culminated in what may have been an unfounded accusation to the Sacred Inquisition of Rome. His criticism of Annibal Caro's* poetic sequence written in praise of the Farnese family and the royal house of France initiated Caro's systematic persecution of Castelvetro, a literary quarrel that further defamed Castelvetro's character in the eyes of his contemporaries. Castelvetro found himself in the position of having to travel to Rome in 1560 to refute the accusation. Threatened with torture, Castelvetro fled Italy, was excommunicated, and remained living in exile for the next ten years of his life.

After leaving Rome, Castelvetro found temporary refuge in Ferrara, Chiavenna, Lyons, Geneva, and, finally, Vienna, where Emperor Maximilian II's patronage provided the opportunity for Castelvetro to publish his most significant literary contribution: his commentary on Aristotle's *Poetics* (1570). In his dedicatory epistle to Emperor Maximilian II, Castelvetro avowed his intent to complete Aristotle's unpolished treatise in order to prescribe rules for writing dramas.

Additional commentaries on Petrarch's *Rime*, published in 1582, and on the first twenty-nine cantos of Dante's *Inferno*, among other textual corrections and considerations of the development of the Italian language, comprise the remainder of Castelvetro's critical endeavors. While still in exile, Castelvetro died on 21 February 1571.

Bibliography

A. Bongiorno, trans., *Castelvetro on the Art of Poetry*, Medieval and Renaissance Texts and Studies, vol. 29, 1984.
H. B. Charlton, *Castelvetro's Theory of Poetry*, 1913.
R. C. Melzi, *Castelvetro's Annotations to* The Inferno: *A New Perspective in Sixteenth Century Criticism*, 1966.

Debbie Barrett-Graves

CASTIGLIONE, BALDESAR (1478–1529)

An Italian author, soldier, and diplomat, Baldesar Castigilone is best known for producing one of the most representative documents of Renaissance aristocratic culture. He was born to a somewhat impoverished, but decidedly distinguished family at Casatico in the Duchy of Mantua. Related through his mother to the Gonzaga of Mantua, he was raised as a familiar of that illustrious family. He received his formal education at the University of Milan, where he studied Latin and Greek, and trained in the martial disciplines appropriate to his class. In 1496 he joined the court of Lodovico Sforza of Milan, where he established a reputation for the scholarly ability, natural grace, and pleasant disposition that were to be the trademarks of his public persona. His father's death and the ousting of Lodovico by the French in 1499 marked the end of Castiglione's service there, and he found himself again in the circles of the Gonzaga. In 1503 he went to Naples in the military train of Marquis Francesco, who had allied himself with the French. The experience proved disappointing, however, and he petitioned his patron to release him to the service of Duke Guidobaldo Montefeltro of Urbino.

Castiglione's decision to move to Urbino in 1504 was a pivotal moment in his public career and, ultimately, his literary destiny. He honed his diplomatic skills in the service of Guidobaldo, who sent him as emissary to Henry VII of England, but it was the court of Urbino and its inhabitants that served as the focus of Castiglione's interest. Largely presided over by Guidobaldo's wife, Duchess Elizabetta Gonzaga, Urbino had become the common ground for some of the most celebrated names of Italian intellectual, literary, and political culture. Steeped in the society of such personalities as Pietro Bembo,* Giuliano de' Medici, and Bibbiena (Bernardo Dovizi), Castiglione would later look back on this company as a working model of gentility and courtly excellence. Although the atmosphere of the court changed after the death of Guidobaldo in 1508, Castiglione remained in the diplomatic and military service of Urbino under Francesco Maria della Rovere until the latter's deposition by the forces of Pope Leo X* in 1517.

Castiglione returned to Mantua, where he married Ippolita Tovelli and settled down in semiretirement until 1519, when he was sent again to the papal court in the service of Federico Gonzaga.* He was still in residence there when Ippolita died after giving birth to their third child in 1520, ending a brief but deeply affectionate marriage. He remained in Rome until Clement VII appointed him papal nuncio to Spain in 1524. The commission, however, was fraught with difficulties. Relations between the pope and Charles V* were deteriorating rapidly, and when imperial troops sacked Rome in 1527, Clement clearly laid some blame on his ambassador. A reconciliation was eventually reached, but illness and exhaustion had worn down the pope's emissary. In 1529, shortly after being appointed bishop-elect of Ávila, Castiglione died in Toledo, Spain. The news of his passing prompted Charles V's succinct and oft-quoted eulogy: "Yo os digo que es muerto de los mejores caballeros del mundo" (I tell you that one of the finest gentlemen in the world is dead).

The pursuit and perfection of gentility had always been central issues in Castiglione's life, and the vehicle he found to express them was to become one of the principal literary works of his age. Castiglione wrote *Il cortegiano* (The Courtier) as a semifictitious retrospective of the court of Urbino when it was at its height in 1506, exploring in dialogue form the composition of the model participants of aristocratic society. In so doing, he made the book a dramatized compendium of Renaissance thought and ideals, covering a diversity of topics from correct rhetorical usage to the virtues of platonic love. Castiglione composed the first draft of the book between 1508 and 1518, mostly while on diplomatic assignment in Rome. The manuscript was later circulated among his friends and acquaintances, some of whom (like Bembo) were principal characters in the work. The book was enthusiastically received, but Castiglione refrained from publishing it until 1528, when he received word that Vittoria Colonna* and others who were in possession of portions of the manuscript were about to do so without authorization. In print, *Il cortegiano* was an enormous success both within and beyond Italy, especially in England, where Sir Thomas Hoby's* translation, published in 1561, had a significant impact on the ideals of Elizabethan courtly society.

Bibliography

P. Burke, *The Fortunes of the Courtier*, 1995.
B. Castiglione, *The Book of the Courtier*, trans. George Bull, 1967.
R. Roeder, *The Man of the Renaissance*, 1933.

Michael J. Medwick

CASTILLEJO, CRISTÓBAL DE (c. 1490–1550)

Cristóbal de Castillejo, a poet of the Spanish Renaissance, led the poets of the traditional school in opposition to Italian innovations favored by their contemporaries. Born in Ciudad Rodrigo, Spain, Castillejo dedicated his life to the service of the Habsburgs. He became a page to Emperor Charles V's* brother, Archduke Ferdinand, at the age of fifteen. He later became a Cistercian priest, a fact that apparently did not diminish the importance of love and women in his life, nor did it prevent him from fathering a child by one of these women. In 1539 he traveled to Venice to join the household of the Spanish ambassador Diego Hurtado de Mendoza. When Ferdinand, his former patron, became king of Austria, Castillejo returned to serve him in Vienna. However, this patronage apparently reaped no personal benefits for Castillejo.

Castillejo's principal contribution is to be found in the realm of poetry. He defended and produced traditional Spanish verse forms, such as the ballad and the *villancico*, at a time when Italian meters were gaining in popularity. Because of his belief that the Italian meters did not represent the Spanish spirit, Castillejo's meter of preference remained the traditional octosyllabic. In his collection *Contra los que dejan los metros castellanos y siguen los italianos* (Against those who leave Castilian meters and follow the Italian ones) he also inserted several Italianate sonnets in order to mock the new style. Ironically, critics have noted his clever use of the Italian meter as an instrument to critique that very form. Although he did not succeed at rendering the Italian meters less popular, he probably did contribute to the conservation of traditional Spanish meters.

Thematically, one might divide his works into the following three categories: moral and devotional (e.g., *Dialogo entre la verdad y la lisonja* [Dialogue between truth and flattery]), courtly love poetry (e.g., his poem to Ana de Aragon), and his more conversational or informal writings (e.g., *Dialogo que habla de las condiciones de las mugeres* [Dialogue on the qualities of women]). Castillejo also completed various classical translations, all of which demonstrate the depth of his humanistic culture.

The complete works of Castillejo were first edited and published by J. López de Velasco in a censored version dated 1573. His well-known works include *Dialogo de la vida de corte*, *Contra los que dejan los metros castellanos*, and *Sermon de amores*. Recently, a manuscript of thirty-three additional compositions was discovered in Spain. Bibliography dealing with Castillejo has been fairly limited in recent years. In particular, very few comprehensive studies have appeared.

Bibliography

C. Guzmán, "Antifeminism in the Cantigas de Santa Maria and the Dialogo de mujeres of Cristóbal de Castillejo," in *Studies on the Cantigas de Santa Maria: Art, Music, and Poetry*, 1987: 279–86.

Lydia Bernstein

CASTRO Y BELLVÍS, GUILLÉN DE (1569–1631)

Guillén de Castro y Bellvís, a Spanish dramatist of the school of Lope de Vega,* successfully adapted popular legends and history to Golden Age drama, culminating in *Las mocedades del Cid* and its sequel, *Las hazañas del Cid*. Born in Valencia of aristocratic origin, Castro y Bellvís is generally considered a soldier turned man of letters. He served for a time as captain of the coastguard and was appointed a knight of Santiago in 1623. He was married twice: first, unhappily, to the Marquesa Giron de Rebolledo in 1595, followed by a happier marriage to Ángela Salgado in 1626.

The greatest contribution of Castro y Bellvís is his poetic reworking and adaptation to Golden Age drama of the *romancero*, epic and chivalresque material, myth, history, and legend. The former is epitomized by *Las mocedades del Cid* (The youthful deeds of the Cid), a play in two parts first published in 1618. This work and *Las hazañas del Cid* (The feats of the Cid) were the first dramatizations of the Cid legend and served as the model for subsequent plays about the hero, including the first great French classic tragedy, Pierre Corneille's *Cid*. Other successful plays of Castro's include *El conde de Irlos* (The Count of Irlos) and *El conde Alarcos* (The Count of Alarcos), both based on epic and chivalresque material. Castro also adapted several works of Cervantes* for the theater: *Don Quijote de la Mancha, El curioso impertinente*, and *La fuerza de sangre*. His mythological plays *Progne y Filomena* and *Los amores de Dido y Eneas* have also achieved considerable renown.

Following an earlier edition, the first licit edition of Castro's works appeared in Valencia in 1618, entitled *Primera parte de las comedias*. The *Segunda parte* appeared in Valencia as well, in 1625. Seven of his plays were edited by Ramón Mesonero Romanos in 1857. The most complete edition of his works produced in the twentieth century is his *Obras*, edited by E. Julía in three volumes, 1925–27. Recent articles on Castro have not been particularly plentiful but have been quite revealing in terms of both genre and analysis of individual plays.

Bibliography

M. Ratcliffe, "Powerless or Empowered? Women in Guillén de Castro's 'Las mocedades del Cid' and 'Las hazañas del Cid,' " *Bulletin of the Comediantes* 44 (1992): 261–67.

W. E. Wilson, *Guillén de Castro*, 1973.

Lydia Bernstein

CELLINI, BENVENUTO (1500–1571)

Benvenuto Cellini was an Italian goldsmith, sculptor, and author of treatises on sculpture and goldsmithing and of a celebrated autobiography. Cellini was born in Florence on 3 November 1500. Unwilling to follow in the footsteps of his father, Giovanni, a musician and maker of musical instruments, he chose instead to study the art of goldsmithery, receiving training from the Florentine goldsmith Marcone (Antonio di Sandro) and Francesco Castoro of Siena. The years 1519 until 1540 were spent chiefly in Rome, in the service of Popes Clement VII and Paul III, where Cellini found inspiration in the models of Michelangelo* and Raphael.* Nearly all of Cellini's masterpieces in jewelry and goldsmith's work have been lost, with the exception of the medallions of Clement VII and Alessandro de' Medici and the elaborate gold and enamel saltcellar (1540–44) that he created for François I* (Kunsthistorisches Museum, Vienna).

Because of his quarrelsome nature, Cellini was involved continually in brushes with the law, some of which led to his imprisonment. In 1529 he killed a man in order to avenge the murder of his brother, but received pardon from the pope. In 1538, however, he was accused of stealing jewels from the papal treasury of Paul III and was subsequently imprisoned in Castel Sant' Angelo. As a result of the intercession of powerful friends, not the least of whom was François I, Cellini was released from prison in 1540. From then until 1545 he was employed at Paris and Fontainebleau in the service of the French court. It was during this period that he achieved recognition as a sculptor and produced what is believed to be his greatest achievement, the bronze relief of the *Nymph of Fontainebleau* (1543–44, Paris, Louvre).

In 1545 he returned to his native Florence, under the patronage of Duke Cosimo I de' Medici,* where he remained until his death in 1571. Among the sculptures that remain of his final period are *Bust of Cosimo I* (1545–48), *Ganymede* (1545–47), *Perseus* (1545–54), and *Apollo and Hyacinth* (1546), all in Florence; *Bust of Bindo Altoviti* (c. 1550, Boston); and his marble *Crucifix* (after 1556, Escorial).

During the latter part of his life, Cellini took on a new role, writing treatises on both sculpture and the art of goldsmithery (Florence, 1568). But of all his artistic achievements, the one that has secured him the greatest fame is his autobiography, written between 1558 and 1562 and circulated in manuscript. The first printed edition, in Italian, was published in Naples in 1728 (*Vita di Benvenuto Cellini*, 1728), with subsequent translations appearing in English (1771), German (1796), and French (1822). A highly impassioned, albeit embellished, account of Cellini's life as artist and adventurer, it gained attention during the romantic period and later served as a model for nineteenth-century historical novelists like Sir Walter Scott and Alexandre Dumas. The *Life* is remarkable for its enduring power to capture the imagination of modern readers, as it presents a stunningly vivid portrait of life in sixteenth-century Italian society. The poet Johann Wolfgang von Goethe, who translated the *Life* into German, wrote, "I see the whole century in more real terms in the confused apprehensions of an individual than in the clearest historical account."

Bibliography

B. Callin, *The Autobiography of Benvenuto Cellini*, trans. George Bull, 1956.
John Pope-Hennessy, *Cellini*, 1985.

Patricia A. White

CERVANTES SAAVEDRA, MIGUEL DE (1547–1616)

Miguel de Cervantes Saavedra, a Spanish novelist, dramatist, poet, and short-story writer, achieved world acclaim, particularly for his *Don Quijote*, not only the first modern novel but probably also the greatest. Born in Alcalá de Henares to a poor surgeon, and into a family once prosperous, Cervantes moved often as a child. Little is known of his education. He apparently studied as a child in Valladolid, then possibly with the Jesuits in Seville, and finally with the humanist Juan López de Hoyos in Madrid. In 1569 he departed for Italy in the service of Cardinal Claudius Acquaviva, becoming a soldier in 1570. He lost the use of his left hand in the Battle of Lepanto in 1571. After recovering,

Cervantes participated in other military campaigns until he was taken prisoner and brought to Algiers by a renegade pirate. He remained in captivity for five years before being ransomed in 1580.

Upon his return to Spain, Cervantes began an unhappy marriage to Catalina de Salazar y Palacios (1584), fathered an illegitimate daughter, and, convinced of his inability to earn a living as a writer, became a purchasing agent for the navy. His troubles were numerous and included at least two imprisonments for debt or bookkeeping errors. In 1605 Cervantes and his family were implicated and later exonerated in the death of a nobleman. After the immediate success of the first part of *Don Quijote*, he moved with the court to Madrid, beginning his most productive literary period until his death in 1616.

Best known as the author of the first modern novel, *Don Quijote*, and his *Novelas ejemplares* (Exemplary Tales), Cervantes was a prolific writer in many genres. He often experimented with genre or blended previously distinct genres or styles. His *Don Quijote*, for example, reconciled the epic and romance traditions and combined elements of chivalric romance, poetry, the pastoral novel, the Byzantine romance, and the Moorish novel, among others. Cervantes is also known for having adapted to his writing elements of Erasmian humanism such as the exaltation of reason, harmony, the overcoming of appearances, common sense, human dignity, and prudence. On the other hand, he appears to abhor ignorance, affectation, pedantry, and arrogance. His writings also reflect his strong belief in free will and personal responsibility.

There were no significant genres of the time with which Cervantes did not involve himself. Although he is not particularly known as a poet, he did write some poetry of interest, including the *Viaje del parnaso* (Voyage to Parnassus) (1614), 3,000 verses based on a poem of the same title by Cesare Caporali. It was not until the twentieth century that his poetry became well regarded.

Before Lope de Vega,* Cervantes was the greatest Spanish playwright. Much of his theater still holds a great deal of relevance and appeal in numerous languages. His early *El trato de Argel* (The Commerce of Algiers) recounts intrigues of life in Barbary and is said to be at least partially autobiographical. *El cerco de Numancia* (Numantia), written during the same period, presents an entire community as patriotic hero and willing to die to preserve its dignity and autonomy when confronted with the unjust and cruel actions of the Romans. It exalts an empire inspired by virtue and faith. This tragedy is often considered a precursor to Lope de Vega's *Fuente Orejuna*.

Cervantes's later drama appeared in 1615 in *Ocho comedias y ocho entremeses nuevos* (Eight plays and eight new interludes). Among these are *El gallardo español* (The gallant Spaniard), *Los baños de Argel* (The Baths of Algiers), and *La gran sultana doña Catalina de Oviedo* (The Grand Sultan Catalina), all of which are based on tensions or themes of captivity between Moors and Christians. Perhaps most successful among his theatrical works were Cervantes's *entremeses*, or short humorous interludes. Two of these, *La elección de los alcaldes de Daganza* (The election of the mayor of Paganza) and *El rufián viudo* (The Widowed Pimp), are in verse, and the others are in prose.

It is his prose for which Cervantes is most appreciated. *La Galatea* (1585), his first attempt at a novel, follows the pastoral tradition adapted from Italy, where it was popularized by Jacopo Sannazaro.* It contains some Neoplatonic ideas and promises a second part, which never appeared. Part one of *El ingenioso hidalgo Don Quijote de la Mancha* met immediate success upon its publication in 1605. The *Segunda parte del ingenioso cavallero Don Quixote de la Mancha* appeared ten years later, after the publication of an illicit sequel by one Alonso Fernandez de Avellaneda. The novel was the newest genre and thus the most wide open for experimentation. Cervantes incorporated most other genres within it, as well as stories and poems that could stand on their own. The work contains a new literary self-consciousness. The characters detach themselves and comment on the stories, as does the author in his dual role as creator and critic. Humanistic values and the exaltation of free will abound.

In the novel, Cervantes re-creates the reality of life in all of its complexities and contradictions. What appears to be a simple dichotomy between the idealistic, crazy, but virtuous Don Quijote and his realistic, grounded, and ignorant squire Sancho Panza becomes far more complicated and less straightforward, as when the two appear to change roles in the second volume. The *Don Quijote* also deals with the Shakespearean boundaries between life and literature, or art in general. Although the distinction must be made, and Don Quijote errs in treating life like literature, the two constantly interfere with one another. Cervantes shows that life, like literature, is susceptible to various interpretations and that only by interpreting experience or literature with virtue and reason can one hope to avoid grave errors. Truth itself is not ambiguous, but human access to it is often limited.

In 1613 the *Novelas ejemplares* (Exemplary tales) appeared in print. These novellas, or short stories, were exemplary in terms of their adaptation to Spanish or experimentation with various genres, including the Italianate novel, the picaresque, satire, and the realistic tale. Cervantes's creations were quite unique and opened the doors for subsequent short prose.

Cervantes's last work, *Persiles y Sigismunda*, appeared posthumously in 1617 but was probably begun in 1609. It is clear that Cervantes was rushing to finish the work before his death. Perhaps posterity would have viewed this work more generously had Cervantes had ample health and time to finish it as he might have planned. In any case, the novel follows the Byzantine style and attempts to illustrate the spiritual quest of humans by means of the varied adventures depicted in the novel.

The bibliography concerning Cervantes and his works is immense and ongoing. Many of these works deal with *Don Quijote*, a work that has meant different things at different times and in different places. Many editions of his complete works are available as well.

Bibliography

M. Duran, *Cervantes*, 1974.
J. V. Ricapito, *Cervantes's Novelas ejemplares: Between History and Creativity*, 1996.
E. C. Riley, *Don Quixote*, 1986.

Lydia Bernstein

CHAMBERLAIN, JOHN (1553–1628)

Regarded as the best letter writer of his time, John Chamberlain, through his extant letters written from 1597 to 1626, describes life from the end of the Tudor period through the Jacobean period. The son of an ironmonger and alderman, the weak and sickly Chamberlain lived a protected life, never marrying. He attended Cambridge but obtained no degree and traveled little, preferring never to stray far from London, where he lived with family and friends not far from St. Paul's all his life. He was of the middle class himself, and his circle of friends included Thomas Bodley, diplomat and later founder of the Bodleian Library; Sir Rowland Lytton and the Fanshawes; William Thomas Allen, mathematician and antiquary; Sir William Gilbert,* physician to Queen Anne; Lancelot Andrewes,* bishop of Ely and then of Winchester; William Camden,* historian; and Inigo Jones, architect and masque writer.

Dudley Carleton, a diplomat for James I* made Lord Dorchester under Charles I, and Sir Ralph Winwood, secretary of state under James I, were Chamberlain's most intimate friends. Most of his letters were written to Carleton. In his forties, Chamberlain became a news gatherer for Carleton, and with his connections at court, his access to the news and intrigue of London, and his eye for detail, Chamberlain was a great benefit to his friend. Chamberlain lived his life near Old St. Paul's and walked in Paul's Walk every day, where he gathered material for his letters. Not simply the cathedral's nave, this spot was the mart where lords, gentry, and men of all professions gathered and conversed. Chamberlain made his occupation that of the spectator, and his letters, marked with consideration and frankness, show a disinterestedness, a mark of a good correspondent. To read his letters is to understand life in the period. From gossip at plays to courtship, fashion, and the plaque, from the murder of Sir Thomas Overbury* to the Gunpowder Plot, Chamberlain reveals the ordinary life of court, city, and countryside and provides a discriminating picture of the end of the reign of Elizabeth* through the beginning of that of Charles I.

Bibliography

J. Chamberlain, *The Chamberlain Letters*, ed. E. Thomson, 1965.

Megan S. Lloyd

CHAPMAN, GEORGE (c. 1559–1634)

A complex poet and innovative playwright, George Chapman was also a respected scholar, a supporter of writers and artists, and, most famously, a translator of Homer. Chapman was the second son in a well-connected and prosperous family, but his fate was marked by a lifelong struggle against poverty. He studied for a while at Oxford and perhaps Cambridge, but never obtained a degree. Instead, he spent time in the service of Sir Ralph Sadler's household and took part in military campaigns in the Netherlands.

His first published work, the allegorical poem *The Shadow of the Night*, dates from 1594. At that time, Chapman belonged to Sir Walter Raleigh's* circle of young erudites, whose interest in the occult earned them the nickname "the School of Night." His poem sparked a parodic literary war with William Shakespeare* and, later, Thomas Nashe.* Another tribute to Raleigh was Chapman's prefatory poem to an account of the explorer's Guiana expedition. Chapman also published a continuation of Christopher Marlowe's* unfinished *Hero and Leander* (1598)—a testimony to his friendship to the deceased poet, closely associated with Raleigh's group.

By the time of this publication, Chapman was already respected as a dramatist. He wrote a number of comedies for the public stage, among them comedies of "humors," so called after the dominant passions that distorted human personality in a particular direction. Although the genre was first theorized by Ben Jonson,* it was Chapman's *A Humorous Day's Mirth* (1597) that inaugurated this comic fashion.

During Chapman's later theater career, he found his talents more suited to the satirical tastes of the select audiences of the private theaters. With *The Gentleman Usher* (c. 1602) and *Monsieur d'Olive* (c. 1604), he introduced another new genre to the English stage, the romantic tragicomedy. He also wrote realistic urban comedies, like *Eastward Ho!* (1605), in collaboration with John Marston and Jonson, and bitter satires, like *The Widow's Tears* (c. 1605). The rest of his stage career was devoted to tragedies, based on his experience of the world of politics and knowledge of contemporaneous French history.

Though they were extremely popular, Chapman's works got him into trouble. Some mocking allusions toward the Scots and the recent Virginia expeditions in *Eastward Ho!* landed him in jail. *The Conspiracy and Tragedy of Charles, Duke of Byron* (1608) roused the ire of the French ambassador, and Chapman barely escaped imprisonment. His poem *Andromeda Liberata* (1614), celebrating the marriage of his patron Robert Carr to Frances Howard, brought upon him accusations of slander against the earl of Essex. Even his monumental translation of Homer's works never earned him the financial reward promised to the poet by Prince Henry at his deathbed, but it did earn him a monument in his honor, fashioned by the famous architect Inigo Jones.

Bibliography

C. Spivack, *George Chapman*, 1967.

Kirilka Stavreva

CHARLES V (1500–1558)

Charles V served as holy Roman emperor from 1519 to 1556, ruling over a vast territory that included Spain, Burgundy, and numerous German and Italian states. He vehemently defended Catholicism against Martin Luther* and the growth of the Protestant Reformation, and he maintained Habsburg dynastic policies in the face of external threats from the papacy, France, and the Ottoman Empire.

Charles was born on 24 February 1500 in Ghent, Flanders, to Philip the Handsome, the son of Emperor Maximilian I, and Joanna the Mad, daughter of Ferdinand and Isabella. He spent his youth in Burgundy influenced by Adrian of Utrecht in religious matters and Guillaume de Croy, sieur de Chievres, who helped him develop chivalrous and missionary tendencies. Charles possessed a medieval character favoring dynastic politics and Catholicism, and he enjoyed an affinity for traditional Burgundian culture. Later influential figures who furthered his dynastic outlook were Cardinal Francisco Ximenes in Spain and Mercurino Gattinara, his close political advisor.

Charles became duke of Burgundy in 1515 and the following year became king of Spain. He traveled to Spain in 1517 and was not well received since he was from Burgundy. In 1519, with financial backing from German bankers, Charles was unanimously elected holy Roman emperor and was crowned at Aachen on 23 October the following year. He remained in Germany for only a short time, however, as he was forced to return to Spain in 1522 to put down a revolt by a group of Castilian cities supported by the nobility. Charles remained in Spain from 1522 to 1529, where he ultimately gained the support of the Spaniards.

The major problem Charles faced during his reign was the emergence of Protestantism. He confronted Luther at the Diet of Worms in 1521 and vowed to defend the Catholic faith against Lutheran Protestantism. Charles had difficulty dealing with Protestantism due to several major external pressures and ultimately allowed his brother, Ferdinand, to focus on issues within the empire.

Dynastic politics forced Charles into conflict with François I,* king of France. Charles wanted to regain the hereditary territories of Burgundy and Milan, and François understandably feared Habsburg encirclement. Fighting between Charles and François began in 1521 and resulted in a French defeat at Pavia in 1525. At the same time Charles was at war with France, he was also experiencing problems with the papacy because it opposed his push for the formation of a church council to manage the threat of Protestantism. Pope Clement VII believed that his authority was being threatened and therefore did not cooperate with Charles. François allied with Clement against Charles and, in 1527, Charles sent forces to sack Rome, resulting in Clement's capture and increased imperial control in Italy. Clement was captured and released in 1528, and Charles and François agreed to the Peace of Cambrai in 1529. Charles renounced claims to Burgundy, and François gave up Milan and Naples. François did not remain idle long, for in 1536 he allied with the Turks—who also posed occasional threats to Charles throughout his reign—and invaded Savoy. François turned down a personal combat with Charles and agreed to peace in 1538. Fighting resumed in 1542, and Charles pushed his forces close to Paris. The Peace of Crépy was concluded in 1544, which maintained the status quo.

Charles's campaign against Protestantism continued throughout his reign but achieved limited success. Although Clement had eventually crowned Charles in Bologna in 1530, the last pope to crown a holy Roman emperor, he still refused Charles's request to call a council to discuss Protestantism. Clement's successor, Paul III, cooperated with Charles and convened the Council of Trent in 1545. The council failed to produce the reforms Charles wanted, and ultimately, papal fear of Spanish control of Italy prevented papal and imperial cooperation toward the suppression of Protestantism.

Charles still continued his attacks on Protestants and was victorious at the Battle of Mühlberg in 1547. At the Diet of Augsburg (1547–48), he allowed Lutherans to return to Catholicism and granted them Communion and clerical marriages. Both Lutheran and Catholic princes feared Spanish domination over Germany, and several prominent German princes deserted Charles and joined Henri II. Charles was driven from Germany in 1552 and in 1553 eventually turned over German affairs to his brother, Ferdinand; both eventually adhered to the Peace of Augsburg in 1555. Lutheranism and Catholicism were deemed equal, and the religion of the regional authority would be the religion of the land. In October 1555 Charles gave control of the Netherlands to his son, Philip,* and in January 1556 abdicated his rule over Spain in favor of Philip. Charles died on 21 September 1558 in Spain.

Charles remained medieval in outlook throughout his reign, defending his territories from external threats and supporting the church against the rise of Protestantism. Although the Reformation caused a decline in the arts, Charles's popularity was seen in numerous artistic forms. Albrecht von Brandenburg constructed Neue Stift at Halle, a reaffirmation of Catholicism, which contained a silver bust of Charles on the high altar. Medallions of Charles were found on tombs signifying imperial ties, medalists such as Christoph Weiditz, Hans Reinhart, Hans Kels the Younger, and Hans Schwarz showed their support of Charles, and portraits by Hans Daucher, Hans Memling, and Titian* showcased Charles's greatness. He was viewed as a great man because of the issues he faced, and he garnered a great deal of support throughout the Holy Roman Empire.

Bibliography

E. Armstrong, *The Emperor Charles V*, 1902.
K. Brandi, *The Emperor Charles V*, 1939.
J. C. Smith, *German Sculpture of the Later Renaissance, c. 1520–1580*, 1994.

Paul Miller

CLEMENS NON PAPA, JACOBUS (c. 1510/15–1555/56)

Jacobus Clemens non Papa was a prolific composer of both sacred and secular music, including over 230 motets, 2 magnificats, 15 masses, approximately 80 French-texted songs, 8 in Dutch, and 8 textless compositions. He also composed 159 psalms on the Dutch Psalter, the *Souterliedekens*.

His place of birth is unknown but was presumably in present-day Belgium. He was employed at Bruges cathedral in 1544–45, was then at the court of Charles V* until 1549, and in October to December 1550 was employed by the Marian Brotherhood in 's-Hertogenbosch. He seems also to have worked in Ieper, where he died, and he also probably lived in Leiden for a time. His death has been determined by a date of 21 April 1555 for his motet *Hic est vere martyr*, marked as his "ultimum opus" in a manuscript, and by the dedication by the printer Phalese in his first book of masses in 1556. He may also have left the *Souterliedekens* unfinished, as the printer Tylman Susato composed ten works in the collection. A *déploration* on Clemens's death by Jacobus Vaet was published in 1558. The reason for his unusual name remains unclear. Most likely it originated as some kind of joke. Less likely are the traditional reasons that it distinguishes him from the poet Jacobus Papa or Pope Clement VII.

Clemens's musical style for his Latin sacred works is typical of his time: thickly textured works based on fuguelike imitative structures. His secular works are also much like those of his contemporaries, revealing him to be a good and skilled composer. Clemens is best known for the publication in 1556–57 of the *Souterliedekens*, the first polyphonic (part-song) settings in Dutch of the Psalter, printed in Antwerp by Tylman Susato. These are in three voices on metrical texts presumably by Willem van Zuylen van Nijevelt, originally printed in 1540 by Simon Cock, also in Antwerp. They are composed in a traditional fashion, employing the popular tunes named by Cock in either the tenor (middle) or upper voice, while the other parts are freely composed. The *Souterliedekens* clearly holds a prime position in the development of a sacred repertory in the vernacular.

Bibliography

W. Elders, "Jacobus Clemens Non Papa," in *The New Grove Dictionary of Music and Musicians*, ed. S. Sadie, vol. 4, 1980: 476–80.

Mitchell Brauner

CLOUET, JEAN (c. 1485–1540/41) and FRANÇOIS (c. 1516–1572)

The Clouets, father and son, dominated the production of portraiture in drawing and painting in sixteenth-century France. Probably influenced by Italian art, they exploited the possibilities of colored chalk to achieve more lifelike effects. Their portraits, produced to meet an increasing demand, provide a uniquely extensive visual record of the royal family and courtiers.

Jean Clouet was court painter to François I.* His individual style first appears in portrait heads decorating illuminated manuscripts. Jean also produced independent portraits, primarily bust-length drawings, although a few documented painted portraits exist. Clouet typically made sketches from life and then produced highly finished drawings (incorporating different colors of chalk) in the studio.

Clouet's drawings, known as *crayons*, were frequently copied. Demand for portraits at court increased during the Renaissance. Catherine de' Medici,* whose handwriting identifying the sitter appears on some drawings, actively promoted dynastic marriages for her children. Portraits were exchanged as part of such negotiations. Collectors also sought portraits for inclusion in albums. Jean Clouet painted portraits near the end of his career. One of the best known— possibly influenced by Hans Holbein's* portrait of Desiderius Erasmus*— depicts the humanist scholar Guillaume Budé* (New York, Metropolitan Museum). Holbein and Clouet may have met during one of the former's trips to the Continent.

François Clouet assumed his father's position in 1540. To satisfy demand, he ran a large workshop with many assistants. Although this workshop continued to produce *crayons*, the younger Clouet made significant large-scale painted portraits, including an equestrian *François I* (Paris, Louvre), as well as allegorical portraits, such as *Lady in Her Bath* (Washington, D.C., National Gallery of Art).

The Clouets moved portraiture from the manuscript to the independent drawing to large-scale painting. They developed the potential of the chalk medium and extended the boundaries of the portrait genre. The extensive number of drawings by the Clouet circle document the personalities of the French court in the Renaissance.

Bibliography

A. Blunt, *Art and Architecture in France, 1500 to 1700*, 1973.
L. Campbell, *Renaissance Portraits*, 1990.
P. Mellen, *Jean Clouet: Complete Edition of the Drawings, Miniatures, and Paintings*, 1971.

Sheila ffolliott

CLOVIO, GIULIO (1498–1578)

Giulio Clovio, called by Giorgio Vasari* the "new and miniature Michelangelo," was the greatest manuscript illuminator of the sixteenth century in Italy. Born in Croatia, Clovio traveled to Italy at the age of eighteen to practice his art. He entered the artistic circle of the important Grimani family and trained under Giulio Romano.* Around 1523 he left Italy and worked for Louis II of Hungary, but after the Turkish invasion of 1526, he returned to Rome.

Following his experiences as a prisoner during the sack of Rome in 1527, Clovio took holy orders and joined a monastery in Mantua, but left following an injury in 1530. Cardinal Grimani helped the artist obtain that dispensation, and Clovio then spent several years with Grimani in Perugia and produced the *Stuart de Rothesay Hours* (British Museum), among other works. He came to the attention of Alessandro Farnese, the most important patron of the arts in mid-sixteenth-century Rome. For Farnese, Clovio produced his masterpiece, the *Farnese Hours* (New York, Pierpont Morgan Library), the fruit of twelve years' labor, and the *Towneley Lectionary* (New York Public Library), a missal for the Sistine Chapel. He traveled with the Farnese entourage and worked also for the Medici at Florence.

Clovio is remembered for his ability to translate the styles of Michelangelo,* Raphael,* and the Mannerists into miniature form. He was highly esteemed by his contemporaries and associated with Vasari, Michelangelo, Vittoria Colonna,* and El Greco,* who painted his portrait (Naples, Capodimonte). Some of Clovio's later drawings were engraved by Cornelius Cort.

Bibliography

C. Robertson, *Il Gran Cardinale: Alessandro Farnese, Patron of the Arts*, 1992.
W. Smith, ed., *The Farnese Hours*, facsimile ed., 1976.

John Marciari

COECKE VAN AELST, PIETER (1502–1550)

The Flemish artist Pieter Coecke van Aelst was not only a painter but also a sculptor, a designer of tapestries and stained glass, and a translator of the works of the Roman architect Vitruvius and the Italian architectural theorist Sebastiano Serlio. With these translations, he introduced his countrymen to Italian Renaissance architecture and its classical origins. His painting was strongly influenced by Italian Mannerism, with a tendency to exaggerate form and movement.

In 1527 Coecke joined the Antwerp painters' guild and set up his own workshop, which was a busy one, producing a great number of stereotypical religious paintings on subjects such as the Madonna and the Adoration of the Magi. But his most popular painting was his very Mannerist *Last Supper*, in which the figures of the disciples, in an elaborate setting and grouped in pairs, converse with violent movements: even the furniture seems to be moving. Coecke's workshop made no fewer than forty-one copies of this *Last Supper*, continuing to produce them until well after Coecke's own death.

The Dutch biographer Karel van Mander wrote that Coecke learned the art of tapestry design, a major component of his career, from Bernaert van Orley, whose pupil he was. Although many drawings for tapestries survive, few actual tapestries can be assigned to Coecke today. Probably in connection with tapestry commissions, he visited both Rome and Constantinople; drawings done on the journey to Constantinople were issued as woodcuts after his death.

Coecke was the father-in-law of the great Flemish painter Pieter Bruegel the Elder*; what is less certain is whether Coecke was also Bruegel's teacher, as van Mander claims, for Bruegel's style shows no resemblance to that of Coecke.

Coecke's importance, however, lies also in his translations, which furthered the understanding of Italian Renaissance architecture in northern Europe.

Bibliography

J. Snyder, *Northern Renaissance Art*, 1985.
W. Stechow, ed., *Northern Renaissance Art, 1400–1600: Sources and Documents*, 1966.

Rosemary Poole

COLET, JOHN (c. 1467–1519)

An English educator, clergyman, and humanist, John Colet founded St. Paul's School, London. The son of Sir Henry Colet, a merchant twice lord mayor of London, Colet matriculated at Oxford around 1483 and went to France and Italy to further his studies in 1493. While studying law and Greek there, he became acquainted with some humanists and was especially interested in their new ideas about education and the revival of classical learning.

By 1496 he returned to England and became a lecturer at Oxford. Although he was not ordained a priest until 1498, he began his lectures on St. Paul's Epistles at Oxford in 1496. In place of the detailed analytical exegesis and allegorical interpretation characteristic of his theological predecessors, the Scholastics, Colet presented a more human commentary on Paul's text, placing it in its historical context and aiming to make its message mean more to Colet's audience personally. As a humanist, he praised classical Latin, and Platonic and Neoplatonic concepts influenced his thought. Colet knew about the humanism of Marsilio Ficino, Politian, and Pico della Mirandola, and his lectures, in which he often refers to their works, illustrate early attempts to bring the ideas of the Italian Renaissance to England.

In 1504 Colet became dean of St. Paul's and held that position until he died. When his father died in October 1505, he used much of his inheritance to found St. Paul's School, with William Lily, another prominent English humanist, as headmaster. Colet supervised the school's curriculum carefully and specified that Greek and Latin classics be taught along with traditional moral training. With Lily, Colet wrote a Latin grammar, which Desiderius Erasmus* revised, and it remained a standard textbook for two hundred years.

Colet vigorously criticized the Catholic church and thus opened the way for the Reformation. From the pulpit, he preached against luxury and corruption in the lives of the clergy, and he rejected beliefs in relics and pilgrimages. His "Convocation Sermon" of 1512 reprimanded priests for ignorance and immorality. As a result, he was suspected of heresy, but Archbishop William Warham dismissed the charges. Because Colet did not advocate breaking from the Catholic church, he remained in favor with it. He died in London on 16 September 1519. Colet's effect on learning, especially on methods of interpreting Scripture, was significant, and his relationship with other humanists, such as Thomas More,* helped to plant the seeds of the Renaissance that would come to fruition in England.

Bibliography

J. B. Gleason, *John Colet,* 1989.

Al Geritz

COLONNA, VITTORIA (1492–1547)

One of the most celebrated women of the Italian Renaissance, Vittoria Colonna was famous for her poetry, her close friendship with Michelangelo,* and her connection with the Italian reform movement. She was a member of the illustrious Colonna family from Rome. Her father, Fabrizio Colonna, a famous military general, was one of the interlocutors in Niccolò Machiavelli's* *Art of War.* Her mother, Agnese de Montefeltro, was the sister of Duke Guidobaldo of Urbino, whose court was the setting for Baldesar Castiglione's* *The Courtier.* When Vittoria was seventeen, she was married to the marquis of Pescara, a marriage intended to ally the Colonna family to Pescara's powerful Neapolitan family. Pescara was also a military man and was away at battle during most of their marriage. Colonna passed the time in extensive traveling and writing; many of her poems focus on the loneliness of separation.

As Colonna's poetry gradually became known, she made the acquaintance of many other authors who paid tribute to her in their works. She was particularly close to Pietro Bembo,* the famous humanist and poet who later became a cardinal with Vittoria's influential help. Bembo encouraged Colonna's writing, and she dedicated a sonnet to him. Through Bembo, Colonna met Castiglione, who asked for her opinion of his manuscript of *The Courtier.* In her enthusiasm for the work, Colonna began to share it with her friends; fearful that a corrupt edition might be published, Castiglione quickly published the book himself in 1528. She also met Ludovico Ariosto,* who singled out her poetic talents for special praise in *Orlando Furioso.*

When Colonna was thirty-three, her husband was killed in battle; she lived in various convents for the rest of her life and never remarried. Colonna became interested in matters of church reform and developed many close friendships with some of the leading reformists and religious figures of the day, especially Cardinal Reginald Pole. She also continued to encourage and inspire writers and artists, especially Michelangelo. Colonna served as both muse and critic for Michelangelo during the many years of their close but platonic relationship.

Colonna's own creative output resulted in a book of poems, *Rime spirituali,* published in 1538. This collection of almost four hundred poems comprises sonnets on both human and spiritual love and a long poem in terza rima about Christ, the Virgin Mary, and Mary Magdalene. Her great friend Michelangelo was at her side when she died in 1547.

Bibliography

R. Bainton, *Women of the Reformation in Germany and Italy,* 1971.
J. Gibaldi, "Vittoria Colonna: Child, Woman, and Poet," in *Women Writers of the Renaissance and Reformation,* ed. K. M. Wilson, 1987.

Jo Eldridge Carney

COORNHERT, DIRCK VOLKERTSZOON (1522–1590)

Dirck Volkertszoon Coornhert was a Dutch humanist, scholar, engraver, and vigorous proponent of religious tolerance. His life and writings were intimately bound up with the political and religious struggles that dominated the Netherlands during the second half of the sixteenth century.

Although Coornhert was born into a prosperous Amsterdam family, he lost his inheritance after a marriage that his parents refused to accept. He then moved to the nearby city of Haarlem, where he earned his living as a skillful etcher and engraver; he also associated with the Haarlem school of painters, a group that had been influenced by the Italian Renaissance. In Haarlem Coornhert linked himself to the ruling patriciate, first as a notary and then in 1564 as secretary for the city. It was in this context that he came into contact with William of Orange, the leader of the Dutch revolt against Spain. Because of his involvement with the revolt, Coornhert spent most of the period from 1568 until 1576 in exile in Germany; he then returned to his native land and lived much of the rest of his life in conflict with the orthodox Calvinist ministers of the Netherlands. He died in Gouda in 1590.

Largely self-taught, Coornhert was deeply influenced by the humanist tradition of the Renaissance. His literary production included translation, poetry, plays, polemical works, and moral and religious treatises. Early in his career Coornhert translated classical authors such as Cicero and Seneca, and his first major work was a verse translation into Dutch of the first twelve books of the *Odyssey;* this translation (1561) can be considered a significant product of the early Dutch Renaissance, and throughout his life Coornhert remained a strong advocate for the Dutch language. Coornhert's writings also demonstrate his preoccupation with moral and ethical issues, as can be seen in his major prose work, *Zedekunst, dat is Wellevenskunst* (Ethics, or the Art of Living Well), produced in 1586. In this treatise on moral philosophy, which reflects the classical tradition, Coornhert places a strong emphasis on virtue and the fact that virtue, or the good life, can be achieved through the guidance of human reason. One sees in *Zedekunst* both Coornhert's rejection of the Christian doctrine of original sin and his emphasis on human perfectibility.

Another major theme in Coornhert's writings—and that for which he is best known—is his strong defense of religious tolerance and freedom of conscience. Coornhert was opposed to all forms of religious persecution and believed that religion consisted largely of ethical teachings. He rejected all doctrinal systems and the need for external religious institutions. Both Catholic and Protestant reformers were suspicious of his religious beliefs, but in Holland he primarily attracted the attention and anger of the Reformed church. Coornhert especially rejected the Calvinist doctrine of predestination and was not above the strong use of invective to attack his opponents, a strategy that cost him some of his support. In the end, the influence of Coornhert's highly individual religious beliefs is difficult to trace; however, his commitment to tolerance and religious freedom is undeniable.

Bibliography

H. Bonger, *Leven en Werk van D. V. Coornhert,* 1978.
R. P. Meijer, *Literature of the Low Countries,* 1971.

Michael A. Hakkenberg

COPERNICUS, NICOLAUS (1473–1543)

With *On the Revolutions of the Celestial Spheres,* Nicolaus Copernicus initiated a shift in scientific thinking often now described as the "scientific revolution." Although the details of the heliocentric theory of the universe were disproved long ago, its central claim that the earth is but one of many objects orbiting the sun without a doubt changed the theory and practice of astronomy and physics within the course of a single century.

The son of prosperous parents from Torun in Poland, Copernicus was educated early both at home and elsewhere. At the age of twelve, following the deaths of his parents, he became the ward of his uncle Lucas Waczenrode, the bishop of Varmia. He first attended the cathedral school and later entered the University of Cracow in 1491. Upon the urging of his uncle, Copernicus was elected a canon to the cathedral chapter at Frombork in 1497. An eight-year educational sojourn in Italy solidified his training in law, medicine, mathematics, and astronomy. After study at the Universities of Bologna, Padua, and Ferrara, Copernicus returned to Varmia for good around 1504 and served the cathedral chapter with distinction for his remaining years.

Most of Copernicus's life was occupied by duties having little to do with his scientific achievements, but he is justly renowned for his heliocentric understanding of the universe: "The earth moves while the sun stands still." His scholarly output was limited, and even though he made no secret of his views, he opposed publication of his theory, bowing to the pressure of his friends only in the last years of his life. His delay can hardly be attributed to fear. He circulated a draft report of his new system as early as 1514, and by 1533 Pope Clement VII approved publication of his views. *On the Revolutions of the Celestial Spheres* was complete by 1540, and the work appeared in 1543, the year of the author's death.

Although some ancient philosophers had posited heliocentricity, Copernicus was the first to elaborate upon it systematically. He did so in the face of significant resistance, since the strength of tradition and academic habits secured the dominant positions of Aristotle and Ptolemy within astronomy. In the second century, Ptolemy described a geocentric model of the universe by relying upon the basic tenets of Aristotle's *Physics.* Accordingly, the earth was the fixed center of the universe, and all bodies fell "naturally" to the earth. Since the heavens did not fall, they were of a qualitatively different substance than the earth, one that exhibited the qualities of perfection, not the least of which was perpetual and, therefore, circular (rather than linear) motion. But the problem for Aristotle was that the heavenly bodies displayed disturbingly irregular behavior to the observer on earth. They sometimes moved at different rates of speed or displayed varying degrees of brightness, and, in particular, they sometimes moved in a retrograde fashion, that is, they sometimes went backward. Ptolemy elegantly tackled this problem in a theory that posited the existence of large and small circles. The planets moved first along the small circles positioned around imaginary points in space (equants) that were themselves moving along the large circles. Although inaccurate, this model, minus the equants, is in essence how modern astronomers understand the movement of moons around planets, in small orbits, and the sun, in large orbits. But centuries of observations had eroded the reliability of ancient thought on the heavens. The problem of explaining the speed, brightness, and retrograde motion of the planets remained.

Copernicus's own observations, along with those of others, led to his dissatisfaction with received wisdom and to his desire to replace it with something simpler and more accurate. His central argument can be easily summarized, although the mathematics used to justify its claims cannot be. The earth rotated daily around an axis; furthermore, it circled annually around the sun. By implication, the sun was the center of the universe around which the other heavenly bodies moved.

The chief significance of Copernicus's views lies not so much in his own conclusions as in the implications they raised—new problems that other astronomers set themselves to solving. Copernicus was clearly right about the centrality of the sun, but he produced a model that was hardly less complex and barely more accurate than the accepted one. But he had vigorously attacked the Ptolemaic system and seriously challenged the physics of Aristotle underlying it. He had broken the traditional paradigm. In the following decades, like-minded philosophers of the natural world would follow. The empirical work of Galileo* would lay bare the physical nature of the heavens, and the theoretical work of Johannes Kepler* would accurately describe the complexities of planetary motion. Both rightly acknowledged their debts to Copernicus.

Bibliography

H. Blumenberg, *The Genesis of the Copernican World,* 1987.
O. Gingerich, *The Eye of Heaven,* 1993.

Edmund M. Kern

CORREGGIO, ANTONIO (ANTONIO ALLEGRI)
(c. 1490–1534)

Antonio Correggio was the most important painter of the High Renaissance in northern Italy outside of Venice; his art combined technical control with a profound expressive effect that exercised a strong influence on the development of baroque art.

Born in a provincial backwater, the town of Correggio in north central Italy, Correggio seems to have appeared out of the blue. His training and education are unknown, although it has been suggested that he may have apprenticed with a pupil of Andrea Mantegna. In 1519 he moved to Parma, where he worked until 1530. There he painted a series of panels and frescoes that create an extraordinary effect on the viewer.

Correggio's first impressive work is a fresco decoration, 1520–25, in the dome and apse of San Giovanni Evangelisti in Parma. The decoration is not a cycle, but a single event—the vision of St. John the Evangelist on Patmos—painted with all the illusionistic techniques and dramatic energy the artist could muster. The success of this work led to the commission for a fresco in the much larger dome of Parma Cathedral (1526–30). Although the subject is different—the Assumption of the Virgin—Correggio uses the same illusionism, agitation, and naturalism that served him so well in San Giovanni. Both frescoes reveal an artist who tries to draw the spectator into the religious event, physically and emotionally.

At the same time, Correggio painted a series of altarpieces that work to involve the viewer. They are characterized by active figures, intense feeling, and strong light effects. Rather than traditional symmetry and clear space, he uses asymmetrical compositions and sharp foreshortenings to convey an air of excitement.

From the 1520s on Correggio also produced a number of mythological paintings for private collectors, the most famous of which is *Jupiter and Io* (Vienna, Kunsthistorisches Museum, c. 1532). These lush and tactile paintings deal openly with human sexuality; arousal, pleasure, and sensory stimulation are all suggested by Correggio's naturalistic forms, dramatic light, and dynamic compositions.

Correggio was obviously familiar with the art of Leonardo da Vinci, Michelangelo,* Raphael,* and Titian,* but the effect of his work goes beyond what these High Renaissance masters attempted. His intensity of expression and form can only be defined as protobaroque.

Bibliography

D. Ekserdjian, *Correggio,* 1997.
C. Gould, *The Paintings of Correggio,* 1976.

Jane C. Long

CORYATE (or CORYAT), THOMAS (1577?–1617)

Thomas Coryate was the most famous English traveler and travel writer of the early seventeenth century. Born in Somersetshire about 1577, Coryate attended Oxford, but like many young men not intending a career in the church, he left without taking a degree. After several years, probably spent rather aimlessly, he made his way to King James I's* court and soon became popular for his comic intelligence, verbal dexterity, and willingness to be the butt of other courtiers' jokes.

In May 1608 Coryate embarked on an almost 2,000-mile tour of the European continent, much of which he completed on foot. The result of his travels was the huge comic work on which his future fame would rest, *Coryats Crudities:*

Hastily Gobled up in Five Moneths Travells (1611). The *Crudities* contains many humorous passages and is marked by an erudite wit throughout, but it also provided future travelers (and in an age of very limited opportunities to voyage abroad, many would-be travelers) with a compendium of practical and sometimes rare information on continental travel. Moreover, his work also became something of an elaborate in-joke among English writers and members of court, since over one hundred pages of its nearly eight hundred are taken up with humorous dedicatory verses and mock panegyrics by some of contemporary England's greatest literary wits, including Ben Jonson.*

Encouraged by the success of his *Crudities* and two shorter sequels, Coryate set off on a second voyage in 1612, this time traveling to Greece, Asia Minor, the Holy Lands, and even India. Several of his letters were published during his absence and were well received in England, but Coryate died in India in 1617.

Bibliography

M. Strachan, *The Life and Adventures of Thomas Coryate,* 1962.

                                                                Thomas G. Olsen

COSIMO I DE' MEDICI (1519–1574)

Cosimo I de' Medici, powerful duke of Florence and grand duke of Tuscany, guaranteed the glorious reputation of his reign through his vigorous patronage of art and architecture. His father was Giovanni delle Bande Nere, the famous condottiere, and his grandmother was the indomitable Caterina Sforza; his mother, Maria Salviati, was the granddaughter of Lorenzo the Magnificent. Given his illustrious and ambitious ancestry, it is perhaps no surprise that Cosimo was chosen the next duke of Florence (1537) when his predecessor, his distant relative Alessandro de' Medici, was murdered. Cosimo proved to be a mercurial but capable ruler, establishing Florence's independence from Spain, conquering Siena and its territories, and eventually becoming grand duke of Tuscany in 1569.

When Cosimo was twenty, he married Eleanora of Toledo,* the daughter of the Spanish viceroy of Naples. Though both the duke and the duchess were said to be willful and temperamental, they were devoted to each other; their marriage was a happy one and produced several children. They were both zealous art patrons, though some scholars have argued that Cosimo was primarily interested in art for its propagandistic potential. Bronzino* served as court artist for several years, creating several paintings of Cosimo, his wife and children, and even his dwarf Morgante. Giorgio Vasari* succeeded Bronzino as official painter; he was also commissioned to redecorate the Palazzo Vecchio with a series of frescoes celebrating the Medici dynasty and to oversee work on the Uffizi Palace. Cosimo also commissioned the bronze statue *Perseus with the Head of Medusa* (1543–53) from Benvenuto Cellini* for the Piazza della Signoria. Cosimo was interested in beautifying the entire city of Florence to glorify the achievements of the Medici dynasty; to that purpose he employed numerous artists and architects.

When Eleanora died in 1562, Cosimo was devastated, and he abdicated two years later in favor of his son, Francesco; the last decade of his life was marked by ill health. His legacy, however, is rich and enduring; it was due to his powerful patronage that many of Renaissance Florence's great works of art and architecture were created.

Bibliography

J. R. Hale, *Florence and the Medici: The Pattern of Control*, 1977.

Jo Eldridge Carney

COTTON, SIR ROBERT BRUCE (1571–1631)

Robert Bruce Cotton was an English antiquary and book collector who, through the acquisition and interpretation of an unprecedented mass of historical material, greatly influenced politics and the study of history in early-seventeenth-century England. Born in Huntingdonshire, England, Cotton was the eldest son of Thomas Cotton of Connington, a rich country gentleman. Cotton began his education at Westminster School, and his interest in antiquities was encouraged and refined by the school's second master, William Camden.* After Westminster he proceeded to Jesus College, Cambridge, where he received a bachelor of arts in 1585, and then entered the Middle Temple in 1588. By age seventeen he had begun his historical researches, collecting materials toward establishing a history of his home county of Huntingdonshire. Cotton assisted Camden in founding the Society of Antiquaries in 1586, along with other lawyers and heralds who were interested in antiquities, such as Henry Spelman, John Stow,* Francis Thynne, John Speed, and Richard Carew. Cotton presented himself at court in 1603 and was knighted by James I,* primarily as a reward for Cotton's efforts to legitimize the new king's claim to the throne through his antiquarian research.

Cotton's growing collection of manuscripts, books, public and private records, coins, and other historical artifacts became a valuable resource in the years 1604–28. Figures such as Ben Jonson,* John Dee,* Sir John Davies,* and Francis Bacon* often used the library, and Cotton was increasingly consulted to legitimize various political agendas. His advice was sought on everything from ceremonial tradition to legal history and precedents in state policy. After the death of James I and the succession of Charles I in 1625, Cotton and his library became the target of envy, suspicion, and political maneuvering. Charges that he had circulated a tract supporting absolute monarchy were brought against him; he was confined, and his library became closed to him. Although he was released soon after, Cotton was banned from his own library until late 1630; by the time Charles relented, Cotton had fallen ill, and he died in May 1631.

Cotton's library was his greatest achievement, both as a contemporary resource for national and international scholars, politicians, men of letters, and antiquaries and as a material legacy. His collecting and scholarly activity provided a model and a catalyst for the major advances in historical and historiographical methods in late-seventeenth-century England.

Bibliography

K. Sharpe, *Sir Robert Cotton, 1586–1631: History and Politics in Early Modern England,* 1979.

Richard J. Ring

COVERDALE, MILES (c. 1488–1569)

Miles Coverdale was a translator of the Bible and bishop of Exeter. He was most likely born in York. After becoming an Augustinian friar, he went on to be educated at Cambridge. Later in life he received further education from the universities at Wittenberg and Tübingen. Although he had taken holy orders, by 1528 he had rejected priest's vestments, which he would continue to do throughout his life, and began preaching against the Mass, confession, and image worship. He soon left England for Europe and in 1534 received a commission from a merchant in Antwerp for a translation of the entire Bible into English, which he completed in 1535. He relied on various sources for his work, including the Vulgate, the Zurich translation of 1531, Martin Luther's* translation, and the work of William Tyndale,* whom he had assisted with his translation of the Pentateuch. The first Coverdale Bible was transported to England, where it met with approval; in 1539 Coverdale revised his work, thus forming the basis for the Great Bible, which would be distributed in churches throughout England.

Coverdale went once more into exile in 1540 after his supporter Thomas Cromwell was executed. Around this time he married Elizabeth Macheson, a Scottish exile, and they traveled first to Denmark and then to Germany, where Coverdale was appointed assistant minister and headmaster of the town school in Bergzabern. After the death of Henry VIII,* Coverdale returned to England, where he enjoyed royal favor. In August 1551 he was appointed bishop of Exeter, an office he held until Mary I* ascended the throne. When she attempted to imprison him on charges of unpaid debts, the king of Denmark appealed on Coverdale's behalf, and he was released into exile once more. He returned to England during the reign of Elizabeth I* and remained there until his death in 1569. His work has been widely recognized as the first complete English translation of the Bible and helped form the basis for the King James,* or Authorized Version, in 1611.

Bibliography

J. F. Mozley, *Coverdale and His Bibles,* 1953.

Jean Akers

CRANACH, LUCAS, THE ELDER (1472–1553)

German painter and printmaker Lucas Cranach, along with rival artist Hans Burgkmair,* is credited with inventing the chiaroscuro woodcut, a medium Cranach perfected. Born in Kronach, Lucas succeeded several generations of painters, including his father, Hans Maler, who trained the artist. Settling in Vienna, a humanist center, Cranach painted an extraordinary pair of marriage portraits of Dr. Johannes Cuspinian and his wife, Anna Cuspinian. Set in a landscape depicting the four elements—air, earth, water, and fire—various motifs allude to the humanist Cuspinian's interest in cosmography, as well as Christian symbolism.

Cranach moved to Wittenberg to become court painter to Frederick the Wise, elector of Saxony, who was Martin Luther's* benefactor. Luther became a close friend, serving as witness to Cranach's wedding in 1525 and godfather to his children, an honor Cranach reciprocated. After returning from a diplomatic mission to the Netherlands, Cranach painted a large altarpiece of the *Holy Kinship* for Frederick, no doubt influenced by Quentin Massys's* Antwerp altarpiece of the same subject. The painting represents the genealogy of the holy family enacted by the imperial family, including likenesses of Frederick, his brother Duke John the Steadfast, and Emperor Maximilian. As part of another major court commission, Cranach contributed eight pages to the grandiose Prayerbook of Maximilian.

Cranach was in Wittenberg on All Saints' Eve in 1517 when Luther posted his ninety-five theses. After his excommunication at the Diet of Worms in 1521, Luther returned to Wittenberg in the guise of Jonker Jorg, an aristocratic knight, and was arrested there on Whitsuntide. Among Cranach's many likenesses of Luther, one of his most compelling is his representation of the Protestant leader as Jonker Jorg, in woodcut and panel. Cranach played a more direct role in the Protestant Reformation in 1519 when he designed the first Reformation broadsheet, the ''Furhwagen'' (Chariot to Heaven and Chariot to Hell). Cranach also illustrated the Book of Revelation for Luther's first edition of his translation of the New Testament, the ''September Testament'' in 1522, with woodcuts inspired by Albrecht Dürer's* *Apocalypse* woodcut series.

A new subject reflecting Protestant views originated in Cranach's workshop. *Allegory of the Law and the Gospel,* painted in 1529, illustrates Luther's tenet of redemption through faith, defining the Law under Moses as one of judgment and punishment, while under the Gospel, as forgiving and merciful. In the altarpiece, bifurcated by a central tree, dead branches and a nude man damned to hell for his sin of idolatry symbolize the Old Law under Moses. On the right side, the tree rejuvenates into the Tree of Life, and the same nude man is redeemed through Christ's sacrificial crucifixion. Cranach is equally renowned for his depictions of mythological subjects, developing a distinctive idealized version of the female nude—soft and willowy, the antithesis of the classical nude—who emanates both innocence and sensuality.

Cranach continued to immortalize the Saxon court in portraits throughout his life. After Charles V* defeated and imprisoned John Frederick, a leader of the Schmalkaldic League, in 1547, Cranach remained loyal to the Saxon noble, following him to Weimar upon his release, where the artist died at the age of eighty-one in 1553.

Bibliography

A. Stepanov, *Lucas Cranach the Elder,* 1997.

Susan H. Jenson

CRANMER, THOMAS (1489–1556)

Thomas Cranmer, the archbishop of Canterbury during the reigns of Henry VIII* and Edward VI, was at the helm of much of the English Reformation, but he was eventually executed during the reign of Mary I.* Cranmer was born in Nottinghamshire and went on to be educated at Jesus College, Cambridge. In 1529 he encountered Henry VIII's secretary and almoner at Waltham Abbey and told them that he thought that the king should take the matter of his divorce before scholars of divinity at the universities to bypass the lengthy process in Rome. The idea pleased Henry, and from then on Cranmer was increasingly drawn into the king's favor. In 1530 he became archdeacon of Taunton and traveled in 1532 on a diplomatic mission to the holy Roman emperor in Germany. He married a woman named Margaret, but kept their marriage secret until 1548, when Parliament voted to legalize clergy marriages. When he returned to England early in 1533, Henry appointed him archbishop of Canterbury, and after taking his vows Cranmer renounced his allegiance to the pope in favor of the Crown. In May he pronounced the king's marriage to Catherine of Aragon null and void and declared the marriage between Henry and Anne Boleyn to be valid. Cranmer formed a solid relationship with the new queen and enjoyed her patronage until her death; he remained sympathetic to her family. Throughout Henry's subsequent marital proceedings, Cranmer lent religious authority and legitimacy, although at times he was not averse to questioning the king's reasoning.

By and large, Cranmer remained a steadfast and loyal supporter of Henry VIII until the king's death and operated as the highest ecclesiastical authority in the land. He assisted in the publication of the *Bishops' Book* in 1534, the first printing of the English Bible in 1537, and the catechism *A Short Instruction into Christian Religion* in 1548 and, in his most lasting contribution, edited the first *Book of Common Prayer* in 1549. After Henry's death, Cranmer continued his role as church primate, but during the reign of Edward VI, sharp differences between religious conservatives and reformers became more contentious. Cranmer may have been concerned for the future of the evangelical movement; he consistently sought to maintain the integrity of the English church and at the behest of critics revised the *Book of Common Prayer* for a new edition in 1552.

After Edward's death in 1553, Cranmer supported the brief reign of Lady Jane Grey,* but when Mary I ascended to the throne, she had him imprisoned in the Tower of London, where he remained for two years. The authorities considered charging him with treason, but Cardinal Reginald Pole eventually condemned him for heresy on 14 December 1555, and he was subsequently stripped of his ecclesiastical vestments and authority. As the day of his execution neared, Cranmer seems to have become increasingly desperate and recanted his evangelical beliefs and activities of the past twenty-five years six separate times. On 21 March 1556, in his last words, he disavowed his recent recantations, depriving the Catholics of their joy at having converted him. As fires were set beneath him at the stake, he thrust his right hand, which had written the recantations, into the fire and denounced its treachery. He was known thereafter as a martyr of the Protestant Reformation.

Bibliography

D. MacCulloch, *Thomas Cranmer,* 1996.

Jean Akers

CRENNE, HÉLISENNE DE (c. 1510–1552)

Hélisenne de Crenne is the pen name of one of the most important female authors of the French Renaissance. She wrote the first novel of romantic passion in French, a collection of letters, a dream allegory, and a translation of Virgil.

Verifiable biographical facts about Hélisenne are few. She was born Marguerite de Briet in Abbeville, a small village in Picardy. Around 1530 she married Philippe Fournel, a country squire who was seigneur of the area of Crasnes; they had a son, Pierre. A 1552 document attests to her legal separation from her husband, though the separation probably occurred much earlier. Additional information about Hélisenne's life is problematic since most of it has been derived from her two major literary works, which appear to be part fiction and part autobiography.

Her first major work, *Les angoysses douloureuses qui procedent d'amours* (The Torments of Love), describes the marriage of a girl named Hélisenne whose family arranges for her to be married at a young age. After her marriage, Hélisenne falls in love with another man; her husband spies on her, beats her, and ultimately imprisons her. The Hélisenne of the novel eventually dies of a fatal illness. This long semiautobiographical novel is also indebted to the popular literary tradition of tragic love tales. Upon its publication in 1538, *Les angoysses* was immediately successful, but it was also criticized for an excessive and pretentious style.

Though the author had put Hélisenne to death in her first work, she continued to write and publish under that pen name. In 1539 her second work appeared, *Les epistres familieres et invectives* (Personal and invective letters), a series of eighteen letters that again recounts the story of her marriage, the publication of *Les angoysses,* and her husband's furious reaction to that novel. Scholars consider this work a significant contribution to the debate about women that took place in sixteenth-century France. Her third work, *Le songe de Madame Hélisenne* (The Dream of Madame Hélisenne) was published in 1540. In the tradition of the allegorical dream vision of fifteenth-century writer Christine de Pizan, Hélisenne's dream describes a debate over questions of virtue and dignity in men and women. Hélisenne's final publication, *Les quatres premiers livres des*

Eneydes (The first four books of the Aeneid, 1541), was the first known unabridged translation of these books into French. Her works were reprinted frequently in her lifetime, but after the sixteenth century her writings fell into
obscurity.

Bibliography

Hélisenne de Crenne, *A Renaissance Woman: Hélisenne's Personal and Invective Letters,*
     trans. M. Mustacchi and P. Archambault, 1986.
Hélisenne de Crenne, *The Torments of Love,* trans. L. Neal and S. Rendall, 1996.

Jo Eldridge Carney

CRESPIN, JEAN (c. 1520–1572)

Jean Crespin was a lawyer and a publisher who achieved fame as a Protestant
martyrologist. He was born into a noble family in Arras. He received a humanist
education and studied law at Louvain and Paris. He returned to Arras and married in 1544, but was banished from that town in the following year under
suspicion of heresy. He fled to Strasbourg and subsequently made the acquaintance of Theodore Beza.*

Crespin moved to Geneva in 1548 and set up a publishing house there. Both
John Calvin* and Beza published some of their works through Crespin. Crespin
quickly became one of the major publishers in Geneva. He had fonts to accom-
modate a variety of languages and published grammars in Greek, Hebrew, Italian, and Latin and works in French and German. He also published the Geneva
Bible for the Marian exiles from England. While Crespin did print the classics,
the majority of his output consisted of Bibles, biblical commentaries, and liturgical works. He published the only two editions of the church fathers in Geneva
before 1570. Although Crespin printed Lutheran works, his own theological
adherence was primarily Calvinist. He published attacks on the Lutherans in the
Lutheran-Reformed debates over the Last Supper.

Crespin also wrote the famous *History of the Martyrs,* a collection of stories
in French about Protestant martyrs. It was first published in 1554 and saw sixteen editions in forty years. It soon became a classic of the Reformed tradition
and was read and imitated in all the major Protestant communities of Europe.
Crespin died of the plague in 1572.

Crespin's martyrology created a genre of literary works about Protestant martyrs. It especially helped provide the French Protestants with a common sense
of identity. As late as the eighteenth century, it continued to be read aloud to
recount the lives of those who suffered persecution and death at the hands of
the Catholics.

Bibliography

A. G. Dickens and J. M. Tonkin, *The Reformation in Historical Thought,* 1985.
J.-F. Gilmont, *Jean Crespin, un éditeur réformé du XVI siècle,* 1981.

Andrew G. Traver

D

DANIEL, SAMUEL (1563–1619)

Samuel Daniel was a successful and respected poet and playwright. He influenced the development of several genres, including sonnets, tragedies, and prose history. Daniel, the son of a music master, entered Magdalen Hall of Oxford University at age nineteen. Before receiving his degree, Daniel left Oxford and eventually became the tutor for William Herbert, the son of Mary Sidney,* the countess of Pembroke. Daniel secured the patronage of the countess, and she was the most influential of his supporters. Other patrons who supported Daniel were Fulke Greville, a courtier and poet, and Charles Blount, earl of Devonshire.

Delia (1592), a collection of sonnets distinguished for their beauty and purity of language rather than their passion, was dedicated to the countess of Pembroke, although there is no indication that Daniel knew her when he composed the sonnets. *Cleopatra* (1594), a neoclassic tragedy, was written in response to the countess of Pembroke's drama *Antonie*. There is speculation that Daniel began writing tragedies due to influence from within the countess's literary circle.

With the accession of James I* to the English throne, Daniel wrote *Panegyric Congratulatoire* (1603) with the intention of gaining favor with the new ruler. Daniel competed with Ben Jonson* and Thomas Campion* to have his masques performed at court. *The Vision of the Twelve Goddesses* (1604) and *Tethys' Festival* (1610) were among the masques written for Queen Anne, King James's consort.

In 1604 Daniel was appointed as licenser for the Children of the Queen's Revels, but left this position in April 1605. It is believed that Daniel resigned due to the production of his play *Philotas* (1604), which contained possible allusions to the earl of Essex, a controversial courtier executed as a traitor in 1601. Daniel was called before the Privy Council and continued to deny any references to the earl of Essex in his play.

Daniel's major prose work, *Defense of Ryme* (1603), was a treatise written in response to Thomas Campion's *Observations in the Art of English Poesie*, which attacked the literary convention of rhyming. *The Civil Wars* (1594–1609), Daniel's famed epic poem, was written in installments and depicted the Wars of the Roses. During the last years of his life Daniel studied history, publishing before his death *The History of England* (1618), a prose chronicle tracing England's history from the Romans to Edward III.

Bibliography

J. Rees, *Samuel Daniel*, 1964.

Barbara Boyle

DAVIES, SIR JOHN (1569–1626)

John Davies was an English poet, jurist, and civil servant whose contribution to literature was secondary to his influence on English law and Anglo-Irish relations and policies in the crucial years following the death of Elizabeth I.* Born in Wiltshire, England, Davies was the third son of a Welsh tanner and began his education at Winchester, where his interest in literature developed. After spending eighteen months of Oxford University, Davies entered the Middle Temple in London in 1588 and was called to the bar in 1595. Disbarred in 1598 for publicly assaulting his friend and fellow member of the Middle Temple Richard Martin, Davies was reinstated by petition in 1601.

Following the death of Elizabeth I in March 1603, Davies went to Scotland with a group led by Lord Hunsdon to inform and pledge loyalty to the new monarch, James I* of England. James recognized Davies as the author of *Nosce teipsum* (Know Thyself, 1599) and was sufficiently impressed with him that in 1603 he knighted Davies and appointed him the solicitor general of Ireland. Three years later he was elevated to attorney general and was created sergeant-at-law. While Davies was in Ireland, he dispensed English justice, surveyed and mapped counties, worked to establish schools, attempted to transfer feudal loyalty to the new English king, and was active in the Protestant settlement of Ulster. In 1612 he published a tract in which he attributed the problems of English rule in Ireland to the failure to establish a system of territorial law (as opposed to personal law), entitled *A Discoverie of the True Causes Why Ireland Was Never Entirely Subdued Nor Brought under Obedience of the Crowne; untill the Beginning of His Majesties Happie Raigne.*

Davies entered the newly formed Irish Parliament in 1613 and was elected speaker. In his trips to London he became associated with Sir Robert Cotton* in reestablishing the Society of Antiquaries, originally founded by Cotton's mentor, William Camden.* Davies was recalled to England in 1619, was elected to Parliament in 1621, and rode the assize circuit until 1626. He died the day that he was to take up a new appointment, chief justice of the King's Bench, granted by Charles I.

Davies's writings are of interest primarily because they reflect the assumptions and concerns of his time. His poetry was popular, if not innovative, and served to help propel him into a position to influence the formation and interpretation of English common and civil law.

Bibliography

J. Sanderson, *Sir John Davies*, 1975.

Richard J. Ring

DEE, JOHN (1527–1608)

John Dee, both feared and respected in Elizabethan England, was a teacher-philosopher whose range of studies encompassed mathematics, philosophy, and geography in both the natural and celestial worlds. Influenced by Platonic and Hermetic philosophies, Dee was imprisoned by Mary I,* admired by Elizabeth I,* and scorned by James I.*

Born on 13 July 1527, Dee studied and taught mathematical concepts, emphasizing their ability to move freely between the physical and immaterial worlds. Imprisoned under Queen Mary in June 1555, Dee was accused of "lewde vayne practices of calculing and conjuring." By 1558, however, he gained the reputation of a learned scientific teacher and a favorite of Queen Elizabeth. Intrigued by Dee's claims to alchemy, the ability to turn base metal into gold, the queen appointed Dee court astrologer. He divined the best date for her coronation, advised on navigational matters, and was approached to revise the Julian calendar. Dee's lectures and teachings were sought by the curious in England for twenty-five years.

By 1570 Dee had established a home at Mortlake that drew distinguished visitors, students, and guests until late 1583. At that point Dee embarked upon a failed trip abroad, and he returned to Mortlake by 1589. There he found his home ransacked and his library severely damaged. Through Queen Elizabeth's favor, Dee became warden of Manchester College in 1595. With the accession of King James, however, Dee quickly fell from royal favor.

Dee's suggestions to Queen Mary, such as the institution of a royal library, were not wasted on Queen Elizabeth. She and members of her court frequented Dee's abode at Mortlake, and he became a valued advisor. His *Mathematical Preface* to Euclid as well as his geographical studies on newly found lands were indispensable in the Elizabethan era.

The humanist education emphasized during the Reformation ran counter to Dee's desire for his studies to have practical application. Mathematics was considered a diabolical study in Dee's day by some, and he sought to prove its theories useful and relevant in the natural world. This focus upon application of knowledge led to the development of the scientific method and ultimately gave birth to technology.

Whispers of black magic plagued Dee during and after his lifetime. These tales apparently surfaced after a stage performance of Aristophanes in which Dee's use of stage mechanics was too realistic. Dee was considered a magician-philosopher, and his ambiguous reputation still persists today. In a diary called

Liber Mysteriorum, Dee's seances at Mortlake with a man first called Mr. Talbot and later Edward Kelly are recorded. Kelly, claiming to be a seer or skryer, interpreted celestial images seen in a mirrored glass for Dee. Reports of angels and these divinations through seance brought the two and their wives to the unsuccessful 1583 trip abroad.

The old traditions that Dee studied at Mortlake were taught not only to Queen Elizabeth but to many of the most influential people in England at the time. While common folk in England doubted and feared Dee and his sorcery, his quest for and application of once-feared topics like alchemy and mathematics brought abstract investigation out of the shadows and into the royal spotlight. His applications of machination and navigation have helped, to an immeasurable degree, to bring Western culture to the stage of technical development that it enjoys today.

Bibliography

P. French, *John Dee: The World of an Elizabethan Magus*, 1972.
W. Sherman, *John Dee: The Politics of Reading and Writing in the Renaissance*, 1995.

Karolyn Kinane

DEKKER, THOMAS (c. 1570–c. 1632)

Thomas Dekker, termed the "Dickens of the Elizabethan Age," was a collaborative playwright best remembered for his observations of London life expressed through his pamphlets.

No information about his education or family survives, and his life is generally masked in mystery. There is evidence that Dekker had knowledge of the Dutch language, and some historians believe that he served his country in the Netherlands. There is record of a Mary "Decker" dying in 1616, but at Dekker's death, his wife's name was given as Elizabeth. Three baptismal records survive that suggest that Dekker did have children.

Philip Henslowe's* diary first mentions Dekker in 1588. The payment was for a lost piece, *Phaethon*, written for the Lord Admiral's Men. The diary records that between 1598 and 1602 Dekker wrote and collaborated on about forty plays, most of which are lost. The last payment to Dekker is recorded in 1604 for his work with Thomas Middleton* on *The Honest Whore*.

Dekker, after a brief term in debtor's prison in 1598, reached his peak in 1599 and the following years with such pieces as *The Shoemaker's Holiday*, *Old Fortunatus*, and later *Satiro-Mastix* and pamphlets like *The Wonderful Year* and *The Seven Deadly Sins of London*. He was then again confined to debtor's prison for a long spell from 1613 to 1619. Upon his emergence, Dekker found that a new crop of writers had established themselves in London and that he was now displaced.

In his own words, Dekker addressed the reader who wanted to be "amused and startled." Mingling simplicity with realism and romance, Dekker produced genial observations of London life. His sometimes-weak plots are tempered with a sweetness that exposes a deep knowledge of common humanity. Some critics state that his pamphlets are exaggerations of London life, but most credit Dekker with delivering the finest reports of life in early-seventeenth-century London.

Bibliography

G. Price, *Thomas Dekker*, 1969.

Karolyn Kinane

DELLA CASA, GIOVANNI (1503–1556)

Giovanni Della Casa, a humanist-educated courtly writer, advanced Catholic reform efforts for the papacy in Venice and authored a handbook on manners titled *Il Galateo*. Della Casa, born in Mugello and raised in Rome, returned to Florence in 1524, where he began humanistic studies under Ubaldino Bandinelli. In 1525 at the University of Bologna he preferred poetry and the classics over law. He studied also at Padua, where he learned Greek. By 1531 he decided, for practical rather than spiritual reasons, on a career in the church, entering papal service and participating in the Accademia dei Vignaioli in Rome. There he composed *Sopra il forno, Quaestio lepidissima an uxor sit ducenda*, and *La formica*, youthful, licentious works later judged obscene. After securing a post as a clerk in the Apostolic Camera, he became a member of the literary Accademia della Virtù and sought the patronage of Cardinal Alessandro Farnese. In 1544 he became archbishop of Benevento, a role he exercised in absentia.

Later that summer he was named to the important post of papal nuncio for Venice and was entrusted with diplomatic missions, the care of ecclesiastical privileges, and the enforcement of Counter-Reformation policies in the Veneto, where he introduced the Inquisition and the Index of Prohibited Books. The most important case heard by the Holy Office was that of Pier Paolo Vergerio, who escaped to Germany and launched accusations against Della Casa, to which the latter responded in beautiful humanistic Latin charging the exile with all manner of crimes. Della Casa's diplomatic efforts were ineffectual despite a humble oration addressed to Emperor Charles V* to restore Piacenza and an *Orazione per la lega*.

After the death of Pope Paul III, Della Casa returned to private life and wrote biographies of Pietro Bembo* and Gaspare Contarini, Latin lyrics in honor of Marguerite de Navarre,* and poetry, epigrams, and orations. With the election of Pope Paul IV, he returned to Rome, hoping to become a cardinal. The nomination was blocked by Della Casa's enemies, who recalled his youthful poetry.

Della Casa enjoyed a hospitable, literary, and courtly life in palatial environs among influential friends, including Pietro Bembo. He was no stranger to the company of noble women nor to Venice's cultured courtesans, and he fathered a child by a common prostitute. He knew the painters Giovanni Battista Franco (Semolei) and Titian.* He generously oversaw the education of his nephews, to whom he recommended humanistic rhetoric for its practicality and eloquence.

In 1546 he wrote *Tractatus de officiis inter potentiores et tenuiores*, which explains the relationship between superiors and inferiors at court and advises the latter in utilitarian terms rather than those of Stoic duty. His most enduring work, *Il Galateo* (c. 1551), often compared to Baldesar Castiglione's* *The Courtier*, is a handbook for civilized, courtly comportment. It deals with more practical matters and pragmatic advice for contemporaries, however, while offering the modern reader a realistic understanding, not simply a prescriptive model, of the level of civility in the sixteenth century.

Bibliography

M. Mazzeschi Porretti, *Il monsignore: Vita e opere di Giovanni Della Casa*, 1990.

Luci Fortunato DeLisle

DELLA PORTA, GIAMBATTISTA (1535–1615)

One of the most versatile scholars of the Italian Renaissance, Giambattista Della Porta was well known in his day as both a scientist and a playwright. Born into a noble family in Naples, Della Porta received a broad education in humanism and the sciences; he was also extremely interested in magic and the occult. Later in his life, he became a member of the scientific Accademia de' Lincei, of which Galileo* was also a member. His early scientific writings were *L'arte del ricordare* (The art of memory, 1556) and *Magiae naturalis* (Natural magic, 1558). Later works included treatises on fruit growing, trees, physiognomy, hydraulics, chemistry, and alchemy. A particularly important work was *De refractione* (On Refraction, 1593), a work on optics that contributed to the debate over the invention of the telescope. One of his most famous, if unsuccessful, scientific investigations was his relentless pursuit of the philosopher's stone.

Many of his scientific studies were undertaken while he was under the patronage of Cardinal Luigi d'Este in Ferrara. Della Porta emphasized the importance of observation in scientific inquiry and was concerned about practical application; nonetheless, much of his scientific work was considered suspect. In the 1570s he was brought to the attention of the Inquisition for his interest in the occult, but was released with the understanding that he would devote more time to literature and less time to science. In spite of his attempts to appear more orthodox in his research, Della Porta could not abandon his passion for magic and fortune-telling, which led to further accusations of sorcery by French author Jean Bodin*; however, he also attracted the great admiration of Holy Roman Emperor Rudolf II*, himself an amateur alchemist and astronomer.

Della Porta considered his literary pursuits secondary to his scientific interests, but his dramatic works are what ensured his reputation. Although he had been writing drama since his youth, his first play was not published until 1589; by the time of his death in 1615, he had completed twenty-nine comedies, three tragedies, and a tragicomedy, as well as several translations of the comedies of Plautus. Of his many plays, seventeen are extant: a tragicomedy, a secular tragedy, a religious tragedy, and fourteen comedies. Of the comedies, *La sorella*

(The Sister, 1589) and *Gli duoi fratelli rivali* (The Two Rival Brothers, 1601) were especially popular. Other important works include the tragicomedy *Penelope* (1591), the tragedy *L'Ulisse* (Ulysses, 1614), and the religious play *Il Georgio* (St. George, 1611). Della Porta's popularity extended beyond Italy; in his lifetime, several of his works were translated for the French and English stage.

Bibliography

L. Clubb, *Giambattista Della Porta*, 1965.

Jo Eldridge Carney

DELONEY, THOMAS (1543?–1600)

One of the most voraciously read writers of the Elizabethan Grub Street, Thomas Deloney was a translator, an epic poet, a fiction writer, and the king of the London ballad makers. Deloney's career is an example of Elizabethan middle-class versatility. His grammar-school education grounded him in Latin and French, introduced him to contemporary literature, and versed him in crisp writing. A silk weaver by trade, he penned historical, moral, and religious ballads for a living. Yet his trademark was protojournalistic balladry concerning journalistic events, such as "A Joyful Song of the Royal Receiving of the Queen's Majesty into Her Camp at Tilbury" (1588), registered the very day after the event, or the "Lamentation of Page's Wife of Plymouth" (1591), a "human-interest story" about a husband-murderer. In 1593 he collected his ballads in *The Garland of Good-Will*, which was soon followed by a second popular collection, *Strange Histories* (1602).

Yet Deloney was not simply a vulgar, profit-driven entertainer. He voiced the cries of the working Londoners, urging, in 1595, protection against the apprenticeship malpractices of immigrant weavers. A year later, he wrote against the scarcity of grain in England. For this, he got in trouble with the lord mayor of London and had to escape to the countryside. There he gained firsthand knowledge of local customs, dialects, stories, and the settings for his novels.

These four novels, *Jack of Newbury*, the two parts of *The Gentle Craft*, and *Thomas of Reading*, are Deloney's chief claim for remembrance. Written between 1597 and 1600, they glorify the English artisan. His characters are busy city folk, jolly men and women, and there is always a solid foundation of fact in their dramatic portrayal. Deloney's novels went through multiple seventeenth- and eighteenth-century editions, while contemporary dramatists borrowed from his plots.

Bibliography

E. P. Wright, *Thomas Deloney*, 1981.

Kirilka Stavreva

DESPORTES, PHILIPPE (c. 1546–1606)

An imitator of Italian poets such as Petrarch and Ludovico Ariosto,* Desportes exploited well-known myths, a certain musicality, and his wit to pen love

poetry, foreshadowing the *précieux* poetry of the seventeenth century and enabling him to supersede Pierre de Ronsard* as court poet of France. Desportes
was born into a family of rather distinguished merchants in Chartres. His early
education was devoted to studies in Latin and Greek. After his father's death in
1562, Desportes moved to Paris, where he worked as a clerk until he lost his
position because of his employer's suspicions about Desportes's relationship
with his wife. He left Paris for Avignon, where he secured employment with
the bishop of Le Puy and accompanied him to Rome. There he devoted a certain
amount of time to reading the Italian poets before returning to France in 1567.
Desportes's recitation of a poem about the duke of Anjou at the performance
of Jean-Antoine de Baïf's* *Le brave* in 1567 resulted in the publication of his
Premières oeuvres (1573), which included *Les amours de Diane* and *Les amours
d'Hippolyte*. The duke of Anjou invited Desportes to join him on a trip to Poland
in 1573, from which he returned to France in 1574 when the duke of Anjou
succeeded Charles IX as Henri III. *Cléonice, dernieres amours* was published
in 1583.

Succeeding Ronsard as royal court poet, Desportes enjoyed a life characterized by financial gifts, privileges, and success. Desportes's lucid assessment of
the political climate in France after Henri III's assassination by Jacques Clément
in 1589 led him to side with the Catholic League, helping to defend Rouen from
Henri IV's troops in 1592. Later, Desportes negotiated the surrender of some
places held by the League in Normandy, an act that led Henri IV to give him
the Abbey of Bonport, where he retired to write his translations of the Psalms
before his death in 1606.

Bibliography

A. Prescott, *French Poets and the English Renaissance: Studies in Fame and Transformation*, 1978.

Nancy Erickson Bouzrara

DES ROCHES, CATHERINE (1542–1587) and MADELEINE (c. 1520–1587)

The Dames des Roches, mother and daughter, were members of France's
upper middle class who hosted a salon, or gathering of scholars and artists. They
were authors of epistolary poems, verse dialogues, and lyric and narrative poems
that exhibit their knowledge of classical authors as well as current debates.

Both Madeleine and Catherine were born and lived their lives in and around
the French city of Poitiers. The mother, Madeleine, instructed herself and her
daughter, Catherine, in the arts and sciences of the time. In order to better pursue
a life of learning with her mother, Catherine des Roches chose not to marry,
despite her many suitors. The *salon* gatherings attracted suitors among the many
writers and scholars in attendance.

Madeleine des Roches wrote three particularly noteworthy pieces: "Epistle to
the Ladies," "Epistle to My Daughter," and an "Ode." In the "Epistle to the

Ladies," she describes a community of educated women readers, perhaps associated with the court of the queen mother Catherine de' Medici.* She warns the
ladies against heeding the virtue of silence in women, a virtue that was highly
admired by many people of the time. Instead of silence, she argues, women's
honor should be associated with reason, which distinguishes humans from animals and is articulated through speech. It is this same advice she passes on to
her daughter in the "Epistle to My Daughter." This letter to her daughter is
written in verse and wishes her the best in her scholarly endeavors. Peppered
with numerous classical references, her "Ode" further discussed the current *querelle des femmes*, in which the virtues and vices of the female gender were hotly
debated. Madeleine encourages the implied female reader to undertake learning
despite considerable opposition she will encounter due to gender expectations.

Madeleine's daughter, Catherine, wrote about a wide variety of gender-based
topics, from Amazons to distaffs to dialogues concerning family relations. In
her poems on Amazons, Catherine resurrects this classical myth about women
warriors from a female point of view. Her Amazons are chaste and learned as
well as strong, virtues she may well have possessed herself. In a poem written
to her distaff, she compares the two instruments—her distaff and her pen—
equally and favorably. The distaff, or spindle, represents the traditional female
occupation of spinning, whereas the pen, which was not a traditionally female
implement, receives equal honors. This poem, like others she wrote, can be read
as conciliatory in the *querelle* about women's roles: women can embrace both
conventional roles and scholarship.

Unlike some other women writers, but like their Lyon contemporary, Louise
Labé,* the Dames des Roches were published in their lifetime: *Les oeuvres*
(1578 and 1579), *Les secondes oeuvres* (1583), and *Les missives* (1586). Madeleine was fervently nationalistic; France was superior to all other nations. Both
mother and daughter opposed the Protestant Reformation, yet they maintained
friendly relations with Protestant humanists.

Bibliography

A. Larsen, "Les Dames des Roches," in *Women Writers of the Renaissance and Reformation*, ed. K. M. Wilson, 1987.

Ana Kothe

DIANE DE POITIERS (1499–1566)

Diane de Poitiers was the mistress of King Henri II of France. Married in
1515 to the grand seneschal of Normandy, Louis de Brézé, Diane was the mother
of two daughters at the time of her husband's death in 1531. She first met King
François I's second son, the dauphin Henri, in 1530, when he was only eleven.
Soon after her husband's death, Diane began an association with Henri that was
viewed by some as maternal in nature, even as late as 1547. Indeed, Henri had
married Catherine de' Medici* in 1533, when both were aged fourteen. Still, it

seems likely that the relationship between the dauphin and Diane became sexual by the mid-to-late 1530s.

Diane's importance at the French court was enhanced in 1536 when Henri's older brother and heir apparent François died unexpectedly. Henri assumed the throne after the death of his father in 1547, and according to more than one contemporary observer, Diane played a key role in the new monarch's decision making. Henri would share a regular noon meal with his informal advisor and sounding board, and she became adept at balancing the rival factions at court. The impact of her influence on the new king was immediate: Diane's son-in-law Robert de La Marck was made a marshall of France, while three of her nephews were elevated to bishoprics during the first few years of the new reign. In addition, the king's mistress was granted a number of valuable properties, some of them seized from his late father's mistress Anne de Pisseleu. Diane's avaricious nature was noted by contemporaries, and by the early 1550s she had become the major recipient of the king's patronage.

Diane was a keen benefactor of the arts and literature. She supported poets, artists, and architects during her years at court. She was also thought to be responsible for the dissemination of the last medieval romance, *Amadis de Gaule*, which was first translated into French in 1540. The king was eager to restore the tournament to court life, even participating in a number of jousts, and the romantic tales of knight-errantry in *Amadis de Gaule* appealed to both king and mistress.

One of the most important features of the reign of Henri II was the rise of Protestantism within France. All of the king's closest advisors, including Diane, were conservative Roman Catholics, and the king, who was not interested in the religious affiliations of potential foreign allies, was concerned to stamp out Protestant heresy in his own kingdom. In 1558 the papal nuncio to France reported that Diane was steadfast in her desire to see French Protestants punished with their lives. Both king and mistress worked tirelessly to intensify the prosecution and punishment of Protestants. After the death of Henri in 1559, Diane retired to her country estates and devoted herself to a quiet life of charitable works.

Bibliography

F. J. Baumgartner, *Henry II: King of France, 1547–1559*, 1988.

William Spellman

DOLET, ÉTIENNE (1509–1546)

Étienne Dolet's unflagging pursuit of his own Ciceronian and Aristotelian intellectual ideals and his reckless disregard for the opinion of others in the dangerous time of the Inquisition led to his death in the Place Maubert in Paris. By then, however, he had managed to write and print several of his own works and translations, including important texts on language, and had edited and printed an impressive number of works by French, Latin, and Greek authors whom we now associate with the central debates of the early Renaissance and Reformation in France.

Dolet was born in 1509 in Orléans, France, where he received a liberal education. At the age of twelve he traveled to Paris, where he studied rhetoric, particularly Cicero, whose work he admired and emulated throughout his life. Five years later Dolet journeyed to Italy, where he studied at the University of Padua for three years and in Venice for one year. The time spent in Padua had a profound impact on Dolet. There he studied with Aristotelian scholars who opposed Christian doctrine by rejecting belief in the immortality of the individual soul. Along with Cicero's opinions, the ideas of the Aristotelians appealed to Dolet, who passionately opposed medieval superstition. Many of the rationalist opinions Dolet learned in Italy later led his enemies to condemn him, despite no evidence of real atheism in his writings.

Dolet then returned to France to study law at the University of Toulouse, where he became known as an outspoken proponent of freethinking. Elected the official orator of the group of French students from the north, the Nation française, Dolet delivered two orations against what he called the stupidity, bigotry, and cruelty of the inhabitants and leaders of Toulouse. For Dolet, Toulouse, the seat of the Inquisition in France, represented medieval jurisprudence and theology in their most narrow-minded form. Dolet's speeches were so inflammatory that the authorities had little trouble bringing charges of heresy against him. Arrested and imprisoned, he was liberated by protectors and was then banished from the city. Heading for Italy, he passed through Lyon, where he immediately began working as reader and corrector for the printer Sebastian Gryphius.

While learning the trade with Gryphius, Dolet published his two speeches against Toulouse, the *Orationes duae in Tholosam* (1534). Soon thereafter, Dolet became a printer in his own right, having received the *privilège royal*, or king's authorization, in 1538. He remained a printer and editor in Lyon for the rest of his life. At his own press, Dolet published works he wrote, those he translated, and many texts by French, Greek, and Latin authors, including Clément Marot,* François Rabelais,* Jacques Lefèvre d'Étaples,* Galen, Sophocles, Seneca, Cicero, the Psalms, and the Bible in French.

The *Commentarii linguae latinae* (Commentary on the Latin language, vol. 1, 1536, vol. 2, 1538), a sort of etymological dictionary of Latin, reflects Dolet's humanist background and belief in the value of studying classical languages and literature. Over the course of his life and work, Dolet, like many other humanists of his day, began increasingly to favor the use of the vernacular in printed texts. To counter his commentaries on the Latin language, Dolet envisioned a work of a similar scale in French, *L'orateur françoys*. We have only the first part of the project, entitled *La manière de bien traduire d'une langue en autre*, published in 1540, which marks the beginning of a long, important debate about language, spelling, translation, and imitation in the French Renaissance.

Dolet's intellectual convictions, along with a passionate and even aggressive personality, contributed to a prolific printing career, but also to a turbulent life and violent death. Not long after settling in Lyon, Dolet was involved in a fight with a man who apparently wanted to kill him. After mortally wounding his assailant, Dolet fled to Paris to ask for King François I's* pardon, which he received. He returned to Lyon, but in 1542 was arrested again and condemned for publishing heretical texts, probably at the instigation of vindictive fellow printers in Lyon, whom Dolet had criticized. Once again, Dolet sought and received the king's pardon. Dolet made many enemies, however, who continued to plot against him. Arrested once again, in 1544, for distributing heretical books in Paris, Dolet escaped his captors and fled to Italy. Returning too quickly to France, he was caught and imprisoned in Paris, where he was burned in 1546, along with a pile of his books, in the Place Maubert.

Bibliography

R. Christie, *Etienne Dolet, the Martyr of the Renaissance, 1508–1546*, 1899.
C. Longeon, ed., *Bibliographie des oeuvres d'Etienne Dolet; Écrivain, éditeur, et imprimeur*, 1980.
V. Worth, *Practicing Translations in Renaissance France: The Example of Extreme Dolet*, 1988.

Karen S. James

DONNE, JOHN (1572–1631)

Known as the father of metaphysical poetry, John Donne was an English poet, essayist, and theologian who served as dean of St. Paul's Cathedral. Born in London in 1572, Donne was named for his father, a successful ironmonger. His mother Elizabeth Heywood was the grandniece of Catholic martyr Sir Thomas More.* Donne was raised a Catholic, and issues of faith are prominent in his writing. Donne attended Oxford (1584) before matriculating to Lincoln's Inn to study law (1592). Donne's writings prove him ambitious and eager for advancement. It is believed that a number of Donne's *Songs and Sonnets*, elegies, paradoxes, and epigrams were written during his years at Lincoln's Inn and were circulated among a coterie of friends. Donne's poetry is characterized by intellect and wit and has been labeled "metaphysical." Metaphysical poetry also employs unusual conceits and relies on irony or paradox. Such characteristics are featured in the body of Donne's work.

In 1596 Donne accompanied the earl of Essex's expedition to Cadiz, and in 1597 he joined the expedition to the Azores. He became secretary to Sir Thomas Egerton, the lord keeper, in 1597. Though Donne's career looked promising, his success was short-lived. Donne secretly married Ann More, Egerton's niece, in December 1601. As a result, Donne was thrown in jail and dismissed from Egerton's service. Though Donne's prison stay was brief, his sufferance was not. He never regained his position, and the couple faced the next fourteen years relying on the kindness of Donne's friends and patrons. His most notable patrons included Robert Drury; Lucy, countess of Bedford; and Magdalen Herbert, mother of George Herbert. Donne's patrons were well connected at court, but

Donne could not secure employment. He continued to write during these years, and the majority of Donne's religious lyrics are attributed to this time. Meanwhile, his family was increasing, beginning with the birth of his first son, John, in 1604. More gave birth to a total of twelve children until her own death in childbirth in 1617.

Donne finally attracted the attention of King James's* court with the publication of *Pseudo-Martyr* (1610) and *Ignatius His Conclave* (1611), both texts actively Anglican. James I encouraged him to take holy orders, and Donne was ordained as an Anglican priest in 1615. Donne's motives for conversion to the Protestant church are unclear: did he experience a spiritual awakening, or was he desperate for employment? In the year of his ordination, he was made a royal chaplain, deacon and priest at St. Paul's Cathedral, and doctor of divinity at Cambridge. Donne was frequently invited to deliver sermons before the king and members of the royal family. He was appointed dean of St. Paul's in 1621. Donne preached his last sermon there on 25 February 1631 and died in March of that year.

Donne has been called the "unidentifiable Donne" because his writings reveal a complexity of thought and character. From the erotic elegies of his youth to the tortured inquiries of his *Divine Meditations*, Donne's work is celebrated for its intellect and its immediacy. His contemporary Ben Jonson* thought him "the first poet in the world in some things," and Thomas Carew crowned him king of the "universal monarchy of wit." The metaphysical aspects of Donne's work, along with his intense explorations of faith, significantly influenced the work of George Herbert, Richard Crashaw, Henry Vaughan, and Thomas Traherne.

Bibliography

R. C. Bald, *John Donne: A Life*, 1970.
J. Carey, *John Donne: Life, Mind, and Art*, 1981.

Michele Osherow

DOWLAND, JOHN (1563–1626)

John Dowland was the foremost composer of English lute music. From an artisan family, the seventeen-year-old Dowland went to Paris in the service of the ambassador to France, Sir Henry Cobham, possibly in order to study music. He apparently married young—his son Robert, also a musician, was born about 1586—but little is known about his wife or other children. In 1588 Dowland earned his bachelor's degree in music from Oxford (on the same day as Thomas Morley*) and was playing music at court by 1590. In 1594 he applied without success for a position as one of Queen Elizabeth's* musicians and then set off on a European tour. From the Continent he wrote to Elizabeth's secretary, Sir Robert Cecil, claiming to have been converted to Catholicism in his youth in France (influenced by "these most wicked priests and Jesuits") and offering to return to the true religion of Her Majesty. As his first two European hosts were staunch Protestants, as was his son's godfather Sir Robert Sidney, Dowland's supposed conversion from Catholicism may have been a ploy to attain Elizabeth's favor. In 1597 Dowland published the first of his several collections of lute music, *The First Booke of Songs*, and the following year he was appointed lutenist at the court of Christian IV of Denmark. *My Observations and Directions Concerning the Art of Lute-Playing* was published in 1604. His other publications were *The Second Booke of Songs* (1600), *The Third and Last Booke of Songs* (1603), *Lachrimae or Seaven Teares* (1604), and *A Pilgrimes Solace* (1612). From 1606 he was given various court appointments in England. Considered proud, irritable, and melancholic, Dowland was admired by Thomas Campion.* Dowland's lute music has been much performed and recorded in the twentieth century, and several pieces were adapted by Benjamin Britten.

Bibliography

D. Poulton, *John Dowland: His Life and Works*, 1972.

Jean Graham

DRAYTON, MICHAEL (c. 1563–1631)

Michael Drayton's contemporaries set him in company with Edmund Spenser* and Philip Sidney* for his contributions to the creation of an English literature. Probably born in Hartshill, Warwickshire, of yeoman stock, Drayton is thought to have studied under a tutor and may have completed his education at the Inns of Court. He was in the service of the Gooderes of Polesworth and Lucy Harington, countess of Bedford. His literary career was framed with religious writings, since his first printed work was *The Harmony of the Church* and his final publication was *Divine Poems* (1630), a compilation of verse from throughout his career that included *Moses His Miracles* (1604) and *Noah's Flood*.

Drayton is more widely known for his poetry, especially *Poly-Olbion*, the first part published in 1612 and the second in 1621–22. Drayton drew extensively from William Camden's* *Britannia* and other chronicles as well as Arthurian romance, John Wilson's *English Martyrologie*, Nicholas Rosacarrock's manuscript lives of British saints, William Harrison's* *Description of Britaine*, and Christopher Saxton's maps of Great Britain to construct thirty songs recording local history, mythology, culture, recreation, and traditions. Drayton's other extant works run to five volumes in their modern edition and include numerous odes and elegies as well as *Idea, the Shepheardes Garland; Ideas Mirrour*, and *England's Heroicall Epistles*, featuring versions of *Rosamund and King Henry II, The Barons Warres, King John and Matilda*, and *Queen Isabella and Mortimer*. While none of his drama survives, Philip Henslowe's* *Diary* indicates that Drayton collaborated with Henry Chettle, Thomas Dekker,* Richard Hathaway, Thomas Middleton,* Anthony Munday, Wentworth Smith, and Robert Wilson from 1597 to 1602 as a playwright for the Lord Admiral's Men. Lawsuits suggest that Drayton worked with the Children of the King's Revels from

1607 to 1608, possibly as a manager or as one of many collaborating play-wrights.

Throughout his career, Drayton relied upon a number of patrons. Anne Good-eres provided the model for "Idea," the beloved woman in *Idea, the Shepheardes Garland*, and Lucy, countess of Bedford, offered inspiration for Drayton's ver-sion of Queen Matilda in the *Heroicall Epistles*. Other dedicatees of his works included Walter Aston; Robert Dudley; Lady Jane Devereux; Mary Sidney,* countess of Pembroke; and Henry, Prince of Wales.

Bibliography

B. Newdigate, *Michael Drayton and His Circle*, 1961.

Karen Nelson

DU BARTAS, GUILLAUME DE SALLUSTE, SEIGNEUR (1544–1590)

Guillaume de Salluste Du Bartas was an important Huguenot poet, statesman, and warrior. His most famous work, *La première semaine ou la création du monde* (1578), is an epic poem recounting the Genesis creation story. It was translated into several languages and influenced the writings of authors such as John Milton, Sir Philip Sidney,* and Torquato Tasso.*

Du Bartas was born in Montfort, near Auch, in Gascony, into a rich merchant family. In 1563–64 he began his law studies at Toulouse at the same time that he pursued his poetic proclivities. In 1565 he won a prize in the Jeux floraux, an annual poetry competition in existence since the fourteenth century. That same year his father, Joseph Sallustre, purchased the château and domain of Bartas, thus acquiring a noble title of sieur Du Bartas. Upon the father's death in 1566, Du Bartas inherited the domain and title. A year later Du Bartas ob-tained his doctor of law degree and by 1571 had refurbished his château, had married Catherine de Manas, a young noblewoman from his province, and had bought himself a judgeship in Montfort.

Under the protection of Jeanne d'Albret* (daughter of Marguerite de Navarre* and mother of Henri de Navarre, who would become King Henri IV of France), Du Bartas continued his literary aspirations. Asked by the Protestant queen to write poetry of biblical inspiration, Du Bartas turned away from the themes of pagan antiquity so favored by Pléïade poets such as Pierre de Ronsard.* He produced instead works of epic proportion designed to bear witness to God's glory as it manifests itself in the universe. No longer construed as an amusing diversion, poetry for Du Bartas became a didactic enterprise designed to lead his readers to a life of righteousness and to propound the doctrines of the Hu-guenot faith. His first moral epic poem was *La Judit*, based on the biblical story of Judith and Holofernes. In 1574 that poem, along with *Le triomphe de la foi* and *Uranie*, was published in Bordeaux in a collection called *La muse chré-tienne*. In his preface Du Bartas proclaims himself the first French writer to deal with sacred matter in a long poem.

Du Bartas's fame blossomed further with the 1578 publication in Paris of *La première semaine ou la création du monde*. Its hexameric theme takes the form of a series of long poems, each describing the successive days of the creation of the world as recounted in Genesis. An encyclopedic inventory of the abundance and variety of nature, *La première semaine* can be read as a compendium of knowledge of the world and man. The 65,000-verse poem offers a vast storehouse of information on topics such as astrology, scientific and philosophical questions of the day, and notions of what constitutes a good king. By 1584 more than twenty-five editions had been published, and the work was translated into many languages. Du Bartas's fame became so great that for a period of time it threatened to outstrip Ronsard's. Detractors of Du Bartas point to a writing style characterized by digressions, neologisms, bizarre metaphors, and violent imagery. Modern critics often describe his style as baroque. In 1584 the first two days of *La seconde semaine ou enfance du monde* were published in Paris. Intended to represent the history of humanity up to the Last Judgment, the long poem remained incomplete. When the final version was published posthumously in 1603, it contained only four days.

Du Bartas greatly influenced the English Renaissance vogue for biblically inspired poetry. His work was enthusiastically received, and many English translations followed. They included those by Thomas Hudson (*Historie of Judith*, 1584), James VI* (*Urania*, 1584), and Joshua Sylvester (*The Triumph of Faith*, 1592). In 1608 Sylvester published a complete translation of the first and second *Semaines*. John Milton was a reader of Du Bartas, and phrases from the *Semaines* can be found in *Paradise Lost*.

Du Bartas entered public life in 1576. In 1586 he was in the service of the king of Navarre, and his diplomatic missions included travels to England, Scotland, and Denmark. In Scotland he was received warmly by James VI and was knighted by him in 1587. Although Du Bartas was more moderate than other Huguenots, he fought as an officer in the Wars of Religion. Several weeks after writing a poem celebrating the victory at Ivry (*Cantique d'Ivry*, 1590), he fought against the Catholic League at Condom and died of wounds sustained in previous battles.

Bibliography

M. P. Hagiwara, *French Epic Poetry in the Sixteenth Century: Theory and Practice*, 1972.

A. Prescott, *French Poets and the English Renaissance: Studies in Fame and Transformation*, 1978.

D. B. Wilson, ed., *French Renaissance Scientific Poetry*, 1974.

Dora E. Polachek

DU BELLAY, JOACHIM (1522–1560)

Joachim Du Bellay's *Deffense et illustration de la langue françoyse* (A defense and illustration of the French language, 1549) proclaimed the doctrine of the French Pléïade poets, including Du Bellay, Pierre de Ronsard,* and Jean-Antoine de Baïf.* Du Bellay's early poetry reflects the literary models of Greece, Rome, and Italy. Du Bellay's later works, however, reject these models in favor of more personal experiences and themes, signaling a shift in attitude and taste in the latter half of the sixteenth century in France. In this respect, Du Bellay is also a precursor of later lyric poetry that focuses on the self and the expression of the poet's state of mind.

Not long after his birth in 1522 at the Château de la Turmelière in Anjou, France, Du Bellay's parents both died, leaving his older brother in charge. Du Bellay spent his childhood in the country, where his education was neglected. As a young man, he probably began his studies at the University of Poitiers. By 1547 he was a student at the Collège de Coqueret in Paris, where he learned Latin and Greek and read the great literature and philosophy of antiquity and of modern Italy under the tutelage of the humanist Jean Dorat. Soon thereafter, Du Bellay and six other poets, including Ronsard and Baïf, formed the school of French poets known as the Pléïade.

Du Bellay's *Deffense et illustration de la langue françoyse* served as the group's manifesto, asserting the dignity of the French language, in keeping with Renaissance humanists' growing support for the vernacular, and calling on poets to enrich the French language so that it, along with French literature, might rival that of the ancients. According to Du Bellay and his compatriots, the poet was not only an inspired artist, but also a skilled artisan who must find nourishment and inspiration in classical and Italian models, then transform them into something new, capable of enhancing the glory of the French language. The Pléïade upheld a lofty ideal of poetry's sake and of the poet as one who expresses universal truths. Du Bellay's first collection of sonnets, *L'Olive*, published in an edition of 50 sonnets in 1542, then in an expanded edition of 155 sonnets in 1550, reflects the ideals put forth in the *Deffense* and incorporates many classical and Petrarchan themes and stylistic elements.

In 1553 Du Bellay traveled to Rome as secretary to his relative, the cardinal Jean Du Bellay, Henri II's envoy to the pope. Once he was in Italy, the poet's humanist enthusiasm soon faded to nostalgia for his homeland, disillusionment with the pretensions of the papal entourage, and painful reflection on the fallen grandeur of Rome and the vanity of all earthly glory. These and other personal emotions inspire the poetry he wrote while he was in Italy and published following his return to France in 1557. Upon his return home, Du Bellay was beset by family legal matters, and his deafness worsened. He died in 1560 at the age of thirty-seven.

The *Antiquités de Rome* (The Antiquities of Rome, 1558) conveys Du Bellay's reactions to the decadence of Rome, his somber reflections on grandeur and decadence and on the inexorable passage of time. Inspired in part by classical models dealing with similar themes, Du Bellay's sonnets nonetheless convey a very personal sense of disappointment, grounded in his nostalgia for France. In addition to treating the same themes of disillusionment with Rome and absence from the homeland, the *Regrets* (1558) also includes messages to friends, sonnets on poetic inspiration, and poetic reflections on the journey home. In the *Regrets*, Du Bellay seeks inspiration in daily experience and in the emotions of one who suffers far from home. The *Jeux rustiques* (1558) also rejects the grand ambition of the *Deffense*, replacing the poet's belief in and quest for eternal glory with the search for individual happiness founded on simplicity.

Bibliography

J. Du Bellay, *Les regrets, precédé de Les antiquités de Rome et suivi de La déffense et illustration de la langue françoyse*, ed. S. de Sacy, 1967.
L.C. Keating, *Joachim du Bellay*, 1971.
V. L. Saulnier, *Du Bellay, l'homme et l'oeuvre*, 1951.

Karen S. James

DUDITH, ANDREAS (1533–1589)

Andreas Dudith is renowned as a man versatile in many disciplines, ranging from literature and rhetoric to astrology and mathematics. The consummate Renaissance man, Dudith involved himself with political, religious, scholarly, and scientific matters while maintaining an active part in academic and aristocratic circles.

Born of combined Hungarian and Italian lineage, Dudith was educated in the typical Hungarian method, humanistic study based on the teachings of Desiderius Erasmus.* Dudith began his religious career as a Roman Catholic priest and was later appointed bishop of Fünfkirchen. Soon after, he attended the Council of Trent during the years 1562–63 as a noted theologian and in the ensuing period was appointed to the bishopric of Pecs. Dudith also executed several diplomatic missions in the names of the emperors Sigismund II and Maximilian II around the years 1563 to 1567.

Dudith's life was marked by a long series of religious conversions, beginning with his stay in Poland and his meeting of Regina Straszowna, for whom he left the Catholic church in order to marry. Following her death, Dudith remarried and once more changed his religious affiliation. Despite Dudith's flexible attitude toward his faith—converting from Catholicism to Lutheranism to Socinianism to Calvinism during his lifetime—he remained in good favor among the elite due to his benevolent and amiable personality.

Both the disciplines of mathematics and medicine appealed to the interests of Dudith, but these gave way to his writing of *De cometarum significatione commentariolus*, a commentary on the comet of 1577. This work generally called for a more scientific approach to celestial phenomena rather than the superstitious analyses typical of that time. In essence, Dudith proposed a school of natural astrology based on empirical data similar to modern conventions of astronomy.

Dudith, an ardent scholar, also collected numerous Greek mathematical manuscripts and printed books, many of which have now found their way into libraries at the Vatican, Paris, Leiden, and several Swedish institutions. In addition, Dudith translated Greek and was an excellent Latinist, an enthusiastic Ciceronian as well as a gifted orator and ambassador. A product of his times, Dudith immersed himself in all manner of study, influenced the intellectual elite, and traveled extensively. As his friend the celebrated Polish poet Jan Kochanowski* remarked, Dudith was "a man filled with knowledge and experience, equally able with pen and eloquence, the emissary of kings."

Bibliography

S. Fiszman, ed., *The Polish Renaissance in Its European Context*, 1988.
P. Rose, in *Dictionary of Scientific Biography*, ed. C. Gillispie, vol. 4, 1971: 212–15.

Christopher D. Roebuck

DU GUILLET, PERNETTE (c. 1520–1545)

Pernette Du Guillet's *Rymes* (1545) project a unique lyric voice in the history of French poetry of the Renaissance. Published soon after the poet's death at the age of twenty-five, her work examines her experiences with love in the light of Neoplatonic and Petrarchan traditions, both familiar to Renaissance readers, and reveals a young woman carefully constructing her own poetic identity in the face of her beloved's impressive learning and eloquence and the patriarchal world he represents.

A slim volume of the seventy poems left behind upon Du Guillet's death, *Rymes* was first published in 1545 by Jean de Tournes, one of the most important printers in sixteenth-century Lyons. Biographical details are scarce, but we do know that Pernette Du Guillet was well educated, married, and part of an active circle of poets that included Maurice Scève* and Louise Labé.* She undoubtedly benefited from the unusually high level of support for women writers in Lyons in her day. In the prefatory letter to the *Rymes*, addressed to the ladies of Lyons, editor Antoine Du Moulin stresses Du Guillet's knowledge of music and languages—her skill with several instruments, her knowledge of Italian and Latin, and her studies of Greek, for example—and calls his readers' attention to the poet as an exemplary model of learning linked with chastity and purity.

Du Guillet is believed to have been the inspiration for Scève's *Délie*, published in 1544 in Lyons and she herself inscribed Scève's name anagrammatically in her verse. The works of both poets met with success in the Renaissance; four editions of Du Guillet's *Rymes* appeared before the end of the century. After several ensuing centuries of relative obscurity, *Rymes* has once again become increasingly important to readers of French literature, in part for the strategies Du Guillet devised as a woman writing in a firmly patriarchal society and responding to its literary conventions, as well as for the combination in her poetry of admiration of the beloved's intellectual qualities, spirited critiques of the lover, and an examination of her role as participant in poetic exchange and Neoplatonic union.

Rymes employs a variety of popular medieval and Renaissance poetic genres, including epigrams, songs, epistolary verse, and elegies. Her preference for short poems is clear in the predominance of eight- or ten-line epigrams. Her vocabulary generally reflects an abstract spirituality, but the poet also captures the essence of everyday encounters and very human emotions, including jealousy. The contrast between day (the life-giving light of the beloved) and night (the darkness in which she found herself before meeting him and before beginning to love and to write) is the central metaphor of the collection, although Du Guillet uses a variety of mythological images sparingly but effectively.

Du Guillet drew much of her inspiration from Neoplatonism, but also, to a lesser degree, from the Petrarchan tradition. In her poetry, chaste love and the Neoplatonic "Good" generally triumph over Petrarchan suffering and desire, although the poet clearly recognizes the latter's force and charm. At times sensuality becomes a subtext for the song of chaste, platonic love. While she recognizes the tension between the two forces, her ultimate goal remains a spiritual and intellectual union with the beloved, a goal she recognizes may only come about in verse.

Bibliography

F. Charpentier, ed., *Louise Labé, Oeuvres poétiques, précédées des Rymes de Pernette Du Guillet*, 1983.

A. Jones, "Pernette Du Guillet: The Lyonnais Neoplatonist," in *Women Writers of the Renaissance and Reformation*, ed. K. M. Wilson, 1987.

Karen S. James

DU PLESSIS-MORNAY, PHILIPPE (SEIGNEUR DU PLESSIS-MARLY) (1549–1623)

Philippe Du Plessis-Mornay was a French Protestant or Huguenot leader, statesman, political theorist, and prominent spokesman for the Protestant cause during the French Wars of Religion (1562–98). Born in Buhy, Normandy, under his Protestant mother's influence he studied law and Hebrew in Heidelberg and while in Cologne wrote two *Remonstrances* (1571–72) exhorting the Netherlands to resist Spanish rule. After his father's death, his family became Protestant in 1559, and after study in Paris and service under de Condé in the Second War of Religion, he escaped the 1572 St. Bartholomew's Day Massacre by fleeing to England. He served over the next decade as a military leader in the Huguenot cause and as a diplomat for William of Orange and Henri de Navarre. He encouraged and supported the Synods of the French Reformed church and sought a wider union of all Protestant communions under the leadership of James I.* In 1589 he was appointed governor of Saumur, where he built a Protestant church and in 1593 established a Protestant academy. Despite the conversion of Henri IV, to whom he was a counsellor, in 1593, he continued to seek religious toleration and was instrumental in having the Edict of Nantes, guaranteeing religious liberty to Protestants, promulgated in 1598. He engaged in public debate with Bishop Jacques Davy Duperron before Henri IV at Fontainebleau on the nature of the Mass in 1600. However, after the renewal of persecution under Louis XIII, he was deprived of his governorship of Saumur and retired to his castle at Poitou, where he died.

Du Plessis-Mornay wrote important political tracts, including *Discours au Roi Charles* (Discourse to King Charles) and *Remonstrances aux estats pour la paix* (Remonstrances on the Conditions for Peace, 1572). The most important tract, though its authorship is disputed, was *Vindiciae contra tyrannos* (A Defense of liberty, 1579), a classical Protestant political tract that posits a contract between the ruler and the ruled and the right of the latter to revolt if the sovereign becomes tyrannical or rejects true religion. He was also an able theologian apologist for the Huguenot cause, publishing while in London in 1578 his *Traité de l'église* (published in English the following year as *Treatise on the Church*), and in 1579 his *De la vérité de la religion chrétienne* appeared in Antwerp (in English in 1587 as *Concerning the Truth of the Christian Religion*). His major theological work was the treatise on the Eucharist, *De l'institution, usage, et doctrine du saint sacrement de l'eucharistie en l'église ancienne* (Concerning the Institution, Usage, and Doctrine of the Holy Sacrament in the early church), which appeared in 1598 and was the occasion for the public debate two years later. In 1611 he published at Saumur his *Mysterium iniquitatis seu historia papatus* (The Mystery of Iniquity, or History of the Papacy), in which he attacked the positions of Caesar Baronis and Robert Bellarmine and which swiftly appeared in French (1611) and English (1612) editions. He was chosen to represent French Protestants at Dort in 1618, but King Louis XIII forbade his attendance.

Bibliography

J. Figgis, *Studies of Political Thought from Gerson to Grotius, 1414–1625*, 1907.
Q. Skinner, *The Foundations of Modern Political Thought*, 1978.

Iain S. Maclean

DÜRER, ALBRECHT (1471–1528)

Albrecht Dürer, a native of Nuremberg and the son of a goldsmith, emerged as the greatest of the German artists who worked in the period leading up to the Reformation. His fame stretched far beyond Germany and far beyond his own lifetime. It was Dürer more than any other artist who interpreted and introduced the ideas and techniques of the Italian Renaissance to northern Europe. He was also a consummate businessman who took full advantage of the print medium, selling his prints throughout Europe.

What we know of him and his life is largely taken from his own copious writings, a family chronicle, letters, diaries, and treatises, all of which illustrate the extraordinary breadth of his interests. Dürer was apprenticed to Michael Wolgemut of Nuremberg when he was fourteen, and it was in Wolgemut's workshop that he learned the art of the woodcut. Nuremberg was a center of printing, and this craft would serve the young artist well. After his apprenticeship, he traveled on his traditional *Wanderjahre* to Colmar and Basel, but unlike many young artists of his time, he also twice visited Italy. He would have become aware of Italian art through prints, which were by his lifetime widely available in the north.

Setting up his workshop in Nuremberg around 1500, Dürer painted three self-portraits that give one a glimpse into his character. We see the handsome young Dürer on the occasion of his engagement, holding a sprig of eryngium, and another portrait of a splendidly dressed young Dürer in clothes of the latest fashion, probably bought in Italy. But one portrait in particular shows his aware-ness of the great gift he possessed, the self-portrait of 1500 in imitation of Christ. He saw his talent as a gift from God.

Dürer's intelligence and belief in his own worth shine out in these early portraits and in his writings. He was a simple and devout man with a friendly disposition, though possibly a little vain as to his looks, who enjoyed his fame yet never seemed to regard it as his due. This general understanding of the worth of the individual led Dürer to form strong connections with the German humanists, particularly his old friend Willibald Pirckheimer,* who had encour-aged his visits to Italy, but also Conrad Celtis, librarian to Emperor Maximilian I, and others.

Dürer's greatest artistic achievements were undoubtedly in the print medium, a medium that he preferred to painting in oils. His subject matter initially was largely religious, such as the *Large Passion* and *Apocalypse* series, both of 1498, but his insatiable curiosity is also evident throughout his career, whether it was aroused by the sight of a walrus, a monstrous pig, or a simple piece of turf. He also led the way in botanical illustrations with exquisite watercolors of birds and animals. Most of Dürer's earliest prints are woodcuts, made with an almost incredible delicacy and skill, but he was equally a master of engraving.

During his second Italian visit, he was commissioned to paint an altarpiece for the German merchants in Venice, the *Rosenkrantz Madonna* (*Feast of the Rose Garlands*): he commented to Pirckheimer that he might have earned more money if he "had not undertaken to paint the German picture" but instead had sold his prints. These prints, which he took with him wherever he traveled, and his success in selling them made him a wealthy man and enabled him to buy a house in Nuremberg; the house still stands today beneath the castle walls.

Probably his most admired engravings are the three known as the Master Prints that date from the years 1513–14: *Knight, Death, and the Devil; St. Je-rome in His Study*: and *Melancolia I*. These are complex works, the first two symbolizing the contrast between the militant Christian and the contemplative Christian; the third print is by far the most enigmatic and is also the most Italianate, seeming to refer to the predicament of the Melancholy Humor, per-sonified as a winged woman, which was believed to control the personality of the artist, awaiting inspiration.

Dürer had great admiration for Martin Luther* and was apprehensive of the dangers that surrounded Luther, as was vividly illustrated in the outburst in his diary for 17 May 1521, on hearing the news of Luther's supposed arrest, news that turned out to be erroneous. In 1520 he wrote of receiving a book by Luther, sent him by the elector of Saxony, and had asked a friend to send him anything written by Luther "in German," at the same time encouraging Frederick the Wise to take Luther under his protection. Another man to whom he looked for moral and spiritual guidance was the Dutch scholar and theologian Desiderius Erasmus.*

Dürer's synthesis of Christian thought and the Italian Renaissance is perhaps best shown in his pair of paintings known as the *Four Apostles*, made for the town hall in Nuremberg and not for a church. The four were St. John the Evangelist with St. Peter (a symbol of Rome) behind him in the left panel, while St. Paul stands in front of St. Mark in the right panel. These four figures with their monumental, Italianate forms also symbolize the four temperaments, sanguine and phlegmatic on the left, melancholic and choleric on the right. Below the feet of the Apostles are translations by Martin Luther of passages from their writings. This was Dürer's last great painting, completed in 1526, two years before his death.

Bibliography

E. Panofsky, *The Life and Art of Albrecht Dürer*, 1971.
R. Wittkower and M. Wittkower, *Born under Saturn*, 1963.

Rosemary Poole

E

ELEANORA OF TOLEDO (1519–1562)

As the wife of Duke Cosimo de' Medici* of Florence, Eleanora of Toledo became renowned as a patron of Renaissance artists, especially Bronzino,* who decorated her eponymous chapel in the Palazzo Vecchio in Florence. As the daughter of the viceroy of Naples, Eleanora attracted the attention of Cosimo de' Medici, who wedded her in 1539. The spectacular celebrations of the marriage involved the participation of many Renaissance artists, and the central theme emphasized Eleanora's role as the future mother of Medici heirs. Eleanora and Cosimo enjoyed a true love match, and within a year Eleanora gave birth to the first of seven children, among them five sons. Cosimo entrusted Eleanora with state affairs in his absences, but her abiding interest was as a patron of the arts. Their court thus became a center for the artistic and literary geniuses of the Renaissance.

Work on her chapel began in 1540 and was completed by 1545. Bronzino portrayed Eleanora as the embodiment of motherhood and identified her with the goddess of matrimony, Juno. The chapel reflected these themes, along with piety and dynastic continuity; its decoration also revealed her affinity for things Spanish and her devotion to the Jesuits. Along with the decoration of the chapel, Bronzino made a number of portraits of the ducal family, and these portraits show Eleanora's physical decline over the years of her marriage.

Eleanora was most likely a victim of tuberculosis by the 1550s, and by 1560 her public appearances came to an end. In an attempt to seek a more temperate climate, the ducal couple embarked on a tour; their three youngest sons contracted malaria, and two of them subsequently died within days of each other. Having previously lost a daughter, Eleanora was broken by this latest tragedy and was unable to rally from a last attack of her illness. She died on 17 December 1562, and a heartbroken Cosimo brought her body back to Florence for an elaborate funeral. Eleanora did much to shore up the reputation of her husband's family as patrons of the arts, and her death, in many ways, signaled the beginning of a decline in this avocation of the Medici.

Bibliography

C. Booth, *Cosimo I, Duke of Florence*, 1921.
J. Cox-Rearick, *Bronzino's Chapel of Eleonora in the Palazzo Vecchio*, 1993.

Connie S. Evans

ELIZABETH I (1533–1603)

Henry VIII* broke with the Catholic church to marry Anne Boleyn in 1533, hoping that the child she carried would be a boy. Instead, it was his second daughter, Elizabeth. Though Henry was deeply disappointed and had Anne executed for adultery in 1536 and Elizabeth declared illegitimate, in 1558 Elizabeth became queen and was to rule England for nearly forty-five years. Elizabeth's intellectual and literary abilities are evident in her letters and speeches as well as her poetry and translations.

Only days after Anne's execution, Henry married Jane Seymour and finally had a son, the future Edward VI. Though he never reversed the illegitimacy of either Elizabeth or her older sister Mary, he did place them in the succession after Edward. Elizabeth received an excellent humanist education with Roger Ascham.* Ascham placed great emphasis on literary and rhetorical studies and on language study. In her teens Elizabeth became fluent in Italian, French, and Latin and had a working knowledge of Greek. When Elizabeth was queen, Ascham was her Latin secretary, and they continued to do translations as a means of relaxation for her.

After Henry VIII's death in January 1547, Elizabeth lived with his last wife, Catherine Parr. Parr became upset with the familiarity that developed between Elizabeth and her new husband, Thomas Seymour, and suggested that Elizabeth leave and set up her own household. Elizabeth and Parr parted on good terms, however. After Parr's death in childbirth, Seymour was arrested and executed for his treasonable activities, which included the plan to marry Elizabeth. Elizabeth herself was subjected to a rigorous examination and spent the rest of Edward's reign living quietly.

Elizabeth survived the dynastic crisis of 1553 in support of Lady Jane Grey,* but her Catholic sister, Mary I,* began to doubt Elizabeth's loyalty, and Elizabeth was imprisoned in the Tower after Thomas Wyatt's failed rebellion of 1554. There was no evidence of Elizabeth's involvement, however, and in November 1558 Elizabeth peacefully ascended the throne upon Mary's death.

Though Elizabeth was Protestant, she did all she could to heal the religious wounds in England caused by the previous reigns and looked for as broadly based a religious settlement as possible. As her reign progressed, however, she found herself with problems both from Catholics and from the growing Puritan movement, which had support in Parliament and among her advisors. She had loyal men in service to her, including William Cecil, eventually Lord Burghley; Sir Francis Walshingham; and Sir Robert Dudley.

As well as religion, another significant issue for Elizabeth was the succession. At the beginning of her reign her Council hoped that she would solve this problem, and the anomaly of a woman ruler, by marrying and then having a son. But while Elizabeth used courtship as a political tool, she refused to either marry or name an heir. Elizabeth had many suitors, including the Habsburg Archduke Charles and the sons of Catherine de' Medici,* both Henri, duke of Anjou (later Henri III), and François, duke of Alençon, later duke of Anjou. Robert Dudley, to whom Elizabeth eventually gave the title earl of Leicester, was also a forceful suitor for her hand. For years rumors swept around Elizabeth and Dudley, particularly after the mysterious death of his wife, Amy Robsart, in 1560.

The problems of religion and the succession became more acute as the reign progressed, especially in 1568, when Mary Stuart,* by right of primogeniture the next heir, who had been forced to abdicate the throne of Scotland in 1567, fled to England. Elizabeth kept Mary in confinement for the next nineteen years as plots to assassinate Elizabeth, free Mary, and place Mary on the English throne in a Catholic revival continued. The Babington plot of 1586 finally convinced Elizabeth to sign Mary's death warrant; she was executed on 8 February 1587. The execution of Mary Stuart and Elizabeth's support of the Protestants in the Netherlands convinced Philip II* of Spain to send his armada in an attempt to conquer England in 1588, but English naval skill and bad weather defeated the Spanish.

The final fifteen years of Elizabeth's reign were difficult. The English economy suffered from bad harvests, inflation, and the long and expensive struggle to dominate Ireland. At Elizabeth's court, as her advisors died off, there was a power struggle between Robert Devereux, earl of Essex, and Robert Cecil, son of William. In 1599 Essex led a disastrous campaign in Ireland. Disgraced by that failure, he staged a rebellion against Elizabeth in 1601. Its failure led to Essex's execution.

But Elizabeth's reign in its final years was also marked by the great literature and drama of such men as William Shakespeare,* Christopher Marlowe,* and Edmund Spenser.* Music, art, and architecture were also flourishing. Interest in expansion, colonization, and overseas trade began to develop, though this would eventually mean England's involvement in the slave trade.

Elizabeth aged visibly after the Essex rebellion. Her health began to fail, and she died on 24 March 1603. She had never named an heir, claiming that God would take care of England, and indeed there was a peaceful transition to her cousin, James VI* of Scotland, the son of Mary Stuart. Under Elizabeth, England had survived and strengthened as an independent country, not dominated by any foreign power and not wracked by civil war. Though her reign had problems, most historians agree that Elizabeth, one of the best known of all English monarchs, will be remembered more for her successes than her failures.

Bibliography

C. Levin, *The Heart and Stomach of a King: Elizabeth I and the Politics of Sex and Power*, 1994.
W. MacCaffrey, *Elizabeth I*, 1993.
A. Somerset, *Elizabeth I*, 1991.

Carole Levin

ELYOT, SIR THOMAS (c. 1490–1546)

Ambassador, scholar, and humanist, Thomas Elyot advocated humanist education and through his writings and translations brought classical works to the literate English. The only son of Richard Elyot, Thomas Elyot learned English common law, was educated at the Middle Temple, and rode with his father as one of the justices of assize for the Western Circuit. In 1525 Cardinal Thomas Wolsey appointed Elyot to a senior clerkship on King's Council. This led him to a short-lived ambassadorship at the court of Emperor Charles V,* a nephew to Catherine of Aragon. Upon Henry VIII's* instruction, Elyot was to "fish out and know what opinion the Emperor is of us," or, in other words, discover the emperor's opinion of the king, especially concerning Henry VIII's divorce from Catherine. Although Elyot was an advocate of Catherine of Aragon—his 1540 *The Defence of Good Women* includes veiled praise of the queen—a religious conservative, and a critic of the Crown, he was not a martyr and worked to maintain his position and keep his head.

Governmental service and private life after 1532 saw Elyot a member of Parliament and a reluctant sheriff. With an impressive public career that led to his being knighted in 1530, Elyot used his works to bring to England classical ideas previously unavailable. Elyot's work *The Castel of Helth* (1536) popularized the ancient theory of the humors for an English audience. Printed in 1538, his *Latin-English Dictionary* was the first such dictionary to appear in English based on humanism and served to give the English language a new standard on which to be based. Probably his most familiar work, *The Boke Named the Governour* (1531) was a training manual for the prince and advocated instruction from moral, religious, intellectual, and physical perspectives. Written to influence Henry VIII, *The Boke Named the Governour* recommended that a good ruler's manners, education, and virtues be grounded in the classics. His translation of Isocrates, *The Doctrinall of Princis* (c. 1533), was probably the first from Greek into English. Through his writing, grounded in Renaissance humanism, Elyot brought new ways of learning to the literate English.

Bibliography

S. E. Lehmberg, *Sir Thomas Elyot: Tudor Humanist*, 1960.

Megan S. Lloyd

ERASMUS, DESIDERIUS (1467–1536)

Dutch scholar, writer, and humanist Desiderius Erasmus was the greatest classicist of the Renaissance in northern Europe. Living amid violent social, economic, and religious upheavals, Erasmus responded to these controversies with moderation. As national and religious factions divided Europe, Erasmus sought peace and unity through his attempts to reconcile faith and reason and bring together Christianity and classical culture.

Erasmus was probably born in October 1467 in Gouda. From 1475 to 1483 he attended school at Deventer under the Brethren of the Common Life, whose *devotio moderna* emphasizing personal piety and charitable works influenced him. He became an Augustinian canon at the abbey of Steyn in 1486. In 1492 he was ordained a priest, but throughout life he received a dispensation enabling him to leave the cloister. After he was granted leave to become secretary to the bishop of Cambrai, Henry of Bergen, in April 1492, he never returned to the monastery. With the bishop's patronage, he entered the University of Paris in 1495 and obtained a bachelor of arts in theology in 1498. His pupil, William Blount, Baron Mountjoy, became his patron, and Erasmus accompanied him to England in 1499.

The first of many visits to England doubtless marked a turning point in Erasmus's life. He became friends with leading English humanists such as John Colet,* Thomas More,* Thomas Linacre,* and John Fisher.* Erasmus was greatly influenced by Colet, whose lectures on St. Paul stimulated his desire to pursue biblical and patristic studies. On another visit, Fisher persuaded Erasmus to lecture on Greek at Cambridge and gave him a chair of Greek and theology (1511–14). From these times on, Erasmus worked steadfastly toward two goals: reclaiming Latin and Greek literature from neglect and returning to early Christian ideals through restoring and publishing the text of the New Testament and the works of the church fathers.

In 1500 he returned to Paris and published the first edition of *Adagia* (Adages). Back in the Low Countries in 1503, he compiled *Enchiridion militis christiani* (The Handbook of the Christian soldier), his statement of the spirit of simple piety. By 1505 he returned to England, renewing contacts with More and Colet, gathering Greek manuscripts, and beginning his *Novum instrumentum*, an edition of the Greek text of the New Testament with a parallel Latin translation, which superseded the Vulgate and was printed in 1516. From England, Erasmus traveled to Italy, where he received a doctorate in divinity from the University of Turin. He also went to Venice and met the great printer Aldus Manutius. With Henry VIII's* accession in 1509, Erasmus returned to England, staying at More's Chelsea home, where he composed a masterpiece of humor, satire, and irony, *Moriae encomium* (Praise of Folly). In 1512 he published *De duplici copia rerum ac verborum* (On Abundance of Things and Words), a textbook intended to aid students in developing rhetorical skills that would affect every serious writer of the English Renaissance.

Erasmus moved to Basel in 1514, where Johann Froben, thereafter his publisher, printed the complete *Novum instrumentum*. Because it underscored the Vulgate's deficiencies and was accompanied by commentary on the church's condition, it became a means of advancing the Protestant cause. An edition of

Jerome was followed by editions of works by other church fathers—Irenaeus, Ambrose, Augustine, Chrysostom, Basil, and Origen.

From 1517 to 1521 Erasmus was at the University of Louvain and learned of Martin Luther's* revolt against the church. Here he wrote the *Colloquia* (Colloquies), in which he satirized the church, society, and politics. By 1521 he returned to Basel where he lived and worked for several years at the printing house of his friend, Johann Froben.

Perhaps the Franciscans of Cologne devised the saying "Erasmus laid the egg that Luther hatched." Although Erasmus shared many Reformers' ideas, he remained loyal to the church. Some Reformers, especially Luther, used his writings (particularly the *Colloquia*) to support measures far more radical than Erasmus could sanction. In 1529 the brutality of the confrontations in Basel between opposing groups forced Erasmus to flee to Freiburg in Breisgau. He continued to write, hoping that his pleas for peace would end the violence. Erasmus returned to Basel in 1535 and died there on 12 July 1536, faithful to the church that would declare him a heretic at the Council of Trent in 1559.

Although Erasmus influenced both Catholics and Reformers, the Reformers really owe him the most. William Tyndale* used his Greek text and Latin translation of the Bible for his English version. Erasmus's biblical paraphrases encouraged private interpretation of the Bible, a characteristic of Protestant humanism during the English Renaissance. His idea of a simple personal imitation of Christ also had profound influence on religious writings throughout the century. It is virtually impossible not to see Erasmus's rhetorical theories and practices, in particular the notions of the copious use of a variety of words and devices, in the literary and polemical works composed during the English Renaissance.

Bibliography

L. Halkin, *Erasmus: A Critical Biography*, trans. John Tonkin, 1993.
J. McConica, *Erasmus*, 1991.

Al Geritz

ERCILLA Y ZÚÑIGA, ALONSO DE (1533–1594)

Alonso de Ercilla y Zúñiga, a Spanish soldier and poet, wrote the epic poem *La Araucana*, the first important literary work inspired by and written in the Americas. Born in Madrid of noble parentage (and possibly of *converso* origin), Ercilla first served as a page to Philip II.* He later enlisted in the army of Don García Hurtado de Mendoza, which was engaged in the conquest of Chile. Chile had proven itself the most difficult American province to conquer because of the unrelenting resistance of the Araucanian Indians. Ercilla traveled to America not to fight the Indians but to help squelch the rebellion of Francisco Hernández. He fell gravely ill in 1560 but recovered and returned to Spain, where he married well and found great success and honor at court.

Ercilla's most significant contribution to world culture lies in his writing of

La Araucana, his only work except for four minor poems. Typical of the epics of the time, this poetic narration of the struggles between the Spanish conquerors and the Araucanian Indians was written in *octavas reales*. Critics laud the brilliant description of the landscapes, battles, and chiefs. The poet glorifies the Araucanian chiefs Caupolican and Lautaro and emphasizes the moral purity of the natives. He fuses historical and personal elements within a complex ideological context. He portrays not just the war between the Spanish and the Araucanians but various internal struggles as well. For example, he accuses various conquerors (e.g., Pedro de Valdivia) of greed as an inappropriate motive for war while simultaneously exalting the nobility, honor, and bravery of the Chilean natives. He goes so far as to equate them with classical heroes such as Dido and Lucretia. By the same token, Ercilla presents the war against the Araucanians within a Spanish context as one of many national wars, likening it to the Battle of Lepanto and the war with Portugal. Themes of justice and patriotism abound, and the text gives a poetic voice to the empire. *La Araucana* appeared in three parts in 1569, 1578, and 1589. A complete version was published posthumously in 1597. Ercilla's text inspired numerous subsequent works.

Bibliography

R. Bauer, "Colonial Discourse and Early American Literary History: Ercilla, the Inca Garellaso, and Joel Barlow's Conception of a New World Epic," *Early American Literature* 30 (1995): 203–32.

Lydia Bernstein

ESTE, ISABELLA D' (1474–1539)

Isabella d'Este distinguished herself during the Italian Renaissance as a consummate politician and an avid patron of the arts. Isabella was born in the independent city-state of Ferrara, which was ruled by the Este family; her arranged marriage to Francesco Gonzaga, the son and heir to the ruling dynasty in Mantua, served to gain an advantageous political alliance for the state of Ferrara.

During her lifetime, Isabella successfully steered the Gonzagas' fortunes through the many political upheavals that resulted from the Italian Wars (1494–1559), as the French house of Valois competed with the Spanish house of Habsburg for control of the Italian peninsula. Always on the lookout for an alliance that might prove expedient for the Gonzagas, Isabella cultivated the good will of the most influential figures of her time. Isabella followed the policy that Mantua would remain neutral no matter what the political situation was. In doing so, she prolonged the survival of Mantua as an autonomous state in spite of the conflicts that ravaged the Italian peninsula.

Isabella had the satisfaction of seeing Holy Roman Emperor Charles V* bestow a dukedom upon her eldest son, Federico II Gonzaga.* On behalf of her second son, Ercole, Isabella received from Pope Clement VII the office of a cardinal. Her third son, Ferrante, chose a military career, serving in Charles V's army. Charles's German mercenary forces eventually gained control over the Italian peninsula.

Just as influential in her patronage of the arts as she was in her role as a political activist and advisor, Isabella amassed with the help of numerous agents a private collection that comprised antiquities as well as contemporary master-pieces. Isabella supported the new printing industry, ordering and purchasing books from Aldus Manutius's acclaimed Aldine Press in Venice. Manutius, the humanist turned printer, made classic works by Ovid and Petrarch available to an educated public. A lover and patron of the arts, Isabella also delighted in works by contemporary authors, taking special pleasure in the poet Ludovico Ariosto's* work. In recognition of her patronage, Ariosto paid Isabella a visit to present her personally with a copy of his famous poem *Orlando Furioso* (1532).

Variously referred to as a "Machiavelli* in skirts" and as the "First Lady of the Renaissance," Isabella d'Este endeavored to live her life on her own terms. Cultivating the recognition and admiration of popes, statesmen, artists, and writ-ers, Isabella pursued her passion for political intrigues and cultural patronage with exceptional vigor.

Bibliography

J. Cartwright, *Isabella d'Este: Marchioness of Mantua, 1474–1539*, 2 vols., 1923.
G. Marek, *The Bed and the Throne: The Life of Isabella d'Este*, 1976.

Debbie Barrett-Graves

ESTIENNE (STEPHANUS), ROBERT (1503–1559)

A French biblical scholar and printer to François I,* Robert Estienne was born in Paris, the son of Henri Estienne and father of Henri, Robert II, and François, all of whom were notable printers. In 1526 he took over his father's printing business and married the daughter of Josse Badius Ascensius, the great Paris publisher. Despite criticism from the Sorbonne, royal patronage (he was appointed by François I as royal printer in Hebrew, Latin, and Greek) kept his books from the Index until the ascension in 1547 of Henri II. His annotated editions of Scripture had provoked criticisms from the Sorbonne, and to avoid proscription, he moved to Geneva in 1550, though keeping his publishing busi-ness in Paris, and became a member of the Reformed church in 1551.

He is recognized for his pioneering Latin dictionary (*Thesaurus linguae La-tinae*, 1531) and his vernacular French dictionary. His Latin editions of the Bible, edited and printed by himself, became famous as examples of critical textual scholarship, particularly his 1528, 1532, and 1540 editions, which fol-lowed the text of St. Jerome. In 1557 he printed another Latin Bible coedited with Theodore Beza.* His Hebrew versions of the Old Testament came out between 1539 and 1546, and in 1544 he began printing in Greek, using the famed Garramond type in his edition of Eusebius's *Historia ecclesiastica*. He proceeded to issue numerous editions of the church fathers, many being the first printed editions of such works. The most influential Greek version of the New Testament he printed was that of 1550, the first edition to contain a critical textual apparatus and the first with verse divisions. He was the publisher of works by Desiderius Erasmus,* Ulrich von Hutten* and Huldrych Zwingli* and in 1553 of John Calvin's* *Institutes* and in 1554 of Beza's tract *De haereticis a civili magistratu puniendis* (Heretics to be Punished by the Civil Magistrate).

Bibliography

E. Armstrong, *Robert Estienne, Royal Printer*, 1954/1986.
D. Starnes, *Robert Estienne's Influence on Lexicography*, 1963.

                                                                    Iain S. Maclean

EUSTACHI, BARTOLOMEO (c. 1500–1574)

Bartolomeo Eustachi edited and translated medical works from ancient Greek and Arabic authors, practiced medicine, and served as a professor of anatomy. His early works included defenses of Galen, but he is best known for his treatises and anatomical illustrations of various organs, including the ear, one part of which still bears his name.

The son of a physician and well trained in classical languages, Eustachi is believed to have studied medicine at Rome, but it is not known when. He served as the personal physician to the duke of Urbino and Cardinal Giulio della Rovere before joining the medical faculty at the Archiginnasio della Sapienza in Rome in 1549. Because Eustachi was affiliated with two hospitals, he was able to procure and dissect cadavers of adults, infants, and fetuses. In 1552, with the help of the artist Pier Matteo Pini, Eustachi prepared a series of anatomical illustrations for a book that was never published. Most of these illustrations were lost from the time of his death until the early eighteenth century, a loss that probably slowed the development of the science of anatomy, given the quality of the engravings and the accuracy of his observations. In 1561 Eustachi published two works that attempted to refute the attacks made upon the medical theories of the classical Greek anatomist Galen. Between 1562 and 1564 Eustachi published a series of treatises on the kidney, the ear, the venous system, and the teeth. In each of these, his precise observations added to contemporary understanding of human anatomy. His important contributions include his descriptions of the suprarenal gland, the eustachian tube, the azygos vein, the thoracic duct, and the sympathetic nervous system, as well as detailed accounts of the hard and soft structures of teeth.

Bibliography

C. D. O'Malley, in *Dictionary of Scientific Biography*, ed. C. Gillespie, vol. 4, 1981: 486–88.

                                                                       Tim McGee

EWORTH, HANS (c. 1515/20–c. 1575)

One of the most influential portrait painters of the sixteenth-century English court, Hans Eworth developed a new, more sophisticated style of portraiture copied by numerous artists of the period. Little is known about Eworth's life prior to his career in England. A Dutch native, Eworth became a resident alien in London by 1549, and official records cite him as living primarily in Southwark. Most of what survives of his work are his portraits, marked by his distinctive monogram "HE," including those of his most famous subjects, the Tudor monarchs, especially Edward VI and Mary I.* He also captured on canvas the most important political figures of the day, among them the duke of Northumberland, Lord Burghley, and Lady Jane Grey.* A striking similarity appears among his sitters, and he apparently favored specific family types and characteristics such as those exhibited by the Brandons, the Seymours, and the Greys.

Though Eworth's early work eschews excess, by the 1560s elaborate costumes, jewelry, and heraldic arms are more prominent in his portrayals. Eworth's oeuvre ranged from the full-length to the miniature and included outdoor settings and allegorical themes as well as the more formal portraits on which his fame rests. Eworth was also a designer for the court's Office of the Revels; notations from a volume of transactions related to the office document that he was paid for drawing up patterns for masques given by Elizabeth I* through 1574.

Eworth's last attributed portrait is dated 1570, but his court work extended to 1574, and several works in his style are found up to 1574. As with his origins, there is no record of the place and time of his death, though the end of his working career in 1574 probably coincides with his death shortly thereafter. In the end, Eworth's major contribution to English portraiture of the age must be his establishment of a very specific physical type that was essentially English in nature, a type that was instantly recognizable. Eworth is thus a major contributor to the iconography of the Tudor age.

Bibliography

L. Cust, "The Painter HE ('Hans Eworth')," *Walpole Society* 2 (1912–13): 1–17.
K. Hearn, ed., *Dynasties: Painting in Tudor and Jacobean England, 1530–1630,* 1995.
E. Mercer, ed., *English Art, 1553–1625, Oxford History of English Art,* Vol. 7, 1962.

Connie S. Evans

F

FALLOPIO, GABRIELE (1523–1562)

Gabriele Fallopio, an Italian anatomist, advanced Renaissance medicine with his descriptions of the ear, the reproductive organs, and the musculature of the head and by refuting ancient authorities such as Aristotle and Galen. Born in Modena, Fallopio was first educated in the classics, but later studied medicine. After a brief and unsuccessful practice in surgery, he continued his medical studies at Ferrara, where he was appointed to the chair of pharmacy. In 1549 he took the chair of anatomy at the University of Pisa, where he was falsely accused of practicing human vivisection. In 1551 he accepted the prestigious chair of anatomy at Padua as successor to Matteo Colombo and Andreas Vesalius.*

Numerous works attributed to Fallopio were actually lecture notes that were edited for publication after his death and therefore may not be fully authentic. However, his *Observationes anatomicae* (Anatomical Observations) of 1561, a commentary on the *De humani corporis fabrica* (On the Structure of the Human Body) of Vesalius, is important because it corrects some observations of his predecessor. By dissecting cadavers of infants and fetuses, he advanced the understanding of the ossification of the occiput and sternum, as well as the origin and development of primary and secondary teeth. He improved Vesalius's account of the structure of the ear and provided detailed accounts of the muscles of the face and scalp, as well as the muscles for chewing and those governing the larynx. He correctly opposed erroneous ancient views regarding blood flow, but denied Vesalius's correct account of venous valves.

In addition to works on anatomy, he wrote about syphilis, surgery, and the production of drugs. His detailed accounts of female anatomy contributed greatly to the understanding of reproduction. He coined the word "vagina" and disproved popular misconceptions about coition. His accurate description of the tubes connecting the uterus and ovaries resulted in their name.

Bibliography

C. D. O'Malley, in *Dictionary of Scientific Biography*, ed. C. Gillespie, vol. 4, 1981: 519–21.

Tim McGee

FENTON, SIR GEOFFREY (c. 1539–1609)

Geoffrey Fenton was an Elizabethan translator, colonial administrator, and advocate of severity against the Irish. Little is known about his early years until 1567, when he dedicated his *Certaine Tragicall Discourses Written oute of Frenche and Latine* to Mary Sidney, the mother of the poet Sir Philip Sidney.* From this point, Fenton began a career first as a translator and then as an administrator within the growing Elizabethan state bureaucracy. The subject matter of *Certaine Tragicall Discourses*, a work originally written in Italian by Matteo Bandello* to which Fenton added many of his own moral interpolations, is culturally significant. His translation was only one of several such projects in the 1560s and 1570s, when Italian *novelle*, short prose tales, enjoyed a tremendous vogue among Elizabethan readers and creative artists, including William Shakespeare.*

Fenton continued to translate a wide variety of works throughout the 1570s, mainly from French works. In 1579, again using a French source, he published an English version of Francesco Guicciardini's* *History of the Wars of Italy*. It is a sign of his position and ambitions that he dedicated *History of the Wars of Italy* to Queen Elizabeth.*

In 1580 he began a longer career in administration, mostly in Ireland, which was in the late sixteenth century the site of a politically contentious and often-brutal English campaign to subdue the Irish. During this period Fenton associated with many important Elizabethan political figures, as well as with literary figures such as Edmund Spenser.* He served in the Irish Parliament, as a secretary in the colonial administration, and as an envoy between Ireland and London, often arguing in vigorous terms for severity against the Irish and the earl of Tyrone in particular. In 1589 he was awarded a knighthood. He died in Dublin in October 1609.

Bibliography

R. L. Douglas, "Introduction," in *Certain Tragical Discourses of Bandello*, by Geoffrey Fenton, 1967.

Thomas G. Olsen

FIRENZUOLA, AGNOLO (1493–1543)

Agnolo Firenzuola was a Florentine lawyer, writer, and poet of the cinquecento. He is best remembered for *I ragionamenti d'amore* (*Tales of Firenzuola*, 1548), an unfinished series of tales set within a frame in the tradition of Boccaccio's *Decameron*, and the dialogue *Delle bellezze delle donne* (On the Beauty of Women, 1558), a treatise on the beauty of the ideal woman.

Firenzuola was born Michelangelo Girolamo in Florence, of a family that had a long record of public service to the house of Medici. At the insistence of his family, he was sent to study law at Siena and Perugia, where he earned his degree in 1518. That same year, Firenzuola entered the monastic order of Vallombrosa, once again in accordance with his family's desire to secure for their son a prosperous and stable career. As a monk, he traveled to Rome, where his services were engaged as procurator to the papal court of Leo X* and later to Pope Clement VII. He cultivated many friendships within Rome's literary community, which included Pietro Aretino,* Pietro Bembo,* Annibal Caro,* and Giovanni Della Casa.* As the legal profession, however, held little interest for him, Firenzuola redirected his energies toward writing. His early works include *I ragionamenti d'amore*; his adaptation of Apuleius's *Golden Ass* (1550); and an assortment of love poetry. He gained fame through his writing, which, although never published during his lifetime, was circulated widely in manuscript. But while his early work earned him critical acclaim, it would not prove sufficient to sustain a lasting place among Italy's literati. In 1526 he obtained release from his monastic vows by Clement VII and withdrew from public life.

It was during this time that Firenzuola endured a long illness, and from 1526 until 1538 he endeavored to restore his health. In 1538 he abandoned Rome for what he believed to be the more wholesome climate of Prato and resumed his monastic work by assuming the duties of abbot of the monastery of San Salvatore until his death in 1543. In Prato, Firenzuola began writing again, producing *La prima veste dei discorsi degli animali* (The first version of the animals' discourses, 1548), a series of fables derived from the ancient Sanskrit collection, the *Panchantantra*. He also wrote the dialogue *Delle bellezze delle donne*, a work that has enjoyed continued critical success for its accurate portrayal of mid-sixteenth-century Italian society that remains of compelling interest to modern scholars for its progressive ideas regarding issues of sexual equality. All of Firenzuola's works were published posthumously.

Bibliography

A. Firenzuola, *On the Beauty of Women*, trans. K. Eisenbichler and J. Murray, 1992.
A. Firenzuola, *Tales of Firenzuola, Benedictine Monk of Vallombrosa*, 1889, rpt., 1987.
T. Riviello, *Agnolo Firenzuola: The Androgynous Vision*, 1986.

Patricia A. White

FISHER, JOHN (1469–1535)

John Fisher, English prelate and humanist, was executed for treason during Henry VIII's* reign. Born at Beverly, Yorkshire, Fisher was educated at Cambridge, where he received the bachelor of arts in 1487 and the master of arts in 1491. He was also ordained as a priest in 1491. In 1501 he was awarded the doctorate. Elected chancellor of Cambridge in 1504, he held that office for life. He became chaplain and confessor to Lady Margaret Beaufort, mother of Henry

VII, and encouraged her patronage of Cambridge. In 1504 Fisher became bishop of Rochester.

Determined to incorporate humanistic ideas into the curriculum of Cambridge, Fisher brought Desiderius Erasmus* there to teach Greek, and he supported Erasmus's work on the New Testament. Fisher, an orthodox Catholic loyal to the papacy, preached and wrote against Martin Luther* and won respect as a theologian, both in England and on the Continent.

As confessor and confidant to Catherine of Aragon, Fisher opposed Henry VIII's desire to divorce her and spoke against it in the legate court of 1529. His opposition to Henry's ecclesiastical policies further angered the king. When Henry asked the clergy to recognize him as supreme head of the church in England in 1531, Fisher refused to acknowledge Henry's supremacy under the Act of Succession. Despite his age and failing health, Fisher's goods were forfeited, and he was imprisoned in the Tower of London, where Thomas More* was held on similar charges. Thomas Cromwell urged Fisher to yield, but he refused. In May 1535, when Pope Paul III created Fisher a cardinal, Henry became enraged and demanded Fisher's trial on charges of treason. At the 17 June trial, Fisher was condemned to death; he was beheaded on Tower Hill on 22 June. Pope Leo XIII beatified him in 1886; Pope Pius XI canonized him on 19 May 1935. Although Fisher wrote against Luther and published sermons in English, his main contribution to the Renaissance and the Reformation lies not in his writings but in his influence as a humanist scholar and teacher and as a defender of Catholicism.

Bibliography

R. Rex, *The Theology of John Fisher*, 1991.

Al Geritz

FLETCHER, JOHN (1579–1625)

It is hard today to realize that John Fletcher, the playwright who succeeded William Shakespeare* as chief dramatist to the King's Men, was once thought to be as great as or greater than his incomparable predecessor. In truth, Fletcher's greatest gift as a dramatist was his unerring sense of the apt social topic and moment in his drama. His tragedies *Bonduca* and *Valentinian* and his satirical tragicomedies with Francis Beaumont,* such as *Philaster*, explore the capriciousness of power and its corrupting influence, offering figures who comment upon the court of King James* and its sensibilities. His conscious development of the mixed genre tragicomedy is his most enduring contribution to English dramatic theory and practice. His play *The Faithful Shepherdess*, a pastoral tragicomedy, announces both its function as a tragicomedy and the playwright's right to determine the role and function of his art.

John Fletcher, born at Rye, England, on 20 December 1579, was not a stranger to controversy or public disregard, whence no doubt his instinct for political drama. His father, Richard, served as bishop of London until his second marriage caused him to lose favor with the queen and leave his family in penury when he died shortly thereafter. The playwright, who was at Cambridge University from his matriculation in 1591 and was intended perhaps for a religious vocation, took a different direction somewhere between his arrival at the university and 1606, when *The Woman Hater*, the first work of his extensive canon, was written. His associations during that time brought him into the acquaintance of Francis Beaumont, with whom he collaborated on that first play. According to a famous passage by John Aubrey, the two young dramatists formed an intense bond altered only upon Beaumont's marriage in 1613. The two "lived together on the Banke side and . . . lay together; had one wench in the house between them . . . the same cloathes and cloak, etc, between them." Together in those first six years of Fletcher's career they produced, either individually or in collaboration, thirteen plays.

Fletcher's output continued to be prolific. The first folio of his works (1647) contains thirty-four plays, the second (1679) eighteen, including works Fletcher wrote on his own, many of his plays with Beaumont, and others done with Philip Massinger, his most extensive collaborator. He collaborated as well with Shakespeare (*The Two Noble Kinsmen* and *All Is True, or Henry VIII*), whose company he joined following Beaumont's retirement and death. According to legend, he died of the plague in 1625 while waiting in London for the delivery of a suit.

Bibliography

P. Finkelpearl, *Court and Country Politics in the Plays of Beaumont and Fletcher*, 1990.
C. Leech, *The John Fletcher Plays*, 1962.
G. McMullan, *The Politics of Unease in the Plays of John Fletcher*, 1994.

Robin Farabaugh

FLORIO, JOHN (c. 1553–1625)

John Florio, a scholar and linguist, is known primarily for his translation of Michel de Montaigne's* *Essais* and for his affiliation with the circle of the earl of Southampton, William Shakespeare's* patron. Florio was the son of Michelangelo Florio, an Italian Protestant refugee who moved to England and became the tutor of Lady Jane Grey.* John was born in London, but shortly after his birth, he and his parents were forced into exile on the Continent when the Catholic queen Mary I* ascended the English throne. John Florio later returned to England, attended Oxford, and published two widely used Italian grammars, *Florio His Firste Fruites* (1578) and *Florios Second Frutes* (1591). In 1598 Florio published the work that guaranteed his reputation as a scholar: his impressive Italian-English dictionary, *A World of Wordes*, a revised edition of which appeared in 1611 as *Queen Anna's New World of Words*.

Florio was also the Italian tutor of the earl of Southampton when the earl began to function as patron for Shakespeare. It was in this capacity that Florio most likely came to know of Shakespeare. Literary scholars have noted Shakespeare's indebtedness to Florio's linguistic works and translations, but it has also been suggested that Shakespeare lampooned Florio in the character of Holofernes, the pedantic scholar in *Love's Labour's Lost.*

Florio's other notable achievement is his 1603 translation of Montaigne's *Essais.* This translation is still widely read and used by Montaigne scholars. There are more recent translations of Montaigne's essays, most notably that of Donald Frame, but many continue to use Florio's translation. Florio's contributions to the culture and life of the sixteenth century are therefore quite significant in that Florio's name is associated with two of the leading figures of his century.

Bibliography

F. Yates, *John Florio*, 1934.

Jeffrey A. Bell

FLORIS, FRANS (1515–1570)

Frans Floris was the most influential history painter of his time in the Spanish Netherlands. He was a member of a family of artists from Antwerp, but he trained in the Romanist workshop of Lambert Lombard in Liège, where he learned to paint in the fashionable, monumental "Italian manner." Floris returned to Antwerp, which had a thriving art market, to set up his own workshop in 1540. His brother Cornelis became a successful Antwerp sculptor and architect.

In Antwerp Floris ran a busy workshop with many assistants organized along highly cooperative lines. His Romanist style was much admired in Italy as well as in the Netherlands. His figures are idealized and heroic and are strongly influenced by such works as Michelangelo's* *Last Judgment* wall of the Sistine Chapel, which he saw and studied at its unveiling in 1541 when visiting Rome. His colors too show a probable Venetian influence.

A good example of Floris's style is his own *Last Judgment* of 1565, where every figure is highly idealized and contorted, muscles bulging and straining. While he did not overpopulate nor distort to the extent of the more Mannerist painters, he did use extreme foreshortening as well as some elongation of forms to create exciting, if unbelievable, scenes.

Frans Floris was regarded as an "official" painter, capable of executing demanding civic commissions for the decoration of public buildings. His subject matter was varied, primarily history paintings based on classical themes, including mythology, allegory, and religion. He was also sought after for his portraits, one of the best known of which is the charming *Falconer's Wife* of 1558. Finally, Karel van Mander, the Dutch biographer, wrote that many an aspiring young Antwerp painter was trained by Frans Floris.

Bibliography

C. Cuttler, *Northern Painting from Pucelle to Bruegel*, 1968.

Rosemary Poole

FONTANA, LAVINIA (1552–1614)

Lavinia Fontana is credited with being the first female painter in Italy to enjoy a successful career as an artist working in an urban context. Lavinia accepted private and public commissions, painting numerous portraits and public altarpieces. Lavinia had the advantage of being trained by her father, Prospero Fontana, a painter regarded as one of the leading artists in Bologna. Lavinia also had the good fortune to be born in Bologna, an important Italian artistic center.

Lavinia was best known as a portraitist, but her oeuvre included a wide range of subject matter. Her works frequently drew on biblical and mythological settings, which incorporated numerous figures, including male and female nudes. Another of Lavinia's significant accomplishments included earning the degree of *dottoressa* from the University of Bologna in 1580.

Breaking artistic ground, Lavinia accepted and completed several large-scale public commissions. The Spanish court provided her with her first opportunity to execute a large-scale religious commission of the *Holy Family* (c. 1589). Lavinia's altarpiece painting of the *Holy Family with the Sleeping Christ Child*, which is in the Escorial, the Spanish royal palace located near Madrid, is still considered a masterpiece.

Lavinia's international reputation earned her the patronage of a succession of popes. Lavinia, along with her artist husband, Gian Paolo Zappi, whom she had married in 1577, and their family, moved to Rome in 1603 in response to a papal invitation. The best-known public commission she executed in Rome, her painting of *The Stoning of St. Stephen Martyr* for the altarpiece in the church of S. Paolo Fuori le Mura, an important pilgrimage church in Rome, proved a disappointment for her contemporaries upon its completion (1603–4). It was destroyed in a fire in 1823, making it impossible to judge the success or failure of this significant work today.

A portraitist and a producer of religious paintings, Lavinia Fontana enjoyed a successful career as a respected artist who achieved international fame. In 1611 a medal was struck in honor of Lavinia's artistic accomplishments. Her contemporaries and patrons, such as Pope Gregory XIII and Pope Clement VIII, held her in high regard, so much so that she was elected to membership in the Roman Academy. Of the over one hundred works she is credited with producing, only thirty-two signed and/or dated works can be securely attributed today.

Bibliography

A. S. Harris and L. Nochlin, *Women Artists, 1550–1950*, 1976: 111–14.
C. Murphy, "Lavinia Fontana: The Making of a Woman Artist," in *Women of the Golden Age*, ed. E. Kloek, N. Teeuwen, and M. Huisman, 1994: 171–81.

Debbie Barrett-Graves

FORMAN, SIMON (1552–1611)

Simon Forman was a prominent astrologer and medical practitioner of his day. His extensive diaries provide an invaluable record of Elizabethan medical practices and perceptions.

In the village of Quidhampton in 1552, Forman was born into a family that could not support his ambitions. He received some elementary schooling, but his father's death in 1563 interrupted Forman's formal education. In 1579 Forman settled on a career in physic and magic. After practicing in various locales, Forman moved to London in 1589. He acquired a significant clientele for whom he combined astrological practice with herbal remedies. Forman also performed astrological readings, interpreted dreams, and provided magical paraphernalia for his clients.

In 1593 the Royal College of Physicians called Forman's qualifications and practices into question. He was subjected to numerous examinations, fines, and periods of imprisonment. Forman abandoned London in 1601, setting up practice in Lambeth. The choice of Lambeth seems a result of Forman's marriage to Anne Baker of Lambeth in 1599. The couple had two children, Dorothy (1605), and Clement (1606); Forman was also accused of siring others. The Lambeth practice was extremely lucrative, and Forman found the means to earn a practitioner's license from Cambridge. At the time of his death on 8 September 1611, he was officially known as "Doctor Forman."

Forman's is the most complete autobiography of the Elizabethan period. His topics range from thoughts on the New World to reactions to William Shakespeare's* plays. His copious professional notes provide biographical information on members of various social classes, including Frances Howard, countess of Hertford, and Aemilia Lanyer.* A legend in his own time, Forman is referred to by name in a number of Elizabethan plays and was the inspiration for Ben Jonson's* *Alchemist*.

Bibliography

S. Forman, *The Autobiography and Personal Diary of Dr. Simon Forman*, ed. J. O. Halliwell, 1849.

A. L. Rowse, *Sex and Society in Shakespeare's Age: Simon Forman the Astrologer*, 1974.

Michele Osherow

FOXE, JOHN (1517–1587)

John Foxe was a zealous proponent of the English Reformation, renowned as the compiler of *Acts and Monuments of These Latter and Perilous Days* (first edition, 1563), known popularly as *The Book of Martyrs*. This monumental collection influenced the formation of English Protestant identity and the development of nationalistic fervor during and after the reign of Elizabeth I* (1558–1603).

After receiving the bachelor of arts degree in 1538 and the master of arts in 1543, Foxe was expelled from Magdalen College, Oxford, because he opposed the vow of celibacy and membership in religious orders required of permanent fellows. He began to chronicle church history under the patronage of the staunchly Protestant duchess of Richmond. With the accession of the Catholic queen Mary I* in 1553, Foxe followed other Protestant ideologues in fleeing to the Continent to avoid persecution. Finding haven at Strasbourg, Frankfurt, and Basel, he followed John Bale's* practice of compiling documents concerning the persecution of Protestant "saints" (fervent believers) and martyrs both in England and abroad. His initial Latin publications, *Commentarii rerum in ecclesia gestarum* (1554) and *Rerum in ecclesia gestarum* (1559), afford the foundation for *Acts and Monuments*, published largely in the vernacular after the death of Queen Mary. Foxe followed the recommendation of fellow exiles, notably Edmund Grindal, later archbishop of Canterbury, that he chronicle the Marian persecutions in close detail.

Printed by the zealously Protestant publisher John Day, *The Book of Martyrs* enjoyed considerable success and underwent four editions in Foxe's lifetime alone. In contrast to the representation of saints as superhuman figures in medieval legends, Foxe offers grisly accounts of the faithful perseverance and death of low-born and high-born people who testified to their religious faith to the point of death. A common thread emphasizes testimonials of faith by lowly artisans, workers, and theologians who denied the efficacy of the doctrine of good works and the salvific force of allegedly magical feats, miracles, paranormal cures, and relics typical in medieval hagiographies.

Among the best-known martyrologies are the examination and burning of Anne Askew* under Henry VIII* and accounts of the death of John Rogers, the first Marian martyr; the suffering of John Hooper, bishop of Gloucester; the reaffirmation of faith and subsequent burning of Thomas Cranmer,* archbishop of Canterbury; and the double execution of Nicholas Ridley and Hugh Latimer. The famous woodcut for the last-named martyrdom is inscribed with Latimer's last words, which were to become a rallying cry of the English reformation: "Be of good comfort, Master Ridley, and play the man. We shall this day light such a candle by God's grace in England, as I trust shall never be put out."

Editions of *The Book of Martyrs* proliferated after its initial publication. By order of convocation, a copy of the 1570 edition was placed in every church in England. It has become a truism that if Protestant households in seventeenth- and eighteenth-century England or New England contained only two books, they would have been the English Bible and some version of Foxe's *Book of Martyrs*. Protestant families conducted assiduous readings from both texts.

Bibliography

D. Loades, ed., *John Foxe and the English Reformation*, 1997.
J. F. Mozley, *John Foxe and His Book*, 1940.
W. Wooden, *John Foxe*, 1983.

John N. King

FRACASTORO, GIROLAMO (c. 1478–1553)

Girolamo Fracastoro, a prominent Italian humanist, taught logic at the University of Padua and later practiced medicine in Verona. He is most famous for his study of syphilis, penning a narrative poem in Latin, *Syphilis sive morbus Gallicus* (1530), and writing *De contagione* (1548), both of which describe the nature of syphilis, how diseases are spread, and possible cures for diseases.

Fracastoro was born in Verona to an influential family that eventually sent him to the academy in Padua. He studied literature, mathematics, astronomy, philosophy, and medicine, and he became a lecturer in logic at Padua in 1501 and *conciliarius anatomicus* in 1502 and was elected to the College of Physicians in 1505. Fracastoro retreated to Incaffi in 1510 after an outbreak of the plague, where he practiced medicine to support his family.

While Fracastoro was in Incaffi, he began writing his famous poem *Syphilis*. He applied this name to the pox more commonly known as the French disease. Many contemporaries believed that the disease had been brought back from the Americas by Columbus, had been spread throughout Spain and France, and had been brought to Italy with the invasion of Charles VIII in 1494. Fracastoro disregarded this theory and found evidence that the disease had existed in classical times but had been forgotten. He believed that the disease resurfaced because of certain astrological conditions. Fracastoro linked his world view to his writings on syphilis and contagion. He disputed the theories of Galen and Aristotle and gained a reputation as an iconoclast. He believed that syphilis was spread by "seeds" in the air as well as through physical contact. Some historians view this as the forerunner to the germ theory.

In *De contagione* Fracastoro links sympathy to contagion. The underlying feeling between two elements, or sympathy, is the principle behind the spread of disease. According to his theory, the body is made up of numerous invisible particles that are passed in contagion, corrupting the new body. Fracastoro believed in three types of contagion: contagion by touch, contagion through fomites, where particles are able to survive for periods of time in inanimate objects, and contagion by a glance. He placed syphilis in the second category. The seeds remained dormant for a long period of time until astrological conditions enabled the outbreak to occur. The seeds originated in the air, entered the body, germinated, and became ready for contagion. Fracastoro believed that the disease could be cured by destroying the seeds and therefore advocated the use of cold, drying-out medicines such as guaiacum, first made known by Ulrich von Hutten* in 1519.

Fracastoro's discussion of syphilis and other contagious diseases changed medical thinking by trying to explain contagion and what exactly was being transmitted. Fracastoro enjoyed a wide circle of friends, including Pietro Bembo,* an influential Venetian noble and cardinal, and Pope Leo X,* to whom he dedicated his second book on syphilis. He even garnered a role in the Council of Trent by having it moved from Trent due to an outbreak of the plague, which was to the advantage of Pope Paul III. Fracastoro's major works were published posthumously in *Opera omnia* in 1555.

Bibliography

J. Arrizabalaga, J. Henderson, and R. French, *The Great Pox*, 1997.
G. Eatough, *Fracastoro's Syphilis*, 1984.

Paul Miller

FRANCIS DE SALES (1567–1622)

Francis de Sales, a leader in the Catholic Reformation and Roman Catholic bishop of Geneva, declared a doctor of the church and a saint, was noteworthy for his devotional writings, his concern for women's education, and his cofounding the Order of the Visitation for nuns. Born to a noble family in Savoy, Francis de Sales was educated at the Jesuit college of Clermont in Paris and the University of Padua, Italy, in accordance with his father's wishes that he pursue law. He received a doctorate in law in 1591 and soon after received a doctorate in theology. He practiced law briefly, but then turned to a life in the church, being ordained a priest in 1593 in Annecy in his native Savoy. Annecy had been the bishop's see of Geneva since 1535, when the Protestants had expelled the bishop and the monasteries. Francis chose to take on missionary work in Chablais, a district of Savoy that had broken away for a time and turned Calvinist. Francis labored virtually alone for four years, slowly winning back the majority of the population to Catholicism. In 1602 he was consecrated bishop of Geneva. Two years later he met Jane Frances Fremyot de Chantal, a young widow with four children, and became her spiritual director through an extensive correspondence. Together they founded the Order of the Visitation of the Holy Mary at Annecy in 1610. A contemplative order, it was open to widows and those with health challenges who could not meet the austere ascetical practices of religious orders of the time. His devotional classic *Introduction to a Devout Life* (1609) emphasized that spiritual devotion was possible for the laity leading busy lives and was not restricted only to those in religious orders. This concern was repeated in *Treatise on the Love of God*. Francis de Sales died in 1622 and is buried at the Visitation Convent at Annecy. He was beatified in 1661 and named a doctor of the church in 1877.

Francis de Sales is best remembered for his writings on spirituality and cofounding the Visitation Order of nuns. He was named the patron saint of writers, both because of his style and because of his message that the spiritual life was for laity as well as clergy and religious. His concern for women's education reflected his recognition of the influence women had on the spiritual life of their families and associates. He stressed that women should be treated with respect and not scorn and should be taught piety. His influence was extensive and personal. He directed Angelique Arnaud, the young abbess of Port Royal, in the reform of her convent. The granddaughter of Jane de Chantal was the famous letter writer Madame de Sévigné. The Visitation Order grew to have 13 chapters by the time of Francis's death and 164 in 1767, the year Jane de Chantal was beatified.

Bibliography

E. Stopp, *A Man to Heal Differences: Essays and Talks on St. Francis de Sales*, 1997.

Elaine Kruse

FRANCO, VERONICA (1546–1591)

Veronica Franco was famous in her time as one of the leading female poets of the Italian Renaissance and as one of Venice's most illustrious courtesans. Franco was born into a respectable subpatriciate Venetian family. At a young age she was married to a physician, but the marriage was short-lived. Following in her mother's footsteps, Franco became one of the city's *cortegiane oneste*, or honored courtesans, a group of women whose brilliant salons, elaborate wardrobes, intellectual gifts, and conversational abilities granted them a status superior to that of other prostitutes. Franco remained in her profession all of her life and never remarried, though she had six children, three of whom died in infancy. A prominent Venetian nobleman, Andrea Thon, fathered one of the children.

During the 1570s Franco became associated with the literary circle of poet and patron Domenico Venier, an affiliation that fostered Franco's literary production and reputation. In 1575 Franco compiled a collection of poems that included nine of her own sonnets as well as works by other poets; she also published some of her poems in other anthologies. During the same year she published *Terze rime*, her own book of love poems, which she dedicated to Guglielmo Gonzaga, duke of Mantua. In 1580 Franco published a collection of her personal letters, one of the first such publications by a woman. A particularly interesting letter is one in which Franco urges a woman not to allow her daughter to become a courtesan. Although Franco's position as a *cortegiana onesta* granted her some intellectual and social advantages, she was aware that courtesanship was often an abusive and oppressive profession, and she criticized Venetian society for exploiting impoverished young women who had few other ways in which to support themselves. In 1577 Franco petitioned the government to establish a home for women who needed financial assistance to live honest, chaste lives.

Franco knew many of the important artistic, intellectual, and political figures of her day. She met Henri III of Valois in 1574 when he was on his way from Poland to France to be crowned king. After he visited her, she wrote two sonnets to celebrate the occasion. She was also the subject of a painting by Tintoretto* and sent a copy of her published letters to Michel de Montaigne.* Her life, however, was not entirely glamorous; she was responsible for supporting not only her children but, after her brother's early death, his children as well. Franco had to defend herself from public attacks, including slanderous poems and charges of heresy, which she did with dignity and eloquence. Veronica Franco died in Venice at the age of forty-five.

Bibliography

V. Franco, *Poems and Selected Letters*, ed. A. Jones and M. Rosenthal, 1998.
M. Rosenthal, *The Honest Courtesan: Veronica Franco, Citizen and Writer in Sixteenth-Century Venice*, 1992.

Jo Eldridge Carney

FRANÇOIS I (1494–1547)

François I, king of France (1515–47) was a humanist, a patron of the arts, and a gallant military figure. François, the son of Charles de Valois-Orleáns and Louise of Savoy, became heir presumptive upon the accession of his cousin Louis XII in 1498. Educated in the humanist tradition, he studied the classics but preferred arms to letters. Both François's mother, with whom he lived until 1508, and his elder sister, Marguerite de Navarre,* exerted tremendous influence over him his entire life.

From 1512 to 1513 François gained experience on the battlefield defending France's borders as well as influence with foreign ambassadors. Shortly before his death, Louis XII married his young daughter Claude to François, who on 1 January 1515 became king.

Within the first year of his reign, François invaded Italy in order to recover Milan. At the bloody battle of Marginano, François defeated the Swiss mercenaries of Massimiliano Sforza and his ally Pope Leo X.* Anxious to appease François, Leo X negotiated the Concordat of Bologna with François, giving him the privilege of nominating prelates in exchange for upholding ecclesiastical privileges. In 1520 François attempted to arrange an Anglo-French alliance but was unsuccessful despite his efforts to secure Henry VIII's* trust on the Field of the Cloth of Gold.

In 1521 the French loss of Milan marked the onset of twenty-seven years of warfare between François and Emperor Charles V.* When François pressed his mother's claim to inherit Bourbon lands, he incited a Bourbon invasion of Provence. François routed the attackers and pursued them into Italy, where French troops laid siege to Pavia, a disastrous affair, for in 1525 François was wounded in battle and captured by Charles V's army.

The emperor imprisoned François in Madrid and demanded an exorbitant ransom for his freedom. François considered abdication, but his advisors finally persuaded him to sign the Treaty of Madrid in 1526. The surrendered French provinces, however, refused to abandon their king. The emperor was outraged with François and held his eldest two sons hostage until 1530, when François's mother negotiated the more realistic Treaty of Cambrai with Margaret of Austria, the emperor's aunt. In 1533 François married his second son, Henri, to Catherine de'Medici,* the niece of Clement VII, and in 1536 the dauphin died, supposedly poisoned by the emperor's agents. François achieved one last diplomatic coup, the Franco-Turkish alliance against Charles V, before his death of a wasting illness in 1547.

François I maintained a Renaissance court, attractive to noblemen, poets, musicians, and scholars alike. He was known for his elegant manners, athletic abilities, and sexual escapades; he curtailed the abuses of overly ambitious nobles, entertained the court with lavish processions, and wrote heartbreaking poems, songs, and letters to his subjects during his imprisonment. François encouraged religious tolerance: he admired Desiderius Erasmus,* acted as patron to François Rabelais,* and delayed the extermination of the Waldensian sect until his death. Notwithstanding his continuous and costly struggles with the emperor, François remained the beloved *grand roi François*.

Bibliography

R. J. Knecht, *Renaissance Warrior and Patron: The Reign of Francis I*, 1996.
Whitney Leeson

G

GABRIELI, GIOVANNI (c. 1555–1612)

Giovanni Gabrieli served as organist at the Basilica of St. Mark in Venice for over two and a half decades, but it was his stature as a composer and teacher that made him one of the most important figures in European music at the turn of the seventeenth century. He was born in Venice, the nephew of Andrea Gabrieli, a prolific composer who served from 1566 as organist at St. Mark's. Like his uncle before him, Giovanni sojourned at the court of Duke Albrecht V in Munich, where he doubtless studied with Orlando di Lasso.* In 1585 he became organist of both St. Mark's and the religious confraternity of San Rocco in Venice, posts he retained for the rest of his life.

An uncommonly high proportion of instrumental music distinguished Gabrieli's oeuvre. In over sixty compositions for the organ he developed the styles and genres (canzona, ricercare, and toccata) cultivated by his uncle. He also composed about fifty canzonas and sonatas for the large contingent of virtuoso brass and string players at St. Mark's. But following the death of his uncle in 1585, Giovanni became the principal composer of large-scale Venetian ceremonial motets, and it was in this genre that he exerted his greatest influence. The majority of his nearly one hundred motets distribute their performing forces among two or more choirs and thus belong to the tradition of polychoral motets cultivated by Lasso and earlier Venetian composers. The significance of Giovanni's contributions to this tradition derives from their dramatic contrasts of texture, timbre, and meter. Instrumental doubling of vocal parts was common in the late sixteenth century, but in some of his later motets Gabrieli wrote lines specifically intended for instruments. His compositions assumed an exemplary status, and he became the most famous musician in a city known for the splendor of its music. The many students he attracted included Heinrich Schütz, the greatest German composer of the seventeenth century.

Bibliography

D. Arnold, *Giovanni Gabrieli and the Music of the Venetian High Renaissance*, 1979.

David Crook

GALILEI, GALILEO (1564–1642)

Renowned for his astronomical observations with a telescope, Galileo Galilei also defined the central tenets of a new scientific method followed by others in succeeding centuries. Condemned for heresy in 1633 because of his defense of heliocentricity, he is emblematic, as are few others, of the "scientific revolution" in human thought.

Born in Pisa, Galileo was the son of a respected if impecunious musician, Vincenzio Galilei.* He began his education at a monastery school in Vallombrosa, but his father withdrew him before he could complete his novitiate. In 1581 he began to study medicine at the University of Pisa, where his attention turned to mathematics and physics. Although he left the university in 1585 without a degree, he continued his scientific work, publishing on the hydrostatic balance in 1586 and the center of gravity in solids three years later. These works led to his appointment as lecturer in mathematics at Pisa in 1589.

Galileo's tenure there proved short-lived. Attacked as an upstart by traditionalists, he moved to become professor of mathematics at the University of Padua, where he remained for eighteen years in a friendlier intellectual atmosphere. He championed a new physics, disproving Aristotle's long-accepted theory that objects of different weights fall at different speeds. Although accounts of Galileo dropping spheres from the tower in Pisa are colorful stories, they are little more than legendary. Galileo became a proponent of Nicolaus Copernicus's* heliocentricity, writing in support of it to Johannes Kepler* in 1597.

Made aware of the invention of the telescope in 1609, Galileo engaged in the astronomical observations that made him famous. In *The Starry Messenger* he announced his discoveries of the irregularity of the surface of the moon, the vastness of the Milky Way as an assemblage of stars, and the existence of four satellites orbiting Jupiter. Each was contrary to accepted astronomical theory, tended to support the Copernican system, and drew strong negative reactions. Nonetheless, Kepler strongly endorsed his discoveries in his *Reply to the Starry Messenger*.

In 1610 Galileo was appointed philosopher to the grand duke of Tuscany in Florence. Within three years Galileo made additional discoveries and mounted a systematic defense of heliocentricity. He observed the oval shape of Saturn and described the phases of Venus. Following his discovery of the existence of spots on the sun, Galileo systematically defended Copernicus for the first time in print in his *Letters on Sunspots*.

Galileo also initiated the central failure of his career. He refused to engage Kepler's brilliant description of the elliptical motion of the planets around the sun, published already in 1609. Because of this failure, Galileo's empirical work tended only to militate against the ideas of Ptolemy and Aristotle, rather than to support Kepler's discoveries. Throughout his life Galileo clung to the mistaken notion that planetary orbits had to be circular.

The publication of Galileo's *Letters on Sunspots* brought him into conflict with the church for the first time. Although Galileo was favorably received by some in the Catholic church, by 1616 Cardinal Robert Bellarmine had declared Copernicanism erroneous and instructed Galileo to avoid open support of it. Galileo entered semiretirement for the next few years until the publication of *The Assayer* in 1623, a defense of his methods. The work was dedicated to Pope Urban VIII, long a friend to Galileo. The next year Urban gave him permission to publish on the Ptolemaic and Copernican systems, but he prohibited any conclusive findings. Galileo composed his *Dialogue Concerning the Two Chief World Systems* and published it with the approval of church censors in 1632.

Presented as an intellectual exercise, the book was in fact a thinly veiled yet strident defense of Copernicanism. Immediately celebrated throughout Europe as a tremendous achievement, it also attracted the attention of the church authorities. Believing that he had been made a fool, the pope ordered a trial of Galileo in 1633. On the basis of a "new" document from 1616 ordering Galileo not to defend heliocentricity, which Galileo claimed not to remember, he was found guilty of heresy and forced to recant his views. More recently scholars have claimed that the real issue in the trial was Galileo's defense of atomism—a theory of matter that challenged the church's doctrine of the Eucharist. Regardless, in 1634 Galileo was placed under house arrest at an estate outside Florence. There he wrote his last great work, *The Two New Sciences*, examining the strength of materials and the mechanics of motion. Completely blind by 1638, Galileo received friends and pupils as visitors until his death in 1642.

Although Galileo is best known for his use of the telescope, the significance of his life and work should be found in his understanding of scientific inquiry and his new method for it. This method stood in contrast to traditional forms of science, which resembled the study of literature, history, and theology. When his defense of Copernicus was attacked as contrary to Scripture, he replied with an eloquent description of the independent realms of science and religion. By 1615 his famous *Letter to Grand Duchess Christina* argued that neither Scripture nor science could be false. The allegorical truth of biblical passages withstood all new scientific discoveries, and only the natural world was the proper domain of the scientist. His contributions to astronomy, physics, and mechanics were considerable, but his most important legacy stemmed from his method. As had no other scientist before him, Galileo emphasized empirical observation, reproducible experimentation, and mathematical modeling as the keys to understanding the natural world.

Bibliography

M. Biagioli, *Galileo, Courtier*, 1993.
P. Redondi, *Galileo Heretic*, 1987.

J. Reston, *Galileo*, 1994.
M. Sharratt, *Galileo*, 1994.

Edmund M. Kern

GALILEI, VINCENZIO (1520–1591)

Vincenzio Galilei was a professional musician and merchant who advanced musical theory of the mid-sixteenth century; credited with devising the formula for tuning lutes and viols to a tempered scale, he played an important role in the move from musical polyphony to harmony. He also helped revolutionize natural philosophy because of his profound influence upon the thinking of his famous son, Galileo Galilei.*

Vincenzio Galilei studied under Gioseffe Zarlino, a musical theorist of the old school, in which mathematics strictly governed musical theory, and theory controlled contemporary practice. The introduction of new instruments in the sixteenth century revealed some contradictions in contemporary theory, which had long been based upon ancient notions of arithmetic proportion; consequently, the mismatch between the discontinuous integers of arithmetic and the continuum of musical sounds needed to be resolved. In 1558 Zarlino attempted to resolve the growing crisis with his *Harmonical Institutions*, a treatise that revised the ancient theories, but persisted in privileging mathematical theory over the perception of sound. In 1578 Vincenzio Galilei wrote a defense of tuning practices that departed from those recommended by Zarlino, thereby arguing for the primacy of sound over the rule of mathematics. Zarlino discouraged the printing of Galilei's book, but an expanded version was published in 1581. Zarlino countered in 1588 with *Sopplimenti musicali* (Musical supplements). Galilei fought back in 1589 with a treatise based not simply upon theory and observed practice, but upon actual experiments that he conducted to produce consonance and dissonance by varying lengths of strings and columns of air. This and some subsequent unpublished treatises he passed on to his son, Galileo Galilei, who incorporated his father's experimental method into his own examinations of the physics of sound, thereby revolutionizing contemporary science.

Bibliography

S. Drake, *Galileo Studies*, 1970.

Tim McGee

GAMBARA, VERONICA (1485–1550)

A quintessential Renaissance woman, Veronica Gambara was a patron of musicians, painters, poets, and scholars; she also produced an impressive body of her own poetry. Born in 1485, Gambara was connected to numerous aristocratic families. Her great-aunt was the famous humanist Isotta Nogarola, and her aunt, Emilia Pia, was celebrated in Baldesar Castiglione's* treatise on courtly life, *The Courtier*. Gambara received a solid humanist education in Greek, Latin, philosophy, theology, and poetry.

When she was twenty-four, Gambara was married to Count Giberto X, ruler of the Correggio region. Gambara enjoyed her life as contessa of a beautiful estate where poets and political figures gathered for social and intellectual interchange. The Casino, their castle of 360 rooms, included an impressive library and was lavishly decorated; guests were drawn there because of the comfort and opulence of the palace, but also because of Gambara herself. Though she was not a great beauty, she was said to be quite vivacious; she loved beautiful clothing, sumptuous decor, painting, and sculpture.

When Gambara was only thirty-two, her husband died. Although her grief was sincere, her reaction was somewhat theatrical. She withdrew from society for several months; when she emerged, she insisted that all of her rooms be decorated in black cloth to match her own mourning clothes and that her carriage horses be black as well. She never remarried, but she took over the management of Correggio, a task for which she proved to be well suited. She worked to improve literacy among her people and helped women and children who had lost husbands and fathers in the various wars Italy then suffered. She defended her city against invaders, found rations for the villagers during a period of famine, and wrote to political leaders of the day, especially her friend Charles V,* urging peace.

Gambara also continued to welcome artists and intellectuals to her estate, especially the painter Antonio Allegri, now known as Correggio.* Among other well-known figures who frequented her salon were Pietro Bembo,* Pietro Aretino,* and Isabella d'Este.* Even the famous monarchs François I* and Charles V, both great patrons of the arts themselves, visited Gambara's estate.

Gambara was herself a poet as well as a patron. Her extant work comprises about eighty poems on various subjects, including the effects of war on Italy, pastoral descriptions, spiritual matters, and dedicatory poems to Vittoria Colonna,* but most of them are love poems to her husband. Gambara was also a lively correspondent; approximately 150 of her letters are extant.

In 1550 Gambara died at the age of sixty-four. She was buried next to her husband in a church near their estate, but in 1556 her tomb, the church, and her beloved Casino were all destroyed by an invasion of Spanish soldiers.

Bibliography

M. Jerrold, *Vittoria Colonna, with Some Account of Her Friends and Her Times*, 1912, rpt., 1969.
R. Poss, "Veronica Gambara," in *Women Writers of the Renaissance and Reformation*, ed. K. M. Wilson, 1987.

Jo Eldridge Carney

GARNIER, ROBERT (c. 1545–1590)

Considered by his contemporaries and by modern literary historians as France's foremost writer of tragedy in the sixteenth century, Robert Garnier engaged in the humanist enterprise of imitating exemplary classical sources in order to establish French as a national language that could rival Latin and Greek. Born in La Ferté-Bernard near Le Mans, Garnier developed his literary procliv- ities and his legal career simultaneously. While he was in law school in Tou- louse, he entered the Jeux floraux, a yearly poetry competition whose origins date back to the fourteenth century. In 1566 he garnered first prize for his *Plaintes amoureuses*. These lyric poems were his first publication; even though they are mentioned by his contemporaries, no editions have come down to us. Some of the early poetry, however (e.g., the 1567 *Hymne de la monarchye*) has survived. An edition of his complete works appeared in 1585; a new two-volume edition was published in Paris in 1923. In 1567 he became a lawyer in the Parlement of Paris. Two years later he assumed the post of magistrate in Le Mans, and in 1574, through the king's influence, he became deputy president of the city's assembly, as well as chief justice for the entire district of Maine. In 1586 Garnier returned to Paris, where, by King Henri III's request, he became a member of the royal judicial body, the Great Council. Poor health and penury characterized the end of his life; he died on 20 September 1590.

Garnier's legal career involved him in the politics of his day. An ardent Catholic, he lived during a period of civil unrest. From 1562 to 1598 the French Wars of Religion pitted Catholics against Huguenots and ravaged the country. These facts help to explain his choice of subject matter for his plays. It seems no coincidence that the seven tragedies of Garnier that appeared between 1568 and 1583 have civil war as their backdrop, with the consequences of war and rebellion as a major theme. Three take place during the fall of the Roman Empire: *Porcie* (1568), *Cornélie* (1574), and *Marc Antoine* (1578). Three take their inspiration from Greek mythology: *Hippolyte* (1573), *La Troade* (1579), and *Antigone* (1580). One, *Les Juives* (1583), takes its inspiration from a biblical source. Garnier makes clear the parallels he sees between events in these plays and the woes befalling France. In the explanatory title to *Porcie*, for example, he writes that the cruel and bloody times of the Roman period provide a fitting mirror for the misfortunes of contemporary times. His dedication to *Cornélie* describes the play as a poem that is sadly appropriate, given France's current misfortunes. His plays deal with the uses and abuses of authority and the pitfalls of tyranny and rebellion.

The continental vogue for neoclassical historical drama as a means of drawing parallels to current political troubles became fashionable in Elizabethan England, in large part due to translations of Garnier into English, which spurred trans- lations of works on related subjects by other authors and subsequently influenced the subject matter of Elizabethan drama. Mary Sidney* Herbert, countess of Pembroke and sister of Sir Philip Sidney,* translated *Marc Antoine*. Appearing in 1592, its influence is seen in William Shakespeare's* *Antony and Cleopatra* (c. 1606). Descriptions of battles in Elizabethan dramatist Thomas Kyd's* *Span- ish Tragedy*, performed in 1592, bear witness to his familiarity with Garnier's *Cornélie*. The interest in neoclassical tragedy and Garnier subsequently spurred

Kyd to translate this play. The dedication to the countess of Suffolk proclaims his intention to follow with a translation of *Porcie*, a project that did not come to fruition.

Bibliography

G. Jondorf, *Robert Garnier and the Themes of Political Tragedy in the Sixteenth Century*, 1969.

Dora E. Polachek

GASCOIGNE, GEORGE (1539–1577)

George Gascoigne was an English poet and dramatist as well as a politician, courtier, and soldier of fortune who is chiefly remembered for successfully importing and domesticating foreign literary genres. Born in Bedfordshire, England, and educated at the University of Cambridge and Gray's Inn, Gascoigne was the eldest son of Sir John and Margaret Scargill Gascoigne of Cardington. He developed an early fascination with court life that continually drained his finances. He married Elizabeth Bacon Breton in 1561, who was in fact already married, and the process of extracting her from her first marriage combined with the litigation that followed also contributed to the drain on his fortune. In need of money, Gascoigne joined Sir Humphrey Gilbert's forces in 1572 in support of William of Orange in the Dutch wars against the Spaniards. He returned within a year, no better off than before, and decided to use his writings and his connections to gain advancement.

Gascoigne continually sought royal favor and finally received it by assisting with the entertainments of Elizabeth I* on her visits to Kenilworth and Woodstock in 1575. In 1576 he was granted an appointment by her advisor, William Cecil, Lord Burghley, was sent to Holland as an agent, and returned with a report of the siege of Antwerp by the Spanish, entitled *The Spoil of Antwerp, Faithfully Reported, by a True Englishman, Who Was Present*—one of the first examples of war correspondence in English.

Gascoigne was greatly interested in proving that English was a language fit for poetry, and many of his works can be seen as serving that end. He wrote the first Greek tragedy to be presented on the English stage (*Jocasta*, performed in 1566), the first prose comedy translated from Italian into English (*Supposes*, 1566), the first treatise on prosody in English ("Certayne Notes of Instruction" in *The Posies of George Gascoigne*, 1575), and one of the earliest formal satires in English (*The Steele Glas*, 1576). Finally, Gascoigne's *A Hundreth Sundrie Flowres* (1573) foreshadowed later English sonnet sequences.

Bibliography

C. T. Prouty, *George Gascoigne: Elizabethan Courtier, Soldier, and Poet*, 1942.

Richard J. Ring

GELLI, GIAMBATTISTA (1498–1563)

Giambattista Gelli was a self-taught Florentine linguist, moralist, and scholar of Dante and Petrarch whose life and writings link Renaissance humanism and the Counter-Reformation in Italy. Gelli passed his life in his native Florence and its environs, taking only one trip possibly as far as Pisa. He made his living as a shoemaker, the craft in which his father, a vintner, had him trained. His participation in Florentine political life was restricted to minor administrative positions he held occasionally and that he owed to Medici patronage. It was rather in the realm of scholarship that Gelli figures as an important contributor to Florentine cultural life.

Gelli was formally trained only in the rudiments of Latin, but in his twenties he determined to study that language and classical and vernacular literature more seriously on his own. He frequented the meetings of the circle of the Orti Or-ecellari in his youth and in 1540 was among the first affiliates of the Accademia degli Umidi, which in the following year became the Accademia Fiorentina. There, from 1541 to 1551, he distinguished himself in a series of public lectures on Dante's *Divine Comedy* and on Petrarch and engaged in discussions about language, championing the use of the vernacular.

Gelli's principal creative works include the moral dialogues *I capricci del bottaio*, the first seven of which appeared in 1546 and the remainder in 1548, and *La Circe* (1549). The *Capricci*, a colloquy between Giusto Bottaio (the just cooper) and his soul, offers insights both into Gelli's own psychology and the culturally conscious mentality of Florence's literate, if not learned, artisan class; while it recognizes the necessity of the practical crafts, the soul ultimately per-suades the cooper that the higher aim of human perfection can be attained only through study and the knowledge of truth. Gelli believed that knowledge could and should be disseminated as widely as possible, and to this end, though he trained himself as a humanist in classical languages in order to read Greek and Roman philosophy and history in the original, he argued in favor of the trans-lation of works into the vernacular in *Della lingua che si parla e scrive in Firenze* (1551). In *La Circe*, composed in imitation of Plutarch and possibly Niccolò Machiavelli,* Gelli presents eleven men who have been turned into animals. Given the choice to accept their metamorphoses or return to human form, all but one posit the superiority of animal existence; only the eleventh, with arguments drawn from Pliny and Aristotle as well as ancient and Renais-sance Neoplatonic literature, sees the human condition as more felicitous be-cause man alone can reason and seek to understand divine truth. Gelli's defense of the vernacular and of clear reasoning, his opposition to Scholastic philosophy, his sympathy with the Lutheran emphasis on scriptural authority, and his ad-miration for the legacy of Girolamo Savonarola led him to be brought errone-ously under suspicion of heresy and resulted in *I capricci* being placed on the Index more than a decade after it first appeared.

Of minor importance are the comedies *La sporta* (1543) and *Lo errore* (1556), which offer psychological and stereotypical snapshots of a widow and two el-derly Florentine men. In Gelli's own view, these comedies serve as a mirror of private and civic customs of the daily life of Florence. Gelli also wrote a brief collection of lives of Florentine artists and historical treatise, *Dell'origine di*

Firenze. He translated the biographies of ten famous men by Paolo Giovio and three works by Simone Porzio.

Bibliography

A. De Gaetano, *Giambattista Gelli and the Florentine Academy: The Rebellion against Latin*, 1976.

Luci Fortunato DeLisle

GEMMA FRISIUS, REINER (1508–1555)

Reiner Gemma Frisius, highly respected as a practicing physician, was a leading theoretical mathematician of his day whose work in practical trigonometry modernized surveying and earned him a name in the field of geography as well. Gemma was born in 1508 in Dokkum, Netherlands; the poverty-stricken district of Friesland in which this small town was located was the source of his nickname, Frisius, or "the Frieslander." Gemma excelled in his premedical courses at Louvain, the only university of the Low Countries, but it took him eight years instead of the usual six to complete his degree because he was too consumed by his interest in the fields of mathematics and geography to attend to his medical studies.

In 1529, while still a student, Gemma revised and published a new edition of one of the standard textbooks of his day, *Cosmographicus liber Petri Apiani mathematici*. His first original work, *Gemma Phrysius de principiis astronomiae et cosmographiae*, was published in less than a year and later translated into several languages.

The globes, maps, and astronomical instruments designed by Gemma were renowned throughout Europe, and the income they provided enabled him to marry in 1534. His son and later biographer, Cornelius, was born in 1535; the next year Gemma received his medical degree and began his practice. Gemma's abilities were held in high esteem by Louvain, his alma mater, and sometime between 1536 and 1539 he was appointed to the university's medical faculty.

Two of Gemma's contributions to the earth sciences are particularly noteworthy. The principle of triangulation, a trigonometrically based surveying procedure used to measure inaccessible sites, was first proposed in a chapter he added to the *Cosmographicus* in 1533. Gemma was also the first to suggest the use of portable clocks for determining longitude at sea, a method that was excellent theoretically but could only be put into practice when a suitable timepiece was invented in the late eighteenth century.

Gemma was also known for mentoring Gerardus Mercator,* who later became the leading mapmaker of his time. Gemma's contemporary, the anatomist Andreas Vesalius,* spoke of Gemma as "famous as a physician, and as a mathematician comparable to but a few."

Bibliography

G. Kish, *Medicina, Mensura, Mathematica: The Life and Works of Gemma Frisius, 1508–1555*, 1967.

Heather J. Murray

GENTILESCHI, ARTEMISIA (1593–1652/53)

Artemisia Gentileschi was the first female Italian artist determined to compete with the male artists of her time; she claimed to have "the spirit of Caesar" in the soul of a woman. Artemisia deserves recognition as a transmitter of Caravaggio's* ideas to Florence, Genoa, and Naples.

Artemisia, the daughter of Orazio Gentileschi, a follower of Caravaggio, enjoyed the benefits of having as her teacher a painter of significant stature. Drawing on mythological subjects and biblical themes, Artemisia's paintings often feature unusually striking depictions of female nudes. The subject for which she has been most celebrated is her dramatic study of *Judith and Holofernes*. An intense focus on individual characters is a hallmark of Artemisia's pictures. Her most successful paintings, executed prior to 1630, incorporate Caravaggesque realism and chiaroscuro, a painting technique using varied tones of light and dark paint for dramatic intensity. While Artemisia's contemporaries praised her skill in portrait painting, only one portrait remains today that can be attributed with confidence to Artemisia: *Portrait of a Condottieri* (1622).

In 1612 Artemisia had to endure what became a sensational trial when her father accused Agostino Tassi, the artist he had hired to teach his daughter perspective, of repeatedly raping her. After five months of being subjected to periodic torture from metal rings being tightened around her fingers to extract a confession of guilt from her, Artemisia refused to recant her story. Tassi spent eight months in prison, but he was ultimately acquitted of all charges. When the trial ended, Artemisia married a Florentine by the name of Pietro Antonio di Vincenzo Stiattesi to avoid further shame. The couple probably moved their household to Florence shortly after being married. Ultimately, the marriage proved to be a failure, and Artemisia with characteristic determination struck out on her own.

Throughout her career, Artemisia used her unique position as a woman, allowing her ready access to female models, to great advantage. A lucrative commission to paint a nude figure, *The Allegory of Inclination* (c. 1615), for Michelangelo Buonarroti the Younger suggests his admiration and recognition of Artemisia's talent in depicting the female nude.

While Artemisia was in Florence, she also enjoyed the patronage of the Medici family, the dynastic rulers of Florence. Artemisia's aristocratic patrons probably facilitated her ready acceptance into the Florentine Accademia del Disegno, originally founded by the artist Giorgio Vasari* and others in 1563. Artemisia became an official member of the academy in 1616, an extraordinary event since it had received no women as members since its inception.

Artemisia is believed to have spent time in Genoa when her father worked there between 1621 and 1624. She also executed commissions in Venice during the 1620s. By 1622 Artemisia had returned to Rome, where she remained working on commissions until the end of the decade. In her surviving letters, Artemisia claims to have executed commissions for the kings of France, Spain, and England. Artemisia is documented as taking up residence in England by 1638, where she helped her father complete work on Queen Henrietta Maria's palace, called the Queen's House, at Greenwich. After 1641, Artemisia would reside in Naples for the remainder of her life. While she produced many paintings during this period, most of them are less engaging than her earlier works.

Bibliography

M. D. Garrard, *Artemisia Gentileschi: The Image of the Female Hero in Italian Baroque Art*, 1989.
N. Heller, *Women Artists*, 1987.

Debbie Barrett-Graves

GESUALDO, CARLO (c. 1561–1613)

Carlo Gesualdo, prince of Venosa, was both a member of the high Neapolitan nobility and a composer of madrigals and other vocal music. A controversial figure, he is remembered today for his highly expressive chromatic compositional style as well as for the notorious double murder of his first wife and her lover. Gesualdo married his cousin, Maria d'Avalos, in Naples in 1586. The murder took place in 1590 and plunged Gesualdo deeper into a melancholia that affected him throughout his life. In 1594 he married Leonora d'Este, the niece of Alfonso II, duke of Ferrara. This second marriage was of great importance for his development as a musician in that it brought him into contact with many of the musicians at Ferrara. There he met Luzzasco Luzzaschi, a composer who profoundly influenced Gesualdo, and Nicola Vicentino, a music theorist whose *arcicembalo*, an experimental keyboard instrument, permitted performance of chromatic and microtonal intervals. While at Ferrara, Gesualdo had his first four books of madrigals published. These early works won him a reputation as a skilled composer and marked the development of his mature personal style.

The most recognizable aspect of Gesualdo's style is his use of chromaticism and dissonance for expressive effect. His works are complex, are irregular in form, and display the composer's concern to set each verbal image with its own unique musical representation. Gesualdo typically avoided pastoral and narrative texts, preferring short epigrammatic poems that allowed him to focus upon elaborate musical settings. With his attention directed primarily toward the music, selecting poems of the highest literary quality became a secondary consideration for him.

Gesualdo's compositions consist of six books of five-voice madrigals, two volumes of motets (the *Sacrae cantiones*), and a collection of responsories for Holy Week. His works, including both secular and sacred compositions, generally seem to be directed toward audiences with somewhat esoteric tastes and to be intended for private, aristocratic performance situations.

The music of Gesualdo seems to have had little immediate impact upon the history of music. His works, though admired by many, were too extreme in style to form the basis for future developments. These compositions, however, make up a remarkable body of work, often strikingly beautiful and strange. This is music of a composer highly skilled in contrapuntal technique, and it demonstrates the potential for intense chromaticism within the linear practice of the sixteenth century. It is music of an eccentric artist whose individual style marked the end of the late Renaissance.

Bibliography

S. Sadie, ed., *The New Grove Dictionary of Music and Musicians*, 1980.

Tucker Robison

GIAMBOLOGNA (GIOVANNI BOLOGNA or JEAN BOULOGNE) (1529–1608)

Giambologna was born in Flanders and apprenticed there to the sculptor Jacques Du Broeucq. As his Italianized name indicates, he spent his career as a sculptor in Italy. As a young man, Giambologna took the almost obligatory artist's journey to Italy (1550–52), where he encountered not only Michelangelo's* work but also the master himself. Michelangelo apparently criticized the younger artist for doing a finished and polished sculpture without working out the poses of the figures first. Giambologna subsequently took up the practice of making multiple models, or *bozzetti*, for all of his works. Many of these models are still extant; they provide an insider's view of the evolution of Giambologna's formal progress.

In 1552 Giambologna stopped in Florence on his way home to Flanders. There he found favor with rich patrons of the arts who were well placed to introduce him to the ruling Medici family, for whom Giambologna was shortly to become official court sculptor. Though he lost the competition for the Neptune fountain in Florence in 1560 to Bartolomeo Ammanati, he went on to do numerous works in both bronze and marble for the Medici and Florence. Many of these works were inspired by Michelangelo, whose serpentine twists and dramatic musculature were not merely copied but rather reinterpreted by Giambologna.

Bologna claimed Giambologna's attention in the mid-1560s when that city needed a Neptune fountain and remembered Giambologna's unsuccessful but critically acclaimed model for Florence a few years earlier. The famous statue of Mercury was also done for the first time in Bologna. In Giambologna's treatment of the messenger of the gods, Mercury is shown in action, delicately balanced on the ball of one foot and rather tenuously supported by a bronze breath of wind beneath that foot. The High Renaissance ideas of balance and stability have here been challenged.

Giambologna's best-known work today is *Rape of a Sabine*, completed in 1582 and now in the Loggia dei Lanzi next to the Uffizi in Florence. The subject was more theoretical than narrative, having been originally conceived as two men of different ages and a young woman in a dramatic yet unified composition. Michelangelo's serpentine compositions are here accelerated and pave the way for Bernini's intensely dramatic compositions of the seventeenth century.

Though Giambologna's earlier work was mostly concerned with mythological or legendary subjects, the Counter-Reformation and its rules about art did have an effect upon the subject matter of his later work. After 1580 he did a number of religious narratives in bronze, including the Passion and the lives of the saints. He continued working for the Medici, providing equestrian statues of several of the grand dukes (that of Cosimo I* is in the Piazza della Signoria in the center of Florence), as well as equestrian statues of other European royalty, statuettes, and naturalistic bronze studies of animals. Though his prominent role was that of a sculptor, he also worked as an architect. He submitted a wooden model for the facade of Florence Cathedral and designed his own funeral chapel in SS. Annunziata, Florence.

Bibliography

Co. Avery, *Giambologna: The Complete Sculpture*, 1987.

Lynne E. Johnson

GILBERT, WILLIAM (1540–1603)

William Gilbert was a physician and scientist whose *De magnete magneticisque corporibus et de magno magnete tellure physiologia nova* (On the Lodestone and Magnetic Bodies and on the Great Magnet the Earth, 1600), the first major study of physical science published in England, won international renown and praise from such luminaries as Sir Francis Bacon,* Galileo,* and Johannes Kepler.* Born in Essex on 24 May 1540, eldest son of Hierome Gilbert, recorder of Colchester, he received from St. John's College, Cambridge, the B.A. (1560), M.A. (1564), and M.D. (1569), becoming a fellow (1561) and then senior fellow (1569). Establishing a successful medical practice in London in 1573, he became a fellow of the Royal College of Physicians in 1576, serving as censor and treasurer before election as president in 1600. He helped begin the *Pharmacopoeia Londinensis* (published in 1618). In 1601 Queen Elizabeth* appointed him as her physician; thereafter he resided at court. At her death in 1603 she left money to support his research. James I* retained Gilbert as royal physician, but Gilbert died on 30 November 1603.

A bachelor, Gilbert had a well-stocked library and laboratory at his St. Peter's Hill residence, where he held monthly meetings that were an early predecessor to the Royal Society (founded in 1662). Influenced by mathematician Henry Briggs, compass maker Robert Norman, and instrument maker and theorist Edward Wright, his account of magnetism is methodical, thorough, and based on extensive empirical research, including observations of metallurgists and hundreds of experiments with small lodestones. He accurately described the properties of magnets, recognized that the earth is a magnet and has a metallic core, introduced the term "electricity," understood the application of his discoveries to determining latitude (though erring in some particulars), and reportedly invented two useful navigational instruments. Rejecting Aristotle's physics and Ptolemy's celestial mechanics, Gilbert accepted a rotating earth but otherwise was torn between the theories of Nicolaus Copernicus* and Tycho Brahe.* Influenced by Hermeticism, he believed in a living earth and spontaneous generation of life. A collection of his papers, *De mundo nostro sublunari philosophia nova* (A new philosophy of our sublunar world), was published posthumously.

Bibliography

A. McLean, *Humanism and the Rise of Science in Tudor England*, 1972.

William B. Robison

GIRALDI CINTHIO, GIAMBATTISTA (1504–1573)

Giambattista Giraldi was a prolific and influential Italian author noted for a collection of short prose tales, nine tragedies, and numerous works of literary criticism. In keeping with a tradition in academic circles, Giraldi adopted a Latin name, Cynthius: thus the addition of "Cinzio" or "Cinthio" to his name. In his own time, he was often referred to simply as "Il Cinzio."

Giraldi received a broad humanist education and was also trained as a physician. In 1532 he was hired to teach medicine at the university in his native town of Ferrara, and in 1541 he assumed the professorship of rhetoric, a post he held until 1562. In addition to his teaching duties, Giraldi devoted much of his time to writing; he preferred the vernacular for most of his works.

Throughout his life, Giraldi wrote short tales, or *novelle*, which he ultimately published in 1565 as *Gli hecatommithi* (The Hundred Tales). This collection of tales is in the tradition of Boccaccio's *Decameron*; here the storytellers are passengers on a ship to Marseilles escaping the sack of Rome. Unlike Boccaccio's work, however, Giraldi's stories exhibit an undercurrent of moral intent. The plots of several of the stories were used by playwrights, including William Shakespeare* in *Measure for Measure* and *Othello*.

Giraldi also based several of his own tragedies on these tales; the most influential of these, *Orbecche*, appeared in 1541 and was the first Italian tragedy to be performed on the stage. Giraldi's admiration of the Senecan tradition is evident in the play's emphasis on horror and violence. His other tragedies appear to have been composed for stage performance as well, in contrast to his contemporaries' Greek tragedies that were written primarily for readership. As a protégé of Duke Ercole II d'Este, Giraldi produced plays to provide entertainment for the ducal court. He also wrote several works of theoretical guidelines for comedy, tragedy, romance, and epic. His arguments on the epic placed him at the center of an ongoing literary debate in which he defended the contemporary romance epic represented by Ariosto's* *Orlando Furioso* against the more traditional proponents of the Homeric epic, such as Gian Giorgio Trissino.* Although Giraldi's dramatic theory was not always in keeping with his own practice, he advocated the idea of *tragedia mista*, a concept similar to tragicomedy, or tragedy with a happy and morally satisfactory ending. His theories of drama had a significant impact on dramatic practice in the latter part of the sixteenth century both inside and outside of Italy.

Bibliography

M. Herrick, *Italian Tragedy in the Renaissance*, 1965.

Jo Eldridge Carney

GIULIO ROMANO (c. 1499–1546)

As a painter and architect, Giulio Romano was Raphael's* heir and a founder of Mannerism. Romano was born in Rome, but as sources list his age at death as either forty-seven or fifty-four, his exact birth date is unknown. If the widely accepted date of 1499 is correct, Romano must have been a precocious talent, as he became Raphael's chief assistant at little more than sixteen years of age. Under Raphael, Romano worked on the frescoes in the Vatican's Stanza dell'Incendio and on oil paintings like *Joanna of Aragon* and *St. Margaret* for the king of France. He became so important that at Raphael's death in 1520, Romano was listed with Giovanni Penni as the artist's chief heir. Romano and Penni finished a number of works that their master had left incomplete, including the largest of the Vatican rooms, the Sala di Constantino. Romano also did some original work, such as the Naples *Madonna*.

Moving to Mantua in 1524, Romano avoided a scandal for which Marcantonio Raimondi,* who made a series of obscene engravings from Romano's drawings, was imprisoned. In Mantua Romano created one of his most important works, the Palazzo del Te, for Duke Federigo Gonzaga.* One of the first examples of Mannerist architecture, the palace retains ancient Roman forms while being so full of surprises that it parodies Donato Bramante's neoclassicism. The Mannerist concept, in which the artist emphasizes his aesthetic idea over the imitation of nature, can be seen in that all elements vary slightly from the expected. For example, the building is a square block around a central court, with a garden opening off at right angles to the dominant axis, a departure from the standard practice of placing the main portal centrally to stress the building's main axis. The Sala dei Giganti provides an example of the unusual room decorations. The continuous scene painted in this square room, in which Jupiter throws his thunderbolts from the ceiling, makes the spectator feel like one of the giants being repulsed as they try to storm Olympus. A streak of cruel obscenity, which often lurks beneath the surface of Romano's work, can be seen in the subject.

In later years Romano built himself a Mannerist version of Raphael's house (1544–46) and began rebuilding Mantua's cathedral (1543 onward). His work on the Reggia dei Gonzaga's Sala di Troia looks forward to the baroque's illusionistic ceiling decorations and may have been inspired by Andrea Mantegna's work on the Camera degli Sposi.

In designs like that of the Palazzo del Te, Romano flouted classical rules of stability, symmetry, and order in ways deliberately designed to shock the observer. His devices contributed greatly to Mannerism's emerging repertoire of characteristic features.

Bibliography

F. Ambrosio, *Giulio Romano*, trans. R. Sadleir, 1991.

Kevin Lindberg

GLAREAN, HEINRICH (1488–1563)

Heinrich Glarean, known also as Glareanus, was a Swiss humanist, music theorist, poet, philosopher, and theologian. A friend of Desiderius Erasmus* of Rotterdam, Glarean argued against the ideas of the Reformation.

Born in the canton of Glarus, Glarean attended the University of Cologne, where he studied philosophy, theology, music, and mathematics. In 1510 Glarean received his license to teach and in 1512 was crowned poet laureate by Emperor Maximilian I. In 1514 he moved to Basel, where he directed a boarding school and later lectured at the university. It was in Basel that he first met Erasmus. It was also here that he formed his opposition to the Reformation, despite his admiration for Martin Luther* and Huldrych Zwingli.* In 1529 he took a post at the university at Freiburg im Breisgau, where he served as professor of poetry and of theology. He helped organize a Swiss Catholic Hochschule in 1558 and served as an advisor for the revision of school curricula at Freiburg, Lucerne, and Solothurn. He remained in Freiburg, bothered by blindness late in life, until his death.

Like his friend Erasmus, Glarean sought to use the Christian faith to illuminate the ideas and wisdom of the ancient Greeks and Romans, and he eagerly studied the literature of antiquity. Inspired by Boethius's great work *De musica*, Glarean developed his own comprehensive theory of music. He published his ideas in the *Dodecachordon* of 1547, a three-volume set that was to become his best-known musical work. In this work he elaborates a theory of twelve modes, an expansion of the old medieval theory of eight modes. Perhaps his most important contribution was the recognition of the Ionian and Aeolian modes, those that correspond to our major and natural minor scales, as important for the music of his day. The ideas developed by Glarean greatly influenced later music theorists, such as Gioseffe Zarlino, and had a profound impact upon Renaissance composers. Several composers, including Claudio Merulo and Giovanni Gabrieli,* wrote instrumental pieces (toccatas or ricercares) that demonstrated the twelve different modes. Glarean's musical works are of value not only because of his original theoretical ideas but also because of the wealth of biographical information he provides, the numerous musical scores that he includes as examples, and his clear description of contemporary polyphonic method as used by the great Franco-Flemish composers.

Bibliography

C. Miller, "Heinrich Glarean," in *The New Grove Dictionary of Music and Musicians*, ed. S. Sadie, vol. 7, 1980: 422–24.

Tucker Robison

GOÍS, DAMIÃO de (1502–1574)

Damião de Goís, a Portuguese diplomat, humanist, and composer, is best remembered for his histories, *Chronica do felicissimo rei Dom Emanuel* (1566–67) and *Chronica do Principe Dom Ioam* (1567). He is also noted for his travels and friendships with such humanists as Cornelius Grapheus and Desiderius Erasmus.*

Goís, born into a noble Portuguese family, spent his early childhood years in the court of King Manuel I. In 1523 he was appointed to a secretarial post in a port trading establishment in Antwerp by John III, Manuel's successor. His diplomatic duties occupied him from 1528 to 1531, enabling him to travel extensively throughout Europe. He studied at the University of Louvain and for a time was able to combine scholarship with his diplomatic duties. Refusing the post of treasurer in 1533, he returned to Flanders to dedicate himself to the life of Erasmian humanism.

Goís had the means to travel and engage in intellectual pursuits. His many travels allowed him contact with different Protestant groups and contributed to his variety of ideas concerning Christianity. He met Erasmus through his associations with his close friend and teacher Cornelius Grapheus. In 1534, after being a guest of Erasmus for five months, Goís married and began a life of scholarly work. His work was interrupted by the French invasion of 1543, during which he was taken prisoner. Once he was freed by John III, he was summoned back to Portugal with his wife and three sons.

Upon his return to Portugal, Goís entered into his new post as chief keeper of the National Archive and was then chosen to write the official chronicle of King Manuel I, which he completed in 1567. His earlier associations with Protestants now came to haunt him, and in 1571 he was imprisoned by the Inquisition. Abandoned by family and friends, he died in 1574, two years after being convicted as a heretic.

Bibliography

E. Hirsch, *Damião de Goís: The Life and Thought of a Portuguese Humanist, 1502–1574*, 1967.

Catherine C. Pontoriero

GÓNGORA Y ARGOTE, LUIS DE (1561–1627)

Luis de Góngora y Argote was known as the poet of light and dark because of his contradictory, bizarre, and richly metaphorical style of poetry called *culteranismo*. This style was highly admired by a group of Spanish surrealist poets in the 1920s that included Federico García Lorca; they named themselves the "Generation of 1927," a year chosen to mark Góngora's death three hundred years earlier.

Born to a prominent family in Córdoba, Spain, Góngora grew up with a voluminous library at his disposal. However, he never finished his formal studies at the University of Salamanca, where he had entered and had begun to write poetry at the age of fifteen. A gentleman poet, he shunned the printing press and never took his work to be published. Nevertheless, by the time he was nineteen, some of his work had found its way into print, and his fame was on the rise. Several years later his friend Pedro Espinosa published a series of his poems in a 1605 miscellany entitled *Flowers of Illustrious Poets*, presumably without Góngora's permission. But it was not until 1610 that Góngora began to write his more ambitious poems, notably the *Fable of Polyphemus and Galatea* and *Solitudes*. In the literary salons he frequented, parts of these poems were circulated and read.

Although Gongora usually circulated his poetry in manuscript, he was preparing it for print when he died. Only thirty-seven works were published in scattered collections in the course of his lifetime. Immediately after his death, his poems were published by López de Vicuña and subsequently by a long series of publishers who were not very scrupulous in separating Góngora's poetry from others' poems that had gotten mixed in with the manuscripts he had circulated. But it was not until the twentieth century that a more accurate edition appeared, called *Chacón*. Góngora is best known for his earlier stage of writing, which was one of extravagance, obscurity, and unintelligibility. At this stage his style became known as *culteranismo*: full of arcane diction and twisted syntax. It is a heightening of the Renaissance style that hearkens back to antiquity and includes the excessive use of Latin-based words and archaic syntax and metaphors. *Góngorismo* is an extreme and personal development of *culteranismo*. It is profoundly difficult to read in Spanish and immeasurably troublesome to translate into other languages. It is musical and intense, colorful and sumptuous, almost surreal. Hence Góngora's poetry influenced poets such as Lorca three hundred years later. Two of the seventeenth-century writers who were most influenced by Góngora were Baltasar Gracián and Sor Juana Inés de la Cruz.

Bibliography

J. Beverly, *Aspects of Góngora's Soledades*, 1980.
M. Woods, *Gracián Meets Góngora: The Theory and Practice of Wit*, 1995.

Ana Kothe

GONZAGA, FEDERICO II (1500–1540)

Federico II Gonzaga distinguished himself in two spheres: political and cultural. Successive military commands led to his becoming the first duke of Mantua, while his patronage of leading Italian artists bequeathed to posterity imposing architectural masterpieces and decorative achievements.

Born in Mantua, Italy, Federico II—the heir of Francesco II, the marquis of Mantua, and Isabella d'Este*—spent his formative years at the court of Pope Julius II* as a guarantor for his father's loyalty. In 1515 Federico went to Milan to pay his respects to François I,* who invited Federico to France for a visit. Federico remained in France for two years. Upon Federico's return from France in 1517, his parents arranged a marriage contract with Maria Paleologa. When

Maria died in September 1530, negotiations for the marriage of Federico II and Maria's younger sister, Margherita, went forward. The couple wed on 3 October 1531.

During the Italian Wars (1494–1559), as the French house of Valois competed with the Spanish house of Habsburg for control of Italy, Federico's political alliances initially appointed him captain of the church on 1 July 1521; however, Federico knew that Holy Roman Emperor Charles V* would decide the future of Mantua. While still papal captain, Federico permitted imperial forces to pass through his realm. Charles V rewarded Federico's loyalty, appointing him as captain general of the imperial forces in Italy on 21 September 1529 and elevating him to a dukedom in 1530. From Margherita, Federico inherited the duchy of Monferrato in 1536.

Along with enhancing the Gonzagas' dynastic fortunes, Federico added to the cultural preeminence of Mantua. His patronage of Giulio Romano* resulted in two impressive architectural monuments, The Palazzo del Te and the Appartamento di Troia. Possibly intended as a retreat for Federico and his mistress, Isabella Boschetti, The Palazzo del Te's building history (c. 1527–34) commenced when Romano began improvements to existing structures on a piece of land west of Mantua. Giorgio Vasari's* account of the building describes the classical orders of the facade and its elegant rooms, ornamented with mythological decorations. Duke Federico personally supervised the addition of a new suite of rooms, called the Appartamento di Troia (c. 1536–38), to the ducal palace. Each of the rooms had a decorative theme. One of them, known as the Cabinet of the Caesars, for which Duke Federico commissioned Titian* to paint a series of Roman emperors, reflects Federico's passion for imperial themes.

The scope of Duke Federico's artistic patronage remains without parallel. Unfortunately, an eighteenth-century fire in Spain consumed Titian's paintings of the emperors. When King Charles I of England purchased the Gonzaga treasures around 1628, the collection was broken up, although fortunately many pieces have survived. In addition, the tapestry factory that Duke Federico established (c. 1539), headed by Nicholas Karcher, was destined to provide a wealth of decorative designs for posterity.

Bibliography

C. M. Brown, G. Delmarcel, and A. M. Lorenzoni, *Tapestries for the Courts of Federico II, Ercole, and Ferrante Gonzaga, 1522–63*, 1996.
D. Chambers and J. Martineau, eds., *Splendours of the Gonzaga*, exhibition catalog, 4 November 1981–31 January 1982, Victoria and Albert Museum, London, 1981.
E. Verheyen, *The Palazzo del Te in Mantua: Images of Love and Politics*, 1977.

Debbie Barrett-Graves

GONZAGA, GIULIA (1513–1566)

Giulia Gonzaga was a noblewoman from the illustrious Gonzaga family of Mantua who became an important patron of the Italian reformist movement.

When she was fourteen, Gonzaga was married to Vespasiano Colonna, a widowed prince from southern Italy. Two years later Colonna died, bequeathing his vast property at Fondi to his young wife. Giulia had many admirers and suitors, but she never remarried. Her villa at Fondi became a salon for religious figures, artists, and writers, many of whom paid tribute to her in their works. Sebastiano del Piombo* and Titian* were among those who painted her portrait, and Ludovico Ariosto* and Torquato Tasso* were only two of the many authors who praised her in their poetry.

Surrounded by creative and intellectual figures, Giulia seemed quite content in her early widowhood, but her peaceful life was soon interrupted by a tragic incident. Hearing of her beauty, the notorious pirate Barbarossa decided to kidnap Gonzaga as a gift for Suleiman II's harem. During a raid on the Italian coast, Barbarossa massacred many of the villagers near Fondi and then advanced toward Gonzaga's castle, but Gonzaga escaped to a nearby fortress. In his fury, Barbarossa continued his murderous assault until he was finally stopped by an Italian army. In the aftermath of this tragedy, which caused numerous deaths and vast destruction, Gonzaga devoted herself to restoring order and repairing damage.

In 1534 Gonzaga moved near Naples to a monastery where she lived the remainder of her life, though she did not take the veil. She became connected with the Italian reformist movement through two of its leaders, the charismatic preacher Bernardino Ochino* and the Spanish humanist Juan de Valdes,* who dedicated a number of his works to her. Gonzaga dedicated her life to performing charitable works and carrying on Valdés's teachings after his death. When many of the reformists fled to Geneva to escape persecution from the Roman Inquisition, Gonzaga refused to leave. She supported the exiles, however, sending financial and emotional support to her friend Isabella Bresenga and others for years. The Italian inquisitors had long suspected Gonzaga of heresy; after her death some of her letters were brought to the attention of Pope Pius V, who proclaimed, "Had I known of this, she would have been burned alive."

Bibliography

C. Hare, *A Princess of the Italian Reformation*, 1912.

Jo Eldridge Carney

GÓRNICKI, ŁUKASZ (1527–1603)

One of the most important writers of the Polish Renaissance, Łukasz Górnicki is most known for his Polish version of Baldesar Castiglione's* *Courtier*. Born in Oświecim in a burgher's family, Górnicki was sent at the age of eleven to his uncle, Stanisław Gasiorek of Bochnia, a court poet, to study in Cracow at St. John's Parish School. In 1545 Górnicki went to Pradnik to the court of Bishop Maciejowski; he then went to Padua for the next several years.

Górnicki returned to Poland and in 1559 entered the court of King Zygmunt August (Sigismund Augustus), where as librarian and secretary in the royal chancellery he joined the luminaries of Renaissance Poland, including Jan Kochanowski,* Nidecki, Frycz Modrewski, Kromer, and Zamoyski. He was raised to the rank of nobleman in 1561 and gradually acquired offices and possessions. It was during his years at court that, at the encouragement of the king, he translated the Italian writer Castiglione's *Il cortegiano* (The Courtier). The fruit of several years of work, *Dworzanin polski* (The Polish Courtier) was not a mere translation. Górnicki adapted the Italian text, transplanting its main ideas into the mainstream of Polish court culture. In his version, Górnicki's major achievement was to produce in Polish the rich, reflective language characteristic of the original.

Górnicki is recognized as a master of Polish Renaissance prose, even if he is not a writer of great originality. Other publications include *A Conversation between a Pole and an Italian on Polish Freedoms and Laws*, published in 1587, and *History of the Polish Crown from 1538 to 1572*, published in 1637.

Bibliography

M. Mikoś, *Polish Renaissance Literature: An Anthology*, 1995.

Michael J. Mikoś

GOSSON, STEPHEN (c. 1554–1624)

The most famous among the attackers of poetry and the theater in Elizabethan England, Stephen Gosson started out, ironically enough, as a poet, playwright, and actor, then turned to pamphlet and fiction writing, and finally settled into a clerical career. He was born into the family of a humble joiner, and his life is a case study of the growth of an English humanist. His solid education at the King's School at Canterbury was followed by four years of studies at Corpus Christi College, Oxford. But Gosson never showed up for the final ceremony of determination, probably because he lacked the money to keep himself at Oxford without a fellowship. Instead, he left for London, hoping to find patronage for his pastoral and elegiac poetry. He also tried his hand at the more profitable trade of playwrighting and acting.

When he published the antitheatrical pamphlet *The Schoole of Abuse* in 1579, this involvement with the theater must have caused him some embarrassment. But in a brilliant journalistic move, Gosson reclaimed his defection from the stage as moral awakening. He followed his first blast against the stage with another pamphlet, *Plays Confuted in Five Actions* (1582), starting a long-lasting pamphlet war between the theater opponents and its defenders.

The turn to satirical pamphleteering changed Gosson's fortunes. From an impoverished actor and poet, he became a tutor, then probably a government agent on the Continent. By his thirties, he had taken holy orders and had embarked on a promising clerical career. His pugnacious sermons won him the affection of his parishioners and the respect of Richard Bancroft, bishop of London. In 1600 he reached the peak of his career as the rector of one of the wealthiest London churches, St. Botolph, where he remained until his death.

Bibliography

W. Ringler, *Stephen Gosson: A Biographical and Critical Study*, 1942.

Kirilka Stavreva

GOUDIMEL, CLAUDE (1514/20–1572)

Claude Goudimel was a French composer of sacred and secular music. His psalm settings in particular were important in the development of Protestant musical styles. Goudimel's compositional career began in Paris while he was a student at the university, and his first chansons were published there in 1549. Over the course of his life he composed more than seventy chansons. A number of these were settings of texts by Pierre de Ronsard,* whom Goudimel knew personally. In 1551 he began work as a proofreader for the Parisian publisher Nicholas du Chemin, and from 1552 to 1555 he was a partner in the business. He spent the years 1557 to 1567 in the city of Metz, a Huguenot stronghold. During this time he converted to Protestantism. Goudimel's final years were spent in Lyons. He met his death in August of 1572, a victim of the St. Bartholomew's Day Massacre.

Psalms were an important component of the Protestant musical tradition, especially in the music of the Calvinist church. Metrical versions in the vernacular (known as the Geneva Psalter) were a staple of congregational singing, and the tunes associated with them were well known. Between 1551 and 1556 Goudimel published eight books of psalm settings (some sixty in number) in a style similar to the contemporary motet. After his conversion, he produced two complete settings of the Geneva Psalter. One comprises simple chordal settings appropriate for domestic singing, while the other is in a more elaborate style. The former was translated into German and published in 1573. It had a strong influence on Lutheran worship traditions.

Bibliography

P.-A. Gaillard, "Claude Goudimel," in *The New Grove Dictionary of Music and Musicians*, ed. Stanley Sadie, vol. 7, 1980: 578–79.

Russell E. Murray, Jr.

GOUJON, JEAN (c. 1510–1565)

Jean Goujon was the major force in sculpture, particularly in relief, in mid-sixteenth-century France. His court-related commissions, often executed in collaboration with other artists and architects, define French Renaissance sculpture.

Goujon's earliest work is in Rouen. Traditionally attributed to him are columns in the Church of St. Maclou that feature an authentic classicism rather alien to France in the 1540s. It is assumed that Goujon played a design role in other works there, including the large wall tomb of Louis de Brézé, seneschal of Normandy (1544), most likely commissioned by his widow, Diane de Poitiers.*

By 1544 Goujon was working in Paris in partnership with the architect Pierre Lescot, with whom he would associate himself for the rest of his career. Goujon's distinctive low-relief figural style emerges in sculptures intended for the rood screen at St. Germain l'Auxerrois (now in the Louvre). One of these, *The Deposition*, demonstrates his assimilation of classical forms and draperies via the Italian Renaissance (as represented in prints or by artists active in France), while emphasizing decorative surface patterns. This work led to commissions in 1545 from Anne, duc de Montmorency and grand constable of France, for his château at Ecouen. Specific details regarding Goujon's work there are lacking.

Goujon returned to Paris to work on the triumphal entry of the new king, Henri II, in 1549. For this event he made the Fontaine des Innocents, his best-known and most complex work, incorporating architecture (probably by Lescot) and sculpture in relief. As originally built, between 1547 and 1549, its rectangular structure abutted a corner; an eighteenth-century restoration left it free-standing. Goujon's large-scale decorative reliefs feature elegant classically draped nymphs standing in contrapposto poses and carrying urns from which water poured into the fountain.

In 1550 Goujon collaborated further with Lescot, providing sculptural decoration for the new Cour Carrée at the Louvre, both for the facade (subsequently altered) and for the interior. Inside—in something totally new for France—Goujon produced four classically inspired, but proportionately more lithe, caryatids (sculpted in the round) to hold up a balcony. Indicative also of his expertise in classical forms, Goujon provided illustrations for the influential French translation of the only surviving ancient architectural treatise, that of Vitruvius (Paris, 1547). Because he was a Protestant, Goujon left France at the outbreak of the first religious war (1562). Records imply his presence in Bologna in 1563, but no further artworks are known. Goujon was the most important sculptor of the French Renaissance, and his work uniquely embodies his thorough grounding in the antique tempered by his propensity for elegance.

Bibliography

A. Blunt, *Art and Architecture in France, 1500 to 1700*, 1970.
N. Miller, *French Renaissance Fountains*, 1977.
J. Thirion, "Jean Goujon," in *The Dictionary of Art*, 13, 1996: 225–27.

Sheila ffolliott

GRAZZINI, ANTON FRANCESCO ("IL LASCA") (1503–1584)

Anton Francesco Grazzini was an academic and writer whose short stories and dramas composed in the Florentine vernacular explore themes of social life in the tradition of Boccaccio. Grazzini's academic and literary interests in his native city of Florence led him to become one of the founders of the Accademia degli Umidi in November 1540, in which he was given the pseudonym "Lasca" that he retained for the remainder of his career. In the following year the circle changed its name to the Accademia Fiorentina, and Grazzini remained affiliated with this group close to the court of Cosimo I* and held several offices in it until 1547, when he was expelled because his linguistic theories differed from those espoused at court. He was finally readmitted in 1566 and went on in 1582 to become one of the founders of the Accademia della Crusca. The vicissitudes of Grazzini's career must be understood against the climate of the granducal court of Tuscany, whose aesthetic values became increasingly linked with established classical idioms, in contrast to Grazzini's more urban, vernacular, naturalistic, and experimental interests.

Grazzini wrote religious, Petrarchan, and pastoral verse, but more notably his interest in urban spectacle inspired carnival songs and madrigals with a particularly Tuscan flavor and often comical good humor. In this same vein he edited a number of books, including *Primo libro dell'opere burlesche del Berni e di altri* in 1548, *I sonetti del Burchiello, et di messer Antonio Alamanni* in 1552, and finally an edition of *Tutti i trionfi, carri, mascherate ossia canti carnascialeschi* from the time of Lorenzo the Magnificent to 1559. His satiric wit is displayed in poems addressed to literary adversaries such as Giambattista Gelli.*

Grazzini is best known for his *novelle* and his comedies conveyed in the vivid Florentine speech of his day. In imitation of and counterpoint to Boccaccio's *Decameron*, Grazzini creates a frame for his tales in which, instead of the verdant villa environs of Boccaccio's brigata, the five young men and five women who narrate Grazzini's tales do so from the familiar setting of the mercantile city of Florence in winter during the last three days of carnival. The *Cene*, as the collection of twenty-two completed tales is titled, moves toward a crescendo, building from small and simple tales toward grand ones over the three nights' dinners. In keeping with his anticlassical sentiments against the pedantry that had crept into Florentine culture through its imitation of antiquity, Grazzini's *novelle* are conveyed in simple, lively, and humorous fashion drawn from more local and contemporary conditions.

Grazzini's comedies *Il frate, La gelosia, La spiritata, La strega, La pinzochera, La sibilla, I parentadi, L'arzigogolo,* and *La monica* (of the last of which only the prologue survives) also convey his preference for the Florentine and the modern over the models of Aristotle, Horace, and Terence. In one play he pointedly draws his readers' attention to the setting of the plot in the shadow of Brunelleschi's dome and prefaces another with the reminder that "in Florence, in Pisa, in Lucca one does not live as they did in ancient times in Rome and in Athens."

Bibliography

R. Rodini, *Antonfrancesco Grazzini, Poet, Dramatist, and Novelliere, 1503–1584*, 1970.

Luci Fortunato DeLisle

GRECO, EL (1541–1614)

After his apprenticeship in Venice and Rome, El Greco moved to Toledo, Spain, where he lived most of his life. In Toledo he painted some of the most important Mannerist works produced in Europe. Born Domenico Theotocopuli in Crete, which was then a colony of Venice, El Greco moved to Venice in 1560, where he became a disciple of the painter Titian.* From there, he moved to Rome, where he entered the Academy of San Lucas. It was in Italy that he learned the Mannerist style of painting that he took with him to Spain. Mannerism can be distinguished from High Renaissance art by its use of uncanonical proportions and tension in its figures, contrasting or unusual colors, and often a strangeness in its subject matter. El Greco's style underwent significant changes in Spain. His new style was characterized by a rejection of Renaissance geometrics, which became increasingly diminished by the heightened attention he gave to a sense of pathos. His characteristic style can be described as a cross between realism and mysticism.

In 1577 El Greco arrived in Toledo, where he met Jerónima de las Cuevas, who possibly became his wife. Although there are no records of their marriage, she was the mother of their son, Jorge Manuel, born in 1578, the same year he received his first commission from the Church of Santo Domingo el Antiguo. The result of this commission is *Expolio* (1579), which depicts Jesus on Calvary at the moment his magnificent red tunic is being taken away from him. In this painting, Jesus has an elongated torso; this type of elongation will characterize the rest of El Greco's figures. This same year, King Philip II* visited Toledo, saw *Expolio*, and commissioned El Greco to paint *The Martyrdom of St. Maurice* for El Escorial, his new palace-monastery near Madrid. However, due to El Greco's increasingly unusual style, the resulting painting of St. Maurice was not to the king's liking and was rejected. Ironically, El Greco was eventually commissioned by the community of El Escorial to paint a memorial portrait of Philip II after his death. *The Dream of Philip II* (1598–1604), which depicts the kneeling monarch caught between a hellish earthly existence and the promise of heaven, hangs above Philip's sepulchre in El Escorial.

After *The Martyrdom of St. Maurice*, El Greco undertook one of his most famous paintings, *The Burial of Count Orgaz* (1586–88). Its theme is the burial of Count Gonzalo Ruiz, who died in 1323. During his life, Gonzalo Ruiz had given generously to the Augustinian order and had established a new church dedicated to St. Stephen. Legend had it that during Gonzalo Ruiz's burial, St. Stephen and St. Augustine descended from the heavens and laid him to rest with their own hands. The painting depicts this miraculous moment. The canvas is divided into two levels, a celestial realm and an earthly one. The lower, earthly level is painted with vigorous realism, which contrasts with the supernatural moment of the two saints appearing. Besides the two saints, several illustrious members of Toledan society attend the burial along with a few figures of El Greco's own time, perhaps including El Greco himself. Most of these figures are in a row behind the saints and are dressed in black, which makes the central figures of the saints and Don Gonzalo stand out; the central trio appears particularly striking due to the rich, golden tones of their garb. A subtle web of gazes among the figures below invite the viewer to gaze upward at the spiritual world.

The upper level is depicted in El Greco's typically spiritual style. Christ as judge appears in the middle of the upper level in a white tunic. At his feet, forming a diamond-shaped composition, are Mary and St. John, interceding on Don Gonzalo's behalf. Directly below them is an angel carrying the vaporous form of the count's soul. At either side of the upper trio is a host of angels and saints, among whose company the viewer might find Philip II. This painting, located in the Church of St. Tomé in Toledo, may be one of El Greco's most complex works.

In a manner and mood quite different from any of his religious paintings, El Greco also painted a series of "gentleman" portraits between about 1584 and 1594, among which *The Gentleman with His Hand at His Breast* (1580–85) is perhaps the most widely known. The portraits, most now in the Prado Museum in Madrid, are of unknown officials residing in Toledo. They are all serious in mood; the men's bodies, clad in black, can barely be distinguished from the dark background, rendering the pale face, which is set apart from the body by an elegant white ruffle around the neck, suspended in the middle of the canvas.

El Greco's other secular paintings include classical and picaresque or "generic" themes. El Greco's figures, particularly his female ones, tend to appear somewhat ambiguously gendered. His classical painting *Laocoön* shows the unfortunate father and sons, naked and pale, being attacked by the sea serpent of myth. El Greco used Toledo to depict the trio's city, Troy, in the background. Toledo was also used as a backdrop for *St. Martin and the Beggar* (c. 1597–99), which along with *Laocoön* hangs in the National Gallery of Art in Washington, D.C.

El Greco's religious paintings can be seen as part of the Counter-Reformation's reaffirmation of iconographic religious themes, although his secular themes, such as the picaresque and classical paintings and the "gentleman" portraits, indicate a more complex artistic inclination. While El Greco's original style had no immediate descendants in Spanish painting, his emphasis on expression over realism resonated in Francisco Goya's "dark period" over two hundred years later.

Bibliography

J. Gudiol, *El Greco, 1541–1614*, trans. K. Lyons, 1987.
J. Morales y Marín, *El Greco*, 1997.

Ana Kothe

GREENE, ROBERT (1558–1592)

A pamphleteer and dramatist, Robert Greene was a central figure in the English literary community of the late sixteenth century. Greene, who was born in Norwich, entered St. John's College, Cambridge, in 1575 as a sizar, or poor working student. He received his B.A. in 1578 and his M.A. in 1583 and was incorporated M.A. from Oxford in 1588. A 1586 marriage produced at least one child, but Greene deserted his family and went to London. There he became notorious for heavy drinking, financial irresponsibility, and associating with prostitutes and cutpurses.

Greene's academic credentials earned him a place among Christopher Marlowe,* George Peele, and Thomas Nashe*—the so-called University Wits. One of England's first professional authors, he produced more than thirty-five works between 1580 and 1592. Beginning with moral writings, he proceeded to pastoral romances, including *Pandosto* (1588), the source of William Shakespeare's* *Winter's Tale*. Greene has at times been linked with forty plays, although modern scholars assign him just five. Of these, only *The History of Orlando Furioso* (c. 1591, published in 1594) bore his name during his lifetime. Another, *The Scottish History of James the Fourth* (c. 1591, published in 1598), anticipates Shakespeare's *Midsummer Night's Dream* with its fairy lore and tragicomic form.

Around 1590 Greene began to write didactic works with autobiographical content. Many of these, like *Greenes Never Too Late* (1590), are prodigal-son stories in which a youth ignores his father's advice, sows wild oats, and returns humbled and penitent. *Greenes Groatsworth of Wit* (1592) expresses concern for the immorality and atheism of Marlowe, Nashe, and Peele. It also contains the first printed reference to Shakespeare, who is attacked as "an upstart Crow, beautified with our feathers, that with his *Tygers hart wrapt in a Players hyde*, supposes he is as well able to bombast out a blanke verse as the best of you: and being an absolute *Johannes fac totum*, is in his own conceit the onely Shakescene in a countrey."

In 1592 Greene wrote several exposés of London conycatchers, or swindlers, including *A Quip for an Upstart Courtier*, which attacks scholar Gabriel Harvey.* Soon after, Greene became ill from a meal of pickled herring and Rhenish wine and died alone and penniless. That his friends failed to dispute Harvey's subsequent malicious description of Greene's vices and death in *Four Letters and Certain Sonnets* (1592) confirms Greene's dubious moral character; despite this, he was a popular writer who provided Shakespeare with a dramatic model of comedy and romance.

Bibliography

C. W. Crupi, *Robert Greene*, 1986.

Kevin Lindberg

GREY, LADY JANE (1537–1554)

Jane Grey, for nine days queen of England in 1553 and dead by the executioner's hand before she was seventeen, was a young woman of extraordinary learning and courage. She was the granddaughter of Henry VIII's* younger sister Mary and the eldest daughter of Frances Brandon and her husband, Henry Grey. She was born in October 1537 about the same time as her cousin, the future Edward VI. Before Henry VIII's death in 1547, he made a will that placed the descendants of his younger sister Mary in the succession after his own children. This closeness to the throne made her a valuable commodity.

Because of the impact of humanism on the education of upper-class women, by the time Jane was seven, she had begun instruction in Latin and Greek. In 1550 the humanist Roger Ascham* met Jane. He described her extraordinary commitment to learning and to the Reformed faith. The pleasure Jane took in reading Plato in the original Greek amazed Ascham. Jane explained to him that she found solace in study: her tutor John Aylmer treated her well, while her parents were critical and cruel.

In the summer of 1553 people close to Edward VI realized that he was dying. Edward decided to disinherit his two sisters, Mary* and Elizabeth,* in favor of Lady Jane Grey. The idea for this change in the succession may well have been that of John Dudley, duke of Northumberland, since that spring Jane's parents had forced her, over her vehement objections, to marry Northumberland's youngest son, Guilford. When Edward died in July, Northumberland kept his death secret for two days in hopes of securing Mary and Elizabeth. Both sisters managed to elude capture, and Northumberland was forced to proclaim Jane as queen while the dead king's sisters were still at large. The country rallied behind Mary as the legitimate heir, and only nine days after Jane was proclaimed queen, Mary became England's legitimate ruler. On 14 November 1553 Jane was arraigned for treason with her husband, and both were sentenced to die. Mary, however, wishing to spare her cousin, suspended the sentences while she kept them both, separately, in the Tower. In the Tower during the last few months of her life, Jane produced most of the slender body of writing for which she is known: a letter to someone fallen from the faith (probably her first tutor, Harding), a prayer, letters to her father and sister Catherine when she knew she was condemned to die, and her speech from the scaffold.

At the beginning of 1554 her father joined Thomas Wyatt in rebelling against Mary's proposed marriage to Philip of Spain.* While Wyatt was interested in proposing Elizabeth as an alternate queen, Jane's father again proclaimed his daughter. Mary was able to stifle the rebellion and agreed that for the safety of her realm the death sentence on Jane and her husband Guilford must be carried out.

Mary still hoped that Jane might be converted to the Catholic faith and arranged for her confessor, Dr. Feckenham, to see Jane. In an attempt to convert Jane, Feckenham persuaded her to publicly debate matters of doctrine inside the Tower. Though neither convinced the other, both were eloquent, and Jane ended the debate with an appreciation of Feckenham's kindness to her. She then in earnest prepared to die and the night before her execution wrote letters to her sister Katherine and her father, who was also soon to be executed. Jane was beheaded on 12 February 1554. To the last moments of her life Lady Jane Grey stayed true to her Protestant ideals. Her youth and courage impressed the witnesses, a number of whom wrote movingly about her execution.

Bibliography

C. Levin, "Lady Jane Grey: Protestant Queen and Martyr," in *Silent But for the Word: Tudor Women as Patrons, Translators, and Writers of Religious Works*, ed. M. Hannay, 1985.
A. Plowden, *Lady Jane Grey and the House of Suffolk*, 1986.

Carole Levin

GRÜNEWALD (MATHIAS GOTHART NEITHART) (c. 1475–1528)

The identity of the painter known as Grünewald was for many years a mystery. Even the name Grünewald by which we know him today is incorrect, the result of an attempt by Joachim von Sandrart, in his *Teutsche Academie* of 1672, to discover his identity. His fame today rests largely on a single work, the great Isenheim altarpiece painted for the Antonite monks at Isenheim in Alsace between 1512 and 1516. It was only in the nineteenth century, when the Isenheim altarpiece was first shown to the public, that interest in the painter grew and his probable identity was revealed. His name was not Grünewald, but Mathias Gothart Neithart, and he was born in Würzburg around 1475. He died in Halle in 1528.

The altarpiece is a complex work of art, including not only the triple wings of nine panels with a predella, painted by Grünewald, but also a carved interior shrine by the sculptor Nicolas Hagenau of Strasbourg. Grünewald's contribution was the series of wings that unfold to expose this central shrine. The wings are a painterly masterpiece, a magical burst of color and form, their inspiration probably mystical in nature, for Grünewald was known to have been a deeply religious man. The altarpiece, which was placed in the monastery hospital, had a very special function—to give hope to the sick.

The Antonite monks specialized in treating skin diseases, such as ergotism and the plague, and the plague saints St. Anthony and St. Sebastian, intercessors for the sick, are shown on both the exterior and the interior of the altarpiece. They flank the crucified Christ on the exterior, a terrible figure covered with skin blemishes, blood, and wounds; in the inner set of wings, Christ is seen ascending to heaven in a burst of light, his skin luminous and clear, giving hope to the sick that they too might be cured of their disfiguring diseases, if not in this world, then in the next.

Grünewald worked for several patrons, including the powerful archbishop of Mainz, Albrecht of Brandenburg. Sandrart mentions three altar panels painted for the Mainz Cathedral; according to him, all were lost in a shipwreck when they were being taken to Sweden in the mid-1600s. Grünewald collaborated with Albrecht Dürer* on the Heller altarpiece, supplying the grisaille wing panels. Unlike Dürer, he did not work in the print medium, though his surviving black chalk drawings are much admired. He was also recorded as holding civic engineering and hydraulic jobs in Mainz, designing city fountains and even engaging in paint and soap manufacture.

Unfortunately, Grünewald fell on hard times during the period of the Peasants' Revolt of 1525. Sympathizing with the rebels and the Protestant cause, he left the service of Albrecht of Brandenburg, who, though tolerant of the Reformers at first, would become an implacable opponent of Martin Luther* and his supporters. Even though Albrecht eventually pardoned Grünewald, he never returned to the archbishop's service, leaving Mainz for Frankfurt and then Halle, where he died in 1528.

Bibliography

A. Hayum, *The Isenheim Altarpiece: God's Medicine and the Painter's Vision*, 1989.
W. Stechow, ed., *Northern Renaissance Art, 1400–1600: Sources and Documents*, 1966.

Rosemary Poole

GUARINI, GIOVANNI BATTISTA (1538–1612)

Giovanni Battista Guarini, a native of Ferrara, the Renaissance Italian city-state ruled by the influential Este family, served in the court of Duke Alfonso II as both a diplomatic functionary and a court poet. Guarini's primary literary contribution is the highly acclaimed pastoral drama *Il pastor fido*.

Descended from a long line of influential humanists—among them Guarino da Verona (1374–1460), a prominent founder of Renaissance letters—Giovanni Battista Guarini was born at Ferrara, Italy, in 1538. In his youth, Guarini studied at Pisa and Padua. When he returned to Ferrara, he became a professor of eloquence and enjoyed the reputation of a poet among his friends and family. Through his marriage with Taddea di Niccolò Bendidio, Guarini affiliated himself with a noble Ferrarese family.

Guarini earned Annibal Caro's* praise for his early sonnets. Alfonso's court poet, Torquato Tasso,* the author of the pastoral drama *Aminta* (1573) and the poem *Gerusalemme liberata* (Jerusalem Delivered, 1581), befriended the young Guarini before a quarrel over a lady ended their friendship.

Disdaining a life devoted only to literary pursuits, Guarini actively sought the advantages associated with the life of a courtier. Alfonso II, the duke of Ferrara, employed Guarini on numerous diplomatic missions: to Venice, to congratulate the new doge; to Rome, to pay homage to the new pope, Gregory XIII; and to Poland, in support of Henri of Valois's election to the crown. After Henri of Valois's accession to the throne of France, Alfonso II dispatched Guarini to negotiate what turned out to be his unsuccessful election to the Polish throne. Alfonso acknowledged Guarini's diplomatic endeavors on his behalf by knighting him.

After Tasso's disgrace, Guarini served as the poetic authority at the Este court, although, writing in 1595, he claimed that "poetry has been my pastime, never my profession." Written in emulation of Tasso's *Aminta*, Guarini's pastoral drama *Il pastor fido* was composed sometime between 1580 and 1585 and was published in 1590, and its popularity and controversial nature assured its wide publication. In its defense, Guarini insisted that hints in Aristotle's *Poetics* authorized his decision to mix genres in the construction of his pastoral tragicomedy. *Il pastor fido*'s strengths included a strong plot, realistic characters, humor, and candid sensuality. *Il pastor fido*, the principal monument of Guarini's poetic genius, exerted tremendous influence on his contemporaries in Italy, France, and England. Numerous editions and translations of the play appeared in Guarini's lifetime.

Bibliography

G. Grillo, *Poets at the Court of Ferrara: Ariosto, Tasso, and Guarini*, 1943.
B. Weinberg, *A History of Literary Criticism in the Italian Renaissance*, 2 vols., 1961.

Debbie Barrett-Graves

GUICCIARDINI, FRANCESCO (1483–1540)

Francesco Guicciardini, a Florentine aristocrat and statesman, served as ambassador and administrator for the Medici for many years; from his privileged vantage point within diplomatic circles, he also wrote highly perceptive analyses of Florentine and Italian history. Born in the benevolent reign of Lorenzo de' Medici, Guicciardini in his youth saw the expulsion of the Medici from Florence, as well as the short-lived populist regime of the fiery preacher Girolamo Savonarola that ended with the friar's death in 1498.

After receiving his law degree, Guicciardini made an ambitious marriage that placed him firmly in the ranks of the highest aristocracy of Florence. He first received communal honor at age twenty-eight as ambassador to the king of Aragon. Recalled from Spain in 1514, he then served the Medici in their capacity as the restored rulers of Florence and was in the employ of the Medici popes Leo X* and Clement VII. By 1527, however, his career had suffered on both fronts: the league he had helped to negotiate against the holy Roman emperor had failed, and Rome had been sacked mercilessly by German mercenaries; and the Florentines had risen in revolt, had expelled the Medici, and had established a new republic. In voluntary retirement at first, Guicciardini was eventually labeled a rebel and an enemy of the new republic during its brief life.

When a coalition of imperial and papal forces restored Medici rule in Florence, Guicciardini too reentered the city, where he proceeded to prosecute leaders of the rebellious republic vigorously. He left the city briefly to serve as papal governor of Bologna, then returned to Florence as close advisor to the Medici duke Alexander. When the duke was assassinated in 1537, Guicciardini saw that he had no further part to play in Florentine politics and retired to compose his masterpiece, *Storia d' Italia* (The History of Italy).

Guicciardini's own life illustrated the limited choices and upsets of fortune available even to the wealthy and well-connected. So too do his many writings. As a youth he had already composed his memoirs and his first draft of the *Storie fiorentine* (History of Florence). In his first ambassadorial post in Spain, Guicciardini began his *Ricordi politici e civili* (Political Maxims), terse and cryptic statements about human nature and the mutability of circumstances. In these and his later *Storia d' Italia*, Guicciardini noted the influence of particular individuals as well as that of coalitions and larger interests. Though allied with the Medici politically, Guicciardini preferred republican government, but one in which learned aristocrats like himself played a prominent part. Ultimately shut out of real political life, he managed nonetheless in his trenchant writings to indicate what fundamentally had caused the ruin of Florentine republicanism and of Italian independence: the lack of wise rulers, or, at the very least, wise advisors like Francesco Guiccardini to whom these rulers listened.

Bibliography

F. Gilbert, *Machiavelli and Guicciardini: Politics and History in Sixteenth-Century Florence*, 1965.

M. Phillips, *Francesco Guicciardini: The Historian's Craft*, 1977.

Alison Williams Lewin

H

HAKLUYT, RICHARD (1552–1616)

Richard Hakluyt was an English author and geographer who compiled and wrote *The Principal Navigations, Voyages, and Discoveries of the English Nation*, which contains most of what we know about early English voyages to North America. Born in London, Hakluyt was the second child of Margery and Richard Hakluyt. He was educated at Westminster School and Christ Church, Oxford, and took his master of arts degree in 1577. His interest in geography and travel was sparked when, as a young student, he visited his cousin (another Richard Hakluyt), who was a lawyer in the Middle Temple. The elder Hakluyt had connections among merchants, geographers, and explorers, as well as books with maps and travel tales, which caught the young Hakluyt's imagination. After taking his master of arts, he began reading every voyage narrative he could acquire and developed his linguistic skills so that he could read Greek, Latin, Italian, Spanish, Portuguese, and French narratives as well as those in English. Hakluyt was ordained in 1580, and though he was always conscientious in his religious duties, his passion continued to be geography and travel.

In 1582 he published the *Divers Voyages Touching the Discoverie of America*, a collection of documents in support of the priority of England's claim to America, including suggestions to Englishmen who might want to further such claims. Hakluyt spent the years 1583–88 between Paris and London, consulting with sea captains, merchants, sailors, and exiles who had been to America and reading their manuscript accounts. Accusations abroad of English laziness toward colonization combined with an impressive European competition in acquiring knowledge of the New World led Hakluyt to beg for the establishment of a lectureship in navigation in London. His *Discourse on Western Planting*, a secret memorandum finished in 1584 but not published until 1877, was written at Sir Walter Raleigh's* request and was given to the queen to support Raleigh's Virginia plans. Before leaving Paris, Hakluyt also edited an edition of Peter

Martyr d'Anghiera's* *De orbe novo* (On the New World, 1587) in order to inform his countrymen of the Spanish experiences in the New World.

War broke out with Spain in 1588, and on his return to London, Hakluyt began the *Principall Navigations*, which appeared in 1589 as a stout folio produced by the queen's printer. In 1590 Hakluyt was appointed rector at Wetheringsett, Suffolk, and he married Duglesse Cavendish (a relative of Thomas Cavendish, the circumnavigator), who bore him his only child, Edmond, in 1593 and died four years later. The greatly enlarged second edition of the *Principall Navigations* appeared in three volumes between 1598 and 1600. After being granted the prebend at Westminster, Hakluyt began consulting for the East India Company and other colonial interests. He married Frances Smithe in 1604, became a rector of Gedney, Lincolnshire, in 1612, and died in London the same year as William Shakespeare,* in 1616.

Hakluyt's influence on Elizabethan colonial efforts and on the much later nineteenth-century imperial agenda of England cannot be overstated. His associations with figures such as Sir Humphrey Gilbert and Martin Frobisher (seekers of a passage to the east), Abraham Ortelius and Gerardus Mercator* (famous mapmakers), and Lord Burghley, Sir Francis Walsingham, and Sir Robert Cecil (powerful political figures in England), as well as the influence of his *Principall Navigations*, make Hakluyt the most important English promoter of geographical knowledge of his time.

Bibliography

G. Parks, *Richard Hakluyt and the English Voyages*, 1928.
D. Quinn, ed., *The Hakluyt Handbook*, 2 vols., 1974.

Richard J. Ring

HALL, JOSEPH (1574–1656)

Joseph Hall, an English bishop and controversialist during the reigns of James I* and Charles I, was an opponent of John Milton, a moral philosopher, and a churchman of some importance. Born in Leicestershire, Hall was educated at the staunchly Puritan Ashby School and later at Emmanuel College of Cambridge, where his satires attracted attention. Feeling called to the ministry, he accepted Sir Robert Drury's offer of Hawstead's rectory in Suffolk in 1601. He continued to write satires, including the Latin *Mundus alter et idem* (c. 1605), which would influence *Gulliver's Travels*, and began a lifetime of meditative writing with *Meditations and Vows Divine and Moral* (1605). In 1608 he left Hawstead to become one of Prince Henry's domestic chaplains and curate of Waltham Holy Cross, Essex. In 1616 Hall was named dean of Worcester; in 1617 he went with King James to Scotland; and in 1618 he served the king at the Synod of Dort.

In 1627 Hall was consecrated bishop of Exeter. To assuage Archbishop William Laud, who suspected him of Puritan sympathies, Hall wrote against Puritan attacks on church government in *Episcopacy by Divine Right* (published in

1640). In 1641 Hall engaged the Puritans in a battle of pamphlets and became an opponent of John Milton. In this conflict the moderate Hall, who underestimated the Puritans' passion, urged compromise concerning church government and liturgy in the interest of peace.

In 1641 Hall was translated bishop of Norwich, but before entering his new see he was imprisoned in the Tower of London with the other bishops for four months. Stripped of most revenues in 1643, Hall was eventually ejected from his palace. He retired to Higham, where he died on 8 September 1656.

In his own time Hall was known for his satires and his Christian adaptation of Stoicism in such works as *Heaven upon Earth* (1606). In the twentieth century scholars became increasingly interested in his moral and meditative work.

Bibliography

F. L. Huntley, *Bishop Joseph Hall, 1574–1656: A Biographical and Critical Study*, 1979.

Kevin Lindberg

HARINGTON, SIR JOHN (1560–1612)

Godson of Queen Elizabeth I,* John Harington was granted opportunities both at court and on the battlefields of Ireland. However, his literary efforts brought him his greatest success as a poet, translator, and chronicler of his age.

Harington, often called Harington of Kelston, was the firstborn son of John Harington of Chestnut and Stepney and Isabella Markham, gentlewoman to Elizabeth I. The Haringtons were a noble family whose descendants obtained significant wealth for the capture of Henry VI at the Battle of Hexham (1464). Harington enjoyed a life of privilege. He attended Eton (1570) and King's College, Cambridge (1575). Harington received the master of arts degree in 1581 and went to Lincoln's Inn to pursue law. These studies were cut short by the death of Harington's father in 1582; shortly thereafter Harington took over his father's estate at Kelston Manor at Somersetshire. Harington married Mary Rogers, or "Mall," as he affectionately called her, in 1583. The couple's first child was born in 1589. Rogers gave birth to a total of eleven children. It was shortly after his marriage that Harington began spending more time at court as courtier to Elizabeth I. His court activities came to a halt in 1588 when Elizabeth I punished Harington for translating some bawdy passages from Ludovico Ariosto's* *Orlando Furioso*. When Elizabeth got hold of the material, she sent for Harington and ordered him to return to the country and not come before her again until he produced a complete version of the poem, which he did.

Harington's *Orlando Furioso* brought him tremendous respect from his contemporaries. The translation was published in 1591 and became an immediate success. His literary activities continued throughout the 1590s with his satirical epigrams, which were circulated at court. Many of these epigrams were written to amuse his wife and jest at his mother-in-law's expense. The epigrams were not published in his lifetime, but Harington did publish a pamphlet titled *A New Discourse of a Stale Subject, Called the Metamorphosis of Ajax* in 1596. This work, on the indelicate subject of domestic sanitation, had a stormy reception; the scandal surrounding this publication resulted in another court hiatus for Harington.

Harington was pardoned by Elizabeth I in 1599 when he was invited to join the earl of Essex in his mission to stifle the earl of Tyrone's rebellion in Ireland. During this eventful campaign, Essex used his power as viceroy to knight Harington and numerous others. When Essex returned to England later that year, he found the queen displeased with his activities both on and off the fields. Harington, as a member of Essex's mission, was also treated coldly upon return. Elizabeth I requested a visit from Harington in 1602, but he never again enjoyed security at court.

Upon James I's* ascension in 1603, Harington sought favor from the new king and greeted his arrival to the throne with a celebratory elegy. Harington's situation seemed more promising toward the end of that year when the king invited him to court. Harington began sending gifts to Prince Henry, including Harington's own translation of *The Aeneid*, book 6 (1604), and a copy of his epigrams (1605). Though Harington petitioned for various posts, he never obtained a position. Harington died in November 1612, survived by his wife and seven of his children.

By Harington's own admission, he played the fool too often, which thwarted his advancement at court. In addition to his fine translation of *Orlando Furioso*, he authored a collection of writings featuring humorous and candid views of domestic life and critiques of court. The opinions expressed in his letters reveal popular attitudes toward manuscript and print cultures and the literature of his day. He applauded Philip Sidney's* *Astrophel and Stella, Arcadia*, and *Defense of Poesy*, along with Edmund Spenser's* *Fairie Queene*.

Bibliography

D. H. Craig, *Sir John Harington*, 1985.
J. Harington, *The Letters and Epigrams of Sir John Harington*, ed. N. E. McClure, 1930.

Michele Osherow

HARRISON, WILLIAM (1534–1593)

William Harrison was a historian and topographer known for his *Description of Britaine* in Raphael Holinshed's* *Chronicles* (1577, 1587), but he is also important for his recently rediscovered manuscript, "Great English Chronology." Born in London on 18 April 1534, Harrison attended St. Paul's and Westminster schools, receiving the bachelor of arts (1556) and master of arts (1560) from Christ Church, Oxford, and the bachelor of divinity from Cambridge (1571). He took Catholic orders in 1556 but, influenced by the Oxford Martyrs, rejected popery before Elizabeth I's* accession in 1558. Harrison became chaplain to William Brooke, Lord Cobham, who made him rector of Radwinter, Essex (1559–93). He also held St. Olave, Silver Street, London (1567–71), Wimbish, Essex (1571–81), and St. Thomas Apostle, London (1583–87), and was a canon of Windsor (1586–93). He died still working on his "Chronology" and left a manuscript dated 1587 on weights and measures.

The *Description* includes his own work on England and his English translation of John Bellenden's Scottish translation of Hector Boece's description of Scotland in *Historia gentis Scotorum a prima gentis origine* (1527). It is a lively account of topography, people, buildings, customs, institutions, products, and so on. Harrison attributed greater significance to his "Chronology," a world history from creation to 1593. Central to his view is the ongoing conflict between the True Church and the satanic Church of Cain (i.e., Catholicism). Past, present, and future form a continuum revealing God's plan, which Harrison sought to discern through an accurate chronology. A moderate Puritan, he believed the struggle against popery more urgent than further Anglican reform, doubted the state's ability to accomplish the latter, thought the apocalypse imminent, and emphasized the scriptural covenant line as a guide to behavior. Though he rejected Hermeticism, he remained unscientific, believing that reason applies only when nature is explained by Scripture.

Bibliography

F. J. Levy, *Tudor Historical Thought*, 1967.
G. J. R. Parry, *A Protestant Vision: William Harrison and the Reformation of Elizabethan England*, 1987.

William B. Robison

HARVEY, GABRIEL (1550–1631)

Gabriel Harvey was an English writer and scholar, an intimate friend of Edmund Spenser,* and a vocal critic noted for his war of words with Thomas Nashe.* The eldest child of John and Alice Harvey, Gabriel Harvey was born in Essex, England. His father was a successful master ropemaker and was able to send Harvey to grammar school and then to Christ's College, Cambridge. After receiving his bachelor of arts in 1570, Harvey was elected a fellow of Pembroke Hall, where he met the young Edmund Spenser. Harvey was a popular teacher at Pembroke and became famous for his talent at disputation as well as his devotion to the pedagogy of Petrus Ramus.* Socially awkward and intellectually independent, Harvey became a fellow of Trinity Hall, Cambridge, in 1578, but failed to be elected master there and was prevented from pursuing a doctorate. He completed his doctorate in civil law at Oxford University in 1585.

In 1579 the publication of Spenser's *Shepheardes Calender* afforded Harvey some renown as the character Hobbinal, Colin Clout's (Spenser's) close friend. In 1580 Harvey and Spenser published a series of letters in which Harvey satirized certain Cambridge professors; this marked the beginning of a long and damaging quarrel with a group of London writers including John Lyly,* Robert Greene,* Thomas Nashe, and (marginally) Christopher Marlowe.* The publication of his brother Richard's discourse on astrology in 1583 and subsequent attacks on it drew Harvey into further controversy. Eventually Harvey found himself in an ever-widening loop of criticism and countercriticism with other authors, consisting of personal, professional, and philosophical attacks. These became so virulent and abusive that in 1599 Archbishop John Whitgift and Bishop Richard Bancroft, the official licensers of the press, ordered the confiscation and destruction of the works of Harvey, Nashe, and other authors of satire. After a final conflict with his sister Mary in 1608 regarding nonpayment of monies to her from their father's estate, Harvey lived the last twenty years of his life in relatively quiet retirement and obscurity.

Bibliography

V. Stern, *Gabriel Harvey: His Life, Marginalia, and Library*, 1979.

Richard J. Ring

HEEMSKERCK, MAERTEN (or MAARTEN) VAN (1498–1574)

Maerten van Heemskerck was born to be a farmer in the village from which he takes his surname. His work includes painted portraits, religious altarpieces, and mythological scenes, as well as graphic works, often with allegorical meaning inspired by Dutch humanists such as Dirck Coornhert* and Hadrianus Junius. Heemskerck's monumental style, focusing on human anatomy and modeled on that of Michelangelo* and Giulio Romano,* influenced the development of Mannerism in the northern Netherlands.

Heemskerck initially trained in Delft and then between 1527 and 1532 with Jan van Scorel,* a well-known Haarlem artist who introduced his Italian style to Heemskerck. Before leaving for Rome in 1532, Heemskerck painted one of his most masterful works, *St. Luke Painting the Virgin*, for the Haarlem Painters' Guild Chapel in St. Bavo. Heemskerck's depiction of this favorite subject of artists is unusual in its low viewpoint, sharp, unnatural light, and humanistic treatment of the subject. The painting includes a classical muse that some scholars consider a self-portrait peering over the artist's shoulder, a robust torch-bearing angel resembling an antique Victory figure, and a Michelangelesque Madonna and Child.

During his Rome sojourn, from 1532 to 1536/37, Heemskerck sketched antique statuary and architectural ruins and works of Raphael* and Michelangelo and painted several mythological scenes on canvas. He also participated in decorating the triumphal arch for Charles V's* joyous entry into Rome on 5 April 1536 and met the Italian art historian Giorgio Vasari,* who mentions Heemskerck in his *Lives of the Artists*.

Returning to Haarlem, Heemskerck joined the painters' guild of St. Luke, becoming dean in 1554. As well as painting numerous altarpieces, Heemskerck continued to paint and design prints of mythological scenes with humanist themes. An accomplished portrait painter, in a 1553 self-portrait he depicted himself in a noble three-quarters bust view before the ruins of the Roman Colosseum.

Unfortunately, Heemskerck lived to see some of his religious work destroyed by iconoclasts, zealots who considered depictions of sacred figures anathema to their beliefs. Other works were lost when the Spanish besieged Haarlem in 1572 and took some of Heemskerck's paintings to Spain.

Heemskerck's fame spread through his numerous engravings of religious, mythological, historical, and allegorical subjects, some with Latin verses composed by the humanist Hadrianus Junius. Rembrandt owned a number of them, and much of seventeenth-century Dutch iconography and allegory in art is indebted to Heemskerck's work.

Bibliography

I. M. Veldman, *Maarten van Heemskerck and Dutch Humanism in the Sixteenth Century*, 1977.

Susan H. Jenson

HENRY VIII (1491–1547)

Henry VIII, the king of England whose policies established the independence of the Church of England, was born on 28 June 1491, the second son of his predecessor Henry VII and Elizabeth of York. Henry became heir to the throne upon the death of his brother Arthur in 1502, ascended the throne in 1509, and soon married Arthur's widow, Catherine of Aragon, daughter of Ferdinand and Isabella of Spain. Henry is best known in popular history for his six marriages, and his marriage trials did affect the constitutional and religious history of England.

Royal patronage of Renaissance culture combined with traditional political policies to characterize the first decades of Henry's reign. Allied with Spain, Henry fought a war with France and Scotland in 1512–14, gaining minor victories. Catherine had several pregnancies, but only one surviving child, a girl named Mary,* born on 18 February 1516. In 1521, against the backdrop of the Lutheran controversies, Henry published a defense of traditional Catholic teachings entitled *Assertio septem sacramentorum* and was rewarded by the pope with the title Fidei Defensor (defender of the faith). The lack of surviving children in Henry's marriage, specifically a male heir, began to bother the king's conscience sometime around 1525. By 1527 Henry was convinced that the death of his children was a judgment by God on an illicit union. Henry sought to have his marriage to Catherine annulled on the grounds of her prior marriage to his brother Arthur. The annulment proved elusive, as the papacy delayed in making a pronouncement. Early in 1533 Henry secretly married his second wife, Anne Boleyn, prior to the newly appointed archbishop of Canterbury, Thomas Cranmer,* annulling the first royal marriage in April. Anne gave birth to a daughter named Elizabeth* on 7 September 1533.

Between 1533 and 1536 parliamentary legislation promoted by royal advisor Thomas Cromwell severed the traditional relationship between the Church of England and the See of Rome, proclaiming "the King's Highness to be Supreme Head of the Church of England." Having given Catholic Europe a reason to unite against his realm, Henry began to dissolve the monasteries, using much of their wealth for military preparations. His last years saw a government confiscation of chantry endowments. However, despite these actions, the English church maintained a Catholic theology and liturgy.

In 1536 Anne Boleyn was executed for adultery, incest, treason, and witchcraft. Henry went on to have four subsequent wives; the third, Jane Seymour, produced a male heir named Edward on 12 October 1537. However, none of the king's subsequent marriages had the constitutional impact of his first two. Henry fought a further war with France and Scotland in the 1540s. Henry's will named his three surviving children as heirs to the throne, giving English political and religious history its main characteristic in the later sixteenth century. Henry died on 28 January 1547 and is buried in St. George's Chapel at Windsor Castle.

Bibliography

J. J. Scarisbrick, *Henry VIII*, 1968.
L. B. Smith, *Henry VIII: The Mask of Royalty*, 1971.

Gary G. Gibbs

HENSLOWE, PHILIP (c. 1550–1616)

Builder of theaters and financier of companies, Philip Henslowe was a theater impresario whose "diary" or account book kept for the Lord Admiral's Men is an indispensable resource about playhouses, playwrighting, and theatrical life of the period. Son of the master of the game in Ashdown Forest, Sussex, Henslowe was apprenticed to a dyer of cloth and later married his master's widow. His marriage gave him enough money to finance acting companies, delve into moneylending and pawnbroking, and build theaters such as the Rose (1587) and Fortune (1600). In 1594 the Lord Admiral's Men, later the Queen's Men, took up residence at the Rose, led by actor Edward Alleyn, with Philip Henslowe, Alleyn's father-in-law, as the company's manager. Henslowe already owned a large number of plays, especially those of Christopher Marlowe,* which benefited the company. Under James I,* Henslowe became royal bear-master and in 1614 built the Hope, a multipurpose playhouse and baiting house. He died in 1616.

In addition to owning theaters and financing companies, Henslowe's greatest legacy was his recordkeeping. Referred to as his "diary," Henslowe's accounts for the Lord Admiral's Men from 1592 until his death in 1616 serve as a primary source documenting theatrical life of the Elizabethan period. Primarily financial, the diary includes daily entries for plays performed, box-office accounts, Henslowe's licensing fees for the playhouse, loans to the players to buy costumes, payments to writers, and Henslowe's system of fines for players who came to rehearsal late or drunk. Although more than half of the plays named in his records have vanished, they reveal that Henslowe processed over three hundred plays between 1592 and 1600, his company performed as many as thirty-five plays in a year, and up to forty different plays were performed in London to satisfy theatergoers. Except for William Shakespeare,* most of the dramatists of the period sold work to Henslowe. Payments to his writers suggest that plays were written in six or seven weeks and were put on in an even shorter time; from acquisition to performance could be as little as three weeks.

Bibliography

P. Henslowe, *Henslowe's Diary*, ed. R. A. Foakes and R. T. Rickert, 1961.

Megan S. Lloyd

HERRERA, FERNANDO DE (1534–1597)

Fernando de Herrera, a Spanish poet and precursor of Luis de Góngora's* pure poetry, or *culteranismo*, also established himself as the father of Spanish literary criticism with his *Anotaciones* of Garcilaso de la Vega's* works. Born in Seville of a family considered socially marginal, Herrera seldom left his city of birth. He was basically self-educated, for example, attending a *tertulia* (an artistic salon) for lack of a local university. It was there that he encountered writers, artists, humanists, and editors. Around 1599 he supposedly met and fell in love (platonically) with the countess of Gelves, who subsequently became the principal object of his poetry. In any case, he wrote little poetry after her death in 1581, and the limited prose he wrote during that period was mostly lost. The priest's minor orders he took provided him with the time to dedicate his life to study and writing.

Herrera's contributions to Western culture hinge partially on his poetry and its anticipation of *culteranismo*, but more on the theoretical norms he established with his *Anotaciones* to his 1580 edition of the *Obras de Garcilaso de la Vega*. His poetry has often been defined as mannerist and erudite. It strives for perfection of form and sound, employs many adjectives and much rhetoric, uses a cultured vocabulary, and appears unconcerned with expression of sincere feeling. His best-known poetry is his Neoplatonic love lyrics, in which Leonor embodies beauty and perfection and leads her love spiritually upward. Herrera also composed patriotic poems such as "La canción por la victoria de Lepanto" and "La canción por la pérdida del rey Don Sebastián." He utilized a great variety of meters, particularly those Italianate forms adapted previously by Juan Boscán and Garcilaso. The only edition of his poetry that Herrera himself published was his *Algunas obras* (1582). In 1619 a more inclusive posthumous edition appeared.

His 1580 *Anotaciones* of Garcilaso's poetry explains the theory behind Herrera's own poetry. This commentary also helps legitimize the use of the vulgar language for aristocratic literature and raise Spanish poetry to the level of Italian poetry. These commentaries codified Garcilaso's poetry and defended his use of a variety of models by emphasizing Garcilaso's triumph over his predecessors. At the same time, Herrera used his commentaries subversively in order to revise Garcilaso's place in the literary canon. For example, he attacked the myths of the courtier-poet, highlighting the need for men exclusively dedicated to letters. In general, he presented Garcilaso as the most recent and quite worthy but not last figure in the tradition, thereby leaving open room for successors, perhaps including himself.

Bibliography

A. Bianchini, "Herrera: Questions and Contradictions in the Critical Tradition," *Caliope* 1 (1995): 58–71.
I. Navarette, "Decentering Garellaso: Herrera's Attack on the Canon," *PMLA* 106 (1991):
Lydia Bernstein

HEYWOOD, JOHN (c. 1497–1578)

John Heywood was an epigrammatist, dramatist, poet, and writer of interludes, music, and entertainments for the early Tudors. Nothing is known about Heywood's birth or parentage, but he was probably born in London around 1497. His appointments at court ranged from a singer to a "player of the virginals" to a life appointment as steward to the royal chamber. Part of Thomas More's* circle, Heywood married Eliza Rastell, More's niece. Heywood's Catholic sensibilities led him to participate in a plot to overthrow Archbishop Thomas Cranmer,* for which he was imprisoned in 1543. In 1544 Heywood recanted. Heywood was a favorite of Mary I*; however, with the accession of Elizabeth I, in 1558, he resigned his position as steward. By 1564 Heywood and his son Ellis, English Catholics, left England for France. Thomas Wilson visited Heywood in 1574 and brought forgiveness from Queen Elizabeth* and permission to return to England. Heywood never returned. By 1576 he was living in Antwerp. More religious upheaval removed Heywood to Louvain, where he died sometime in 1578.

Deemed a mad, merry wit, Heywood experimented with comic subplots and current events and ideas and reflected real people in his work. His interludes include *The Four P's* (c. 1545), a farce about a Palmer, Pardoner, and Pothecary, who ask a Pedler to judge which of them is most important, and *The Play of the Weather* (1533), which considers the problem of the ruler of state through the guise of Jupiter, who asks his subjects to petition him to establish a certain weather pattern. Other works include *A Dialogue Conteinying the Nomber in Effect of All the Proverbes in the Englishe Tongue* (1546) and a long allegorical poem, *The Spider and the Flie*, infused with mock-heroic wit, published in 1556 but begun twenty years earlier. Heywood himself identifies Queen Mary as the Maid in the poem who solves problems between the Protestant spiders and Catholic flies by squashing the spiders and removing their webs.

Bibliography

R. C. Johnson, *John Heywood*, 1970.
Megan S. Lloyd

HEYWOOD, THOMAS (c. 1575–1641)

The most prolific and versatile writer of the age of William Shakespeare,* Thomas Heywood, according to his own boast, had a hand or at least a "main finger" in more than two hundred plays. He composed in most of the major genres of the era, from topical pamphlets and epic verse to prose history.

Born in Lincolnshire, Heywood spent some time at Cambridge before going to seek his fortune in London. Throughout his life, he was involved with the theater as an actor, shareholder, and dramatist. Heywood wrote for the whole gamut of London theaters, from the riotous down-market Red Bull through the intimate clublike theater within St. Paul's Cathedral to the court stage. He also composed annual pageants for London's lord mayor.

Heywood's belief in the dignity of actors and acting found expression in his *Apology for Actors* (1612), the first English defense of the stage. He is best known for his domestic dramas (*A Woman Killed with Kindness*, 1607), adventure romances (*The Fair Maid of the West*, 1631), and comedies of low life (*The Wise-Woman of Hogsdon*, 1638). The strong female characters in these plays anticipate the appeal of the heroines of Henrik Ibsen and Bertolt Brecht. Several of his prose works were also devoted to strong historical women: *Gunaikeion* (1624), reprinted after his death as *The General History of Women* (1657), *The Exemplary Lives and Memorable Acts of Nine the Most Worthy Women of the World* (1640), and a biography of the early years of Queen Elizabeth* (1631).

Contemporary life was not Heywood's sole interest. He started his career with chronicle-history plays and finished it with a dramatic reproduction of Greek mythology in *The Four Ages* (1611–32). His nondramatic works likewise ranged from the didactic poem *The Hierarchy of the Blessed Angels* (1635) to translations of Latin writers from antiquity and the Renaissance.

Bibliography

B. Baines, *Thomas Heywood*, 1984.

Kirilka Stavreva

HILLIARD, NICHOLAS (c. 1547–1619)

Nicholas Hilliard, the son of an Exeter goldsmith, was the first native-born English painter to achieve prominence in the field of portraiture, and in particular the portrait miniature. Hilliard became painter and goldsmith to Queen Elizabeth I* in 1572, immortalizing the queen and her courtiers in exquisite, delicately painted portrait miniatures, usually in a jewelled setting of his own making.

Hilliard's father Richard had supported the Protestant cause in a Catholic uprising against the Reformed prayer book during the reign of Edward VI. In 1553, when the Catholic sovereign Mary I* came to the throne, and fearing retribution for his Protestant sympathies, Richard Hilliard sent his son out of England in the household of staunch Protestant supporter John Bodley, whose eldest son Thomas founded the Bodleian Library at Oxford. Bodley and a group of reformers went first to Wesel in Germany and then for two years to Frankfurt, where they joined John Knox* and other Protestant refugees. Bodley's group moved on to Geneva in 1557 and finally returned to England in 1559. In Calvinist Geneva, Nicholas Hilliard not only met members of the English aristocracy who had fled Mary I's tyranny, contacts that would benefit him later in life, but also Huguenot refugees from Paris and Rouen, among whom was the goldsmith Pierre Oliver, whose son Isaac Oliver* would become Hilliard's most gifted pupil.

Hilliard's art, known to his contemporaries as "limning," first developed in the Netherlands, growing out of religious-manuscript illumination. The first miniature painters at the English court, Levina Teerlinc* and Luke Hornebolte,* were from Flanders. Hans Holbein,* who had learned the craft from Hornebolte, was from Augsburg, and it was his work especially that was to be the main source of inspiration to Hilliard, who wrote in his *Arte of Limning* that Holbein's "manner of limning I have ever imitated."

The small size of portrait miniatures, seldom more than two inches in diameter and often oval in shape, made them highly desirable as gifts, particularly in a jewelled setting. Their expensive nature restricted their possession initially to the royal court and nobility. Hilliard may also have painted life-size portraits of Queen Elizabeth I, but his fame rests on his miniatures and on his book *Treatise Concerning the Arte of Limning* (1600). Among his miniatures, the elegant and courtly *Young Man among Roses* (c. 1598) evokes the Shakespearean sonnets of his time, expressing a lover's devotion: in this case, the lover may have been the earl of Essex, and the lady the queen herself.

Unlike his pupil Isaac Oliver, Hilliard did not use any chiaroscuro, relying instead on a purity of line. His backgrounds are usually of ultramarine blue, and skin colors are of great delicacy. He was highly inventive with his techniques, incorporating the use of gold and silver and often including inscriptions. Trained as a goldsmith, he made his own jewelled settings. Nicholas Hilliard brought the portrait miniature to its highest point in English art, a visual counterpart to the poetry of his contemporary, William Shakespeare.*

Bibliography

M. Edmond, *Hilliard and Oliver*, 1983.
N. Hilliard, "Treatise Concerning The Arte of Limning," intro. and notes by P. Norman, *Volume of the Walpole Society* 1 (1912): 1–54.

Rosemary Poole

HOBY, SIR THOMAS (1530–1566)

Traveler, diplomat, and Italianist, Sir Thomas Hoby translated into English early modern Europe's most important conduct book, *The Courtier* of Count Baldesar Castiglione.* Hoby was born into a prominent Herefordshire family in 1530 and at the age of fifteen matriculated at St. John's College, Cambridge. Though he did not take a degree, in his two years at Cambridge Hoby came into contact with some of the leading English humanists of the sixteenth century, including the Protestant reformers John Cheke and Roger Ascham.*

In 1547 Hoby set off for the Continent as an educational traveler, no doubt intending to follow in the steps of his half brother Sir Philip Hoby, an established diplomat. In France he stayed with the Protestant theologian Martin Bucer,* whose polemic against Bishop Stephen Gardiner Hoby later translated into English. Hoby then made his way to Italy, where he remained until 1550, traveling extensively and gaining fluency in the Italian language.

Two important literary endeavors came from his European sojourn: a record of his travels and his famous 1561 translation of Castiglione's *Il cortegiano*, which Hoby rendered as *The Courtyer of Count Baldessar Castilio, Divided into Foure Bookes*. His journal, *A Booke of the Travaile and Life of Me, Thomas Hoby*, which was not published until the twentieth century, documents many aspects of educational travel in the sixteenth century and is one of the best firsthand accounts of conditions in Italy during this period.

Hoby's translation of Castiglione's book was hugely influential in Renaissance England. The work went into five editions by the end of the Elizabethan period and inspired numerous imitations and adaptations well into the next two centuries. It became the central text in a decades- or even centuries-long cultural debate to define the grace, duty, and morality essential to the ideal courtier. Though Hoby was an able linguist, his translation does not always convey the grace, playfulness, and deliberate ambiguity of Castiglione's original. Nonetheless, scholars have tended to concur that he successfully anglicized a work and a social ideal that needed some degree of domestication in order to take root in England.

In the 1550s and 1560s Hoby continued to travel in various diplomatic capacities, and in March 1566 he was knighted in preparation for a mission to France. He died unexpectedly during that embassy, in Paris on 13 July 1566.

Bibliography

S. J. Masello, "Thomas Hoby: A Protestant Traveler to Circe's Court," *Cahiers Élisabéthains* 27 (1985): 67–81.

E. Powell, "Introduction," in *The Travels and Life of Sir Thomas Hoby, Kt. of Bisham Abbey, Written by Himself, 1547–1564*, Camden Miscellany 10, no. 2, 1902.

Thomas G. Olsen

HOLBEIN, HANS, THE YOUNGER (1497/98–1543)

Hans Holbein the Younger was born in Augsburg in 1497/98. His subsequent career, however, linked him more closely with Basel in Switzerland and, finally, London. Born some twenty-five years after the great Albrecht Dürer,* Holbein lived at a time of religious turmoil as well as artistic change, both of which affected his career. He became court painter to England's Henry VIII,* and his portraits of the king and his court created images that have ensured Holbein's fame.

Holbein was a member of a family of painters that included his father, Hans Holbein the Elder, his older brother Ambrosius, and the painter and printmaker Hans Burgkmair,* who, according to an early tradition, may have been his uncle.

Holbein's training began in his father's workshop, where he quickly showed his prodigious talent. In 1515 the Holbein brothers went to Basel, where they entered the workshop of a minor artist, Hans Herbst. For Hans Holbein, the move to Basel was to have far-reaching consequences, for the city was not only a center of printing and thus an important source of commissions for painters, but also a place of intellectual freedom, a center of humanism where the thinkers of the time met and discussed the need for reform in the church.

Desiderius Erasmus,* the Dutch humanist, also arrived in Basel in 1514 to oversee the publication of his Greek New Testament and found a city that was much to his liking, a gathering place of intellectuals, where many spoke Latin, Greek, and even Hebrew. Sebastian Brant's famous book *The Ship of Fools* was printed in Basel, and it was the printers of Basel who also gave Holbein early experience of designing woodcuts for books by commissioning forty-one illustrations for the popular tract *The Dance of Death*, which he completed between 1523 and 1526.

As Hans Holbein matured, he began to receive commissions for paintings, notably a double portrait of the mayor of Basel, Jacob Meyer, and his wife, Dorothea Kannengieseer, for whom he would later also paint an altarpiece. In 1517 Holbein moved to Lucerne, where he painted frescoes on both the interior and exterior walls of a mansion built by a prominent citizen. It was while he was working in Lucerne that he made his only visit to northern Italy, traveling for a few weeks to Milan and Mantua to study the work of Italian Renaissance artists such as Leonardo da Vinci and Andrea Mantegna.

Returning to Basel in 1519, Holbein took out citizenship, joined the painters' guild, and married the widow of a tanner, Elsbeth Schmid. The 1520s were a profitable and busy time for Holbein, but as the Reformation gained strength, and religious paintings went out of favor, it became increasingly difficult for painters to get commissions other than for portraits. In 1526 Holbein made his first trip to England, armed with letters of introduction, including one from Erasmus to Sir Thomas More*; his success in England eventually persuaded him to return there in 1532.

It was in London in 1533 that Holbein painted what has become one of his best-known works, *The Ambassadors*, a double portrait that shows the French ambassadors to both the court of Henry VIII and the Vatican. It is a masterful display of technical virtuosity, including symbols of the new Renaissance learning of the two men and a strange anamorphic, or stretched, skull across the lower portion. The painting marked the beginning of the period of Holbein's greatest success in England, leading to his appointment in 1536 as court painter to Henry VIII.

Holbein painted not only full-scale portraits of Henry VIII and others but also, encouraged by Luke Hornebolte,* miniature portraits. His miniatures were later greatly admired by Nicholas Hilliard.* Holbein's paintings of possible brides for Henry included those of *Christina of Denmark* (1538) and *Anne of Cleves* (1539). The latter was to create a problem, for the king, on finally meeting Anne, found her less attractive than Holbein had shown and quickly divorced her. Holbein does not seem to have been blamed. Being a servant of Henry VIII had its dangers, and Holbein saw three of his major patrons, Sir Thomas More, Anne Boleyn, and Thomas Cromwell, lose their heads. Holbein himself survived until 1543, when he died in London, possibly of the plague.

The paintings of Henry VIII himself, with his great bulk, proud stance, and extravagent displays of precious jewels and splendid fabrics, are pure royal propaganda. To this day the name of Henry VIII conjures up Holbein's images, a tribute to the skill of this most successful of court painters.

Bibliography

A. G. Dickens, ed., *The Courts of Europe: Politics, Patronage, and Royalty, 1400–1800*, 1977.
D. Wilson, *Hans Holbein*, 1996.

Rosemary Poole

HOLINSHED, RAPHAEL (d. 1580)

An English chronicler and historian, Raphael Holinshed was the principal editor of Elizabethan England's most important domestic history. Holinshed's early years cannot be reconstructed with any certainty, but he probably was educated at Cambridge in the mid-1540s. By the early Elizabethan period he was associated with Reginald Wolfe, a printer who was compiling a universal history and cosmography—an unrealistically ambitious project later abandoned in favor of a more restricted enterprise, a descriptive history of England, Scotland, and Ireland from the earliest times to the present day.

The result of this venture was published in 1577 as *The Chronicles of England, Scotlande, and Irelande* (the full title is considerably longer, and scholars often call it simply "Holinshed's *Chronicles*"). Though not the first attempt to chronicle the history of the British Isles, Holinshed's project was the most extensive, detailed, and systematic of its genre. Holinshed's *Chronicles* certainly falls short of modern historical standards, but it was in many respects a remarkably documented and often self-critical enterprise for its age. A massive two-volume folio containing over three million words, copiously illustrated and indexed, the *Chronicles* became the principal source of English, Scottish, and Irish history and legend to generations of readers, including William Shakespeare* and other early modern dramatists.

Though the *Chronicles* has come to be associated with Holinshed as if he "wrote" it, it was in fact the work of many contributors and editors working over a period of about two decades. An expanded and updated three-volume edition appeared in 1587–88, almost a decade after Holinshed's death. It is this edition that Shakespeare used as a source for his plays. Like the first edition, this one provoked considerable controversy and was several times found objectionable by the Privy Council or powerful aristocrats and clergymen disturbed by the *Chronicles*' reporting of politically and culturally sensitive topics. It is some measure of the *Chronicles*' importance as a de facto "official history" of the British Isles that most of these conflicts concerned nearly contemporary events or matters of English policy in Ireland and Scotland.

Holinshed's *Chronicles* has long attracted scholarly attention because Shakespeare used it as a source, albeit with many modifications, for no fewer than thirteen of his plays, most notably his English histories. In recent years, however, scholars have begun to look at the *Chronicles* on its own terms, finding in it a complex, significant, and influential Elizabethan document that can be analyzed independently of its value as a source for other creative artists.

Bibliography

W. G. Boswell-Stone, *Shakespeare's Holinshed*, 1896.
A. Patterson, *Reading Holinshed's "Chronicles,"* 1994.

Thomas G. Olsen

HOOKER, RICHARD (1554–1600)

Richard Hooker was a scholar and theologian of considerable ability whose principal work is the most eloquent defense of the Church of England of its time as well as one of the finest examples of Elizabethan prose. Hooker was born in or near the city of Exeter, where he attended grammar school and acquired an early reputation as a capable student. Possibly through his uncle's influence, he came to the attention of John Jewel, bishop of Salisbury and author of the *Apologia Ecclesiae Anglicanae* (Apology for the Church of England), who sponsored Hooker's studies at Corpus Christi College, Oxford, from 1568 to 1571. His time at Oxford brought Hooker into contact with a diversity of theological backgrounds, but he would follow his principal influences in the paths of conservative ecclesiastical reform. Izaak Walton, Hooker's early biographer, gives us the picture of a gifted scholar with retiring manners and a deep love of the contemplative life. His personal shyness notwithstanding, he was fully capable of intelligently and vigorously defending his work and beliefs when necessary.

In 1581 Hooker took holy orders and preached his first sermon at St. Paul's Cross in London, lodging with a prosperous merchant, John Churchman, whose daughter he would marry seven years later. In 1585 Hooker was given a vicariate in Drayton-Beauchamp, but after three months he was appointed master of the Temple Church in London's center of legal studies. The post embroiled him in a public dispute over doctrinal issues of the Anglican church with Walter Travers, the assistant master of the Temple Church and a principal exponent of English Puritanism. Hooker, critical of Puritanism as dangerous to civil and ecclesiastical order, met sharp opposition from Travers, particularly on his interpretation of predestination and human will. In 1586 Travers was silenced by the archbishop of Canterbury, but continued his criticism of Hooker in his appeal to the Privy Council, which circulated in print that same year. Hooker's own reply was not published until 1612. It is worth noting that in spite of their differences, Hooker and Travers avoided the bitter exchange of invective common to polemical controversy at the time.

It may have been this dispute, and certainly the Anglican/Puritan tensions that engendered it, that prompted Hooker to undertake his landmark work, *The Laws of Ecclesiastical Polity*. A highly articulate appeal to civil law, philosophy, and theology, the book defends the Anglican administrative structure and use of ceremony against Puritan criticism, which regarded such conventions as emulating too closely the errors of Roman Catholicism. Central to Hooker's argument is his belief in the ability of human reason to develop certain laws useful to ecclesiastical and civil order without sole reliance on scriptural authority, a point deeply inimical to the Puritan stance. Hooker saw five of the book's eight volumes into print before his death in 1600, continuously working throughout subsequent ecclesiastical appointments at Boscombe (1593) and Bishopsbourne (1595). The remaining three volumes were published between 1648 and 1662 and continue to generate debate about their textual integrity and authenticity. Theological issues aside, Hooker's book was praised in its own time for its clarity and stylistic elegance. His other surviving works, including sermons, correspondence, and some fragmentary writings, were also published posthumously.

Bibliography

S. Archer, *Richard Hooker*, 1983.
R. K. Faulkner, *Richard Hooker and the Politics of a Christian England*, 1981.

Michael J. Medwick

HORNEBOLTE, LUKE (c. 1490/95–1544)

Luke (or Lucas) Hornebolte (variously spelled Horenbout, Hornebaud) was a member of a prominent family of artists from Ghent, where his father Gerard was in 1515 appointed court painter to Margaret of Austria, regent of the Netherlands. However, around 1525 Gerard Hornebolte moved his family and workshop to England, possibly because of Lutheran sympathies as well as for economic reasons. His son Luke found employment at the court of Henry VIII* as a painter of portraits and, in particular, of portrait miniatures. In 1534 Luke Hornebolte was appointed to the honored position of painter to the king, a position that he held until his death in 1544. His father, Gerard, either died or returned to Flanders in the 1530s.

While Gerard Hornebolte had specialized in the illumination of religious manuscripts, Luke Hornebolte worked in the field of portraits and portrait miniatures. The importation of Flemish artists into England, many of whom had been trained as illuminators (corrupted to "limners" in English), was important to the development of the English portrait miniature. Luke Hornebolte himself taught the craft of the portrait miniature to his great contemporary and colleague Hans Holbein.* Hornebolte and Holbein were both employed as painters to Henry VIII during the same period; indeed, some portraits attributed to the better-known painter Holbein may well be by Hornebolte. Henry VIII, unlike many of his princely contemporaries in the Renaissance, was not a connoisseur of art. His need was simply for accurate portraits that displayed his majesty; as a result, the court portraits of his period tend to be stiff stereotypes. But the portrait miniatures are very different, with their small size, jewel-like colors, rich settings, and imaginative poses. Hornebolte in particular can be credited with introducing the portrait miniature to English art, paving the way for Holbein, Nicholas Hilliard,* and Isaac Oliver.*

Bibliography

H. Paget, "Gerard and Lucas Hornebolte in England," *Burlington Magazine*, 1959, 396–402.

R. Strong, *The Tudor and Stuart Monarchy: Pageantry, Painting, Iconography*, 3 vols., 1995–98.

Rosemary Poole

HOTMAN, FRANÇOIS (1524–1590)

François Hotman was a French legal scholar and historian who strengthened the case for resistance to kings by writing about the elective nature of the early Frankish monarchy. A native Parisian who received his doctorate in law at Orléans, Hotman converted to Protestantism in 1547 and pursued a career teaching law. With the outbreak of the French Wars of Religion in 1562, Hotman took up his pen to criticize members of the powerful Guise family, the principal Catholic advisors of King Charles IX. In the wake of the 1572 St. Bartholomew's Day Massacre, in which upwards of thousands of Protestants (called Huguenots by their opponents) in the city of Paris and a dozen other cities were murdered by Catholic mobs, Hotman fled to Geneva and finally settled in Basle.

Hotman's greatest work, the *Francogallia* (1573), was a constitutional history of France that offered support to emerging Protestant theories of resistance to the monarchy. The author accomplished this second goal by presenting historical evidence for the elective nature of the early French monarchy. He also emphasized the integral nature of a public advisory council that represented the interests of the entire population.

In Hotman's day that council was the Estates General, but the *Francogallia* insisted that this and earlier councils held ultimate power in the French state. Councils could create and depose monarchs, shared in the most important decisions relating to the kingdom, including taxation, and participated in the regulation of religious matters. According to Hotman, the Roman Catholic church had exercised a malign influence on the public council in recent centuries, distorting the original mandate in the interests of the majority religion.

Hotman's legal antiquarianism placed the author within the mainstream of humanist scholarly researches. The study of ancient texts and state documents, which in Hotman's hands established the origins of a "mixed constitution" in early Frankish culture, provided contemporaries with a justification for political action against the centralizing state in an age of religious and civil conflict. By arguing in favor of an elective monarchy, Hotman provided Protestant opponents of the French Catholic monarchy with historical precedent for their cause.

Bibliography

D. Kelley, *François Hotman: A Revolutionary's Ordeal*, 1973.

William Spellman

HOWARD, HENRY, EARL OF SURREY (c. 1517–1547)

In his *Arte of English Poesie* (1589), George Puttenham gave Henry Howard, earl of Surrey, the title of being among "the first reformers" of English poetry for having "greatly polished" its "rude and homely manner." Though the subsequent revival in literary reputation of Surrey's predecessors like Chaucer has led to a modification of Puttenham's evaluation, Surrey still remains an important figure in English literary history for his role in introducing new verse forms into English, in particular, blank verse and the sonnet form later made famous by William Shakespeare.*

Born into a noble family in Norfolk, England, Surrey continually lived in close proximity to royal power. At Henry VIII's* request, Surrey took up residence in 1529 at Windsor Castle to be companion to the king's illegitimate son Henry Fitzroy, the duke of Richmond. Though Surrey married in 1532, he was deemed too young to live with his wife and thus maintained his residence with the duke of Richmond until the two young men were sent to the French court for a year while Henry VIII's effort to divorce Catherine of Aragon gained momentum. In 1536, however, three years after their return from France, the duke of Richmond died, leaving Surrey to grieve for years afterwards. Many of Surrey's most affecting poems refer to these young years at Windsor.

The year 1536 was a time of other important events in Surrey's life. In May he acted the part of earl marshal at the trial of Anne Boleyn, Henry VIII's second wife. In the autumn a rebellion against the king's policies known as the Pilgrimage of Grace broke out, and though Surrey and his father, the duke of Norfolk, were clearly sympathetic to some of the reforms demanded by the rebels, they helped as ordered to repress the rebellion. One Lord Darcy, however, who had played a prominent role in the rebellion and was thus condemned to death, alleged in his final testimony that Surrey and Norfolk's true loyalties were to the rebels. The charge so infuriated Surrey that he struck Lord Darcy on royal premises, the punishment for which was normally the loss of one's right arm. Through the intercession of Thomas Cromwell, Henry VIII's chief minister at the time, the punishment remained limited to four months' confinement at Windsor.

Although by 1541 Surrey had introduced blank verse into English in his translation of the second and fourth books of Virgil's *Aeneid*, he was made a knight of the Garter that year by Henry VIII mainly for his continued military service. Indeed, for several years following, military service most engaged his life, particularly in connection with hostilities against France. The year 1545 marked the pinnacle of his military career when he was appointed lieutenant general of the king on sea and land for England's continental possessions. In the very next year, however, a military debacle in a battle near Saint-Étienne in France led to his losing his title of lieutenant general and to his effective retirement from military service.

Surrey's life ended tragically soon thereafter. In the fall of 1546 trumped-up charges of conspiring against the king were brought against Surrey and his father based on resemblances of their family coat of arms to the king's. Though his father was spared his life, Surrey was found guilty as charged and was executed in January 1547.

All except one of Surrey's poems were published posthumously, most importantly in a volume called Richard Tottel's *The Book of Songs and Sonnets* (known as Tottel's *Miscellany*) in 1557 that staked something of a claim to breathing new life into English poetry. Insofar as Surrey, along with Sir Thomas Wyatt,* brought continental forms like the sonnet into English while inventing others, he did indeed revitalize English poetry.

Bibliography

W. A. Sessions, *Henry Howard, Earl of Surrey*, 1986.

Yu Jin Ko and Lisa Hinrichsen

HUTTEN, ULRICH VON (1488–1523)

Ulrich von Hutten gained prominence with his poetical and satirical polemics against the papacy and continued support of German national solidarity. He was considered a humanist and German patriot and associated with such intellectual and theological figures as Desiderius Erasmus* and Martin Luther.*

Born into the knight class in Franconia, Hutten was sent to a convent in Fulda at age eleven and left in 1505 to become an itinerant scholar. He spent the next five years at universities in Cologne, Erfurt, Frankfurt, Leipzig, Griefswald, and Wittenberg, during which time he gradually became disenchanted with scholastic endeavors and became keenly aware of the cultural and economic decline of his class. Humanists such as Mutianus Rufus and Rhagius Aesticampianus influenced Hutten during his university days, which led to his disavowal of Scholasticism. He included in his early tracts not only defenses of humanism but also a sense of German pride in an attempt to restore the greatness of the knightly class. Hutten's *Exhortation*, written to Maximilian I, was a political poem praising German literary and military greatness that was based upon Tacitus's description of Germany. Maximilian, duly impressed, began to use Hutten, as he had Conrad Celtis, for political reasons in order to promote and justify Habsburg expansion, and he even named Hutten poet laureate in 1517.

Visits to Italy in 1512 and Rome in 1515 greatly shaped Hutten's view of the papacy, and ultimately, his view found expression through his writings.

While Hutten was in Italy, he incited German students to riot, and he killed a Frenchman for speaking poorly of the emperor. He became overly critical of papal Scholasticism and the lack of religiosity found in Rome. His poem *Nobody* reflected his growing distaste for the papacy and support of the Christian humanism of Erasmus. Hutten attacked Scholastic theologians, however, not church doctrine. He also became involved in the Reuchlin feud (Johannes Reuchlin was a defender of Jewish learning), which gave him the perfect opportunity to defend humanism and attack the papacy. He and Crotus Rhubeanus produced *Letters of Obscure Men* between 1515 and 1517, which was a satirical, but fictitious, dialogue between the opponents of Reuchlin. Hutten and Crotus successfully ridiculed conservative theologians while creating a new satirical genre. The attack on the papacy continued during this period with such polemics as *Concerning the Sword of Julius, Fever the First, Fever the Second*, and *Roman Trinity*, or *Vadiscus*. The famed knight Franz von Sickingen protected Hutten during this period. Hutten refused to recant his writings and became an open enemy of the papacy. When his writings were printed in German in 1521 in the form of *Dialogues*, they greatly expanded his audience. He continued to promote German greatness and mobilization against Roman tyranny, but his political aspirations proved unrealistic. His pamphleteering on behalf of the empire aided in supporting Habsburg dynastic ambitions but failed to motivate people to action.

Hutten eventually attached his cause to that of Martin Luther. He did not understand Luther's spiritual arguments but fully appreciated his displeasure with the church. Hutten included in his polemics programs for church reform, but his last hope of encouraging a political movement ended after the close of the Diet of Worms in 1521. The various German leaders returned to their homes without heeding Hutten's call to arms against papal tyranny.

Support for Hutten waned as it became evident to many Germans that he only promoted the resurgence of his own class, and that he possessed no realistic political agenda. In *Expostulation* (1522) Hutten turned against his former idol, Erasmus, claiming that he was too inactive in the struggle against the papacy, and he attacked those German princes and cities that resisted the Reformation. Hutten remained under the protection of Sickingen until his defeat in battle in 1523, and Huldrych Zwingli* subsequently gave him asylum in Switzerland. Hutten's battle with syphilis ended in 1523 when he died at age thirty-five on an island in Lake Zurich.

Hutten produced numerous polemics against papal tyranny and proudly supported his German heritage. Contemporaries viewed him as an equal to Erasmus, Celtis, and Luther, but due to the unrealistic nature of his political programs, he did not command the following of an Erasmus or a Luther. Both influential leaders admired Hutten's poetry and polemics but ultimately differed over his political and religious agenda. Hutten was most successful as a humanist patriot espousing the greatness of the German empire for the holy Roman emperor in contrast to the unabated tyranny of the papacy.

Bibliography

H. Holborn, *Ulrich von Hutten and the German Reformation*, 1937.
K. Stadtwald, *Roman Popes and German Patriots*, 1996.
H. Watanabe-O'Kelly, ed., *The Cambridge History of German Literature*, 1997.

Paul Miller

I-J

IGNATIUS OF LOYOLA (1491–1556)

Ignatius of Loyola founded the Society of Jesus (the Jesuits), the religious order responsible for returning large portions of Europe to the Catholic church after the Reformation. The Society of Jesus, trained by Ignatius's *Spiritual Exercises*, epitomized the spirit of the Catholic Counter-Reformation. It was a disciplined and obedient spiritual army ready to defend and serve the church.

In 1521 serious battlefield injuries precipitated a complete religious conversion in Ignatius. During his long convalescence, he read spiritual classics. Since he was a gentlemen soldier who subscribed to the romantic ideals of medieval chivalry, he understood Christ and the saints to be more heroic, spiritually speaking, than the most valiant knights. Ignatius resolved to imitate the deeds of his spiritual heroes as a soldier of Christ.

As he fought with himself to leave behind his old way of life, he wrote the first draft of the *Spiritual Exercises*, a manual of self-discipline whose purpose was to root out vice and instill virtue. After several years of study, Ignatius obtained his master's degree in Paris in 1534. While he was in Paris, he vowed to live in poverty and chastity with several of his companions. When his group could not go to the Holy Land as they had hoped, they went to Rome to work as preachers, teachers, and hospital chaplains. They were officially recognized as the Society of Jesus in 1540 by Pope Paul III.

Ignatius's constitutions broke with the traditional forms of religious life. The Jesuit way of life did not call for the observance of set times for communal prayer nor for special religious garb. Ignatius wanted his men to take a fourth vow of obedience to the pope, in addition to the three traditional religious vows of poverty, chastity, and obedience. Inspired by military ideals in creating the Jesuits, Ignatius prized obedience over all other virtues. Ignatius hoped that discipline and respect for authority, joined with the conviction that prayer was found in work and action in the world, would prepare the Jesuits to revitalize the church and fight the advance of Protestantism.

Elected the first general of the Jesuits in 1541, Ignatius served in that capacity until his death. When he died in 1556, the Society of Jesus had over one thousand members. He was declared a saint of the Catholic church in 1622. Ignatius's *Spiritual Exercises* continue to exert a great influence on the Catholic understanding of the spiritual life.

Bibliography

P. Caraman, *Ignatius Loyola: A Biography of the Founder of the Jesuits*, 1990.

Evelyn Toft

INGLIS (KELLO), ESTHER (1571–1624)

Esther Inglis was a calligrapher and miniaturist; she made exquisite illuminated manuscripts of religious verses for numerous aristocrats and monarchs. Inglis was born of French Huguenot parents who had fled France in the atmosphere of religious persecution that culminated in the St. Bartholomew's Day Massacre. Her father, Nicholas Langlois, and her mother, Marie Presot, established a French school in Edinburgh. Esther received an excellent education from her parents; her mother also taught her the art of calligraphy. When she was in her twenties, Esther married a minister, Bartholomew Kello, who also performed some administrative services for Queen Elizabeth.* Esther did not assume her husband's last name for the purposes of her work; she anglicized her father's name to Inglis. Though Esther and her husband were constantly plagued by poverty, their marriage seems to have been a happy one. They had six children, four of whom survived to adulthood.

Inglis's talents as both a calligrapher and a miniaturist are evident in over fifty extant manuscripts that she presented to various wealthy patrons, including Queen Elizabeth, King James,* Prince Henry, Prince Charles, the earl of Essex, and the Sidney and Herbert families. Most of the manuscripts are religious verses or translations; the great achievement of the works is their artistic presentation. The books are miniature in size, often only a few inches wide, with intricate borders of foliage and animals, and they are bound in leather, silk, or velvet. The calligraphy is exquisite, extremely detailed, and often microscopic. Inglis was capable of producing over forty styles of the various scripts described in sixteenth-century handwriting treatises.

In many of the dedications of her manuscripts, Inglis apologizes for her temerity in presenting her work since she is only a woman, yet she also takes evident pride in her labors, finishing off several manuscripts with the motto "Vive la plume." She also includes self-portraits in several of her manuscripts, a sign of ownership of the very works she would then present to potential patrons. In spite of the patronage she received, Esther Inglis was in serious debt when she died in 1624 at the age of fifty-three. Her portrait, painted in 1595 by an unknown artist, now hangs in the Scottish Portrait Gallery.

Bibliography

J. Goldberg, *Writing Matter: From the Hands of the English Renaissance*, 1990.
A. H. Scott-Elliot and Elspeth Yeo, "Calligraphic Manuscripts of Esther Inglis (1571–1624): A Catalogue," *Papers of the Bibliographical Society of America* 84 (March 1990):11–85.

Jo Eldridge Carney

JAMES VI AND I (1566–1625)

James was king of Scotland as James VI from 1567 and the first Stuart monarch in England as James I from 1603. Though derided as the "wisest fool in Christendom," he was a genuine scholar and patron of the Authorized or King James Version of the Bible (1611).

James was born on 19 June 1566 in Edinburgh, the only child of Mary Stuart* (Mary Queen of Scots) and Lord Darnley, who was murdered in 1567. Mary then married the earl of Bothwell but, facing rebellion, abdicated the throne and in 1568 fled to England, becoming Elizabeth I's* prisoner until her execution (1587). A turbulent regency in Scotland lasted until 1578, the same year that Presbyterianism was established there. In 1579 James fell under the influence of Esmé Stuart, later duke of Lennox, and in 1582 he was kidnapped by the radical Presbyterian Ruthven Raiders, who opposed Lennox's pro-French, Catholic influence. After escaping in 1583, James assumed real power, though he faced further challenges in the 1590s from sorcerer and would-be kidnapper Francis Stewart, earl of Bothwell, and from the Catholic northern earls of Angus, Erroll, and Huntly, acting in collusion with Philip II* of Spain. He dealt with them all in 1595–96 but was kidnapped briefly again in the Gowrie Conspiracy of 1600. Meanwhile, he gradually asserted authority over the Kirk (Scottish church), virtually independent under the radical Andrew Melville, and the Scottish Parliament. In 1589 he married Anne of Denmark, who gave birth to Henry (1594), Elizabeth (1596), and Charles (1600).

While James was highly effective in Scotland, his regime in England traditionally has been regarded as incompetent, though recently some historians have tried to rehabilitate that reputation. Certainly the reign was not without turmoil, beginning with his feud with Puritans at the Hampton Court Conference (1604), the Gunpowder Plot (1605), the refusal of his first English Parliament (1604–10) to approve the union of England and Scotland, and fiscal problems that the earl of Salisbury's abortive Great Contract (1610) failed to solve. English disdain for Scots was compounded by James's generous patronage to Scottish supporters. He had a penchant for unpopular favorites like Robert Carr, earl of Somerset (1607–14), and George Villiers, duke of Buckingham (1614–25). His pro-Spanish foreign policy aroused opposition, as did his refusal to enter the Thirty Years' War on the Protestant side. The Addled Parliament of 1614 accomplished nothing, and the Parliaments of 1621 and 1624 were acrimonious, with impeachment of Sir Francis Bacon and the Commons Protestation marking the former, impeachment of the earl of Middlesex and conflict over Arminianism in the latter, and disputes over foreign policy, monopolies, and Buckingham in both. James died on 27 March 1625.

James's contributions to Western culture are considerable. The arts and scholarship flourished in Jacobean England, thanks partly to royal patronage (William Shakespeare* being a prominent example). James's own famous works (c. 1598–99) are *Basilitkon Doron*, a manual on kingship written for Prince Henry, and *The True Lawe of Free Monarchies*, a defense of divine-right monarchy, rejecting the resistance theories of John Knox* and George Buchanan.* He also wrote essays on poetry, scriptural commentaries, a treatise on demonology, an attack on tobacco, and an apology for the oath of allegiance that sparked controversy between Cardinal Robert Bellarmine and Bishop Lancelot Andrewes.* Perhaps his most important legacy is the King James Bible, a translation uniquely revered by Protestants throughout the English-speaking world, a literary masterpiece even if viewed from a purely secular perspective, and one of the most powerful formative influences on the development of the modern English language.

Bibliography

M. Lee, Jr., *Great Britain's Solomon: James VI and I in His Three Kingdoms*, 1990.
R. Lockyer, *James VI and I*, 1998.

William B. Robison

JODELLE, ÉTIENNE (c. 1532–1573)

Étienne Jodelle was a member of the Pléïade in addition to Jean-Antoine de Baïf,* Joachim Du Bellay,* Rémy Belleau,* Jacques Peletier Du Mans, Pierre de Ronsard,* and Pontus de Tyard. His most famous literary achievement remains the creation of the first modern French tragedy, *Cléopâtre captive* (Cleopatra in captivity), which was performed before the court of Henri II in 1552.

Born in Paris in 1532 of humble origins, Jodelle, like Belleau, attended the Collège de Boncourt in Paris, where he studied with Marc-Antoine Muret,* Ronsard's commentator, and George Buchanan,* whose Latin tragedies were often imitated. Jodelle began writing poetry in 1549, but it is the publication and warm reception of the representation of the first modern French tragedy, *Cléopâtre captive*, in 1552 for which he is best known. Jodelle's application of the principles set forth by the Pléïade distinguished his play from medieval passion and mystery plays and foreshadowed the works of Pierre Corneille and Jean Racine. His dramatic production was completed by the composition of a comedy, *Eugène* (1552), and a second tragedy, *Didon se sacrifiant* (1555).

The city council of Paris invited Jodelle to organize a large party in honor of King Henri II and the duke of Guise's recapture of Calais from the English in

1558. Jodelle's hastily organized party had a classical theme, the story of Jason and the Argonauts, and elaborate decorations of inscriptions, mottos, and proverbs in addition to musical and poetical performances. Unfortunately, this event was a miserable failure, casting Jodelle into disfavor among possible patrons of his works. It did, however, result in the publication of *Recueil des inscriptions* (1558), which Jodelle prefaced by a rather long explanation of the reasons for the lack of success of the celebration and his original intentions for the event. He never again enjoyed a success equal to that of his early years, and although he did receive money from Charles IX for a poem about the St. Bartholomew's Day Massacre, he lived out his life in relative poverty, dying in Paris in 1573. His remaining dramatic and poetic works were collected and published by his friend Charles de La Mothe as *Oeuvres et mélanges poétiques d'Étienne Jodelle* (1574) and include his love sonnets, *Les amours et Les contr'amours*.

Bibliography

F. Charpentier, "Invention d'une dramaturgie: Jodelle, La Peruse," *Littératures* 22 (Spring 1990): 7–22.

Nancy Erickson Bouzrara

JONSON, BEN (1572/73–1637)

Although Ben Jonson began his literary career as a playwright, he successfully marketed himself as England's first professional poet. He produced plays and poems sufficient to fill eleven volumes in the Oxford edition. Although he has been treated as a model for the intellectual, he was influenced by legends of Maid Marian and Robin Hood as well as by the Greek and Latin classics.

According to his own report, Jonson was the posthumous son of an Anglican clergyman of Scottish ancestry by the name of Johnson. An anonymous benefactor enabled young Ben to attend the elite Westminster School, but financial constraints prevented him from continuing his education at Oxford or Cambridge. Instead, he served as an apprentice to his stepfather, a bricklayer, eventually becoming a journeyman. Particularly in his youth, he was known for drunken brawls and affairs with married women, siring at least one illegitimate child. Jonson fought in the Low Countries in his late teens, later boasting of having killed a Spanish infantryman in a duel. He married Anne Lewis in 1594, when he was only twenty-two, presumably for love. The union was soon affected by financial struggles, long separations, and the loss of all four of their children between 1601 and 1611. According to Jonson, he and Anne separated permanently around 1614.

In 1597 Jonson became an actor with the Earl of Pembroke's Men and then began writing plays for that company. With Thomas Nashe,* he satirized the court in *The Isle of Dogs*, now lost. Nashe escaped, but Jonson and several of the players were imprisoned, and the company was banned from London. The incident caused mutual ill feeling, and less than a year later, in mysterious circumstances, Jonson killed Gabriel Spencer, one of the actors who had been imprisoned. Because Jonson was able to prove knowledge of Latin, he escaped execution for murder and was instead branded on the thumb. By his own account, he converted to the Catholic faith while in prison, returning to Anglicanism when the Gunpowder Plot of 1605 made it dangerous to be a Catholic in England.

Jonson's first success as a writer was the comedy *Eastward Ho!* (1605), a collaboration with John Marston and Thomas Dekker* that went through three editions in one year. It was less popular with James I,* who jailed the collaborators for mocking Scottish courtiers; Jonson apparently appealed for help to powerful friends who secured their release. Jonson soon gained James as one of his many patrons; the royal family commissioned masques and entertainments from Jonson, who usually collaborated with the prominent set and costume designer Inigo Jones. For a time Jonson acted as tutor to Sir Walter Raleigh's* son Wat, who carted his drunken tutor around Paris during Mardi Gras. Jonson considered himself primarily a poet, and his plays and masques as forms of poetry. His inclusion of plays in his 1616 *Works of Benjamin Jonson* was the first treatment of popular plays as serious literature and set a precedent for the 1623 publication of William Shakespeare's* plays (with a tribute by Jonson, "To the memory of my beloved, The Author Mr. William Shakespeare," which includes the infamous complaint that Shakespeare had "small Latin and less Greek"). After publishing his works, Jonson was awarded a royal pension, making him the unofficial poet laureate of England.

If Jonson was notoriously contentious and eventually alienated both Marston and Jones, he inspired devotion in his disciples. Young poets like Robert Herrick and Thomas Carew called themselves "sons of Ben" and engaged with Jonson in literary discussions, usually in the Apollo Room of the Devil Tavern. Jonson was also granted much official recognition, including an honorary degree from Oxford (1619), the offer of a knighthood (an expense he declined), and the office of master of revels. His last years were marked by misfortune: a 1623 fire that destroyed much of his library and several unpublished manuscripts, a decrease in royal commissions after Charles I ascended the throne, failures in the public theater, and in 1628 a stroke that left him paralyzed. Despite these setbacks, he continued writing poetry; in 1630 he successfully petitioned for an increase in his pension. He was visited by many friends during his confinement, and his 1637 funeral was attended by most of the aristocracy.

Jonson survived competition with Shakespeare and Christopher Marlowe* to become a prominent English playwright; his career paralleled and contributed to the modern idea of the author; and his stylistic influence has been felt by generations of poets. Among his best-known dramatic works are *Volpone* (1606), *Epicoene, or the Silent Woman* (1609), and the masques *The Masque of Blackness* (in which Queen Anne performed in blackface, 1604) and *Oberon* (1613). His many poems anthologized and studied today include "To Penshurst," the seat of the Sidney family, "On My First Daughter," "On My First Son," and "Song: To Celia" from *Volpone*.

Bibliography

R. Dutton, *Ben Jonson: Authority: Criticism*, 1996.
D. Riggs, *Ben Jonson: A Life*, 1989.

Jean Graham

JOSQUIN DES PREZ (JOSSEQUIN LEBLOITTE DIT DES PREZ) (c. 1455–1521)

Josquin des Prez was considered by his contemporaries and succeeding generations to be the most important composer of the Renaissance. Significantly, he has remained a shadowy figure whose biography and canon of works have been in much dispute.

We now know that he was born in the region near Condé-sur-Eschaut where he grew up and later died. He has evidently been confused with another musician, a Josse de Kessellia, who was employed at the cathedral and the ducal court of René of Anjou in Provence from 1475. At René's death he may have come into the employ of King Louis XI of France. From 1484 he worked for Cardinal Ascanio Sforza, an association that may have lasted for fifteen years or longer. From 1489 to at least 1495 Josquin was a member of the papal chapel, the Cappella Sistina. Sometime afterwards, perhaps by 1497, he was at the French court of Charles VIII and Louis XII, though not formally in royal employ. His *Nymphes des bois*, written on the death of Johannes Ockeghem (d. 1497), was probably composed there. He was definitely at the French court in 1501 and again in 1503. From April 1503 to March 1504 Josquin was maestro di cappella to Duke Ercole I d'Este in Ferrara. He returned in 1504 to Condé as provost of the cathedral, an appointment perhaps engineered by Philip the Fair, duke of Burgundy and king of Castile. Josquin remained in Condé for the rest of his life.

Josquin's fame and reputation seem to have been the cause of the many misattributions of works to him. Early printers seem to have used his name for marketing purposes, and Martin Luther's* avowed love of Josquin's music gave license to his followers to put the composer's name on any number of works. Heinrich Glarean* also falsely ascribed numerous works to Josquin and passed on many apocryphal anecdotes about his life.

The actual numbers of his works are in dispute, as is the chronology of these works. We can be sure that he wrote approximately sixty motets for three to six voices, about a dozen masses, twenty French chansons, perhaps three Italian-texted works, and five instrumental or untexted pieces. Although he is sometimes given sole credit for transforming the style of composition, he should be recognized as the leader of his generation, which did indeed completely change the way music was written. The new style inaugurated by Josquin and his contemporaries included the use of voice pairs in fuguelike imitation as the principal compositional device. They introduced the technique of incorporating the whole four-voice texture of a model as the basis of the composition of mass ordinary cycles (called imitation or parody masses). They paralleled this with paraphrases of chants in all voices when chants were used as models. In secular music Josquin's generation presided over the end of the medieval fixed forms of French chansons and the beginnings of a new simpler style, and also the reemergence of Italian-texted part songs. In Josquin's personal style one finds tight concentration of musical motives and gestures that he uses to spin out his melodies, a kind of continuous variation technique. Among his most highly regarded works are the motet *Ave Maria . . . virgo serena, a 4*, probably written in the early 1480s; the large setting of Psalm 50, *Miserere mei Deus, a 5*, commissioned by Ercole d'Este and imbued with the teachings of Savonarola; and the *Missa Pange lingua*, based on the Marian hymn.

Bibliography

Josquin des Prez, *Werken*, ed. A. Smijers et al., 1921–69.
G. Reese and J. Noble, "Josquin Des Prez," in *The New Grove Dictionary of Music and Musicians*, ed. S. Sadie, vol. 9, 1980: 713–38.

Mitchell Brauner

JUAN DE LA CRUZ, SAN (c. 1542–1591)

San Juan de la Cruz, also known as St. John of the Cross, is arguably the preeminent author of mystical poetry and prose of the Western Christian tradition. San Juan expressed with lyric intensity the sufferings and joys that accompany the spiritual journey to union with God in this life. On the basis of his three major poems alone, *The Dark Night, The Spiritual Canticle*, and *The Living Flame of Love*, he is acclaimed as one of the finest lyric poets of the Spanish language; his poetry was published posthumously in 1618.

Under the leadership of Teresa of Ávila,* the founder of groups of reformed Carmelite nuns in Spain, San Juan initiated the reform of the Carmelite friars. He was imprisoned for nine months because of the conflicts that developed between the reformed Carmelites, who chose a stricter rule of religious life, and those who did not. Although his imprisonment was a traumatic experience, during it he composed his poem *The Spiritual Canticle*. A leader in the Teresian reform, San Juan became known for his life of prayer and his ability to guide others in their journey toward union with God. He wrote commentaries on his three major poems to describe the experiences encountered on the way. These treatises focus on contemplative spirituality, a spiritual path whose goal is mystical union or the direct unmediated experience of God.

Juan was an advocate of inner renewal and reform in the Catholic church, and his teaching became suspect when the church began to stress active piety and apostolic endeavors due to the Protestant Reformation and a general climate of religious unrest within Spain. He was declared a saint in 1726 and a doctor of the church in 1926. Juan de la Cruz's spiritual writings now are acknowledged as masterpieces of Western Christianity's mystical tradition.

Bibliography

God Speaks: The Life, Times, and Teaching of St. John of the Cross, 1991.
Poems of St. John of the Cross, trans. K. Krabbenhoft, 1999.

Evelyn Toft

JULIUS II (1443–1513)

Credited with strengthening the temporal authority of the church in Italy, as well as launching some of the principal artistic commissions of his time, Julius II presided over one of the most militaristic and culturally ambitious periods of the Renaissance papacy. He was born Giuliano della Rovere at Albissola, near Savona, and received his education and holy orders from the Franciscans at Perugia. When he was twenty-seven, his uncle Pope Sixtus IV made him a cardinal, and for many of the next thirty years he was a politically prominent member of the Sacred College. His enmity with Rodrigo Borgia led to his self-imposed exile from Rome between 1493 and 1503 when the latter became Pope Alexander VI. During this time he aligned himself with France and supported Charles VIII's invasion of Naples (1494), but his hopes of using the French to engineer Alexander's deposition failed to coalesce. After the death of Pius III in 1503, he advanced his papal candidacy for the third time and secured the election through an unprecedentedly swift campaign that did not shrink from open bribery, a practice he proscribed during his own pontificate.

The new pope immediately took steps to reinforce papal authority over the compromised territorial integrity of the Holy See. Julius began by subduing Cesare Borgia, the son of his old enemy Alexander VI, dispossessing him of his lands and imprisoning him for a time. In 1506 he scandalized Christendom by donning armor and successfully leading papal forces against the tyrants of Perugia and Bologna. Julius, however, recognized Venice as his principal adversary and vigorously opposed its annexation of significant portions of the Romagna in 1503. An alliance with France and Germany to counter the Venetian threat eventually matured with the formation of the League of Cambrai, which the pope formally joined in 1509. The league, backed by a papal bull of excommunication and interdict, obliged Venice to surrender the last of its appropriated holdings in 1510. The war, however, left France firmly ensconced in northern Italy, and thereafter Julius dedicated himself to ridding the peninsula of foreign encroachment. In 1511 he formed the Holy League with Venice, Spain, and England to expel the French and succeeded after entering an alliance with the Swiss the following year. He then went on to lead his troops against France's Italian allies, but the effort consumed his remaining vitality. After a series of illnesses, Julius died in February 1513, both praised and criticized for his single-minded determination to strengthen and expand the Papal States by any means necessary.

Intractable, easily enraged, and delighted by military activity, Julius's personality lent itself well to his temporal ambitions, but was less suited to serious ecclesiastical reform. His primary endeavor in this regard was the convocation of the Fifth Lateran Council (1512), but its activities were mostly concerned with countering the schismatic, French-sponsored Council of Pisa. He was far more successful in advancing the dignity and grandeur of the papacy through his extensive patronage of the arts; it is in this capacity that he made his most enduring achievements. He appointed Donato Bramante to oversee reconstruction of St. Peter's, partially financing the massive endeavor through indulgence sales, an issue that would haunt his successor, Leo X.* Julius also employed Raphael,* who brilliantly decorated in fresco the Vatican *stanze*. His most dramatic and tumultuous artistic affiliation, however, was with Michelangelo,* whom he commissioned to paint the Sistine Chapel ceiling. In spite of his difficult personality and the scope of his military and artistic undertakings, Julius's administration left the papacy temporally powerful, financially solvent, and aesthetically enriched, if decidedly poorer in spiritual clout.

Bibliography

C. Shaw, *Julius II: The Warrior Pope*, 1993.

Michael J. Medwick

K

KEPLER, JOHANNES (1571–1630)

Employed as an astrologer by Habsburg emperors, Johannes Kepler is best remembered for his discovery of the elliptical orbits of the planets. He was relentless in pursuit of universal harmonies, and his magical conception of the cosmos led him to reject both the Ptolemaic and Copernican systems. Through observation, mathematics, and reason, he discovered those harmonies known to posterity as Kepler's laws of planetary motion.

Kepler was born in the predominantly Catholic town of Weil der Stadt in Germany to Lutheran parents. He attended local elementary schools before a religious education at the Lutheran seminary in Maulbronn and the University of Tübingen. After taking a master's degree, Kepler continued his studies, guided by the astronomer Michael Maestlin, who taught the heliocentric ideas of Nicolaus Copernicus.* Suspected of Calvinist leanings, he halted his theological training in favor of astronomy.

In 1594 Kepler set out to teach mathematics at the Lutheran grammar school in Graz, in the Habsburg duchy of Styria, a land increasingly subject to pressures of the Counter-Reformation. His reputation protected him from serious threat, and in Graz he was able to compose his first great theoretical work, *The Cosmographic Mystery* (1596), which brought the attention of Tycho Brahe,* imperial astronomer of Rudolf II.* By 1600 pressures forced him from Styria and into the employ of Brahe in Prague. Within a year Brahe was dead, and Kepler had inherited both his post and his compilation of astronomical observations.

This inheritance proved essential to Kepler. Working with Brahe's superior data, Kepler set about solving problems found within the Copernican system. Often distracted by calendar making and astrology, by 1609 Kepler outlined his first two laws of planetary motion in *The New Astronomy*. A year later his *Reply to the Starry Messenger* supported Galileo's* use of the telescope and explained the optical principles behind it.

By 1612, however, when Catholic reform came to Bohemia, Kepler moved to Linz in Upper Austria, spending fourteen years as provincial mathematician and remaining in Habsburg employ. Astronomical works followed: *The Epitome of Copernican Astronomy* (1618), a definitive textbook; *The World Harmony* (1619), which introduced Kepler's third planetary law; and *The Rudolfine Tables* (1627), a mathematical description of the cosmos based on Brahe's observations and Kepler's chief task as imperial astrologer.

Forced by the Thirty Years' War to leave Linz in 1626, Kepler continued the last years of his unsettled life attached to Albert von Wallenstein, moving to the duchy of Sagan and feeling an unwelcome outsider. While traveling to secure payment for *The Rudolfine Tables*, he fell ill and died in Regensburg in 1630.

Throughout his life Kepler contributed to fields of knowledge other than astronomy; optics was a particular love. His *Dioptrics* described comprehensively the behavior of light passing through lenses, and *The Optical Part of Astronomy* applied his findings. Additional works came on the human eye and the theory of regular solids. He completed an important early work on logarithmic analysis and infinitesimal calculus. *The Six-sided Snowflake* and *The Dream* are small masterpieces of crystallography and science fiction.

Brought into the world among religious and financial uncertainties, Kepler never entirely escaped. His entire life was marked by suspicion from religious partisans, precarious postings, a near-constant pursuit of funds owed to him, and diverse insecurities, including his mother's prosecution for witchcraft around 1620. Despite these realities, Kepler built a reputation as a brilliant astronomer who reshaped generations' views of the universe.

Kepler's chief significance lies in his astronomical theories, a curious blend of the mystical and the rational. This style of thought can best be seen in his *Cosmographic Mystery*, rejected by modern scientists in every detail, but clearly inspiring brilliant later discoveries. Convinced that God had not created a chaotic universe, Kepler suggested that distances among the then-known planets displayed ratios corresponding to the five perfect solids known to the ancients. The idea is difficult to describe, but elegant in concept: the orbit of each planet is the circumference of a circle formed by each of the five polyhedrons and a sphere extending, in a certain order, outward from the sun. Kepler depicted Mercury within an octahedron (eight equilateral triangles), Venus within an icosahedron (twenty equilateral triangles), earth within a dodecahedron (twelve pentagons), Mars within a tetrahedron (four equilateral triangles), Jupiter within a cube (six squares), and Saturn within a sphere encompassing the entire system.

Although ultimately rejected by Kepler himself (despite its remarkably small margin of error), the theory represents the painstaking pursuit of universal harmonies that led him to less fanciful mathematical modeling. The results were his three laws of planetary motion outlined in *The New Astronomy* and *The World Harmony*. The first law states simply that a planetary orbit is an ellipse with the sun as one of the foci. The second stipulates that the radius of a planetary orbit, drawn from the sun, sweeps equal areas in equal periods of time.

Thus, as a planet speeds up approaching the sun, the area swept by its orbital radius, in a given interval of time, is equal to the area swept by the radius as the planet slows down departing the sun, for the same length of time. The third law outlines the relation between a planet's mean distance from the sun and the time required for it to complete one orbit. Sometimes referred to as the 3/2 ratio, the law stipulates that the cube of the distance is proportional to the square of the time.

Kepler's science was a natural theology, the relentless discovery of the mind of God in the cosmos. Shunned by some, most notably Galileo, for its mystical qualities, his work nonetheless clearly directed the course of astronomy and physics for years to come. Without Kepler, Newton's explication of the laws of gravity and motion would be hardly imaginable. Dubbed an astronomer's astronomer by one biographer because of his mathematical precision, Kepler was surely the first modern scientist to illustrate the "laws of nature."

Bibliography

J. B. Brackenridge, *The Key to Newton's Dynamics*, 1995.
M. Caspar, *Kepler*, 1993.
O. Gingerich, *The Eye of Heaven*, 1993.
J. R. Voelkel, *Johannes Kepler and the New Astronomy*, 1999.

Edmund M. Kern

KNOX, JOHN (c. 1514–1572)

A Scottish Protestant adversary of Mary Stuart* (Mary Queen of Scots) and England's Elizabeth,* John Knox wrote *The First Blast of the Trumpet against the Monstrous Regiment of Women* (1558) and *History of the Reformation of Religion within the Realme of Scotland* (1587). Born around 1514 in Haddington, East Lothian, he attended grammar school and St. Andrews University and took holy orders, but converted to Protestantism in the early 1540s. He spent nineteen months in French galleys for joining Cardinal David Beaton's besieged murderer in St. Andrews Castle in 1547. Traveling to England in 1549, he preached at Berwick and Newcastle, became Edward VI's chaplain (1551), and persuaded Archbishop Thomas Cranmer* to include the "black rubric" concerning Communion in the 1552 *Book of Common Prayer*. During Mary I's* reign he pastored English exiles in Frankfurt before feuding with Richard Cox (1555), preached secretly in Scotland, then took over Geneva's English congregation (1556). *First Blast* targeted Mary but antagonized Elizabeth, effectively barring him from England. In 1559 he incited Scottish Protestants against the regent Mary of Guise and promoted a godly (Calvinist) commonwealth in Scotland, helping prepare the *First Book of Discipline* and a confession of faith. But he feuded with the Catholic Mary Queen of Scots until her fall in 1567 and thereafter found his influence nullified because James VI's* regents had to mollify Elizabeth. He died on 24 November 1572.

Knox regarded female rule as unscriptural and the Mass as idolatrous, identifying himself with Jeremiah and Mary I with Jezebel. Thinking that a Protestant nation violated its covenant by observing the Mass, he concluded in *The Appellation to the Nobility and Estates* (1558) that resistance to a ruler who sanctioned such blasphemy was lawful, distinguishing divinely established monarchy from its holder. He later applied this principle to Mary Queen of Scots.

Bibliography

R. L. Greaves, *Theology and Revolution in the Scottish Reformation: Studies in the Thought of John Knox*, 1980.

J. Knox, *On Rebellion*, ed. R. A. Mason, 1994.

R. A. Mason, ed., *John Knox and the British Reformations*, 1999.

William B. Robison

KOCHANOWSKI, JAN (1530–1584)

Jan Kochanowski, the greatest lyric poet of the Polish Renaissance and one who wrote in the vernacular as well as Latin, was born in Sycyn, near Radom, into a noble family of average means. In 1544 he began his studies at Cracow Academy, where he studied for several years. In 1551 Kochanowski went to Königsberg and the following year to Italy, where he spent his formative years, studying and traveling. In 1559, after visiting France, where he probably met Pierre de Ronsard,* Kochanowski returned to Poland.

Kochanowski spent the next fifteen years at the courts of influential magnates and bishops; in 1564 he became secretary and courtier to King Zygmunt August (Sigismund Augustus). During this period Kochanowski participated in major political and intellectual debates and was strongly influenced by the literary milieu of the royal court and of Cracow, the capital of Renaissance Poland. In 1575 Kochanowski composed several panegyrics in Latin to celebrate the election of Stefan Batory, and later he wrote a triumphal ode to commemorate the king's victories. His Latin elegies and epigrams appeared in the volume *Ioann. Cochanovi Elegiarum libri IIII, eiusdem Foricoenia sive Epigrammatum libellus*, published posthumously in Cracow in 1584.

Kochanowski married Dorota Podlodowska in 1575, settled in his country estate in Czarnolas, and devoted himself to poetry. In 1579 this most happy and productive period of his life was interrupted by the death of his daughter Ursula and soon after of her sister Hanna. This personal loss is described in the moving poems of *Treny* (Laments, 1580). Five years later, at the age of fifty-four, Kochanowski died suddenly in Lublin; he was buried in Zwoleń.

Kochanowski was a master of lyric poetry. Throughout his life he wrote light poems called the *Fraszki* (Trifles, 1584); this collection of several hundred poems describes his thoughts, impressions, and activities, transforming ordinary sentiments and experiments into poetry. In the *Songs* (1585), more profound and meditative, Kochanowski borrowed some formal devices and general ideas from the Horatian tradition to proclaim his moral philosophy as well as give artistic expression to feelings inspired by love, beauty of nature, and patriotic exultation.

The goal of enriching Polish poetry with new genres and promoting the use of the national language inspired Kochanowski to undertake other artistic challenges. His largest work, a poetic version of *David's Psalter* (1578), gave Polish literature the elevated language and diction that were capable of expressing deep religious emotions. He also wrote the first modern Polish drama, a play in the classical mold, *The Dismissal of the Greek Envoys* (1578), which brought to the stage numerous allusions to the political situation in the country.

Kochanowski was the most prominent Slavic poet until the nineteenth century. He was steeped in the great traditions of the ancient world, namely, Greek mythology, Greek and Latin literatures, and the Bible. He was familiar with the programs and achievements of Italian humanists and the poets of the French Pléïade. He also reached out to his native heritage and language, especially Polish country life, folk culture, and customs. Out of these deep sources of inspiration Kochanowski created modern Polish poetry, widening its thematic range and setting a course for its growth.

Bibliography

M. Mikoś, *Polish Renaissance Literature: An Anthology*, 1995.

Michael J. Mikoś

KYD, THOMAS (1558–1594)

"Industrious Kyd" was how Thomas Kyd's contemporaries referred to the father of the revenge tragedy. Yet this influential Elizabethan playwright, translator, poet, and pamphleteer was so humble that he rarely signed and at the most initialed his works. A scrivener's son, Kyd grew up in a thriving commercial quarter of London. At seven he enrolled in the Merchant Taylors' School. Its remarkable headmaster, Richard Mulcaster, used languages, music, acting, and Latin as well as English books to teach his students "good behavior and audacity." This wide education influenced the range of Kyd's writing career. His first work was a translation from the Italian of Torquato Tasso's* *Householder's Philosophy* (1588). His last work was a translation from the French of Robert Garnier's* *Pompey the Great, His Fair Cornelia's Tragedy* (1594).

Young Kyd probably began his career as a dramatist writing for the Queen's Company. We can only speculate, however, about Kyd's part in building the troupe's repertory. His incredibly popular play *The Spanish Tragedy* (1592), admired and imitated for decades in England, Germany, and the Netherlands, does not appear to have been written for that company. He may have also authored a pre-Shakespearean *Hamlet* to which Thomas Nashe* alludes, but the play is not extant.

In 1587–88 Kyd entered the service of a lord as a tutor or secretary, commenting with some condescension on playwrighting. He appears to have written some verses on Queen Elizabeth's* escape from the Tychborne conspiracy. Patronage, poetry writing, and pamphleteering, however, did not pay enough for sustenance, and late in 1591 we find the two most prominent pre-Shakespearean tragedians, Kyd and Christopher Marlowe,* sharing a room and possibly writing together. In the following year *Soliman and Perseda* was registered, a tragedy so similar to *The Spanish Tragedy* in dramatic technique, plot, style, and versification that most scholars today treat it as part of Kyd's canon.

On 12 May 1593 Kyd was apprehended for writing libelous pamphlets against foreign residents of London, but the charges got much more serious when the search of his lodgings yielded heretical writings. He claimed that the papers belonged to Marlowe and was soon released, but only after severe torture. He also lost the protection of his patron. To clear his name, Kyd sent letter after letter to Sir John Puckering, keeper of the great seal of England, but no amount of explaining the irreligious opinions of his already-dead roommate Marlowe could restore him to favor with his patrons. He died at thirty-six, broken in spirit, single, and destitute.

Bibliography

A. Freeman, *Thomas Kyd: Facts and Problems*, 1967.

Kirilka Stavreva

L

LABÉ, LOUISE (c. 1520–1566)

One of the finest lyric poets of the French Renaissance, Louise Labé was famous for her passionate love sonnets. Labé was raised in the French city of Lyons, a vibrant hub of artistic, commercial, and publishing activity that was influenced by Italian Renaissance ideas before most other cities, including Paris. Labé's father, Pierre Charly (called Labé), was a prosperous ropemaker; her mother, Etiennette, was his second wife. Labé's father gave her an excellent education; she knew Latin and Italian and probably Spanish and Greek also. In one poem, Labé refers to her skill at horsemanship and arms, as well as needlework, and she may even have participated in a tournament held for Henri II. Around 1543 Labé was married to Ennemond Perrin, a ropemaker at least twenty years her senior. A volume of her works was printed in 1555, containing twenty-four sonnets (one in Italian), three elegies, and a prose dialogue, *Le débat de Folie et d'Amour* (Debate Between Folly and Love). It is dedicated to Clémence de Bourges, daughter of a Lyonnese nobleman; the dedicatory letter defends women's education and rejects their alleged inferiority. Labé died several years after her husband in 1566.

Although readers still speculate, the identity of the beloved addressed in Labé's sonnets remains unknown. Her poems depart from tradition because they are spoken by an overtly passionate female lover who desires a more mutual love than convention usually provided. She knew or met many celebrated poets of her day, including those of the Pléiade—Joachim Du Bellay,* Pierre de Ronsard,* and Pontus de Tyard—and Lyonnese poets Pernette Du Guillet* and Oliver de Magny, and had a sort of literary salon at her home. Some critics suggest that Magny is Labé's beloved, as he wrote several poems praising her, used lines from her second sonnet in one of his, and wrote an ode satirizing her husband. Labé drew criticism from some for her renown, public role, and passionate poetry. A scurrilous poem calling Labé "la belle cordiere" (the beautiful ropemaker) and accusing her of sleeping with numerous men circulated in 1557. In a letter, John Calvin* called her a common whore, but modern scholars discount these charges, viewing them as hostile reactions to a talented, unconventional woman.

Bibliography

A. Jones, *The Currency of Eros*, 1990.
L. Labé, *Louise Labé's Complete Works*, ed. E. Farrell, 1986.

Gwynne Kennedy

LA BOÉTIE, ÉTIENNE DE (1530–1563)

A magistrate in the Bordeaux Parlement, humanist, poet, and political writer, Étienne de La Boétie is best known for the role he played in the life of Michel de Montaigne.* Montaigne celebrates their friendship in "De l'amitié," one of the most famous chapters of the *Essais*. After the untimely death of La Boétie, Montaigne undertook the project of having his friend's work published.

Born in Sarlat in Périgord, La Boétie came from a family whose ancestry dated back to the fourteenth century. He followed in his father Antoine's professional footsteps by studying law. He received his degree in 1553 from the law faculty of the University of Orléans. A year later he became one of the youngest *conseillers* admitted to the Bordeaux Parlement. It is believed that he and Montaigne met in 1557 when Montaigne became a member of the Bordeaux Parlement.

An accomplished humanist scholar, La Boétie translated Greek texts into French, including Plutarch's *Lettre de consolation*, dedicated to his wife, Marguerite de Carle, upon the death of her child, and from the *Oeconomicus, Le Mesnagerie de Xenophon*. These translations, along with others, were published in 1571. The volume also included Latin and French poetry composed by La Boétie. What has become La Boétie's most controversial work, a treatise entitled *Discours de la servitude volontaire* (also known as the *Contr'un*), was originally intended to be the centerpiece of the first book of *Essais* by Montaigne, published in 1580. Montaigne planned for it to follow immediately the twenty-eight essay, "De l'amitié," describing the deep friendship the two shared. Believed to have been written in response to the 1548 revolt against the salt tax and the brutal repression of the popular uprising, La Boétie's treatise against tyranny was put to use by the Huguenots to attack the monarchy. After the St. Bartholomew's Day Massacre, they printed long extracts of it in their publication *Reveille-matin*. At a time when the Wars of Religion were dividing France, Montaigne defended his late friend against accusations of being a Huguenot sympathizer, characterizing the treatise as a schoolboy exercise. Nevertheless, Montaigne chose not to publish what had become a politically charged pamphlet and substituted instead twenty-nine sonnets of La Boétie.

La Boétie died unexpectedly of dysentery at the age of thirty-three. In a letter Montaigne wrote to his father, most likely shortly after La Boétie's death, and published in 1570, he describes at great length the death of his cherished soul mate. Numerous references to La Boétie in the *Essais* attest to the important role he played in Montaigne's life. It is generally believed that the need to fill the void left in Montaigne's life after his friend's death was a major factor in Montaigne's writing the *Essais*. Apart from the notoriety his political treatise achieved because of its co-opting by the Huguenots, La Boétie was not redis-covered until the nineteenth century. In the last decade his life and works have been given closer attention in their own right.

Bibliography

A. Cocula, *Etienne de la Boétie*, 1995.
E. de la Boétie, *Oeuvres complètes d'Estienne de La Boétie*, ed. L. Desgraves, 1991.

Dora E. Polachek

LANYER, AEMILIA (1569–1645)

Aemilia Lanyer was a poet and advocate for women's equality in early mod-ern England. Lanyer's social position differed markedly from that of other well-known women writers of the time, such as Mary Wroth* or Elizabeth Cary.* They were members of the aristocratic classes, whereas Lanyer's family mem-bers were middle-class professionals who made their living as artists or providers of entertainment. Lanyer's father was Baptist Bassano, a Jewish lutenist from Venice and one of Queen Elizabeth's* musicians; her mother, Margaret Johnson, was English. Lanyer became the mistress of Lord Hunsdon, the queen's lord chamberlain. Because Hunsdon was a patron of William Shakespeare's* acting company, one critic believes that Lanyer is the "dark lady" of Shakespeare's sonnets; there is little evidence to support this speculation. When she became pregnant, Lanyer was married for appearance's sake to Alfonso Lanyer, another of Elizabeth's musicians, in 1592. Her son, Henry, followed family tradition to become a court flutist. A daughter, Odillya, died at nine months.

Both Lanyer and her husband were ambitious for social advancement. In addition to his court employment, Alfonso participated in the earl of Essex's expedition to the Azores and Irish campaign in the hope of financial and social rewards. He eventually received some income from a patent granted by James I.* Aemilia, on the other hand, took to writing. Her *Salve Deus Rex Judaeorum* (1611) contains dedications to a number of prominent noble and royal women, including Queen Anne. In some copies, dedications are in different orders or omitted, suggesting that they were tailored for different recipients. Alfonso gave one to the lord chancellor of Ireland. There is no evidence that such appeals for patronage succeeded, however, and after Alfonso's death in 1613, Aemilia's financial position grew precarious. She fought her husband's family over the patent in the courts for more than twenty years; her attempt to support herself by running a school ended in legal disputes after a short time. Lanyer died in 1645 at the age of seventy-six.

Salve Deus is remarkable for many reasons. Lanyer's multiple dedications to potential female patrons are highly unusual in women's writings. Its "To Cook-ham" is the first English country-house poem. Like other nonnoble writers seek-ing the patronage of social superiors, Lanyer had to prove herself worthy of their favor. *Salve Deus* displays both a desire to be among the elite and anger at her exclusion. Lanyer's claims to have been at Cook-ham with the countess of Cumberland and to have known the countess of Kent in her youth have not been substantiated. "To the Vertuous Reader" is a defense of women against male (and female) detractors; it belongs to the "woman controversy" or *querelles des femmes* tradition. The longest section both narrates the Passion of Christ and praises the spiritual virtues of Margaret, the countess of Cumberland. It argues not only for women's central role in Christian biblical history, but also for their spiritual superiority to men; Lanyer's account of the Passion emphasizes women's empathy with Jesus and makes men responsible for his death. Lanyer, like many early modern writers, offers her own interpretation of Adam and Eve's fall. Lanyer's is more radical than most. She argues that Pilate's responsibility for Christ's death more than cancels out Eve's sin, and thus women's submission to men (one consequence of the Fall) should cease.

Bibliography

M. Grossman, ed., *Aemilia Lanyer*, 1998.
A. Lanyer, *The Poems of Aemilia Lanyer*, ed. S. Woods, 1993.

Gwynne Kennedy

LAS CASAS, BARTOLOMÉ DE (1484–1566)

Bartolomé de Las Casas was an early Spanish missionary to the newly dis-covered Americas and Caribbean islands. Born in Seville, Spain, he witnessed Columbus's return after the first voyage to the New World. He accompanied the Spanish governor Nicolás de Ovando to Hispaniola (Haiti) in 1502 as a lawyer, but the treatment of the American Indians by the Spanish settlers led him to denounce such behavior and to seek ordination as a missionary priest. Ordained in 1507, probably in Rome, he returned in 1510 to Hispaniola, from where he accompanied Panfilo de Narváez as a chaplain in the Spanish conquest of Cuba. There he became convinced that the whole pattern of Spanish conquest was unjust. He joined the Dominican order in 1522, was consecrated bishop of Chiapa in Mexico in 1543, and left the diocese in 1547 for Spain, where he spent the rest of his life defending the humanity and rights of the Indians. This he did in the Americas and in Spain, both through writing and by opposing the current Spanish colonial practices. Despite strong and often-violent opposition from the colonists, he successfully defended the rights of the native American Indians, presenting the case for their natural rights before Emperor Charles V* in 1515 and again in 1542 through his *Brevísima relación de la destrucción de las Indias* (A short account of the destruction of the Indies, written in 1542, published in 1552), which he read before the emperor. This latter case led to the promulgation of the *New Laws of the Indies* (1542), which limited the practice of granting hereditary encomiendas and other colonial abuses of the native American Indians.

His most famous case was his debate with Juan de Sepúlveda in 1555, in which he argued against Sepúlveda's position that the native American Indians were less than human and could therefore be enslaved. The philosopher John Major (1469–1550) was among the first European thinkers to argue, on the basis of Aristotle's *Politics*, that there exist two classes of persons, the free and the "natural slave." The former, if they occupy the latter's territory, are therefore entitled to rule and to enslave the inhabitants. This was the line of argument developed by Las Casas's great opponent Sepúlveda, himself a commentator on Aristotle and one who clearly regarded the native American Indians as barbarians lacking in virtue who could therefore be subjugated, by force if necessary. Las Casas won the debate, which resulted in a papal declaration of the humanity of the native American Indians and the prohibition of their enslavement.

Las Casas's works achieved fame and notoriety for the image portrayed of Spanish cruelty toward the native American Indians. In particular, his works *Brevísima relación* and his later ethnological study, *Apologética historia de las Indias*, powerfully argued for the humanity of the native American Indians and against the cruelty of the Spaniards. His works so powerfully described such abuse that they shaped Protestant Europe's image of Spanish colonial policy, creating what became known as the *leyenda negra* ('black legend'). Rejecting the dominant interpretation of Aristotle on biblical grounds and favoring St. Augustine, Las Casas argued for the unity, equality, and freedom of all peoples. His activity led to the promulgation of numerous imperial laws protecting indigenous rights and forbidding slavery. While Las Casas was an advocate for Indian rights, initially he did not extend such rights to Africans, suggesting the importation of slaves to ameliorate the pressures on the Indian populations of the New World, an opinion he sharply rejected later when in his great *History of the Indies* he condemned the African slave trade. Contrary to most mission practices of the time, he argued that "persuading the understanding through reason" is the only acceptable approach to mission.

Bibliography

G. Gutierrez, *Las Casas: In Search of the Poor of Jesus Christ*, 1993.
L. Hanke, *Aristotle and the American Indians: A Study in Race Prejudice in the Modern World*, 1959.
H. R. Wagner, *The Life and Writings of Bartolomé de Las Casas*, 1967.

Iain S. Maclean

LASCO (or ŁASKI), JOHN À (1499–1560)

A Polish Reformer, proponent of Protestant church union, Bible translator, and friend of Thomas Cranmer,* Desiderius Erasmus,* and John Calvin,* John à Lasco was born at Łask to Jaroslav and his wife Susanna of Bakova-Gora. Under the patronage of his uncle, John Łaski, primate of Poland, he attended

Bologna University, became canon of Cracow and Plock, was ordained priest in 1521, and became dean of Gnesen. From 1523 to 1525 he lived in Basel with Erasmus and met numerous Reformers whose views he adopted. Returning to Poland, he became bishop of Vesprim in 1529, provost of Gnesen, and in 1538 archdeacon of Warsaw. In 1538 he left for Frankfurt and Emdem, becoming a Reformed pastor in the latter Frisian town from 1540 to 1546. Here he published his catechism and befriended Richard Hooker,* who made him well known in England. Thus he was invited by Cranmer to England in 1548 for discussions of Protestant union at Lambeth. Becoming superintendent of the London church for foreign Protestants, he reorganized it on a Protestant model, the first Presbyterian form of church government in England. He deeply influenced the court of Edward VI and Cranmer's revision of the prayer book, and in addition he assisted in the revision of the ecclesiastical laws of 1551 and debated Martin Bucer* at Cambridge on the nature of the Sacrament. In 1552, after the decease of his first wife, he married Catherine, by whom he had five children. In 1553 he sought to return to Poland, eventually arriving in 1556 and becoming secretary to the king. He became general superintendent of the Reformed churches in Little Poland and one of the eighteen divines who translated the Bible into Polish, an edition that appeared in 1563. He remained intensely involved in union schemes for Reformed and Protestant churches, traveling widely outside of Poland to facilitate such unions, none of which entirely succeeded. He died in Calish, Poland, on 13 January 1560.

Bibliography

D. Rodgers, *John à Lasco in England*, 1994.

Iain S. Maclean

LASSO, ORLANDO DI (1532-1594)

A cosmopolitan master of all the important vocal genres of his age, Orlando di Lasso became the most published composer of the sixteenth century. He was born in Mons, the capital of the province of Hainaut in present-day Belgium. By the time of his birth, singers employed by the churches of Hainaut and its neighboring territories and choirboys trained in the schools attached to these churches were sought by churches and courts throughout Europe. Samuel Quickelberg, Lasso's first biographer, reported in 1566 that the composer received his early education at such a school in Mons and was three times abducted on account of the beauty of his voice. Twice his parents secured his return; the third time he remained with his abductor, Fernando Gonzaga, viceroy of Sicily and general in the army of Emperor Charles V.* Following the Peace of Crépy in 1544, Lasso traveled through France to Mantua, Sicily, and Milan with Gonzaga, whom he served until after the age of sixteen, when his voice began to change. In 1549 he traveled to Naples, where he remained for approximately three years in the service of Giovanni Battista d'Azzia, Marchese della Terza, whose poem *Euro gentil* he set to music. In late 1551 Lasso moved to Rome, where by 1553 he had become choirmaster at the Church of St. John Lateran, the same post Giovanni Pierluigi da Palestrina* assumed in 1555. Having learned that his parents were gravely ill, Lasso returned to Mons in 1554, only to find that both parents had already died.

Following sojourns in England and France, he settled in Antwerp, where he enjoyed the support of a circle of prominent citizens. His first compositions were published there and in Venice in 1555, and during the next forty years his music appeared in over 530 publications. In 1556 Lasso became tenor in the court chapel of Duke Albrecht V of Bavaria in Munich. From the beginning his salary exceeded that of his superior, the choirmaster Ludwig Daser, and in 1562 Lasso replaced Daser. His duties required him to provide music both for the liturgical services of the duke's chapel (mainly for the Mass and vespers) and the secular entertainments of the court. Despite his increasing international fame and offers of employment from King Charles IX of France in 1574 and Prince August of Saxony in 1580, Lasso chose to remain in Munich for the rest of his life. Several months before his death in 1579, Duke Albrecht had guaranteed Lasso four hundred gulden annually for the rest of his life; in 1587 Lasso received from Albrecht's successor, Wilhelm V, an additional guarantee that his wife would receive one hundred gulden per year in the event he preceded her in death. Two of Lasso's sons became composers and served in the Bavarian court chapel.

Lasso's unparalleled international popularity derived from his mastery of diverse genres, stylistic versatility, and ability to mirror in his music the sense of his verbal texts, whose themes range from the frivolous and obscene to the most profound expressions of Counter-Reformation piety. His enormous oeuvre includes around 150 French chansons, around 200 Italian madrigals, around 90 German lieder, around 70 masses, 101 magnificats, and over 500 motets.

Bibliography

J. Haar, "Orlande de Lassus," in *The New Grove High Renaissance Masters*, 1984.

David Crook

LEFÈVRE D'ÉTAPLES, JACQUES (c. 1455–1536)

Jacques Lefèvre d'Étaples, a Renaissance humanist dedicated to the pursuit of authenticity, blazed the trail that led from Renaissance to Reformation. His contemporaries, including Desiderius Erasmus,* Martin Luther,* and John Calvin,* praised him for his accurate translations of and commentaries on the text of the Bible.

Born in Étaples, France, Lefèvre went to Paris as a student, graduated with a master of arts in theology, became an ordained priest, and then taught philosophy and mathematics at the Collège du Cardinal Lemoine until 1508. In his earnest pursuit of authenticity, which he located at the source, Lefèvre fearlessly criticized scholars at the University of Paris for their complacent use of corrupt

Aristotelian texts. To remedy the situation, Lefèvre dedicated himself to preparing critical Latin translations of Aristotle's works in 1492.

His diligence as a scholar and teacher quickly earned Lefèvre a reputation of being first among contemporary men of letters. It was a reputation reaffirmed not only by his translations, commentaries, and annotations of the Aristotelian corpus but by the prodigious number of carefully edited volumes he produced on mathematics, philosophy, the Hermetic writings, the works of Dionysius the Areopagite, and the texts of mystical authors like Ramon Lull, Jan van Ruysbroeck, and Nicholas of Cusa. As his career advanced, Lefèvre became increasingly interested in biblical exegesis. In 1507 Lefèvre published a critical edition of *De fide orthodoxa* (The Orthodox Faith) by John of Damascus, and in 1509 he argued for the primary of Scripture in his *Quincuplex Psalterium* (Fivefold Psalter). With its five different Latin versions, including Lefèvre's own revision of the Vulgate, the *Quincuplex Psalterium* was a pioneering essay in textual criticism and practical hermeneutics.

For the remainder of his life, Lefèvre expended tremendous energy writing scriptural commentaries and translating the Bible into French. He also encouraged and directed the publication of numerous other scholarly projects devoted to the exposition and translation of the Scriptures. In spite of efforts by his adversaries at the Sorbonne to censure his ideas, Lefèvre continued to strongly advocate a number of reforming doctrines, such as justification by faith and not works, that he had developed independently through intensive study of the Bible. Lefèvre's rigorous scholasticism earned him many enemies, but the powerful patronage of François I* and Marguerite de Navarre* enabled him to live the remainder of his life, from 1526 onwards, free from political and religious persecution.

Bibliography

P. E. Hughes, *Lefèvre: Pioneer of Ecclesiastical Renewal in France*, 1984.

Whitney Leeson

LE JEUNE, CLAUDE (c. 1528–1600)

Claude Le Jeune, a prolific and influential Protestant French composer, was an advocate of *musique mesurée à l'antique* and an outspoken participant in France's religious controversies. Born in Valenciennes, Le Jeune produced his first known publications in 1552. During his career after 1560, he enjoyed the protection and support of many Huguenot nobles such as William of Orange and Henri of Navarre. He quickly developed an international reputation to rival that of his fellow composers, Jacobus Clemens non Papa* and Orlando di Lasso.* By 1564 he had settled in Paris. Because of his opposition to the Catholic League, Le Jeune was forced to flee Paris and take refuge at La Rochelle in 1589. His return to Paris is indicated by references to his service to Henri IV in the king's records from 1596 and 1600.

Le Jeune participated in the Académie de poésie et de musique, an intellectual group dedicated to humanist ideals and to the search for a balanced union of poetry and music. The Academie, in an attempt to revive the manner of ancient Greek music, developed a style in which music closely followed the natural rhythms of its text. Le Jeune's *Revecy venir du printemps* is perhaps the best known example of this *musique mesurée* style. Music theory was also of interest to Le Jeune. He experimented with tetrachords drawn from Greek music theory and employed the theoretical ideas of Gioseffe Zarlino in the organization of several of his works. His *Dodecacorde* consists of twelve psalm settings, each psalm based upon a different one of Zarlino's twelve modes.

Le Jeune's compositions include both sacred and secular works and range in style from traditional Flemish polyphony to the more experimental *musique mesurée*. Among his works are 347 psalm settings, 146 airs, sacred and secular chansons, Italian madrigals, motets, a mass, and three instrumental fantasias.

Le Jeune's contribution as a composer was manifold. His significance to French Protestantism can be seen in the lasting popularity of his psalm settings, which were used throughout the seventeenth century. His compositions served as an inspiration for much later French sacred music. And his innovations in handling the relationship between text and music provided a model not only for French music but also for Claudio Monteverdi in his *Scherzi musicali*.

Bibliography

S. Sadie, ed., *The New Grove Dictionary of Music and Musicians*, 6th ed., 1980.

Tucker Robison

LEO X (1475–1521)

The pontificate of Leo X (1513–21) was a period of intense cultural activity and was exemplary of the heights of Renaissance extravagance. Born Giovanni de' Medici in December 1475, the future Leo X was the intelligent second son of the illustrious Lorenzo de' Medici of Florence. Tonsured at the age of seven, Giovanni was intended by his father to become the vehicle of Medicean and Florentine interests in the Sacred College. He was tutored by some of the leading scholars of the time—Politian and Marsilio Ficino among them—and later studied canon law at Pisa before his formal elevation to the College of Cardinals in 1492. Following the exile of the Medici from Florence in 1494, the cardinal traveled throughout Europe, eventually returning to Rome six years later, where he took up a relatively pious, modest, but thoroughly urbane mode of life. He distinguished himself politically under Pope Julius II,* who appointed him papal legate for Bologna and Romagna in 1511. In 1512 he accompanied the papal army against the French at Ravenna and finally saw the restoration of the Medici to Florence that same year.

Leo's election to the papacy after Julius's death in 1513 was unexpected, but not unwelcome to those who looked forward to a more cultured pontificate. As a product of the intellectual and artistic ferment of his father's court, the new pope launched an extravagant program of patronage that attracted to Rome some of the brightest lights of the day. Both Michelangelo* and Raphael* were in his employ, although the latter soon became the artistic centerpiece of his court. Leo's fondness for belles lettres drew into his service such famous literati as Pietro Bembo* and Pietro Aretino,* as well as a galaxy of less noteworthy talents. The pope's devotion to scholarship and the culture of antiquity also helped finance the University of Rome, an academy of Greek studies, and many other erudite projects. In addition to these high-minded pursuits, Leo delighted in lavish amusements, theatrical and musical performances, buffoonery, and hunting. His generosity and enthusiasms, however, were too widespread to be sustained; within two years of his accession the papal finances were in a state of crisis.

The pope's genial personality was less apparent in his political affairs. His general strategy was to unify central Italy (preferably under Medicean control) against France and Spain. Although his initial efforts were moderately success-ful, the French victory at Marignano in 1515 obliged him to make significant territorial and investiture concessions to François I* in return for the revocation of the Pragmatic Sanction of Bourges. Leo's allegiances continued to shift freely with the changing political landscape, however, earning him a not-undeserved reputation for duplicity and diplomatic opportunism. He also became mired in a costly and unpopular private war (1516–17) to install his nephew as the duke of Urbino. Burdened by debt and the cost of the reconstruction of St. Peter's, Leo frequently resorted to outright simony to raise funds. In 1516 his fiscal dealings with Albrecht of Brandenburg brought into light the worst abuses of the sale of indulgences and set in motion the first stages of Martin Luther's* revolt against Rome. Leo's own attempts at church reform through the Fifth Lateran Council had been minor and ineffectual, and he never truly appreciated the scope of disaffection caused by papal policy. He excommunicated Luther in 1521 and died, possibly of malarial fever, later that same year, leaving the Roman church financially unstable and irrevocably compromised by the growing momentum of the Reformation.

Bibliography

L. Pastor, *The History of the Popes*, vols. 7–8, 1908.
H. M. Vaughan, *The Medici Popes*, 1908.

Michael J. Medwick

LEO AFRICANUS (c. 1488–1552)

The Arab name of the author known to Europeans as Leo Africanus and famous for his book on Africa was al-Hassan Ibn-Mohammed al-Wezaz al-Fasi. He was born in Granada. In the late 1490s his family left for the city of Fez, where he received a fine education. From the time he was in his late teens, he did a great deal of traveling, most of which was professional. He appears to have traveled with merchants, to whom possibly he acted as a clerk or notary, reducing their transactions to writing, keeping their accounts, and generally assisting in the legal part of their business. He also acted in this capacity for government functionaries. Al-Hassan was entrusted with diplomatic missions at an early age and also on occasion served as a soldier. Before his capture, al-Hassan seems to have had an impressive career engaged in trade, serving his king both in diplomacy and as a soldier.

Probably sometime between 1518 and 1520, he was returning from what appears to have been a second voyage to Istanbul when he was captured by Christian pirates, who brought him to Rome and presented him to Pope Leo X.* Leo was impressed by his slave's learning and his familiarity with many countries and decided to free him once he had converted to Christianity. He was baptized John Leo, and the pope was his godfather. Hereafter he was known as Leo Africanus.

For the next few years al-Hassan, now called Leo, lived in Rome and interacted with many intellectuals and the literary elite. It was while he was in Rome around 1526 that Leo wrote in Italian the work that brought him his fame, *The History and Description of Africa and of the Notable Things Therein Contained*. It was based on a diary or draft of a book of his travels that was with him when he was captured. The final book was not simply a translation of the diary. In it Leo also refers to events that occurred in Rome and to authors he would not have known before he came to Rome and studied Latin. Leo continued to live in Rome for a number of years. However, he was no longer living there in 1550 when a wealthy Italian collector, John Baptista Ramusio, secretary of state of Venice, acquired his history and had it published. Leo's history was also translated into French and Latin and in 1600 into English. In the 1550 edition Ramusio says of Leo that he lived for a long time in Rome but is no longer a resident there, and this was repeated in the edition of 1554. But subsequent editions affirmed, though without any authority being given, that not only did Leo live in Rome, but never set foot out of it for the rest of his life. Another contemporary, however, reported that Leo eventually left Rome and took up residence in Tunis, resuming his Moslem faith, and died there in 1552.

Bibliography

Leo Africanus, *The History and Description of Africa and of the Notable Things Therein Contained, Written by al-Hassan Ibn-Mohammed al-Wezaz al-Fasi, a Moor, Baptised as Giovanni Leone, But Better Known as Leo Africanus*, 1896.
C. Levin, "Backgrounds and Echoes of Othello: from Leo Africanus to Ignatius Sancho," *Lamar Journal of the Humanities* 22, no. 2 (Fall 1996): 45–68.

Carole Levin

LEÓN, LUIS DE (1527–1591)

An Augustinian Scripture scholar, theologian, and poet, Luis de León epitomizes the Spanish Renaissance. One of the most important lyric poets of Spain's Golden Age, Fray Luis is also considered the father of Spanish literary prose.

Fray Luis is closely associated with Salamanca. He began his studies at the

University of Salamanca at the age of fourteen and spent most of his life there as a professor. His academic career was not without controversy. He spent almost five years in prison while being investigated for heresy by the Inquisition before being exonerated and released. A renowned Hebrew scholar, he was accused of preferring the Hebrew text of the Bible to the Latin Vulgate translation. He was also denounced for composing a literal translation of the Song of Songs for his cousin, a Carmelite nun. His difficulties arose as the Catholic church began to distrust Renaissance humanism after the Reformation.

Fray Luis defended the importance of providing religious materials in the vernacular, given that the Bible was only available in Latin in Catholic countries. *De los nombres de Cristo* (On the Names of Christ, 1583) and *La perfecta casada* (The Perfect Wife, 1583), his two most important prose works, are grounded in the Bible. By writing these books in Spanish, he greatly advanced the use of Spanish in expository prose and gained acceptance for its use in writing about theological topics. Fray Luis repeatedly expressed his desire to escape conflict through solitude and communion with nature. He prepared a translation with commentary on the Book of Job. In his *Exposición del libro de Job*, written over a twenty-year period, he interprets Job's misfortunes in terms of his own. His best-loved poems, "Vida retirada" and "Noche serena," also express his desire to escape the intrigues of enemies. In seeking refuge from city life, he hoped to be elevated spiritually by the contemplation of nature.

Fray Luis's work blends influences of classical antiquity and the Italian Renaissance with the Jewish and Christian traditions. He combined the humanistic spirit of the Renaissance with religious faith at a time when Spanish society and the Catholic church cast doubt on such a possibility.

Bibliography

M. Duran, *Luis de León*, 1971.

Evelyn Toft

LEONI, LEONE (c. 1509–1590) and POMPEO (c. 1533–1608)

Leone Leoni and his son Pompeo were Italian sculptors and medalists whose most famous works were done for the Habsburg monarchs, particularly Holy Roman Emperor Charles V* and his son, Philip II* of Spain. Leone was born in northern Italy; with his wife and son, Pompeo, he moved to Venice around 1533 and established himself as a goldsmith and a medalist. Through his kinsman, the writer Pietro Aretino,* Leone met another important man of letters, Pietro Bembo,* for whom he executed a portrait medal. Employment at the papal mint took Leone to Rome in 1537, where he became acquainted with various artists, including Michelangelo*; in 1542 Leone moved to Milan as a medalist for the royal mint. In the late 1540s Leone began fulfilling commissions from Charles V and his sister, Mary of Hungary,* for statues and portrait busts: the dazzling, monumental bronze *Charles V and Fury Restrained* (Madrid,

Prado, 1549–55); the bronze busts *Charles V Supported by an Eagle* (Madrid, Prado, 1551–55) and *Mary, Queen of Hungary* (Vienna, Kunsthistorisches Museum, 1550–53); and bronze statues of several of the Habsburgs (Madrid, Prado, 1549–55). Pleased with Leone's work, Charles gave the sculptor a knighthood and a house in which to work.

Leone's personal life was as colorful as it was productive. Early in his career, accusations of counterfeiting cost him a job. In Rome he became embroiled in an argument with Benvenuto Cellini,* another famous goldsmith: Cellini was suspected of pilfering some of the papal jewels during the 1527 sack of Rome, and Leone bore witness against him. Cellini retaliated by charging that Leone had tried to poison his food. Leone also stabbed the pope's jeweler, for which he was first sentenced to lose his hand, but was instead ordered to serve as a galley slave, which he did for a year until the admiral Andrea Doria obtained his release.

In 1558 Charles V died, and henceforth Leone's significant work was for Italian patrons, including his impressive monument statues for Gian Giacomo de' Medici, Ferrante Gonzaga, and Vespasiano Gonzaga. In the late 1560s he began restoration of the residence Charles V had given him, referred to as the Casa degli Omenoni, or House of Big Men, for the imposing statues that decorate the front of the building.

Leone returned to the Habsburgs for his last significant work, fifteen colossal bronze statues for the Escorial. As with many of his other works, Leone enlisted the help of his son Pompeo for this enormous project. Pompeo, a talented sculptor in his own right, was also in the employ of the Habsburgs for much of his life. Though his royal patrons were apparently unable to prevent his one-year imprisonment by the Inquisition for harboring heretical views, they undoubtedly appreciated his work, given the long list of commissions he received from them. After completing the statues for the Escorial begun by his father, Pompeo turned to the final project of his life, effigies of Charles V, Philip II, and several other Habsburg monarchs.

Both Leonis were also enthusiastic art collectors. Leon's collection comprised several plaster casts of both ancient and contemporary works and several drawings and paintings by Leonardo da Vinci, Michelangelo, Titian,* Tintoretto,* and Parmigianino.* Pompeo also owned several paintings and, most notably, the notebooks and papers of Leonardo da Vinci.

Bibliography

J. Pope-Hennessey, *Italian High Renaissance and Baroque Sculpture*, 1986.

Jo Eldridge Carney

LINACRE, THOMAS (c. 1460–1524)

A principal figure of late-fifteenth- and sixteenth-century English humanism, Thomas Linacre was a proponent of Greek scholarship as a means of recovering the medical knowledge of antiquity. A lack of documentary evidence leaves particular facts about his life uncertain. He was born around 1460 in Canterbury, where he seems to have attended the school of Christ Church Monastery. By age twenty he was at Oxford and became a fellow of All Souls College in 1484. Three years later he journeyed to Florence to study Greek under Politian and Chalcondylas in the company of William Grocyn and William Lily. After a brief stay in Rome, he took up medical studies at the University of Padua and received his doctorate in 1496. Thereafter, Linacre fell in with the circle of scholars surrounding the printer Aldus Manutius of Venice, whom he assisted in the preparation of a Greek edition of the works of Aristotle.

By 1499 Linacre was back at Oxford, where his degree from Padua was officially recognized. His scholarly reputation led to an appointment as the tutor of Henry VII's son Arthur, to whom he dedicated his translation of Proclus's *De sphaera*. He also gave private instruction in Greek to a body of students, including Sir Thomas More.* In 1509 Linacre became royal physician to Henry VIII,* and his practice extended to such notable clients as Cardinal Thomas Wolsey, William Warham, and Desiderius Erasmus.*

The improvement of contemporary medicine through the accurate translation of classical medical texts became one of Linacre's primary concerns in later life. With the publication of *De sanitate tuenda* (1515), he began a series of Latin translations of the works of Galen that continued to appear on European presses well after his death. Although his work had greater impact abroad, he continued to oppose popularized and erroneous medical practice in England by promoting its regulation. The principal accomplishment of his life came in 1518 with his involvement in the foundation of the Royal College of Physicians, which held the power of licensure of physicians in and around London. He served as president of the college until his death in 1524.

Bibliography

F. Maddison, M. Pelling, and C. Webster, eds., *Essays on the Life and Work of Thomas Linacre, c. 1460–1524*, 1977.
C. D. O'Malley, *English Medical Humanists*, 1965.

Michael J. Medwick

LODGE, THOMAS (1558–1625)

A poet, dramatist, prose romancer, translator, and pamphleteer who became a Roman Catholic physician, Thomas Lodge pioneered many literary forms in English, paving the way for later Renaissance writers. Variety well describes Lodge's life as the son of Anne and Sir Thomas Lodge, lord mayor of London, a prominent citizen. He attended the Merchant Taylors' School and Trinity College, Oxford, taking a degree in 1577. In 1579 his anonymous reply to Stephen Gosson's* *Schoole of Abuse* in defense of plays launched his literary career, which included experimentation with drama (*The Wounds of Civil War*, 1594, and *A Looking Glasse, for London and England*, in collaboration with Robert Greene,* 1594), satirical poems (*A Fig for Momus*, 1595), historical romances

(*The Famous, True, and Historicall Life of Robert Second Duke of Normandy*, 1591), and the first Ovidian minor epic in the Elizabethan period (*Scillaes Metamorphosis*, 1589). Around 1586 he accompanied Captain John Clarke on a voyage to the Canaries and Azores. Later he traveled with Sir Thomas Cavendish around the world. While traveling in the Canaries, he wrote "to beguile the time with labor" and penned his prose romance *Rosalynde* (1590), on which William Shakespeare's* *As You Like It* is based. An experiment in literary form, *Rosalynde* was written in the style of John Lyly's* *Euphues*. Lodge transformed the prose narrative, and Shakespeare took the story to create his own dramatic romance. Lodge was able to infuse his prose with a variety of elements, from pastoral to chivalric episodes, lyrics, ornate narrative, and poems, not only making *Rosalynde* a popular work—eight editions appeared during Lodge's lifetime—but also one that brought prose fiction of the romance genre to its highest development. In 1596 his life changed when he replaced literature with medicine and converted to Roman Catholicism. From then until his death in September 1625, most probably of the plague, he wrote translations, medical documents, and treatises, among them *The Famous and Memorable Works of Josephus* (1602) and *A Treatise of the Plague* (1603). Marked with experimentation and dedication, Lodge's writing reflects the popular genres of the period.

Bibliography

N. B. Paradise, *Thomas Lodge: The History of an Elizabethan*, 1931.

Megan S. Lloyd

LOTTO, LORENZO (c. 1480–1556/57)

An itinerant artist in sixteenth-century northern Italy, Lorenzo Lotto possessed an inventive artistic power that expressed itself in original and expressive paintings. While Lotto was born in Venice, Italy, he spent only brief interludes there. His artistic style responded to his peripatetic lifestyle, constantly changing as he reacted to the artistic scene around him. Lotto incorporated aspects from Venetian colorism to Roman and Emilian Mannerism without losing his own style, which embodied an inventiveness, expressiveness, and rich and vibrant colors. By 1503 he was in Treviso, Italy, a city located on an important trade route to southern Germany, where he began to mature, considering art from a wider range of examples, such as Albrecht Dürer.* In 1509 he traveled to Rome, where he painted a ceiling, now destroyed, in the Vatican Palace. The period between 1513 and 1525 in Bergamo was extremely productive. Lotto soon showed his skill in the painting of altarpieces and also proved himself to be a gifted frescoist. In further recognition of his talent and creativity in Bergamo, Lotto received a commission to provide the designs for sixty-eight intarsia panels for the Church of Santa Maria Maggiore. Lotto's inventiveness may be seen in his *Annunciation* (Recanati, Pinacoteca, 1527), in which he showed an anxious Mary facing away from the angel, and in the *Saint Lucy Altarpiece* (Jesi,

Biblioteca) with its intensity of emotions and lack of narrative solution in the central scene.

A talented and original portraitist, Lotto used objects and settings to provide a great deal of information about the sitters, portraying their character and telling stories about them, sometimes even revealing their inner feelings. In 1554 Lotto entered the religious community of the Holy Sanctuary at Loreto, where he died two years later. Although Lotto worked on the artistic margin of Venice, his independent and distinctive art that embodied his very character was in demand throughout northern Italy.

Bibliography

Peter Humfrey, *Lorenzo Lotto*, 1997.

Mary Pixley

LUCAS VAN LEYDEN (c. 1489/94–1533)

According to the early seventeenth-century art historian Karel van Mander, Lucas van Leyden was precocious, engraving his first works at age nine and becoming equally accomplished in painting, glass painting, and engraving. Born in Leiden, Lucas trained first with his father, Hugo Jacobsz, and later with Cornelis Engebrechtz.

Mohammed and the Monk Sergius, a subject taken from the fourteenth-century *Travels of Sir John Mandeville*, is Lucas's earliest dated work signed with his "L" monogram. Influenced by the German master printmaker, Albrecht Dürer,* *Mohammed and the Monk Sergius* in turn inspired the background of Italian engraver Marcantonio Raimondi's* print after Michelangelo's* *Battle of the Cascina*. Another early print, the 1510 *Ecce Homo*, set in Leiden's city square, inspired Rembrandt in his later treatment of the subject.

Van Mander considers an engraved portrait of Emperor Maximilian to be Lucas's most outstanding work, while the sixteenth-century Italian art historian Giorgio Vasari* praises Lucas for his 1509 engraving, *The Conversion of St. Paul*, declaring it better than Dürer in capturing subtle, realistic light effects and in its delicate technique. More significant in terms of content are his 1514 and 1517 woodcut series of *The Power of Women*, depicting women betraying or triumphing over men.

Lucas showed similar virtuosity in his painting. His *Last Judgment* triptych, for the Church of St. Peter in Leiden, depicts hell in the manner of his fellow Dutch artist, Hieronymus Bosch, with fantastic devils and monsters. Here Lucas excels in his idealized treatment of the nude figure, his vibrant color, and his rationally conceived perspective. Another late work, *Healing of the Blind*, anticipates the development of seventeenth-century landscape painting with its low horizon line.

Lucas worked most of his life in Leiden, except for two trips to the southern Netherlands, where he met Dürer in 1521 and Jan de Mabuse and other Flemish artists in 1522. Unfortunately he contracted an illness during the last trip and spent much of his last six years in bed, where he continued to paint and engrave with specially adapted tools, according to van Mander. Lucas van Leyden died in 1533, eulogized by the poet Dominicus Lampsonius in a Latin poem for bringing fame to his birthplace, Leiden.

Bibliography

E. S. Jacobowitz and S. L. Stepanek, *The Prints of Lucas van Leyden and His Contemporaries*, 1983.

E. L. Smith, *The Paintings of Lucas van Leyden: A New Appraisal with Catalogue Raisonné*, 1992.

Susan H. Jenson

LUTHER, MARTIN (1483–1546)

Martin Luther, one of the most famous Reformers of the Christian church, was a monk, pastor, theologian, and professor. His theology and life's work continue to affect the Christian churches to this day.

Martin Luther was born in 1483 in Eisleben, Germany. He attended school in Mansfeld, Magdeburg, and Eisenach and entered the University of Erfurt in 1501. He obtained both the bachelor of arts (1502) and the master of arts (1505) degrees. He began to study law, but broke off his studies and, after a traumatic experience in a thunderstorm, entered the monastery of the Augustinian friars in Erfurt and became a monk. Ordained a priest in 1507, he studied for his doctorate in theology, which he gained in 1512. After a journey to Rome in 1510–11, Luther moved to the Augustinian monastery in Wittenberg and taught at the university there. He remained there the rest of his life.

Luther was plagued by the question of how sinful humans could ever be reconciled to a righteous God. Unsatisfied with the answers that the Catholic church, late medieval theology, and his own monastic lifestyle offered him, he continued to seek an answer to his question. He finally found his answer in Paul's Epistle to the Romans in the doctrine of justification by grace through faith. Luther believed that humans are justified (set right) with God not by anything they do, think, or decide, but solely by God's gift of the forgiveness of sins. God sees the sinner as righteous, not on the basis of the sinner's life, but rather for the sake of what Jesus Christ has done. God's grace, the forgiveness of sins, is received by faith.

In 1517 Luther wrote his ninety-five theses, a protest against the Catholic church's practice of selling indulgences. Luther protested that God's mercy was free and could not be bought. Intended to serve as the basis of an academic disputation and thus written in Latin, the theses were soon translated into German and distributed all over Germany. They struck a chord with many people tired of abuses in the Catholic church. The *Heidelberg Disputation* of 1518 afforded Luther an opportunity to expound his theology of the cross.

In 1520 Luther published three major treatises. *The Babylonian Captivity of the Church* was an attack on the medieval sacramental system. *The Freedom of a Christian* laid out Luther's views on the inner freedom of the Christian from sin and death and defined the Christian life as one of service to others. *An Appeal to the German Nobility* attacked the notion that the "religious" (popes, bishops, priests, monks, and nuns) were a separate class of people worthy of special privileges and advanced Luther's notion that all Christians were priests, though only some actually functioned publicly as priests.

By now excommunicated, Luther was granted safe conduct to the Imperial Diet at Worms in 1521. Asked to renounce his views before the emperor, Luther refused to do so. On his return to electoral Saxony, his prince had him kidnapped and hidden in the Wartburg castle. Here Luther translated the New Testament into German, an event that helped shape the modern German language. After his return to Wittenberg from the Wartburg in 1522, Luther was largely occupied with institutionalizing his reformation. He reformed the Latin liturgy (1523) and wrote the *Small Catechism* and the *Large Catechism* (both 1529) for instructing lay people and pastors in the basics of the Christian faith. In 1525 Luther opposed the peasant uprisings in Germany. Though he sympathized with the peasants' grievances, he believed that they used the Christian gospel improperly to advocate their cause. Thus he encouraged the ruling princes to use violent force to put down the uprisings. Also in 1525 Luther married Katharina von Bora, a former nun. The couple had six children.

Unable to attend the Diet of Augsburg (1530), Luther nevertheless put his stamp of approval on the Augsburg Confession, the statement of beliefs that became the constitutive document for the Lutheran church. In the 1530s Luther was active as a pastor, professor, and expositor of the Bible. His lectures on Galatians (1531, published in 1535) provide a complete statement of his mature theology. Lectures on Genesis (1535–45) occupied the last years of his life. Although his literary output dropped during this time, his *Smalcald Articles* (1537) provided another summation of his theology. *On the Councils and the Church* (1539) contained Luther's views on ecclesiology. The 1530s and 1540s were also a time when Luther was subject to a number of different pressures from political, social, and ecclesiastical sources. During this time Luther is also particularly known for his harsh polemics against his opponents—in particular, Roman Catholics, Jews, and Anabaptists. Luther died in 1546 while on a visit to Eisleben.

Luther wanted to reform the theology and practice of the Christian church to reflect his central insight that humans were justified with God by faith in God's forgiveness of their sins. Luther never intended to form his own church, but the effect of his movement was to split the Christian church in Europe. The Lutheran churches of the world look upon Luther as their leading figure.

Bibliography

M. Brecht, *Martin Luther*, 3 vols., 1993–99.
J. Kittelson, *Luther the Reformer*, 1986.

B. Lohse, *Martin Luther: An Introduction to His Life and Work*, 1986.
H. Oberman, *Luther: Man between God and the Devil*, 1992.

Mary Jane Haemig

LYLY, JOHN (c. 1554–1606)

John Lyly authored prose narratives, plays for the private Elizabethan stage, and religious tracts. Born in Canterbury, Lyly attended King's School, Canterbury, before matriculating at Magdalen College, Oxford, in 1569. He received his bachelor of arts in 1573 and his master of arts in 1575. He briefly pursued an academic career before turning to work under the patronage of Edward de Vere, earl of Oxford, for whom he served as secretary after 1580. Later, Lyly sat on four Parliaments, as the member for Hinden in 1589, for Aylesbury in 1593, for Appleby in 1597, and for Aylesbury in 1601.

Lyly is best known for two of his prose narratives, *Euphues: The Anatomy of Wit* (1578) and *Euphues and His England* (1580), which served as stylistic models for English prose in the early 1580s. Both use carefully structured sentences that rely heavily upon rhetorical figures such as antithesis, epigram, alliteration, and rhetorical questions. This style became very fashionable during the 1580s and was ridiculed afterwards, especially in the 1590s, but the continued popularity of Lyly's work is reflected by their publication history, since *The Anatomy of Wit* was reprinted nineteen times from 1578 to 1638, and *Euphues and His England* was published fourteen times from 1580 to 1609. Lyly also wrote his plays for the Boys' Companies of the Blackfriars Theater beginning in 1583; these include *Campaspe, Sappho and Phao, Galatea, Endymion, Midas, Love's Metamorphosis, Mother Bombie*, and *The Woman in the Moon*. Readers of religious controversies see Lyly's authorship in controversial tracts; Gabriel Harvey* attributed *Pap with a Hatchet*, one of the responses to Martin Marprelate, to Lyly; and other anti-Martinist tracts have been credited to Lyly, Thomas Nashe,* or a team of the two.

Bibliography

M. Pincombe, *The Plays of John Lyly: Eros and Eliza*, 1996.

Karen Nelson

M

MACHIAVELLI, NICCOLÒ (1469–1527)

Niccolò Machiavelli was an Italian historian, statesman, and political philosopher. Machiavelli's political theory has turned his name into a synonym for amoral deception and cunning in pursuing one's goals.

Machiavelli was born in Florence on 3 May 1469. He began his influential career in politics when he became a clerk for the newly proclaimed Florentine Republic in 1498. In the new republic, Machiavelli served as secretary of the ten-man council that conducted diplomatic negotiations and supervised the military operations of the republic. Machiavelli's duties included, among other things, missions to the French king (1504, 1510–11), the Holy See (1506), and the German emperor (1507–08). While Machiavelli was involved with these diplomatic missions, he became acquainted with many rulers and was able to study the methods they used in governing. The most significant such ruler that Machiavelli studied was Cesare Borgia.

In 1512, when the Medici, a Florentine family, regained power in Florence and the republic was dissolved, Machiavelli was removed from office, and the Medicis temporarily arrested him for allegedly conspiring against them. Once he was released from prison, Machiavelli spent much of the rest of his life on his estate near Florence. It was during this period that Machiavelli wrote his most important works, including *The Prince* (published in 1532) and *The Discourses* (published in 1534). Machiavelli was never able to curry political favor with the Medicis, and consequently he never regained his former prominent place in the political life of Florence. To make matters worse, when the Florentine Republic was temporarily reinstated in 1527, Machiavelli was suspected of being too closely allied with the Medicis to regain his former post. In Florence, on 21 June of the same year, Machiavelli died.

Machiavelli is considered by many to be the father of modern political theory. In his book *The Prince*, Machiavelli argued that a ruler is justified in using whatever means necessary to secure power. A ruler should not be too tyrannical, for this might enflame the hatred of the governed; yet the ruler should not seek to be too kind or beneficent, for without fearing the prince, the governed may pursue selfish ends that are ultimately to the detriment of the state and the prince. Within these parameters, however, Machiavelli claimed that the most successful rulers (rulers he studied while on diplomatic missions) were those who could, through deception and cunning, foster the love, respect, and fear of the citizens. Some have interpreted *The Prince* to be a satire that should be read as a critique of absolutist rulers such as the Borgias. This reading would emphasize the importance of liberty and the role of government in protecting the liberties and rights of its citizens—hence the reason Machiavelli is often cited as the initiator of modern political theory, for much of modern political theory is concerned precisely with detailing the manner in which a government or ruler is legitimate only if it protects the rights and liberties of the governed. However, this reading of Machiavelli fell largely into doubt when, in 1810, a letter by Machiavelli was discovered in which he reveals that he wrote *The Prince* to endear himself to the ruling Medici family of Florence. Read in light of this letter, *The Prince* emerges as a justification for strong governments, even absolutist if necessary, as a means of reducing the influence and threat of foreign powers.

Although Machiavelli's name has become a pejorative term, these associations should not lead one to minimize the importance of Machiavelli as a political theorist. Regardless of the motives that led him to write *The Prince*, many of Machiavelli's observations and analyses of political tactics, the role chance and *fortuna* play in restricting political policy, and many other points stand on their own as important contributions to the theoretical study of political strategy and tactics. Machiavelli is also an important figure in the resurgence of humanism and the Italian Renaissance. Since Machiavelli, political theorists have turned their attention to the human condition, to human nature, and to structuring a government that is based upon conclusions regarding these issues (Hobbes is a case in point). This is in direct contrast to the ancient and medieval tradition of imposing an ideal form upon human beings and molding and raising people who are best accommodated to this form. It is this turn to humanism in political theory that is perhaps Machiavelli's greatest contribution to Western culture.

Bibliography

S. de Grazia, *Machiavelli in Hell*, 1989.
J.G.A. Pocock, *The Machiavellian Moment*, 1975.
R. Ridolfi, *The Life of Niccolò Machiavelli*, 1963.

Jeffrey A. Bell

MARENZIO, LUCA (1553/54–1599)

Luca Marenzio was a leading composer of secular music in the late sixteenth century, composing over four hundred madrigals. His music was popular throughout Europe and had a strong influence on the next generation of Italian composers as well as on the English madrigal composers.

Marenzio was born near Brescia in northern Italy and may have studied with Giovanni Contino there and in Mantua. From 1574 to 1586 he was in Rome, serving as a singer first for Cardinal Christoforo Madruzzo and then for Cardinal Luigi d'Este. It was in Rome that Marenzio's compositional career began in earnest, and he published some thirteen collections of secular pieces during this period. From 1586 to 1588 he visited various Italian cities, including Verona, where he made the acquaintance of Count Mario Bevilacqua, whose Accademia Filarmonica was one of the most important musical institutions of the period. His 1588 collection of madrigals was dedicated to Bevilacqua.

By early 1588 Marenzio was in Florence to help provide music for the wedding festivities of Ferdinando de' Medici and Christine of Lorraine in 1589. The most important musical event was a series of *intermedi* presented between the acts of Girolamo Bargagli's play *La pellegrina*. These pieces played an important role in the development of dramatic music in the late Renaissance. Marenzio set the second and third *intermedi* with texts by Ottavio Rinuccini,* who would later write the libretto for the first fully sung opera, Jacopo Peri's* *Dafne* of 1598. In 1589 Marenzio returned to Rome, and in 1595 he embarked on an extended trip to Poland. By 1598 he was back in Rome, where he died within a year.

Marenzio's madrigals were marked by inventive use of musical techniques to illustrate the text. In his later works, this was often accomplished by the use of surprising and original harmonies. The complexity and intellectual quality of his writing often reflected his texts, which came from writers as diverse as Francesco Petrarch and Giovanni Battista Guarini.*

Bibliography

S. Ledbetter and R. Jackson, "Luca Marenzio," in *The New Grove Dictionary of Music and Musicians*, ed. Stanley Sadie, 1980.

Russell E. Murray, Jr.

MARGUERITE DE NAVARRE (1492–1549)

Queen of Navarre and elder sister of François I* of France, Marguerite de Navarre was a patron of the arts, an author, a sponsor of religious Reformers, and a beneficent ruler. Marguerite was born on 11 April 1492 to Louise of Savoy and Charles de Valois-Orléans. Louise encouraged Marguerite to devote herself to her brother, and throughout her life, Marguerite strove to fulfill that expectation; she and her brother were extremely close. As a child, she studied theology, history, classics, and philosophy, as well as several languages, including both Hebrew and Latin.

In 1509 she was married to Charles, duc d'Alençon, to settle an inheritance dispute. The marriage was unhappy, and once François assumed the throne in 1515, she spent most of her time at the court, acting as his hostess and receiving foreign ambassadors. In 1517 her brother gifted her with the Duchy of Berry, a present that accorded her financial independence from her husband as well as jurisdiction over the University of Bourges, a center of classical learning and law that she supported. During this time she also encouraged the humanist Guillaume Budé* in his efforts to persuade François to endow royal lectureships in such subjects as Greek, Hebrew, and mathematics. This project would eventually lead to the foundation of the Collège de France in Paris.

Marguerite also became involved in spiritual matters, acting as a patroness to the fledgling Protestant movements. Over the years, she corresponded with Reformers such as John Calvin* and protected men like Jacques Lefèvre de'Étaples* and Clément Marot.* Marguerite's personal religious beliefs are difficult to determine; although she protected the Protestants, evidenced a belief in mysticism, and skirted the bounds of heresy, she remained a Catholic all of her life.

In 1525, when the king of Spain, Charles V,* took her brother captive at the Battle of Pavia, Marguerite was one of the people named as regent for the king. Furthermore, she went to Spain in an attempt to negotiate a peace treaty and François's release. While she was there, she nursed her brother back to health and helped to plan his escape. She was forced to flee back to France when Charles learned of their plans.

Her husband, the duc d'Alençon, died shortly before her trip to Spain. Accordingly, after François's return to France, he arranged for her marriage to Henri d'Albret, king of Navarre. Although he was eleven years Marguerite's junior, they were initially happy in the marriage, and in November 1528 their daughter Jeanne* was born, their only child to survive infancy. Unfortunately, relations between Henri and François became strained when François failed to regain the lands of Navarre that had been lost to Spain, and Marguerite was increasingly torn between the two.

Isolated from the court at Paris, Marguerite created her own court at the city of Nérac. There she continued her role as patron both of the arts and of religious Reformers. Furthermore, Marguerite effected economic and social reform in her lands, sponsoring cloth manufacturing, reforming the courts, and founding orphanages and a hospital.

In addition, Marguerite also composed numerous religious poems exploring her spiritual ideas. When one of her works, a long mystical poem called *Mirror of a Sinful Soul*, was condemned by the Sorbonne for heresy in 1531, François furiously forced the institution to apologize. (Interestingly, the work would later be translated into English by Queen Elizabeth I*.) In 1547 she arranged to have a collection of her poetry called *Pearls of the Pearl of Princesses* published, and after her death, scholars discovered a number of her poems.

The work for which she is best known, however, is her collection of seventy-two short stories, the *Heptameron*, an imitation of Boccaccio's *Decameron*, except that she based her stories on factual events. Although Marguerite died before she could complete her planned one hundred tales, through her use of character and theme, she creates a web of symbiotic relationships that reflect an intriguing picture of life in Renaissance France. *The Heptameron* was published posthumously in 1558.

Marguerite died of an illness on 21 December 1549 after being exposed to a chill. Her last years were sad ones. François, the source of her lifelong devotion, had died, and she was isolated from court. Her remaining family brought additional grief; she was estranged from her husband and, to a large extent, from her daughter as well.

For many years Marguerite was dismissed as a minor author of the Renaissance. Recent scholarship has resurrected her reputation, and there are numerous works providing analysis of the various complexities of her themes of love and the relations between men and women as well as of her religious ideas and convictions. Her literary works provide a unique view of French aristocratic life during the Renaissance. Furthermore, her contributions to the culture and politics and her legacy of religious tolerance serve as a sterling example of a Renaissance monarch. Her accomplishments exemplified the potential strength and gifts of a female ruler, for which she was celebrated throughout Europe.

Bibliography

C. J. Blaisdell, "Marguerite de Navarre and Her Circle," in *Female Scholars: A Tradition of Learned Women before 1800*, ed. J. R. Brink, 1980.
P. F. Cholakian, *Rape and Writing in the "Heptameron" of Marguerite de Navarre*, 1991.
G. Ferguson, *Mirroring Belief: Marguerite de Navarre's Devotional Poetry*, 1992.

Erin Sadlack

MARGUERITE DE VALOIS (1553–1615)

As the daughter of Henri II and Catherine de' Medici* and, later, wife to Henri IV, Marguerite de Valois found herself at the center of French politics and religion during the tumultuous sixteenth century. Beautiful, willful, and extravagant, Marguerite was brought up at a court acknowledged as the most brilliant in Europe. By 1570 she was betrothed to the Huguenot prince Henri de Navarre, despite Marguerite's own Catholicism. Catherine, the queen mother, used the lavish wedding ceremony as the opportunity to convince her son, Charles IX, to order a general massacre of the Huguenots. Though Henri de Navarre and his closest associates were spared, the St. Bartholomew's Day Massacre on 24 August 1572 left thousands of Huguenots dead.

The marriage was a loveless one, and the couple reached an understanding that both could pursue discreet affairs. Marguerite established a cultured court at Navarre, but her many affairs shocked her husband's courtiers. A blatant liaison in the early 1580s led to a separation from Henri; returning to France, she alienated both her brother and her mother, which eventually resulted in her imprisonment. Marguerite escaped and set up court in one of her dower lands. In August 1589 Henri de Navarre became Henri IV of France and agreed to convert to Catholicism, but insisted upon an annulment from Marguerite, which was granted in December 1599. Marguerite was given a generous settlement and began to lead a relatively circumspect life. Henry IV was assassinated in 1610; Marguerite found herself a confidante of Queen Marie de' Medici, the regent for Henri's son, Louis XIII, and enjoyed this preeminence until her own death in March 1615. A woman ahead of her time, Marguerite was determined to live life on her own terms and established a notion of sexual equality that was indeed rare for a woman of the sixteenth century, making her, perhaps, one of the world's earliest feminists.

Bibliography

E. R. Chamberlin, *Marguerite of Navarre*, 1974.
C. Haldane, *Queen of Hearts: Marguerite of Valois ("La Reine Margot"), 1553–1615*, 1968.

Connie S. Evans

MARLOWE, CHRISTOPHER (1564–1593)

The brightest star among the Elizabethan dramatists before William Shake-speare,* Christopher Marlowe was also a gifted lyric poet, an adventurer, and a secret agent whose services were appreciated by the queen herself. His quick temper was matched by an intellectual curiosity and originality that bore no respect for orthodoxy.

Marlowe grew up in the quarrelsome and litigious family of a Canterbury shoemaker whose disposition he apparently inherited. He rose up in society thanks to a scholarship-sponsored education first at the King's School at Canterbury and later at Corpus Christi College, Cambridge. At Cambridge he was reported to have been a "rare scholar" who excelled in Latin versifying, but whose academic discipline was far from perfect. When he supplicated for the master's degree in 1587, the academic authorities proposed to withhold the degree because of his prolonged absences from campus. They yielded only after Queen Elizabeth's* Privy Council testified to Marlowe's "good service" to Her Majesty during these absences.

Instead of going on to a traditional career in either the church or the academy, the new master of arts joined the lively group of the University Wits in London. These were university-educated playwrights and poets who penned exciting new works for the commercial theaters. By 1591 Marlowe's name was mentioned among the group of intellectuals and bohemians associated with Sir Walter Raleigh* and Thomas Walsingham. The members of this circle, nicknamed "the School of Night," devoted themselves to philosophical and scientific speculation and were reputedly intrigued by the occult.

Such was the intellectual and cultural climate in which Marlowe wrote his works. From Cambridge, he brought to town his classical translations of Ovid's *Amores* (1585) and the first book of Lucan's *Pharsalia* (1585) and two plays, *Dido, Queen of Carthage* (1586), and the first part of *Tamburlaine the Great*

(1586). *Tamburlaine*'s instant popularity encouraged Marlowe to write a sequel. The *Tamburlaine* plays (published in 1590), whose central "atheist" character drew the wrath of Robert Greene,* already demonstrated the signature qualities of Marlowe's innovative drama. Like his other plays, *The Jew of Malta* (1589), *Edward II* (1592), *Doctor Faustus* (1592), and *The Massacre at Paris* (1593), *Tamburlaine* displayed the dramatist's fascination with violence, sensuousness, and power. The central character of this double feature was the first in a series of diabolical rebels. *Tamburlaine*'s philosophical idiom and its blank-verse form also set the mode for dramatic speech in English Renaissance drama.

Marlowe's life in London was almost as action packed and violent as his plays. In 1589 he fought a duel with one William Bradley. Bradley's quarrel seems to have been with the poet Thomas Watson, who, like Marlowe, was under the patronage of Thomas Walsingham. Watson stabbed Bradley fatally, and the two friends were arrested and imprisoned in Newgate until they eventually succeeded in pleading self-defense. Marlowe spent only two weeks in prison, Watson several months.

More troubles with the authorities followed. Early in 1592 Marlowe was accused of money counterfeiting and treason by one Richard Baines, a Cambridge graduate and, like Marlowe, a secret-service agent. Nothing came of this accusation, but later in the year he was reported to have threatened the safety of two constables of Shoreditch and to have fought a Canterbury tailor in the street "with staff and dagger." Yet all of these misdemeanors paled in comparison to the accusation leveled against Marlowe by his chamber fellow, the playwright Thomas Kyd.* In May 1593 Kyd had been arrested, and the search of his room yielded a heretical manuscript. On the rack, he asserted that the manuscript belonged to Marlowe. Marlowe was apprehended at the home of his patron Thomas Walsingham at Scadbury. Unlike Kyd, he was released immediately with the understanding that he was to report daily to the authorities until further notice. The case was never resolved in court, however, for on 30 May Marlowe was stabbed to death in a brawl at Eleanor Bull's tavern in Deptford, following a dinner with associates from the Walsingham circle. The circumstances and interests served by his death remain open to speculation and controversy.

Like his violent death, Marlowe's critical heritage poses significant problems. His brilliant narrative poem *Hero and Leander* (1593) was left unfinished. We are not sure of the order in which his plays appeared. Only two of his plays were published in his lifetime, and the texts of all are badly corrupted. Yet their synthesis of intellectual significance, expressive spectacle, breathtaking action, and psychologically complex characters of unforgettable stature marked the beginning of the greatest age of the English theater.

Bibliography

D. Cole, *Christoper Marlowe and the Renaissance of Tragedy*, 1995.
R. Sales, *Christopher Marlowe*, 1991.

Kirilka Stavreva

MAROT, CLÉMENT (1496–1544)

Clément Marot, court poet for François I* of France, was an innovative, witty, and prolific poet, author, and translator who commemorated myriad historical events and provided satiric criticism of various institutions; his controversial religious beliefs, however, eventually forced him to flee France because of charges of heresy. Marot's childhood and education are little known; it is certain that his father was the court poet to Anne of Brittany, the wife of Louis XII, and that in 1514 Marot himself was placed as a page to Nicolas de Neufville, a secretary of finance. In addition, Marot trained as a law clerk. At this juncture, Marot began to write poetry and make translations from Latin and Greek in hopes of gaining patronage; King François I received him well and recommended him to his sister Marguerite de Navarre.* Marot became one of the first and most famous poets she sponsored; she appointed him valet de chambre, court poet, and her secretary. His works, which commemorated various diplomatic missions, court events, and military exploits, demonstrated his elegant wit and deft ability to weave courtly flattery with a sense of underlying importance of the events.

In 1526 Marot was imprisoned at Châtelet for a religious infraction. Hints in Marot's writing suggest that he was denounced for eating meat during Lent, but modern historians question the veracity of this story. It is certain that he was vulnerable to attack because of Marguerite's absence; she was in Spain negotiating the release of François I, who had been captured by the Spanish. Upon François's return, he released Marot and restored him to popularity. Unfortunately, Marot fell ill during the winter of 1531–32 and afterward was imprisoned again for a brief period, apparently for a similar offense. His court connections again obtained his release and showered further rewards upon him; his fame continued to grow.

However, in 1534 the king turned against the idea of religious reform. Marot, who was known for his attacks on the conservative religious views of the Sorbonne as well as for his reformist convictions, was in danger. When his home was raided, searchers found a translated copy of the Bible and other forbidden tracts. These were hanging offenses, but Marot had already fled to Marguerite's court at Nérac, a shelter for those with Protestant beliefs. However, Marguerite was unable to shield him for long, as she herself came under suspicion. She arranged for him to go to Italy, to the court of her cousin, Renée of Ferrara.*

Although Marot found happiness at Ferrara, a cultural center of Italy, Renée's husband, a staunch Catholic, eventually began to cause trouble for him and the other refugees. This time, Marot went to Venice, known for its tolerance. However, he returned to France in 1536 after François declared an amnesty for all religious offenders. After performing a humiliating ceremony of abjuration, Marot returned to court and for a brief time enjoyed his former popularity. The king even requested that Marot make translations of the Psalms into French as a gift for Charles V.* However, when once again François reversed his position, these translations, as well as his other writings, became grounds for another accusation of heresy, and Marot was forced to flee again.

This time, Marot went to Geneva, where John Calvin* welcomed him and urged him to continue his translations. However, Marot was uncomfortable with the austere atmosphere of Geneva and left unhappily, longing for France. He wandered throughout Europe, seeking patronage, and finally died in exile in Turin in September 1544.

Scholars disagree as to the depth of Marot's religious commitment. Some maintain that his religion was inextricably interwined with his politics, and that while he certainly possessed reform convictions, his reputation as a Protestant may have been inflated by circumstance. Others contend that his was, in fact, a true religious zeal, and that his writings reflect that fact.

Marot left a legacy of innovative poetical forms and styles, such as the ec-logue and the coq-à-l'âne, and his use of the epigram continued to inspire later generations of poets. In addition, he wrote the first epithalamion in French and what was most likely its first sonnet. He published several collections of poetry and other writings that contain a humorous but insightful view into court life, satiric commentary, and, especially in his later works, his moving explorations of religion and death. Ultimately, he left behind a reputation as France's fore-most poet of the Renaissance.

Bibliography

G. Joseph, *Clément Marot*, 1985.
M. A. Screech, *Clément Marot: A Renaissance Poet Discovers the Gospel*, 1994.

Erin Sadlack

MARY I (1516–1558)

Mary I was queen regnant of England (1553–58). Her reign sought to undo Protestant influences in both church and society. Born on 18 February 1516, Mary was the only surviving child of Henry VIII* and Catherine of Aragon. Educated according to the theories of the Spanish humanist Juan Luis Vives,* Mary studied languages, music, and history. Never formally invested with the title "Princess of Wales," by age nine Mary lived near the Welsh Marches with a household appropriate for the heiress to the throne. Early marriage negotiations established short-lived betrothals, especially with Charles V,* but no marriage followed.

Mary's life began to change in 1527–33 when Henry sought an annulment of his marriage to Catherine. Her father's marital intrigues led to the national independence of the English church. While canon law would have allowed for Mary to retain legitimate status, political concerns about the succession dictated that she be decreed illegitimate. During her father's life Mary endured periods of favor and disfavor, but none as dangerous and devastating as the period 1533–36, when Mary was threatened with arrest and trial for refusing to acknowledge her own illegitimacy. Mary swore an oath acknowledging Henry's supremacy over the church and her own bastardized status in 1536.

During the reign of her brother, Edward VI (1547–53), Mary opposed the government's Protestant policies as illegal because of the minority of the king. Mary continued to observe the Latin Mass, and after an entry into London in March 1551 with her household displaying rosaries in sight of the crowds that had come to greet her, the Privy Council lessened its demands for Mary's conformity.

Mary became queen after her brother's death and a contested succession in July 1553. Two issues dominated her reign. One was the restoration of Catholic worship and the 1554 reconciliation with the Holy See. In 1555 Mary's government began the burning of heretics, martyring over three hundred individuals within three years and earning her the label "Bloody Mary." The second important issue of Mary's reign was her marriage to Philip II* of Spain. Opposition to the Spanish alliance produced Thomas Wyatt's rebellion, which was defeated in 1554. Mary and Philip were married in Winchester Cathedral in late 1554, but Philip became king in title only. He influenced Mary to declare war against France in 1557, which resulted in the English loss of Calais. Mary I died on 17 November 1558.

Bibliography

D. Loades, *Mary Tudor: A Life*, 1989.

Gary G. Gibbs

MASSYS (METSYS), QUENTIN (c. 1466–1530)

Quentin Massys, founder of the Antwerp school of painting, blended the medieval Flemish tradition with the style of the Italian Renaissance. Inspired by Leonardo da Vinci, Massys utilized architectural settings, richer ornamentation, and broad sunlit landscapes in his compositions. He also painted scenes from everyday life in a straightforward and realistic manner.

Born in Louvain in 1466, Massys decided to become a painter instead of a blacksmith like his father and his older brother. His apprenticeship remains a matter of conjecture, but it is probable that he did receive formal training under the direction of one of the sons or other followers of the great Dirk Bouts of Louvain. Massys had evidently moved his family to Antwerp by 1491, for in that year he registered as a master with the St. Luke Guild of painters. From at least 1495 to 1510 Massys accepted apprenticeships to assist him in painting two large-scale, five-panel altarpieces: the *St. Anne Altarpiece* painted for St. Peter's in Louvain (1507–9), and the *St. John* or *Lamentation* commissioned by the joiners' guild for their chapel in the Cathedral of Antwerp (1508–11). After 1510 Massys no longer took on apprentices. Since he had turned from the public arena of large-scale religious painting to the private sphere of smaller-scale portrait and votive-panel painting, Massys required less assistance. Also, what help he needed came from his two sons, Cornelius and Jan, who worked under him in an undeclared apprenticeship. Both sons simultaneously achieved the status of master painter upon the death of their father in 1531.

One of Massys's greatest achievements was his experimentation with color. Compared with the relatively uniform and solid blocks of color used in the fifteenth century, the variable and broken colors used by Massys in *The Moneychanger and His Wife* (1514) are electrifying. Massys was also an innovator in the field of portrait painting, and his brushstrokes captured the humanistic quality of men like *Erasmus of Rotterdam** (1517) and *Petrus Aegidius* or *Pierre Gillis* (1517). With the adoption of portraitlike half-lengths in his later years, Massys gave his figures emotional intensity. Whether they are repulsive, like the secular figures of *The Old Woman* (c. 1520–21) or *The Ill-matched Pair* (c. 1523–24), or comely, like the sacred figure of the *Rattier Madonna* (1529), the viewer is captivated.

Bibliography

L. Silver, *The Paintings of Quinten Massys with Catalogue Raisonné*, 1984.

Whitney Leeson

MEDICI, CATHERINE DE' (1519–1589)

Catherine de' Medici's childhood provided no indication of her later central position on the European stage as queen of France in the turbulent years of the Wars of Religion. The subject of controversy during her lifetime and thereafter, she worked tirelessly in her children's interests, to maintain monarchical authority, and to neutralize the sectarian strife that divided the country.

Catherine, the daughter of Lorenzo, duke of Urbino, and a French princess, was the first member of her Florentine family to be nobly born. Orphaned shortly after her birth, she grew up under the guardianship of relatives, sometimes living in convents. In 1533 her cousin, Pope Clement VII, arranged her marriage to Henri, duc d'Orléans, the second son of François I* of France. Although Catherine was supported by her Italophile father-in-law, her husband greatly favored his mistress, Diane de Poitiers.* Compounding Catherine's situation, the young couple had difficulty conceiving and produced no children during the first ten years of their marriage, although they eventually had ten, of whom seven survived.

An improbable series of events brought—and kept—Catherine close to the throne. First, her husband's older brother died, leaving him heir apparent. Henri became king—and Catherine queen—in 1547. He was killed accidentally twelve years later and succeeded by François II, aged fourteen. In 1560 he too died, followed by Charles IX, who had not yet reached his majority. Catherine served as regent and began pacification efforts between opposing religious factions, but they failed, and in 1562 the first of the Wars of Religion broke out.

Catherine spent the rest of her seventy-year life working in her children's interests. She sought advantageous marriages for all and snared the crown of Poland for the future Henri III. She tried unsuccessfully to wage peace through mediation. This required constant travel, which she undertook even in advanced age. Catherine also staged lavish court entertainments that effected allegorical reconciliation between Catholics and Protestants. One, celebrating the marriage of her youngest daughter, Marguerite de Valois,* a Catholic, to Henri de Navarre, the Protestant heir to the throne, brought many Protestants to Paris. It turned into the St. Bartholomew's Day Massacre, during which over two thousand Huguenots were killed in Paris, and more in the provinces.

Catherine de' Medici has been painted as one of history's greatest villains, accused of any number of poisonings and masterminding the St. Bartholomew's Day Massacre, but some accounts are exaggerated due to gender bias and xenophobia. She can be credited with working to shore up French monarchical authority and to defuse religious strife. As an architectural patron, she built the Valois Chapel—the first independent tomb chapel to be appended to the Church of St. Denis, the French royal mausoleum—and two Parisian houses, the Tuileries and the Hôtel de la Reine.

Bibliography

S. ffolliott, "The Ideal Queenly Patron of the Renaissance: Catherine de' Medici Defining Herself or Defined by Others?" in *Women and Art in Early Modern Europe: Patrons, Collectors, and Connoisseurs,* ed. Cynthia Lawrence, 1997.
M. P. Holt, *The French Wars of Religion, 1562–1629,* 1995.
R. J. Knecht, *Catherine de' Medici,* 1998.
N. M. Sutherland, *Catherine de' Medici and the Ancien Régime,* 1966.

Sheila ffolliott

MELANCHTHON, PHILIP (1497–1560)

Author of the Augsburg Confession and the subsequent *Apology,* Philip Melanchthon is regarded as one of the main leaders of the Reformation, and his theology served as the focal point for most strains of Protestantism emerging from that age. Melanchthon's early love of Latin and Greek led him to translate his birth name of Schwartzerd into its Greek equivalent, Melanchthon. Influenced by William of Occam, he came to doubt many of the traditional teachings of the Catholic church. As a professor at the University of Wittenberg, he became a close acquaintance of Martin Luther*; already an evangelical, Melanchthon readily accepted the idea of justification by faith alone and by 1519 had rejected the Catholic belief in transubstantiation.

Melanchthon grew even more convinced that Scripture was the basis for belief, and not church tradition. His relationship with Luther was a complementary one, and he was neither the spokesperson for his colleague nor his tool. Indeed, Melanchthon's humanist beliefs put him at odds with Luther in many respects. They did collaborate on several pamphlets, most notably *Freedom of a Christian Man,* and when Luther refused to recant his beliefs at the Diet of Worms in 1521, Melanchthon wrote a defense of his friend. Responding to Catholic criticism of the evangelicals, Melanchthon issued *Loci communes* in April 1521, which was a systematic exposition of Protestant thought up to that point.

Melanchthon also turned his energies in 1524 toward the establishment of a public school system in Germany based on evangelical principles and reorganized the faculty at Wittenberg to train future teachers for that task; the university thus abandoned its Scholastically based curriculum in favor of one based on the humanities. Melanchthon believed that a lack of education led to a decline in piety, and that a humanities curriculum could more effectively weld education to true Christian doctrine. For his efforts, Melanchthon earned the title "Preceptor" (teacher) of Germany.

The Protestants did not seem able to reach a consensus on the major doctrinal issues, and two diets at Speyer also failed to effect a conciliation with the Catholics, leading Emperor Charles V* to call the Diet of Augsburg in early 1530. Melanchthon headed up the Protestant delegation that found itself having to issue an unequivocal response concerning its doctrines. Drawn up by Melanchton, this statement, known as the Augsburg Confession, was essentially a Lutheran confession of faith. It was presented to the emperor in June and was refuted by Johann Eck, and it soon became clear that no compromise could be reached on the major issues, despite Melanchthon's conciliatory attitudes. Luther wanted the negotiations broken off, but Melanchthon wished to avoid a religious war, leading some of the evangelicals to question his devotion to the faith.

Falling to reach agreement, the German Lutheran princes formed the Schmalkaldic League to prepare for hostilities, and Melanchthon issued *Apology*, which was essentially a defense of the Augsburg Confession. The emperor's demand that the princes renounce their heretical beliefs by April 1531 meant the beginnings of a cold war between the two sides, solidified by the Council of Trent in 1545. Melanchthon carried the pamphlet torch in the aftermath of Luther's death in 1546, and when the Schmalkaldic War broke out in 1547, he made further futile attempts to conciliate with the Catholics. When the Peace of Augsburg ended the war in 1555 and allowed the German princes to determine the religion in each of their territories, Melanchthon was hopeful that a final resolution was in sight.

After the death of his wife in 1557, Melanchthon entered a period of physical decline and passed away in April 1560. Buried next to Luther, Melanchthon took his rightful place, in death as in life, as one of the primary leaders of the Reformation, whose theology provides the underpinnings for most evangelical Protestantism today.

Bibliography

C. L. Manschreck, *Melanchthon, the Quiet Reformer*, 1975.

Connie S. Evans

MERCATOR, GERARDUS (1512–1594)

Gerardus Mercator, a transforming figure in the history of cartography, devised the projection that bears his name when he created his world map of 1569 that revolutionized both mapmaking and, by extension, the way people came to view the world. Mercator was born in Flanders near Antwerp and studied astronomy, geography, and geometry at the University of Louvain. Mercator, like his mentor, Reiner Gemma Frisius,* became a well-known surveyor—he drew an acclaimed map of Europe in 1541—as well as a master engraver, making astrolabes, globes, and scientific instruments along with maps and charts. He also introduced italic type to northern Europe. However, in 1544 he ran afoul of the Inquisition.

Escaping punishment, Mercator moved in 1552 to Duisburg in the Rhineland, at that time a center of geographic study and a place where religion was less heated than in the Low Countries. There, under the patronage of William, duke of Cleves, he made another map of Europe in 1544—which reduced the size of the Mediterranean from Ptolemy's representation by ten degrees of latitude—and his celebrated map of the world five years later.

For his magnum opus, Mercator incorporated the European "discoveries" that had been made since the first decade of the sixteenth century. Thus the map more accurately depicted the western coasts of America and the southern coasts of Asia, although it retained the mythical Terra Australis.

However, its greater significance lay in the way in which it portrayed that knowledge. Sixteenth-century seafarers wanted to chart their courses by drawing a straight line between two points, without having to constantly reset their compasses. Mercator, almost literally, had to square a circle to meet this need. Portraying the rhumb lines—the curves of a course on a globe—as straight lines perpendicular to the equator enabled him to set latitudes parallel to the equator, with the lines of longitude, still inexact in Mercator's lifetime, intersecting latitudes at right angles. The result was a fundamentally more reliable map, although distortion of land masses increases the closer they are to the poles. Mercator also conceived of compiling a series of maps between two covers. He was working on such an atlas when he died, but an edition based on his plates edited by Jodocus Hondius first appeared in 1607.

Bibliography

J. N. Wilford, *The Mapmakers*, 1981.

Louis Roper

MICHELANGELO (1475–1564)

Born Michelangelo Buonarroti, Michelangelo was the dominant artist of the Italian High Renaissance, arguably the greatest sculptor in the history of Western art, as well as a notable painter, draughtsman, and architect. Born in Caprese in central Italy, Michelangelo was the son of a minor Florentine government official. Against his father's wishes, he determined to become an artist and at the age of thirteen apprenticed to the workshop of the popular Florentine painter Domenico Ghirlandaio. He seems to have found the shop or the painting uncongenial, for he left the studio before completing his apprenticeship and moved to the Medici household in 1490, where an "art school" was being established by Lorenzo de' Medici. There he was exposed to the collection of ancient and contemporary sculpture, to other sculptors—most notably, Bertoldo di Giovanni, pupil of Donatello—and to the highest circles of humanist intellectual discourse. He later claimed to have taught himself how to carve stone; his sculptures from this period (*Madonna of the Steps* and *Battle of Lapiths and Centaurs*, Florence, Casa Buonarroti, c. 1490–92) reveal a young artist of enormous talent who has not yet totally conquered issues of space, anatomy, and composition.

When Lorenzo died in 1492, Michelangelo went in search of new patronage, first to Bologna, then by 1496 to Rome, where he immediately achieved success and received important commissions. His first *Pietà* (Rome, St. Peter's, 1498–1500) revealed him as an outstanding master of the High Renaissance style. Its character of idealized naturalism and the beauty of its carving established the artist's reputation. He returned to Florence in 1501 to begin work on the *David* (Florence, Accademia, 1501–4). Colossal, classicizing, naturalistic, and filled with an awesome psychological tension that was peculiar to the artist, the *David* ensured that Michelangelo would be seen as a peerless master who had surpassed the achievements of antiquity.

As he finished the *David*, Michelangelo was commissioned to paint a fresco of *The Battle of Cascina* (1504) in the town hall of Florence; Leonardo da Vinci had earlier received a commission for another battle fresco in the same room, so this work put the young artist into direct competition with the greatest artist known to Florence. Michelangelo was eager to show off his skill, but he never completed the commission, for he received a more tempting offer: a project to carve the most elaborate tomb ever designed for Pope Julius II* at St. Peter's. This expensive, time-consuming project would bedevil the artist for most of his life, as the patrons repeatedly canceled and reinstated the commission.

In 1508 Julius II decided that Michelangelo could serve him better by painting the ceiling of the Sistine Chapel; under the strongest protests, the sculptor turned to the massive fresco program, which he designed and painted almost entirely on his own in the years 1508–12. Within and around a painted architectural framework, Michelangelo depicted nine scenes from Genesis, twelve prophets and sibyls, and dozens of subsidiary scenes and figures. Taking the male nude as his primary subject, he described a heroic, grandiose world where God's plan for salvation was initially revealed.

Michelangelo continued to work intermittently on Julius's tomb after the Sistine Chapel, but his next major project was a mausoleum for the Medicis to be added to the family church of San Lorenzo in Florence. The artist designed the architecture, ornamentation, and sculptural ensembles of the "New Sacristy" between 1519 and 1534. At the same time, he also designed a new library for the same church. Michelangelo's architecture could not be called classicizing; he used forms in unexpected ways, avoided balance and harmony, and made the viewer aware of spaces in an expressive way.

In 1534 Michelangelo moved to Rome, where he spent the rest of his life.

Commissioned to paint the *Last Judgment* on the altar wall of the Sistine Chapel (1536–41), he rejected his earlier notions of grandeur and heroism to create a vision of the end of that time that was profoundly pessimistic. He was strongly affected by the Reformation and produced an image that was markedly unbalanced, whose figures were distorted and often ugly, and whose overall focus was on sin and damnation rather than salvation. It retained his characteristic profound expression, but no longer accepted the idealization of High Renaissance art.

As his strength waned, Michelangelo produced fewer sculptures in his old age; his primary preoccupation from 1546 to his death was designing the Church of St. Peter. Building on the ideas of Donato Bramante, in particular, he sought to produce a centralized structure on a huge scale that would be monumental, impressive, and unified. The complex structure was topped by a gigantic dome that created a dramatic, upward emphasis on both the interior and exterior of the church.

The most famous sculptor in history during his own lifetime, Michelangelo has continued to be the model of artistic talent to the current day. His enormous skill goes without saying; it is his originality, his dedication, and his profound understanding of human experience that make his art so powerful. The modern notion of the artist as a solitary genius and the concept of artistry as a combination of intellect, individuality, proficiency, and inventiveness are exemplified by Michelangelo's career.

Bibliography

H. Hibbard, *Michelangelo*, 1985.
C. de Tolnay, *Michelangelo*, 5 vols., 1947–60.

Jane C. Long

MIDDLETON, THOMAS (1580–1627)

With a prolific writing career that almost exactly spanned the Jacobean era, Thomas Middleton is perhaps the most representative figure of Jacobean drama. Born into a middle-class London family, Middleton was educated at Oxford. There he wrote his earliest poems, marked with Elizabethan stylistic exuberance. They also demonstrate a strong satiricial impulse that was to become the hallmark of his drama. Two satirical pamphlets about London life followed, showing Middleton's advance along the road of realism.

His career as a playwright began with collaborations with Thomas Dekker* and John Webster,* marked by keen interest in citizen life and the portrayal of living historical characters. The most famous of these is *The Roaring Girl* (1611), whose title character was London's own Mary Frith, a celebrated cross-dresser. Middleton's reputation as a dramatist was established through his brilliant city comedies, composed for the fashionable boys' companies. After their closure, Middleton went on to write moral comedies for adult companies. From 1613 on, he devoted much time to writing and producing civic entertainments informed by the militant Protestantism that marked the rest of his work. In 1620 he was appointed London's chronologer, a position he held until his death.

Middleton's tragicomedies from 1614 to 1616 (*The Witch, A Fair Quarrel*) and tragedies (*Women Beware Women*, c. 1621, and *The Changeling*, 1622) share the moral concerns of his comedies, but humor here has turned sinister. His last work for the theater was the most controversial political play of the era, *A Game of Chess* (1624). The play's expression of the English hatred of Spain and Catholicism ensured it a phenomenal consecutive nine-day run before it was closed after vehement protests by the Spanish ambassador. Middleton avoided arrest by discreetly disappearing. For one last time, the playwright whose plays were produced at court, the man whom King James* accepted as his ghostwriter, demonstrated his attraction for politically self-conscious theater.

Bibliography

M. Heinemann, *Puritanism and Theatre: Thomas Middleton and Opposition Drama under the Early Stuarts*, 1980.

Kirilka Stavreva

MONTAIGNE, MICHEL EYQUEM DE (1533–1592)

Michel Eyquem de Montaigne is famous for his essays, a genre of writing he largely originated, and for the honest, frank observations found within these essays. Montaigne also served as the mayor of Bordeaux and was friends with Henri of Navarre, later King Henri IV of France.

Montaigne was born on 28 February 1533 in the family domain of Montaigne in Périgueux, in southwestern France. As a child, Montaigne was tutored at home in accordance with his father's ideas of pedagogy. This included the use of Latin as the only language that was spoken in the presence of the young Michel. Latin was considered the language educated people should know, and thus the young Michel was raised speaking Latin as his first language; he was not exposed to French until he was six years old. He later continued his education at the Collège de Guyenne, where he was studying to practice medicine. Montaigne found university life extremely boring, and the instructors he described as abhorrent; he later transferred to the University of Toulouse, where he studied law. After his studies, Montaigne continued in the tradition of his father and grandfather by entering public service. He entered the magistrature, where he became a member of the Board of Excise—the tax court of Périgueux. When this board was disbanded in 1557, Montaigne then served in the Parlement of Bordeaux, one of the eight regional parliaments that constituted the French Parlement, the highest national court of justice.

It was while Montaigne was serving on the Parlement of Bordeaux that he met Étienne de La Boétie.* La Boétie and Montaigne became close friends. La Boétie was a humanist and scholar, and he and Montaigne engaged in many extended conversations. When La Boétie died of dysentery in 1563, Montaigne was disconsolate, so to appease his grief, he began writing his essays in an effort to recapture the conversations he had once had with his friend. In 1570 Montaigne sold his seat in the Parlement of Bordeaux and retired to his estate to devote time to reading, writing, and compiling and preparing the posthumous publication of La Boétie's works.

The essays Montaigne wrote in honor of his friend are what have given Montaigne his fame, and they continue to be a source of information and insight regarding sixteenth-century culture. Montaigne's essays, along with his travel journals, provide a rare glimpse into the daily life of people in the sixteenth century, and for this reason historians continually refer to these essays as a primary source. Philosophers and literary theorists also find in Montaigne the beginnings of what has been called the modern era, whether it be modern philosophy or modern literature. The essays were composed primarily during Montaigne's period of retirement, between 1571 and 1580. The first two books of the *Essays* were published in Bordeaux in 1580. After their publication and a lengthy period of time at home, Montaigne left on the travels that would lead to the travel journals. While traveling in Italy, Montaigne found out that he had been elected mayor of Bordeaux, a position his father had once held. Although he was reluctant to accept the post due to ill health—Montaigne long suffered from kidney stones—he returned to Bordeaux and served as mayor for two terms, until 1585. While serving as mayor, Montaigne fought to keep Bordeaux loyal to the Protestant king, Henri IV, though he faced much opposition from the Catholic majority. After serving his tumultuous second term, Montaigne returned home to his reading and writing. He died at his home on 13 September 1592. The essays Montaigne left behind after his death, although they were prompted by the tragic loss of his friend, are nevertheless something for which anyone interested in sixteenth-century culture will be forever thankful.

Bibliography

B. Bowen, *The Age of Bluff: Paradox and Ambiguity in Rabelais and Montaigne*, 1972.

D. Frame, *Montaigne: A Biography*, 1965.

H. Friedrich, *Montaigne*, 1991.

Jeffrey A. Bell

MONTEMAYOR, JORGE DE (c. 1520–1561)

Jorge de Montemayor is most famous for his pastoral novel, *Diana* (c. 1559), which signaled the decline of the chivalric romance and became the new style of novel in Spain. It may have been the source of Sir Philip Sidney's* *Arcadia*.

Born near Coimbra, Portugal, Montemayor took the name of his birthplace, translated it into Spanish, and made it his surname. His original surname is unknown. He became Spanish of his own free will, which did not sit well with his compatriots, who at one point banned his works in Portugal. Musically inclined, he was a singer in the chapel of Princess Maria and later Princess Juana, both daughters of the monarch Charles V.* When Princess Juana married the Portuguese Prince Juan, Montemayor went with her to Portugal. When the prince died, he returned with the princess to Spain. It was then that he began to gather his religious and secular poems in *Cancionero*, or poetic anthology, which he published in 1554. The Inquisition banned his religious poems on theological grounds. His secular ones achieved a degree of success and saw seven editions before the turn of the century. Montemayor went to Flanders and possibly England as a part of King Philip II's* retinue when the monarch went intending to marry Mary I.* He returned to Spain in 1559 and died two years later in a duel, possibly over jealousy.

Although *Diana* is his most famous work, Montemayor wrote poems, translated poetry, and wrote other prose works as well. *Diana* first appeared in print in Valencia in 1558 or 1559. It blends the pastoral with the fantastic, mythology with portraits, real life with fancy. It was enormously successful: it saw seventeen editions in Spanish before the end of the century and was translated into French, English, Italian, and German four times. In Spain, a *Second Part of the Diana* was published in 1564, and in the same year Gaspar Gil Polo published *Diana in Love*. The novel influenced Honoré d'Urfé's* novel *L'Astrée* and possibly Philip Sidney's *Arcadia*. True to its genre, *Diana* is a sentimental love story about courtiers disguised as shepherds. It appealed to Cervantes's* Don Quixote even on his deathbed. Don Quixote's preference for this novel over his previous affinity for chivalric romances registered the change in taste among Spanish readers. Although the pastoral was intended for a more elite audience, *Diana* enjoyed great popularity, as attested to by its censure by moralists who attacked its extended love scenes. After the *Diana*, Spaniards saw at least forty bucolic novels published over the next sixty years.

Bibliography

B. Damiani, *Montemayor's* Diana, *Music, and the Visual Arts*, 1983.
E. Rhodes, *The Unrecognized Precursors of Montemayor's* Diana, 1992.

Ana Kothe

MONTEVERDI, CLAUDIO (1567–1643)

Claudio Monteverdi was a composer of sacred and secular music, the most important Italian composer during the transition from the Renaissance to baroque style. His operas are the first masterpieces in the genre. Monteverdi was born in Cremona and began his musical studies at the cathedral there. His compositional career began at an early age, and he published his first pieces, a collection of three-voice motets, at the age of fifteen. By 1591, when he went to Mantua to serve as a musician for the Gonzaga court, he had already published books of "spiritual madrigals" (1583), canzonettas (1584), and his first two books of madrigals (1587 and 1590). In Mantua he continued writing madrigals, and in 1607 he produced his first work in the new genre of opera, a setting of *Orfeo*. The next year he produced his second opera, *L'Arianna* (now lost), to celebrate the wedding of Francesco Gonzaga and Margaret of Savoy. Along with these works, he published three more books of madrigals. He was dismissed from his position, along with a number of other musicians, in 1612.

In 1613 Monteverdi was appointed maestro di cappella at St. Mark's Cathedral in Venice. At that time, the musical quality of the cathedral had diminished, and much of his energy was taken up in rebuilding it. He still had time, however, to fill commissions for dramatic music from the new duke of Mantua and sacred music for various religious organizations in Venice. During this time he also published his last four books of madrigals. He remained in Venice for the rest of his life, writing music in all genres, including his final opera, *L'incoronazione di Poppea* (1642).

Monteverdi's role in the musical transition of his time is twofold. In his madrigals he wrote in a style that he called the *seconda prattica*, a description he used to separate himself from the more conservative tradition of Giovanni Pierluigi da Palestrina* and his contemporaries. Here, the meaning of the text controlled nearly every aspect of the musical setting. This often led to violations of the accepted rules, a fact that caused the theorist Giovanni Maria Artusi to excoriate Monteverdi and other "moderns." Far from willfully repudiating the rules, however, Monteverdi used these new techniques to create an enormous depth of meaning in his pieces. In doing so, he was following the path of an earlier generation led by Cipriano de Rore.*

At the same time, composers were beginning to abandon complex polyphony to concentrate on a simpler texture of voice and chordal accompaniment. This style, called monody, was cultivated in Florence but soon became the primary means of musical expression, especially in opera. Monteverdi made effective use of this style, and in his operas and other dramatic works he was able to go beyond simple text expression and to explore the psychological aspects of the characters he portrayed. Variety in harmony and the immediate expression of the single voice became impressively flexible tools for composers, and Monteverdi exploited them to their fullest potential in his operas. Monteverdi was neither a revolutionary nor a pioneer. His place in musical history rests on his ability to realize fully the possibilities of musical expression.

Bibliography

D. Arnold, *Monteverdi*, rev. ed., 1975.
P. Fabbri, *Monteverdi*, trans. T. Carter, 1994.

Russell E. Murray, Jr.

MOR (MORO), ANTONIO (1519–1576)

Antonio Mor was a Dutch artist who earned his reputation as a portrait painter, primarily for the Habsburg monarchs in the Netherlands and Spain. Born in Utrecht, Mor served an apprenticeship under the painter Jan van Scorel,* though he soon established himself independently. By 1549 he was in Antwerp, in the employ of Antoine Perrenot de Granvelle, one of Philip II* of Spain's most influential counsellors; Mor's portrait of Granvelle (Vienna, Kunsthistorisches

Museum) from this time has been compared to Titian's* similar portrait of the same subject. Granvelle's patronage provided Mor an entrée to the Habsburg court established in the Netherlands. In the fall of 1549 the Habsburgs convened in Brussels to officially acknowledge Philip as heir to the Netherlands; on this occasion, Mor was commissioned to execute several portraits of the monarchs. Mor's ability to render his subjects convincingly was admired by his royal patrons.

In 1550, at the command of Philip's aunt, Mary of Hungary, the current regent of the Netherlands, Mor was sent to Spain and Portugal to produce portraits of other members of the Habsburg family, among them *Maximilian of Austria* (Madrid, Prado, 1550) and his consort, *Mary* (Madrid, Prado, 1551). By 1554 Mor was recognized as the official court painter of Philip II, with whom he enjoyed a close friendship; during this year he went to England with Philip to paint what would become one of his most famous works, the portrait of *Mary Tudor* (Mary I*) (Madrid, Prado, 1554), Philip's second wife. For the next several years Mor traveled between the Netherlands and Spain, continuing to paint various members of the royal family; several works on religious subjects as well as Mor's *Self-Portrait* (Florence, Uffizi, 1558) also date from this period. Mor returned to the Netherlands around 1561; though he still painted for the Habsburgs, he turned to other subjects, including prosperous merchants and acquaintances from humanist circles. He was working on a painting for the cathedral of Antwerp when he died there in 1576.

Mor paid homage to the teaching of his master, Jan van Scorel, in a bust portrait (London, 1559). Scholars have also pointed to Titian's influence on Mor's work; but while Mor may have assimilated some of the techniques of these predecessors, his work evinces his own style, characteristically austere and formal but realistic.

Bibliography

M. J. Friedlander, *Antonis Mor and His Contemporaries*, 1975.

Jo Eldridge Carney

MORALES, CRISTÓBAL DE (c. 1500–1553)

A singer and choirmaster, Cristóbal de Morales became the greatest Spanish composer of the early sixteenth century. Morales received his early musical training in Seville, a city with a rich musical tradition by the time of his birth there. Like most composers of his age, he was employed primarily as a singer. In 1526 he assumed the post of choirmaster at Ávila Cathedral, and by 1535 he had joined the papal choir in Rome, where he remained for the next ten years. As a baritone in that ensemble, Morales was given a monthly salary of eight ducats, a servant, and, when he traveled in the papal retinue, a horse. Gifts received for performances before visiting dignitaries and at special events supplemented the singers' incomes. For one such event—festivities celebrating a peace treaty between François I* and Emperor Charles V* negotiated by the pope in 1538—Morales composed the motet *Jubilate Deo omnis terra*, whose text praises all three men. His earliest published music dates from the following year, and during the early 1540s a large number of his compositions appeared in print. At the same time, his health began to decline, and as the dedications to two books of masses published in 1544 make clear, he was actively seeking a more lucrative post. In 1545 he returned to Spain, where he served as choirmaster at Toledo Cathedral (1545–47), to the duke of Arcos in Marchéna (1548–51), and at Málaga Cathedral (1551–53). During these last years he suffered from poor health and discipline problems with the singers and the choirboys in his charge.

Morales was almost exclusively a composer of Latin sacred music; his output includes sixteen magnificats, over two hundred masses, and over one hundred motets. No other Spanish composer of the century attained a comparable level of international popularity: his music spread beyond Spain and Italy to France, Germany, the Low Countries, and even Mexico and Peru.

Bibliography

R. Stevenson, *Spanish Cathedral Music in the Golden Age*, 1961.

David Crook

MORE, SIR THOMAS (1477/78–1535)

Known throughout the world for his authorship of *Utopia*, Thomas More wrote humanist, polemical, and devotional works in Latin and English. Lawyer, politician, humanist, statesman, and lord chancellor, he was executed on grounds of treason and died a martyr. The Roman Catholic church canonized him in 1935.

Son of judge Sir John and Agnes Graunger More, More was educated at St. Anthony's School, London. He spent two years of his youth as a page in the house of Cardinal John Morton. With Morton as his patron, he went to Oxford, where he studied under Thomas Linacre* and William Grocyn. Back in London to study common law in 1494, he was admitted to Lincoln's Inn in 1496 and called to the bar in 1501. While at Lincoln's Inn, he tested a vocation to the priesthood by living at a Carthusian monastery; there habits of prayer, fasting, and penance became parts of his life. Having decided against the monastic life, in 1505 he married Jane Colt, who bore him three daughters and a son. On her death in 1511, he married Alice Middleton.

More's Chelsea home became a center of intellectual life. Since 1499 he had been friends with Desiderius Erasmus*; Hans Holbein* was his guest, John Colet* another friend. Erasmus and More produced Latin translations of some of Lucian's Greek works during Erasmus's second visit to England. At More's Chelsea home, on his third visit in 1509, Erasmus wrote *Moriae encomium* (Praise of Folly), the title of which plays on More's name.

In 1504 More entered Parliament and won Henry VII's disapproval by opposing his financial demands. With Henry VIII's* accession in 1509, he gained the king's favor and began to rise rapidly in public life. From 1510 to 1518 More was undersheriff in London and earned a reputation for being impartial and protecting the poor. In 1515 he was sent as a diplomat to Flanders to settle a dispute in the wool trade; here he wrote book 2 of *Utopia*. He became privy councillor and master of requests in 1518, accompanied Henry to the Field of the Cloth of Gold in 1520, and was knighted in 1521. The king's favor seemed without bounds, and More became speaker of the House of Commons (1523), chancellor of the Duchy of Lancaster (1525), and lord chancellor (1529).

More's fall from favor came rapidly. When the king decided to divorce his wife, Catherine of Aragon, who had given him no male heir, so he could marry Anne Boleyn—a position involving him in disputes with Emperor Charles V* (Catherine's nephew) and Pope Clement VII—More refused to support Henry. After years of futile negotiations, Henry, despite his opposition to Martin Luther's* Reformation, repudiated papal authority, named himself head of the church in England in 1531, had his marriage to Catherine declared invalid, and married Anne.

More resigned the chancellorship in 1532 and by doing so lost nearly all his income. He refused to attend Anne Boleyn's coronation and was one of those accused of complicity with Elizabeth Barton, the nun of Kent, who opposed Henry's break with Rome. In 1534 More refused to swear to the Act of Succession, which made Henry and Anne's children legitimate heirs to the throne, and was imprisoned in the Tower of London. He remained there for fifteen months, until Richard Rich, solicitor general, acting as prosecutor at More's trial, brought a charge of treason against him on 1 July 1535. On 6 July 1535, fourteen days after John Fisher's* execution, More was beheaded on Tower Hill. Pope Leo XIII beatified him in 1886; Pope Pius XI canonized him in 1935.

Because More played so many parts so well—lawyer, judge, civil servant, political figure, statesman, humanist, critic, intellectual, jester, man of wit, storyteller, poet, husband, father, friend, host, educator, polemicist, ascetic, man of conscience, defender of the Catholic faith—it is sometimes difficult to find unity in his writings as a whole. His work in Latin and English helped to shape early-sixteenth-century humanism in England and on the Continent. Although he left some works unfinished, his canon was enormous. The largest part of it was polemical, and his defense of Catholicism against the Protestant Reformers, mainly Luther and William Tyndale,* is historically and culturally important. His literary reputation, however, depends on his humanist pieces and the letters and devotional tracts he wrote as a prisoner in the Tower. Written at the request of the bishop of London, Cuthbert Tunstall, *Responsio ad Lutherum* (Response to Luther), *Dialogue Concerning Heresies, Supplication of Souls, The Confutation of Tyndale's Answer, The Apology, The Debellation of Salem and Bizance, The Answer to a Poisoned Book*, and some letters comprise his polemical works. His humanist works include English verses, Latin and English versions of *The History of King Richard III*, a translation of the *Life of Pico*, some Latin epigrams, and letters in defense of humanism. *Utopia* (completed 1516), his humanist masterpiece, an enigmatic description of an imaginary society that has provided the name for and model of a literary form, was written in Latin and found its place as a classic of English literature after Ralph Robinson translated it in 1551. Of his devotional treatises, *A Dialogue of Comfort against Tribulation*, which he wrote in the Tower as he contemplated his fate, stands as one of his noblest pieces and the finest English prose of its time.

Bibliography

R. W. Chambers, *Thomas More*, 1935.
A. Fox, *Thomas More: History and Providence*, 1983.
R. Marius, *Thomas More*, 1984.

Al Geritz

MORLEY, THOMAS (1557–1603)

Thomas Morley was an English composer particularly known for his madrigals and other secular dance music. Little is known about his early life. He was a pupil of William Byrd,* from whom he purchased a royal monopoly to print music and music paper, and an Oxford classmate of John Dowland,* earning his bachelor's degree in music on the same day in 1588.

Some of his surviving music explicitly celebrates the Virgin Mary, indicating probable composition for Roman Catholic patrons. Morley played the organ first at Norwich Cathedral and then at St. Paul's before joining the Chapel Royal musicians, who played at court. However, Morley is known less for religious compositions than for his secular dance music in forms imported from Italy: the madrigal, the canzonet ("little song"), and the ballett (derived from the dance). In addition to seven collections of these dances (1593–1603), Morley published music for ensembles of mixed instruments in *The First Booke of Consort Lessons* (1599) and a book of music theory with the deceptive name of *A Plaine and Easie Introduction* (1597). His final collection of madrigals, *The Triumphes of Oriana*, was published in honor of Elizabeth I.* Morley may have spied for Elizabeth during continental travels; although he was a Catholic himself, he apparently used his time in the Low Countries to discover information about Catholics in England, presumably because even the Church of England was preferable to rule by Catholic Spain. In his composing, Morley was particularly interested in the madrigal's basis in dance and poetry. Some have admired his experimentation with the madrigal and its related forms. Others have charged that his compositions rely too heavily on continental work, and even that he may have deliberately put his name to the work of others.

Bibliography

D. C. Jacobson, "Thomas Morley and the Italian Madrigal Tradition: A New Perspective," *Journal of Musicology* 14 (Winter 1996): 80–91.

Jean Graham

MÜNSTER, SEBASTIAN (1488–1552)

Sebastian Münster was a German Renaissance scholar with broad interests: one of the most important Hebraists of his age, he was also a theologian, astronomer, cartographer, and geographer. Born in Ingelheim on the Rhine, Germany, Münster, at an early age, came to Heidelberg, where he entered the Franciscan order in 1505. He studied philosophy, Greek, and Hebrew at the monasteries of Heidelberg, Louvain, Freiburg, Rufach (Alsace), and Pforzheim. Ordained priest in 1512, Münster taught philosophy in the monastery of his order in Tübingen and at Basel, where he began in the early 1520s his literary career with translations from Latin into German, among them some works by Martin Luther* and the medieval *Speculum sapientiae/Spiegel der Wyssheit* (Mirror of Wisdom), a collection of medieval fables. From 1521 on, he devoted himself to Hebrew-language studies. After 1524 he taught at the University of Heidelberg. In 1529 he left his order after having been offered a chair for Hebrew and theology at the reformed University of Basel, whose rector he became in 1547/48. He died of the plague in 1552.

Though Münster worked in many fields, he achieved fame in two areas: his study of Hebrew and his geographical studies. Together with Johannes Reuchlin and Konrad Pellikan, Münster was the third great Christian Hebraist of that period. The range of his interests and his scholarly output were enormous. He published over sixty works, and by the end of the sixteenth century over 100,000 volumes were in circulation, ranging from grammars, dictionaries, and textbooks to commentaries, editions, and original works. In his work he often incorporated the work of the eminent Jewish scholar Elia Levita. Münster's most important achievement was the Hebrew edition of the Old Testament, the *Biblia Hebraica* (1534–35), with a new Latin translation and commentary. Münster also published several missionary works aimed at the Jewish community, including a translation of the Gospel of Matthew into Hebrew, the first such translation of any part of the New Testament. In addition, he devoted himself also to the study of Aramaic, the language of the Apostles, authoring a dictionary and grammar in that language.

While his Hebraic books and studies, important as they are, were limited to a small circle of scholars, his astronomical and geographical works established his fame throughout Germany and Europe. His astronomical works became great publishing successes, especially his calendars and his instructions on how to build sundials and astronomical instruments. His principal reputation, however, rests on his *Kosmographey* (Cosmography, 1544), a geographical-historical description of the whole world known at the time. It was translated into Latin (1550), French (1552), Czech (1554), and Italian (1558). Using ancient, medieval, and modern sources and relying on a network of coworkers from all over Europe as well as his own excursions to southern Germany and Switzerland, Münster's work was the first serious attempt at a scholarly but at the same time popular description of the total geographical knowledge of his time. Richly illustrated with maps and woodcuts, it was published in numerous editions in the sixteenth century.

Bibliography

K. H. Burmester, *Sebastian Münster: Versuch eines biographischen Gesamtbildes*, 2nd ed., 1969.
J. Friedman, *The Most Ancient Testimony: Sixteenth-Century Christian-Hebraica in the Age of Renaissance Nostalgia*, 1983.

Eckhard Bernstein

MURET, MARC-ANTOINE (1526–1585)

Marc-Antoine Muret, a learned French humanist and member of the Pléïade, taught classics and included among his admiring pupils the noted essayist Michel de Montaigne.* Muret was born in 1526 in Limoges, France. Muret's father, a famous jurist, inspired in him a love of study and sent him to Poitiers for formal study, but he could not stand having teachers, so at the age of twelve he took charge of his own studies. In 1545, at eighteen, he became a professor at Auch, but he continued his peripatetic ways, moving on to being a private tutor to a wealthy family, then returning to Poitiers to resume his legal studies, where he formed his friendship with the poet Joachim Du Bellay.* While he was teaching at the Collège de Guyenne in Bordeaux in 1547, he put on his Latin tragedy, *Julius Caesar*, in which Michel de Montaigne played a role. Muret personally tutored Montaigne until the latter left at the age of thirteen. Montaigne later said of Muret that he was "the best stylist of his age."

In 1551 Muret moved to Paris, teaching at the Collège du Cardinal Lemoine and the Collège Royal. While he was in Paris, he joined the famed poetic group the Pléïade through his connection with Du Bellay. The members of the Pléïade, headed by Pierre de Ronsard,* distinguished themselves as champions of the French language based on classical models of poetry. Muret wrote a *Commentary* on Ronsard's *Amours*, explaining the mythological allusions in the poems. He became famous for his orations, frequented by the French king and queen, Henri II and Catherine de Medici.*

But Muret's career was marred by scandal; whether this was due to envious rivals or actual excesses is unclear. He left Paris after having been incarcerated in the Châtelet for unnatural vices; he had resolved to die from hunger, "but God had pity on his soul." He moved to Toulouse, where he was accused of being a Huguenot and a sodomite. His enemies burned him in effigy, but he escaped in disguise.

He lived in Venice, Padua, and Ferrara, eventually becoming the official orator for Cardinal Ippolito d'Este and the French at the papal court in Rome. Muret made a point of his "implacable hatred" of heretics in an oration at the funeral of Pius V in 1572. Later that year he glorified the St. Bartholomew's Day Massacre before the new pope, Gregory XIII: "During the night I imagine the stars shone more brilliantly and the Seine had greater waves to carry and vomit the bodies of the impure men into the sea more quickly." After having held the chair of humane letters for many years in Rome, he retired in 1584 and died the following year. Pope Gregory XIII called him "the torch and pillar" of the Roman school.

Muret is best known as a learned French humanist and celebrated Latin stylist. In addition to the play *Julius Caesar*, he is remembered for his French commentary on the *Amours* of Ronsard, his editions of classical authors, and his multivolume *Variae lectiones*.

Bibliography

C. Dejob, *Marc Antoine Muret: Un professeur françois en Italie*, 1881, rpt., 1970.

Elaine Kruse

N

NASHE, THOMAS (1567–c. 1601)

"Young Juvenal," as Thomas Nashe's friends called him, was a satirist who shocked and delighted literary London with his polemical tracts, pamphlets, extravaganzas, comedies, literary criticism, and descriptive pieces. Born into a clerical family, Nashe graduated with a bachelor of arts from Cambridge, but withdrew before obtaining the coveted degree of master of arts. After his father's early death, he moved to London to join the lively group of Oxford and Cambridge graduates with literary ambitions known as the University Wits. The city welcomed Nashe kindly. Shortly after his first work, *The Anatomy of Absurdity* (1589), appeared, he was invited by the popular Robert Greene* to write a preface to his romance *Menaphon* (1589). Nashe's first public triumph was his brilliant defense (1590), solicited by the episcopacy, against the pseudonymous Puritan satirist Martin Marprelate. Yet he had little luck courting patrons and soon realized that his living depended on his popularity with the reading public. To gain it, Nashe would occasionally venture into disreputable genres, as with his pornographic poem "The Choice of Valentines."

Nashe's first popular success, *Pierce Penniless His Supplication to the Devil* (1592), was a controversial pamphlet that satirized England's sins and follies. Surprisingly, it won him the patronage of the archbishop of Canterbury, for whom he also wrote his one surviving comedy, *Summer's Last Will and Testament* (1592). But *Pierce Penniless* also ignited Nashe's scandalous controversy with the Cambridge scholar Gabriel Harvey,* which eventually caused the bishops to ban both of their works.

As Nashe's productivity grew, so did his troubles with the authorities. In September 1593 his historical protonovel *The Unfortunate Traveler* was registered. The same month saw the registration of *Christ's Tears over Jerusalem*. But the thinly veiled charges about the corruption of London's civic leaders in this pamphlet angered the lord mayor. The satirist only escaped prison through the intervention of the captain general of the Isle of Wight, at whose home he took shelter. Shortly after Nashe's return to London, *The Isle of Dogs* (1597), a comedy he coauthored, was declared seditious. Facing charges of treason, the author fled to Yarmouth. The hospitality of Yarmouth's citizens inspired his last work, *Nashes Lenten Stuffe* (1599), a mock praise of the city's main product, kippered herring. The circumstances of the death of this forerunner of today's journalism, who first gave the lie to the myth of the Elizabethan golden age, remain unknown.

Bibliography

C. Nicholl, *A Cup of News: The Life of Thomas Nashe*, 1984.

Kirilka Stavreva

NERI, ST. PHILIP (1515–1595)

Canonized by Pope Gregory XV in 1622, St. Philip Neri was venerated in his lifetime on account of his ministry through the confessional and his role in cofounding the Confraternity of the Most Holy Trinity of Pilgrims and Convalescents (1548) and founding the Congregation of the Oratory (c. 1564). The former order, as its name indicates, focused on ministry to the poor and often-indigent pilgrims who arrived in Rome.

Born into a Florentine merchant family, the youngest child of Francesco Neri and Lucrezia Soldi, he moved to Rome in 1533 to study and teach philosophy, giving away his books three years later in order to devote himself to austere spiritual discipline, primarily prayer, in the Catacombs of St. Sebastiano on the Appian Way. In 1544 he experienced his heart becoming enlarged, a mystical experience often compared to the stigmata of St. Francis of Assisi. In 1551, after having been ordained priest, he lived with a community of priests in San Girolamo, where the repute of his confessional spread and he cultivated the practice of prayer. Out of these communal practices emerged the Congregation of the Oratory, which was recognized by Pope Gregory XIII in 1574. His fame grew to such an extent that he was nicknamed the "Apostle of Rome," and popes and kings sought his advice. He acted as intermediary in the conflict between the pope and France by persuading Pope Clement VIII in 1593 to withdraw the excommunication of Henri IV. The Oratory, named for its emphasis on prayer, spread rapidly among clergy in Italy and France, including among its members Cardinal Pierre de Bérulle, Nicholas Malebranche, and the famous preacher Jean-Baptiste Massilon.

Bibliography

M. Trevor, *Apostle of Rome: A Life of Philip Neri, 1515–1595*, 1966.
P. Turks, *Philip Neri: The Fire of Joy*, 1995.

Iain S. Maclean

NOSTRADAMUS (MICHEL DE NOTREDAME) (1503–1566)

Nostradamus, a renowned French physician, astrologer, and prophet in his own time, is best remembered for his *Centuries*, a collection of astrological predictions in rhymed quatrains. His predictions earned him the favor of Kings Henri II and Charles IX of France, as well as a solid place in their employment.

Michel de Notredame was born in St. Remi to a family of Jewish descent that had converted to Roman Catholicism. He studied in Avignon and received his medical degree in 1529 at the prestigious University of Montpellier. During his early practice he met the famed humanist Julius Caesar Scaliger* in Agen, where he eventually settled and married. After the death of his wife and two children, most likely of the plague, he returned to his native Provence. He lived in Aix, receiving a salary from the city for his services during the plague of 1546. As a physician, his ministrations during the outbreaks of plague in Aix and Lyons were renowned; the formula for his remedy for the plague survives to this day. He later traveled to Salon de Craux, where he married for the second time and had more children.

In 1555 his prophetic *Centuries* was published, and the following year he was invited to the court of Henri II and Catherine de' Medici.* The queen later sent him to the Château de Blois to predict her children's future. He reportedly told her that all of her sons would be kings, a prediction that would turn out to be partially true, in that three of the four princes would successively become king of France.

There are several other legendary predictions that would eventually prove to be true. A stanza in Nostradamus's *Centuries* predicted that King Henri II would die in a joust; four years later Henri died after being pierced through the eye during a jousting tournament, as Nostradamus had written. Another famous tale involves Nostradamus kneeling before an undistinguished young monk and addressing him prophetically as His Holiness. In fact, the young monk would indeed go on to become Pope Sixtus V. These anecdotes aside, there is still not enough evidence to prove whether Nostradamus was a true prophet or a charlatan.

Nostradamus retired in 1557 to his home in Salon. In 1564 Charles IX appointed him royal physician and provided him with a pension; two years later Nostradamus died quietly in his sleep. He was looked upon as an oracle by many of the noble and educated people of his time and was greatly respected for his supernatural knowledge.

Bibliography

P. Brind'Amour, *Nostradamus Astrophile*, 1993.
C. Ward, *Oracles of Nostradamus*, 1940.

Catherine C. Pontoriero

O

OCHINO, BERNARDINO (1487–1564)

Bernardino Ochino was an Italian theologian and itinerant preacher who converted to Protestantism and influenced many radical Reformers by his nontraditional views. Bernardino de Domenico Tommasini was born in Siena in 1487. The nickname Ochino originated in the fact that he was born in the quarter of the city named Oca (goose). At an early age he entered the Order of the Observant Friars, the strictest sect of Franciscans. He rose to be the order's general, yet he desired a stricter monastic rule and had himself transferred to the newly founded order of Capuchins in 1534. In 1538 Ochino was elected vicar general of the Capuchins.

Ochino was renowned as a popular preacher who traveled throughout Italy delivering sermons; his popularity as a preacher soon prompted papal regulation of his appearances. In 1536 he met the Spanish religious writer Juan de Valdés* in Naples. Along with Peter Martyr Vermigli, Ochino began to spread the teachings of Valdés from the pulpit. Ochino seems to have hoped that all of Italy would embrace evangelical reform. But his summons to Rome in 1542 led him to suspect his arrest. He fled to Geneva and almost immediately published a series of sermons reflecting rigid Calvinist orthodoxy. Ochino married in Geneva and then traveled first to Basel and then to Augsburg (1545), where he became the minister of the Italian Protestant community there. When the imperial forces of the Schmalkaldic League occupied the city in January 1547, he was forced to abandon this position.

After brief stays in Basel and Strasbourg, Ochino accepted the invitation of the Archbishop Thomas Cranmer of Canterbury and visited England. Here he received a prebend and wrote his chief work, *A Tragoedie or Dialoge of the Unjuste Usurped Primacie of the Bishop of Rome, and of All the Just Abolishyng of the Same*, which some have viewed as a precursor to John Milton's *Paradise Lost*. Events preceding Mary I's* accession to power forced Ochino to leave

England in 1553. He traveled to Geneva, arriving there on the day of the execution of the Antitrinitarian Michael Servetus.* Ochino next went to Zurich, where he became pastor of the Italian congregation there.

Ochino's tenure at Zurich witnessed his greatest period of literary activity. When his work started to stir up doctrinal controversy within the Swiss congregations, the Zurich authorities warned him not to publish. In 1563, however, he published his *Thirty Dialogues*. His critics argued that in this work Ochino justified polygamy, condemned the use of force against heretics, and questioned the traditional interpretation of the Trinity. Ochino was condemned and expelled from Zurich. He then traveled to Poland and was forced to flee yet again after a royal edict expelled all non-Catholic foreigners. Ochino lost three of his children to a plague and died in ignominy at Austerlitz in 1564. Ochino's legacy bears witness to his own religious individuality. Although he was a peaceful Reformer, contemporary Protestants and Catholics alike found his teachings intolerable.

Bibliography

E. Gleason, ed. and trans., *Reform Thought in Sixteenth-Century Italy*, 1981.

Andrew G. Traver

OLIVER, ISAAC (c. 1565–1617)

Isaac Oliver, French by birth, became well known as a "limner," a painter of miniature portraits, receiving his training from the greatest of the Tudor miniaturists, Nicholas Hilliard.* He took the art of the miniature beyond its Elizabethan models, making use of such Italian Renaissance techniques as chiaroscuro, but also in the process losing some of the poetry of the miniatures of Hilliard.

Born in Rouen, Isaac Oliver was a member of a French Huguenot family that had fled France for Geneva in 1557 while he was still a child, arriving in that city at the same time as the young Nicholas Hilliard, who was to become his teacher. In 1568 his father, Pierre Olivier, transferred his family to England, anglicized their name to Oliver, and settled in London, joining the large expatriate group of European artists there.

Oliver joined the workshop of Nicholas Hilliard at the age of fourteen on an informal basis to learn the art of "limning," but unlike Hilliard, he did not receive a goldsmith's training. His apprenticeship lasted some seven years, his first signed miniatures appearing in 1587–88. His style proved to be radically different from that of his teacher, sturdy and realistic, showing some European influence, and without the stylization and symbolism so loved by the Elizabethan courtiers.

Ushering in the new Stuart era, Oliver's first court appointment in 1605 was not to King James I,* but to his consort, Queen Anne of Denmark, a connoisseur of art, and to her son, Henry, Prince of Wales, then heir to the throne (Henry would die in 1612 before succeeding his father). This gave Oliver the sole right to paint their portraits, among them the well-known miniature of the queen dressed for a masque. Her son, Prince Henry, was also shown in a new rectangular form of the miniature, like a full-sized portrait but much reduced in scale. Nicholas Hilliard meanwhile continued as painter to the king until his own death in 1619; Oliver was never to succeed him in this coveted position, for he died before Hilliard in 1617.

Oliver never forgot his French Huguenot roots, living among and marrying into the French and Flemish expatriate communities in London. His second wife connected him with the prominent Flemish Gheeraerts and de Critz families, portraitists and serjeant-painters to both the Tudor and Stuart courts. Perhaps because of his closeness to the European community in London, Oliver's style showed a new realism, a European influence not present in the work of Hilliard. Together, Oliver and Hilliard brought the era of the great miniature painters of the Tudor and Stuart periods to its highest point and culmination.

Bibliography

M. Edmond, *Hilliard and Oliver*, 1983.

Rosemary Poole

OVERBURY, SIR THOMAS (1581–1613)

Thomas Overbury was the murder victim in a plot that scandalized the English royal court and a writer from the same circles as Ben Jonson* and John Webster.* Overbury's poem "The Wife" enjoyed great popularity in Stuart England.

Born in 1581 in Warwickshire to Sir Nicholas Overbury and his wife Mary, he received the bachelor of arts at Queen's College, Oxford (1598), and studied law at the Middle Temple. In 1601 he befriended Robert Carr, later James I's* favorite (1607–14), viscount of Rochester (1611), and earl of Somerset (1613). Overbury profited thereby, being appointed sewer to the king and being knighted in 1608. During Rochester's affair with Frances Howard, Overbury wrote letters and poems for him to give her. However, when she sought to divorce the earl of Essex and Rochester planned to marry her, Overbury, afraid of being displaced, objected, antagonizing Rochester, the Howards, the king, and Queen Anne (one historian has suggested that Overbury and Rochester were lovers). Frances's great-uncle, the earl of Northampton, urged James to offer Overbury a diplomatic post overseas, and the king, jealous of his influence over Rochester, agreed. Overbury's refusal of the position landed him in the Tower of London on 26 April 1613. That is the traditional account; however, it has been argued that Overbury was incarcerated because his Protestant views on foreign policy fell afoul of the pro-Spanish faction at court. Again, tradition has it (probably correctly) that Frances instigated a scheme whereby Overbury was gradually poisoned, dying on 15 September, though some have sought to exonerate her or even implicate Overbury. Two years later, with George Villiers ascendant at court, Somerset and his new bride were condemned for Overbury's murder in a trial prosecuted by Sir Francis Bacon,* but though several lesser plotters were executed, the pair were merely imprisoned and in 1621 exiled from court. It was perhaps poetic justice that their marriage was unhappy.

Overbury's literary reputation may have benefited from his notorious death, but Jonson thought him responsible for enhancing the Jacobean court's appreciation of the arts. According to Jonson, Overbury wrote "The Wife" because of his infatuation with the countess of Rutland (Sir Philip Sidney's* daughter), a matter that cost Overbury Jonson's friendship, though others claim that he wrote it to dissuade Rochester from marrying Frances. Initially published in 1613, it went through many editions and inspired numerous imitations, including Jonson's poem "The Husband" (1614). Overbury authored other poems; dozens of character sketches ranging from "A Wise Man" and "A Good Woman" to "A Golden Asse" and "A Very Whore"; and "Observations upon the XVII Provinces (the Netherlands) As They Stood A.D. 1609." His death inspired works by Jonson, Webster, and others and influenced Nathaniel Hawthorne's *Scarlet Letter*.

Bibliography

C. Dunning, "The Fall of Sir Thomas Overbury and the Embassy to Russia in 1613," *Sixteenth Century Journal* 22, no. 4 (Winter 1991): 695–704.
A. Somerset, *Unnatural Murder: Poison at the Court of James I*, 1997.

William B. Robison

P

PALESTRINA, GIOVANNI PIERLUIGI DA (1525/26–1594)

Giovanni Pierluigi da Palestrina was the leading Roman composer during the second half of the sixteenth century. Because his music became a paradigm of Catholic church music in the centuries following his death, his influence on later generations exceeds that of all other Renaissance composers.

Palestrina probably received his earliest musical training at the Roman church of S. Maria Maggiore; a document of 1537 lists him among the choirboys there. By 1544 he had accepted a position as organist and maestro at the cathedral in nearby Palestrina, the town from which his name derives and his presumed place of birth. There he met Lucrezia Gori, whom he married in 1547 and with whom he had three sons, and Cardinal Giovanni Maria del Monte, bishop of Palestrina, who became his first and most powerful patron. Following del Monte's election as Pope Julius III in 1550, Palestrina returned to Rome to become maestro of the Cappella Giulia. In 1554 he dedicated to Julius his first book of masses, and at the beginning of 1555 the pope ordered Palestrina's admission to his official music chapel, the Cappella Sistina, without examination or the consent of the other singers, and in violation of the chapel's prohibition against the admission of married singers. Following the death of Julius three months later, enforcement of the rule on celibacy led to Palestrina's dismissal. During the next fifteen years he served as maestro di cappella for three prominent Roman institutions: St. John Lateran (1555–60), S. Maria Maggiore (1561–66), and the Roman Seminary (1566–71). In 1571 he was reappointed maestro of the Cappella Giulia, a post he retained until his death. His stature had increased steadily: in 1568 he had declined Emperor Maximilian II's invitation to become kapellmeister in Vienna; in 1577 he was one of two men entrusted by Pope Gregory XIII with the revision of the Roman chantbooks. But these were also years of personal loss. Following the deaths of his brother, two of his sons, and in 1580 his wife, Palestrina made plans to enter the priesthood. Instead, he married the wealthy widow of a Roman fur merchant. He took a lively interest in her business and enjoyed a level of financial security previously unknown to him. At his death he left about one hundred masses and over three hundred motets in addition to madrigals (both sacred and secular), hymns, magnificats, and other liturgical music.

Palestrina was already revered and emulated by Roman composers of the next generation such as Felice Anerio, Ruggiero Giovannelli, and Francesco Soriano, but his stature assumed mythic proportions in the centuries following his death. At a time when the music of his contemporaries had fallen into obscurity, his music became the model for composers seeking to invoke the *stile antico* of the Renaissance, and the study of "counterpoint in the Palestrina style" became the focus of a venerable pedagogical tradition that found its classic expression in J. J. Fux's *Gradus ad Parnassum* (1725). The unique reverence accorded Palestrina derived in part from his legendary status as the "savior of church music": earlier scholars mistakenly believed that his composition of the Pope Marcellus Mass had dissuaded the Council of Trent from banning polyphony in church. Today Palestrina appears as only one of a number of composers who in diverse ways worked to bring the polyphonic tradition into conformity with the ideals of the Catholic Reformation. These revisions of his historical position, however, have done little to diminish his stature as a composer. For many, his music remains a model of contrapuntal elegance, expressive restraint, and technical mastery.

Bibliography

L. Lockwood, "Palestrina, Giovanni Pierluigi da," in *The New Grove High Renaissance Masters*, 1984.
N. O'Regan, "Palestrina, a Musician and Composer in the Market-place," *Early Music* 22 (1994): 551–72.

David Crook

PALISSY, BERNARD (c. 1510–1590)

As a ceramic artist, Bernard Palissy's technical experimentation pushed the medium beyond its traditional practice. His unique inventions gained him patronage at the highest level, and his style was widely imitated. An autodidact amateur philosopher and Huguenot, he wrote books advocating his position on religion and science.

Palissy's early life is not well documented. Born in the Agenais, he spent the period before 1536 traveling in southwest France, working as an artisan and land surveyor. Settling in Saintes on the Charente River, Palissy explored the illusionistic possibilities of ceramic glazes to imitate the Italian majolica prized in France and minerals like jasper. He combined these innovations with his observation of nature, made while surveying, to create a new form of pottery he called *rustiques figulines*: basins decorated with naturalistic plants, shells, and aquatic animals. These works attracted patronage from, among others, the influential Anne de Montmorency, constable of France.

Palissy's adherence to Protestantism meant that he was harassed. When Catholic forces sacked Saintes in 1562, Palissy was eventually imprisoned and his studio devastated. His influential patrons obtained his release and a royal appointment. In 1563 Palissy published his *Recepte veritable*, a Protestant polemic contained within a discussion of garden design. Despite this daring move, Catherine de' Medici* brought him to Paris to design a grotto, comprised of his remarkable naturalistic glazed terracotta forms, for her new Tuileries Palace.

After the St. Bartholomew's Day Massacre, Palissy went to Sedan, a Protestant haven, where he set up his "Little Academy" in 1575. Here Palissy composed his *Discours admirable*, a dialogue in which Practice is pitted against Theory, the former always winning the points. In 1587 renewed prosecution resulted in his arrest, and he died in the Bastille.

Palissy's distinctive ceramic style continued to be imitated through the nineteenth century. As a self-taught polymath without a classical education, he was pragmatic: his experiments with ceramics and his written reflections on nature were both based on practice, not theory.

Bibliography

L. N. Amico, *Bernard Palissy: In Search of Earthly Paradise*, 1996.
J. McNab, "Bernard Palissy," in *The Dictionary of Art*, 23:849–50.
B. Palissy, *Recepte veritable*, 1563.

Sheila ffolliott

PALLADIO, ANDREA (1508–1580)

Andrea Palladio was among the most significant sixteenth-century Italian architects and almost unquestionably the most influential figure in Western post-Renaissance architectural theory. Palladio was born Andrea di Pietro della Gondola in Padua in 1508. As a young man, he benefited from the encouragement of a number of patrons, including Gian Giorgio Trissino,* who helped launch the young stonemason's career as an architect and who gave him the sobriquet "Palladio." Even in his formative years, Palladio had a penchant for the symmetrical, hierarchical principles of design that would later make his reputation, as evidenced by his sketches, which often rationalize and harmonize the less orderly structures of classical antiquity he viewed as he traveled throughout northern Italy and Rome.

Palladio's career can be divided into two major phases. From the late 1530s he worked largely on aristocratic palaces and villas in the Veneto, a rich agricultural area east of Venice that during this period was under Venetian political control. The "Palladian villas" that still grace the countryside around the Italian city of Vicenza were the product of a unique combination of Palladio's architectural talents and larger economic and political forces. Palladio's neoclassical designs precisely suited aristocratic patrons eager to assert their wealth and status by appealing to classical antiquity, but they were also sought because they were pragmatic and relatively inexpensive to build. Palladian villas could be built in stages, as the patron's finances permitted, and they were rarely designed with expensive stone carvings or other embellishments. In a climate of intense competition for impressive architectural self-promotion and in an uncertain economy, Palladio's designs appealed aesthetically and pragmatically. In addition, during this period he also worked on several civic projects, most notably the magnificent basilica in Vicenza (1549).

Palladio continued to design villas and palaces, including the famous Villa Rotonda near Vicenza (1566–70) that has inspired imitations across the world, but from 1560 he began also to design ecclesiastical buildings, many of them in Venice. In the early sixteenth century, church architecture had stagnated, but the impetus of the Council of Trent and the general atmosphere of Catholic reforms freed ecclesiastical architects to experiment with new ideas. Palladio applied many of his by-then-trademark neoclassical motifs and techniques to sacred buildings: symmetry, simplicity, and order, as well as a distinctive attentiveness to interior light and colors. His designs marked a radical departure from the dark, sometimes-cluttered Gothic designs of previous centuries.

Palladio's influence upon Western architecture can hardly be overstated. With the publication of his *Quattro libri dell'architettura* (The Four Books of Architecture) in 1570, builders and designers across Europe, without the expense and difficulties of traveling to the Veneto, had ready access to the principles of Palladian architecture: symmetry and hierarchy, proportion, harmony, and an intense, mathematical concern for the relation of individual elements to each other and to the whole design. *I quattro libri* became the single most influential work of neoclassical architectural theory and inspired generations of disciples, imitators, and simplifiers whose works can be seen in neoclassical edifices throughout Europe and North America and, indeed, across the globe.

Bibliography

J. S. Ackerman, *Palladio*, 1966.
L. Puppi, *Andrea Palladio*, trans. Pearl Sanders, 1975.
R. Wittkower, *Palladio and Palladianism*, 1974.

Thomas G. Olsen

PARACELSUS (1493–1541)

A German physician, alchemist, and magician, Paracelsus is renowned for establishing the role of chemistry in medicine. Although his theories qualify as magical, his insistence upon experiential learning in the face of received tradition redirected the practice of medicine following his death.

Born Philippus Theophrastus Bombastus von Hohenheim in Einsiedeln in the Swiss canton of Schwyz, Paracelsus spent his early years in Villach, Carinthia, with his father, an alchemist and physician. He began his lifelong wanderings in 1507, studying in Vienna and most likely attending the Italian universities of

Padua and Ferrara until about 1516. Thereafter, accounts of his service as a military physician have him traveling through Europe and the eastern Mediterranean.

By 1525, after a brief stay in Salzburg, where Paracelsus angered authorities with his rebellious sympathies for the German Peasants' War, he traversed southern Germany before establishing a successful medical practice in Strasbourg. Although there is some dispute regarding his completion of an academic degree, he was called to Basel in 1527 and was appointed municipal physician and professor of medicine. This position proved to be short-lived. Finding himself again under the scrutiny of authorities after he publicly burned several works of traditional medicine, he was forced to flee the following year and again took up a life of wandering. He spent the rest of his life engaged in medical research and publishing a wide variety of works. Always a controversial figure, he found asylum in Salzburg near the end of his life and died there in 1541.

There is little doubt that Paracelsus sought to redefine medical theory and practice. Good evidence for his medical views can be found in the very name "Paracelsus" that he chose for himself. Meaning "above" or "beyond" Celsus (the first-century Roman physician), the name is consciously emblematic of his new ideas and rejection of tradition.

Paracelsus's views are a curious mixture of the magical and the practical, certainly out of step with received wisdom, but reflecting the Renaissance notion of Neoplatonic universal harmonies ordering the world. Derived at least in part from this context, his greatest work displays a keen awareness of causation, which he usually cast in terms of the analogous association between the microcosm (the individual) and the macrocosm (the universe). Although his theory is magical and astrological, it was nonetheless drawn from empirical practice and experiential learning. The medical doctor was to learn from nature.

His more practical achievements derived from the role of chemistry in his medical theory. They include an excellent clinical description of syphilis, as well as a course of treatment for it using mercury compounds, and a recognition of the etiology of the "miners' disease" of silicosis, a condition caused by the inhalation of metal dust. He can also be credited with the discovery of the connection between goiter and mineral compounds and an explanation of the role of acids in digestive functions.

Paracelsus's new conception of the nature of disease, drawn from his magical conception of the universe, led to more practical results. Gone, for the most part, is the ancient notion that disease was a condition of the body caused by imbalances among the bodily humors, and in its place is a theory emphasizing the external causes of most illnesses. Diseases, according to Paracelsus, had their own substantial being as agents themselves, introduced into the body, occupying a particular place within it, and causing certain, predictable forms of impairment.

From Paracelsus's new conception followed new modes of therapy: "what makes a man ill also cures him" and "nature will heal the wound all by herself." Paracelsus foresaw the curative effects of small doses of disease-causing substances, and he outlined the need for minimalist, noninvasive forms of treatment, calling for basic hygiene and nursing as the most effective treatment for traumas to the body. His most famous explication of therapeutic practices came in his most important work, *The Great Surgery Book* of 1536.

A Paracelsian movement spread through Europe within decades of his death. Compelled by a desire to replace ineffective treatments with better ones, many of medical science's most important pioneers found inspiration in the alchemist's works.

Bibliography

A. Debus, *The Chemical Philosophy*, 1977.
C. Webster, *From Paracelsus to Newton*, 1982.

Edmund M. Kern

PARÉ, AMBROISE (c. 1510–1590)

Ambroise Paré was a French physician whose exceptional contributions to the medical field have earned him current recognition as one of the fathers of modern surgery. Paré was born around 1510 in the village of Bourg-Hersent, France. After an apprenticeship to a barber-surgeon, he served for three years at the Hôtel-Dieu, the Parisian hospital where he acquired much of his practical knowledge. Paré later established a private practice in Paris; he became a master barber-surgeon in 1541 and a member of the College of St. Cosmas in 1554.

For thirty years Paré divided his life between serving in the army in times of war, where he gained extensive experience in military surgery, and caring for the sick of Paris during times of peace. The professional acclaim he earned led him to be chosen as surgeon to four French kings: Henri II, François II, Charles IX, and Henri III.

Paré is perhaps best known for rejecting the common practice of cauterizing gunshot wounds with boiling oil. These discoveries were announced in 1545 in his landmark book, *The Method for Treating Wounds Made by Harquebusses and Other Firearms*, the first surgical publication in the French language. Paré's other contributions include promoting the ligature rather than the cauterization of blood vessels and popularizing various improvements in the treatment of fractures. He devised numerous surgical and orthopedic devices, including artificial limbs, and made significant advancements in the field of obstetrics. He also compiled *On Monsters and Marvels*, a collection of curiosities and human and animal aberrations.

Paré was essentially a man of practice, trusting experience if his observations were not in accord with contemporary theory. Paré was noted for his humility and dedication, recording his own achievements with modest satisfaction: "I treated him, but God cured him." Paré died in Paris on 2 December 1590.

Bibliography

J. F. Malgaigne, *Surgery and Ambroise Paré*, trans. from the French and ed. W. B. Hamby, 1965.

A. Paré, *On Monsters and Marvels*, trans. J. L. Pallister, 1982.

Heather J. Murray

PARMIGIANINO (GIROLAMO FRANCESCO MARIA MAZZOLA) (1503–1540)

Francesco Mazzola, best known from the late sixteenth century by the diminutive "il Parmigianino" after his native Parma, was one of the premier Italian Mannerist painters and draftsmen of the generation of artists to follow Raphael* and Michelangelo* who rejected the fundamental empirical principles of Renaissance painting. Parmigianino's artistic career began in Parma, where he was born into a family of artists. Although little is known about his formal training, his precociousness is evident, resulting in the decoration of two chapels in S. Giovanni Evangelista by the age of twenty. Parmigianino developed a highly expressive, distinctively personal style marked by elongated proportions, distorted perspectives, and a polished refinement that has come to exemplify grace, elegance, and a sensual sophistication that had a wide influence in Italy and beyond, particularly on the French Fontainebleau school. His frescoes for the Rocca Santivale for Galeazzo Santivale, count of Fontanellato, reveal an early interest in the trompe l'oeil effects and optical distortions that would mark his mature work. Parmigianino's portraits from this period display a facility with the relatively new half- and three-quarters-length formats, exploiting the possibilities they accorded for pose and the inclusion of revealing accoutrements, but are most notable for his ability to convey the personality of his subject with a striking intensity. His own *Self-Portrait in a Convex Mirror* of 1524 illustrates his experimentation with the expressive possibilities of optical manipulation.

During this time he was profoundly affected by the achievements of Correggio,* who was also working in Parma, an encounter that gave birth to an intense rivalry with Correggio and to an insecurity in his own abilities that Parmigianino would carry with him throughout his life, and that motivated him to leave Parma for Rome sometime around 1524. His drawings from there display an interest in classical antiquity and the work of Michelangelo and Raphael. In Rome he also became involved with graphics, producing designs for others to translate into prints. Some years later, settling in Bologna after the 1527 sack of Rome, he produced his own graphic works, becoming the first major Italian artist to practice etching. The affected elegance and thinly veiled eroticism that have come to be seen as the hallmarks of his mature style are readily evident in the *Madonna of the Rose* (c. 1529–30) and his impish *Cupid Cutting His Bow* (c. 1531–32) from around this time. In 1531 Parmigianino returned to his native Parma, where he remained until his death by an unknown cause in 1540 at the age of thirty-seven. There he painted two of his best-known and most intensely charged paintings, the *Madonna with the Long Neck* (1535) and a portrait of a young woman, *Antea* (c. 1535–37), but also experienced one of the darkest episodes of his life when he failed to complete a commission for Santa Maria della Steccata for which he was contracted and was briefly incarcerated.

Bibliography

S. J. Freedberg, *Parmigianino: His Works in Painting*, 1950.
C. Gould, *Parmigianino*, 1994.

Rachel Hostetter Smith

PATINIR (PATINIER), JOACHIM (c. 1480–1524)

Joachim Patinir was born in Dinant or Bouvignes in the Meuse River valley. His greatest contribution to art was his development of landscape painting as an independent subject. Patinir may have trained with the Bruges artist Gerard David, and documents tell us that he collaborated with Joos van Cleve and Quentin Massys,* who worked in Antwerp, the thriving artistic and economic center of the Netherlands in the sixteenth century. Patinir entered the painters' guild in Antwerp in 1516, which, according to the artist's biographer, the early art historian Karel van Mander, is where great painters went because "artists desire to be near wealth."

In his collaborations as well as his own independent works, Patinir was primarily responsible for painting the landscape background, in which he used a three-color formula to suggest deep recession in depth: brown forms in the foreground, blue-green in the middle ground, and a light blue in the background. The artist was more concerned with depicting immense vistas and panoramic views showing the grandeur of nature than with the activity of its human inhabitants. To achieve this wide-angle view, or *Weltlandschaft*, the artist employed a bird's-eye view with a high horizon line, as though the viewer were standing on a mountain ledge peering out over the landscape from above. Incongruously, he showed the vertical elements in the painting—houses, trees, and figures—as though they were seen straight on, making the whole painting appear more coherent and legible to the viewer. These landscapes were not cartographic, however, but rather were constructed partly from elements in nature, from arrangements of craggy rocks brought into the studio, and were woven as a whole through the artist's imagination. Although Patinir's *Landscape with Flight into Egypt* borrows motifs from Gerard David's painting of the same subject in the National Gallery of Art in Washington, D.C., he was probably more influenced by the earlier Hieronymus Bosch's fantastic landscapes, particularly in his painting *Charon Crossing the River Styx* in Madrid.

Despite his major contribution to Netherlandish-language painting, very few works remain by Patinir—only twenty are extant that are attributed to him. Of these, Philip II,* the Spanish monarch, owned four, probably some of Patinir's last works. The humanist poet Dominicus Lampsonius eulogized Patinir, noting in his poem that the great German artist Albrecht Dürer* admired Patinir's landscapes and drew a portrait of the artist.

Bibliography

R. L. Falkenburg, *Joachim Patinir: Landscape as an Image of the Pilgrimage of Life*, 1988.

Susan H. Jenson

PERI, JACOPO (1561–1633)

Jacopo Peri, a Florentine composer, singer, and instrumentalist, is best known as the creator of dramatic recitative, a form of monody that made possible the development of opera. Born in Rome, Peri moved to Florence at a young age. From as early as 1573 he held a number of posts in Florence as both singer and organist. In 1588 he was employed by Grand Duke Ferdinando I for service in the Medici court. During the 1580s it is possible that he participated in discussions with the Florentine Camerata at Giovanni de Bardi's home. The ideas this group expressed concerning the revival of ancient Greek practices in music and drama certainly influenced Peri's experiments in operatic recitative.

Recitative is a musical style that lies somewhere between speech and song. In Peri's recitative, the roles of voice and accompaniment are adjusted in a way that allows the music to follow the natural pacing of its text. This form of music fueled the development of opera in that it provided a vehicle for narrative verse, dialogue, and other text forms that require rapid delivery, all of which are necessary for a dramatic production.

Most of Peri's compositions are in some way related to music theater, and he frequently worked in collaboration with other Florentine artists, in particular the poet Ottavio Rinuccini.* Peri provided music for Rinuccini's pastoral *Dafne* in 1598. Shortly thereafter they again collaborated in a pioneering effort to produce the opera *Euridice* (1600), the earliest surviving example of its kind. This influential work, written for the wedding celebration of Maria de' Medici and Henri IV of France, contains many examples of Peri's characteristic recitative style.

Peri's contribution to musical form had a profound impact upon music after 1600. Baroque opera, church music, and even chamber monody are all shaped by his innovations. His many imitators include the composers Giulio Caccini and Claudio Monteverdi.*

Bibliography

W. Porter, "Jacopo Peri," in *The New Grove Dictionary of Music and Musicians*, ed. S. Sadie, vol. 14, 1980: 401–405.

Tucker Robison

PERUZZI, BALDASSARE (1481–1536)

Baldassare Peruzzi, sometimes better known as an associate of Raphael,* was a painter, draughtsman, stage designer, and especially an architect in his own right. His early work has been called typical of the High Renaissance in Italy, while some of his later buildings introduce the complex visual ideas associated with Mannerism.

Born in Ancaiano near Siena, Peruzzi spent his early life and presumably received his artistic training in Siena. The source of this training, however, remains unknown; Giorgio Vasari* reported that Peruzzi studied with an unnamed goldsmith. Vasari also noted that Peruzzi was less well known than he could have been because of the artist's innate timidity. He was reported to have painted a series of frescoes in Siena Cathedral (1501–2), but these are no longer extant. The Sienese elite, however, began taking advantage of his architectural skills early in the sixteenth century. The Chigi family of bankers, merchants, and later popes commissioned a villa outside of Siena from Peruzzi in 1500. The villa's plan was a U-shape and owed much to the influence of his fellow Sienese, Francesco di Giorgio Martini.

Peruzzi traveled to Rome in 1503, perhaps because Pius III, a Sienese pope of the Piccolomini family, had just been elected, and the prospects for important commissions looked promising. By 1506 at the latest, Peruzzi was given another Chigi commission, this time in Rome. Agostino Chigi, banker to the pope, wanted a villa outside of town. Now referred to as the Villa Farnesina (the Farnese family purchased it in the seventeenth century), it has a U-shaped plan much like that of Peruzzi's earlier work in Siena. Peruzzi used classical motifs in the architecture, and the structure as a whole conveys a sense of High Renaissance harmony and balance. The interior decoration was mostly done by Raphael* and his workshop, but Peruzzi himself painted the Sala delle Prospettive (perspective room), in which he displayed his mastery of illusionism. The walls of the frescoed room seem to be painted away to reveal ancient Roman sites through the painted columns. During this period Peruzzi also collaborated with Raphael in the Vatican *stanze* for Pope Julius II.* It has been suggested that the ceiling of the Heliodorus Room showing Old Testament scenes of salvation was done by him. Peruzzi received numerous other commissions in Rome and elsewhere, and at the death of Raphael in 1520 he was put in charge of the building of St. Peter's. What precisely he contributed to that grand and polyglot structure is unclear.

The sack of Rome in 1527 found Peruzzi imprisoned by the armies of Emperor Charles V.* Fortunately, he was ransomed by the Sienese and became architect to the Republic of Siena, where he used much of what he had learned and observed in Rome to design fortifications and churches. In 1532 Peruzzi returned to Rome, where he again worked on St. Peter's. His last work was the Palazzo Massimo alle Colonne, begun in 1532 and finished after his death. This house presented numerous problems, not the least of which was the already-existing curved street. In a total break with High Renaissance ideas of the architectural plane, Peruzzi curved the facade of the house around the curve of the street. He also used the system of progression of almost flat engaged pilasters at the outsides of the facade toward freestanding columns at the center to accentuate the curve and thereby made one of the earliest structures in Italy to be called Mannerist.

Bibliography

M. Fagiolo and M. L. Madonna, eds., *Baldassarre Peruzzi: Pittura, scena, e architettura nel cinquecento*, 1987.

Lynne E. Johnson

PHILIP II, KING OF SPAIN (1527–1598)

During Philip II's reign Catholic Spain was often at war, frequently for religious reasons. Though his father was King Charles I of Spain, he was far more known as Holy Roman Emperor Charles V.* When Charles abdicated in 1556, he divided his enormous realm between his younger brother and his son. Philip's desire to have a suitable resting place for his father's remains was the impetus for El Escorial, the huge monastery-palace in the hills north of Madrid built under Philip's personal direction. Philip was the first Habsburg king to be truly identified with Spain.

Philip married four times but had difficulty producing a suitable heir. In his brief first marriage to his Portuguese cousin Maria he had one son, Don Carlos, but his bizarre behavior made him incapable of ever ruling. It was a relief when he died in 1568. Philip had no children from his second marriage to Mary I* of England, also his cousin. Though he was known for his mistresses, Philip eventually came to love and be faithful to Elisabeth of Valois; they had two daughters before her death in 1568 after eight years of marriage. With another cousin, Anna of Austria, who died after ten years of marriage, he had three sons who died in childhood, but another, Philip III, lived to survive his father. During Philip II's reign Spain fully established its empire in Mexico, Central America, and the Philippines. In 1580 Philip also seized Portugal, which did not regain its independence until 1604, several years after his death. Spain gained great wealth but dissipated much of it on war.

Philip II's reign encompassed what has been called the Golden Age of Spain. Though some Spanish intellectuals feared that Spain was more interested in war than in the arts, the empire Spain had amassed did have a great influence on its intellectual development. The wealth that poured in made owning art attractive. Philip was particularly interested in the works of Italian and Flemish painters; he commissioned many works by the Venetian artist Titian* and invited Antonio Mor* from the Netherlands to come to Spain as his court painter. Though there was censorship and a decree that forbade education abroad, thousands of Spaniards traveled through Europe and the rest of the world and learned about other cultures.

Philip fought hard to keep control of the Netherlands; his motives were not only dynastic but also religious, as part of Dutch nationalism was conversion to Protestantism. Philip was especially outraged that Elizabeth I* and the English supported their Dutch coreligionists. Though for a long time Philip was cautious, he eventually decided to lead a holy crusade against Protestant England, but the Spanish Armada of 1588 was a disaster for Spain and hinted at a future when Spain would be in decline and the Dutch and British would have greater world influence. When Philip died a decade later in 1598, the world was already changing.

Bibliography

H. Kamen, *Philip of Spain*, 1997.
G. Parker, *Philip II*, 3rd ed., 1995.

Carole Levin

PIRCKHEIMER, CARITAS (1467–1532)

Caritas Pirckheimer, abbess of the Convent of St. Clare in Nuremberg, was noted by her contemporaries for her leadership, learning, and virtue and was recognized by German humanists as a female patron of German learning. Educated at the Convent of St. Clare from the age of twelve, Pirckheimer received training from literate nuns and from Franciscan preachers and confessors affiliated with the convent. She edited a *Chronicle* of the history of the Order of St. Clare in Europe and in Nuremberg that included many excerpts from original source material. Pirckheimer also benefited from her family's close ties to the humanist movement in Germany. Her brother, Willibald Pirckheimer,* corresponded with many northern European humanists and helped establish Caritas's reputation as a scholarly woman. His efforts, along with her own correspondence with humanists such as Sixtus Tucher, Conrad Celtis, and Christopher Schuerl, led to numerous dedicatory epistles and odes honoring Pirckheimer's erudition. Her convent also recognized her superior skills; she became abbess in 1503.

As abbess, Pirckheimer successfully resisted Lutheran efforts to close the Convent of St. Clare in Nuremberg. She used her knowledge of theology, along with her political connections, to preserve the convent as a community of academic study and spiritual retreat for women. Among those she persuaded were her brother Willibald, originally opposed to monastic life, and Philip Melanchthon.* Melanchthon convinced the Council of Nuremberg to maintain all of the convents in the district, although none were allowed to accept novitiates. Pirckheimer recorded her efforts by constructing a final chapter for her *Chronicle* that documented her letters and her opponents' responses.

Bibliography

P.S.D. Barker, "Caritas Pirckheimer: A Female Humanist Confronts the Reformation," *Sixteenth Century Journal* 26, no. 2 (1995): 259–72.

Karen Nelson

PIRCKHEIMER, WILLIBALD (1470–1530)

Willibald Pirckheimer was an important German humanist, responsible for significant translations of classical texts. He is best known today as the closest friend of the artist Albrecht Dürer.* Pirckheimer was born on 5 December 1470 to Dr. Johannes Pirckheimer and Barbara Löffelholz, members of wealthy patrician families from Nuremberg. He was their only surviving son. He was educated at the Universities of Padua and Pavia. Pirckheimer studied in Italy for a total of seven years, but left school before acquiring a degree, apparently because the Nuremberg city council frowned upon excessive education. He served on the city council from 1496 until his death, with only a few years' interruption while he traveled to Italy. Pirckheimer wed Crescentia Rieter on 13 October 1495. After bearing six children, Crescentia succumbed to childbirth fever in May 1504. Pirckheimer never remarried.

As a member of the inner circle of Emperor Maximilian I, Pirckheimer became acquainted with the leading humanists of the day, including Conrad Celtis, the first poet laureate of Germany. Celtis and Pirckheimer engaged in a lifelong enterprise to change the nature of education in Germany via a humanist revival of the classical literature of Greece and Rome. Pirckheimer's scholarly pursuits included extensive translations of Greek texts by Xenophon, Lucian, Isocrates, Plutarch, and Plato into Latin. In addition to translating Ptolemy's *Geography*, Pirckheimer introduced the study of historical geography in German schools. He also wrote an early history of Germany, an account of the Swiss War (in which he participated), and an autobiography. He translated the Roman historian Sallust from Latin into German and many writings by the early church fathers, such as Gregory of Naziarzus, John of Damascus, St. Nilus, and St. Fulgentius of Ruspe.

Pirckheimer was an active defender of Johannes Reuchlin and Martin Luther.* He was suspected of being the author of a satirical polemic against Luther's papist adversary, Johann Eck. For this reason he was included in the excommunication bull issued against Luther in 1521; however, Eck granted Pirckheimer absolution prior to publication of the bull. Pirckheimer became disillusioned with the Reformation following civil disturbances of the 1520s and also because of Luther's rejection of the concept of free will.

It is often remarked that Albrecht Dürer would never have achieved fame and international celebrity were it not for his associations with Willibald Pirckheimer. Pirckheimer and his circle of humanist friends made available to Dürer literary texts that the artist could not have read on his own. Furthermore, Pirckheimer's friendship with the artist introduced Dürer to a level of society that the artist would otherwise not have achieved. Finally, the eulogy that Pirckheimer wrote for "my best friend" Albrecht Dürer testifies to their abiding friendship. He followed his friend in death on 5 May 1530.

Bibliography

J. Hutchinson, *Albrecht Dürer: A Biography*, chap. 5, "Willibald Pirckheimer," 1990.
G. Strauss, *Nuremberg in the Sixteenth Century*, 1966.

Cheryl Smart

PONTORMO (JACOPO CARUCCI DA PONTORMO) (1494–1557)

Pontormo was the leading master of the Florentine Mannerist style of painting in the second quarter of the sixteenth century. Born in a small town outside Florence, Pontormo was trained primarily by Andrea del Sarto* in the High Renaissance style of idealized naturalism. Although he produced a few portraits and mythological paintings, the majority of his works were religious frescoes and altarpieces; in addition, close to four hundred drawings from his hand survive. His early independent works, for example, *Visitation* (Florence, S. Annunziata, c. 1515), display his understanding of the Renaissance methods for representing the real world through anatomy, perspective, and lighting effects, but they also reveal an idiosyncratic approach in the choice of asymmetrical compositions, unusual figure types, unexpected palette, and strangely nervous expressions.

By about 1517 a close study of the art of Michelangelo* and northern European artists such as Albrecht Dürer* appears to have led Pontormo to abandon the classicizing approach of the High Renaissance to concentrate on the development of the more personal aspects of his style. *Joseph in Egypt* (London, National Gallery, c. 1518) forsakes a spatial and anatomical logic to create oddly unsettling dislocations of setting and form. A series of frescoes of the Passion (Florence, Certosa del Galluzo, 1523–26) creates a haunting impression on the viewer with their compressed space, dissonant colors, and expressive figures. Pontormo's mature style is most effectively seen in his decoration of the Capponi Chapel in S. Felicita in Florence (525–28). The *Deposition* is a supreme example of Mannerist art, in which High Renaissance notions are overturned. Balance and harmony give way to instability and unpredictability. Instead of clarity, there is confusion: scholars are divided on the exact iconography, and sculpturesque forms exist in a setting whose three-dimensionality cannot be established. Figures are equally irrational: their clothing, whose colors could not be found in the real world, resembles no known costumes, contemporary or historical; their poses are preternaturally graceful; their mood can best be described as anxious.

In his late works Pontormo continued to experiment with complex poses, indecipherable spaces, and sharp colors. His remarkable originality led him to create images that always had a striking impact on the viewer, but his art was so eccentric that his influence failed to last beyond the end of the sixteenth century.

Bibliography

J. Cox-Rearick, *Dynasty and Destiny in Medici Art: Pontormo, Leo X, and the Two Cosimos*, 1984.

Jane C. Long

PRAETORIUS, MICHAEL (c. 1571–1621)

Michael Praetorius stands as the most versatile and prolific Lutheran composer of the first two decades of the seventeenth century. As a chronicle of contemporary musical fashions and practices, his treatise *Syntagma musicum* is without peer.

Praetorius was born in Creuzburg an der Werra, near Eisenach, the son of a Lutheran theologian. His brother became a professor of theology, and he himself authored a number of theological tracts no longer extant. He received his education at Torgau, Frankfurt an der Oder, and Zerbst and served for three years as organist at St. Marien in Frankfurt before moving to Wolfenbüttel, where he served from 1595 as court organist and from 1604 as kapellmeister to Duke Heinrich Julius of Brunswick-Wolfenbüttel. From 1604 until the death of Heinrich Julius in 1613, Praetorius enjoyed a period of extraordinary productivity, during which he published the majority of his surviving music. Under Heinrich Julius's successor, Praetorius retained his post but spent much of his time away from Wolfenbüttel. Three years at the electoral court in Dresden, where he came into contact with Heinrich Schütz and the latest Italian music, were followed by sojourns in Magdeburg, Leipzig, and other German cities. By the time he returned to Wolfenbüttel, he had suffered a serious decline in health, and in 1620 he was relieved of his duties.

During his short lifetime Praetorius produced an oeuvre of astonishing size and diversity. Above all, however, it was the Protestant hymn that defined and directed his activity as a composer. His more than one thousand hymn-based compositions, which range from diminutive duets to massive polychoral works for voices and instruments, provide a veritable encyclopedia of styles and procedures applicable to this most Lutheran of musical material. At the same time, his enthusiasm for foreign developments imbues publications such as *Polyhymnia exercitatrix* (1619–20), which he published to give choirboys practice in the new Italian manner, and *Terpsichore* (1612), which presents over three hundred dances as performed by French dancemasters. His three-volume *Syntagma musicum* (1614–19) contains invaluable discussions of contemporary instruments, genres, and performance practices.

Bibliography

W. Blankenburg, "Praetorius, Michael," in *The New Grove Dictionary of Music and Musicians*, ed. S. Sadine, vol. 15, 1980: 188–92.

David Crook

PRIMATICCIO, FRANCESCO (1504–1570)

Francesco Primaticcio was the most influential Italian artist working in France in the sixteenth century. Born and trained in Bologna, where the influence of Raphael* was preeminent, Primaticcio worked as a painter, stuccoist, and architect. He was invited to Paris in 1532 by François I,* who hoped to introduce the Renaissance to French art, and spent the rest of his career as a court artist. Primaticcio was installed at the royal château of Fontainebleau, where he proceeded to develop a Mannerist style influenced by Correggio,* Michelangelo,* and Parmigianino.* His primary responsibility was to direct the decoration of the château. He produced architectural ornamentation in both paint and stucco; few of the paintings have survived, but many of the stuccos are preserved in good condition. The Gallery of François I, decorated in partnership with Rosso Fiorentino* (1530s), combines painting and sculpture in an elaborate program of mythological scenes. Typical elements of Mannerist art, such as elongated figures, unreadable space, and serpentine poses, are found in both narratives and framing elements. The style is highly sophisticated, artificial, and erotic.

Works of the 1540s (e.g., the Gallery of Ulysses, late 1540s, destroyed 1738) appear to have continued the taste Primaticcio established in his first works at Fontainebleau. Ornate and complex, they reveal the artist adding illusionism and drama to his mannered compositions. By the 1550s Primaticcio was established as the leading court artist, and his work was more and more limited to direction rather than execution. Seen primarily as a decorator, he was highly influential in the introduction of Italian and antique aesthetic ideas to French artistic circles.

Bibliography

S. Béguin, *Fontainebleau: L'art en France, 1528–1610*, 1973.

Jane C. Long

R

RABELAIS, FRANÇOIS (c. 1494–1553)

François Rabelais was a French humanist and a prominent figure in the French Renaissance. Rabelais's most famous work is the satirical prose novel *Gargantua and Pantagruel*. Little is known about the life of Rabelais. There is disagreement, for example, regarding when he was born. An entry in the records of a Paris church says that Rabelais died in 1553 at the age of seventy; however, many scholars contest this evidence, for this would imply that Rabelais had his three illegitimate children while in his late forties and early fifties, and that he did not even begin to write his books until his fifties. Most scholars generally accept 1494 as a more probable birth date. What is known of Rabelais is that he was a priest in the Franciscan order, though later he transferred to the Benedictine monastery of Saint-Pierre de Maillezais. The abbot of this monastery, Geoffroy d'Estissac, the bishop of Maillezais, became Rabelais's first patron. In 1527 or 1528 Rabelais gave up the monk's robe and directed his energies toward medicine, and in 1530 he enrolled in the Faculty of Medicine of Montpellier.

Rabelais later moved to Lyons, where he continued to practice medicine and began writing and editing books. While he was in Lyons, he met Jean Du Bellay, the bishop of Paris. Du Bellay was an important force in Rabelais's life and enabled Rabelais to enter the Benedictine monastery in the capacity of a doctor. Du Bellay was also instrumental in the publication of Rabelais's masterpiece, *Gargantua and Pantagruel* (1532–34), a book that immediately brought fame to Rabelais. In the last couple of years of his life, Rabelais had frequent battles with the king and then the pope regarding his books, and on more than one occasion his books were banned. In the midst of such a battle to keep his books from being banned, Rabelais died sometime in 1553.

In many ways, Rabelais is an enigmatic figure. Not only is little known about his personal life, but there is also little consensus on the significance or meaning of his work. Some see Rabelais's writing as the rantings of a drunken buffoon or as a case for a psychoanalytic interpretation; others see in Rabelais the highest expression of humanism and an overflowing exuberance and joy for worldly things and life. What is accepted is that Rabelais had a mastery of language that was and perhaps is still unequaled. Rabelais's style was certainly unique, and his studies of excess and largess have forever left their mark on the cultural mind-set with such words as "gargantuan" and "Rabelaisian." This emphasis upon the joys and excesses of earthly pleasures places Rabelais squarely into the tradition of the French Renaissance. Rabelais was to become a major influence upon the French philosophes of the eighteenth century, for example, Voltaire, Jean-Jacques Rousseau, Montesquieu, and Julien Offray Ide La Mettrie. An emphasis on what humans can do and on the power of the mind and body in this world, as opposed to the more medieval view that stresses the priority of God's judgment and the life hereafter: this view, as found in Rabelais, has been a constant theme throughout the modern era. The wide popularity of Rabelais while he was alive must deserve some of the credit for this shift in world view. Consequently, regardless of how one may view the quality of Rabelais's works, few dispute the claim that Rabelais exemplifies a shift in perspective, the results of which are still with us to this day. The sixteenth century is a critical period in the history of Western culture, for it is a pivotal turning point to the world view that led to the explosion of scientific knowledge and technologies. In compiling a list of crucial figures about this new world view, Rabelais most certainly deserves to be included.

Bibliography

D. Frame, *François Rabelais*, 1977.
A. L. Prescott, *Imagining Rabelais in Renaissance England*, 1998.

Jeffrey A. Bell

RAIMONDI, MARCANTONIO (c. 1480–c. 1534)

Marcantonio Raimondi, the most prolific engraver of sixteenth-century Italy, is remembered for his reproductions of the later works of Raphael.* In his native Bologna Raimondi learned niellowork from the painter and goldsmith Francesco Francia and then took up copper engraving, copying paintings of contemporaries. By 1504 his skill was acknowledged in *Viridario* by his fellow Bolognese, Giovanni Philoteo Achillini, who is assumed to be the subject of Raimondi's early print of his own design, *The Guitar Player*.

In Venice (c. 1505–09) Raimondi was employed in the De Jesu brothers' workshop, where he transposed Albrecht Dürer's* woodcuts of the *Life of the Virgin* into copper engravings, a practice about which Dürer complained in person to the Venetian Senate in 1506. Stylistically, Raimondi learned Dürer's system of crosshatching, which he adapted to his own technique. Giorgione's *Tempesta* may have influenced a curious engraving titled *Raphael's Dream*, whose nightmare imagery recalls that of Hieronymus Bosch.

In 1508 or 1509, in Florence and en route to Rome, Raimondi saw the cartoons for Michelangelo's* lost *Battle of Cascina* and *The Bathers*, which provided models for future engravings. In Rome his technique matured. Baldassare Peruzzi's* paintings inspired engravings on the Third Punic War and Orpheus and Euridice. Most important was Raimondi's close affiliation with Raphael, whom he convinced of his abilities with an incised study, *Lucrezia* (1511–12). Raimondi's Lucrezia exemplifies his preference for the human figure set against classical architectonic elements rather than landscape settings, which here are simply borrowed from Lucas van Leyden.* Lucrezia herself imitates the twisted human torsos in Raphael's Stanza della Segnatura and may be directly related to an antique statue excavated in Rome in 1500.

While the precise dynamics of Raimondi's collaboration with Raphael have proven difficult to reconstruct, it is clear that he worked from the painter's drawings to reproduce the effects of chiaroscuro and night light for the first time in prints. The most important engravings based on Raphael are *Morbetto, The Massacre of the Innocents, The Judgment of Paris*, and *Apollo and the Muses*. Raimondi incised a full-figure portrait of Raphael himself, who, in turn, included the engraver's likeness in the fresco *The Expulsion of Heliodorus* in the Vatican alongside his own as a bearer of Pope Julius II's* gestatorial chair. After Raphael's death in 1520, Raimondi associated with Baccio Bandinelli* and Giulio Romano.* Reproduction of the latter's sketches to illustrate Pietro Aretino's* pornographic sonnets, *I modi*, resulted in Raimondi's imprisonment by the pope. Thanks to Bandinelli, he was released to copy the mannerist *Martyrdom of St. Lawrence*. Marcantonio's good fortune ended with the sack of Rome in 1527, after which he returned to his native Bologna, where he died poor and in obscurity.

Bibliography

L. Lawner, ed. and trans., *I Modi: The Sixteen Pleasures: An Erotic Album of the Italian Renaissance: Giulio Romano, Marcantonio Raimondi, Pietro Aretino, and Count Jean-Frederic-Maximilian de Waldeck*, 1988.
I. H. Shoemaker and E. Broun, *The Engravings of Marcantonio Raimondi*, 1981.

Luci Fortunato DeLisle

RALEIGH, SIR WALTER (c. 1552–1618)

The consummate courtier, Sir Walter Raleigh was the epitome of the Renaissance man, being a skilled poet, an overseas explorer, a military adventurer, and an effective parliamentarian. After devoting his early years to military adventures, Raleigh set to work creating an image of himself as a master of the sword and the pen. Deciding to take a commission in Ireland, he helped reimpose English rule there, and his success brought him to the attention of Elizabeth I.* Raleigh quickly became one of her favorites, extolling her virtues as the "Virgin Queen" in song and verse. The queen rewarded him with monopolies and leases, and his growing power and influence became increasingly resented by other members of the court.

In 1584 Raleigh was granted a patent for North American colonization, and settlement began on Roanoke, but the venture ended in disaster for the settlers. Raleigh's—and England's—attention was soon diverted by the launching of the Spanish Armada against England in 1588, with Raleigh part of the fleet that eventually defeated it.

The revelation of a secret marriage with one of the queen's ladies-in-waiting proved his undoing with the notoriously jealous Elizabeth, who had him arrested in May 1592. This mistake led to five years of disgrace and banishment from the court, but by 1593 he was starting his climb back to favor, in part through his skills as a parliamentarian. Raleigh cast about for a solution to his shredded reputation and began to dream of a great adventure—to acquire the mythical kingdom of El Dorado in South America. He believed that it would restore him everything he had lost, but his first venture there was abortive. In 1596 his participation in a preemptive strike against Spain damaged its morale, and he regained some favor with Elizabeth. A subsequent expedition against Spain to acquire treasure—the ill-fated "Islands Voyage"—was a disaster from start to finish, but Raleigh was able to remain in the queen's good graces.

When Elizabeth died in March 1603, it was apparent that her successor, James I,* harbored deep suspicions against Raleigh, and James began to deprive him of some of his monopolies and estates. Raleigh found himself embroiled in a conspiracy of others' making, and he was arrested for treason in July 1603, found guilty, and sentenced to die on 13 December. Raleigh petitioned men of influence in the hopes of averting his fate, and James commuted his sentence to life imprisonment in the Tower. During the next twelve years the imprisoned Raleigh produced some of his greatest poems and treatises and perhaps his most enduring work, *The History of the World.*

James, sorely in need of funds, decided to reopen the expedition to find El Dorado; he released Raleigh from prison in 1615 to oversee the construction of the fleet, but did not pardon him. The voyage went badly from the start, and a group of his marauding sailors disobeyed orders and attacked a Spanish fort, killing some of its inhabitants, while the mythical treasure was left undiscovered. Raleigh, determined to salvage his honor with the King, was not given a chance to defend himself publicly, and his execution was ordered for 29 October 1618. In many ways, Raleigh was being sacrificed to appease Spain, and he resigned himself to his fate. Dressed magnificently, he made a final speech on the scaffold that refuted his "treason" before he laid his head on the block.

In the end, Raleigh became a victim of his own stellar rise to the top of the early modern English political world. He was too intricately involved in the issues of the day to be entirely guiltless of whatever charges might be laid at his door, and he paid the price for that knowledge.

Bibliography

S. Coote, *A Play of Passion: The Life of Sir Walter Raleigh,* 1993.
R. Lacey, *Sir Walter Raleigh,* 1974.

Connie S. Evans

RAMUS, PETRUS (PIERRE DE LA RAMÉE) (1515–1572)

Petrus Ramus broke with the medieval philosophical dependence upon Aristotle, developing an inductive logical method that became common not only in philosophy and Protestant (Reformed) theology, but also in other disciplines. A French humanist from Picardy, Ramus studied at Cuts and the College of Navarre in Paris, receiving his master of arts degree in 1536. In 1543 he published *Aristotelicae animadversiones* (Aristotelian observations) and *Dialecticae institutiones* (Dialectical instructions), in which he sharply attacked the traditional Aristotelian approach then dominant in the University of Paris. The debate this opinions aroused became so strong that François I* forbade him to teach. However, his influential patrons, the Cardinals Charles de Bourbon and Charles de Lorraine, helped remove the ban and assisted him in becoming president of the College of Presles in 1545 and in 1551, professor of rhetoric and philosophy at the Collège Royal. He became a Calvinist in 1561 and left for Germany, returning to Paris in 1571, only to die the following year in the St. Bartholomew's Day Massacre.

Ramus sought to develop a new method of logic and rhetoric that would use logic in disputation, its two parts being invention, the discovery of proofs for the thesis, and disposition, which ordered the materials gained in the first part. This was to enable the ordered, reasoned, and systematic presentation of any subject. His work in logic and method was to deeply influence English and later American Puritanism. In particular, his method of maintaining a unity between theology and ethics powerfully influenced Puritan understandings of epistemology, theological method, and conceptions of nature and literature. His method is reflected in the theology of Johannes Piscator (1546–1625), Amandus Polanus von Polansdorf (1561–1610), William Perkins (1558–1602), William Ames (1576–1623), and Richard Baxter (1615–1691). He applied his method to theology in his posthumous *Commentariorum de religione christiana libri quatuor* (Commentaries on the Christian religion, 1576). His logic was influential throughout the sixteenth and seventeenth centuries.

Bibliography

P. Miller, *The New England Mind: The Seventeenth Century*, 1939.
W. J. Ong, *Ramus, Method, and the Decay of Dialogue*, 1958.

Iain S. Maclean

RAPHAEL (RAFFAELO SANTI or SANZIO) (1483–1520)

Raphael was an outstanding master of Italian High Renaissance art. Working chiefly as a painter and occasionally as an architect, he synthesized classicism, idealization, and naturalism to create a consummate Renaissance style.

Born in Urbino, a small independent duchy on the east coast of Italy, Raphael was the son of a court painter. His earliest training under his father exposed him not only to modern painting techniques and ideas, but also to the humanist intellectual concerns that circulated in Urbino. His father died in 1494, and sometime thereafter Raphael was sent to the workshop of Perugino, the most successful artist in central Italy. His early paintings, such as *Coronation of the Virgin* (Vatican, c. 1502–4) and *Marriage of the Virgin* (Milan, Brera, c. 1504), reveal considerable reliance on the older master; indeed, it is often difficult to distinguish the two artists' works.

From 1504 to 1508 Raphael lived in Florence; this period proved decisive in the maturation of his career, as exposure to the art of Leonardo da Vinci and Michelangelo* led him to develop a grandiose, powerful approach. Still very young, he received no significant public commissions in Florence. Instead, he concentrated on rather small private works—paintings of the Madonna and Child and portraits—to explore a variety of artistic ideas. Works such as the *Madonna of the Meadow* (Vienna, Kunsthistorisches Museum, c. 1505), the *Madonna of the Goldfinch* (Florence, Uffizi, c. 1506) and *Maddalena Doni* (Florence, Uffizi, c. 1507) reveal his use of geometry, balance, ideal form, and naturalism to create impressive, moving, believable images.

In 1508 Raphael moved to Rome, where he spent the rest of his life. Like Michelangelo, he had been summoned by Pope Julius II* and was employed in redecorating the Vatican to suit the pope's notions of an appropriate setting for the seat of Christianity. He painted three rooms of the pope's private apartments from 1508 to 1517. The first, the Stanza della Segnatura (1509–11), is his most famous. *The School of Athens* and *Disputa* show the artist's mastery of composition in a large-scale, public format. The frescoes are balanced, harmonious, and naturalistic. Figures' anatomies and poses are believable, and space and light are clear, but the overall impression is of a perfect world, where human and divine beings act with the utmost nobility and monumentality. In the later two rooms, the Stanza d'Eliodoro (1511–14) and the Stanza dell'Incendio (1514–17), Raphael strove to add drama and complexity to his ideal world. Increasingly he relied on assistants to carry out his designs.

After the Stanza della Segnatura, Raphael's popularity was ensured; he was inundated with commissions, both public and private, from the highest levels of Roman society. His portrait *Julius II* (London, National Gallery, 1512) and the *Sistine Madonna* (Dresden, 1513), both painted for the pope, showed him returning to the painting types of his Florentine years in a transformed style; now he moved beyond artistic formulas to probe the psychology of both his figures and his viewers, creating powerful impressions of personality. He was commissioned by Pope Leo X* to design a set of nine tapestries to decorate the Sistine Chapel (London, Victoria and Albert Museum, 1515–16); their clarity and monumental calm served as the classic model for depicting historical narrative until the nineteenth century. He painted a number of fresco decorations in Roman churches and private homes as well.

Raphael also worked as an architect. He designed two chapels for Agostino Chigi, an influential Roman banker, between 1512 and 1516. Normally the building of a new chapel would be parceled out to specialists, but Raphael controlled the whole commission, planning the architecture and devising the two-dimensional and three-dimensional decoration. Thus he established the concept of the artist as the master who managed an entire design rather than the craftsman for hire who produced what his patron demanded. This new role allowed him to determine how his art was experienced.

Raphael's last major work was still incomplete at his death. The *Transfiguration* (Vatican, 1518–20), a huge altarpiece commissioned by the Medici, took the static altarpiece formula of Renaissance art and converted it into dynamic narrative. The clarity of the psychological relationships is typical of Raphael, while the complexity of the poses and irregularity of the space suggest the seeds of the Mannerist style that would dominate Italian painting after his death.

Until the nineteenth century Raphael's works served as the paradigm of great art for Western civilization. Clear, skillful, and grand, they symbolized the artist as a rational intellect whose art was didactic and ennobling. His popularity has declined with the modern concept of the artist as a tortured genius, but there is no mistaking the richness of his invention or the power of his presentation.

Bibliography

R. Jones and N. Penny, *Raphael*, 1983.
J. Pope-Hennessy, *Raphael*, 1970.

Jane C. Long

REJ, MIKOŁAJ (1505–1569)

Mikołaj Rej was one of the most important and prolific writers of the Polish Renaissance; he is often referred to as the father of Polish vernacular literature. He was born into the family of a well-off nobleman. He had little formal education; he attended local parish schools and then studied one year at Cracow Academy. Between 1525 and 1530 he was secretary at the court of Andrzej Tęczyński, the voivode of Sandomierz; afterwards he settled in the village of Topole. In 1541 Rej converted to Protestantism, participated actively in numerous synods, and organized congregations and schools. He obtained a position at the court of Zygmunt I (Sigismund I) and later became secretary to Zygmunt Augustus (Sigismund Augustus). By the end of his life, he had acquired considerable property, including two small towns, several villages, and a house in Cracow.

In addition to his busy public and social life, Rej was a popular and prolific writer. Major works of his earliest period include religious songs, moralistic and satirical dialogues, and translations of the Psalms as *David's Psalter* (1546). In his political treatise *Short Conversation between Three Persons, a Squire, a Bailiff, and a Parson* (1543), Rej shows the tensions between the three estates.

Other important works include *Postilla* (1557), a religious treatise that champions the teachings of John Calvin* and criticizes Rome and Christian morals, and *A Faithful Image of an Honest Man* (1568) and *The Mirror* (1568), two works that focus on several cultural and moral issues then current in Europe. *The Life of an Honest Man*, which constitutes a part of *The Mirror*, records

Rej's views on married life, military service, education, farming, and household activities. Three books (youth, middle age, and old age) describe in detail the biological cycle of life and major occupations of a Renaissance man. Rej also compiled a *Bestiary* (1562), a collection of approximately seven hundred epigrams that include animal fables and portraits of outstanding figures from antiquity and from contemporaneous Poland. In a lighter vein, Rej wrote satirical poems in a ribald style, called *Trifles* or *Pranks*.

Bibliography

M. Mikoś, *Polish Renaissance Literature: An Anthology*, 1995.

Michael J. Mikoś

RENÉE OF FERRARA (1510–1575)

Renée of Ferrara was the second daughter of King Louis XII of France and the wife of the duke of Ferrara, Italy. She was a patron of Protestant Reformers and a supporter of a number of religious refugees during the Wars of Religion in France. When King François I* of France began a campaign against religious dissent in 1534, a number of recent converts to the Reformed faith, including the youthful John Calvin,* fled the country. Although we do not know the nature of her own religious opinions at the time, Renée allowed a number of French Calvinist refugees to settle in Ferrara. In 1536 Calvin himself was a visitor, and although the author of the *Institutes of the Christian Religion* ultimately settled in Geneva, Calvin and Renée maintained a lifelong correspondence.

In 1547 Renée intervened with her husband on behalf of an Italian Protestant named Fanino Fanini, but her appeals were in vain, and Fanini was executed. She had already been examined by the Italian Inquisition in 1543, and ten years later, King Henri II of France sent inquisitors from his court in order to convince Renée of her need for repentance. Much to the disappointment of Calvin, Renée capitulated and publicly returned to the Roman Catholic fold in 1555.

Returning to France upon the death of her husband and establishing her court at Montargis, east of Orléans, in 1560, Renée extended her earlier efforts in support of Protestant Reformers. She befriended Gaspard II de Coligny, head of the Huguenot army in France, but she was also mother-in-law to Francis, duke of Guise, leader of the Catholic forces in the French religious wars. Although she attempted to maintain neutrality during the long conflict, the patronage of women like Renée was key to the survival of the Reformed cause during the Wars of Religion (1562–98); she was joined in this work by a number of other powerful noblewomen. Calvin sent spiritual advisors from Geneva, but they quarreled with Renée because she wanted to attend meetings of the synod or council of church elders.

Renée's work of granting refuge and repose to those who suffered during the decades of religious conflict was part of a larger movement by aristocratic women to forward the cause of the Protestant Reformers. Of the thirty-seven women arrested at a Protestant demonstration in Paris in 1557, half were of noble birth.

Bibliography

R. H. Bainton, *Women of the Reformation in Germany and Italy*, 1971.

William Spellman

RICCI, MATTEO (LI MADOU) (1552–1610)

Matteo Ricci, superior of the mission of the Society of Jesus in China from 1597 until his death and a regimental officer in the society's global offensive in the war for souls during the Counter-Reformation, played a central role in the effort to bring Catholicism to China. From his observations of the country, where he arrived in 1583, and as an extension of the Jesuit emphasis on "top-down" conversion, he quickly identified mandarins and other important people as the keys to mission success. Knowing the respect his targets had for learning, he used a common interest in science, mathematics, cartography, memory arts, and printing to bridge the cultural chasm with Chinese intellectuals. Ricci also pursued the controversial Jesuit policy of employing indigenous practices and beliefs, when they were not regarded as being in violation of Roman Catholic teaching, in order to further conversion.

Born in Macerata, Italy, in the Papal States, Ricci became a novice of the Society of Jesus in 1571 and studied at the Jesuit colleges in Florence and Rome. With a gift for languages and a keen desire to expand the "true faith," he was recruited for a campaign to reinvigorate the East Asian missions. Ricci's works include the *Treatise on Friendship* (1595), a "memory palace" (1596) that sought to mesh Chinese ideographs with Christian teachings, *The True Meaning of the Lord of Heaven* (1603), *Twenty-five Sayings* (translated from Epictetus, 1605), a translation of the first six books of Euclid's *Elements of Geometry* (1607), and *Ten Discourses by a Paradoxical Man* (1608). He also made a map of the world that was published in China in 1602 and began a *Historia* of his career in China.

Ultimately, Ricci did baptize a small number of the circle in which he operated. However, implacable hostility from many officials and the social and political upheaval that preceded the collapse of the Ming in 1644 frustrated Ricci's hopes of a Christian China. The Jesuits' scientific and intellectual activity, rather than their faith, made the most enduring imprint on seventeenth-century China.

Bibliography

J. D. Spence, *The Memory Palace of Matteo Ricci*, 1984.

Louis Roper

RICH, BARNABE (1542–1617)

Captain Barnabe Rich was a notable personality of his day, famous for his military service and his literary successes. Rich described himself as a gentleman, though he had no university education. During the course of his fifty-five-year military career, Rich fought in France, the Low Countries, and Ireland. Rich began writing prose and poems in the early 1570s. He took careful notes of military maneuvers and described the trials and tribulations of fighting men. The first of his two best-sellers was titled *Riche His Farewell to Militarie Profession* (1581); his second was *The Honestie of This Age* (1614). Both texts enjoyed numerous reprintings in the author's lifetime. While Rich was in Ireland, he authored a pamphlet exposing the negligence of the Irish clergy. This work, published in 1589, caused a scandal, and Rich suffered from numerous attacks for his critique.

Ireland was also the site of the most devastating episode of Rich's military career. In 1585 his company was executed in a bloody massacre. His service was rewarded with a small pension from Elizabeth I* in 1587. In the same year, Rich married Kathryn Easten. He later sought preferment in London. In 1595 he was assigned the task of training new recruits and later was involved in intelligence work. While Elizabeth I praised Rich and provided some compensation, it was James I's* court that recognized Rich with ample reward for his military service, bestowing a gift of one hundred pounds in 1616. Rich died shortly thereafter, in 1617. He had no fewer than twenty-six publications to his name.

Rich had a reputation as a fine military strategist, satirist of the Irish, and celebrated figure of his day. His patrons included Elizabeth I, James I, and Lord Mayor Thomas Middleton.* He was friendly with the writers Thomas North, Thomas Lodge,* and George Gascoigne.* The popularity of Rich's tales is best evidenced by those who read and referenced his work; it is believed that William Shakespeare* borrowed from one of Rich's plots, as did John Webster,* Thomas Heywood,* and Thomas Dekker.*

Bibliography

T. M. Cranfill and D. H. Bruce, *Barnaby Rich*, 1953.

Michele Osherow

RINUCCINI, OTTAVIO (1562–1621)

Ottavio Rinuccini, born in Florence and active there for most of his life, was a librettist, poet, and courtier. He was of a noble Florentine family and received a good classical education. At an early age he became a member of the Accademia Fiorentina and also of the Accademia degli Alterati, in which he took the name "Il Sonnacchioso" (The Somnolent One). The speculative discussions at the latter academy centered around the relations of dramatic theory and music, especially the adaptation of pastoral drama to a musical setting. It was thought that music was natural to shepherds, who lived close to nature and whose poetic utterances were reechoed by woods and mountains.

Rinuccini experimented first in the composition of *intermedi*, or interludes, which glorified the power of ancient music. Out of one of these, which depicted the struggle between Apollo and the python taken from Ovid's *Metamorphoses*, Rinuccini drew the opening scene of his first operatic text, *Dafne*. It is indebted in its subject matter to the plots of the great pastoral dramas of the period, especially *Il pastor fido* of Giovanni Battista Guarini.*

The originality of Rinuccini consisted in his fashioning of a new verse form that was well adapted to the new style of singing, the *recitativo*, or recitation on musical tones. Rather than the blank verse of spoken tragedy or the strict metrical units of traditional lyric forms, he used a combination of seven- and eleven-syllable verses, *versi a selva* (woodland verses). The rhetorical style of his poetry lent itself to the heightened declamatory style of the new music. This first opera, for which Jacopo Peri* wrote the music, was performed in the Palazzo Corsi in Florence in the pre-Lenten carnival of 1598. The text is divided into a prologue and six scenes or tableaux. The text was published in 1600 and therefore survives, but Peri's music, save for the prologue and one aria, is no longer extant.

The next collaboration with Peri was *Euridice*, taken once again from Ovid's *Metamorphoses*, but also with borrowings from Virgil's famous narration of the tale of Orpheus in the fourth *Georgic* and Politian's *Orfeo*, accounted as the first verse drama on a secular theme. The opera was performed in the Boboli gardens in Palazzo Pitti in Florence on 6 October 1600 to celebrate the wedding of Maria de' Medici and Henri IV of France. In the preface Rinuccini apologizes for the *lieto fine* (happy ending), which he introduced in view of the joyous occasion.

The dramatic organization of this opera lies behind the more famous *Favola d'Orfeo*, with the libretto by Alessandro Striggio and the music by composer Claudio Monteverdi.* Rinuccini later collaborated with Monteverdi for the opera *Arianna*, but unfortunately it is lost save for the wonderful lament of Ariadne, abandoned by Theseus, expressing her outrage, despair, and obsession with death, "Lasciatemi monre" (Let me die). It became one of the most popular operatic excerpts of the century and gave rise to a specific type of aria in countless operas.

Rinuccini is thus the creator of the first operatic libretto. He was an able versifier, if not a great poet, and a creative man of the theater.

Bibliography

N. Pirrotta, *Music and Culture in Italy from the Middle Ages to the Baroque*, 1984.

Charles Fantazzi

RONSARD, PIERRE DE (1524–1585)

An aspiring humanist and member of the literary circle La Pléïade, Pierre de Ronsard was the official court poet during the reign of Henri II and later under François II. A staunch Catholic and nationalist during a time of much religious upheaval in France, he is best known for his Petrarchan-style sonnets.

He was born around 10 September 1524 in the castle of the Possonniére near

Orléans. His parents were of minor nobility, and Ronsard spent his childhood in the family castle, tutored by his uncle, the clergyman Jean de Ronsard, who would will Pierre his library. In 1536 he entered the royal court as page to the dauphin Francis. He accompanied one of the dauphin's sisters, Magdalene, to Scotland when she married James V in 1537. Upon his return to France in 1540, he served under the duke of Orléans, whom he accompanied to Alsace on a diplomatic mission to reach an accord between Protestants and Catholics. However, he was unable to further pursue a diplomatic or military career after a fever left him hard of hearing.

Ronsard had by then already begun composing verses, first in Latin, then in French, and he was leaning toward humanist studies. After his father died, the duke of Orléans invited Ronsard to live in his home in Paris, where he would tutor and be companion to the duke's son, Jean-Antoine, seven years Pierre's junior. Both were tutored in ancient Greek, and Ronsard became a Grecophile. In court circles he met Cassandre Salviati, the daughter of a Florentine banker living in France. She was fourteen, he was twenty-one. He wrote verses to her, despite her marriage in 1546 to Jean de Peigné. Thus Cassandre became the idealized, inaccessible woman.

After joining the political group called La Brigade, which later became La Pléïade, Ronsard published his *First Four Books of Odes* in 1550. In 1552 he published his sonnets, *The Loves*, dedicated to Cassandre, along with the fifth book of the odes. These Petrarchan sonnets sold out in six months.

While staying in the Loire Valley in 1555, Ronsard met a fifteen-year-old country girl, Marie Dupin. His verses became earthier and more realistic in his next publication, *Continuation of the Loves*. That same year his *Hymns* was published; these poems consist of political, religious, and philosophical themes. The publication of *Hymns* coincided with his undertaking of a French version of the *Aeneid* entitled *La Franciade*, which turned out to be his greatest literary failure. However, nine other works appeared, among them a continuation of the *Hymns* and the *Loves*.

Upon his official naming as court poet, Ronsard composed *Sonnets to Sinope*, who was an unknown younger woman. In 1559 Henri died, but Ronsard continued in his post under François II. Under the new king, Ronsard wrote patriotic and religious anti-Protestant poems. François II died in 1560, but Ronsard continued as court poet under his successor, Charles IX, who was ten years old. He was faithful to the regent, Catherine de' Medici,* and more poems appeared about unknown women: Genèvre and Isabel de La Tour.

Ronsard wrote his *Discourse on the Calamities of Our Time* as a consequence of siding with the king in the civil war against the Huguenots in 1562. In Geneva, Protestants insulted him in print, accusing him of frivolity, deafness, syphilis, pederasty, and atheism. He responded with equal passion, blaming Protestants for the fragmentation of national unity. His zeal was rewarded with the Priory of Saint-Cosme, near Tours. However, he moved to Vendômes in 1566, where he published nine books, got a fever, and consequently gave up the priory. He returned to court in 1570.

A few days after the St. Bartholomew's Day Massacre in 1572, his *First Four Books of the Franciade* were published but were poorly received. Two years later, Charles IX died, and Henri III, the last Valois, ascended the throne. Unfortunately for Ronsard, Henri III preferred the poetry of the younger and more modern Philippe Desportes,* who replaced Ronsard as court poet. Ronsard retired to Saint-Cosme and to Croixval, where he published his complete works in seven volumes (1578). These volumes included his *Sonnets for Hélène* and *Sonnets and Madrigals for Astrea*. The sonnets for Hélène were destined for Hélène de Surgères, who outlived him. In his fifties, he fell in love with this inaccessible and erudite lady, and the poems reflect his suffering and his return to Petrarchism. The themes of these poems include those of inaccessible love, life that brings death, the gaze that blinds, and the wound that heals. The book is filled with mythological references and abundant Latin- and Greek-based words. Hélène is compared to Helen of Troy, who had been blamed for starting the Trojan War. The historical Hélène de Surgères was a lady in the court of Catherine de' Medici. After her lover, Jacques de la Rivière, died in a duel, she took to wearing gray. Around 1570 she frequented the literary salon of her cousin, where she possibly met Ronsard. She was quite learned and fond of reading Latin and Italian as well as French literature. Although published late in life, Ronsard's sonnets to her have become his best known. After a year of fighting grave illness, Pierre de Ronsard died on 27 December 1585 at the age of sixty-one.

Bibliography

R. Bruneau, *Ronsard, gentilhomme vendômois*, 1985.
A. Prescott, *French Poets and the English Renaissance*, 1978.

Ana Kothe

ROPER, MARGARET MORE (1505–1544)

Margaret More Roper, the "ornament of Britain," enjoyed contemporary renown as a classical scholar and a woman of letters. The eldest daughter of Sir Thomas More* and Jane Colt, Margaret, along with her sisters Elizabeth and Cecily, her brother John, and others attached to the More household, received a first-rate humanist education. The students' classical education included Latin and Greek, astronomy, medicine, philosophy, theology, rhetoric, grammar, and logic. More employed numerous tutors, including John Clement, the Greek scholar and physician, and Nicholas Kratzer, the astronomer, both of whom served at the Tudor court of Henry VIII.* By the time Juan Luis Vives* published his *On the Instruction of a Christian Woman*, in which he praised the learning of More's daughters, the girls were already accomplished scholars. Their fame continued to grow, until finally King Henry VIII of England invited them to dispute before him.

The works Margaret wrote that have not survived included epistles and orations in Latin, a treatise on the *Four Last Things* (c. 1522), and a translation of Eusebius from Greek to Latin. She is also credited with having written poetry. Margaret Roper's most important surviving work is her English translation of Desiderius Erasmus's* *Precatio dominica in septem portiones distributa* (1523). Her translation, with its sensitive rendering of Latin meanings into English, provides evidence of a high level of scholarly achievement. Richard Hyrde's important groundbreaking argument in defense of the education of women, which prefaces Margaret's published translation, *A Devout Treatise upon the Pater Noster* (1526), holds a prominent place in the history of women's studies.

Margaret's connections with Erasmus and his humanist network were probably firmly established by 1524. Referring to Margaret as the "ornament of Britain," Erasmus dedicated one of his works to her in 1523, upon the birth of her child. Erasmus also accepted and used in his edition of St. Cyprian's work Margaret's emendation of a corrupt passage. Margaret's ability to emend the corrupt passage demonstrates how fully developed her critical scholarship was. Margaret More married her husband, William Roper, on 2 July 1521. The Roper's household, along with More's, was arguably the most literate in Tudor England.

Along with her translation of Erasmus's treatise, some of Margaret Roper's letters have survived. The letters Margaret sent to her father while he was in the Tower of London were written in English, further indicating her mastery of English as well as Latin. One extraordinary letter, on which Margaret and her father probably collaborated while he was lodged in the Tower—the Alington letter—is a Platonic dialogue in which More analyzes his "case of conscience." A devoted daughter, Margaret preserved the head of her beloved father after his execution in 1535. Family members continued to protect the head until its final interment in the Roper family vault in St. Dunstan's, Canterbury.

In addition to continuing her own studies after her marriage, Margaret Roper provided her children with a humanist education. One of her daughters, Mary Bassett (fl. 1553–58), proved to be especially gifted. Basset translated one of Sir Thomas More's incomplete works, *De tristitia Christi*, from Latin to English, a translation that later appeared in the published 1557 edition of More's works.

Bibliography

E. McCutcheon, "Margaret More Roper," in *Women Writers of the Renaissance and Reformation*, ed. K. M. Wilson, 1987.
E. E. Reynolds, *Margaret Roper: Eldest Daughter of St. Thomas More*, 1960.

Debbie Barrett-Graves

RORE, CIPRIANO DE (c. 1516–1565)

Cipriano de Rore, a Flemish composer active in Italy, enhanced the expressive power of the Italian madrigal by fusing its lyric poetry with a passionate and affective form of musical expression. As a pioneer of the so-called *seconda prattica*, his concern was for music to serve the text.

Rore was born in the Netherlands, but it is assumed that he went to Italy early in his life. During the 1540s he studied in Venice with Adrian Willaert,* maestro di cappella at St. Mark's Cathedral. He assumed the post of maestro di cappella at Ferrara around 1547 and in 1561 traveled to Parma to serve Ottavio Farnese. He briefly succeeded Willaert at St. Mark's in 1563, but soon returned to Parma in 1564, where he remained until his death.

Rore's madrigals are among the finest of the Renaissance. He carefully selected poetry of the highest quality and was particularly fond of setting the sonnets of Petrarch. He strove in his madrigals to make the music serve its text not only by making the words intelligible but by conveying a sense of the text's imagery and emotion in his musical setting. Rore, with his setting of Petrarch's *Vergine belle* as a set of eleven madrigals in 1548, is credited with creating the madrigal cycle, a form that subsequently became very popular for the remainder of the sixteenth century. Although Rore is best known for his madrigals, he also wrote secular Latin motets, French chansons, and sacred masses and motets. Rore had a profound impact upon the work of all madrigal composers who followed him in the sixteenth century. That impact is evident in the work of Claudio Monteverdi.*

Bibliography

A. Johnson, "Cipriano de Rore," in *The New Grove Dictionary of Music and Musicians*, ed. S. Sadie, vol. 16, 1980:185–90.

Tucker Robison

ROSSO FIORENTINO (1494–1540)

Giovanni Battista di Jacopo de Guaspare, known as Rosso Fiorentino, was among the most innovative artists working in Italy and France in the first half of the sixteenth century. The Florentine painter's earliest training remains a mystery, but by 1513 he was working alongside Pontormo* and Andrea del Sarto* at Santissima Annunziata. His *Assumption of the Virgin* there was not well received, and Rosso spent several years working in other Tuscan cities. From this period dates the *Deposition from the Cross* in Volterra, today the artist's most famous work. Its inventiveness led early-twentieth-century critics to treat Rosso as a paradigmatically anticlassical artist, one of the so-called Mannerists who reacted against the classical, normative art of Raphael* and Michelangelo.*

Rosso returned to Florence in 1522 and in 1524 moved to Rome. His works there, such as the *Dead Christ*, now in Boston, show the Mannerist "stylish style" that is a development of Raphaelesque ideas of grace and elegant beauty, rather than a reaction against them. He also designed a series of prints (engraved by Caraglio) that led to the diffusion of this style.

Following the sack of Rome in 1527, Rosso traveled under the protection of

Leonardo Tornabuoni to Umbria and painted several altarpieces. In Venice Pietro Aretino* helped bring Rosso to the attention of King François I,* and from 1530 until his death Rosso worked in France, especially at Fontainebleau. He lived a princely life and was responsible for paintings as well as designs for decorative arts. He is the main artistic personality behind the early stages of the so-called Fontainebleau school.

Bibliography

E. Carroll, *Rosso Fiorentino: Drawings, Prints, and Decorative Arts*, 1987.
D. Franklin, *Rosso in Italy*, 1994.

John Marciari

RUBENS, PETER PAUL (1577–1640)

Rubens single-handedly transformed the character of Flanders from a city where provincial art was created to a major artistic center. He was not only a prolific painter with approximately three thousand works attributed to him, but also an avid art collector, diplomat, and advisor to the infanta Isabella Clara Eugenia, the archduchess of Flanders.

Rubens was born in Westphalia to a Calvinist lawyer from Antwerp. In 1578 his family moved to Cologne, and in 1589, after his father's death, his mother returned with her children to Antwerp. There Rubens apprenticed first with the painter Tobias Verhaecht, his mother's cousin, then with Adam van Noort, and finally with Otto van Veen.

From 1600 to 1608 Rubens was employed by Duke Vincenzo Gonzaga of Mantua as court painter. There he was able to study the works in the duke's collection of Venetian masters, including Titian,* Tintoretto,* and Paolo Veronese,* as well as those by other important Renaissance and Mannerist painters such as Raphael,* Andrea del Sarto,* and Correggio.* The duke encouraged Rubens to travel to other Italian cities to further his education as a painter. Venice, Verona, Padua, Genoa, and Rome were among the cities he visited. Rubens soon adopted the Venetian mode of painting with a lush application of color and an emphasis on the nude and the landscape. Among the works Rubens painted in Italy are his *Madonna and Child with Sts. Gregory and Domitilla* for the high altar at S. Maria in Vallicella, Rome (1606–7), the *Ecstasy of St. Helena, Mocking of Christ, and Elevation of the Cross* for S. Croce in Gerusalemme, Rome (1601–2), and *The Gonzaga Adoring the Trinity, The Baptism of Christ*, and the *Transfiguration* for the Cappella Maggiore in the Jesuit Church by Trinity Sunday, Mantua.

Rubens returned to Antwerp in 1608 after his mother's death. In the same year he was appointed court painter to the infanta Isabella Clara Eugenia and Archduke Albert; sovereigns of Flanders. In the following year he established a large studio with numerous apprentices and married Isabella Brant. Rubens marked this last event by painting a double portrait of himself and his new bride, *The Honeysuckle Bower* (1609–10). Between 1609 and 1614 Rubens was engaged in several important commissions, including his well-known *Raising of the Cross* for the Church of St. Walburga, Antwerp, and *Descent from the Cross* for the Harquebusiers' altar at Antwerp Cathedral. In these works he combined a traditional triptych format with the Italianate elements he had learned in his travels.

Rubens's diplomatic activities began in the 1620s. In 1624 he conducted secret peace negotiations between Spain and the Dutch Netherlands. Rubens was rewarded by the king of Spain for his successful intervention with a title of nobility. In 1628–29 he was knighted by King Charles I of England at Whitehall Banqueting Hall, London, where he would later paint his famous ceiling glorifying King James I* and proclaiming the unification of England and Scotland. By now Rubens had remarried. His new wife, Helena Fourment, appears in several of his works.

Rubens's diplomatic missions led to other important commissions. While he was in Spain, he painted several portraits of members of the royal family, including *Philip IV on Horseback* (1628–29). In 1636 he became court painter to the king's brother, Cardinale Infante Ferdinand, appointed in 1634 as the new regent of the Spanish Netherlands. Rubens was put in charge of the decoration of the Torre de la Parada, Philip IV's hunting lodge in Madrid. This was the largest commission he ever received, carried out mainly by assistants because of the great number of works required. Another major commission Rubens received from royalty was the Medici cycle at Luxembourg Palace, Paris. Marie de' Medici, wife of Henri IV, commissioned this work from the artist in 1622, and the paintings were installed by 1625. They depict the life of the queen, including her birth, education, betrothal to the king, and arrival in France.

In 1640, after an illustrious career that spanned over four decades, Rubens fell seriously ill with gout. He died on 30 May of the same year. His works caused a great impact in the development of art, particularly in the eighteenth century in France when rococo artists like Watteau adopted his loose brushwork, lush application of paint, and sensuous subjects.

Bibliography

J. Held, *Rubens and His Circle*, 1982.
J. R. Martin, ed., *Rubens before 1620*, 1972.
M. Warnke, *Peter Paul Rubens: Life and Work*, 1980.

Lilian H. Zirpolo

RUDOLF II OF HABSBURG, HOLY ROMAN EMPEROR (1552–1612)

Rudolf II, one of history's most eccentric individuals, was a ruler, a madman, an alchemist, and a patron of the arts. Rudolf's historical distinction comes not from his political accomplishments but from the people he brought to his court and from his Kunstkammer, which included collected and commissioned artworks.

Rudolf's own modest childhood education at the court of his uncle, Philip II* of Spain, perhaps prompted him as an adult to bring to Prague some of the greatest minds and talents of his age. Not without his own talent, Rudolf reportedly spoke German, Latin, Spanish, Italian, French, and some Bohemian and Czech; however, as a ruler, he withdrew from much of his political responsibility and chose to fashion his imperial image through the arts.

Crowned king of Hungary in 1572, king of Bohemia in 1575, and holy Roman emperor in 1576 after the death of Maximilian II, his father, Rudolf II established Prague as his royal residence in 1583. Rudolf's patronage made Prague home to scholars, artists, painters, alchemists, craftsmen, architects, and astrologers, among those of name were Tycho Brahe,* Johannes Kepler,* Bartholomaeus Spranger,* Giuseppe Arcimboldo,* Giambattista Della Porta,* and John Dee.* During his life Rudolf acquired a collection of artworks, especially paintings, sculptures, drawings, engravings, sketches, books, manuscripts, scientific instruments, tapestries, gems, stones, fossils, shells, and bones. Aside from his participation in the arts, in his later years Rudolf developed a passion for the occult sciences: alchemy and magic.

Nearing the end of his life, Rudolf II relinquished the Hungarian crown in 1608 and the Bohemian crown in 1611 to Matthias, his brother and successor. After Rudolf's death, Matthias greedily claimed much of the collection, which had been appraised at seventeen million ducats, and transported it to Vienna. With Rudolf's death and the removal of his collection, Prague never reclaimed its artistic notoriety.

Bibliography

R.J.W. Evans, *Rudolf II and His World*, 1973.
E. Fucikova, ed., *Rudolf II and Prague: The Court and the City*, 1997.

Stephanie Witham

RUZZANTE (1496–1542)

Angelo Beolco, more commonly known by his stage name Ruzzante, was a famous actor and playwright in the Venetian and Paduan territories. He was the illegitimate son of Giovanni Francesco Beolco, a member of Paduan high society and rector of the faculty of medicine at the University of Padua. As a young man he was charged with the administration of the country estates of Alvise Cornaro, a wealthy landowner, who became Ruzzante's patron. During this same period Ruzzante founded a dramatic company and performed in comic recitals in the street celebrations of carnival time and in the homes of Venetian patrician families.

His first play, called simply *La pastoral*, first performed in 1518, is a parody of the artificial pastoral drama much in vogue at the time. Instead of the enamored shepherd swain, the protagonist is a rough, almost animalistic peasant who speaks the crude rustic dialect of the Paduan countryside, bristling with obscenities and double entendres. The other characters in the play, in comic contrast, use either a literary, Tuscanizing Italian or other dialects, like the quasi-incomprehensible Bergamask of the doctor.

Ruzzante made a spirited apology for the naturalness of the rustic dialect and the natural, genuine life of the country in an oration delivered at the formal installation of a relative of his patron as bishop of Padua. More blatantly naturalistic is Ruzzante's next theatrical production, *La Betia*, a marriage comedy belonging to a genre called the *mariazo*, performed at rustic weddings. It ends in a happy, country-style *mélange à quatre* between two married couples with the connivance of the lover of one of the spouses. Ruzzante once more pits the realism of his peasant world against the artifices of pastoral poetry and the stylized conversations of the new courts of love, as in Cardinal Pietro Bembo's* *Gli Asolani*, set in a villa near Padua.

In 1529 Ruzzante presented a monologue entitled *Parlamento*, spoken by a peasant who went off to the wars hoping to escape his misery but returns more impoverished than ever and finds that his wife has turned prostitute and repudiated him. In *La Anconitana* Ruzzante makes use of the time-honored device of mistaken identity. Ginevra, a widow from Ancona, falls in love with Gismondo, who turns out to be her own sister, who had been captured by pirates and had assumed male disguise.

Toward the end of his life, under the influence of Ludovico Ariosto,* with whom he collaborated at the court of Ferrara, Ruzzante wrote two comedies based very closely on two plays of Plautus, although they still retained the pungency and naturalism of the Paduan peasantry. It is interesting to note that many of Ruzzante's plays were performed in a theater designed by the famous architect Giovan Maria Falconetto on the classical principles formulated by the Roman writer on architecture, Vitruvius.

On the vigil of a celebration in which he was to play a role in Sperone Speroni's* horrendous tragedy *Canace*, Ruzzante took sick and died. It was as if he could not survive his own stage image nor be completely integrated into the academism of his patrons.

Bibliography

L. Carroll, *Angelo Beolco (Il Ruzante)*, 1990.
N. Dersofi, *Arcadia and the Stage*, 1978.

Charles Fantazzi

S

SACHS, HANS (1494–1576)

A cobbler poet in Nuremberg, Hans Sachs was a major representative of Protestant humanist literature rooted in the popular culture of southern Germany. Sachs's life and literary activities were closely linked to the Free City of Nuremberg, an economic and cultural center and a key player in the political and religious conflicts of the Reformation period. Although Sachs was of humble origins (his father was a tailor), he was able to attend a grammar school until he was fifteen. He was then apprenticed to a local shoemaker and learned the art of *Meistersang*, a highly prescriptive literary and musical genre that allowed the writing of new lyrics to established tunes and the invention of new melodies if one had become a master.

From 1511 to 1516 he traveled as a journeyman throughout Germany, wrote his first poems, tales, and *Meisterlieder*, and taught at several singing schools. After returning to Nuremberg, he married in 1519, inherited his parental home, and subsequently became a master shoemaker and was admitted to the guild of *Meistersinger*, societies of amateur singers who preserved strict codes for the composition and delivery of their religious and narrative songs. Around 1520 Sachs became a follower of the teachings of Martin Luther.* He propagated them through his poems and dialogues—often printed on illustrated broadsheets and as pamphlets—and was actively engaged in the religious debates of his age. His anti-Catholic propaganda brought him into conflict with the authorities, who forced him to tone down his polemics. In the following years he became a prosperous and respected citizen in his hometown and in 1542 was able to purchase a second house. During his leisure hours he produced a voluminous body of poetry and for nearly fifty years was a leading representative of the Nuremberg *Meistersang* tradition. From 1551 to 1560 he functioned as director of a *Meistersinger* stage, and from 1555 to 1561 as juror of a singing school. When his wife died in 1560, he began to withdraw from public life. He remarried in 1561, at the age of sixty-seven, and continued his creative writing until he was seventy-eight.

Sachs was a prolific author in a wide variety of genres. His *Summa all meiner gedicht* of 1567 records over 6,000 works, including 16 books of *Meisterlieder* (2,575 in all), over 1,500 *Sprüche* (tales, chronicles, fables, satires, and epigrams, all in rhymed verse), 213 plays (58 tragedies, 70 comedies, and 85 Shrovetide plays), and a large number of hymns, songs, prose pieces, and dialogues. His education was much inferior to that of the great humanist scholar-poets of his age, and his social status as a shoemaker prevented him from playing a major role in the international republic of letters. However, Nuremberg enjoyed an artistic and intellectual life of the highest order, and Sachs profited greatly from the active cultural scene around him. His knowledge of classical and Italian Renaissance literature was extensive and influenced much of his writing. But all of his works were written in the vernacular, betray a homespun simplicity, and appeal through their humorous depiction of human foibles.

Although Sachs wrote some influential Reformation dialogues and was an undisputed leader in the *Meistersang* tradition, he is best remembered as an author of farces (*Schwänke*) and Shrovetide plays (*Fastnachtsspiele*). Modern editions of these can still be enjoyed by a nonspecialist reader, and amateur performances have delighted many theater audiences throughout the twentieth century. Sachs was a pioneer of the *Schwank* as a literary genre, and his *Fastnachtsspiele* can be seen as *Schwänke* in dialogue form. The medieval tradition of Shrovetide plays was revived in Nuremberg in 1533 and offered Sachs an opportunity to shift from the political and religious concerns of his early works to a more humorous treatment of the human condition. His plays are devoid of any clear dramatic structure and present character types in everyday situations and conflicts. Blending caricature with shrewd observation and coarse humor with witty turns of phrase, they have a freshness and directness that works well even in translation. In contrast, his comedies and tragedies are only of historical interest. Based mainly on biblical, classical, and Germanic mythology, they focus on telling a long and complicated story in dialogue form and are epic rather than dramatic in structure. They were important attempts at translating humanist school drama into vernacular forms and used the *Meistersinger* stage to popularize popular culture; however, due to their untheatrical character and the subsequent development of a baroque and neoclassical aesthetics of drama, these plays were soon forgotten.

Bibliography

R. Aylett and P. Skrine, eds., *Hans Sachs and Folk Theatre in the Late Middle Ages*, 1995.
M. Beare, ed., *Hans Sachs: Selections*, 1983.

Günter Berghaus

SACKVILLE, SIR THOMAS, EARL OF DORSET (1563–1608)

Statesman for Elizabeth I,* Sir Thomas Sackville contributed to *A Mirror for Magistrates* and in collaboration with Thomas Norton wrote *Gorboduc*, the first

English tragedy in blank verse. Born in Buckhurst, Sackville was the only son of Sir Richard Sackville. He attended Oxford, joined the Inner Temple, and married Cicely Baker. Knighted on 8 June 1567 and made a peer, Baron Buckhurst, Sackville was sent on various missions for Queen Elizabeth. His offices under Elizabeth I and James I* included commissioner at state trials, knight of the Garter, lord chancellor of Oxford, and lord high treasurer for life. He died on duty at the council table on 19 April 1608. Sackville's literary career includes contributions to *A Mirror for Magistrates*, a collection of verse in which famous English men and women recount their ruin. Sackville wrote the "Complaint of Buckingham," and his "Induction" to *A Mirror for Magistrates* features Sorrow leading the poet to the dead. On 6 January 1561 *Gorboduc* was performed at the Inner Temple. Thomas Norton, who wrote the first three acts, and Sackville, who wrote the last two, drew their story from the chronicles of Britain and patterned the play after Senecan tragedy.

Bibliography

N. Berlin, *Thomas Sackville*, 1974.

Megan S. Lloyd

SÁ DE MIRANDA, FRANCISCO (1481–1558)

Francisco Sá de Miranda was a Portuguese lyric poet credited with bringing the Italian Renaissance through its verse forms into Portugal. His central position in the history of Portuguese letters is marked by the introduction of the Italian hendecasyllabic line to Portuguese verse, as well as the introduction of the forms in which it most commonly appeared, the sonnet and the eclogue.

Born the illegitimate son of the canon of Coimbra, Sá de Miranda was later legitimized and seems to have suffered no ill effect from his origins. He attended the university at Coimbra and received a degree as doctor of law, a career he never pursued. His earliest poetry was published in the *Cancioneiro geral* (General songbook) in 1516. His extended stay in Italy, from 1521 to 1526, seems to have exerted a profound influence on his poetic production. Upon his return to Portugal in 1527, he voluntarily left the court and retired to the country in Minho. This period marks the most productive stage of his artistic development. Like many Iberian poets, he wrote in both Spanish and Portuguese; over one half of his poetry is written in Spanish.

Sá de Miranda is very much a transitional figure, bridging the medieval and Renaissance traditions. While his verse shows a clear integration and mastery of the new Italianate meters, he nonetheless evinces an independent spirit in the themes expressed. Although love is the principal theme, it is rarely the ennobling and morally uplifting experience of much Renaissance poetry. Rather, Sá de Miranda is more ascetic in tone, viewing man as a victim of his own passions, and love as a destructive force contributing to man's downfall. Similarly, a pessimistic strain runs through many of his works, which are heavily moralistic in tone and focus on the evils of human society. Indeed, his most acclaimed work is the satirical eclogue *Basto*, which implicitly advocates the life of retreat of the ascetic. In addition to his eclogues and love poetry, Sá de Miranda also composed two *comedias* and five satiric epistles. The first complete edition of his works appeared in 1595.

Bibliography

T. F. Earle, *Theme and Image in the Poetry of Sá de Miranda*, 1980.
J. V. de Pina Martins, *Sá de Miranda e a cultura do renascimento*, 1972.

Deborah Compte

SALVIATI, FRANCESCO (1510–1563)

A Florentine painter, Francesco Salviati frescoed highly imaginative and complex decorative systems that extended the possibilities of interior decoration to a new level. Salviati probably received his early training with a goldsmith and in mediocre workshops in Florence. While there, he remained impressed by the work of various Mannerist artists and probably met Giorgio Vasari,* who became a friend and supporter. He arrived in Rome in 1531, and in 1536 he collaborated on the decorations for the entry of Emperor Charles V* into the city. By 1538 he had assumed an important place among the many new painters in Rome, receiving a commission for a fresco of the *Visitation* in the Oratory of St. John the Baptist, which reveals his study of Raphael* and Michelangelo.*

Salviati returned to Florence briefly in 1539 to work on the decorations for the marriage of Cosimo I de' Medici* with Eleanora of Toledo.* Following this, he traveled to Bologna and then went to Venice, where he imported the latest Mannerist innovations of Rome and Florence to northern Italy. In 1543, upon the invitation of Cosimo I, he returned to Florence to work in the Palazzo Vecchio. Salviati's decorative style, with its profusion of ornament, inventive motifs, and compositional liberty, presented an original ornamental splendor. The fame of his work in Florence led to several more decorative commissions in Rome for the Sacchetti and Farnese families, which reveal a new complexity as he played with levels of reality and artifice in a sophisticated fashion. Salviati also occupied himself in painting portraits at various moments, even executing the portrait of King François I* when he visited France in 1555–57. Salviati's creativity, sense of fantasy, skill as a colorist, and Mannerist elongated and elegant figural manner coalesced into a decorative style that made him one of the most popular interior decorators in central Italy.

Bibliography

L. Mortari, *Francesco Salviati*, 1992.

Mary Pixley

SANNAZARO, JACOPO (c. 1458–1530)

Jacopo Sannazaro was a Renaissance humanist and poet who wrote in Italian and Latin. He is most famous for the poem *Arcadia* (1504), which established the literary tradition of the pastoral mode and influenced writers for the next two centuries, most notably the English poet Philip Sidney* and the Portuguese Jorge de Montemayor.*

Born into a distinguished Neapolitan family, Sannazaro was educated in the style of an aristocrat. He was admitted to the prestigious literary academy of Naples around 1478 and, according to the prevailing custom in these circles of assuming Latinized names, was given the academic name of "Actius Syncerus." It is believed that he did much of his writing in Italian during the 1480s, with *Arcadia* being his principal undertaking. *Arcadia* is an elegiac portrayal, written in prose and verse, of lovelorn shepherds who inhabit a world permeated by a profound sense of melancholy. Sannazaro introduces himself into his own poem in the person of its narrator, Sincero, who, unfortunate in love, leaves Naples in order to find respite within the idyllic landscape of Arcadia. The poem circulated widely in manuscript, and a pirated edition was published in 1501; Sannazaro's revised and corrected version was ultimately published in 1504.

By 1490 Sannazaro was engaged in the Latin poetry that he hoped would ensure his reputation. Notable among these works are the *Eclogae piscatoriae* (Piscatorial Eclogues, 1526), in which the *Arcadia*'s plaintive shepherds are reinvented as fisherman on the Bay of Naples, and *De partu virginis* (On the virgin birth, 1526), an epic poem on Jesus' nativity.

Sannazaro lived almost his entire life in his native city, maintaining close ties with the court of Aragon, then rulers of Naples. Thus when Frederick of Aragon was deposed in 1501, Sannazaro loyally followed his king into exile in France. Following Frederick's death in 1504, he returned to his villa in Naples, where he lived the remainder of his life. After the tumultuous period he spent in France, he remained estranged from the social and political life of Naples. Although he refrained from taking part in affairs of state, his writings reflect his continued allegiance to King Frederick and to Naples.

Sannazaro's remains are housed in Santa Maria del Parto a Mergellina, the small church built on the property given to him by King Frederick in 1499. The tomb, which is believed to have been designed by the poet himself, is characterized by both Christian and classical motifs and endures as a fine example of Renaissance art.

Bibliography

C. Kidwell, *Sannazaro and Arcadia*, 1993.
R. Nash, trans., *Jacopo Sannzaro: Arcadia and Piscatorial Eclogues*, 1966.
R. Nash, trans., *The Major Latin Poems of Jacopo Sannazaro*, 1996.

Patricia A. White

SANSOVINO, JACOPO (1486–1570)

A Florentine architect and sculptor, Jacopo Sansovino orchestrated the architectural renewal of the political center of Venice, helping to modernize the city and bring it into the High Renaissance. In Florence, Italy, Jacopo Tatti trained as a sculptor with Andrea Sansovino and subsequently adopted the surname of his mentor. While he was in Florence, he encountered the High Renaissance as it was currently unfolding in the studio and the city. Around 1506 Sansovino went to Rome, where he established himself as an important sculptor whose work was deeply influenced by ancient sculpture and the art of Michelangelo.* Sansovino also continued to pursue his interest in architecture as he studied ancient buildings and eventually received religious and private architectural commissions.

After the sack of Rome, Sansovino moved to Venice in 1527, where he was in demand from the beginning, subsequently becoming famous as an architect. His formation and commissions in Rome and Florence meant that he brought with him the latest artistic and architectural innovations to Venice. In 1529 he was named chief architect of St. Mark's and received the commission to restructure and unify the central piazza of St. Mark, the political, economic, and cultural center of the city. The Roman vocabulary and the scale of his projects there, including the Library, the Loggetta underneath the campanile, various offices, and the Venetian mint, made a tremendous impact. While outwardly modern, Sansovino's buildings responded to the local architectural tradition and Venice's specific construction needs as Sansovino likewise adapted the design to the site and function of the building. Stylistically, his architecture reflects his sculptural formation with a pictorial dynamism owing to the play of light and shade on the surface.

Sansovino also continued to sculpt in Venice, renewing the Venetian and northern Italian sculptural scene there with his sculptures, tombs, and reliefs that embodied his mixture of classical and modern models, as evidenced in his sculptures for the Loggetta. Sansovino simultaneously continued to study fifteenth-century sculpture, especially the work of Donatello, as he sensitively responded to the northern Italian artistic tradition and fused it with central Italian developments. Sansovino worked in Venice for more than forty years, helping to visibly establish the *all'antica* style there with his sculptures and architecture.

Bibliography

B. Boucher, *The Sculpture of Jacopo Sansovino*, 1991.
D. Howard, *Jacopo Sansovino: Architecture and Patronage in Renaissance Venice*, 1975.

Mary Pixley

SANUDO or SANUTO, MARINO (1466–1533)

Marino Sanudo wrote of events in his own life and in his native city of Venice, where he also served in various public offices. Like many other well-born Venetian youths, Sanudo received an excellent classical education. In his *Lives of the Doges* (c. 1520) he relied heavily on his early training, comparing Venice to Rome and hailing a doge of recent memory as "the new Augustus." His loyalty to his city led him to note in 1509, after Venice's crushing defeat at Agnadello, that he would have asked even the Ottoman sultan for help against its foes. He believed that certain powerful unnamed enemies thwarted his own political ambitions; his outspokenness or his relatively modest means may equally have barred his path. Though it is as yet untranslated from the Italian, Sanudo's fifty-eight-volume *Diarii* covering the years from 1496 to 1533 is an essential source for understanding cultural and religious attitudes in Venice, Venetian policies on the mainland, and the particular challenges faced by the Venetian elite during several of the city's more turbulent decades.

Bibliography

D. S. Chambers, *The Imperial Age of Venice, 1380–1580*, 1970.
R. Finlay, *Politics in Renaissance Venice*, 1980.

Alison Williams Lewin

SARPI, PAOLO (1552–1623)

A Venetian cleric and historian, Paolo Sarpi is best known for articulating the rights of the Venetian state against the universal claims of the papacy. Precocious as a child, by age thirteen Sarpi had joined the Servite order, and by eighteen he was a reader in canon law and positive theology. He received his doctorate at Padua in 1576, and at age thirty-three he became procurator general of his order (1585–88). Despite several brushes with the authorities, Sarpi assumed no public role until the city of Venice appointed him as its theological and canonistic consultant.

In the spring of 1606 the papacy placed the Venetian state under interdict for its refusal to withdraw several measures restricting the economic and political power of the clergy in Venice. The clash between the papacy and Venice exposed two conflicting ideals of Christian life: papal supremacy and universal order, on the one hand, and service to God through involvement in an earthly community, on the other. Sarpi's considerable talents served to define and defend the general Venetian sense of independence and pride that had long characterized the republic.

Though in April 1607 the Venetians won on every point of substance with the lifting of the interdict, the strains it had created, together with general economic deterioration, served to tip the once-flourishing republic into a long, irreversible decline. Sarpi perceived the internal weakness of his republic and compared it to a patient who lacked visible symptoms but nonetheless still suffered from disease. Official status and recognition failed to protect Sarpi from his enemies. In October 1607 he was severely beaten and left for dead by unidentified assailants who took refuge in the Papal States; the Curia itself took less violent but still dramatic action in burning his writings. Though he remained in favor in Venice and wrote with great caution in his later years, the papal nuncio in Venice demanded (fruitlessly) after Sarpi's death in 1623 that his body be exhumed and tried for heresy.

Sarpi's longest-lived and most influential writings include his *History of the Interdict* and *History of the Council of Trent*, in which he argued that the council had failed to eliminate corrupt practices from the past, practices that existed not only because of ambitious worldly prelates, but because of general historical conditions. By using the form of a dialogue, Sarpi presented a variety of interpretations of ecclesiastical and human history, many of which emphasize human failings and limitations. He noted with displeasure the clerical bias of the council, and in his tract on benefices he gave full voice to his conviction that a healthy church required the active participation of the laity and of secular governments. On certain points clerical self-interest was certain to collide with genuine reform, and on these points only concerned lay powers could effectively perceive and resolve problems within the church. Many years later, Enlightenment writers from David Hume to Edward Gibbon would praise his insight and judicious reflections, as they would more broadly the republican traditions and liberty of Venice itself.

Bibliography

W. J. Bouwsma, *Venice and the Defense of Republican Liberty: Renaissance Values in the Age of the Counter Reformation*, 1968.
P. Sarpi, *History of Benefices and Selections from History of the Council of Trent*, trans. and ed. Peter Burke, 1967.
D. Wootton, *Paolo Sarpi: Between Renaissance and Enlightenment*, 1983.

Alison Williams Lewin

SCALIGER, JOSEPH JUSTUS (1540–1609)

A French philologist and historian, Joseph Justus Scaliger reformed historical and classical studies during the Renaissance through his careful correction of various ancient chronologies and by a rigorous approach to textual criticism. The son of the French classical scholar Julius Caesar Scaliger,* Joseph began his studies in Bordeaux, moving to Paris in 1559 to study classical Greek and Latin. There he also learned Hebrew, Arabic, Syrian, and Persian, as well as modern languages. Although he claimed to have taught himself these languages, these claims now appear overstated. Nevertheless, his mastery of philology enabled him to eventually classify European languages with remarkable accuracy, positing the existence of eleven mother languages, unrelated to each other, and thereby undermining a widespread belief that all languages had evolved from Hebrew. Related to his linguistic endeavors was his work as a literary critic. However, unlike his father, who promoted a broad Aristotelian view of criticism as judging the merits of literary works, Joseph Scaliger defined criticism as a subdivision of grammar, in which the critic's primary goal was to distinguish between genuine and corrupt versions of classical texts. In 1562 he converted to Protestantism and traveled to Germany, Italy, and France. In 1572, when Protestants were being persecuted in France, he traveled to Geneva, where he taught until he returned to France in 1574. As reports from the New World and the Far East reached him, Scaliger understood that the sophisticated calendars of the Meso-Americans and Chinese provided evidence of civilizations in some ways more advanced than Europe. In 1593 he traveled to the University of Leiden, where he stayed until his death.

Scaliger is best known for his 1583 *Opus novum De emendatione temporum* (Study on the Improvement of Time), in which he compares and corrects the chronologies of various ancient authors, endeavoring to create an accurate and universal system of dating ancient events. His calculations and polemical style got him into trouble with Johannes Kepler* and Tycho Brahe,* and his scholarship was frequently attacked by contemporary Jesuits, due to a mixture of theological partisanship and disagreements over the controversial Gregorian calendar. In the process of editing and commenting upon the writers of antiquity, he came to doubt the widely held belief in a former golden age, believing instead that modern scholars could do better than their ancient counterparts. Another major work is his 1606 *Thesaurus temporum* (Thesaurus of Time), in which he reconstructs the chronicles of Eusebius and combines them with a collection of Greek and Latin remnants placed in chronological order. He also wrote two treatises that established numismatics, the study of coins, as a new and reliable tool in historical research. In the course of his work, Scaliger created powerful tools for understanding manuscript traditions and retrieving accurate information from ancient texts, tools that critics and historians depended upon for the next four centuries.

Bibliography

A. Grafton, *Joseph Scaliger: A Study in the History of Classical Scholarship*, 2 vols., 1983–98.

Tim McGee

SCALIGER, JULIUS CAESAR (1484–1558)

Julius Caesar Scaliger, a French classicist of Italian birth, wrote on such varied topics as botany, zoology, grammar, and literary criticism. He composed a considerable volume of Latin verse, introduced a generation of French scholars to the Greco-Roman classics, and fathered a brilliant classicist, Joseph Justus Scaliger.*

Born in the Republic of Venice, Scaliger claimed, inaccurately, to descend from the Della Scala family who had ruled Verona for centuries. He left Italy in 1525 to become a physician in France. He first achieved fame in 1531 by attacking Erasmus's* *Ciceronianus: O Dello stile migliore* (Ciceronian: A Dialogue on the Best Style of Speaking), a work in which Erasmus had ridiculed the purists for refusing to admit nonclassical terms into their Latin prose. Scaliger's attack indicates that he may not have understood precisely what Erasmus was ridiculing. In 1539 he wrote a commentary on a work by Hippocrates; a year later he wrote *De causis linguae Latinae* (On the Subject of the Latin language), a Latin grammar based on scientific principles. In 1556 he wrote a commentary on an ancient book about plants that had been incorrectly attributed to Aristotle. In 1557 he addressed some of the problems raised by a contemporary natural philosopher, Girolamo Cardano.* Two unfinished commentaries, one on Aristotle, the other on Theophrastus, were published posthumously.

His most influential work was another posthumous book, his *Poetice* (Poetics) of 1561, in which he grounded a theory of literary criticism in the ancient works on rhetoric and poetics, including those of Aristotle. It was this wider conception of "criticism," in which the critic judges the quality of the work, rather than simply argues for the correctness of the text, that was the greatest contribution of the elder Scaliger.

Bibliography

A. Grafton, *Joseph Scaliger: A Study in the History of Classical Scholarship*, 2 vols., 1983–93.

Tim McGee

SCÈVE, MAURICE (1501–c. 1560)

Maurice Scève is best known for his *Délie* (Lyon, 1544), the first sequence of love poetry in France in the tradition of Petrarch's *Canzoniere*. Scève's dense, intellectual style draws imagery and themes from classical, Petrarchan, Neoplatonic, and Christian literature and philosophy.

Born in 1501 into an aristocratic ruling family of Lyons, Maurice Scève played a central role in important intellectual circles throughout his life, along with Étienne Dolet,* Clément Marot,* and others. He was a key figure in the successful circle of Lyonnese poets that included Louise Labé,* Pernette Du Guillet,* and Pontus de Tyard. Little is known about Scève's life as a young man, but tradition assumes an unhappy love affair about 1520, an experience that would form the basis for the love poetry of *Délie*.

While Scève was in Avignon in 1533, he reportedly discovered the tomb of Petrarch's Laura. The Lyonnese printer Jean de Tournes describes this episode in the dedication to his 1545 French translation of Petrarch's *Canzoniere*. Whether or not the account is true, the reported uncovering of Laura's tomb symbolizes the enormous influence of Petrarch on Scève and the vast majority of French Renaissance poets.

In 1535 Scève began his literary career with *La déplourable fin de Flamete*, a French translation of a Spanish novel by Juan de Flores. In 1536 Scève submitted two poems, "Le Sourcil" (The eyebrow) and "La Larme" (The tear), for a competition of *blasons anatomiques* (brief, concrete descriptions of parts of the female anatomy, written in epigrammatic form) called by Clément Marot. The winner, Scève's "Le Sourcil," was published with other entries in 1536 in Lyon. Scève's success with the genre (in 1536 and with three more *blasons* contributed to an edition in 1539) is due to his ability to balance realistic description and abstract qualities in a brief poetic form. Also in 1536 Scève contributed poems in both Latin and French to a collection of verse, commemorating the death of the dauphin Francis, edited by Étienne Dolet.

In 1544 Scève published what is now considered his masterpiece, the sequence of love poetry entitled *Délie object de plus haulte vertu*. Scève's *canzoniere* conveys the progression of the lover, suffering from unrequited love, undergoing separation, experiencing absence and jealousy, slowly mastering desire, and striving for an ascetic goal of "haulte vertu." Scève uses numerous themes familiar to Renaissance poetry drawn from Petrarchan motifs, Greek mythology, Platonic philosophy, and Christian iconography to create the hermetic series of dizains that demand the reader's intellectual engagement. *Délie* is composed of 1 "huitain" (an epigram of eight lines of verse), 449 "dizains" (epigrams of ten lines of decasyllabic verse), and 50 woodcut emblems with mottos. Many theories have been advanced to explain the relationship between emblem (image) and text, as well as the mathematical arrangements of the poems, but none resolve the enigma that characterizes the work and is an important element of its enduring beauty.

Who was "Délie"? That question too has elicited many answers. Délie was probably intended to be an anagram of "l'idée," the Platonic Idea. Sixteenth-century humanists and poets were very familiar with Neoplatonist thought and well versed in the use of anagrams. Uncertain biographical details suggest that Délie is Pernette Du Guillet, the younger poet for whom Scève was mentor, teacher, and platonic beloved. She inscribes his name in anagrammatic form in her *Rymes*, but Scève's *canzoniere* itself yields no clues as to her identity, reinforcing the notion that Délie is an idealized figure, the poetic creation of Scève.

In 1545, following the death of Pernette Du Guillet, Scève contributed three poems to the posthumous edition of her works. After a brief period of retirement in the country, Scève published *La saulsaye, eglogue de la vie solitaire* (The Willow Grove, Eclogue of Solitary Life) in 1547. He was called back to the city in 1548 to lead preparations for the lavish royal entry of King Henri II into Lyons on 23 September 1548. The poet's own account of the events was published by Jean de Tournes in 1549.

We know very little of Scève's later years, during which he composed his last great poem, *Microcosme*, published in 1562. He is believed to have died as early as 1560, when civil war broke out in France, or as late as 1564, when the plague struck Lyons. Sadly, the death of such a prominent civic figure and influential poet seems to have gone unremarked, although his works seem never to have gone unnoticed.

Bibliography

D. Coleman, *Maurice Scève, Poet of Love: Tradition and Originality*, 1975.
R. Mulhauser, *Maurice Scève*, 1977.
D. M. Scève, ed., I. D. McFarlane, *"Délie,"* 1966.

Karen S. James

SCOREL, JAN VAN (1495–1562)

Jan van Scorel, a major painter in the city of Utrecht from 1524 until his death, was largely responsible for the introduction into the northern Netherlands of the ideas of the Italian Renaissance, such as movement, proportion, architectural forms, and perspectives, all of which he had the opportunity to study firsthand during a four-year stay in Rome. A native of Schoorel, near Alkmaar in the Netherlands, van Scorel was illegitimate, the son of a priest. His talent was noticed by Jan van Egmond, who sent him to work with an Alkmaar painter. In 1516 van Scorel moved to Utrecht, a center of Catholicism in the northern Netherlands, in order to study with the late Mannerist painter Jan Gossaert (called Mabuse). In 1519, probably encouraged by Gossaert, he left on a long trip that took him to Venice, the Mediterranean islands, and the Holy Land. Finally making his way back to Rome, he was taken into the household of the Dutch pope Adrian VI, who was himself a native of Utrecht, and who appointed van Scorel curator of the Vatican collections. Adrian VI died in 1523, and van Scorel returned to the Netherlands, settling permanently in Utrecht by 1528.

Little of van Scorel's larger-scale works survives today, though he painted several great altarpieces, all destroyed, but there are enough smaller paintings to give a sense of his style and its influences. His *Death of Cleopatra* is derived from the reclining Venus of Giorgione; his *Presentation of Christ in the Temple* of 1530 shows his debt to Italian architecture; and the calm monumentality of his figures displays none of the frenetic late Mannerism of Gossaert. He was also a fine portraitist in the Flemish tradition, both of single figures and groups, the latter to be an important component of Dutch art in the next century.

Van Scorel's pupils included Maertin van Heemskerck,* best known today perhaps for his drawings of Rome, and Antonio Mor,* a fine portraitist who spent his career working for the Spanish Habsburg court of Philip II.* According to Karel van Mander, van Scorel became famous in the Netherlands for importing a new style of painting, Mannerism, from Italy, which he described as an "extraordinary beautiful and novel manner of painting which made a great impression on everyone."

Bibliography

J. Snyder, *Northern Renaissance Art*, 1985.
W. Stechow, ed., *Northern Renaissance Art, 1400–1600: Sources and Documents*, 1966.

Rosemary Poole

SCOT, REGINALD (c. 1538–1599)

Reginald Scot, a Kentish writer, produced one of the most exhaustive works criticizing the belief in witchcraft to be available in the sixteenth and seventeenth centuries. Scot's ideas were scorned by King James I,* but the English world began to accept them by the mid-eighteenth century.

Scot spent his whole life in southeastern England. His father was a justice of the peace and a member of Parliament. In 1574 Scot published the first book to systematically explore the Kentish industry of hop growing. His practical guide made the cultivation of hops a skill available to a greater number of people.

In 1584 Scot produced his *Discovery of Witchcraft*, in which he aimed to expose the folly inherent in accusations of witchcraft against the innocent. His arguments, which pressed courts to rely on solid evidence and common sense, were ineffectual in his own time, but as the seventeenth century progressed, more and more people accepted his point of view. Scot felt that evidence against witches was based upon impossible circumstance. He believed that magicians were frauds and that belief in witchcraft was in itself a heresy. He related to the courts his rational belief that "no person of psychokinetic powers" and no "separated spirit has the least ordinary ability to work in the physical world."

By using common sense, Scot exposed weak trials whose evidence rested upon absurd assumptions and little or no investigation. Exploring the circumstances around an accusation, Scot drew logical explanations. Pleading on behalf of innocent victims, Scot was convinced that mere superstition brought faithless accusers to force confessions from people. "When the punishment exceedeth the fault," Scot explained, "it is rather to be thought vengeance than correction."

Scot attacked Heinrich Kraemer and Johann Sprenger's widely read *Malleus maleficarum*. His humanitarian approach to the subject stands in stark contrast with *Malleus*'s fiery, fear-inspiring diatribe on witches. Scot used the Bible to urge sympathy for the meek while avoiding bombastic phrasing and unnecessary enthusiasm. His writing was meant less to protect witches than to expose those whose actions were solely meant "to pursue the poore, to accuse the simple, and to kill the innocent."

Scot's book delivered opinions that were difficult for the Elizabethan and Jacobean populace to accept. King James I, renowned for his preoccupation with witchcraft, ordered *The Discovery of Witchcraft* to be burned. The king made reference to Scot's "damnable opinions," but, as Robert West points out, gave little sign of having examined the opinions himself. More than a century passed before England at length accepted Scot's ideas.

Bibliography

R. West, *Reginald Scot and Renaissance Writings on Witchcraft*, 1984.

Karolyn Kinane

SEBASTIANO DEL PIOMBO (c. 1485–1547)

A Venetian painter who migrated to Rome, Sebastiano del Piombo mixed Venetian and Roman artistic manners to create a unique style that found success in sixteenth-century Rome. From Venice, Italy, Sebastiano may have studied painting with Giorgione, as revealed in similarities between their work. According to Giorgio Vasari,* Sebastiano and Giorgione shared another quality: they were both talented musicians. After Giorgione's death, Sebastiano accompanied Agostino Chigi in 1511 to Rome to work in his villa (now called the Villa Farnesina), where he painted beside Raphael* and Baldassare Peruzzi.* Around 1512–13 Michelangelo* befriended the artist, and the two maintained a close relationship for several years and collaborated on several occasions, with Michelangelo providing the preliminary designs and Sebastiano executing the final work. In the *Raising of Lazarus* (London, National Gallery), painted for Cardinal Giulio de' Medici in competition with Raphael's *Transfiguration* (Rome, Vatican), Michelangelo's participation was most likely limited to designs for some of the figures. Their collaborative efforts found success in Rome and established Sebastiano on the artistic scene. This professional and personal relationship had tremendous artistic consequences for Sebastiano, forever changing his painting style as he combined monumental, muscular, and sculptural forms inspired by the art of Michelangelo with a Venetian coloring, soft and refined modeling, and depth of expression. With the death of Raphael in 1520, Sebastiano became the most important painter in Rome and received numerous commissions. Commended by both Michelangelo and Vasari for his portraits, Sebastiano combined a realistic and tangible presence with a monumentality and poise mixed with a sense of intimacy that made him the supreme portrait painter in Rome. In 1531 he received the office of *piombatore*, (Keeper of the papal seal—hence his nickname) in the Vatican for his loyalty to Pope Clement VII. With the secure and handsome income this position provided him, Sebastiano continued painting until his death.

Bibliography

M. Hirst, *Sebastiano del Piombo*, 1981.

Mary Pixley

SERVETUS, MICHAEL (MIGUEL) (1511–1553)

Michael Servetus was a Spanish physician who questioned the Trinity and believed that God is unitary. In Geneva while in flight from persecution in Italy, Servetus was captured and, on orders of John Calvin,* burned at the stake for heresy.

Servetus trained as a physician in Paris, though his many activities included studying theology and being a jurist. During his many travels throughout Europe, Servetus met many religious reformers in Germany and Switzerland. These contacts fueled Servetus's own theological questionings, the result of which was his book *De trinitatis erroribus* (On the Errors of the Trinity, 1531). This book sparked much expected criticism from both Roman Catholics and Protestants. By questioning the Trinity, Servetus immediately brought upon himself the specter of being a heretic. In 1540 Servetus became the first person to describe the pulmonary transit of blood. In 1553 he returned to his theological pursuits and published his main work, *Chrisitianismi restitutio* (Restitution of Christianity, 1553). Although the book was published under the pseudonym Michel de Villeneuve, it was common knowledge that Servetus was the actual author. Servetus was quickly condemned from all sides for his Antitrinitarian heresies, and in 1553 he was arrested in Geneva and, on orders of John Calvin, burned at the stake for his heretical views.

Servetus is cited as a founding figure within Unitarianism. Although Servetus did not himself establish Unitarianism as a separate sect, Unitarians have largely accepted his criticisms of the Trinity. Moreover, Unitariansm continue to accept a diversity of religious views, and they do so largely because they believe that Servetus was wrongly executed for questioning the dogmas of the day. Unitarians, Quakers, and others within the tradition of free, liberal religions find in Servetus a source of inspiration.

Bibliography

R. Bainton, *Hunted Heretic: The Life and Death of Michael Servetus, 1511–1553*, 1953.
                                                                    Jeffrey A. Bell

SHAKESPEARE, WILLIAM (1564–1616)

William Shakespeare was one of early modern England's most successful and celebrated playwrights, and since the eighteenth century he has often been regarded as England's, perhaps the modern world's, greatest writer. There is considerably more legend, opinion, and supposition than there is documentary evidence to sustain anything that could reasonably support a complete biography of William Shakespeare. Since the early eighteenth century Shakespeare's life has been a magnet for eager speculation, tendentious interpretation, and wishful thinking, and each generation has reinvented aspects of Shakespeare on its own terms.

Records of Shakespeare's youth are not plentiful, but scholars have been able to reconstruct a fairly accurate picture of the poet's early years. He was born in Stratford-upon-Avon to John Shakespeare and Mary Arden in late April 1564 (the traditional date of 23 April owes a great deal to nationalistic legend, since that date is also St. George's Day, and St. George is the patron saint of England). The elder Shakespeare was a reasonably successful glover in a provincial town, a tradesman who also held various public offices and was involved in the life of the community—including more than one legal controversy. Like those of his class and era, he probably sent his son to Stratford's grammar school, where the young boy would have been schooled in Latin language and literature and, we can suppose, would have acquired talents and habits that sustained him throughout his professional career.

In November 1582 William married Anne Hathaway, who was twenty-six and three months pregnant. The couple's first daughter, Susanna, was born in May 1583, and in 1585 there followed two more children, twins Hamnet and Judith. In Elizabethan times, marriages after conception were not sanctioned, but the practice was quite widespread, and little should be made of the circumstances of their marriage. This said, however, the fact that Shakespeare spent much of his adult life living apart from his wife and children has provoked considerable speculation about his familial and sexual identity.

The period between 1585 and 1592 is often called "the Lost Years" by scholars because there is little biographical evidence from this time. Shakespeare may have moved to London soon after the birth of the twins, but it seems certain that he was involved in the world of professional theater at least by the late 1580s because he is mentioned, unflatteringly, by the playwright Robert Greene* in a 1592 pamphlet that suggests that Shakespeare had already gained some prominence.

Plague in 1592–93 forced the theaters to close, and during this period Shakespeare wrote two narrative poems based upon classical themes, *Venus and Adonis* and *The Rape of Lucrece*, both dedicated to the young aristocrat Henry Wriothesley, the third earl of Southampton, who may also be the young man addressed in Shakespeare's *Sonnets* (1609). Both poems catered to late Elizabethan tastes for erotic themes and were popular successes. They indicate a pattern in Shakespeare's career: despite his consummate artistry, he was not above catering to prevailing trends and fashions.

When the theaters reopened in late 1593 until about 1600, Shakespeare enjoyed a remarkably prolific and creative period during which he wrote an average of two plays per year, acted professionally, and began acquiring financial interests in London's growing world of professional theater. During these years, in which he was a member of the troupe the Lord Chamberlain's Men, he wrote principally comedies and English history plays, the latter being a theatrical genre he did much to develop.

Professional theater was a precarious business in the late Elizabethan era, and were it not for the protection of powerful aristocrats, Shakespeare and his contemporaries might never have been allowed by city authorities and influential clergyman to produce the plays they did. But even less ideologically motivated forces could have an effect: in 1599 Shakespeare and nine other shareholders lost the lease on their playing space at the Theatre and built the now-famous Globe, which proved a huge success. By the turn of the century and only midway through his career, Shakespeare was already both prominent and well-to-do.

Two developments in the early 1600s may have had an influence on Shakespeare's artistic shift from comedies and history plays to tragedies, dark comedies, and romances. First, King James I,* who came to the throne in 1603, offered his patronage to Shakespeare's troupe, which became known as the King's Men. Second, in 1608 Shakespeare's company acquired Blackfriars, an indoor theatrical space that, it is thought, attracted a more exclusive audience than the outdoor spaces in which his plays had been acted. Between 1600 and 1608 he wrote the great tragedies for which he is perhaps best known, as well as the so-called problem plays—works with comic structures that nonetheless have darker themes and characters than traditional comedies. From about 1609 he began to experiment in a new form that critics have come to call "romances." These four plays (*Cymbeline, The Winter's Tale, Pericles*, and *The Tempest*) defy conventional definitions of tragedy or comedy, but all employ supernatural or coincidental elements, and all end happily. They are usually characterized as mature, reflective works that somehow fuse obviously unrealistic actions and themes with very realistic insights into aspects of the human condition.

For many years, critics attempted to make Shakespeare's life fit an idealized career path that began with youthful experiments in comedy, tragedy, and history and ended with *The Tempest*, which was typically read sentimentally as the poet's "farewell to the theater." More objective scholarship, however, has shown that Shakespeare wrote or collaborated on three plays after *The Tempest*, thus revealing convenient allegories of his career and retirement to be the product of critical imagination more than biographical fact.

Details of Shakespeare's final years and death are only a little better documented than those of his birth and youth. We do know, however, that in March 1616 he revised his will to provide better for his daughter Judith and to organize dispersal of his personal property, including a much-debated clause stipulating that his wife of almost thirty-five years be given his "second-best bed." He died on 23 April, leaving no mention of his literary or theatrical works—an omission quite appropriate to his age but almost incomprehensible to later ages.

With any cultural icon, the production of "biography" depends less on the labors of contemporaries than on those of subsequent generations. Shakespeare's biography is a case in point: although the publication of his collected plays in 1623 and a grave marker and painted bust in Stratford signal some degree of esteem for Shakespeare after his death, the real work of legend formation and critical biography alike belongs to later centuries. Hard facts of Shakespeare's life have been elusive and often contested, but there has probably been more energy, both scholarly and amateur, invested in the pursuit and analysis of these facts than for any writer in history. What can be said with certainty is that he was a performer, dramatist, poet, and theatrical entrepreneur, and that in a career of about three decades, he wrote or collaborated on almost forty plays and wrote narrative and lyric poetry that, on its own, would have earned him a place among the great English writers.

Bibliography

G. E. Bentley, *Shakespeare: A Biographical Handbook*, 1961.
E. K. Chambers, *William Shakespeare: A Study of Facts and Problems*, 1930.
S. Schoenbaum, *William Shakespeare: A Documentary Life*, 1975.

Thomas G. Olsen

SIDNEY HERBERT, MARY, COUNTESS OF PEMBROKE (1561–1621)

The sister of Sir Philip Sidney,* Mary Sidney Herbert, countess of Pembroke, was a proficient poet, translator, editor, and patron of the arts. Mary Sidney's birth in 1561 made her the fourth child born of the powerful Sidney/Dudley alliance. Her father, Henry Sidney, was raised with Edward VI and was knighted by him; her mother, Mary Dudley, was of a family of considerable fortune. She spent most of her youth at the family's estates of Ludlow and Penshurst. She was well educated and was raised in a strongly Protestant home; she attended Queen Elizabeth I's* court in 1575. In less than two years she was married to Henry Herbert, earl of Pembroke. Even after her marriage, the countess of Pembroke aligned herself with the Sidney family, maintaining the Sidney coat of arms. She remained active at court until the birth of her first child, William, in 1580. William was followed by Katherine in 1581, Anne in 1583, and Philip in 1584. Philip's birth coincided with the death of three-year-old Katherine. This was the start of a most tragic period for Pembroke. Her father died in May 1586, and her mother in August of that year. In September her brother Philip Sidney was mortally wounded in the Netherlands, where he was fighting Spanish control in the name of the Protestant cause.

When Pembroke returned to court in 1588, she did so with tremendous pomp. Her mission was to garner honor for her brother. Sidney's memory was exalted by his sister; she depicted him as a virtuous martyr of the Protestant cause. A significant part of Pembroke's glorification of her brother involved the publication of various Sidney texts, including *The Countess of Pembroke's Arcadia* (written by the hero for his sister), *Defense of Poesy*, and the *Astrophel and Stella* sonnet sequence. Pembroke also applied herself to her brother's projects and principles. She continued his practice of translating works advocating religious and political aspects of Protestantism. She is most acclaimed for finishing Sidney's translations of the Psalms, though "finishing" is an understatement. Of the 150 psalm translations, only 43 were completed by her brother. The psalm translations reveal Pembroke to be a virtuoso of poetic voice and form. They were presented to Elizabeth I in 1599. Though the queen is named in the dedication of the collection, Pembroke's dedicatory poems present the work in reverence to her brother. The collection was so revered that verses were composed to honor its creators.

Pembroke's pen was not the only one employed on her brother's behalf. Much of her reputation is founded on her tremendous patronage of the arts. The Pembroke home at Wilton became the cultural hub of the "Sidney circle," consisting of writers, courtiers, philosophers, and educators who had gathered around Sidney and, subsequently, his sister. Poets who sought Pembroke's patronage often attracted her attention by honoring the memory of her brother. Of course, Pembroke herself is a frequent subject of praise, and always she is identified by her relationship to Sidney, a designation she assigned herself in the role of author, authorizer, editor, or general promoter of the Sidney family.

Pembroke produced the majority of her own translations and writings in the 1590s. This decade was also her most active period of patronage, when she and the earl of Pembroke fostered the creation of a plethora of poetry, music, and devotional treatises. Pembroke's power as patron diminished with the death of her husband in 1601. With his loss came other losses: Pembroke's title, much of her wealth, and many court connections. Her son William became the third earl of Pembroke. As a widow, she occupied herself by attending to friends and family and occasionally appearing at court. She died in London on 25 September 1621.

Pembroke's success manifests itself in the fame conferred upon her brother. From her we inherit the literary achievements of Sidney and her own impressive contributions to the Sidney family legacy. This legacy was most readily accepted by Pembroke's niece and goddaughter, Mary Sidney Wroth,* author of *The Countesse of Mountgomeries Urania*. Pembroke's patronage benefited Samuel Daniel,* Edmund Spenser,* Fulke Greville, Nicholas Breton, and other writers of her day.

Bibliography

M. P. Hannay, *Philip's Phoenix: Mary Sidney, Countess of Pembroke*, 1990.
G. F. Waller, *Mary Sidney, Countess of Pembroke: A Critical Study of Her Writings and Literary Milieu*, 1979.

Michele Osherow

SIDNEY, SIR PHILIP (1554–1586)

Sir Philip Sidney was widely eulogized by his contemporaries for his prowess as author, courtier, diplomat, political theorist, religious reformer, and soldier. Well connected from his birth in Kent, England, Sidney was the son of Sir Henry Sidney, advisor to Edward VI and lord deputy governor of Ireland during Elizabeth I's* reign, and Mary Dudley Sidney, whose relations included Lady Jane Grey*; Robert Dudley, earl of Leicester; Ambrose Dudley, earl of Warwick; and Henry Hastings, earl of Huntingdon. King Philip* of Spain, husband of Mary I,* was Sidney's godfather and namesake. Among Sidney's six siblings were Mary Sidney* Herbert, countess of Pembroke, and Robert Sidney, Viscount L'Isle and earl of Leicester. Upon his marriage to Frances Walsingham in 1583, Sidney became son-in-law to Sir Francis Walsingham. The union produced one daughter, Elizabeth (1585–1612).

Sidney was educated at Shrewsbury School and at Christ Church, Oxford, before beginning his apprenticeship as courtier and diplomat with sojourns on the Continent and at Elizabeth I's court. In 1572 Sidney traveled first to France, where King Charles IX made him "gentleman of the bedchamber" and Baron de Sidenay; soon after, he witnessed and escaped the St. Bartholomew's Day Massacre of thousands of Huguenots in Paris. He remained in Europe until 1575, when he returned to Elizabeth's court. In 1577 Elizabeth named Sidney her ambassador to Holy Roman Emperor Rudolf II*; Sidney was also tasked with visiting the Protestant princes of northern Europe to investigate the possibility of a Protestant alliance against Spain and Rome. Sidney then returned to Elizabeth's court, although he withdrew in 1579 to the Wilton estate of the countess of Pembroke after voicing his opposition to the queen's proposed marriage to the duke of Alençon.

Sidney is thought to have produced the bulk of his literary work during this period and in the next few years. His compositions include the various versions of the *Arcadia: The Old Arcadia* (1579–80?), a prose pastoral narrative of five books interspersed with poetic interludes, circulated in manuscript and then forgotten until the early twentieth century, when it was recovered and printed; *The New Arcadia* (1582–84?), the first three books revised into heroic epic; and *The Countess of Pembroke's Arcadia* (1593), a hybrid version created by Mary Sidney Herbert and published after Sidney's death. Sidney also wrote a defense of English prose and poetry, various poems and entertainments, and three political treatises. Over a hundred of his letters survive. He began translations of the Psalms, completed by Mary Sidney Herbert, and of a discourse against atheism by Philippe Du Plessis-Mornay,* completed by Arthur Golding; he also created English versions of Aristotle's *Rhetoric* and Guillaume Du Bartas's* epic creation poem. The publication in 1591 of one of his sonnet sequences, *Astrophel and Stella*, started a trend that inspired Samuel Daniel,* John Donne,* William Shakespeare,* Edmund Spenser,* Mary Wroth,* and many others to write sonnet sequences in English.

As courtier, Sidney served as a member of Parliament for Ludlow in 1581. Warwick asked to have Sidney join him as master of the ordnance in 1583; Elizabeth granted this petition in 1585 and asked Sidney to entertain various visiting foreign dignitaries throughout the early 1580s. During these years Sidney also followed England's exploration of newfound territories with interest and attempted to join Sir Francis Drake's expedition to the West Indies and America in 1585, but Elizabeth thwarted Sidney's efforts.

Sidney supported efforts to reform religion along Calvinist lines both in England and on the Continent. In 1583 he was knighted so that he could serve as proxy for the installation as knight of the Garter of John Casmir, count palatine; Elizabeth proffered titles for both rather than offering financial or military support for the Protestant cause in the Netherlands. In 1585 Elizabeth sent Leicester as general over English forces in the Netherlands; she also named Sidney governor of Flushing. Leicester appointed Sidney colonel of a Zeeland regiment in 1586. At the Battle of Zutphen in 1586, Sidney was wounded by musket fire and died shortly thereafter.

Bibliography

K. Duncan-Jones, *Sir Philip Sidney: Courtier Poet*, 1991.
B. Worden, *The Sound of Virtue: Philip Sidney's "Arcadia" and Elizabethan Politics*, 1996.

Karen Nelson

SKELTON, JOHN (c. 1460–1529)

Primarily known as a poet and satirist of unusual technique, the flamboyant John Skelton was also a scholar and clergyman during the reigns of Henry VII and Henry VIII.* Born around 1460 in Yorkshire, Skelton was laureated by Oxford University and apparently received his special robe from Henry VII, whose service he entered in 1488. Skelton later became the only laureate ever created by Cambridge University. In the king's employ he wrote commemorative poetry and acted as tutor to Prince Henry, later Henry VIII. Memorable poems like "Manerly Margery Mylk and Ale" and the court satire *Bowge of Courte* probably date from this period.

Sometime after 1502 Skelton became rector of Diss. While he left his clerical duties to subordinates and returned to court in 1512, Skelton was in Diss long enough to inspire several racy stories. A typical one involves a sermon by the rector, who in angry response to complaints about his keeping a mistress, strips his illegitimate child before the congregation and argues that the perfection of the child's body absolves him from blame in fathering it. Many of the stories are no doubt apocryphal, yet they portray a character who reflects the witty forthrightness and intolerance of hypocrisy seen in Skelton's poetry.

It was also during this time that Skelton perfected a poetic style known as "Skeltonics." This method uses short, rhythmic, often-bawdy lines and emphasizes common English words and situations. One characteristic example is *The Tunning of Elinor Rumming*, which describes how the title character's beer brewing prompts a rural community's unsophisticated behavior. Poems produced in this style represent some of Skelton's best-known work.

In 1512 or 1513 Skelton was named *orator regius*, a combination court poet and secretary, by Henry VIII. In this capacity Skelton wrote Latin epitaphs, court entertainments, and other poetry. Henry's 1513 victory over the French in the Battle of the Spurs, in which he may have accompanied the king, and the earl of Surrey's over the Scots in the same year at Flodden Field gave Skelton much to write about soon after his appointment. Skelton also wrote several dramas, of which only the political satire *Magnificence* survives.

Magnificence warns the king against the growing power and excess of Cardinal Thomas Wolsey. Skelton continued to attack the cardinal in poems like *Colin Clout* and *Why Come Ye Not to Court?* A story that the poet had to seek sanctuary from Wolsey in Westminster may be true. The two apparently came to terms around 1522, as Skelton's poetry after this compliments the cardinal, and his last known work, an invective against Lutheran heretics, is dedicated to him.

While Skelton's poetry inspired no known disciples, his satiric methods ironically became popular among Protestant Reformers. Late-sixteenth-century poetic theorists scorned him, but playwrights dramatized Skelton as a figure of wit. Colin Clout had come to symbolize the layperson's simple yet astute criticism long before Edmund Spenser's* 1595 *Colin Clouts Come Home Againe*. Such reactions reflect England's complicated response to a complex poet.

Bibliography

N. C. Carpenter, *John Skelton*, 1967.

Kevin Lindberg

SOUTHWELL, ROBERT (c. 1561–1595)

Robert Southwell served as a Jesuit missionary in England, wrote religious tracts and verse, was executed at Tyburn in 1595 for treason, and was canonized by the Roman Catholic church in 1970. Born in Norfolk, England, Southwell was educated at various Roman Catholic schools on the Continent, first at Douai, then as a Jesuit novitiate at Sant' Andrea, and finally at the Jesuits' Roman College. Upon completing his education, he served as a tutor and prefect of studies at the English College of Rome. In 1584 he was ordained priest. Most of Southwell's fame stems from his work as a missionary priest. Along with his superior, Henry Garnet, Southwell was sent to England in 1586 and ministered there until his arrest in 1592. He acted as priest for various Catholic households, including those of William, Baron Vaux of Harrowden, and Anne Howard, countess of Arundel. Once Southwell established a network of patrons, he assisted priests as they negotiated England's anti-Catholic policies.

Southwell viewed writing as an essential aspect of his ministry. He wrote theological tracts and spiritual verse that circulated widely in manuscript and were printed repeatedly, some by Southwell on a secret press. His works include *Mary Magdalen's Funeral Tears, An Humble Supplication to Her Majesty, A Short Rule of Good Life, The Triumphs over Death,* and *An Epistle of Comfort.* Many of these touch upon the importance of active faith and martyrdom and discuss the spiritual rewards for those being persecuted. With his poetry, Southwell hoped to move poetic forms away from their emphasis on sensual topics; he used sonnets and songs to speak of holiness and divine love in *St. Peter's Complaint* and *Moeniae.*

In 1592 Southwell was caught by Richard Topcliffe, a priest hunter. Southwell was tortured but would not admit to being a priest. Eight months after his arrest, he decided that his silence hurt the reputation of the priesthood, so he confessed and asked for release or a trial. He was tried in 1595, found guilty of treason, and executed at Tyburn.

Bibliography

F. W. Brownlow, *Robert Southwell,* 1996.

Karen Nelson

SPENGLER, LAZARUS (1479–1534)

A civic leader and champion of the Reformation in Nuremberg, Lazarus Spengler helped shape that city's political and religious landscapes during a time of momentous change. His father's early death led Spengler to take a job with the government of Nuremberg; in 1507 he became secretary to the city council and functioned as a diplomat who represented the city. He was influenced by the sermons of a number of reformist preachers in Nuremberg, and when Martin Luther* posted his ninety-five theses in 1517, Spengler wrote a spirited defense of him in 1519 that effectively began the Reformation in Nuremberg. Under

Spengler's leadership, the city began to appoint Lutheran preachers and provosts and extended its control over the local monasteries and nunneries.

Spengler wanted to remain loyal to the Holy Roman Empire, but refused to bend on any moral questions issuing from his new religious convictions, which inevitably meant a break with Rome. Spengler argued that the truth from Scripture had to outweigh any civil custom, a position that Nuremberg adopted: the city's clergy were subsequently required to be in conformity with official religious policies. The council continued to rely on Spengler to help it hold the line against the Holy Roman Empire, but Spengler, like Luther, was opposed to any use of force to protect the Reformation. As hostilities between the Lutherans and the Catholics continued to grow, Nuremberg refused to join in any alliance against the emperor, and this refusal meant that the city and Spengler gave up their leading role in the spread of the Reformation and in the affairs of the Holy Roman Empire. By 1534 illness had confined Spengler to his home, and he died there on 7 September 1534, leaving behind a permanent legacy of Protestantism in Nuremberg.

Bibliography

H. J. Grimm, *Lazarus Spengler: A Lay Leader of the Reformation*, 1978.

Connie S. Evans

SPENSER, EDMUND (1552–1599)

Edmund Spenser was the outstanding nondramatic poet of the English Renaissance and Reformation, the author of numerous poetical works, most notably the epic romance *The Fairie Queene* (1590–96). He was known as a "poet's poet"; his verse has influenced generations of later poets, who include the seventeenth-century Spenserians, John Keats, and Alfred Lord Tennyson, among many others. *The Fairie Queene* undergoes parody in William Shakespeare's* *Midsummer Night's Dream*, and Spenser's poetic oeuvre affords rich antecedents to verse by John Milton, including *Lycidas, L'Allegro* and *Il Penseroso*, and *Paradise Lost*, a masterwork that succeeds *The Fairie Queene* as a great English Protestant epic.

Born in London around 1552, Spenser studied at the Merchant Taylors' School under its humanistic headmaster, the militantly Protestant Richard Mulcaster. He received his bachelor of arts (1573) and master of arts (1576) at Cambridge University, where his friendship with Gabriel Harvey* led to experimentation with various theories of poetry and poetic versification. Mulcaster may have recommended Spenser to his first employer, John Young, bishop of Rochester, whom he served as secretary and from whose household he moved to that of his second patron, Robert Dudley, earl of Leicester. During services to Dudley, Spenser claimed intimacy with his nephew, Sir Philip Sidney,* and Sir Edward Dyer, courtiers who promoted reform of English verse. Under the pseudonymous guise of Immerito, Spenser dedicated *The Shepheardes Calender* (1579) to Sidney, but it failed to win unqualified approval in Sidney's *Defense* *of Poesy*. The collection includes satirical eclogues ("May," "July," and "September") that defend Reformation religious principles. The dazzling stanzaic and metrical virtuosity of Spenser's collection of pastoral eclogues heralded innovations associated with the poet's name: the Spenserian sonnet with its distinctive *ababbcbccdcdee* rhyme scheme, used in *Amoretti* (invented by James VI* of Scotland); the adaptation of the Italian *canzone* in *Epithalamion* and *Prothalamion*; and, of course, the Spenserian stanza employed in *The Fairie Queene*, in which a terminal line in iambic hexameter produces an eccentric couplet at the end of a Spenserian sonnet octet (*ababbcbcc*).

One year following publication of *The Shepheardes Calender*, Spenser went to Ireland as aide of Arthur Lord Grey de Wilton, the lord deputy of Ireland. Random visits to England notwithstanding, Spenser spent the remainder of his life as a functionary charged with imposing English Protestant overlordship upon Catholic Ireland. He published the first three books of *The Fairie Queene* in 1590 with a dedicatory letter to his patron, Sir Walter Raleigh,* whose tortuous involvement with Elizabeth I* undergoes allegorization in the episodes involving Timias and Belphoebe (Spenser's figure for the queen as a private person). In the years following, Spenser published *Complaints: Containing Sundry Small Poems of the World's Vanity; Amoretti and Epithalamion*, concerning his courtship and marriage to Elizabeth Boyle; and *Prothalamion*, a wedding poem. Containing three more books out of a projected twelve, the expanded version of *The Fairie Queene* appeared in 1596, and again in 1609 with the addition of the "Mutability Cantos," a fragment of book 7. Following the sacking of Kilcolman Castle in 1598, Spenser returned to England and died in an impoverished state, according to tradition, on 13 January 1599. He underwent interment near Chaucer, to whom he paid homage as the "well of English undefiled," at Westminster Abbey.

Spenser's complex and varied poetic oeuvre is notable for Neoplatonic speculation; stern moral precepts; Reformation ideology, for which Puritans adopted him as one of their own after his death; moral allegory concerning the human quest to achieve "right" action; and fusion of classical, continental, and native British literary traditions. Those elements receive fullest expression in the complicated allegory of *The Fairie Queene*, whose purpose "is to fashion a gentleman or noble person in vertuous and gentle discipline," according to the letter to Raleigh. Each of the six books portrays the growth of a Christian Knight in six distinct virtues: the first three books deal with the private attributes of holiness, temperance, and chastity, whereas the latter three treat the more public virtues of friendship, justice, and courtesy. Book 1 constitutes a full-blown allegory concerning the course of the English Reformation. The romantic epic is an outstanding example of the mixing of an encyclopedic array of genres and modes characteristic of Renaissance masterworks at their best. The work sustains multiple levels of reading, which may involve moral, philosophical, historical, and other allegorical modes. Readers may approach Spenser's often wildly fantastical characters, settings, or objects at one or more levels involving literalistic narrative concerning Faerieland, topical allusion to real personages, or abstract representation of conflict between virtue and vice.

Bibliography

D. J. Gless, *Interpretation and Theology in Spenser*, 1994.
A. C. Hamilton, D. Cheney, and W. Barke, eds., *The Spenser Encyclopedia*, 1990.
J. N. King, *Spenser's Poetry and the Reformation Tradition*, 1990.

John N. King and Mark Bayer

SPERONI, SPERONE (1500–1588)

A versatile and extremely influential man of letters, Sperone Speroni was known for his literary criticism as espoused in the many prose dialogues and treatises he wrote over his long career. He was born in Padua, where he lived most of his life; he taught in various capacities at the city's university and also served in civic offices. His primary devotion was to letters, however, and as such, he was acquainted with the authors Pietro Bembo,* Giambattista Giraldi Cinthio,* and Torquato Tasso* and was the magnetic center of a powerful literary circle in Padua. Following in the footsteps of Giraldi Cinthio's play *Orbecche* (1541), Speroni wrote a Senecan revenge tragedy, *Canace* (1542), which instigated a feud among the literati about the genre of tragedy that went on for decades.

Speroni's literary reputation rests primarily on his *Dialogi* (1542), the numerous dialogues he wrote on subjects ranging from love to rhetoric, history, fortune, family, and classical literature. The dialogues were popular enough to see several reprintings, although they were also called into question by the Roman Inquisition. In response to the Inquisition's charges, Speroni wrote *Apologia dei dialogi* (Apology on the Dialogues, 1574), a detailed defense of the dialogue as a literary genre. His defense was partially successful; although he personally escaped punishment, his works were periodically placed on the Index of Forbidden Books.

Speroni worked on his dialogues and treatises all of his life, and they circulated widely in manuscript; however, he took less care in their publication, which presents difficulty in attributing dates to individual works. One of his most famous dialogues was the *Dialogo delle lingue* (Dialogue on Languages), which advocates the use of the vernacular in Italian literature; the French poets Joachim Du Bellay* and Pierre de Ronsard* were influenced by this work. Another important work was the *Discorsi sopra Virgilio* (Discourses on Virgil), in which he praises Homer at the expense of Virgil, arguing that Virgil was more of a historian than a poet. Also influential were his *Dialogo di amore* (Dialogue on Love), in which he includes the courtesan poet Tullia d'Aragona* as one of his interlocutors, and the *Delle dignità della donne* (On the Dignity of Women), which focuses on whether women are meant to serve men or be served by them. Speroni died in 1588, leaving behind a rich and significant body of literary criticism and theory.

Bibliography

B. Hathaway, *The Age of Criticism: The Late Renaissance in Italy*, 1962.
J. Snyder, *Writing the Scene of Speaking: Theories of Dialogue in the Late Italian Renaissance*, 1989.

Jo Eldridge Carney

SPIEGEL, HENDRICK LAURENSZOON (1549–1612)

Hendrick Laurenszoon Spiegel was a Dutch Renaissance poet and moralist. In the second half of the sixteenth century, Holland emerged as the literary and cultural center of the Low Countries, and Spiegel, a native of Amsterdam, became one of the leading literary figures of the Dutch Renaissance. From an early age Spiegel distinguished himself as a poet, and throughout his life his poetry had a serious and sober tone to it. In Amsterdam Spiegel was closely associated with the De Englantier, an established chamber of rhetoric (*rederijkerskamer*) that functioned as a literary society and a center of literary life. Many of the chambers of rhetoric felt the influence of humanism and the Renaissance in the sixteenth century, and as a leader in De Englantier, Spiegel came under this influence as well.

Spiegel's literary production was quite varied, but he is best known for two major works. The first is the *Twe-spraack vande Nederduitsche Letterkunst* (Dialogue on the Dutch language), published in 1584. This important grammar, the first of its kind, was very influential for the development of the Dutch language and helped to establish a standard Dutch for the Netherlands as a whole. Throughout his life Spiegel remained a strong advocate for the Dutch language. Spiegel's other major work, the *Hertspiegel* (Mirror of the Heart), did not appear until after his death in 1614. This lengthy and not easily accessible poem reflects many of the common elements of the Dutch Renaissance. It was a work of moral philosophy that contained both Christian and Stoic themes, and that emphasized the role of reason, natural law, and virtue in the moral life. Spiegel's poem clearly demonstrated the influence of the classical tradition as well as his own religious vision that emphasized ethics rather than dogma. Spiegel himself never left the Catholic church and did not support Amsterdam's embrace of the Protestant Reformation in 1578.

Bibliography

R. P. Meijer, *Literature of the Low Countries*, 1971.

Michael A. Hakkenberg

SPRANGER, BARTHOLOMAEUS (1546–c. 1611)

Bartholomaeus Spranger, Flemish by birth, was the leading painter at the court of the Habsburg emperor Rudolf II* in Prague. A well-traveled man who visited France, Italy, and Vienna before settling in Prague, Spranger developed a distinctive late Mannerist style that drew on Italian Mannerism, particularly that of Correggio.*

Spranger was born and trained in Antwerp, coming under the influence of the painter Frans Floris.* Spranger's Rudolfine school of Mannerism was more pronounced than that of Antwerp, and his fantastic allegories, with their spirals, diagonal formats, and scenes of exaggerated movement, such as *Rudolf II's Victory over the Turks*, were greatly to the liking of the eccentric emperor. Rudolf II attracted a number of painters to his court, including Giuseppe Arcimboldo,* Jan Bruegel the Elder, and Roelandt Savery, as well as Spranger, but no one of the first rank, unlike other Habsburg courts. Rudolf also employed the great astronomers Tycho Brahe* and Johannes Kepler,* who produced for him the *Rudolfine Tables*, an important work on astronomy.

There were few foreign artists who stayed in Rudolf's Prague for any length of time. Spranger was probably the most talented of those who came and remained in the city, which was in fact a center of the arts generally, was enriched with many new Renaissance buildings, and was the site of art fairs. Spranger married into the burgher class in Prague and became a leader of the guild of painters in the city, never returning to the Netherlands. But Spranger's Mannerist influence was to return to the Netherlands when Karel van Mander, who had met him in Rome, took some of his drawings back to Holland. There they were admired by Hendrick Goltzius, one of the founders, along with van Mander himself, of the Haarlem "academy."

Bibliography

R.J.W. Evans, *Rudolf II and His World*, 1973.

Rosemary Poole

STAMPA, GASPARA (1523–1554)

An accomplished musician and poet of sixteenth-century Venice, Gaspara Stampa used her poetry to chart the anguish of unrequited love. Gaspara's father was a wealthy jeweler of Padua, but after his early death, Gaspara's mother, Cecilia, took Gaspara, her sister Cassandra, and her brother Baldassare to Venice, where she provided them with a fine education in Latin, poetry, history, art, and music. The Stampa home soon became a *ridotto*, or salon, for writers, musicians, artists, and intellectuals; Sperone Speroni* and Giovanni Della Casa* were among the many famous literary figures who gathered there.

Venice enjoyed a reputation as a city of flourishing musical activity; *virtuosi*, or professional musicians and singers, performed frequently for both public and private occasions. Gaspara and her sister were both talented singers and instrumentalists; many contemporary accounts praise Gaspara's angelic voice. Gaspara performed a variety of musical selections, including melodic transcriptions of the poetry of Petrarch, whose works would also influence Gaspara's literary expressions.

In 1548 Gaspara fell in love with the aristocratic Count Collaltino de Collalto, who only partially returned her affection. Their tumultuous love affair inspired Gaspara to write some two hundred poems of praise, complaint, and despair.

She did not publish the poems, but they circulated widely in manuscript among the Venetian literati who appreciated them more than the count, who ended the affair in 1551. After a year of deep depression and ill health, Gaspara recovered and continued to write poetry. She had a brief and peaceful relationship with Bartolomeo Zen, a prominent patrician, but Gaspara again became ill and died on 23 April 1554 at the age of thirty-one.

Following her death, Gaspara's talents as both an accomplished musician and poet were so celebrated by many of her contemporaries that her sister Cassandra decided to publish Gaspara's poetry; she dedicated the collection, *Rime*, to Giovanni Della Casa. The volume was a success, but Stampa's reputation as a poet gradually faded until a descendant of the Collalto family decided to reprint the *Rime* in 1738. While the republication of Stampa's work contributed significantly to the revival of her literary reputation, the accompanying biography, highly romanticized and often erroneous, contributed to many myths about Stampa. Twentieth-century scholars have begun to separate fact from fiction and to focus more on Stampa's literary production, which includes some of the finest lyric poetry in the Renaissance.

Bibliography

F. A. Bassanese, *Gaspara Stampa*, 1982.
A. Jones, *The Currency of Eros: Women's Love Lyric in Europe, 1540–1620*, 1990.

Jo Eldridge Carney

STEVIN, SIMON (c. 1546–1620)

Simon Stevin, an associate of Prince Maurice of Orange, began publishing his numerous and varying works in the late sixteenth century during the Golden Age of the Netherlands. Topics Steven discusses in his works include weights and measures, mathematics, mechanics, music, language, architecture, astronomy, warfare, and civic duty, but he is best known for his work on fractions and the decimal system.

A native of Bruges, Stevin received training as a bookkeeper but became very familiar with mathematics and mechanics. In 1585, in Leiden, Stevin produced his most famous and influential work, *De Thiende* (On Decimals). Later published under the English title the thirty-six-page pamphlet discusses the systematic use of the decimal system, primarily regarding fractions. *De Thiende* was widely read across Europe, and Stevin's ideas influenced mathematicians such as John Napier, inventor of logarithms, and the prominent Dutch mathematician Frans van Schooten. Stevin also argued for the use of the decimal system in weights and measures, but this idea did not begin to gain acceptance until the French Revolution.

Stevin's other accomplishments include his promotion of the Dutch language, especially in science. He believed Dutch to be the best language to express scientific thought, an idea he explained in the introduction to *De beghinselen der weeghconst* (The Art of Weighing) in 1586. By using the Dutch language,

Stevin began creating a scientific vocabulary not yet in existence. *Weeghconst,* apart from the importance of the introduction, discusses geometry, algebra, mechanics, and statistics and uses algebraic notation that served as a transition between old, clumsy notation and modern Cartesian notation. Stevin also further developed Archimedes' ideas on the equilibrium of solid bodies and liquids in *De beghinselen des Waterwichts* (1586), which ultimately influenced integral calculus.

Prince Maurice, excellent at the art of warfare, befriended Stevin, which certainly influenced his later works. He also wrote works on the art of fortification, field encampment, perspective in architecture, heliocentric theory, musical tuning, and civics. Stevin even helped in constructing mills, locks, and harbors and wrote *Havenvindingh* (How to Find the Harbor), which discusses the importance of latitude and declination in finding the right harbor.

From 1604 until his death at The Hague in 1620, Stevin served as quartermaster general of the Netherlands, focusing much of his writing on mathematics. He wrote in the vernacular, but his works were later translated into Latin by Willebrord Snellius and into French by Prince Frederick Henry, Maurice's brother.

Bibliography

D. J. Struick, *The Land of Stevin and Huygens,* 1981.

Paul Miller

STOSS, VEIT (c. 1450–1533)

Veit Stoss was either from the Black Forest town of Horb, in Swabia, or from one of several similarly named towns in Poland; judging from his subsequent career, the former seems more likely. He is first heard of as a sculptor in Nuremberg in 1477, but from then until 1496 he worked in Cracow, both for the Polish king and for the prosperous German commercial community there. He returned to Nuremberg in 1496. Facing competition from other sculptors in stone and bronze, he found work as a woodcarver, becoming one of the great German masters of limewood sculpture.

Among Stoss's major works are the elaborate marble tomb of King Casimir IV Jagiello and a carved polychromed wooden winged retable decorated with scenes from the life of the Virgin, some forty feet high, at St. Mary's in Cracow (1477–89). At St. Lorenzkirche in Nuremberg is one of his most popular wooden sculptures, the suspended openwork carving of the *Annunciation of the Rosary* (1517–18), also polychromed. Later in his career, the unfinished limewood altarpiece in Bamberg Cathedral (1520–23) shows Stoss's response to the growing preference in Germany for unpainted wooden sculpture.

It was with both the Bamberg Cathedral altarpiece and the *Annunciation of the Rosary* that Stoss's career ran into trouble, for his son, Andreas, had originally commissioned the former for the Carmelite monastery in Nuremberg, of which he was prior. Andreas, however, was strongly anti-Lutheran and was banished from the city in 1525 before the altarpiece was finished. It was moved to Bamberg in 1543. Meanwhile, in 1529 the Nuremberg town council declared the *Annunciation of the Rosary* a Marian cult figure and thus offensive to the Reformers; happily, they did not remove or destroy it, but ordered it covered. The fact that Anton Tucher, one of Nuremberg's most powerful citizens, had donated it to the city may have helped to preserve this fine work.

Veit Stoss, with Tilman Riemenschneider and others, represents the high point of the German limewood carvers in the period culminating in the Reformation. Of these sculptors, he also marks the transition from a polychrome to a natural finish in wood sculpture, but his style remained late Gothic, never taking the step into the world of the Italian Renaissance.

Bibliography

M. Baxandall, *The Limewood Sculptors of Renaissance Germany*, 1980.
W. Stechow, ed., *Northern Renaissance Art, 1400–1600: Sources and Documents*, 1966.

Rosemary Poole

STOW, JOHN (1525–1605)

The most accurate sixteenth-century English chronicler, John Stow amassed a huge manuscript collection, part of which is in the British Library's Harleian manuscripts. Born in 1525 in St. Michael Cornhill, London, where his father and grandfather were tallow chandlers, Stow may have attended grammar school, though rumors said that his Latin was poor. He was apprenticed to a tailor and in 1547 was made free of the Merchant Taylors' Company but never took livery or held office. He published an edition of Geoffrey Chaucer (1561) and may have edited John Lydgate and John Skelton's* works. His *Summary of English Chronicles* (1565) provoked bitter rivalry with Richard Grafton, who produced similar pocket histories. His collecting prompted official investigations on suspicion of popery but also brought him Archbishop Matthew Parker's patronage, membership in his Society of Antiquaries (founded in 1572), and acquaintance with fellow scholars. He edited chronicles by Matthew of Westminster (1567), Matthew Paris (1571), Thomas Walsingham (1574), and Raphael Holinshed* (1585–87). He authored *The Chronicles of England* (1580), *Annals of England* (1592, later expanded by Edmund Howes), and the famous *Survey of London* (1598, often reprinted with additions, notably by John Strype in 1720, and still in print). Though his reputation grew, he died in poverty on 6 April 1605.

Most Tudor chroniclers valued the past for moral examples and accumulated facts without assessing their relative importance or meaning. Stow loved English history for its own sake, was conscious of anachronism, used primary sources extensively, and was more concerned with accuracy, though he defended Geoffrey of Monmouth. Stow's later works, which remain useful, reveal William Camden's* influence and suggest that he was evolving from chronicler to historian. Regrettably, his history of Britain, written near the end of his life, was never published, and the manuscript has been lost.

Bibliography

F. J. Levy, *Tudor Historical Thought*, 1967.
J. Stow, *The Survey of London*, ed. H. B. Wheatley with intro. by V. Pearl, 1987.

William B. Robison

STUART, MARY (QUEEN OF SCOTS) (1542–1587)

Mary Stuart (Mary Queen of Scots) has intrigued people for centuries. Accurately described by Elizabeth I* as the "daughter of debate," Mary has been dubbed queen, adulteress, murderess, and conspirator, but her role as poet and writer is of equal importance, although frequently ignored.

Born in Linlithgow Palace, at the age of one week she became sovereign queen of Scotland following the death of her father, King James V. In an attempt to secure a beneficial marriage for her daughter, Mary of Guise arranged a union between Mary and the dauphin, heir apparent to the French throne, and in 1548, at the age of five, Mary left Scotland and sailed to France.

At the French court, Mary received an education suitable for a princess. She wrote in English, French, and Italian, and based upon her libraries' collections at Holyrood and Edinburgh castles, she was probably able to read Latin, Greek, and Spanish. According to contemporary accounts of her French education, Mary was skilled at needlework, dance, singing, music, poetry, and riding. Two French poets, Pierre de Ronsard* and Joachim Du Bellay,* served as her mentors at the Palace of Fontainebleau.

In 1559 Mary became queen of France, and she and François II boldly declared themselves "King and Queen of France, Scotland, England, and Ireland," although within a year François died. Mary returned to her homeland, Scotland, in 1560, where she ruled problematically for less than a decade. By the age of twenty-four, Mary had married three times, to the French king, to her cousin Lord Darnley, and to Lord Bothwell, whom some called her second husband's murderer. Scotland's response to her third marriage led to rebellion, her forced abdication, and her fleeing to England, where she remained for nearly twenty years. Queen Elizabeth, fearing that English Roman Catholics might rally around Mary in rebellion against her own government, had her imprisoned. Several conspiracies did transpire, and in 1586 Mary was found guilty of being party to a plot hatched by one Anthony Babington to assassinate the queen. Mary was executed in 1587. Her son James* later became king of England following Elizabeth's death in 1603.

As a writer, Mary produced a diverse collection of writings: love sonnets to Bothwell, sonnets of supplication to Elizabeth, dedicatory poems to Ronsard, contemplative poems revealing her religious piety, and numerous letters. In the margins of her favorite book, *The Book of Hours*, she drafted her later poems. Although Mary was a skilled writer, she never attempted to publish her works, and aside from a few pieces published by contemporaries, the first publication of her poetry appeared in 1873, nearly three hundred years after her execution. As history records her story, Mary's writings did not achieve great attention during her lifetime or after it. Undoubtedly, she is remembered more for the words written about her than by her.

Bibliography

Mary, Queen of Scots, *Bittersweet within My Heart: The Love Poems of Mary, Queen of Scots*, ed. R. Bell, 1992.
J. Wormald, *Mary Queen of Scots: A Study in Failure*, 1991.

Stephanie Witham

STURM, JACOB (1489–1553)

Jacob Sturm was an influential politician in sixteenth-century Europe. He was born in 1489 in Strasbourg. Educated at Heidelberg and Freiburg, he was destined for a career in the church. Shaped first by the humanism of Jakob Wimpfeling,* he later came under the influence of Desiderius Erasmus* and other reforming currents in sixteenth-century Europe. In the early 1520s he converted to what became Protestantism. He was married in the 1520s; his wife died by 1529.

Sturm became one of the most important political figures of the first half of the sixteenth century in the Holy Roman Empire. In 1526 he became a member of Strasbourg's Privy Council, which dealt with foreign affairs. He worked to promote understanding and cooperation between two branches of the nascent Protestant movement, the Lutheran reform of northern Germany and the Zwinglian reform of southern Germany and Switzerland. In this regard, he played a role at both the Colloquy of Marburg (1529) and the Diet of Augsburg (1530). In the 1530s he was important in the formation of the Schmalkaldic League, a league of Protestant princes and cities, and in both the 1530s and 1540s he sought continuing influence over its structure and policy. After the Schmalkaldic War and the defeat of the Protestant league, he sought reconciliation with Emperor Charles V.* He did not give up his own Protestant views, but saw Catholics as truly Christian.

While primarily concerned with foreign affairs in these decades, Sturm also worked for the reform of the church in Strasbourg. He was also a member of the school board there from 1526 until his death and was particularly concerned with the reform of secondary education. A lessened engagement with the politics of the empire and a greater concern with local issues marked his last years. Sturm died in Strasbourg in 1553.

Bibliography

T. A. Brady, Jr., *The Politics of the Reformation in Germany: Jacob Sturm (1489–1553) of Strasbourg*, 1997.

Mary Jane Haemig

SWEELINCK, JAN PIETERSZOON (1562–1621)

Jan Pieterszoon Sweelinck, the widely acclaimed organist of Amsterdam's Oude Kerk (Old Church), was a gifted composer of keyboard and vocal music as well as one of the most renowned and influential teachers of his day. Born in Deventer, Netherlands, Sweelinck grew up in a musical family. His grandfather, uncle, and father were all organists. His father preceded him in the post at Oude Kerk, and his son, Dirck, succeeded him there in 1621. Records show that Sweelinck held this position from 1580 to 1621, but it is possible that he began work there as early as 1577. Sweelinck's reputation as a teacher attracted many pupils to Amsterdam. Students from Germany, such as Samuel Scheidt, Jacob Praetorius, and Heinrich Scheidemann, went on to found the great North German organ school, which ultimately culminated in the music of J. S. Bach.

As a composer of vocal music, Sweelinck set sacred and secular texts and drew from both Protestant and Catholic traditions. His *Rimes françoises et italiennes* (1612) is a secular collection of French chansons and Italian madrigals. His *Cantiones sacrae* (1619) is a set of motets based upon the Catholic liturgy. Perhaps his most monumental achievement and life's work is his setting of the entire Psalter using French metrical psalms.

Sweelinck's keyboard music includes variations, toccatas, and fantasias. The technically difficult toccatas often seem to have a pedagogical purpose. The fantasias, which frequently employ fugal elaboration of a single theme, led to the development of the monothematic fugue and had a profound impact on the music of Bach. Because of his magnificent keyboard improvisations, Sweelinck was known during his day as the "Orpheus of Amsterdam," but his influence as a composer and teacher carried far beyond his own city and time to shape the finest musical developments of the late baroque.

Bibliography

K. Tollefsen, "Jan Pieterszoon Sweelinck," in *The New Grove Dictionary of Music and Musicians*, ed. S. Sadie, vol. 18, 1980: 406–13.

Tucker Robison

T

TALLIS, THOMAS (1505–1585)

Thomas Tallis was one of the best-known English composers of the sixteenth century. Little is known about his early life, but he began his fifty-year musical career as an organist and choirmaster, first at Dover Priory, then at St. Mary-at-Hill near Billingsgate, then at Waltham Abbey. When the abbey was dissolved in 1540 by Henry VIII,* that monarch made Tallis a gentleman of the Chapel Royal, in which group of musicians he remained during the reigns of Edward VI, Mary I,* and Elizabeth I.* Tallis was known as a mild and quiet man, and this temperament probably enabled him to survive these years at court under both Protestant and Catholic monarchs. Tallis was famed as a teacher as well as a composer. With his most famous pupil, William Byrd,* he was granted a monopoly over printed music and music paper by Elizabeth I in 1575; producing only one book, their unsuccessful joint *Cantiones sacrae* (Sacred songs, 1575), their business was a failure. Tallis was godfather to Byrd's son Thomas, to whom he left his share of the monopoly. Tallis was survived by Joane, his wife of thirty-three years; the couple had no children.

Tallis's Latin works include two masses, two magnificats, a number of lamentations, and fifty-one motets; in English he composed eighteen anthems and numerous other works. He was much respected by his contemporaries; Byrd's elegy for him concludes, "Tallis is dead, and music dies." He is well represented in twentieth-century hymnals, and the ten-person early-music chorus the Tallis Scholars bears his name.

Bibliography

P. Doe, *Tallis*, 1968.

Jean Graham

TARTAGLIA, NICCOLÒ (c. 1500–1557)

A significant contributor to sixteenth-century mathematical scholarship, Niccolò Tartaglia was born into an impoverished family, possibly surnamed Fontana, of Brescia in northern Italy. From his very early years, his life was a document in hardship. His father, a mail courier, died when the boy was about six, and afterward the family fell into poverty. In 1512 Niccolò barely escaped with his life when the French army sacked Brescia, putting much of the population to the sword. The wounds he sustained to his head and mouth, however, left him with a speech defect that earned him the name Tartaglia, from the Italian verb meaning "to stutter."

Despite the family's straitened circumstances, Tartaglia's mother managed to finance her son's early education until lack of funds obliged him to continue his studies on his own. Tartaglia's mathematical aptitude developed rapidly. When he was about eighteen years of age, he became a teacher of the abacus in Verona, where he eventually started a family before moving to Venice in 1534. He was employed as a professor of mathematics in and around that city for nearly the entire remainder of his life.

Given his limited formal schooling, Tartaglia's contributions to mathematical and humanistic scholarship were not inconsiderable. He acquired a favorable reputation for his work in the military sciences, particularly for his treatise on ballistics, *Nova scientia* (1537). Also noteworthy were his translations of the Greek works of Archimedes and of Euclid's *Elements* (1543), the latter being the first translation of that work ever to reach print in a modern language. One of his principal works, the *General trattato di numeri et misure* (1556), became a widely used text in general arithmetic in his time.

Tartaglia, however, is primarily associated with the unfortunate controversy that surrounded his solution for cubic equations, which he achieved in the course of a public academic debate with a pupil of Scipione del Ferro in 1535. News of Tartaglia's accomplishment eventually reached the noted physician and mathematician Girolamo Cardano* of Milan, to whom he confided the solution under an oath of secrecy. When Cardano learned of del Ferro's prior work on the subject, however, he published the solution in his algebraic text *Ars magna* (1545), giving attribution both to Tartaglia and del Ferro. The ensuing dispute produced an exchange of published challenges in mathematics (the so-called *Cartelli*) between Tartaglia and Cardano's pupil Lodovico Ferrari, whose work also appears in the *Ars magna*. The two met in public debate at Milan in 1548; although no official verdict survives, Tartaglia's defeat is suggested by his early departure from the proceedings. He eventually returned to Venice, where he died in 1557, never having achieved the professional justification nor the lasting financial security that he sought.

Bibliography

O. Ore, *Cardano: The Gambling Scholar*, 1953.

Michael J. Medwick

TASSO, TORQUATO (1544–1595)

Torquato Tasso was the most accomplished man of letters in Italy during the late Renaissance. He composed the purest example of Renaissance pastoral drama, *Aminta* (1573), and the most influential narrative poem of his era, *Gerusalemme liberata* (1581). He was also a prolific literary theorist; his *Discorsi del poema eroico* (1594) constitutes a fundamental contribution to the emergence of neoclassical poetics, which dominated European letters for two centuries after Tasso's death.

Tasso was born in Sorrento, the son of a gifted courtier-poet, Bernardo Tasso, whom political allegiance forced into exile. When he was eight years old, Torquato was separated from the rest of his family to accompany his father. Torquato never saw his mother again, and his subsequent career entailed changes of court service and crises of religious conscience indicative of a restless spirit.

Tasso briefly studied law in Padua, but poetry proved an irresistible vocation. At the age of eighteen he published a chivalric romance, *Rinaldo*, and thereafter he continued working on the epic *Gierusalemme* [*sic*], of which he had completed three cantos four years earlier. Innovative poetics enabled Tasso to merge this early project with romance traditions typical of his predecessors at the Este court in Ferrara, Matteo Maria Boiardo and Ludovico Ariosto,* to produce his greatest literary achievement, *Gerusalemme liberata*. He dedicated considerable intellectual energy to articulating the theory behind this feat of composition, and he continued to revise this epic romance, which he ultimately published as *Gerusalemme conquistata* (1593). Ironically, this final version of Tasso's masterpiece, which he deemed authoritative, has never enjoyed the esteem of the *Liberata*. Although the earlier version was published without the author's approval while he was in confinement in Ferrara, it has become canonical and widely influential.

Tasso's reputation as a melancholy genius victimized by a coercive system of court patronage became a romantic legend most famously represented in Johann Wolfgang von Goethe's play of 1790, *Torquato Tasso*. The origins of this legend hark back to Michel de Montaigne's* account of his visit with Tasso during his confinement. In Montaigne's *Apologie de Raimond Sebond* Tasso's fate actually betokens the catastrophic results of intellectual overreaching that skepticism's prudent acceptance of the limits of human intelligence aims to avoid. But Goethe's sympathetic portrait of Tasso as a sensitive soul misunderstood by worldlier sorts made a deep impact. Such poets as George Gordon, Lord Byron, Paul Verlaine, and Charles Baudelaire produced moving lyrics that respond to the pathos of Tasso's legendary misfortunes, and Sigmund Freud briefly analyzed a passage from *Gerusalemme liberata* in *Beyond the Pleasure Principle*.

Although the romantic myth of Tasso's victimization dominates the modern reception of his legacy, his importance as a literary artist and theorist should not be underestimated. Only John Milton's *Paradise Lost* superseded Tasso's *Gerusalemme liberata* as an example of Christian epic fully informed by classical precedents; and Tasso's poem, more than any other, sets the standard by which Milton's measure must be taken in this regard. In *Of Education* Milton recommends Tasso's literary theory to students, who can thereby come to understand the "true laws" of epic poetry, and during his Italian journey, Milton sought out Tasso's first biographer, Giovanni Battista Manso, to whom he subsequently addressed a poem in Latin.

Tasso's *Aminta* is the fountainhead of a dramatic tradition that made itself felt in English pastoral plays and interludes from William Shakespeare* and Ben Jonson* through Milton's *Comus*. Moreover, Tasso's lyrics, and especially his sonnets, provided models for such Elizabethan poets as Edmund Spenser* and Samuel Daniel* during the great sonnet "boom" of the 1590s. Tasso's dual legacy as both an exemplary neoclassicist and a romantic legend ensured the durability of his memory despite the shifting perspectives of literary culture in the centuries after his death.

Bibliography

C. P. Brand, *Torquato Tasso: A Study of the Poet and of His Contribution to English Literature*, 1965.
J. Kates, *Tasso and Milton: The Problem of Christian Epic*, 1983.
L. F. Rhu, *The Genesis of Tasso's Narrative Theory: English Translations of the Early Poetics and a Comparative Study of Their Significance*, 1993.

Lawrence Rhu

TAVERNER, JOHN (c. 1495–1545)

John Taverner was considered the greatest English composer during the first decades of the reign of Henry VIII.* Little is known about his early life, although he may have been born in Lincolnshire, where he was a fellow of Tattershall College before his 1526 appointment as choirmaster and organist at Cardinal College, Oxford, founded the preceding year by Cardinal Thomas Wolsey. In his second year Taverner became involved in an underground Lutheran study group and was briefly imprisoned when Protestant books were found in his possession. Unlike the scholars arrested at the same time, Taverner was quickly released and spent two more years at Oxford. John Foxe's* *Acts and Monuments* (1563) notes Taverner's imprisonment for the Protestant faith and claims that the composer repented for having made "Popish" songs before this time. Taverner left Oxford in 1530 after Wolsey alienated the king by refusing to seek an annulment of Henry's marriage to Catherine of Aragon and his college began to fail. Taverner's location for the following six years is unknown, but his last eight years were spent in Boston, Lincolnshire. In Boston he married a widow with two daughters; Rose Parrowe may have been his second wife, as he had been involved in marriage negotiations in 1525. Taverner became a member and eventually the treasurer of the Gild of Corpus Christi, which maintained a chapel in the town. A few months before his death in 1545, he became an alderman of Boston. Taverner continued to demonstrate Protestant tendencies: he was employed by Thomas Cromwell to look into the local friaries and reported that he had publicly burned a large, ornate cross, presumably as a symbol of his opposition to "idolatry." Taverner also expressed sympathetic concern for the poverty of friars and promised them any aid they required. The only major English composer of the sixteenth century to embrace Protestant doctrine, Taverner wrote in both traditional modes (such as the elaborate *Western Wynde*) and in the new, simple style preferred by Protestants (such as his *Playn Song Mass*).

Bibliography

C. Hand, *John Taverner: His Life and Music*, 1978.

Jean Graham

TEERLINC, LEVINA BENING (c. 1520–1576)

Levina Bening Teerlinc was born in Bruges and was the eldest of five daughters. Her father Simon Bening and her grandfather Alexander Bening were both famous miniaturists, and Levina followed in their footsteps. Levina studied in Bruges with her father and in the late 1530s was becoming well known for her skill. By 1545 she had married George Teerlinc, and the couple moved to England when they were invited by Henry VIII,* who had heard of Teerlinc's gifts as an artist, and whose earlier court artist, Hans Holbein,* had died in 1543.

In 1546 Teerlinc was granted forty pounds per annum as a court painter, the most a court artist received in England until the end of the century; she was paid considerably more than Holbein, today a far more famous artist. Teerlinc was a court painter in the reigns of Henry VIII and all three of his children, Edward VI, Mary I,* and Elizabeth I.* Around 1550 Teerlinc painted a portrait of Elizabeth as a young girl. There is a scholarly dispute, however, as to exactly which portrait this might be.

During Mary's reign she did miniatures of the queen at prayer and portraits of other noblewomen, such as Mary's cousin, Catherine Grey. When Elizabeth became queen in 1558, the new queen confirmed the patent granted by her father to Teerlinc, and Elizabeth greatly valued Teerlinc's work. Teerlinc not only painted individual portraits of Elizabeth but also portraits of Elizabeth on her tours, or progresses, through the countryside, with her knights of the Garter, and participating in various religious ceremonies such as washing the feet of poor women on Maundy Thursday. Elizabeth's first great seal was done from a design by Teerlinc. Royal accounts suggest that Teerlinc was highly respected at the English court and that all four sovereigns for whom she worked appreciated her.

Levina Teerlinc had the status of a gentlewoman. Each year she did a special picture for Elizabeth's New Year's gift, and Elizabeth in return gave her valuable gifts. In 1566 Levina's husband George was granted the lease of a property in Stepney, where he built a new house valued at five hundred pounds. The same year George, Levina, and their son Marcus all received English citizenship. Levina clearly lived in comfortable circumstances and had high social status. She continued as a court painter until her death in 1576. Some scholars suggest that her portrait of a lady is a self-portrait since the sitter is wearing ornamental dice, and the word for dice in Flemish is *teerlinc*.

Bibliography

R. Strong, *Artists of the Tudor Court*, 1983.

Carole Levin

TERESA OF ÁVILA, ST. (1515–1582)

Canonized in 1622, St. Teresa of Ávila fought illness most of her life, but had a will strong enough to reform the Carmelite order despite substantial opposition. She was a mystic, a prolific writer, and an important figure in the Counter-Reformation.

Born Teresa de Cepeda y Ahumada in Ávila, Spain, St. Teresa showed her characteristic trait of fusing spirituality and activism at an early age. At seven, inspired by her reading of saints' lives, she ran away from home in order to become a martyr among the infidels. She was educated in the Augustinian convent in Ávila, which she left, inspired by St. Augustine's *Confessions* and advice given by a nun and her uncle, to enter the convent of the Carmelites at the age of twenty.

The severely ascetic exercises she underwent drained her health and brought her to the brink of death. Had it not been for her father's intervention, she would have been buried alive. Although she regained her health to an extent, she always retained symptoms of her illness in the form of fever, headaches, and insomnia. Alternating between spiritual doubts and mystical highs, Teresa encountered the moment of inner illumination, vividly described in the autobiographical *Book of Her Life*.

One of her visions of hell led her to reform her order toward a basic, austere severity and purity. Thus began her long phase of great activity, for which she would suffer and be punished by those who felt that her method of mystical ecstasy posed a threat to church authority. In 1562 she founded the first convent of the Discalced Carmelites in Ávila. The old Order of Carmelites did not take her reforms well and denounced the *Book of Her Life* to the Inquisition. The denunciation was processed, perhaps due in part to her Jewish ancestry; St. Teresa's father, Alonso, was the son of Juan Sanchez, a converted Jew. Her detractors tried to have her deported to America but ended up confining her to the city of Toledo in order to impede her from founding more convents. But among her supporters were also the famous Fray Luis de León*; her brother of the same order, Fray Juan de la Cruz*; and most important, the Jesuits, who saw her as a powerful ally against the Protestant Reformation. Eventually, her ally in the court of Philip II,* Count of Tendilla, used his powerful influence to get the pope to establish a separate province for the Discalced Carmelites.

Teresa founded seventeen new convents in Castilla and Andalucia. On a trip from Burgos to Ávila at the end of September 1582, she stopped at the Convent of Alba de Tormes, where she died in early October.

All her books are autobiographical, even the most doctrinal, such as *The Way of Perfection* or *The Interior Castle*. Her first book, the *Book of Her Life* (c.

1562), is mostly a detailed description of mystical experiences, which she sees as a result of personal experience. Like St. Augustine, St. Teresa uses an introspective, intimate voice of address. *Book of the Foundations* (c. 1573–82) and *Letters* (c. 1560–79) are continuations of her religious activities begun in the *Book of Her Life*. Of particular interest in *Book of the Foundations* (c. 1573–82) are the numerous portraits of secular and religious people she knew over the course of her industrious life. Her *Letters* gather together epistles directed to various confessors who inspired and advised her work. *The Interior Castle*, also known as *The Dwelling Places*, is a treatise on the soul and its relationship to God. St. Teresa also wrote several religious poems, the most famous of which begins: "I live without living in me / and so high a life do I await / that I die because I do not die."

St. Teresa was among the first Spanish women to be published in print. Her life and her work inspired countless biographies and at least one important sculpture, Gianlorenzo Bernini's *Ecstasy of St. Teresa* (1645–52). This full-figure sculpture depicts her at the moment when she, pierced by an angel's arrow, receives a vision of the Holy Spirit. The order is still strong in and outside of Europe. Currently, at the close of the twentieth century, the Discalced Carmelites—men and women—have 30 convents across Africa, 2 missions in Latin America, 103 convents across Asia and Oceania, and 1 mission in the Middle East.

Bibliography

T. Bielecki, *Teresa of Ávila: An Introduction to Her Life and Writings*, 1994.
J. Bilinkoff, *The Ávila of Saint Teresa*, 1989.

Ana Kothe

THOMAS, WILLIAM (c. 1507–1554)

An English humanist, author, and Protestant martyr, William Thomas was a clerk to King Edward VI's privy council and published the first English history of Italy and the first English-Italian grammar. Little is known of Thomas's early life, but it is probable that he was of Welsh origin, was educated at Oxford, and prospered under Henry VIII's* new Protestant regime. In 1545 he fled England as a fugitive, having embezzled money from his patron. His stay of approximately four years in Italy formed the basis for his most important works: *The Historie of Italie* (1549), *The Principal Rules of the Italian Grammar* (1550), and *The Pilgrim*, a defense of Henry VIII's break with Roman Catholicism that circulated in manuscript in his native country and was published in Italian in 1552 as *Il pellegrino inglese*.

Soon after his return from Italy, Thomas was appointed clerk to Edward VI's privy council. Through this position, he came into contact with some of England's most influential courtiers and administrators, and also with a number of foreign diplomats. During this period he also composed for the young king a collection of "Commonplaces of State," political discourses in the manner of

Niccolò Machiavelli,* whose works were scarcely known in England at this time.

Thomas left the privy council before the death of the king in June 1553 and soon after became actively involved in Thomas Wyatt's rebellion, a failed popular uprising whose object was to dethrone Queen Mary I.* In May 1554 Thomas was executed for high treason. John Foxe* records his death as a Protestant martyr, claiming that he "made a right godly end, and wrote many fruitful exhortations, letters and sonnets, in the prison before his death." None of these, however, has survived. Thomas wrote or translated devotional, political, and scientific works, but his influence in sixteenth-century England was most significant because of his work on Italian history and language.

Bibliography

E. R. Adair, "William Thomas: A Forgotten Clerk of the Privy Council," in *Tudor Studies*, 1924.
G. B. Parks, "Introduction," in *The History of Italy*, by William Thomas, 1963.
S. Rossi, "Un 'Italianista' nel Cinquecento Inglese: William Thomas," *Aevum* 40 (1966): 281–314.

                                                                          Thomas G. Olsen

TINTORETTO (1519–1594)

An important Venetian painter of the later sixteenth century, Tintoretto possessed a highly original, dynamic, and expressive painting style. This powerful style endowed Tintoretto's religious works with a dramatic visionary quality and profound religious spirit.

Tintoretto was born Jacopo Robusti in Venice, and his name derived from his father's profession as a textile dyer, a *tintore*. Initially influenced by the art of Titian,* Tintoretto pursued a more Mannerist approach through the study of the art of Michelangelo,* Giorgio Vasari,* Francesco Salviati,* Giulio Romano,* and Francesco Parmigianino.* His encounter with the art of Schiavone with its fluid pictorial style of flowing and mixed colors provided an important source for Tintoretto in the development of his rapid method of execution, which permitted his expressiveness and fantasy to thrive. Tintoretto came to the forefront of Venetian painting with his *Miraculous Rescue of a Christian Slave by St. Mark* (1548, Venice, Accademia), which rejected all previous models of religious painting. The painting's violent contrasts of light and shade, cursive painting style, use of the diagonal, energetic and curving figures, and exciting foreshortenings surprised the public. Tintoretto's theatrical sense in skillfully creating a spatious and dynamic architectural setting that appears to open in all directions is rooted in the study of architecture and stage scenery. His performance was based on sound study, including designing from life and from plaster casts of ancient sculpture and Michelangelo's work. To understand the effects of light on figures and drapery, according to the seventeenth-century writer Carlo Ridolfi, Tintoretto constructed small stage sets, placed wax figurines in them, and arranged candles in different positions to study how light interacted with figures and drapery.

From the beginning of his career, Tintoretto painted portraits. While they reveal his study of Titian, they lack the older painter's heroic idealization and concern with social position. Instead, Tintoretto concentrated on the character and psychology of the individual while remaining faithful to the sitter's appearance. In 1553 Tintoretto married Faustina de' Vescovi and fathered eight children, some of whom later joined him as painters. The following decade, Tintoretto was entrusted with the decoration of the downstairs room of the Scuola di San Rocco, which he completed in three years. Tintoretto's enormous *Crucifixion* in the Scuola shows the artist's previous experiments on a grander spatial scale, with Christ represented as a triumphant hero. During this period Tintoretto was also called to work in the ducal palace. In 1575 Tintoretto returned to the Scuola to paint the upstairs room with scenes from the Old Testament on the ceiling and the life of Christ on the walls. In this cycle, his image of the *Adoration of the Shepherds* innovatively divided the composition into two levels with the shepherds below and the holy family above in the hayloft. Tintoretto's poetic, spiritual, and dramatic vision was ideally suited to the unsophisticated religiosity of his works, which show a popular vision sympathetic to the renewed Christian religiosity and the desire for reform current at that time.

In the 1580s Tintoretto continued to accept many commissions, and as a result his workshop played a larger role in his later art. His work for another room of the Scuola di San Rocco (1582–87) depended heavily on the workshop, as did his final image of *Paradise* (1588–92), the largest of his career, for the Sala del Maggior Consiglio in the ducal palace. An expressive and imaginative painter, Tintoretto almost seems to have sought the difficult and ignored the traditional in his attempts to endow a new dynamism in narrative painting. His virtuoso fluid technique, innovativeness, and expressive eloquence provided a great influence on seventeenth-century painting.

Bibliography

R. Pallucchini and P. Rossi, *Tintoretto: Le opere sacre e profane*, 1982.
D. Rosand, *Painting in Cinquecento Venice: Titian, Veronese, Tintoretto*, 1982.
F. Valcanover and T. Pignatti, *Tintoretto*, 1985.

Mary Pixley

TITIAN (d. 1576)

Tiziano Vecellio was the most famous painter in sixteenth-century Venice. His dynamic compositions, expressive brushwork, tonal and naturalistic color scheme, and use of color permeated with natural light influenced the development of painting both during and after his life.

Born in Pieve di Cadore, Italy, probably in the later 1480s, Titian studied painting in the shop of Giovanni Bellini. By 1507 he was associated with the studio of Giorgione. Giorgione's art exercised a great influence on Titian, and their contemporaries sometimes had difficulty in distinguishing their paintings. His frescoes for the Confraternity of Saint Anthony of Padua, his first documented work, finished in 1511, show a synthesis of contemporary Venetian art with the latest in central Italian art, in particular that of Michelangelo.* By 1516 he was the outstanding painter in Venice owing to his technical skill, strength of form, fluid touch, clarity of expression, and ability to handle large compositions, as seen in his original, colorful, and energetic *Assumption of the Virgin* for the Church of the Frari (1516–18). Titian's inventiveness also appears in his *Pesaro Madonna* altarpiece in the same church, in which he modernized the nature of such devotional works by organizing the composition along a diagonal, incorporating monumental classicizing architecture, and sacrificing individual elements in the interest of the overall design. Titian's working method was also revolutionary, because he developed his compositions by sketching directly on the canvas instead of relying on full-scale preliminary drawings.

Evidence of his growing fame, the duke of Ferrara, Alfonso d'Este, commissioned Titian to paint a series of mythological paintings for his study (1518–23). In this period, Titian continued to compose in a dynamic fashion, as seen in the now-destroyed *Death of St. Peter Martyr*, one of Titian's most celebrated and reproduced paintings. In 1525 Titian married Cornelia and had two sons and a daughter. Probably through his work for Alfonso d'Este, Titian was commissioned to paint the portrait of his nephew, Federico II Gonzaga,* the marquis of Mantua (Madrid, Prado). Extremely popular as a portraitist, Titian painted portraits of many of the most important people of Venice and elsewhere in the sixteenth century, idealizing them and endowing them with an aristocratic poise to create inventive, heroic, and appealing portraits. The writer Pietro Aretino,* who ardently admired, supported, and publicized Titian's art, helping to spread his name throughout Europe, immediately commissioned a portrait from Titian upon his arrival in Venice in 1527.

Masterpieces from the 1530s include the *Presentation of the Virgin* (1534–38, Venice, Accademia), which displays a naturalism and artlessness thanks to its clarity of composition, casual figural groups, and realism of lighting. The now-destroyed but much-admired *Battle of Spoleto* for the ducal palace provided an important source for later battle scenes. During the 1540s Titian displayed a more active interest in overt rhetoric, massive forms, foreshortening, and twisting poses, perhaps in response to the growing interest in Mannerism. His brushwork also became increasingly free and his use of color more broken in this period. Titian went to Rome in 1543 and painted a portrait of Pope Paul III and his nephews, but the trip left little impact on him. Back in Venice, as the demands on Titian continued to increase, earlier compositions became repeated, and assistants, including his son Orazio, played a larger role in his artistic production.

In 1548 Titian went to Augsburg for eight months to work for Emperor Charles V* and was knighted for his services; the famous portrait *Charles on*

Horseback was executed during this period. Titian also worked for Charles's son, Philip II,* painting various mythological works that reveal a new sumptuousness in his use of color, perhaps motivated by the mature works of Paolo Veronese.* The *Rape of Europa* (c. 1562, Boston, Isabella Steward Gardner) shows a remarkable sense of energy and movement, and the apparent sense of spontaneity here and in other paintings was actually the result of a great deal of work. Titian continued to paint until his death in 1576, leaving his last work, an emotional and moving *Pietà* (Venice, Accademia), probably intended to decorate his own tomb, unfinished. While Titian was the last survivor of the High Renaissance, he nonetheless anticipated some of the principles of baroque art. He exercised a strong influence on the next generation of artists, including Tintoretto* and Veronese, as well as later painters like Peter Paul Rubens* and Diego Rodríguez de Silva Velázquez.

Bibliography

C. Hope, *Titian*, 1980.
Titian, Prince of Painters, exhibition catalog, 1990.
H. E. Wethey, *The Paintings of Titian*, 3 vols., 1969–75.

Mary Pixley

TOMÁS DE JESÚS (1564–1627)

Discalced Carmelite Tomás de Jesús founded the first Carmelite deserts and was responsible for the expansion of the Discalced Carmelite order into Belgium and Germany. After promoting exclusively the contemplative dimension of Discalced Carmelite life in his first twenty years of religious life, he sought to foster a missionary spirit in the order in his later years. He joined the Discalced Carmelites in 1585 in Granada, where Juan de la Cruz* was prior, after reading the autobiography of Teresa of Ávila.* He established in Spain the first houses where friars could live as recluses and devote themselves completely to religious contemplation. These houses were known as Carmelite deserts.

Called to Rome by Pope Paul VI in 1607, Tomás de Jesús promoted the first missionary activity of the Discalced. In 1613 he wrote a treatise to stimulate interest in the missions. His purpose was not only to prepare missionaries to evangelize the indigenous peoples of the Americas, but also to provide them with arguments to refute the convictions of any kind of unbeliever. His focus on missionary activity anticipated the creation of the church's missionary office, the Congregation for the Propagation of the Faith.

Tomás de Jesús also authored several ascetical and mystical texts in Latin and in Spanish. Although some question whether his writings agree with the teachings on the spiritual life he inherited from Teresa of Ávila and Juan de la Cruz, he is the most important Discalced Carmelite theologian of the seventeenth century.

Bibliography

R. Hoffmann, *Pioneer Theories of Missiology*, 1960.

Evelyn Toft

TRISSINO, GIAN GIORGIO (1478–1550)

Gian Giorgio Trissino was a prolific and influential man of letters in sixteenth-century Italy. He was a poet, literary theorist, and dramatist; his most significant contribution to literary history was his play *Sofonisba*, the first modern Italian tragedy.

From an important noble family in Vicenza, Trissino received a fine humanist education and was particularly devoted to Greek studies. He moved to Rome in 1514, where he enjoyed the favor of the papal courts of Leo X,* Clement VII, and Paul III. In 1515 he wrote a play based on Livy's account of the Carthaginian princess, *Sofonisba*. This was considered the first Italian tragedy influenced by Greek models. In addition to its adherence to Greek tragic forms, the literary significance of *Sofonisba* was in its use of unrhymed verse in place of rhymed stanzas. Although *Sofonisba* was not performed on stage until after Trissino's death, it was very popular among readers and scholars, undergoing several reprintings. Trissino later wrote a comedy, *I simillimi* (The Look-alikes, 1548), modeled after Plautus's *Menaechmi*.

Trissino divided his time between Rome and Vicenza, where he had a villa designed by his friend, the architect Andrea Palladio.* In 1529 he published the first part of his important work of literary criticism, *Poetics*, dealing with prosody and linguistics; the last part of the work appeared much later, in 1563. Trissino was also involved in the current literary debate about the use of the vernacular in literature; he wrote a treatise on language and a work urging the reform of the Italian alphabet.

In 1547 he completed the first nine books of his epic, *La Italia liberata da Gotthi* (Italy Liberated from the Goths), which he dedicated to Emperor Charles V.* The following year the remaining eighteen books were published. Critical of the episodic chivalric romance embodied in Ludovico Ariosto's* *Orlando Furioso*, Trissino strove to re-create a heroic epic in the style of Homer. Although Trissino considered *Italia liberata* his finest achievement, readers then and now have found it tedious and pedantic. His literary legacy instead derives from his drama and his literary criticism.

Bibliography

T. G. Griffith, "Theory and Practice in the Writings of Giangiorgio Trissino," *Bulletin of the John Rylands University Library of Manchester*, 69 (1986).
M. Herrick, *Italian Tragedy in the Renaissance*, 1965.

Jo Eldridge Carney

TYE, CHRISTOPHER (c. 1497–1573)

Christopher Tye was an English musician and composer chiefly known for his religious anthems. Little is known about his life. Probably the music tutor to the future Edward VI, Tye dedicated his *Actes of the Apostelles in Meter to Synge* (1553) to that monarch. With a bachelor's degree in music from Cambridge in 1536 or 1537 and doctorates in music from Cambridge and Oxford,

he served for twenty years as a choir director at Ely Cathedral. Tye played with
the Chapel Royal musicians, serving the English royal family and the court. He
was apparently married and had children, as the musician Robert White was his
son-in-law. Also a priest, Tye was held in low esteem as a preacher, but was
applauded by his contemporaries as the "father of the anthem."

Bibliography

D. Price, *Patrons and Musicians of the English Renaissance*, 1981.

Jean Graham

TYNDALE, WILLIAM (c. 1490–1536)

William Tyndale was a translator of the English Bible, Protestant evangelical
Reformer, and martyr. Sometimes known as William Huchyns, he was born
near Gloucestershire, an area with a history of Lollard sympathies. He received
a master of arts in philosophy at Oxford's Magdalen College and also studied
languages and rhetoric. In 1522 Tyndale returned to Gloucestershire to tutor the
children of Sir John Walsh and spent his spare time preaching in the surrounding
villages. He may have also studied the *Novum instrumentum*, Desiderius Erasmus's* recent translation of the New Testament in both Greek and Latin; this
edition challenged the Vulgate, the traditional Latin version used in the Catholic
church. Tyndale became convinced of the need for an English translation of the
Bible so that lay people could read the Word of God for themselves.

He traveled to London, hoping to get approval from Cuthbert Tunstall, bishop
of London, but was denied; instead, Humphrey Monmouth, a wealthy merchant,
befriended Tyndale and financed his trip to Germany in 1524. In Cologne, Tyndale's first translation of the Bible was cut short by a raid on the printing shop,
but a fragment survived and made its way into England. In 1526 he was able
to translate the New Testament from Greek into English; after it was printed in
Worms, it was smuggled into England inside bales of cloth. When church authorities there burned several copies, Tyndale was appalled and began to attack
the church and its abuses; his polemical writings included *The Parable of the
Wicked Mammon, The Obedience of a Christian Man*, which stressed the importance of access to Scripture for all, and *The Practice of Prelates*, a work that
inspired the wrath of Henry VIII* for its conclusion that the king could not
lawfully divorce Catherine of Aragon. In 1530 Tyndale translated the first five
books of the Old Testament, the Pentateuch, from Hebrew into English for the
first time. He also published a reply to Sir Thomas More's* *Dialogue Concerning Heresies*, an attack against Protestant Reformers, particularly Tyndale. In
1535 someone in England hired a man named Henry Phillips to falsely befriend
Tyndale in Antwerp and trick him into a situation whereby he could be arrested.
After his arrest, Tyndale was sent to Vilvorde, Belgium, where he was imprisoned, tried for heresy, and executed on 6 October 1536.

Tyndale's work, especially his 1534 revision, formed the basis for most succeeding versions of the English Bible, including the King James Bible. He au-

thored many of the most recognized phrases of the Bible, such as "In the beginning" and "Let there be light." In addition, his translation is one of the first written records of modern English.

Bibliography

D. Daniell, *William Tyndale*, 1994.

Jean Akers

U–V

UDALL, NICHOLAS (c. 1505–1556)

Nicholas Udall, a humanist scholar, preacher, and schoolmaster, wrote one of the first English comedies, *Ralph Roister Doister*. Udall received his bachelor of arts degree from Corpus Christi College, Oxford, in 1524. Two years later he was arrested for possessing some Protestant tracts; his public renunciation of heresy ended the matter. Although there is no evidence that he was a leader in the reform cause, he was marked thereafter as possessing Lutheran beliefs.

Udall collaborated on some laudatory verses for the coronation of Anne Boleyn and in 1534 published his book *Flowers for Latin Speaking*, a celebrated Latin phrasebook used widely in schools. Shortly after its publication, Udall was appointed headmaster of Eton School and received his master's degree from Oxford one month later. In 1537 he was named vicar of Braintree, an office he served in absentia. He was dismissed from Eton in 1541 after being found guilty of buggery by the Privy Council, was suspected of collusion in the theft of some of the college chapel plate, and was sent to Marshalsea Prison.

Shortly thereafter, he was released and quickly regained royal favor. In the next few years he translated selections from Desiderius Erasmus,* including a collaboration sponsored by Catherine Parr. Udall, appointed canon of Windsor and rector of Calbourne, also received the right to print books. Finally, in 1555 he was appointed headmaster of Westminster School, a post in which he served until one month before his death in 1556.

His most famous play, *Ralph Roister Doister*, probably was first performed around 1552. This play, showing direct classical influence, most notably that of the Roman playwright Terence, serves as one of the first examples of English comedy. In addition, he wrote several other plays, one of which, *Res Publica*, was performed before Queen Mary,* and another, *Ezechias*, before Queen Elizabeth* after Udall's death.

Bibliography

W. L. Edgerton, *Nicholas Udall*, 1965.

E. Pittenger, " 'To Serve the Queere': Nicholas Udall, Master of Revels," in *Queering the Renaissance*, ed. J. Goldberg, 1994.

Erin Sadlack

URFÉ, HONORÉ D' (1567–1627)

Honoré d'Urfé, who lived during the tumultuous reigns of Henri III and Henri IV amid the Catholic-Huguenot wars, wrote the pastoral novel *L'Astrée*, an epic romance inspired in part by some of the events of his own life. Born in 1567, d'Urfé was raised in his grandfather's château in Forez, a cultural center located in Lyon, which encouraged him to learn. Later he attended the Jesuit Collège de Tournon, where he received a humanist education. In addition, he studied the Gospels, philosophy, and ancient and French history and there commenced his writing career.

Upon his return from the university, d'Urfé found that his older brother Anne had married a woman named Diane de Châteaumorand, but was unable to consummate the marriage due to impotency. Honoré fell in love with Diane, who reciprocated his feelings, much to the dismay of his family, who sent him away.

During this period, Honoré, along with his brother Anne, joined the Catholic League, a group of Catholics dedicated to fighting Protestantism. The group mobilized in order to attempt to prevent the accession of the Protestant Henri IV to the throne. Lyon, near the d'Urfé home, became a center of opposition to Henri, and Honoré especially played a significant leadership role, continuing to oppose the king even after his ascension to the throne and his conversion to Catholicism. This leadership twice led to his incarceration in 1595, once by his political enemies and once by a friend's betrayal. At this same time, both Antoine, his younger brother, and the duke of Nemours, d'Urfé's best friend and fellow leader of the Catholic League, died, causing him great grief. In 1596 d'Urfé was freed and subsequently was forced into virtual exile; he stayed in Savoy until 1599. Back in France, he lived in Châteauneuf and in a château in Virieu-le-Grand that he had inherited. There he pursued literary subjects, joining the Academie Florimontane, a society of learned individuals. That same year, his brother Anne's marriage to Diane was annulled, and d'Urfé married Diane the following year. Ironically, the marriage was an unhappy one punctuated by quarrels and separation.

In addition to his writing, d'Urfé's diplomatic career was growing. He was reconciled to Henri IV in 1602, and in 1610 the regent Queen Marie de Medicis sent him on a mission to Savoy. His efforts there were successful and led to the closer alliance between the two lands. In 1625 d'Urfé fought in the conflict between the French and Spanish over the Val Telline; however, in June of that year he died, probably from a case of pneumonia, leaving his novel *L'Astrée* incomplete.

Technically of the pastoral genre, the book, which was probably written in the late 1580s, was published in parts, but never finished. To a great extent, his relationship with Diane provided the inspiration for *L'Astrée*, which explores themes of human love and passion and draws on mythological, romantic, and chivalric traditions. In addition to *L'Astrée*, d'Urfé wrote a pastoral play called *La Silvanire*, completed in 1625, and several pastoral poems. His works also include a collection of his letters, *Epistres morales*, composed during his imprisonment, which explore both his grief and his hope for the future.

Bibliography

L. Horowitz, *Honoré d'Urfé*, 1984.

Erin Sadlack

VALDÉS, JUAN DE (c. 1500–1541)

Juan de Valdés was a Spanish humanist and religious writer who played a significant role in the intellectual and religious framework of Spain and its empire. Valdés was of *converso* descent on both sides; his father was the *regidor* of Cuenca. He had several brothers and was close to an older one, Alfonso, with whom he carried on frequent correspondence. Alfonso later became a Latin secretary to Emperor Charles V*; Juan himself may have been a page to the imperial court.

In 1523 Valdés went to Escalona, where he entered the service of Diego López Pacheco, an Erasmian who encouraged the *alumbrado* (spiritually enlightened) movement. During this time Valdés began to broaden his religious education, reading the Bible and Desiderius Erasmus,* but also some of the works by Reformers such as Martin Luther.*

By December 1527 he had entered the University of Alcalá, where he studied humanities and gained proficiency in Latin, Greek, and Hebrew. Valdés became acquainted with many Erasmian scholars in Alcalá and in 1529 published his *Dialogue on Christian Doctrine*, which highlighted many flagrant religious abuses. This work was not well received by the Inquisition, and Valdés found it prudent to leave Spain.

Valdés arrived in Rome, where he accepted a post from Charles V and obtained the position of papal chamberlain at the court of Pope Clement VII. He spent the rest of his life in Italy, writing in Spanish for an Italian audience. At Clement VII's death in 1534, Valdés moved to Naples and was shortly thereafter appointed inspector of fortifications by the viceroy. In 1535–36 Valdés experienced a deep religious experience perhaps provoked by a Lenten sermon of Bernardino Ochino.* Valdés afterwards moved toward open evangelical belief and created the so-called Valdésian circle at Naples, which consisted of several well-known like-minded associates. Valdés's house soon became a locus for literary and religious discussions; his conversations and his writings stimulated a desire for a spiritual reformation within the church. In 1534 Giulia Gonzaga* went to Naples and made Valdés her spiritual advisor. Several of his works are dedicated to her.

In 1535 Valdés published his *Dialogue on Language*, a philological treatise that circulated only in manuscript form until the eighteenth century. In this work, Valdés combined the Spanish language with his own grace, wit, and common sense in a masterfully humanistic spirit.

Throughout his stay at Naples, Valdés continued to write. He translated the Psalms and commented upon the first forty-one. He also translated and commented upon Matthew, Romans, and I Corinthians. Before his death in Naples in 1541, Valdés allegedly stated that he died in the same faith in which he had lived. He criticized the Protestant Reformers for disrupting the unity of the church, yet he also condemned or toned down certain ceremonies of the Catholic church.

Valdés's death scattered his band of associates. Most of his literary work, however, only became apparent after his death when some of his writings were published and admirers began to popularize his teaching. Valdés remains a difficult character to pinpoint doctrinally and has alternately been labeled a Catholic, an Anabaptist, and an Antitrinitarian.

Bibliography

J. Longhurst, *Erasmus and the Spanish Inquisition: The Case of Juan de Valdés*, 1950.
B. Wiffen, *Life and Writings of Juan de Valdés*, 1865.

Andrew G. Traver

VASARI, GIORGIO (1511–1574)

Giorgio Vasari was an Italian writer, painter, draughtsman, architect, and collector. Born in Arezzo, Vasari remained loyal to his Tuscan roots, placing his fellow Tuscans among those he felt were the best and the most innovative of the artists in the Renaissance in his *Lives of the Artists*. For this book he is often called the father of art history, though his observations are often subjective.

Vasari came from a family of potters (his name is derived from the Italian word for potter, *vasaio*). One should take his biographical data with a grain of salt, as almost all of them are based upon his autobiography. He was well educated in Latin and mythology and began his training as a painter with Guillaume de Marcillat, an artist familiar with Rome and its masterpieces. Vasari's connection with the Medici began in 1524, and he trained in Florence at that time in the workshops of Andrea del Sarto* and others.

After the Medici were expelled in 1527, Vasari went back to Arezzo, where he was influenced by the Mannerist painter Rosso Fiorentino.* He returned to Florence in 1532 and again worked for the Medici, painting portraits of Lorenzo the Magnificent and Alessandro (1534), using complex symbolism to convey personality traits of the sitters. When Alessandro was murdered in 1537, Vasari began working for the monks at Camaldoli. He traveled to Rome and returned to Camaldoli and Florence, where he painted the *Immaculate Conception* for

SS. Apostoli. This painting helped establish the subsequent iconography for the theme in later sixteenth-century and especially seventeenth-century art.

In the 1540s Vasari went to Venice with the writer Pietro Aretino,* for whose play *La talanta* he painted the stage set and the room where it was presented. Vasari also returned to Rome, where he and numerous assistants frescoed the Sala dei Cento Giorni (Room of one hundred days, the name based upon the time of execution), and went on to Naples.

In the late 1540s Vasari began writing the first edition of his *Lives of the Artists* (published in 1550). This work, published in a second edition in 1568, has proven to be his most important legacy. He interviewed contemporaries, looked at artworks of his illustrious predecessors, and provided a framework for the history of Italian Renaissance art that continues—despite serious critiques— to the present. Vasari put Tuscans, especially Florentines and Aretines, at the center of the new art of the Renaissance. He set up a structure of three periods. The first was dominated by Giovanni Cimabue and Giotto, the *primi lume* (first lights) of the late thirteenth and early fourteenth centuries. The second period of Vasari's construct roughly corresponds to the fifteenth century; he thought that these artists, such as Masaccio, improved upon the observation of nature. The third period, according to Vasari, culminated in the work of the master Michelangelo,* who enjoys the longest biography in Vasari's work.

In addition to his writing, Vasari continued working for the Medici after a stable dynasty under Cosimo I,* grand duke of Tuscany, was established in Florence. Cosimo asked Vasari to execute numerous works for the public spaces of sixteenth-century Florence. Most notably, Vasari painted the ceiling of the Sala dei Cinquecento (Hall of the Five Hundred), a meeting room designed at the turn of the century for the new Republic of Florence. The republican decoration by Leonardo da Vinci and Michelangelo had never been completed, and the republican ideas of the original patrons were subsumed in a glorification of the new aristocratic ruler. There are many battle scenes showing the victories of Florentine armies, but in the center there is an apotheosis of Cosimo I.

Vasari also designed the Uffizi, originally an office building for the administration of the Grand Duchy, but today the world-famous art gallery. In his design Vasari manipulated Renaissance architectural themes in a way that was undoubtedly inspired by Michelangelo's later architecture. He also designed the "Vasari corridor," a passage from the Uffizi over the top of the Ponte Vecchio that connected to the Palazzo Pitti on the left bank of the Arno, the new residence of the grand ducal family. Cosimo could therefore walk in safety from home to work without risking attacks from enemies. This gallery, much damaged during World War II, is now the home of the Uffizi's collection of artists' self-portraits.

Vasari was also one of the earliest serious collectors of drawings. Drawings were usually workshop property, used by apprentices to learn the techniques of the master, and thus were often worn to death by repeated handling. Vasari changed this idea by collecting drawings of master artists and mounting them in a book, the *Libro de disegni*. Thus he established the idea that the drawing, the *disegno*, was not just a sketch, but rather a major intellectual articulation of the artist's idea.

Bibliography

T. Boase, *Giorgio Vasari: The Man and the Book*, 1979.
G. Vasari, *Lives of the Artists*, trans. George Bull, 1987.

Lynne E. Johnson

VEGA, GARCILASO DE LA (c. 1501–1536)

Garcilaso de la Vega, a Spanish courtly poet-soldier, in his adaptation into Spanish of Italian meters, styles, and preoccupations, realized the poetic revolution initiated by his friend and predecessor, Juan Boscán. Born in Toledo to a noble family, Garcilaso served the court of Charles V.* He married Elena de Zúñiga in 1525 and had three children with her while addressing the majority of his love poems to the Portuguese Isabel Freyre, his courtly muse. In 1532 he was banished for attending a forbidden marriage without permission and ended up in Naples, where he served Pedro de Toledo, uncle of the duke of Alba. It was there that he completed his humanistic education and wrote his most important poems. In 1536 Garcilaso was fatally injured during an invasion in southern France.

Garcilaso's most significant contribution was his successful adaptation into Spanish of Italian poetry, including the Petrarchan love convention and Neoplatonic love. He thus established the standard and opened the doors for writers who followed. Garcilaso brought to Spanish poetry new rhythms, vocabulary, themes, and metaphorical expression and favored such poetic forms as the sonnet, Horatian ode, elegy, epistle, and eclogue. His poetic trajectory matured from his early *cancionero* works to Petrarchan courtly love poetry and, finally, his later Neoplatonic and classical poetry. Within each of these stages one also finds considerable variation and challenge to convention. His influence was immediate and widespread.

Garcilaso's complete poetry was first published in 1543, along with that of Boscán. It was later reedited with commentaries by El Broncense (1574) and Fernando de Herrera* (1580). The literary canonization of Garcilaso's work took place during that period. Modern editions include that of Elias Rivers (*Obras completas*, 1964) and *Poesías castellanas completas* (in Clásicos Calstalia, 1969). Garcilaso's works and role continue to attract the attention of contemporary scholars.

Bibliography

D. L. Heiple, *Garcilaso de la Vega and the Italian Renaissance*, 1994.

Lydia Bernstein

VEGA, GARCILASO INCA DE LA (1539–1616)

Garcilaso Inca de la Vega was a Spanish-Incan historian of Incan culture and of Spain's colonization of Peru and Florida. Born Gómez Suarez de Figueroa, the son of Spanish conquistador and poet Sebastián Garcilaso de la Vega and Incan princess Chimpu Ocllo, Garcilaso Inca de la Vega lived in his father's household in Peru until 1560. He was educated by his mother's family in the Incan language (Quechua) and culture and by Spanish tutors in Latin and rhetoric. At the age of fourteen, he began training in the military arts, in part as a result of Peruvian civil wars. In 1560 de la Vega traveled to Spain to complete his education. A catalog of his library indicates that he knew Quechua, Spanish, Latin, Italian, and probably Greek. He served as an officer in the Alpujarras wars (1570–71) before residing in Montilla, Spain, where his uncle, Alonso de Vargas, had an estate.

Garcilaso de la Vega is best known for his writing. His early works include *La traducción del indio los tres dialogos de amor de Leon Hebreo* (The translation of three dialogues on love, 1590), a translation of Neoplatonic dialogues; *Relación de la descendencia de Garci Pérez de Vargas* (Account of the Descendants of Garci Pérez de Vargas, 1596), a genealogy; and *La Florida del Inca* (Florida of the Inca, 1605), a history of Florida. His later works gained him the most renown, especially his history of the Incan people, *Comentarios reales de los Incas* (Royal Commentaries of the Inca, 1609). Its sequel, *Historia general del Perú* (General History of Peru, 1617), was published posthumously and continued the work of the *Comentarios* by describing the Spanish conquest and colonization of Peru from the Incan perspective. As a mestizo, de la Vega was particularly adroit at explaining the Incan culture in a way that European readers could understand. His histories were widely reprinted and translated, and he was recognized as the authoritative historian of Peru until the late eighteenth century. More recent scholars have examined his works' relationships to utopian literature, Christian world history, travelogues, historiography, and fiction, as well as to the humanist tradition and to anthropological studies of other Quechua narratives.

Bibliography

M. Zamora, *Language, Authority, and Indigenous History in the "Comentarios reales de los Incas,"* 1988.

Lydia Bernstein

VEGA, LOPE DE (1562–1635)

Credited with having created what is now called "the grand national theater of Spain," Lope Félix de Vega y Carpio wrote well over one thousand works of poetry as well as drama. Lope de Vega was extremely popular and admired by different social classes, perhaps due to having put so many of his works into print during his lifetime.

Lope de Vega was born in Madrid on 25 November 1562, a year after the monarch Philip II* made the city into the seat of the Spanish Empire. Lope's father had abandoned his wife and two sons in Valladolid for a life in Madrid, but his wife eventually followed him to the capital, won him back, and conceived Lope. Lope later alludes to this family adventure in his poem "Epistle to Amarilis." Lope's colleague and biographer Pérez de Montalban wrote that Lope was a brilliant student, far surpassing his classmates, and went on to study at the Jesuit College and later at the Royal Academy. Around 1577–82 Lope, under the patronage of the bishop of Ávila, attended the University of Alcalá, but abandoned his studies there due to "love problems."

An actor's daughter, Elena Osorio, was Lope's first significant love. In his poems, often drawn from life experiences, he alludes to Elena as "Filis." Years later, he resuscitates her in one of his major works, *La Dorotea*, a novel written with a dramatic structure. Elena was married, but her husband was frequently absent, and her family tolerated Lope as long as he kept turning out comedies for her father. After the couple broke up, Elena's father sued him for defamation, which landed Lope in jail and subsequently in an eight-year exile from the court and two-year exile from the kingdom under penalty of death.

After further adventures leading to a hasty marriage with a courtier's daughter, Isabel de Urbina, and a stint with the "invincible armada" at sea, he and Isabel moved to Valencia, where he produced many verse romances and comedies. His fame took off. After his sentence of exile expired, he moved to Toledo, where he became secretary to the duke of Alba and wrote his pastoral novel *La Arcadia*, in which Lope recorded the duke's amorous affairs. His wife, Isabel, died in 1594 while giving birth to their second daughter, who also died shortly thereafter. The poet then moved back to Madrid, where he married a wealthy butcher's daughter, Juana de Guardo. In 1614, after his wife, Juana, had died and his mistress with two surviving children had moved in with him, Lope was ordained a priest.

Like his love life, Lope's social life was fraught with highs and lows. Lope had always aspired to court circles, but despite his many titled acquaintances, connections, and employers, he was never truly accepted among the aristocracy. He was chronically impoverished throughout his life, which might have led in part to his enormous literary production. One of Lope's most ardent followers was the noted playwright Tirso de Molina. Another noted writer, Francisco de Quevedo, was also Lope's friend and commemorated him in *The Laurel of Apollo*. Yet Lope had his detractors, most notably the famous poet Luis de Góngora.* Besides Góngora, the most noted detractor was Cervantes,* who criticized Lope's new style of theater. But Cervantes was seldom publicly judgmental of Lope, despite having joined in Góngora's ridicule of Lope's self-invented family crest. Góngora, who wrote highly complex verse, never admired Lope's unadorned style, which he found vulgar.

Lope de Vega had written about 150 comedies by the turn of the century. Dubbed the "new comedy," his style is formulaic, but the themes are extremely varied. Written in an anachronistic style, often in a lyric present, the comedies are popular and vivacious, not elite. Setting aside the three unities of time, place, and action, Lope's momentum is unceasing, and there are great leaps in time and place. Lope does not separate tears from laughter, nobility from common life; often his comedies lack a marked protagonist. Lope developed a *gracioso*, or clownish figure, possibly based on an impoverished servant-student type frequently found in the universities. Rather than stick to the convention of unified meter, he varied his meter in accordance with the character or situation. His themes range across a wide variety of subjects: religion, mythology, chivalry, history, pastoral fictions, and Spanish legends. Of the last type, his most famous play is *Fuente Ovejuna*, a drama of collective revenge that deals with democracy, the noble character of the lower classes, and the role of the monarchy in disassembling the feudal system of nobility.

Bibliography

A. Flores, *Lope de Vega: Monster of Nature*, 1969.
H. Rennert, *The Life of Lope de Vega, 1562–1635*, 1968.
Y. Yarbro-Bejarano, *Feminism and the Honor Plays of Lope de Vega*, 1994.

Ana Kothe

VERGIL, POLYDORE (1470–1555)

Polydore Vergil was an Italian humanist scholar and antiquary who wrote a history of England that became compulsory in schools and influenced sixteenth-century chroniclers such as Edward Hall and Raphael Holinshed.* Born in Urbino, Italy, and educated in Padua and Bologna, Vergil became an ordained priest and secured a position in the chancery of Pope Alexander VI by 1496. In 1498 he published the *Proverbiorum libellus*, a collection of classical adages. In 1499 *De inventoribus rerum libri tres*, an antiquarian work on the origins of everything from mirrors to prostitution, precious metals, and navigation, appeared. In 1502 the pope sent him to England as a deputy collector of Peter's pence, an annual tax to support the papacy. Vergil was well received by Henry VII, as were most learned Italians who became useful to the advancement of the Tudor state. In 1503 he acquired the living of Church Langston in Leicestershire; in 1507, the prebendary of Lincoln and Hereford; and in 1508, the archdeaconry of Wells. Vergil was naturalized in 1510, became prebendary of St. Paul's in 1513, and began to move in learned circles.

Vergil corresponded with Desiderius Erasmus* and became friends with Sir Thomas More.* At the request of Henry VII in 1505, Vergil began the *Anglicae historiae libri xxvi*, a history of England from its beginnings to the present, which was finished in 1513, but not published until 1534. This work challenged the traditional mythic view of England's founding by the Trojan Brutus, created originally by Geoffrey of Monmouth in the twelfth century. In 1582 the Privy Council made the *Anglicae historiae* required reading in English schools because of its influence on the chronicles of Hall and Holinshed, the latter being a favorite source of William Shakespeare.*

Bibliography

D. Hay, *Polydore Vergil: Renaissance Historian and Man of Letters*, 1952.

Richard J. Ring

VERONESE, PAOLO (1528–1588)

One of Venice's greatest decorative painters, Paolo Veronese invented a Mannerist pictorial language uniquely suited to large-scale decorative styles. Born in Verona, Italy, into a family of artisans, Veronese entered the workshop of Antonio Badile by the age of fourteen. A precocious artist, Veronese was already working on his own four years later. He was working in Mantua in 1552; the art of Giulio Romano,* with its sculptural tendency and dramatic foreshortenings, heavily influenced Veronese's work in the ducal palace in Venice one year later. Not long after, his paintings for the Church of San Sebastiano showed his mastery of illusion by this time and a new and active approach to painted architecture that became united with the subject of the painting. He was a consummate scenic designer, and his architectural constructions reflected not just the architecture of Sanmicheli, but also an awareness of Sebastiano Serlio's recently published work on theatrical scenery. Veronese utilized an artificial and decorative approach to coloring in which accents are produced with contrasting tints frequently possessing pale and acidulous qualities. Not yet thirty, Veronese participated in the decoration of the Marciana Library, and according to tradition, Titian* judged Veronese's work the most beautiful and awarded him a golden chain. In the Villa Barbaro at Maser, designed by Andrea Palladio* for Marcantonio and Daniele Barbaro,* Veronese gave pictorial form to Daniele's complex humanist program exalting the universal harmony of the cosmos as he continued to explore classical culture in many details.

Back in Venice, Veronese worked on several commissions and produced a series of paintings of huge sumptuous feasts showing an unparalleled scenic grandiosity and choral effect. In 1573 Veronese completed his *Feast in the House of Levi* (Venice, Accademia), in which he painted a Venetian feast with soldiers, banqueters, buffoons, and exotic animals. The painting was originally intended as a Last Supper, but Veronese was forced to change the name of the composition to avoid charges of heresy and the destruction of the painting by the Inquisition. Back in the ducal palace after the devastating fires there, Veronese extolled the virtues of the good government of the republic in the Sala del Collegio and painted the *Triumph of Venice* in the Sala del Maggior Consiglio. Veronese's decorative approach to color with its unique synthesis of color and light, his sound sense of design and drawing, his skill in the staging of figural groups, and his incorporation of painted architecture combined to form an artistic language perfectly adapted to such glorifying, monumental decorative projects. As Veronese's fame continued to grow, he received requests from various courts like that of Rudolf II* at Prague. Despite the heavy demands and Veronese's extensive use of workshop assistants, among whom were numbered two of his sons and his brother, the quality of the studio's production remained high. Later in his life, Veronese revealed an increasing religious emotionality in his paintings, which may have resulted from various influences, including the Council of Trent's demand that artists should identify with the emotional themes they represented, the death of one of his sons, and his own declining health.

Bibliography

T. Pignatti and F. Pedrocco, *Veronese: Catalogo completo dei di pinti*, 1991.
W. Rearick, *The Art of Paolo Veronese, 1528–1588*, exhibition catalog, 1988.
D. Rosand, *Painting in Cinquecento Venice: Titian, Veronese, Tintoretto*, 1982.

Mary Pixley

VESALIUS, ANDREAS (1514–1564)

Andreas Vesalius is known to posterity as the founder of modern anatomy. He emphasized dissection of cadavers to acquire anatomical and surgical knowledge rather than relying on established authorities, especially Galen.

Born in Brussels in 1514, Vesalius began attending school in Louvain in 1529. He left to study medicine at Paris in 1533 and soon followed a revived classical school of thought led by Guinter of Andernach and Jacobus Sylvius, both of whom favored Galenic anatomy. Vesalius was forced to return to Louvain in 1536 due to the war between François I* and Charles V,* and in 1537 he received his bachelor of medicine.

From Louvain Vesalius traveled to Padua, which maintained the most renowned medical faculty in Italy. After a few months of impressive study, the faculty allowed him to teach and bestowed upon him a doctor of medicine. Vesalius held the chair of surgery at Padua and consequently improved upon his reputation in the field of anatomy. He continued to follow Galenist tradition, although his *Tabulae anatomicae*, published in 1538, displayed some original thinking. The collection of anatomical drawings combined with text departed from tradition and represented the beginning of a separation from Galenic anatomy. He proved that Galen's description of human anatomy was based on animals, especially the ape. Galen did not have the opportunities to dissect human cadavers as did Vesalius, who had the luxury of dissecting executed criminals in Padua.

Vesalius moved further from Galen in his *Venesection Letter* of 1539, which stressed the importance of dissection rather than blindly following revered authorities. Students and faculty alike admired his new dissection methods, but at a public dissection in Bologna in 1540, many walked out after Vesalius attempted to disprove Galen. Vesalius demonstrated his scientific independence, which attracted younger students but alienated the conservatives in the field. Many medical leaders criticized Vesalius for opposing Galen and the classics.

In 1543 Vesalius journeyed to Basel to publish *De humani corporis fabrica* (On the Structure of the Human Body), which became the most influential and important work of his career. *Fabrica* was an extremely detailed work based on human dissection. It corrected many medieval and Galenic errors in human anatomy, but surprisingly left many uncorrected. *Fabrica* served as one of the first anatomy textbooks aiming to reach those that were not the author's students or did not have access to a cadaver. The illustrations, done by Jan van Calcar, were remarkable for their extraordinary detail, especially regarding skeletal and muscular structure. *Fabrica* received much criticism for disputing Galen, but many contemporaries realized its importance. It influenced physicians to acquire hands-on training through dissection, it added to nomenclature by applying names that describe a body part, and it influenced future comparative anatomists (although Vesalius is not considered a true comparative anatomist). Vesalius began to develop anatomy as a science first and foremost, thus displacing the theological and philosophical elements traditionally attached to anatomy.

Vesalius left Basel in 1543 to present *Fabrica* to Charles V at the imperial court. Charles was sufficiently impressed with Vesalius and his work to appoint him physician to the imperial household, a position he held until Charles's abdication. Vesalius accompanied the emperor on various campaigns, which occasionally gave him the opportunity to lecture at academic centers. In 1546 he published the *Letter on the China Root*, which explains how the China root can be used to treat syphilis. In the letter he also defends *Fabrica* against the Galenist supporters, primarily his former teacher Sylvius. Vesalius continued his anatomical research while he was employed in the imperial service and responded to his critics in a timely manner. He even republished *Fabrica* in 1555, correcting many of his own errors but adding no outstanding discoveries to his prior work.

Charles abdicated in 1556, and Vesalius, previously named count palatine, received a pension with no duties. His medical reputation was evident in 1559 when he was called upon to examine the eventually fatal head injury of Henri II of France. Vesalius went to Spain at this point to become a physician to the Netherlanders at court. He attended upon Philip II* occasionally and was summoned to attend Philip's eldest son, Don Carlos, who sustained an ultimately fatal injury when he fell down a flight of stairs chasing a girl. Vesalius published his last major work, *Examen*, in 1564, which was primarily biographical and holds no scientific importance.

Vesalius left Spain in 1564 to pilgrimage to the Holy Land; however, on his return trip from Jerusalem, he became ill and died on the Greek island of Zante. The most important achievement of his life was the publication of *Fabrica*, which influenced later generations to further develop the science of anatomy through human dissection.

Bibliography

F. J. Cole, *A History of Comparative Anatomy: From Aristotle to the Eighteenth Century*, 1949.
C. D. O'Malley, *Andreas Vesalius of Brussels, 1514–1564*, 1964.
A. Serafini, *The Epic History of Biology*, 1993.

Paul Miller

VETTORI, PIERO (1499–1585)

Piero Vettori stands as one of the foremost representatives of the practice of sixteenth-century classical humanism in Italy. Born in Florence, Italy, Vettori first studied physics and mathematics under the direction of the Carmelite Giuliano Ristorio before turning to the study of Greek and Latin under the tutelage of Andrea Dazzi and Virgilio Adriani. Before finally settling into a career as a classical philologist, he spent some time in 1514 at Pisa engaged briefly in the study of law. Upon his return to his villa at San Casciano in the outskirts of Florence, he took up the humanist activity of commenting on ancient texts that he collected.

Vettori, like Niccolò Machiavelli,* had supported the cause of republicanism in Florence and in that cause had delivered a speech rallying the local militia. As a result, from 1530 to 1532 he came under suspicion by the newly restored Medici regime and cautiously retired from the city to his villa, where he resumed the contemplative life. His scholarly efforts in the fields of dialectics, theology, and natural philosophy in close collaboration with the Neoplatonic philosopher Francesco de Vieri (il Verino) brought him by 1538 to the attention of Duke Cosimo I,* who offered him the post of lecturer of Greek and Latin at the Studio di Firenze, a position Vettori held until two years before his death. During these productive years he became active in the Accademia Fiorentina and traveled occasionally to other Italian cities such as Venice, where he was in contact with scholars of similar mind. His prodigious scholarship in many ways helped fulfill Petrarch's vision to restore the best of Greek as well as Latin classical writing to western Europe. Vettori edited and commented upon Cicero's letters and political writings, Aristotle's works on poetry and rhetoric, and various texts by Aeschylus, Euripides, Plato, Sallust, and Terence. Additionally, he edited the Latin works of his friend and contemporary Giovanni Della Casa.* Vettori's interests, conveyed through his surviving correspondence and published orations (*Epistolarum libri X, Orationes XIV, et liber de laudibus Iohannae Austriacae*, 1586), like those of his humanist contemporaries, focus primarily on moral and ethical concerns identified by Cicero and Aristotle that he saw as germane to issues of his own generation. His broad education and concern with practical matters also led him to compose a work in the Tuscan vernacular on the cultivation of olives (*Trattato delle lodi et della coltivatione de gl'ulivi*, 1569).

Bibliography

G. Fragnito, *Memoria individuale e costruzione biografica: Beccadelli, Della Casa, Vettori alle origini di un mito*, 1978.

Luci Fortunato DeLisle

VICENTE, GIL (c. 1456–1537)

Gil Vicente, a Portuguese dramatist, is a leading literary figure bridging the medieval and Renaissance traditions. A man of many talents, he was overseer of the gold and silver craft in Portugal, master of the royal mint, and a member of the Lisbon town council, as well as a musician, poet, and actor. His works were published for the first time by his son, Luis Vicente, as the *Copilacam de toda las obras de Gil Vicente* (Compilation, 1562).

Of Vicente's forty-four extant plays, sixteen are completely in Portuguese, eleven are completely in Spanish, and seventeen combine both languages. His early works are rather simple and are heavily derivative. Works written after 1520 reveal a greater originality as a definite artistic personality emerges. The later works reflect Vicente's mastery of style, language, and the stage and include chivalric, allegorical, and popular plays.

Vicente's first extant play is the *Visitação* (The visitation, 1502), or *Monólogo do vaqueiro* (Herdsman's Monologue). The *Auto pastoril castelhano* (Castilian Pastoral Play, 1502), the *Auto dos Reis Magos* (Play of the Magi, 1503), and the *Auto de San Martinho* (Play of St. Martin, 1504) reveal his debt to Juan del Encina, the Castilian playwright. The *Auto da Sibilla Cassandra* (The Play of the Sibyl Cassandra, 1513 or 1514) in particular is noted for its fine lyricism. Vicente's celebrated trilogy *Trilogia de las barcas* (The Three Ships, 1516–19) and the *Auto da feira* (The Festival Play, 1525) illustrate his capacity for the social and anticlerical satire of the Erasmian tradition. Vicente's later works reveal his gifts as a mature artist. The *Comédia de Rubena* (The Play of Rubena, 1521) is a fantastic comedy filled with lyricism and pageantry, drawing from popular and folkloric traditions. Vicente's two chivalric tragicomedies, *Dom Duardos* (1522 or 1525) and *Amadis de Gaula* (1523 or 1533), are both in Spanish and represent his most highly developed efforts. Vicente's farces make a major contribution to the development of the theatrical tradition. They combine learned and popular elements designed to entertain the audience with comic caricatures of social types and customs. They include *Farsa de Inés Pereira* (The Farce of Inés Pereira, 1523), *O velho da horta* (The Old Man of the Orchard, 1512), and *Quem tem farelos?* (Who has Bran? 1508 or 1515).

Vicente's finest achievement is the outstanding lyrical expression of popular themes. These transformations of anonymous folkloric motifs into splendid lyrical creations are unrivaled in the theater until the time of Lope de Vega.*

Bibliography

S. Reckert, *Gil Vicente, espiritu y letra*, 1977.

Deborah Compte

VICTORIA, TOMÁS LUIS DE (1548–1611)

Tomás Luis de Victoria was the greatest Spanish composer of the Renaissance. In his life and works, the ideals of the Catholic Reformation found their quintessential musical expression.

Victoria was born in Ávila and received his early musical training there as a choirboy in the cathedral. After his voice broke, he was sent to the Jesuit German College in Rome, where he doubtless came into contact with Giovanni Pierluigi da Palestrina,* who was at that time choirmaster of the nearby Roman Seminary. In 1569 he accepted a part-time position as singer and organist at the Church of S. Maria di Monserrato, and from 1571 he taught music at the German College, where he also served as choirmaster from 1575 to 1577. He entered the priesthood in 1575, and from 1578 until 1585 he held a nonmusical position as chaplain at S. Girolamo della Carità, the church where St. Philip Neri* held his famous religious meetings. With the support of five Spanish benefices conferred by Pope Gregory XIII, he now devoted himself to his priestly duties and charitable works, serving in 1583–84, for example, as visitor of the sick for the Spanish Archconfraternity of the Resurrection. But it was also during these years that he published five deluxe folio editions of his music. In the dedication of his 1583 mass book to Philip II,* Victoria expressed his desire to return to Spain. In response, Philip named him chaplain to his sister, the dowager empress Maria, at the Convento de las Descalzas Reales in Madrid. Following the empress's death in 1603, Victoria remained at the convent, serving as maestro of the choir until 1604 and organist until his own death in 1611.

Victoria's compositions include about fifty motets and over twenty masses in addition to magnificats, hymns, and other liturgical pieces. He wrote only Latin sacred music, and his output, compared to that of William Byrd,* Orlando di Lasso,* or Palestrina, is both small and limited in scope. But in technical refinement and expressive power, he was unsurpassed. In the dramatic intensity of his music, moreover, modern critics have heard a parallel to the spiritual fervor and mysticism of Spanish contemporaries such as El Greco* and St. Teresa of Ávila.*

Bibliography

R. Stevenson, "Tomás Luis de Victoria (ca. 1548–1611): Unique Spanish Genius," *Inter-American Music Review* 12 (1991): 1–100.

David Crook

VIGNOLA, JACOPO BAROZZI DA (1507–1573)

Jacopo Barozzi da Vignola, an Italian painter, architect, and theorist, took the name of his native town. His painting is not well known today, and it has been suggested that his lack of success in that medium was due to poor training. Architecture, however, was another matter entirely. He worked as an assistant to Baldassare Peruzzi* and was also influenced by Sebastiano Serlio. He moved to Rome in the 1530s, spent most of the 1540s working in Bologna (where his plans for the cathedral were undermined by political and intellectual intrigues), and settled again in Rome from 1550 on, executing numerous commissions for the powerful and papal Farnese family. His major architectural monuments are the Gesù (the mother church of the Jesuit order) in Rome and the Villa Farnese in Caprarola, not far from Rome.

The Villa Farnese at Caprarola combined a fortified pentagonal exterior with a circular courtyard inside. In addition to his innovative transformation of an already-fortified structure into a pleasant summer house, Vignola used his skills as an urban planner to facilitate the arrival of guests and to provide extraordinary organized views of the surrounding countryside.

The Gesù (1568–75) was also a Farnese commission. It has a single vaulted nave with side chapels, an idea perhaps adapted from the fifteenth-century Church of Sant' Andrea in Mantua by Leonbattista Alberti. Though Vignola's original version of the Gesù was altered by Giacomo Della Porta, the Counter-Reformation ideas and classical motifs used were most influential in Jesuit churches throughout the world.

Vignola also collaborated on stage sets, notably with Perino del Vega for a production of Niccolò Macchiavelli's* *Clizia* at the Farnese Palace (1541). His intellectual life was centered on the Accademia della Virtù, a private society dedicated to publishing a definitive edition of Vitruvius, the ancient Roman writer on architecture.

It was probably this interest in ancient architectural theory that prompted Vignola to write his two theoretical treatises on architecture. The *Regola delli cinque ordine d'architettura* (Rule of the Five Orders of Architecture, c. 1562) gave a universal rule for the proportions of the five orders (Doric, Ionic, Corinthian, Composite, and Tuscan). The illustrations were very clear, and the text was kept to a minimum. There were more than five hundred editions of this work, with translations into many languages. Vignola's second book, *Le due regole della prospettiva pratica* (The Two Rules of the Practice of Perspective, 1583), explains the Albertian (fifteenth-century) perspectival system as well as another method of achieving the illusion of perspective. At his death, Vignola was buried in the Pantheon in Rome, an honor previously accorded to Raphael.*

Bibliography

W. Lotz and L. H. Heydenreich, *Architecture in Italy, 1400 to 1600*, 1974.

Lynne E. Johnson

VITORIA, FRANCISCO DE (c. 1483–1546)

A Dominican theologian and the founder of modern international law, Francisco de Vitoria constructed a theory of international society and of sovereign, independent nation-states. Vitoria also outlined the rights and responsibilities of the Spanish Empire in its governance of the conquered peoples of the Americas. When he assumed the principal chair of theology at the University of Salamanca in 1526, Vitoria introduced the use of Thomas Aquinas's *Summa theologica*, a text that dominated Catholic theological education into the twentieth century.

Vitoria addressed important political and legal issues of his day over a twenty-year period at the beginning of each academic year. In *De potestate civili* Vitoria examined the scope of power of the rising nation-states. He maintained that civil societies must be complete within themselves, with their own laws and authority, and that citizens should be free to choose the form of government and the leaders of their society.

The rights of the Spanish Crown to colonize the newly conquered lands of the Americas and the question of its dealings with its peoples were hotly debated topics. In *De Indis* Vitoria argued for the property rights of the native Americans. However, he also admitted that the Spanish state might be justified in conquering backward peoples as long as it was in their interests and not principally for the benefit of the Spaniards.

De Indis also dealt with the relationship of sovereign nations to each other, thus defining principles of international law for the first time. Vitoria envisioned the creation of a world organization that would govern the international community and have the authority to impose its will. Vitoria anticipated the thinking that led to the creation of the League of Nations and the United Nations.

Bibliography

L. Getino, *El maestro fray Francisco de Vitoria: Su vida, su doctrina e influencia*, 1930.

Evelyn Toft

VITTORIA, ALESSANDRO (1525–1608)

Best known for his exceptional portrait busts, the Italian sculptor and stuccoist Alessandro Vittoria worked in Venice and northern Italy in the second half of the sixteenth century. Vittoria received his early training as a sculptor in Venice with Jacopo Sansovino,* who led one of the largest and busiest workshops active in the architectural renewal of the city. By 1550 Vittoria was executing his first independent works, which reflect the influence of Sansovino's Tuscan style. As seen in his impressive *St. Jerome* from the Zane altar at the Church of the Frari of 1570, Vittoria later infused his sculptures with the monumental and twisting forms inspired by the art of Michelangelo* and the refined and attenuated figural style of Parmigianino.* The resulting graceful Mannerist style balancing dynamic movement and beautiful forms could also be seen in many of the small bronze statuettes bearing his signature that were widely reproduced in Venice. Vittoria was also in great demand as a portrait sculptor of the illustrious patriciate of Venice. In these images, he did not just portray a likeness of the sitter, but captured the dignity of the figure as he balanced idealism and realism both to reflect the person's appearance and to communicate an image of the sitter.

From 1551 to 1553 Vittoria lived in Vicenza, where he established himself as a stuccoist known for his imaginative and luxurious stucco ornament both there and in Venice. Frequently collaborating with Andrea Palladio,* he worked with Paolo Veronese* in the decoration of the famous Villa Barbaro designed by Palladio. Vittoria maintained an important and influential role in sculpture until his death. His sculpted altars may even be seen as an early manifestation of the baroque with their incorporation of unorthodox architecture and figures that detach from the frame.

Bibliography

B. Boucher, *The Sculpture of Jacopo Sansovino*, 1991.
J. Pope-Hennessy, *Italian High Renaissance and Baroque Sculpture*, 1963.

Mary Pixley

VIVES, JUAN LUIS (1492–1540)

An important sixteenth-century humanist, the Spanish philosopher, scholar, and social reformer Juan Luis Vives also broke new ground in education and philosophy. Born in Valencia, Vives left Spain in 1509 because of the Inquisition. From 1509 to 1514 he lived in Paris and studied at Montaigu College. Here Vives learned about Renaissance humanism and its rejection of medieval Scholasticism, a subject he addresses in *Adversus pseudodialecticos* (Against the Pseudodialecticians, 1519).

Never returning to Spain, Vives moved to Bruges and became a tutor of Guillaume de Croy in 1517. As professor of humanities at Louvain by 1519, Vives met Desiderius Erasmus* and joined his international humanist circle. At Erasmus's behest, Vives published, in 1522, his commentary on Augustine's *City of God*, which criticized clergy and friars and perhaps unintentionally aided in promoting ideas central to the Reformation.

Because Vives dedicated his commentary to Henry VIII,* he was invited to teach at Corpus Christi College, Oxford, where he lectured on philosophy. He also became court counsellor and secretary to Henry's Valencia-born queen Catherine of Aragon. Although he never tutored Henry and Catherine's daughter Mary,* Vives guided her parents about her education. In England, Vives met Thomas More,* involved himself in More's humanist circle, grew disinterested in theological reform, and became more interested in educational, social, and legal change. He spent summers in England and winters in Bruges until, in 1527, he lost Henry's favor when he opposed Henry's divorce and was imprisoned for six weeks. Henceforth he remained in Bruges and devoted himself to writing.

Vives was skilled in Latin, and his dialogues in *Exercitatio linguae Latinae* (School dialogues in Latin, 1538) were utilized in schools throughout Europe; his *De tradendis disciplinis* (The Transmission of Knowledge, 1531) argued for reforming the curriculum at all levels; and his *De institutione feminae Christianae* (On the Instruction of a Christian Woman, 1523) advocated expanding the scope of women's education. *De subventione pauperum* (Concerning the Relief of the Poor, 1526) explored ways to relieve the poor financed by secular authority, and *Aedes legum* (The Temple of the Law, 1519) mocked jargon used in legislation. Although he warned rulers to beware of Turkish aggression, Vives denounced the wars dividing Europe. In *De anima et vita* (The Soul and Life, 1538), he examined emotions and connected their control to order and peace. He also wrote *De veritate fidei* (The True Faith), an apology for Christianity (posthumously published in 1543). The issues Vives championed—rejecting Scholasticism, reforming education, relieving poverty, attaining world peace, and exploring human psychology and ways of learning, among others—all mark his place as a Renaissance humanist who influenced not only his times but ours as well.

Bibliography

C. G. Norena, *Juan Luis Vives*, 1970.

Al Geritz

W

WALDSEEMÜLLER, MARTIN (1470–1518)

Martin Waldseemüller, a mapmaker, book publisher, and canon of the Church of St. Dié in Lorraine, coined the term "America" as the name for the "New World" to honor, erroneously, the Italian navigator Amerigo Vespucci as its "discoverer." In 1507 Waldseemüller both printed the first world map, a woodcut, to incorporate "America" and published his *Cosmographiae introductio* with purported accounts of Vespucci's four voyages. He produced another edition of his map in 1513 that updated its portrayal of the American coastline and dropped "America," supporting instead Columbus's prior claim to "discovery." However, the term had already caught on.

Waldseemüller's quite large (fifty-three by ninety-four inches) and famous map remained the basis for western European perceptions of the world for approximately the next thirty years. Using the latest reports from Spanish and Portuguese voyages, he was able to depict the "New World" in two separate parts that identified all the sightings that had been made from Labrador to Argentina. He also provided a reasonably detailed picture of Africa. But Waldseemüller's maps were, by design, reprints of Ptolemy's *Geographia*. Thus he grossly overextended Asia eastwards and perpetuated Ptolemy's conical projection of landmasses. As a result, the portrayal here of northern latitudes, a problem generated by the curvature of the earth, is, from a modern standpoint, hopelessly distorted. Subsequently, in his *Carta marina navigatoria Portugallen*, Waldseemüller adopted the newly prevalent view of the world and brought the eastern boundary of Asia more into accord with today's knowledge.

Waldseemüller's *Cosmographiae introductio* was likewise linked to the learning of antiquity. Its earth, like Aristotle's, consisted of evenly balanced frigid, temperate, and torrid zones. Waldseemüller was aware of the geographical changes brought about by discovery, but he apparently did not grasp the intellectual and social ramifications of a "New World."

Bibliography

N.J.W. Thrower, *Maps and Civilization*, 2nd ed., 1999.
M. Waldseemüller, *Cosmographiae introductio*, 1507; trans. J. Fischer, 1907.

Louis Roper

WEBSTER, JOHN (c. 1580–c. 1634)

John Webster, a dramatic poet and playwright who flourished during the first twenty years of the seventeenth century, is best known for his melodramatic style emphasizing terror and pity. He was at times a collaborative writer; Webster's two tragedies, *The White Devil* and *The Duchess of Malfi*, contributed to the development of Elizabethan drama as well as the revenge tradition.

Nearly nothing is known about Webster's life, and a great deal of his work has been lost. First mentioned in Philip Henslowe's* diary in 1602, Webster collaborated with many writers, most notably George Chapman* and Thomas Dekker.* During an early apprenticeship he worked with Dekker on such plays as *Northward Ho! Westward Ho!* and *The Famous History of Sir Thomas Wyatt.* By 1604 Webster was writing for William Shakespeare's* company.

Scholars generally argue that Webster's talent as a tragic poet outweighs his merit as a playwright. This talent is clearly presented in his two great tragedies, *The White Devil* (1601–2) and *The Duchess of Malfi* (1613–14). Webster was a follower of the Senecan revenge tradition; his plays wax morbid and brooding, and his characters are motivated by their passions. The duchess, an intriguing heroine, is the victim of revenge. Her death consumes the entire fourth act of the play, displaying a hint of Webster's taste for the horrific. Webster uses supernatural themes, employs horror and gloom, and evokes a great pathos. In the eighteenth century Nathan Drake complimented his "demonic forcefulness of phrase," but Webster's plot construction is at times weak. However, there can be no question of Webster's greatness as a tragic poet.

His obsession with the idea of vengeance changed Elizabethan drama's concept of revenge. Webster's pity lay with the victim, not the avenger. The avenging character is no longer the proper hero but Webster's villain. Revenge falls from a noble calling to a petty excuse. Revenge is a drive that overpowers Webster's characters, not a duty of society. Webster was apparently appreciated in his own time, since publishers often gave his name emphasis on title pages equal to that of Shakespeare. His appeal survives; both *The White Devil* and *The Duchess of Malfi* are still produced today.

Bibliography

M. L. Ranald, *John Webster*, 1989.

Karolyn Kinane

WESTON, ELIZABETH JANE (1582–1612)

Elizabeth Jane Weston, known as "Westonia," was a brilliant poet, scholar, and exile. Her background is ambiguous, and there seems to be some question over whether Elizabeth and her brother John Francis Weston, two years older, were the illegitimate children of a noble.

When her children were infants, Joanna Cooper Weston married Edward Kelley, the assistant of the learned magician John Dee.* Dee and his entourage soon after left England for the Continent. Dee returned to England in 1587, but Kelley and his family stayed on. Kelley received a knighthood from Emperor Rudolf II* in 1589 and soon after removed his family to Jilov. Kelley, himself intellectually gifted, insisted on a fine education for both his stepson and step-daughter. Despite the knighthood, Kelley offended the emperor, and he was imprisoned in 1591 in the town of Most. Joanna and her daughter then moved to Most, where Elizabeth continued her education. By the time she was fourteen, Elizabeth was writing Latin verse and was also fluent in Italian, German, and Czech. Kelley remained in prison until his death in 1597. All his property was confiscated, and the situation of Elizabeth and her mother became even more desperate and tragic when John Francis died in 1600 while still a student. In 1601 Elizabeth and her mother moved to Prague. Elizabeth wrote Latin verse seeking patronage from nobles at the emperor's court as a way to support herself and her mother. Elizabeth was also a skilled calligrapher. Her skill as a poet as well as her reputed grace, wit, and beauty led to her success at finding court patrons and to the publication of some of her poems in 1602.

Though Elizabeth had left England as a small child, English was spoken in her family home, and she had a strong identity as an English woman. Especially after the deaths of Kelley and her brother, she wished to return to England and wrote some poems that she sent in 1603 to the new king, James I.* James, however, was appalled by educated women and suggested that the poems were probably ghostwritten, which deeply hurt Elizabeth.

Her fortunes improved in 1603 when she married Johann Leo, or Lowe, a lawyer and agent of the duke of Braunschweig-Wolfenbüttel at the imperial court, who aided her and her mother in their legal fight with the emperor to have Kelley's estate returned to them. Leo also edited her poetry for publication. Elizabeth revised some of her poems as well as adding new ones for a new edition that was probably published in 1607. Elizabeth had four sons and three daughters in the nine years of her marriage, but she died in Prague on 23 November 1612. Only the three daughters survived her.

Bibliography

S. Bassnett, "Revising a Biography: A New Interpretation of the Life of Elizabeth Jane Weston (Westonia) Based on Her Autobiographical Poem on the Occasion of the Death of Her Mother," *Cahiers Élisabéthains* 37 (April 1990): 1–8.
L. Schleiner, *Tudor and Stuart Women Writers*, 1994.

Carole Levin

WILLAERT, ADRIAN (c. 1490–1562)

Adrian Willaert was a versatile and influential Flemish composer and teacher who spent much of his career in Italy, most notably as maestro di cappella of

St. Mark's Cathedral in Venice. Born most likely in Bruges, Willaert went to Paris to study law, but soon turned his attention to music. He studied with Jean Mouton, a composer at the royal chapel of Louis XII and François I.* Willaert's professional life began with several posts in Rome, Ferrara, and Milan (c. 1515–27) in which he served various members of the powerful Este family. In 1527 he assumed the prestigious post at St. Mark's. There he composed and became teacher to many of Europe's finest young musicians. Among his students were the theorist Gioseffe Zarlino and the composers Cipriano de Rore* and Andrea Gabrieli.

Willaert's versatility can be seen in the wide variety of his music. His sacred works include masses, motets, hymns, settings of the Magnificat, and psalm settings. Of particular interest are his vesper psalms for double chorus, or *cori spezzati*, designed to exploit the two facing balconies of St. Mark's. In the realm of secular music, Willaert composed French chansons, participated in the early development of the Italian madrigal, and contributed to the rise of purely instrumental music with his nine ricercares. His *Musica nova* of 1559, a collection of thirty-three motets and twenty-five madrigals, is considered to be one of his most significant works.

The fluid polyphony of Willaert's mature works is often seen as the culmination of Renaissance *prima prattica* style. His techniques for his text setting, characterized by careful attention to declamation and to creating the appropriate musical mood, laid the foundation for the Renaissance madrigal and for much vocal music of the late baroque period.

Bibliography

L. Lockwood and J. Owens, "Adrian Willaert," in S. Sadie, ed., *The New Grove Dictionary of Music and Musicians*, vol. 20, 1980: 421–28.

Tucker Robison

WIMPFELING, JAKOB (1450–1528)

Jakob Wimpfeling was a conservative German Renaissance humanist who tirelessly worked for educational reforms. Born in the old imperial Alsatian city of Schlettstadt (today Selestat, France), Wimpfeling attended the local Latin school and, at age fourteen, enrolled at the University of Freiburg im Breisgau, where he received his bachelor of arts in 1466. After a brief sojourn at the University of Erfurt, he studied and taught at the University of Heidelberg, obtaining a master of arts in 1471 and the baccalaureate in theology in 1479, and rapidly climbed the academic ladder, becoming the dean of the arts faculty and rector of the university. After the plague put an end to his activities in Heidelberg, in 1483 he moved to nearby Speyer to become a cathdedral canon. He rejoined the faculty in Heidelberg in 1498, answering a call from Elector Philip of the Palatinate to work on university reform. In 1501 he left Heidelberg and spent the next fourteen years in Strasbourg, joining his friends Johannes Geiler von Kayserberg and Sebastian Brant there and founding a literary society around 1508 on the model of the loose associations Conrad Celtis had established earlier in various parts of Europe. In 1515 he moved back to Schlettstadt, where he died.

Although Wimpfeling was a prolific writer working in such diverse fields as literature, church history, politics, and theology, his work is dominated by two major themes: his concern for the correct education of the youth and his historiographical interests. In the former area, his most important works are two educational treatises, *Isidoneus Germanicus* (Guide to German Youth, 1497) and *Adolescentia* (Youth, 1500). Filled with extensive quotations and pragmatic tips for moral living, these works also reveal the very tentative nature of his humanism. In contrast to many other humanists, Wimpfeling did not appreciate ancient literature for its own sake but allowed its study only for the development of a good Latin style and for the moral teachings it offered. For this reason, his choice of Latin authors was very selective and was always filtered through the lenses of his orthodox Christianity. If his interests in pedagogy were one of his concerns, his historical studies, informed by a fierce patriotism, were another. They prompted him to write a number of works, among them a treatise called *Germania* (1501), a rambling work in which he tried to prove that his native Alsace had always been inhabited by Germans. Also inspired by his patriotism was his work *Epithoma rerum Germanicarum* (A Short History of Germany, 1505). It is remarkable for its treatment not only of the military and political matters but also of the cultural history, comprising a veritable hall of fame of theologians, poets, musicians, historians, architects, sculptors, and painters. The work contributed decisively to the development of a German historiography.

Wimpfeling's views and his somewhat cantankerous nature involved him in a number of bitter scholarly feuds: he quarreled with the Augustinians, whom he angered by denying that St. Augustine had been a monk; with the Swiss, whom he blamed for having left the empire; and with the flamboyant humanist Jakob Locher, whom he accused of corrupting the youth.

Though Wimpfeling vehemently attacked ecclesiastical abuses and at first welcomed Martin Luther,* he sharply rejected the Reformer after 1521 when it had become clear to him that the Lutheran movement was leading to a schism of the church. He died a lonely and bitter man in his native town.

Bibliography

E. Bernstein, *German Humanism*, 1983.

J. H. Overfield, "Jakob Wimpfeling," in *German Writers of the Renaissance and Reformation, 1280–1580*, Dictionary of Literary Biography, 179, 1997: 317–25.

Eckhard Bernstein

WORDE, WYNKYN DE (d. 1535)

Wynkyn de Worde was the student and successor of William Caxton, England's first printer, and he produced more than eight hundred editions of almost four hundred titles, more than any other English printer before 1600. Born in either Holland or Alsace, de Worde learned the printing trade and met Caxton in either Cologne or Bruges. De Worde apparently accompanied Caxton when he moved to Westminster in 1476 and inherited the shop and equipment when Caxton died in 1491 or 1492. De Worde did not have the connections to the nobility that his mentor had enjoyed, so he moved the shop from Westminster to Fleet Street in London. The move increased his business sufficiently that by 1509 he was selling from another shop in St. Paul's Churchyard, the center of the London book trade. By the time of his death in 1535 he was counted among the wealthier inhabitants of his parish.

Before the move to Fleet Street, most of the works printed by de Worde were homages to his master in the form of reprints, translations, and new editions of Caxton's books, such as Geoffrey Chaucer's *Canterbury Tales* (1498) and Thomas Malory's *Morte d'Arthur* (1498). After the move he developed new interests and produced grammar books, handbooks, contemporary religious writing, romances, and satires. A change in content also heralded a change in format, and de Worde's productions decreased in size (and, therefore, expense) from large folio volumes to the smaller quarto and octavo sizes.

De Worde had a tremendous influence on the early English book trade. The relative newness of the printed book, the availability of foreign printed books, and the scarcity of English printers at this time combined to make competition a present but not overbearing factor in production. De Worde collaborated with younger members of the trade as well as with foreign printers, and his inexpensive books contributed substantially to the spread of literacy in early-sixteenth-century England.

Bibliography

J. Moran, *Wynkyn de Worde: Father of Fleet Street*, 2nd ed., 1976.

Richard J. Ring

WROTH, LADY MARY (1587–1653?)

One of the most important woman writers in early modern England, Mary Wroth produced the first female-authored romance, pastoral play, and sonnet sequence in English. Wroth's family was well known for its literary accomplishments. Her uncle, Sir Philip Sidney,* was a famous courtier during Elizabeth I's* reign and the author of a popular sonnet sequence, a romance, and literary criticism. Wroth's aunt was Mary Sidney* Herbert, a poet, translator, and distinguished literary patron. Wroth's father, Robert Sidney, also wrote verse. The Sidney name was important to Wroth, who kept her family coat of arms after her marriage.

Wroth participated actively in the artistic and social life of James I's* court. She was chosen twice to perform in court masques, a significant honor. The poet and playwright Ben Jonson* wrote several poems to Wroth and dedicated his play *The Alchemist* to her. She was married in 1603 to Sir Robert Wroth, one of James's frequent hunting companions; the marriage was not particularly happy. Wroth's husband died in 1614, and their only son, James, died in 1616. Wroth spent many years paying off the huge debts left by her husband. Although Wroth was less active in court circles after 1616, she maintained ties with many at court and took part in Queen Anne's funeral in 1619. Between 1614 and 1621 Wroth had two children, William and Catherine, with her cousin William Herbert, the third earl of Pembroke. After 1621 her name appears in documents related to her debts and later to transfers of property or tax payments. The precise year and circumstances of her death are unknown.

Wroth's romance *The Countesse of Mountgomeries Urania* (1621) is an enormous work of nearly 600,000 words; roughly half remains in manuscript. The romance depicts the adventures, courtships, and marriages of a large cast of noble lovers. It defends the right to choose one's spouse and harshly criticizes unions arranged against the desires of either party. As Wroth's contemporaries recognized, the romance alludes to real people and events during James I's reign. Some references are biographical; the relationship between Pamphilia and Amphilanthus, the main characters, parallels in a complex fashion Wroth's experiences with Herbert. Edward Denny's vehement, public reaction to his unflattering portrait in the book caused Wroth to stop its further sale. In a widely circulated poem to Wroth, Denny labels her a "hermaphrodite" for being a woman and a writer, and he makes innuendos linking her "idle" book with her illegitimate children. *Pamphilia to Amphilanthus*, Wroth's sonnet sequence, was printed at the back of the *Urania*. It is the first English sequence in which the unrequited lover-poet is a woman. Wroth's pastoral play (c. 1620), a tragicomedy entitled *Love's Victory*, may have been acted privately. Its main themes of love and desire are explored through the experiences of four couples, each representing a different kind of love.

Bibliography

S. P. Cerasano and M. Wynne-Davies, eds., *Renaissance Drama by Women: Texts and Documents*, 1996.

M. Wroth, *The First Part of the Countess of Montgomery's Urania*, ed. J. A. Roberts, 1995.

M. Wroth, *The Poems of Lady Mary Wroth*, ed. J. A. Roberts, 1983.

Gwynne Kennedy

WYATT, SIR THOMAS (1503–1542)

Thomas Wyatt is credited with having "Englished" the Italian poet Petrarch and more generally with having brought the polish and continental sophistication to English poetry that earned him George Puttenham's commendation in 1598 as one of the "two chief lanterns of light" to subsequent English poets. The other "lantern" was Henry Howard,* the earl of Surrey, with whom Wyatt remains associated, and whose elegy for Wyatt claimed that he "reft Chaucer the glory of his wit."

Wyatt was born in Kent, England, to a father whose loyalty to Henry VII had

placed him in a series of high positions at court. Thomas Wyatt was thus introduced early to courtly life, serving in 1516 at the christening of Princess Mary*
as sewer extraordinary (attendant). After graduating from Cambridge and entering into a disastrous first marriage that ended in early estrangement, Wyatt went
to court and began his lifelong career as courtier under King Henry VIII.* By
1526 Wyatt was esteemed enough to be sent on a special embassy to the French
court and in the following year was sent on another embassy to the papal court.
Traveling in Italy afterwards, he was taken prisoner by Spanish troops near
Ferrara, but was ultimately released. From 1528 to 1532 he was stationed in
Calais and served for a time as high marshall. Wyatt's interest in French and
Italian literature seems to have been greatly stimulated during these years, for
though his reputation as a writer of lyrics was established at court before his
travels, his more famous and influential adaptations of continental writers like
Ludovico Ariosto* and Petrarch probably date from after these trips.

His life as a courtier after returning to England reached something of an ironic
pinnacle in 1533 when he represented his father as chief sewer at the coronation
of Henry VIII's second wife, Anne Boleyn. Within three years Anne was beheaded following charges of adultery with numerous men, including Wyatt
(though prior to her marriage). The charges against Wyatt have never been
substantiated, but one of his most famous poems, an adaptation of Petrarch that
begins "Whoso list to hunt," hints at least at deep erotic interest on Wyatt's part
in the queen. Wyatt did nonetheless suffer imprisonment for over a month, but
was released and then later in the same year was advanced by the king to several
positions, including sheriff of Kent, which ultimately suggests that the king
never took the charges too seriously. The strong bond between them is further
attested by Wyatt's raising 350 men to help suppress a northern rebellion against
the king's policies called the Pilgrimage of Grace.

In 1537 Wyatt was sent for two years to the imperial court to improve relations between Henry and the Holy Roman Empire, which had been under great
strain because of Henry's divorce from the emperor's kinswoman Catherine of
Aragon. The embassy proved a disaster in every way. Wyatt, along with two
other English ambassadors, Edmund Bonner and Simon Heynes, found no success with the emperor, who, meanwhile, had achieved a closer alliance with the
anti-Henry François I* of France. Further, Edmund Bonner filed a litany of
accusations against Wyatt that included being too familiar with "papists" (the
worst and most used slander in Bonner's vocabulary) and spending money "un-
thriftly." Thomas Cromwell, chief minister to Henry VIII, reviewed the charges
but dismissed them. On the brighter side, a collection of lyrics titled *The Court
of Venus* that dates from this period included some of Wyatt's poems.

Shortly after Wyatt's return to England in 1540, Cromwell was arrested and
executed. In the following year, without Cromwell's protection, Wyatt was arrested for treason based on Bonner's previous charges; however, due in part to
a written declaration of his innocence, and perhaps a prepared oration that survives but may never have been delivered, the charges were ultimately dismissed.

Soon thereafter, he regained the favor of the king, eventually being named chief steward of the royal manor at Maidstone and vice admiral of a fleet prepared against France. Wyatt's renewed fortunes were short-lived, as he died on 11 October 1542. Wyatt remains a critical figure in literary history for his role in shaping continental forms for use in a distinctly English style.

Bibliography

S. M. Foley, *Sir Thomas Wyatt*, 1990.

Yu Jin Ko

X–Z

XAVIER, ST. FRANCIS (1506–1552)

Canonized in 1622 by Pope Gregory XV, Francis Xavier led the mission of the Society of Jesus to Asia from 1540 until his death. The force of his personality and vivid accounts of his activities extended Jesuit influence to India, Japan, and China and also made Xavier into the quintessential missionary and a symbol of the Counter-Reformation. As the Jesuits' first superior, he naturally laid the foundations of the overseas missions, a philosophy that the Jesuits transplanted to their operations in the Americas.

A member of the Basque aristocracy, Xavier took a master of arts degree at the University of Paris. There he met Ignatius of Loyola* and by 1533 had accepted the way of life later codified in the older man's *Spiritual Exercises*. On 15 August 1534 Xavier, Ignatius, and their six companions—the founders of the Society of Jesus—vowed to offer their services to the pope and swore themselves to a life of poverty. Xavier was ordained priest in 1537.

The Mediterranean political situation frustrated the companions' plans to visit Jerusalem, but King John III of Portugal, an early supporter of Ignatius, wanted a mission sent to the Indies. The Jesuit leader, after some hesitation, viewed this prospect as vital to the society's political future and to its self-appointed task of furthering Catholic education. He gave Xavier the job, and the missionary arrived in Goa on 6 May 1542.

There he translated prayers into Tamil and other Indian languages, taught the catechism, and led simple prayers. He also attracted other Jesuits and traveled far afield in search of fertile territory for his gospel. By 15 August 1549 he and two comrades were in Japan. Highly optimistic about prospects among the Japanese, a people he regarded as highly moral, Xavier pursued a policy of catering to the elite in order to receive licenses to preach and minister as well as to induce conversion from the top of Japanese society down to the lower orders. He bestowed gifts that demonstrated Western technology upon officials, intellectuals, and other important individuals and generally cultivated Japanese contacts based on a common interest in learning. By late 1551 several thousand Japanese had accepted baptism, and this number increased to some 30,000 by 1570.

Xavier learned of China and spent the last year of his life trying to gain entry into that country. However, he was unsuccessful and died on 3 December 1552 just a few miles away from his goal.

Bibliography

J. W. O'Malley, *The First Jesuits*, 1993.

Louis Roper

ZELL, MATTHIAS (1477–1548) and KATHARINA (1497–1562)

Matthias and Katharina Zell were German Protestant preachers, activists, and Reformers in the city of Strasbourg. After a brief tenure as rector at the University of Freiburg (1517–18), Matthias Zell arrived in the city of Strasbourg in order to serve as Roman Catholic priest of the cathedral parish. He also held the office of *poenitentiarius* (penitentiary), charged with carrying the bishop's right to absolve grave sins. Zell soon found himself attracted by the views of Martin Luther,* and as early as 1521 he began preaching sermons with a Lutheran emphasis. He insisted that he was preaching the "pure Gospel," but the authorities took notice. The bishop of Strasbourg attempted to have the cathedral chapter oust Zell, but the effort failed in the face of the popularity of his sermons. So great was his reputation that the city council decided to extend its protection to the preacher. Clearly the majority in this sovereign city wanted a reform of the church.

Zell led the movement for reform in Strasbourg from 1521 until 1523, when he was joined by Wolfgang Capito and by the former Dominican Martin Bucer.* Following Bucer's example, Zell broke his vow of celibacy and married Katharina Schütz in 1523, an action that resulted in his excommunication at the hands of the bishop. That same year he published a defense of the Reformation titled *Christliche Verantwortung* (Christian Answer). In 1525 Zell published the city of Strasbourg's first evangelical catechism, and he took a principled stand against the use of force in religious matters. Throughout his professional life Zell focused on preaching and pastoral work.

Katharina Zell was Matthias's junior by twenty years. She came from a respected and politically influential Strasbourg family, and she had read Luther's early works before the marriage to Matthias. The priest was immediately attacked as a libertine, but Katharina spoke publicly in defense of her husband, even publishing an attack on priestly celibacy in 1524. She was one of the few women to continue writing lay pamphlets after 1525.

Katharina Zell maintained a high public profile in the city of her birth. She was a tireless worker for the Reformation cause. Strasbourg, as one of the free cities in the empire, became a haven for Lutheran Reformers from nearby lands, especially after the peasant revolt of 1525 was crushed by the authorities. Thousands of refugees flooded into the city of 25,000 in the aftermath of the slaughter.

Katharina played a central role in the relief effort until the fighting stopped and the refugees could return to their homes. She also composed a pamphlet aimed at Lutheran women whose husbands had fled to Strasbourg at this time, and in the 1530s she edited four hymn booklets. When her husband died in 1548, Katharina participated in the service, breaking the traditional injunction that women remain silent in church and separate from the official ministries. In 1557 she published *A Letter to All the Citizens of Strasbourg*, in which she criticized ministers who persecuted Anabaptists and spiritualists. Toward the end of her life she conducted funerals for two women who had been refused clerical services because of their association with sectarians.

Both Zells were exceedingly tolerant of all who suffered from religious persecution. Katharina went so far as to call for the toleration of Roman Catholics and Anabaptists. At times she and her husband alarmed the city authorities with their insistence that charity take precedence over profit and convenience. They lived the conviction that all work must be spiritualized, and their repeated efforts on behalf of countless refugees and nonconformists linked secular tasks with moral duty.

Bibliography

L. J. Abray, *The People's Reformation: Magistrates, Clergy, and Commons in Strasbourg, 1500–1598*, 1985.

William Spellman

ZUCCARO, FEDERICO (1540/42–1609)

Federico Zuccaro, painter and draughtsman, worked throughout Europe in the second half of the sixteenth century. Born in the small town of Sant' Angelo in Vado in the Marches, Zuccaro traveled to Rome while still a young boy and received artistic training in the studio of his older brother Taddeo Zuccaro. Federico's earliest work was as an assistant to his brother, and apart from Federico's work in the Grimani Chapel at Venice, virtually all of his work before the late 1560s was on projects begun by Taddeo. After Taddeo's untimely death in 1566, Federico completed Taddeo's projects in Rome and at the Farnese Villa at Caprarola. He also worked at Orvieto and at the Villa d'Este in Tivoli.

In 1574 Zuccaro began the period of almost continual travel that would last for the rest of his life. He visited the Netherlands and England, where he executed portraits, including the famous drawing of Queen Elizabeth I* (British Museum). By the end of 1574 he was in Florence and completed Giorgio Vasari's* fresco cycle in the cupola of the Duomo, after which he won the prestigious commission to complete Michelangelo's* decoration of the Pauline Chapel in the Vatican. When he was criticized by Gregory XIII's Bolognese advisors, however, Zuccaro responded with the satirical *Porta virtutis* print, for which he was expelled from Rome. He traveled to Venice and to Loreto. Pardoned by the pope in 1583, Zuccaro returned to Rome and finished the Pauline Chapel, but in 1585 he went to Spain and worked at the Escorial. Here too, his cold academic style was criticized. Zuccaro again returned to Rome, where that style was more appreciated, especially by leading Counter-Reformation patrons. One of these patrons, Federico Borromeo, invited Zuccaro to work at Pavia and Arona during the last decade of his life. Zuccaro is also remembered as a writer and theorist whose works include the *Lamento del pittura* (1605) and *L'idea de' pittori, scultori, ed architetti* (1607).

Bibliography

E. J. Mundy, *Renaissance into Baroque: Italian Master Drawings by the Zuccari, 1550–1600*, 1990.

John Marciari

ZWINGLI, HULDRYCH (1484–1531)

Huldrych Zwingli was a Reformation theologian who oversaw Zurich's break with Rome and developed the notion of the spiritual, rather than the actual, presence of Christ in the Eucharist. Zwingli, of peasant stock, received his master of arts in theology by 1506 in Vienna. Influenced by the humanists, Zwingli turned his linguistic talents in Greek to the study of the Bible. After drawing attention for his sermons as a papal chaplain, he became a minister at the Great Minster of Zurich in 1518.

Zurich was dominated by a skillful council, and Zwingli was granted great latitude with his sermons, which, though plain, were very effective. By 1522 Zwingli was an evangelical, holding the Bible as the only source of theological authority. A near-death experience convinced him of the necessity of complete submission to God's will to achieve salvation, and his zeal so impressed the Zurich council that he was appointed canon of the Minster in 1521.

By 1522 Zwingli was beginning the process of breaking ties with Rome and renounced his former humanist leanings. He attacked the church on the issue of indulgences and on clerical celibacy; he pushed the envelope further by taking a bride himself in early 1522. His enormous popularity in Zurich was supported by the city council, but opposition within the Swiss Confederation and the Holy Roman Empire was mounting to such an extent that Zwingli felt compelled to issue a statement of faith in response, the *Apologetica Architeles*. He followed up the statement with a challenge for debate in 1523, essentially to underpin the council's assertion of government control in matters of religious worship. Zwingli was now irrevocably a Reformer.

Zurich's break with Rome was now apparent and was confirmed by its abandonment of the Mass in 1525. Zwingli's *Short Christian Introduction* justified the repudiation of the Mass based on his contention that the Eucharist was only symbolic, not the miraculous transubstantiation espoused by the Catholic church; he also rejected a number of other Catholic practices.

Tensions between Zurich and the Swiss Catholic states were growing, and Zwingli advocated an aggressive defense of the new faith and a solid political plan that would give Zurich dominance within the Swiss Confederation. To assure that his Reformed teaching would survive and spread, Zwingli began to get involved in the political world much more intimately. To that end, he arranged a debate in the city of Berne, and his commanding performance led that city to accept the Reformation. In many ways, this debate saved Protestantism in Switzerland and assured its eventual spread throughout Europe.

Martin Luther* and Zwingli, despite having many shared beliefs, disagreed heartily over the nature of the Eucharist, and it was apparent that the only way to heal the split in Protestantism was to have the two men meet and debate. However, the Marburg Conference, held in October 1529, failed to resolve their differences over the Eucharist, although a feeling of mutual respect was engendered between the two Reformers. Marburg definitively split the Catholics and the Protestants, and it was clear that a violent confrontation was inevitable within the confederation. A short fight in June 1529 was followed by more sustained hostilities in the aftermath of the Diet of Augsburg in 1530 and the formation of the Protestant Schmalkaldic League early in 1531. Zwingli, in the figurative guise of an Old Testament warrior, participated in a preemptive strike by Zurich against the Swiss Catholic states and was severely wounded in a confrontation on 11 October 1531. Captured, he refused a confessor and was then killed; his body was cut up and burned to prevent its use as a Protestant relic. The subsequent peace allowed Zurich's religious freedom, a cause for which Zwingli was no doubt glad to have died, as it meant that the Reformed faith was permanently ensconced in central Europe.

Bibliography

U. Gabler, *Huldrych Zwingli: His Life and Work*, 1986.
G. R. Potter, *Zwingli*, 1976.

Connie S. Evans

Appendix A:
Subjects by Discipline

ANTIQUARIANISM AND PRINTING

Camden, William

Cotton, Sir Robert Bruce

Worde, Wynkyn de

ART AND ARCHITECTURE

Abate, Niccolò dell'

Aertsen, Pieter

Altdorfer, Albrecht

Andrea del Sarto

Anguissola, Sofonisba

Arcimboldo, Giuseppe

Bandinelli, Baccio

Bassano, Jacopo da

Beccafumi, Domenico

Bronzino, Il

Bruegel, Pieter

Bry, Theodore de

Burgkmair, Hans

Caravaggio

Caron, Antoine

Carracci, Ludovico, Agostino, and Annibale

Cellini, Benvenuto

Clouet, Jean and François

Clovio, Giulio

Coecke van Aelst, Pieter

Correggio, Antonio

Cranach, Lucas, the Elder

Dürer, Albrecht

Eworth, Hans

Floris, Frans

Fontana, Lavinia

Gentileschi, Artemesia

Giambologna

Giulio Romano

Goujon, Jean

Greco, El

Grünewald

Heemskerck, Maerten van

Hilliard, Nicholas

Holbein, Hans, the Younger

Hornebolte, Luke

Inglis, Esther

Leoni, Leone and Pompeo

Lotto, Lorenzo

Lucas van Leyden

Massys, Quentin

Michelangelo

Mor, Antonio

Oliver, Isaac

Palissy, Bernard

Palladio, Andrea

Parmigianino

Patinir, Joachim

Peruzzi, Baldassare

Pontormo

Primaticcio, Francesco

Raimondi, Marcantonio

Raphael

Rosso Fiorentino

Rubens, Peter Paul

Salviati, Francesco

Sansovino, Jacopo

Scorel, Jan van

Sebastiano del Piombo

Spranger, Bartholomaeus

Stoss, Veit

Teerlinc, Levina Bening

Tintoretto

Titian

Vasari, Giorgio

Veronese, Paolo

Vignola, Jacopo Barozzi da

Vittoria, Alessandro

Zuccaro, Federico

CARTOGRAPHY

Gemma Frisius, Reiner

Mercator, Gerardus

Waldseemüller, Martin

DRAMA AND THEATER

Beaumont, Francis

Burbage, Richard

Calmo, Andrea

Cary, Elizabeth

Castro y Bellvís, Guillén de

Cervantes (Saavedra), Miguel de

Chapman, George

Daniel, Samuel

Davies, Sir John

Dekker, Thomas

Della Porta, Giambattista

Fletcher, John

Florio, John

Garnier, Robert

Gascoigne, George

Giraldi Cinthio, Giambattista

Gosson, Stephen

Grazzini, Anton Francesco

Greene, Robert

Guarini, Giovanni Battista

Henslowe, Philip

Heywood, John

Heywood, Thomas

Jodelle, Étienne

Jonson, Ben

Kyd, Thomas

Lodge, Thomas

Lyly, John

Marlowe, Christopher

Middleton, Thomas

Ruzzante

Sachs, Hans

Sackville, Sir Thomas

Shakespeare, William

Tasso, Torquato

Trissino, Gian Giorgio

Udall, Nicholas

Vega, Lope de

Vicente, Gil

Webster, John

Wroth, Lady Mary

HISTORY, CHRONICLES, TRAVEL

Acosta, José de

Anghiera, Pietro Martire d'

Camden, William

Chamberlain, John

Coryate, Thomas

Goís, Damião de

Guicciardini, Francesco

Hakluyt, Richard

Harrison, William

Holinshed, Raphael

Las Casas, Bartolomé de

Leo Africanus

Ricci, Matteo

Sanudo, Marino

Sarpi, Paolo

Stow, John

Vega, Garcilaso Inca de la

Vergil, Polydore

Vettori, Piero

HUMANISM AND EDUCATION

Agricola, Georg

Amyot, Jacques

Ascham, Roger

Barbaro, Daniele

Barclay, Alexander

Budé, Guillaume

Camerarius, Joachim

Casaubon, Isaac

Colet, John

Coornhert, Dirck Volkertszoon

Della Casa, Giovanni

Dolet, Étienne

Elyot, Sir Thomas

Erasmus, Desiderius

Estienne, Robert

Gelli, Giambattista

Hutten, Ulrich von

More, Sir Thomas

Münster, Sebastian

Muret, Marc-Antoine

Ramus, Petrus

Roper, Margaret More

Scaliger, Joseph Julius

Scaliger, Julius Caesar

Thomas, William

Vettori, Piero

Vives, Juan Luis

Wimpfeling, Jakob

LAW AND POLITICAL THEORY

Bacon, Francis

Barclay, William

Bodin, Jean

Buchanan, George

Davies, Sir John

Du Plessis-Mornay, Philippe

Guicciardini, Francesco

Hotman, François

Knox, John

La Boétie, Étienne de

Machiavelli, Niccolò

Sturm, Jacob

Vitoria, Francisco de

LITERATURE

Alemán, Mateo

Aragona, Tullia d'

Aretino, Pietro

Ariosto, Ludovico

Bacon, Anne Cook

Baïf, Jean-Antoine de

Bandello, Matteo

Belleau, Rémy

Bembo, Pietro

Brantôme

Camões, Luís Vaz de

Campion, Thomas

Caro, Annibal

Cary, Elizabeth

Castelvetro, Lodovico

Castiglione, Baldesar

Castillejo, Cristóbal de

Cervantes (Saavedra), Miguel de

Chapman, George

Colonna, Vittoria

Crenne, Hélisenne de

Daniel, Samuel

Dekker, Thomas

Deloney, Thomas

Desportes, Philippe

Des Roches, Catherine and Madeleine

Donne, John

Drayton, Michael

Du Bartas, Guillaume

Du Bellay, Joachim

Du Guillet, Pernette

Ercilla y Zúñiga, Alonso de

Fenton, Sir Geoffrey

Firenzuola, Agnolo

Franco, Veronica

Gambara, Veronica

Gascoigne, George

Giraldi Cinthio, Giambattista

Góngora y Argote, Luis de

Górnicki, Łukasz

Grazzini, Anton Francesco

Greene, Robert

Harington, Sir John

Harvey, Gabriel

Herrera, Fernando de

Heywood, John

Heywood, Thomas

Hoby, Sir Thomas

Howard, Henry, Earl of Surrey

Jonson, Ben

Juan de la Cruz, San

Kochanowski, Jan

Kyd, Thomas

Labé, Louise

Lanyer, Aemilia

León, Luis de

Lodge, Thomas

Lyly, John

Marguerite de Navarre

Marlowe, Christopher

Marot, Clément

Montaigne, Michel Eyquem de

Montemayor, Jorge de

More, Sir Thomas

Nashe, Thomas

Overbury, Sir Thomas

Rabelais, François

Raleigh, Sir Walter

Rej, Mikołaj

Rich, Barnabe

Rinuccini, Ottavio

Ronsard, Pierre de

Sachs, Hans

Sackville, Sir Thomas

Sá de Miranda, Francisco

Sannazaro, Jacopo

Scève, Maurice

Scot, Reginald

Shakespeare, William

Sidney Herbert, Mary

Sidney, Sir Philip

Skelton, John

Southwell, Robert

Spenser, Edmund

Speroni, Sperone

Spiegel, Hendrick Laurenszoon

Stampa, Gaspara

Tasso, Torquato

Trissino, Gian Giorgio

Urfé, Honoré d'

Vega, Garcilaso de la

Weston, Elizabeth Jane

Wroth, Lady Mary

Wyatt, Sir Thomas

MATHEMATICS

Cardano, Girolamo

Gemma Frisius, Reiner

Tartaglia, Niccolò

MEDICINE

Cardano, Girolamo

Eustachi, Bartolomeo

Fallopio, Gabriele

Fracastoro, Girolamo

Linacre, Thomas

Paré, Ambroise

Vesalius, Andreas

MONARCHS

Albret, Jeanne d'

Charles V

Cosimo I de' Medici

Elizabeth I

François I

Gonzaga, Federico II

Grey, Lady Jane

Henry VIII

James VI and I

Marguerite de Navarre

Marguerite de Valois

Mary I

Medici, Catherine de'

Philip II

Rudolf II

Stuart, Mary (Queen of Scots)

MUSIC

Arcadelt, Jacques

Bull, John

Byrd, William

Campion, Thomas

Carver, Robert

Clemens non Papa, Jacobus

Dowland, John

Gabrieli, Giovanni

Galilei, Vincenzio

Gesualdo, Carlo

Glarean, Heinrich

Goudimel, Claude

Josquin, des Prez

Lasso, Orlando di

Le Jeune, Claude

Marenzio, Luca

Monteverdi, Claudio

Morales, Cristóbal de

Morley, Thomas

Palestrina, Giovanni Pierluigi da

Peri, Jacopo

Praetorius, Michael

Rore, Cipriano de

Sweelinck, Jan Pieterszoon

Tallis, Thomas

Taverner, John

Tye, Christopher

Victoria, Tomás Luis de

Willaert, Adrian

RELIGION AND THEOLOGY

Agricola, Johann

Agricola, Michael

Andrewes, Lancelot

Askew, Anne

Bale, John

Becon, Thomas

Beza, Theodore

Boehme, Jakob

Briçonnet, Guillaume

Bucer, Martin

Bullinger, Heinrich

Calvin, John

Casaubon, Isaac

Coverdale, Miles

Cranmer, Thomas

Crespin, Jean

Fisher, John

Foxe, John

Francis de Sales

Gonzaga, Giulia

Hall, Joseph

Hooker, Richard

Ignatius of Loyola

Juan de la Cruz

Julius II

Knox, John

Lasco, John à

Lefèvre d'Étaples, Jacques

Leo X

Luther, Martin

Melanchthon, Philip

Neri, St. Philip

Ochino, Bernardino

Pirckheimer, Caritas

Pirckheimer, Willibald

Renée of Ferrara

Ricci, Matteo

Servetus, Michael

Southwell, Robert

Spengler, Lazarus

Teresa of Ávila, St.

Tomás de Jesús

Tyndale, William

Valdés, Juan de

Xavier, St. Francis

Zell, Matthias and Katharina

Zwingli, Huldrych

SCIENCE, ASTRONOMY, AND ASTROLOGY

Agricola, Georg

Agrippa von Nettesheim, Heinrich Cornelius

Bacon, Francis

Brahe, Tycho

Bruno, Giordano

Copernicus, Nicolaus

Dee, John

Della Porta, Giambattista

Dudith, Andreas

Forman, Simon
Galilei, Galileo
Gemma Frisius, Reiner
Gilbert, William
Kepler, Johannes
Münster, Sebastian
Nostradamus
Paracelsus
Stevin, Simon

WOMEN

Albret, Jeanne d'
Anguissola, Sofonisba
Aragona, Tullia d'
Askew, Anne
Bacon, Anne Cook
Bess of Hardwick
Cary, Elizabeth
Colonna, Vittoria
Crenne, Hélisenne de
Des Roches, Catherine and Madeleine
Diane de Poitiers
Du Guillet, Pernette
Eleanora of Toledo
Elizabeth I

Este, Isabella d'
Fontana, Lavinia
Franco, Veronica
Gambara, Veronica
Gentileschi, Artemesia
Gonzaga, Giulia
Grey, Lady Jane
Labé, Louise
Lanyer, Aemilia
Marguerite de Navarre
Marguerite de Valois
Mary I
Medici, Catherine de'
Pirckheimer, Caritas
Renée of Ferrara
Roper, Margaret More
Sidney Herbert, Mary
Stampa, Gaspara
Stuart, Mary (Queen of Scots)
Teerlinc, Levina Bening
Teresa of Ávila, St.
Weston, Elizabeth Jane
Wroth, Lady Mary
Zell, Katharina

Appendix B:
Subjects by Country

DENMARK

Brahe, Tycho

ENGLAND

Andrewes, Lancelot

Ascham, Roger

Askew, Anne

Bacon, Anne Cook

Bacon, Francis

Bale, John

Barclay, Alexander

Beaumont, Francis

Becon, Thomas

Bess of Hardwick

Bull, John

Burbage, Richard

Byrd, William

Camden, William

Campion, Thomas

Cary, Elizabeth

Chamberlain, John

Chapman, George

Colet, John

Coryate, Thomas

Cotton, Sir Robert Bruce

Coverdale, Miles

Cranmer, Thomas

Daniel, Samuel

Davies, Sir John

Dee, John

Dekker, Thomas

Deloney, Thomas

Donne, John

Dowland, John

Drayton, Michael

Elizabeth I

Elyot, Sir Thomas

Eworth, Hans

Fenton, Sir Geoffrey

Fisher, John

Fletcher, John

Florio, John

Forman, Simon

Foxe, John

Gascoigne, George

Gilbert, William

Gosson, Stephen

Greene, Robert
Grey, Lady Jane
Hakluyt, Richard
Hall, Joseph
Harington, Sir John
Harrison, William
Harvey, Gabriel
Henry VIII
Henslowe, Philip
Heywood, John
Heywood, Thomas
Hilliard, Nicholas
Hoby, Sir Thomas
Holinshed, Raphael
Hooker, Richard
Hornebolte, Luke
Howard, Henry, Earl of Surrey
Inglis, Esther
James I
Jonson, Ben
Kyd, Thomas
Lanyer, Aemilia
Linacre, Thomas
Lodge, Thomas
Lyly, John
Marlowe, Christopher
Mary I
Middleton, Thomas
More, Sir Thomas
Morley, Thomas
Nashe, Thomas
Oliver, Isaac
Overbury, Sir Thomas
Raleigh, Sir Walter
Rich, Barnabe
Roper, Margaret More
Sackville, Sir Thomas

Scot, Reginald
Shakespeare, William
Sidney Herbert, Mary
Sidney, Philip
Skelton, John
Southwell, Robert
Spenser, Edmund
Stow, John
Tallis, Thomas
Taverner, John
Teerlinc, Levina Bening
Thomas, William
Tye, Christopher
Tyndale, William
Udall, Nicholas
Vergil, Polydore
Webster, John
Weston, Elizabeth Jane
Worde, Wynkyn de
Wroth, Lady Mary
Wyatt, Sir Thomas

FINLAND

Agricola, Michael

FRANCE

Albret, Jeanne d'
Amyot, Jacques
Arcadelt, Jacques
Baïf, Jean-Antoine de
Belleau, Rémy
Beza, Theodore
Bodin, Jean
Brantôme
Briçonnet, Guillaume
Budé, Guillaume
Calvin, John

Caron, Antoine

Clouet, Jean and François

Crenne, Hélisenne de

Crespin, Jean

Desportes, Philippe

Des Roches, Catherine and Madeleine

Diane de Poitiers

Dolet, Étienne

Du Bartas, Guillaume

Du Bellay, Joachim

Du Guillet, Pernette

Du Plessis-Mornay, Philippe

Estienne, Robert

Francis de Sales

François I

Garnier, Robert

Goudimel, Claude

Goujon, Jean

Hotman, François

Jodelle, Étienne

Josquin, des Prez

Labé, Louise

La Boétie, Étienne de

Lefèvre d'Étaples, Jacques

Le Jeune, Claude

Marguerite de Navarre

Marguerite de Valois

Marot, Clément

Medici, Catherine de'

Montaigne, Michel Eyquem de

Muret, Marc-Antoine

Nostradamus

Palissy, Bernard

Paré, Ambroise

Rabelais, François

Ramus, Petrus

Ronsard, Pierre de

Scaliger, Joseph Justus

Scaliger, Julius Caesar

Scève, Maurice

Urfé, Honoré d'

GERMANY

Agricola, Georg

Agricola, Johann

Agrippa von Nettesheim, Heinrich
  Cornelius

Altdorfer, Albrecht

Boehme, Jakob

Bucer, Martin

Burgkmair, Hans

Camerarius, Joachim

Cranach, Lucas, the Elder

Dürer, Albrecht

Grünewald

Holbein, Hans, the Younger

Hutten, Ulrich von

Kepler, Johannes

Luther, Martin

Melanchthon, Philip

Münster, Sebastian

Paracelsus

Pirckheimer, Caritas

Pirckheimer, Willibald

Praetorius, Michael

Sachs, Hans

Spengler, Lazarus

Stoss, Veit

Sturm, Jacob

Waldseemüller, Martin

Wimpfeling, Jakob

Zell, Matthias and Katharina

HOLY ROMAN EMPIRE

Charles V

Rudolf II

HUNGARY

Dudith, Andreas

ITALY

Abate, Niccoló dell'

Andrea del Sarto

Anghiera, Pietro Martire d'

Anguissola, Sofonisba

Aragona, Tullia d'

Arcimboldo, Giuseppe

Aretino, Pietro

Ariosto, Ludovico

Bandello, Matteo

Bandinelli, Baccio

Barbaro, Daniele

Bassano, Jacopo da

Beccafumi, Domenico

Bembo, Pietro

Bronzino, Il

Bruno, Giordano

Calmo, Andrea

Caravaggio

Cardano, Girolamo

Caro, Annibal

Carracci, Ludovico, Agostino, and
   Annibale

Castelvetro, Lodovico

Castiglione, Baldesar

Cellini, Benvenuto

Clovio, Giulio

Colonna, Vittoria

Correggio, Antonio

Cosimo I de' Medici

Della Casa, Giovanni

Della Porta, Giambattista

Eleanora of Toledo

Este, Isabella d'

Eustachi, Bartolomeo

Fallopio, Gabriele

Firenzuola, Agnolo

Fontana, Lavinia

Fracastoro, Girolamo

Franco, Veronica

Gabrieli, Giovanni

Galilei, Galileo

Galilei, Vincenzio

Gambara, Veronica

Gelli, Giambattista

Gentileschi, Artemesia

Gesualdo, Carlo

Giambologna

Giraldi Cinthio, Giambattista

Giulio Romano

Gonzaga, Federico II

Gonzaga, Giulia

Grazzini, Anton Francesco

Guarini, Giovanni Battista

Guicciardini, Francesco

Julius II

Leo X

Leo Africanus

Leoni, Leone and Pompeo

Lotto, Lorenzo

Machiavelli, Niccolò

Marenzio, Luca

Michelangelo

Monteverdi, Claudio

Neri, St. Philip

Ochino, Bernardino

Palestrina, Giovanni Pierluigi da

Palladio, Andrea

Parmigianino

Peri, Jacopo

Peruzzi, Baldassare

Pontormo

Primaticcio, Francesco

Raimondi, Marcantonio

Raphael

Renée of Ferrara

Ricci, Matteo

Rinuccini, Ottavio

Rore, Cipriano de

Rosso Fiorentino

Ruzzante

Salviati, Francesco

Sannazaro, Jacopo

Sansovino, Jacopo

Sanudo, Marino

Sarpi, Paolo

Sebastiano del Piombo

Speroni, Sperone

Stampa, Gaspara

Tartaglia, Niccolò

Tasso, Torquato

Tintoretto

Titian

Trissino, Gian Giorgio

Vasari, Giorgio

Vergil, Polydore

Veronese, Paolo

Vettori, Piero

Vignola, Jacopo Barozzi da

Vittoria, Alessandro

Zuccaro, Federico

NETHERLANDS

Aertsen, Pieter

Bruegel, Pieter

Bry, Theodore de

Clemens non Papa, Jacobus

Coecke van Aelst, Pieter

Coornhert, Dirck Volkertszoon

Erasmus, Desiderius

Eworth, Hans

Floris, Frans

Gemma Frisius, Reiner

Heemskerck, Maerten van

Hornebolte, Luke

Lasso, Orlando di

Lucas van Leyden

Massys, Quentin

Mercator, Gerardus

Mor, Antonio

Patinir, Joachim

Rore, Cipriano de

Rubens, Peter Paul

Scorel, Jan van

Spiegel, Hendrick Laurenszoon

Spranger, Bartholomaeus

Stevin, Simon

Sweelinck, Jan Pietenszoon

Teerlinc, Lavina Bening

Vesalius, Andreas

Willaert, Adrian

POLAND

Copernicus, Nicolaus

Górnicki, Łukasz

Kochanowski, Jan

Lasco, John à

Rej, Mikołaj

PORTUGAL

Camões, Luís Vaz de
Goís, Damião de
Sá de Miranda, Francisco
Vicente, Gil

SCOTLAND

Barclay, William
Buchanan, George
Carver, Robert
James VI
Knox, John
Stuart, Mary (Queen of Scots)

SPAIN

Acosta, José de
Alemán, Mateo
Castillejo, Cristóbal de
Castro y Bellvís, Guillén de
Cervantes (Saavedra), Miguel de
Ercilla y Zúñiga, Alonso de
Góngora y Argote, Luis de
Greco, El
Herrera, Fernando de

Ignatius of Loyola
Juan de la Cruz, San
Las Casas, Bartolomé de
León, Luis de
Martyr, Peter d'Anghera
Montemayor, Jorge de
Morales, Cristóbal de
Philip II
Servetus, Michael
Teresa of Ávila, St.
Tomás de Jesús
Valdés, Juan de
Vega, Garcilaso de la
Vega, Garcilaso Inca de la
Vega, Lope de
Victoria, Tomás Luis de
Vitoria, Francisco de
Vives, Juan Luis
Xavier, St. Francis

SWITZERLAND

Bullinger, Heinrich
Casaubon, Isaac
Glarean, Heinrich
Zwingli, Huldrych

Bibliography

GENERAL

Brown, Alison. *The Renaissance*. London: Longman, 1988.
Burke, Peter. *The European Renaissance*. Oxford: Blackwell Publishers, 1998.
———. *The Italian Renaissance: Culture and Society in Italy*. Princeton: Princeton University Press, 1986.
Di Cesare, M. A., ed. *Reconsidering the Renaissance*. Binghamton, NY: Medieval and Renaissance Texts and Studies, 1992.
Garin, Eugenio, ed. *Renaissance Characters*. Trans. Lydia G. Cochrane. Chicago: University of Chicago Press, 1991.
Hale, J. R. *The Civilization of Europe in the Renaissance*. New York: Atheneum, 1994.
———. *A Concise Encyclopaedia of the Italian Renaissance*. New York: Oxford University Press, 1981.
Kaufmann, Thomas DaCosta. *Court, Cloister, and City: The Art and Culture of Central Europe, 1450–1800*. Chicago: University of Chicago Press, 1995.
Kerrigan, William, and Gordon Braden. *The Idea of the Renaissance*. Baltimore: Johns Hopkins University Press, 1989.
Koenigsberger, H. G., George L. Mosse, and G. Q. Bawler. *Europe in the Sixteenth Century*. 2nd ed. London: Longman, 1989.
Kristeller, Paul. *Renaissance Thought and the Arts: Collected Essays*. Princeton: Princeton University Press, 1990.
Porter, Roy, and Mikuláš Teich, eds. *The Renaissance in National Context*. Cambridge: Cambridge University Press, 1992.
Trevor-Roper, Hugh. *Renaissance Essays*. Chicago: University of Chicago Press, 1985.
Yates, Frances. *Renaissance and Reform: The Italian Contribution*. Boston: Routledge and Kegan Paul, 1983.

ART AND ARCHITECTURE

Blunt, A. *Art and Architecture in France, 1500 to 1700*. London: Penguin Books, 1957.
Brown, J. *The Golden Age of Painting in Spain*. New Haven: Yale University Press, 1991.

Campbell, Loren. *Renaissance Portraits: European Portrait Painting in the 14th, 15th, and 16th Centuries*. New Haven: Yale University Press, 1990.

Cox-Rearick, Janet. *Dynasty and Destiny in Medici Art*. Princeton: Princeton University Press, 1984.

Harbison, Craig. *The Mirror of the Artist: Northern Renaissance Art in Its Historical Context*. New York: Harry N. Abrams, 1995.

Hearn, Karen, ed. *Dynasties: Painting in Tudor and Jacobean England, 1530–1630*. London: Tate Publishing, 1995.

Hitchcock, H. *German Renaissance Architecture*. Princeton: Princeton University Press, 1981.

Humfrey, Peter. *Painting in Renaissance Venice*. New Haven: Yale University Press, 1995.

Jestaz, Bertrand. *Architecture of the Renaissance: From Brunelleschi to Palladio*. New York: Harry N. Abrams, 1996.

———. *The Art of the Renaissance*. New York: Harry N. Abrams, 1995.

Millon, Henry, A., and Vittorio Magnago Lampugnani, eds. *The Renaissance from Brunelleschi to Michelangelo*. New York: Rizzoli, 1994.

Partridge, Loren. *The Art of Renaissance Rome, 1400–1600*. New York: Harry N. Abrams, 1996.

Pope-Hennessy, John. *Italian High Renaissance and Baroque Sculpture*. London: Phaidon, 1970.

———. *The Portrait in the Renaissance*. Princeton: Princeton University Press, 1989.

Shearman, John. *Only Connect . . . Art and the Spectator in the Italian Renaissance*. Princeton: Princeton University Press, 1992.

Snyder, James. *Northern Renaissance Art*. New York: Harry N. Abrams, 1985.

Stechow, Wolfgang, ed. *Northern Renaissance Art, 1400–1600: Sources and Documents*. Evanston: Northwestern University Press, 1989.

Strong, Roy. *Art and Power: Renaissance Festivals, 1450–1650*. Berkeley: University of California Press, 1984.

THE REFORMATION

Bainton, R. H. *The Reformation of the Sixteenth Century*. Boston: Beacon Press, 1962.

Cameron, Euan. *The European Reformation*. Oxford: Oxford University Press, 1991.

Dickens, A. G. *The Counter Reformation*. New York: Norton, 1979.

Elton, G. R. *Reformation Europe, 1517–1559*. London: Collins-Fontana, 1963.

———, ed. *Renaissance and Reformation, 1300–1648*. 3rd ed. New York: Macmillan, 1976.

Hillerbrand, Hans J. *The World of the Reformation*. New York: Scribner's, 1973.

———, ed. *The Oxford Encyclopedia of the Reformation*. Oxford: Oxford University Press, 1995.

Marshall, Peter, ed. *The Impact of the English Reformation, 1500–1640*. London: Arnold, 1997.

Ozment, Steven. *The Reformation in the Cities*. New Haven: Yale University Press, 1975.

———, ed. *Reformation Europe: A Guide to Research*. St. Louis: Center for Reformation Research, 1982.

Spitz, Lewis W. *The Protestant Reformation, 1517–1559*. New York: Harper and Row, 1985.

————. *The Renaissance and Reformation Movements.* Chicago: Rand McNally, 1971.

Stephens, W. P., ed. *The Bible, the Reformation, and the Church.* Sheffield: Sheffield Academic Press, 1995.

Thompson, Bard. *Humanists and Reformers: A History of the Renaissance and Reformation.* Grand Rapids, MI: William B. Eerdmans, 1996.

Wright, A. D. *The Counter-Reformation.* New York: St. Martin's, 1982.

LITERATURE

Brand, Peter, and Lino Pertile, eds. *The Cambridge History of Italian Literature.* Cambridge: Cambridge University Press, 1996.

Donadoni, Eugenio. *A History of Italian Literature.* New York: New York University Press, 1969.

Dubrow, Heather, and Richard Strier, eds. *The Historical Renaissance.* Chicago: University of Chicago Press, 1988.

Giamatti, A. Bartlett. *The Earthly Paradise and the Renaissance Epic.* Princeton: Princeton University Press, 1966.

Greene, Thomas M. *The Light in Troy: Imitation and Discovery in Renaissance Poetry.* New Haven: Yale University Press, 1982.

Hathaway, Baxter. *The Age of Criticism: The Late Renaissance in Italy.* Ithaca: Cornell University Press, 1962.

Hollier, Dennis, ed. *A New History of French Literature.* Cambridge, MA: Harvard University Press, 1989.

King, John. *English Reformation Literature: The Tudor Origins of the Protestant Tradition.* Princeton: Princeton University Press, 1982.

Krailsheimer, A. J., ed. *The Continental Renaissance, 1500–1600.* Harmondsworth: Penguin Books, 1971.

McFarlane, I. D. *A Literary History of France: Renaissance France, 1470–1589.* New York: Barnes and Noble, 1974.

Meijer, Reinder P. *Literature of the Low Countries.* Assen: Van Gorcum, 1971.

Parker, Patricia, and David Quint, eds. *Literary Theory/Renaissance Texts.* Baltimore: Johns Hopkins University Press, 1986.

Pascal, Roy. *German Literature in the Sixteenth and Seventeenth Centuries: Renaissance, Reformation, Baroque.* New York: Barnes and Noble, 1968.

Prescott, Anne Lake. *French Poets and the English Renaissance: Studies in Fame and Transformation.* 1978.

Wilkins, Ernest Hatch. *A History of Italian Literature.* Cambridge, MA: Harvard University Press, 1974.

THEATER

Aylett, Robert, and Peter Skrine, eds. *Hans Sachs and Folk Theater in the Late Middle Age.* Lewiston, NY: Edwin Mellen, 1995.

Bentley, G. E. *The Profession of Player in Shakespeare's Time, 1590–1642.* Princeton: Princeton University Press, 1984.

Braden, Gordon. *Renaissance Tragedy and the Senecan Tradition.* New Haven: Yale University Press, 1985.

Braunmuller, A. R., and M. Hattaway, eds. *The Cambridge Companion to English Renaissance Drama*. Cambridge: Cambridge University Press, 1990.

Clubb, Louise. *Italian Drama in Shakespeare's Time*. New Haven: Yale University Press, 1989.

Crawford, J. P. *Spanish Drama before Lope de Vega*. Philadelphia: University of Pennsylvania Press, 1967.

Gurr, Andrew. *The Shakespearean Stage, 1574–1642*. Cambridge: Cambridge University Press, 1970.

Herrick, Marvin. *Italian Comedy in the Renaissance*. Urbana: University of Illinois Press, 1966.

————. *Italian Tragedy in the Renaissance*. Urbana: University of Illinois Press, 1965.

Jeffery, B. *French Renaissance Comedy, 1552–1630*. Oxford: Clarendon Press, 1969.

Levin, Carole, and Karen Robertson, eds. *Sexuality and Politics in Renaissance Drama*. Lewiston, NY: Edwin Mellen, 1991.

Montrose, Louis. *The Purpose of Playing: Shakespeare and the Cultural Politics of the Elizabethan Theatre*. Chicago: University of Chicago Press, 1996.

Mullaney, Steven. *The Place of the Stage: License, Play, and Power in Renaissance England*. Chicago: University of Chicago Press, 1988.

Orgel, Stephen. *The Illusion of Power: Political Theater in the English Renaissance*. Berkeley: University of California Press, 1975.

Wells, Stanley. *Shakespeare: A Life in Drama*. New York: Norton, 1995.

Wilson, E. *A Literary History of Spain: The Golden Age of Drama, 1492–1700*. New York: Barnes and Noble, 1971.

SCIENCE

Biagioli, Mario. *Galileo Courtier: The Practice of Science in the Culture of Absolutism*. Chicago: University of Chicago Press, 1993.

Debus, Allen G. *Man and Nature in the Renaissance*. Cambridge: Cambridge University Press, 1978.

Edgerton, Samuel Y., Jr. *The Heritage of Giotto's Geometry: Art and Science on the Eve of the Scientific Revolution*. Ithaca: Cornell University Press, 1991.

————. *The Renaissance Rediscovery of Linear Perspective*. New York: Basic Books, 1975.

Field, J. V., and F. A. James, eds. *Renaissance and Revolution: Humanists, Scholars, Craftsmen, and Natural Philosophers in Early Modern Europe*. Cambridge: Cambridge University Press, 1993.

Hall, Marie Boas. *The Scientific Renaissance, 1450–1630*. New York: Dover, 1994.

Redondi, Pietro. *Galileo Heretic = Galileo eriteco*. Princeton: Princeton University Press, 1987.

Rossi, Paolo. *Francis Bacon: From Magic to Science*. London: Routledge, 1968.

Sarton, George. *Six Wings: Men of Science in the Renaissance*. Bloomington: Indiana University Press, 1957.

Shumaker, Wayne. *The Occult Sciences in the Renaissance*. Berkeley: University of California Press, 1972.

Smith, Alan. *Science and Society in the Sixteenth and Seventeenth Centuries*. New York: Harcourt Brace Jovanovich, 1972.

Vickers, B., ed. *Occult and Scientific Mentalities in the Renaissance*. Cambridge: Cambridge University Press, 1984.

MUSIC

Brown, Howard Mayer. *Music in the Renaissance*. Englewood Cliffs, NJ: Prentice-Hall, 1976.

Caldwell, John. *The Oxford History of English Music*. Vol. 1. Oxford: Clarendon Press, 1991.

Knighton, Tess, and David Fallows, eds. *Companion to Medieval and Renaissance Music*. New York: Schirmer Books, 1992.

Maniates, Maria R. *Mannerism in Italian Music and Culture, 1530–1630*. Chapel Hill: University of North Carolina Press, 1979.

Price, David. *Patrons and Musicians of the English Renaissance*. Cambridge: Cambridge University Press, 1981.

Reese, Gustave. *Music in the Renaissance*. New York: Norton, 1954.

Sadie, Stanley, ed. *The New Grove Dictionary of Music and Musicians*, 29 vols. New York: Groves Dictionaries, Inc. 1980.

Tomlinson, Gary. *Music in Renaissance Magic*. Chicago: University of Chicago Press, 1993.

HUMANISM, PHILOSOPHY, AND SCHOLARSHIP

Bernstein, Eckhard. *German Humanism*. Boston: Twayne Publishers, 1983.

Copenhaver, Brian P., and Charles B. Schmitt, eds. *Renaissance Philosophy*. Oxford: Oxford University Press, 1992.

Eisenstein, Elizabeth. *The Printing Revolution in Early Modern Europe*. Cambridge: Cambridge University Press, 1993.

Garin, Eugenio. *Italian Humanism: Philosophy and Civic Life in the Renaissance*. Trans. Peter Munz. New York: Harper and Row, 1965.

Grafton, Anthony. *Defenders of the Text: The Traditions of Scholarship in an Age of Science, 1450–1800*. Cambridge, MA: Harvard University Press, 1991.

Grafton, Anthony, and Lisa Jardine. *From Humanism to the Humanities: Education and the Liberal Arts in Fifteenth- and Sixteenth-Century Europe*. Cambridge, MA: Harvard University Press, 1986.

Greenblatt, Stephen. *Renaissance Self-Fashioning*. Chicago: University of Chicago Press, 1980.

Gundersheimer, Werner, ed. *French Humanism, 1470–1600*. New York: Harper and Row, 1969.

Kraye, Jill, ed. *The Cambridge Companion to Renaissance Humanism*. Cambridge: Cambridge University Press, 1996.

Kristeller, Paul. *Renaissance Thought and Its Sources*. New York: Columbia University Press, 1979.

Mack, Peter, ed. *Renaissance Rhetoric*. New York: St. Martin's Press, 1994.

Rabil, A., Jr., ed. *Renaissance Humanism: Foundations, Forms, and Legacy*. 3 vols. Philadelphia: University of Pennsylvania Press, 1988.

Schmitt, Charles B., ed. *The Cambridge History of Renaissance Philosophy*. Cambridge: Cambridge University Press, 1988.

Trapp, J. B. *Erasmus, Colet, and More: The Early Tudor Humanists and Their Books.* London: British Library, 1991.

WOMEN AND GENDER

Amussen, Susan. *An Ordered Society: Gender and Class in Early Modern England.* London: Basil Blackwell, 1988.

Anderson, Bonnie, and Judith P. Zinsser. *A History of Their Own: Women in Europe from Prehistory to the Present.* 2 vols. New York: Harper and Row, 1988.

Bridenthal, Renate, Claudia Koonz, and Susan Stuard, eds. *Becoming Visible: Women in European History.* 3rd ed. Boston: Houghton Mifflin, 1998.

Crawford, Patricia. *Women and Religion in England, 1500–1720.* London and New York: Routledge, 1993.

Davis, Natalie Zemon, and Arlette Farge, eds. *Renaissance and Enlightenment Paradoxes.* Vol. 3 of *A History of Women in the West.* Cambridge, MA: Harvard University Press, 1993.

Ferguson, Margaret, Maureen Quilligan, and Nancy Vickers, eds. *Rewriting the Renaissance: The Discourses of Sexual Difference in Early Modern Europe.* Chicago: University of Chicago Press, 1986.

Hannay, Margaret, ed. *Silent But for the Word: Tudor Women as Patrons, Translators, and Writers of Religious Works.* Kent, OH: Kent State University Press, 1985.

Jordan, Constance. *Renaissance Feminism: Literary Texts and Political Models.* Ithaca: Cornell University Press, 1990.

King, Margaret. *Women of the Renaissance.* Chicago: University of Chicago Press, 1991.

Levin, Carole, and Patricia A. Sullivan, eds. *Political Rhetoric, Power, and Renaissance Women.* Albany: State University of New York Press, 1995.

Muir, Edward, and Guido Ruggiero, eds. *Sex and Gender in Historical Perspective.* Baltimore: Johns Hopkins University Press, 1990.

Ozment, Steven. *When Fathers Ruled: Family Life in Reformation Europe.* Cambridge, MA: Harvard University Press, 1983.

Turner, James Grantham, ed. *Sexuality and Gender in Early Modern Europe: Institutions, Texts, Images.* Cambridge: Cambridge University Press, 1993.

Warnicke, Retha. *Women of the English Renaissance and Reformation.* Westport, CT: Greenwood Press, 1983.

Weisner, Merry. *Women and Gender in Early Modern Europe.* Cambridge: Cambridge University Press, 1993.

Wilson, Katharina M., ed. *Women Writers of the Renaissance and Reformation.* Athens: University of Georgia Press, 1987.

Woodbridge, Linda. *Women and the English Renaissance: Literature and the Nature of Womankind, 1540 to 1620.* Urbana: University of Illinois Press, 1986.

Index

Abate, Niccolò dell', **1**, 70

Acosta, José de, **2**

Aertsen, Pieter, **2–3**

Agricola, Georg, **3–4**

Agricola, Johann, **4–5**

Agricola, Michael, **5–6**

Agrippa von Nettesheim, Heinrich Cornelius, **6–7**

Albret, Jeanne d', **7–8**, 117, 242

Alemán, Mateo, **8–9**

Altdorfer, Albrecht, **9–10**

Amyot, Jacques, **10–11**

Andrea del Sarto, **11–12**, 285, 303, 304, 358

Andrewes, Lancelot, **12–13**, 74, 83, 207

Anghiera, Pietro Martire (Peter Martyr d'Anghera), **13–14**, 183

Anguissola, Sofonisba, **14–15**

Aragona, Tullia d', **15–16**, 332

Arcadelt, Jacques, **16–17**

Arcimboldo, Giuseppe, **17–18**, 306, 334

Aretino, Pietro, **18–19**, 359; as career builder, 19, 304, 350; and Pietro Bembo, 19, 138, 154, 229, 231; and Rome's artistic community, 138, 154; and satire, 15, 18; and sonnets, 18, 291; and Titian, 19, 350

Ariosto, Ludovico, **19–21**, 169; influence of, 21, 109, 307, 380; and *Orlando Furioso* (*The Madness of Roland*), 19–21, 91, 133, 163, 184, 352

Ascham, Roger, **21–22**, 127, 177, 193

Askew, Anne, **22–23**, 28, 144

Bacon, Anne Cook, **24–25**

Bacon, Francis, 24, **25–26**, 97, 162, 271

Baïf, Jean-Antoine de, **26–28**, 36, 109, 119, 207

Bale, John, 23, **28**, 32, 144

Bandello, Matteo, **29–30**, 137

Bandinelli, Baccio, **30–31**, 291

Barbaro, Daniele, **31–32**, 364

Barclay, Alexander, **32**

Barclay, William, **32–33**

Bassano, Jacopo da, **33–34**, 66

Beaumont, Francis, **34**, 139

Beccafumi, Domenico, **35**

Becon, Thomas, **35–36**

Belleau, Rémy, **36–37**, 207

Bembo, Pietro, **37–38**, 107; and the church, 38, 91, 145, 229, 307; friends of, 20, 138, 145, 231, 332; and *Gil Asolani*, 19, 37, 307; and the literary community, 76, 138, 154; patrons of, 69, 91

Bess of Hardwick, **38–39**

Beza, Theodore, **39–40**, 102, 133

Bodin, Jean, **40–42**, 108

Boehme, Jakob, **42**

About the Editor and Contributors

JEAN AKERS, Department of History, State University of New York, New Paltz

DEBBIE BARRETT-GRAVES, Department of English, College of Sante Fe

MARK BAYER, Department of English, Ohio State University

JEFFREY A. BELL, Department of History and Government, Southeastern Louisiana University

GÜNTER BERGHAUS, Department of Drama, University of Bristol

ECKHARD BERNSTEIN, Department of Modern Languages and Literature, College of the Holy Cross

LYDIA BERNSTEIN, Department of Foreign Languages, Bridgewater State College

NANCY ERICKSON BOUZRARA, Department of Foreign Languages and Classics, University of Southern Maine

BARBARA BOYLE, Department of English, The College of New Jersey

MITCHELL BRAUNER, Department of Music, University of Wisconsin, Milwaukee

JO ELDRIDGE CARNEY, Department of English, The College of New Jersey

DEBORAH COMPTE, Department of Modern Languages, The College of New Jersey

DAVID CROOK, Department of Music, University of Wisconsin, Milwaukee

LUCI FORTUNATO DELISLE, Department of Modern Languages, Bridgewater State College

CONNIE S. EVANS, Department of History, Auburn University

CHARLES FANTAZZI, Department of Foreign Languages, East Carolina University

ROBIN FARABAUGH, Department of English, University of Maryland

SHEILA FFOLLIOTT, Department of Art History, George Mason University

AL GERITZ, Department of English, Fort Hays State University

GARY G. GIBBS, Department of History, Roanoke College

JEAN GRAHAM, Department of English, The College of New Jersey

MARY JANE HAEMIG, Department of Religion, Pacific Lutheran University

MICHAEL A. HAKKENBERG, Department of History, Roanoke College

LISA HINRICHSEN, Department of English, Wellesley College

KATHERINE HOFFMAN, Department of English, Roanoke College

KAREN S. JAMES, Department of Foreign Languages, Roanoke College

SUSAN H. JENSON, National Endowment for the Humanities

LYNNE E. JOHNSON, Department of Art and Art History, Goucher College

GWYNNE KENNEDY, Department of English, University of Wisconsin, Milwaukee

EDMUND M. KERN, Department of History, Lawrence University

KAROLYN KINANE, Department of English, University of Minnesota

JOHN N. KING, Department of English, Ohio State University

YU JIN KO, Department of English, Wellesley College

ANA KOTHE, Department of the Humanities, University of Puerto Rico

ELAINE KRUSE, Department of History, Nebraska Wesleyan University

WHITNEY LEESON, Department of History, Roanoke College

CAROLE LEVIN, Department of History, University of Nebraska, Lincoln

ALISON WILLIAMS LEWIN, Department of History, Saint Joseph's University

KEVIN LINDBERG, Department of English, Ohio State University

MEGAN S. LLOYD, Department of English, King's College

JANE C. LONG, Department of Art History, Roanoke College

IAIN S. MACLEAN, Department of Philosophy and Religion, James Madison University

JOHN MARCIARI, Department of Art History, Yale University

TIM MCGEE, Department of English, The College of New Jersey

MICHAEL J. MEDWICK, Department of English, University of Nebraska, Lincoln

MICHAEL J. MIKOŚ, Department of Foreign Languages and Linguistics, University of Wisconsin, Milwaukee

PAUL MILLER, Department of History, Louisiana State University

HEATHER J. MURRAY, Department of English, Pennsylvania State University

RUSSELL E. MURRAY, JR., Department of Music, University of Delaware

KAREN NELSON, Center for Renaissance and Baroque Studies, University of Maryland

THOMAS G. OLSEN, Department of English, State University of New York, New Paltz

MICHELE OSHEROW, Department of English, University of Maryland

MARY PIXLEY, independent scholar, McLean, Virginia

DORA E. POLACHEK, Department of Modern Languages, State University of New York, Binghamton

CATHERINE C. PONTORIERO, Department of English, The College of New Jersey

ROSEMARY POOLE, Department of Art History, George Mason University

LAWRENCE RHU, Department of English, University of South Carolina

RICHARD J. RING, John Carter Brown Library, Brown University

TUCKER ROBISON, independent scholar, Charleston, Illinois

WILLIAM B. ROBISON, Department of History and Government, Southeastern Louisiana University

CHRISTOPHER D. ROEBUCK, Department of English, Boston College

LOUIS ROPER, Department of History, State University of New York, New Paltz

ERIN SADLACK, Department of English, University of Maryland

CHERYL SMART, Department of Art History, University of Arizona

RACHEL HOSTETTER SMITH, Department of Art History, Taylor University

WILLIAM SPELLMAN, Department of History, University of North Carolina, Asheville

KIRILKA STAVREVA, Department of English, St. Ambrose University

EVELYN TOFT, Department of Modern Languages, Fort Hays State University

ANDREW G. TRAVER, Department of History, Southeastern Louisiana University

PATRICIA A. WHITE, Department of English, The College of New Jersey

STEPHANIE WITHAM, Department of English, University of Nebraska, Lincoln

LILIAN H. ZIRPOLO, independent scholar, Woodcliff Lakes, New Jersey